SOCIETIES, CHOICES AND ENVIRONMENTS

ISSUES AND ENQUIRIES

Editor: Frances Slater

COLLINS
EDUCATIONAL

© Frances Slater et al., 1991

First published in 1991
by Collins Educational,
a division of HarperCollins Publishers
77 Fulham Palace Road
London W6 8JA

ISBN 0 00 327401 2

Designed by Jacky Wedgwood
Artwork by John Booth and Gay Galsworthy
Picture research by Caroline Thompson

Typeset by Burns and Smith Ltd, Derby
Printed and bound in Great Britain by
Holmes McDougall Ltd., Edinburgh

The cover photograph shows a view of Cortina, a winter
resort in the Dolomites, northern Italy

CONTENTS

INTRODUCTION

In my introduction to *People and Environments* I highlighted certain contradictions which many agree are at work in our world. There are food surpluses and food shortages; severe poverty for many and a superabundance of riches for others; and so it goes on. And the more I think about it, the more convinced I am that the concepts of positive and negative feedback are central to understanding many of the contradictions or issues working themselves out in our world.

I explained these concepts in the following way.

Most natural systems are self-regulating. That is, they are able to respond to changing circumstances by adjusting the way in which they function. The result of this adjustment is usually the return to 'normal working', although some systems will take much longer than others to achieve it. If self-regulation is to occur, a system must be able to check or correct itself. For this to happen, at least one part of the system must be able to compensate for the behaviour of another part. This compensation is known technically as 'negative feedback'. Without it there can never be a return to normal, and self-destruction is virtually inevitable.

A simple example of a self-destructive relationship between three parts of the soil-slope system is shown here:

Suppose that a decrease in the infiltration capacity of the soil (F^*) causes an increase in the amount of surface water running-off the soil (q). In its turn, this increased run-off causes an increase in the erosion of the slope leading to the removal of its soil in the process. Removal of the soil creates a further decrease in infiltration capacity (less soil, hence less capacity) resulting in even more run-off and more slope and soil erosion. In other words, the cycle begins again. Such behaviour exhibits no self-regulating mechanism. In fact, it displays 'positive feedback' where one initial change (the decrease in F^*) sets off a pattern of activity which becomes progressively more acute.

Where physical or natural systems are linked to human activity systems – as, for example, in the case of trampling and erosion – the risk of positive feedback occurring is much increased. This is because human activity may interfere with the normal working of a natural system and prevent negative feedback from playing its compensating role. A very long period of time may be needed for recovery, if it is all possible. For example, poor farming techniques can devastate an area if they initiate a positive feedback

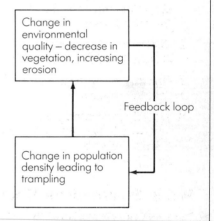

Feedback loop

loop which causes severe soil erosion. The problem is how to manage linked physical and human systems so that a destructive chain of events is not set in motion.

Source: F. Slater (ed.), *People and Environments*, Collins Educational, 1986

Read the article 'The modern parable' on the next page and define positive feedback and negative feedback in its terms. You need to decide what may bring about the achievement of negative feedback in the human system described in the parable.

The modern parable

There was once a factory which employed thousands of people. Its production line was a miracle of modern engineering, turning out thousands of machines every day. The factory had a high accident rate. The complicated machinery of the production line took little account of human error, forgetfulness, or ignorance. Day after day, people came out of the factory with squashed fingers, cuts, bruises. Sometimes a woman would lose an arm or leg. Occasionally someone was electrocuted or crushed to death. Enlightened people began to see that something had to be done.

First on the scene were the churches. An enterprising minister organised a small first-aid tent outside the factory gate. Soon, with the backing of the Council of Churches, it grew into a properly built clinic, able to give first-aid to quite serious cases, and to treat minor injuries. The town council become interested, together with local bodies like the Chamber of Trade and the Rotary Club. The clinic grew into a small hospital, with modern equipment, an operating theatre, and a full-time staff of doctors and nurses.

Several lives were saved. Finally, the factory management, seeing the good that was being done and wishing to prove itself enlightened, gave the hospital its official backing, with unrestricted access to the factory, a small annual grant, and an ambulance to speed serious cases from workshop to hospital ward.

But year by year, as production increased, the accident rate continued to rise. More and more people were hurt

and maimed. And, in spite of everything the hospital could do, more and more people died from the injuries they received.

Only then did some people begin to ask if it was enough to treat people's injuries, while leaving untouched the machinery that caused them.

Source: New Internationalist Publication, January 1985

What is at issue?

Throughout the case studies in this book, I think it will become clear to you that *at issue* in each chapter is the question of what process or processes are operating to bring about for example, coastal management and mismanagement; desertification; water management or mismanagement on mountain slopes. Or what processes operate to create benefits and losses through the aid business, through tourism, through attitudes to women, through transport policies?

Each case study is not there only as an end in itself. It is there to illuminate an issue – something of significance that gives us a general understanding of a possible or negative feedback process which is operating now. That is putting it in very scientific language. It's positive feedback which brings more and more cars into city centres, for example. We could make decisions and policies which would change positive feedback into negative feedback.

Other people (see Introduction to Part I) might not talk of feedbacks. They might use a more humanistic language and think in terms of individual and collective responsibility, of attitudes and value systems (which to my way of thinking can transform negative feedback mechanisms to positive, and vice versa).

Whatever language we use, processes are at work in environments and in societies which we can come to understand through the following case studies in geography. Each case study can be analysed and understood through the use of the Geography 16–19 Route for Enquiry (Figure 1). If you get into the habit of analysing each chapter in terms of the key questions which define the route, you should then have grasped what is at issue in each case study.

Let 'What is at issue here?' be your key, overall guiding question through the case studies illustrating issues in this book.

FRANCES SLATER

Figure 1 *The route for geographical enquiry*

Factual enquiry more objective data	Route and key questions	Values enquiry more subjective data
Achieve awareness of a question, issue or problem arising from the interaction of people with their environments.	OBSERVATION AND PERCEPTION What?	Achieve awareness that individuals and groups hold differing attitudes and values with regard to the question issue or problem.
Outline and define the question, issue or problem. State hypotheses where appropriate. Decide on data and evidence to be collected. Collect and describe data and evidence.	DEFINITION AND DESCRIPTION What? and Where?	List the values held or likely to be held by different individuals or groups with interest and/or involvement. Collect data on action and statements of individuals/groups. Classify values into categories. Assess the actions likely to be linked with each category.
Organise and analyse data. Move towards providing answers and explanations. Attempt to accept, reject or modify hypotheses. Decide whether more or different data and evidence are required.	ANALYSIS AND EXPLANATION How? and Why?	Assess how far the values can be verified by evidence, ie, to what extent are the values supported by facts? Attempt to recognise bias, prejudice, irrelevant data. Identify sources of values conflict.
Evaluate results of enquiry. Attempt to make predictions, to formulate generalisations and, if possible, to construct theories. Propose alternative courses of action, and predict possible consequences.	PREDICTION AND EVALUATION What might? What will? With what impact?	Attempt to identify the most powerful values positions. Consider future alternatives from these positions and recognise preferred decisions. Identify people/groups who could act and assess impacts/consequences.
Recognise the likely decision given the factual background and the values situation. Identify the probable environmental and spatial consequences.	DECISION-MAKING What decision? With what impact?	Recognise the likely decision given the results of the values analysis and the factual background. Identify the probable reactions and responses of those who hold other viewpoints.

PERSONAL EVALUATION AND JUDGEMENT

What do I think? Why?

Determine what values are important to oneself and so decide which values position one would support in this issue.
Identify which decision and what courses of action one could accept personally.
Assess their impact on the situation.
Consider how one would defend and justify this course of action.

PERSONAL RESPONSE

What next? What shall I do?

DECIDE WHETHER AS A RESULT OF THIS ENQUIRY

- to take action oneself or with others on this issue
- to help to initiate action on this issue by contacting those in positions of power

- to take action to change aspects of one's personal lifestyle/actions which may affect future issues
- to take no immediate action, but to follow further enquiries in order to test out one's feelings

Source: Naish, Rawling, Hart, *Geography 16–19: The contribution of a curriculum project to 16–19 education*, Longman Group UK Limited 1987.

PART I

CHALLENGE OF NATURAL ENVIRONMENTS

Choices and ideologies: four views

Some people believe that the human race can always find a way out of its difficulties, whether these are political, scientific or technical. If we create changes in ecosystems and their checks and balances, such people believe human genius and cleverness is great enough to overcome the difficulties created.

Other people believe that the human race has lost touch with nature and is doomed to destroy itself and its environment unless we follow nature's laws and restrict economic development. Such people say they would like to return to a much simpler way of life that fits into a natural ecosystem.

Yet other people believe that economic growth can continue on a large scale and that we should not worry unduly about using up natural resources.

They do feel, however, that the process and direction of economic growth should be managed and directed and to some extent controlled by government. They believe in some regulation to protect resources and the environment.

A fourth group of people argue that large-scale economic growth should be replaced by small-scale activity using intermediate technology, for example. They distrust development which involves large companies and organisations and strong centralised government control. They favour local community developments that involve everyone in decision making. They dislike the way that people today are obsessed with what they own or think they need to have.

?

1 You have to decide to join one of these groups of people. Which one would you choose? Why?

2 Match the description of the four groups to those in Figure 1.

We have here, in fact, four ideological positions in relation to our environment and how we may treat it. Ideologies are bundles of beliefs, opinions, attitudes, values, preferences which we hold together. They help explain a good deal about how we act and behave. These five words or concepts – beliefs, opinions, attitudes, values and preferences – all have slightly different meanings and you need to look them up in a dictionary and begin to sort out the differences.

3 Write out a definition for each word and give examples of it:

a Beliefs **b** Opinions **c** Attitudes
d Values **e** Preferences.

4 This question will also help to make some of the differences in meaning clearer. (This may be an individual or group activity.)
Look at Table 1:

Newspapers are full of reports on things like this. Write down on a piece of paper your initial, gut reaction, your more-or-less spontaneous reaction to the situation. Don't ponder too long. Just think in terms of whether it is a desirable or undesirable situation. Is it generally good or bad?

Table 1

Situation	Reaction	Reason
A polluted river		
An oil spill		
A plant species becoming extinct		
Closing off a public footpath		

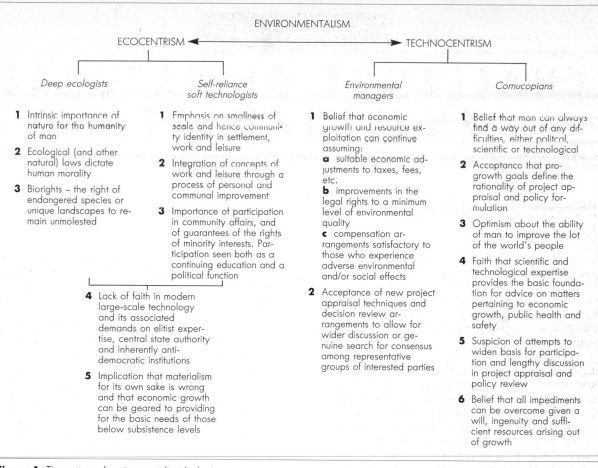

ENVIRONMENTALISM

ECOCENTRISM ← → TECHNOCENTRISM

Deep ecologists

1 Intrinsic importance of nature for the humanity of man

2 Ecological (and other natural) laws dictate human morality

3 Biorights – the right of endangered species or unique landscapes to remain unmolested

Self-reliance soft technologists

1 Emphasis on smallness of scale and hence community identity in settlement, work and leisure

2 Integration of concepts of work and leisure through a process of personal and communal improvement

3 Importance of participation in community affairs, and of guarantees of the rights of minority interests. Participation seen both as a continuing education and a political function

4 Lack of faith in modern large-scale technology and its associated demands on elitist expertise, central state authority and inherently anti-democratic institutions

5 Implication that materialism for its own sake is wrong and that economic growth can be geared to providing for the basic needs of those below subsistence levels

Environmental managers

1 Belief that economic growth and resource exploitation can continue assuming:
  a suitable economic adjustments to taxes, fees, etc.
  b improvements in the legal rights to a minimum level of environmental quality
  c compensation arrangements satisfactory to those who experience adverse environmental and/or social effects

2 Acceptance of new project appraisal techniques and decision review arrangements to allow for wider discussion or genuine search for consensus among representative groups of interested parties

Cornucopians

1 Belief that man can always find a way out of any difficulties, either political, scientific or technological

2 Acceptance that pro-growth goals define the rationality of project appraisal and policy formulation

3 Optimism about the ability of man to improve the lot of the world's people

4 Faith that scientific and technological expertise provides the basic foundation for advice on matters pertaining to economic growth, public health and safety

5 Suspicion of attempts to widen basis for participation and lengthy discussion in project appraisal and policy review

6 Belief that all impediments can be overcome given a will, ingenuity and sufficient resources arising out of growth

Figure 1 The pattern of environmentalist ideologies

Source: from 'Teaching of Geography in Higher Education', *Journal of Geography and Higher Education*, Vol. 5, No. 1, 1981

5 Next, in the third column of Table 1, write down the reasons for your initial reaction. Why did you have such a reaction? What general ideas do you hold to about people and their environments and the way societies of people should relate to their natural and built environments?

Sorting out your reasons is not such an easy task as giving your initial reaction. The reasons probably come closest to expressing your values, ideas which you hold firmly, deeply and consistently. For example, most people in response to seeing a child being severely beaten and wounded by an adult would be angry and disgusted, dismayed and incredulous. Why? Because most of us hold to a notion that values the protection of the weak, values kindness over cruelty, values talk and persuasion over violence, and so on. We are into quite advanced ideas here and so you will have to think hard and discuss with others to decide on your value-laden reasons in question **3**. Keep discussing and thinking, and dig deep.

Why? It is important that we become aware of our values because they explain a lot of what we do and believe. It is just as important to think about what forms our values too. How long a list could you make?

● Your experiences
● Your parents/guardians
● Your friends
● Your teachers
● School
● TV, radio, newspapers...
● Pop stars

The society you live in helps form your values and beliefs. As individuals we live in groups and societies. We treat and mistreat our various natural and human-built environments.

Our natural environment

The chapters in this section focus on how we have interacted and treated or how we are interacting and treating our natural environment today. The challenge is to understand how the environment works, and we certainly cannot do this without understanding how our beliefs, attitudes and values as groups of people lead us to meet and treat environments in different ways. Each of the four groups of people identified above interacts with environments in different ways, from different starting points.

Each of the chapters in this section is about how people and societies have made choices and decisions based on their values and attitudes towards natural environments. You might try to classify ideologically the story each chapter tells – the issues it highlights in relation to coasts, glaciers and so on. Have people in societies been cornucopians, environmental managers, deep ecologists, or self-reliance soft technologists? This is an essential question to answer and understand. What environmental ideological stand do the authors of the chapters seem to take? Does their ideological position affect the way they have organised and written the question? This is a puzzling question but an interesting one to think about.

Grasping ideas

Study skills: making notes

Ideologies and environments are one thing, and certainly a set of quite abstract ideas. First for you as a student, there is the problem of reading through the chapters and grasping the significant facts and points which the author(s) is attempting to make. There is a big leap between studying geography at GCSE and at 'A' level. We know that at 'A' level students often find the amount and level of reading pretty tough. There is so much to read, and that takes a long time, and then it takes even longer to simplify it and get the main points.

I was very interested not long ago to read the extracts alongside in a dissertation which investigated how 'A' level students cope with reading and writing essays.

You should read through them – some important points on how to read a text come up. Too often we teachers take it for granted that you see the organisation of the chapter in the same way as we do. We have had years of practice and forget what it is like trying to sort out the wood from the trees as a beginner.

For this reason I thought I would attempt to give you a lesson in analysing part of a text and making notes on its important points and how it hangs together.

Notes to the teacher

a Get your students reading the excerpts from the research early on in the lesson in order to introduce the lesson on note-taking and the key points involved. Encourage early initial discussion on the questions I have posed and any other questions you may wish to raise.

b Move on to dealing with the case study and my model of note taking.

c Move back to the excerpts and the questions and problems they raise.

The Norfolk Broads (pages 8–11) is an interesting self-contained case study. I first skimmed through it and jotted down on a rough piece of paper the general points I picked up. I was asking myself, what does it seem to be about?

Excerpts from research into an 'A' level attempt to read a text for an essay

D is the student, T is the teacher/interviewer.

The approach to, and focus of, reading

T Now ... how did you get on with reading this?

1 D *I read bits of it, then I wrote about them, then I read bits again and wrote about them. I didn't read it all through in one go.*

T Did you want to read it?

2 D Well ... I read it because I had the essay to write, but I did think it was quite interesting – more so than some of the work, so I think I would have read it anyway once I started ... I didn't find it boring, but I found I was losing track of it a bit as I went on.

T Did you know anything about it as a topic?

3 D I knew vaguely.

T What do you think you got out of it? What was it about?

4 D Well, I think the main thing that struck me was how

the forests had been used up so quickly … and how most of the forests in the world had been used up …

● Was her strategy, not to read it through in one go, a good one?

Awareness of 'sections' and 'headings'

T Now, turning again to how you said you read this, you said you read 'a bit' and then wrote your essay. How far did a bit go?

9 D Usually it's, sort of, a heading. Like in 'The Location of Pulp and Paper Mills' it was about a page … just different headings … different blocks … Normally, with geography, there's always headings inside the chapters and you know what's going to happen. There's different kinds of heading …

T What different kinds of heading are you aware of?

10 D *Well, there's the main heading, like … er … 'Distribution' – where they are – and then it goes on to 'Conservation' and then 'Industry' – the kinds there are*. They're the different main blocks and then there's little side headings, like 'Tropical Hardwood Forest' and so on *and they're all separate bits*.

T When you're reading, do the different kinds of heading help at all?

11 D Er … *When I'm reading, I don't so much think of them as different kinds, I think of them as following on, one type of tree and where it is and then another – and I picture them*, like with *'Tropical Hardwood Forest'* I'd be thinking of low-lying ground, with a monsoon-type climate. I suppose I see it as jungle more than anything else. It's usually very wet and very hot … *It's not so much a place – an area – actually very dense (laughing). It's what it looks like in your mind*, with trees everywhere.

T Did the 'Hardwood' form part of your picture?

12 D No – I didn't think about that really, till later on they mentioned furniture wood like mahogany and teak. It tells you – page 194, the 2nd paragraph. Then I just thought of furniture (laughing).

● Discuss in groups to identify what seems to be the main problem here.

Reading of 'methods … of forest management' section

T Now, we've been talking about headings or sections that you'd particularly noticed or felt were helpful. Is there anything else that you were aware of as you read and that you'd like to tell me about before we move on?

24 D Well – er … there was the bit about conservation (looking), page 204. There were little headings that picked out points. *'Forest Establishment'*, I was thinking of the renewing of the trees that had been used and making up the stock and er … then *'Selective Cutting'* – cutting only parts of the forest at a time so you always save some. When I first read them I took them as all separate, but then after I'd read them they seemed to connect up to conservation and they were numbered too. I already knew about some of them and about the idea of conservation.

T How did they connect up?

25 D I realised that obviously *'Conservation'* was the main heading – protecting the forest – and this was the different ways that people were trying to conserve the forests, so it linked to that heading.

● How often do you aim in your reading to work out how things connect up?

Awareness of maps and tables

T Right, now did the maps and tables figure at all in your reading?

26 D Well – I usually read a block, write about it, and then look at the maps and tables.

T Were there any that you particularly noticed when you did come to look at them?

27 D The one on page 195 was more confusing than anything. There were so many different shadings and there was writing everywhere. I was too confused to take much notice of it really.

● Can you use maps and tables to advantage?

Source: Robson, 1983

The Norfolk Broads: the decline of Broadland

David Brewster and Geoff Philips

The Broads were formed from medieval peat diggings which were abandoned in the 13th–14th centuries due to flooding when sea levels rose. There is little documented history of Broadland until the early 19th century, and evidence gleaned from the writings of naturalists of that time shows that the shallow Broadland lakes were very different from those we see today. The lakes contained *clear water* with an abundant growth of water weeds and a wide variety of aquatic animal life. The growth of water weeds in places became so abundant that it impeded boat movement and had to be removed to maintain navigable channels.

Today the open water of most of the Broads contains no water weeds due to the lack of light penetrating through the *turbid water*. This change is not well documented but probably took place fairly rapidly sometime during the 1950s and early 1960s. Some data from Hickling Broad is available, and from the amount of weed removed (see Figure 2) to maintain navigation it is clear that the decline took place over a fairly short period.

The role of weeds in the ecosystem

In these shallow lakes water weeds played a critical role in increasing the habitat diversity of an otherwise rather uniform environment. They provided cover for a variety of the small planktonic crustacea, preventing their populations from being decimated by fish predation. They offered almost the only stable substratum for eggs to be laid, and they provided a source of food for a wide range of animals. Thus the loss of these plants, important in itself, has had considerable implications for the ecosystem of the Broads.

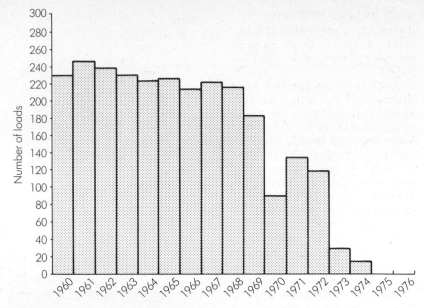

Figure 2 Number of loads (approximately 8 tonnes each) of 'Sponge Weed' removed from Hickling Broad by the Yare, Bure and Waveney Commissioners

The cause of the problem

A great deal of research has been undertaken to establish the cause of these changes and to attempt to reverse them. It is often suggested that the increase in boat numbers may have led to the loss of plants but, although this is clearly an additional pressure, it cannot explain the change, as many of the Broads affected are not subject to boat traffic. Although the exact mechanism involved is still not completely understood, it is clear that the lack of light penetration through the water, caused by the growth of algae (phytoplankton), is the main reason why submerged water weeds no longer grow.

Work carried out in North America during the 1960s convincingly demonstrated that plant nutrients, nitrogen and phosphorus were responsible for this excess of growth of phytoplankton. The process is known as eutrophication and, if the input of either nitrogen or phosphorus from the *catchment* can be reduced, it seems likely that the changes to the Broadland ecosystem could be reversed. The source of nitrogen is primarily from diffuse agricultural sources and is therefore

difficult to control. Even if this could be achieved, many algae have the capability of *fixing* atmospheric nitrogen and could continue to cause problems. In contrast, phosphorus is derived from animal waste products, mainly sewage effluent, and can be controlled by chemical precipitation within a treatment plant. The reduction of the amount of phosphorus discharged to the Broads catchment should therefore result in a reversal of the changes described above.

The initial solution

A major experimental programme to reduce the amount of phosphorus discharged to the River Ant and Barton Broad, the second largest of the Broads, was started in 1977 by Anglian Water. This involved the removal of phosphorus from sewage effluent by chemical precipitation with ferric sulphate. This resulted in a reduction of phosphorus discharged from the works of about 90%. Initially only effluent from Stalham Sewage Treatment Works, because of its proximity to Barton Broad, was treated. When it became clear that this was inadequate, effluent from

North Walsham STW was diverted to a sea outfall and all other significant discharges had phosphorus removal facilities installed.

Look at Figure 3, which shows that by 1980 this action resulted in a 90% reduction in the amount of phosphorus discharged to the River Ant from sewage or industrial discharges. The amount of phosphorus moving along the river was carefully monitored. There was clearly a substantial reduction in the phosphorus load in the upper river at Honing Lock; however, further downstream the effect was considerably less marked. At the inflow to Barton Broad the reduction in phosphorus load was less than 50%.

The hoped-for reduction in phytoplankton growth also failed to occur. Measurement of the chlorophyll content of the water provides a good measure of the amount of phytoplankton in the water, and data collected from the beginning of the experiment illustrated in Figure 4 shows that only a modest reduction in phytoplankton had occurred.

Comparing the total phosphorus concentration of Barton Broad with the chlorophyll concentration (Figure 5) demonstrates that

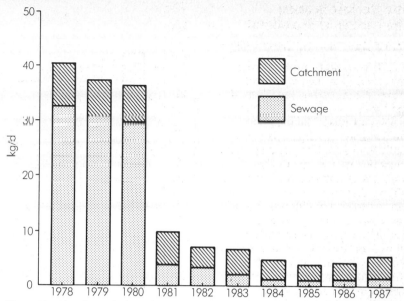

Figure 3 Phosphorus discharged to the River Ant: annual mean load

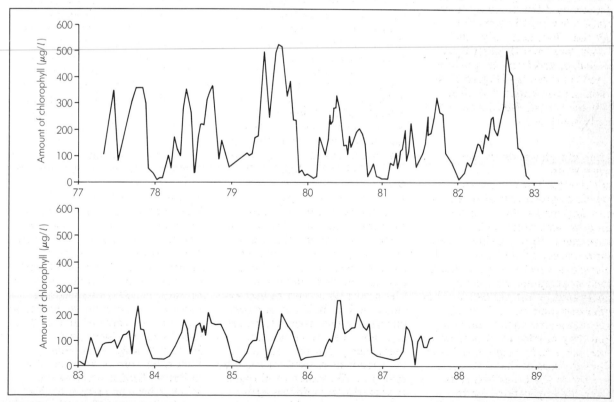

Figure 4 Barton Broad: chlorophyll

phosphorus still remains high in the Broad, despite the changes in the catchment.

Average phosphorus concentrations in Barton Broad were greater than those in the inflow, suggesting that a further source of phosphorus was present. It was subsequently found that the mud in the Broad contained a considerable amount of phosphorus which was being released into the overlying water.

Sediments and their stores of phosphorus

For many years the sediment of Barton Broad has absorbed phosphorus from the water. However, as its absorption capacity was exceeded, phosphorus in the mud became available. This residual load is now apparently preventing the Broad from recovering. The mechanism controlling this release of phosphorus is currently being investigated, and it may be possible to reduce or prevent the release of phosphorus by the addition of chemicals such as ferric sulphate to the lake sediments. However, the effectiveness of this is awaiting further research. At present the only way to overcome the problem is to remove the sediment.

Sediment removal

The effectiveness of sediment removal as a solution to the problem of the release of phosphorus was tested at Cockshoot Broad. This Broad was dammed off from the adjacent River Bure in 1982 and the top layers of sediment were pumped out by a suction dredger. The results of this experiment by the Broads Authority were compared with those from Alderfen Broad which was also isolated from an enriched source of water, but in this case phosphorus-laden mud was left undisturbed.

At Cockshoot Broad up to one metre of phosphorus-rich mud was removed, and the effect of this can be seen in Figure 6. This

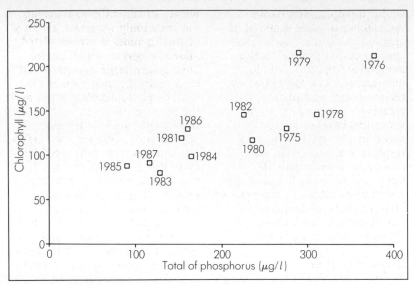

Figure 5 Barton Broad: phytoplankton versus phosphorus

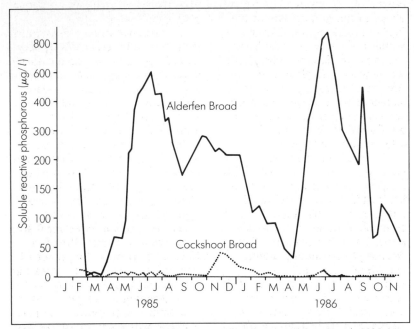

Figure 6 Comparison of soluble phosphorus in Alderfen and Cockshoot Broads 1985–86

graph compares the levels of soluble phosphorus in the water of the two Broads for the years 1985 and 1986. Significantly higher levels can be seen in Alderfen Broad, reflecting release of phosphorus from the sediments. In Cockshoot Broad the levels were very low and, as a result, the growth of phytoplankton was considerably less. The recovery of water weeds, in-

itially slower because the majority of viable seeds had been removed during the suction dredging, has, however, been sustained, and a more varied plant community has developed. The forecast for Cockshoot Broad is now good.

The isolation of Alderfen Broad in 1979 was followed by a period of rapid development of one particular water weed, hornwort (*Ceratophyllum demersum*), whilst phytoplankton declined. As the amount of plant material increased, the surface sediments became de-oxygenated as this material started to break down in mid-summer, and this triggered the release of phosphorus. The increasing concentration in the water itself triggered a resurgence in phytoplankton, which resulted in a decline in the growth of water weeds. The future for Alderfen Broad is now uncertain because the reservoir of phosphorus is fuelling the continued growth of algae and therefore inhibiting recovery.

Biomanipulation

Research has shown that although water weeds dominate under conditions of low nutrient status and algae normally dominate at the higher range, both can exist within the levels of phosphorus found in the Broads today. Both water weed and algae communities are also resistant to change, stabilised by a number of mechanisms which need to be disturbed if a switch from one to another is to take place.

Although the phosphorus concentrations have been reduced to levels where water weeds can exist, Barton Broad is still dominated by phytoplankton. In contrast, experiments with small ponds have demonstrated that, despite phytoplankton adding considerable quantities of nutrients, ponds do not lose their water weeds. Add fish to these ponds and there is a loss of water weeds, and an increase in phytoplankton rapidly takes place. A central role in this mechanism is played by the water fleas (Daphnia species).

For a short period during June, water fleas form large populations. These animals filter the water to obtain their food. At the peak of their population they can filter the entire volume of Barton Broad three times a day. Under these conditions the little animals can rapidly remove phytoplankton and create clear water, which is the explanation of the commonly observed 'clearing' of small ponds. However, shortly after this period, small fish fry have grown large enough to eat these animals; their capacity to remove phytoplankton is lost and the water once again becomes dominated by phytoplankton.

In a lake dominated by underwater plants the feeding efficiency of fish fry is reduced and the water fleas survive, continuing to reduce the phytoplankton and creating conditions more suitable for the plants to grow. The plants also require phosphorus and will absorb significant quantities from the water, reducing the amount available to phytoplankton. In contrast, in a weedless lake, any phosphorus will support additional phytoplankton growth.

A lake containing a substantial growth of submerged plants may be able to maintain these plants due to the mechanisms described above. However, a lake already dominated by phytoplankton, such as the Broads, will not automatically change. If the effect of fish predation on the large water flea (Daphnia) species were reduced by artificially removing the fish, it might be possible for plants to re-establish in a period of much greater water clarity.

To test this an experiment was carried out in Barton Broad in 1987. Pens (1 m × 2 m) made of a very small mesh were placed in the Broad. A variety of plants were placed into the pens and into a similar area outside the pens. A check was made to ensure that no fish were present inside the pens, and regular observations of plant growth, water flea numbers and chlorophyll concentrations were made. Water flea populations inside the pens reached much higher numbers than in the open water immediately outside, almost certainly a result of less fish predation. Inside the pens plant growth was found to be luxuriant, whereas outside the pens no growth could be observed.

The experiment demonstrated that in the shallower areas around the edge of the Broad it should be possible to provide conditions suitable for plant growth if zooplankton numbers can be increased. Clearly the permanent removal of fish from a large Broad would be both undesirable and impossible to achieve. However, the temporary removal of the breeding stock from smaller isolated Broads may provide a window of low phytoplankton growth and, combined with a large-scale planting exercise, may allow the desired change in community structure to take place. Alternatively, in larger sites, connected to the river where external phosphorus loads have been reduced, it might be possible to build much larger fish exclosures to enable plant colonisation to occur.

In 1986 Anglian Water began to remove phosphorus from large sewage treatment plants discharging to the River Bure. This has reduced the phosphorus load in the upper reaches of the River Bure, and some of the Broads in this area are beginning to show marked changes in phytoplankton abundance.

This is the essential first step to the restoration of the Broads situated on this river. In many of these Broads it will also be necessary to control the release of phosphorus from the sediment by chemical methods or by sediment removal and to manipulate the grazing pressure exerted by the large zooplankton through fish abundance. One small lake, Belaugh Broad, has already received this combination of treatments and a much larger one will be treated in 1989 in order to restore a more diverse and interesting community of plants and animals.

Source: The Broads Plan, Broads Authority, Norwich

My notes on the Norfolk Broads case study

To David Brewster, who works for the East Anglian Water Authority, it is important as a wetland area – that is the way he comes to it. Then he tells us where it is – its location – and he hints at its ecosystem – wildlife and use by people.

A bit of history

In the first paragraph he gives a bit of history – flooded peat diggings – interesting – one of the effects of a change in sea level – so it really happens now and again. He's italicised *clear water* to give his readers a hint about its importance, because that is the big change. This clear water had lots of water weeds and other life and sometimes the water weeds got a bit too happy – so we cut them back, managed them for the good of the boaters. That's how I read the paragraph. That is the story so far.

His heading is handy – The Norfolk Broads: wetlands under threat – as it alerts us to the fact that it has changed and he is going to tell us how. OK, get brain ready for picking out changes and perhaps reasons for the changes.

Aha, today the water is turbid, not clear, murky. Figure 2 shows the time (early to mid-1970s) of the dramatic decrease – quite recent really, I think to myself. No, he doesn't give reasons, he goes back to tell us how important water weeds were for sheltering smaller things with big names. (I am not a biologist.)

On to causes

Now he comes on to causes – the heading gives us the help to see where he is going, and I put in my notes, 'Why did the weeds disappear?' That simply raises another question further down which I think he could have put in as a heading for the next paragraph. 'What causes lack of light and excess phytoplankton?' It is too much nitrogen and phosphorus – from agriculture – causing phytoplankton/algae to grow. What can be done? Can we control nitrogen, phosphorus? Phosphorus, yes, how? In a treatment plant, chemical reaction.

As a result of my early skimming of the study, I know that we are going to get the story of some experiments now. It is very interesting to see how the case study is an account of the scientific method. I mean the process by which we set up an hypothesis. Eutrophication, the growth of algae in murky water, might be due to too much phosphorus. That is the first hypothesis – so we experiment by changing the variable, phosphorus, and see what happens.

What was the experiment?

Right, so let's find out about the experiment and make more notes. What was the experiment? We get the detail of the stages. Essentially, the supply of phosphorus was cut to a minimum by diversion of effluent and chemical treatment of effluent. But the phytoplankton stays. Help! The hypothesis is not upheld. What else is going on, we have to ask ourselves? David Brewster tells of the next stage in the thinking and the experiment. The scientists measure the amount of phosphorus coming in (they know that has been reduced) and the amount in the Broad. There is still a lot of phosphorus and chlorophyll (phytoplankton) in the Broad. Why? Is there another source of phosphorus which has not been turned off? Exactly, yes, and it is stored in the mud. And when the mud cannot store any more, the phosphorus stays in the water.

Now we get detail on how it might be possible to control the release of phosphorus chemically, but this needs more research. In the meantime, remove the mud. Seems a good idea, a good hypothesis. So we get the details of that experiment. At Cockshoot Broad, mud is dredged and water weeds come back. More complicated story in Alderfen Broad where mud left undisturbed – ugh, lots of details and connections. How does it all fit together? Let's have a try.

In Alderfen Broad with its phosphorus-laden mud undisturbed, a water weed comes back and phytoplankton declines. But in mid-summer a chemical effect of plants on surface water (de-oxygenation) triggers release of phosphorus, more phytoplankton grows and water weed declines.

The story continues, however. Slight complication is that both algae (phytoplankton) and water weeds can exist in the phosphorus levels present now. And now there the phytoplankton tends to stay even in reduced phosphorus levels – a good example of inertia perhaps.

The scientists keep on experimenting and ask another question. It has been noticed that small ponds, *without* fish but with phosphorus added, do not lose their water weeds. Put in fish as well and water weeds *do* disappear. Aha! So what have fish to do with the interactions in the ecosystem? Well, it's more to do with fleas than fish. (It is getting awfully detailed!)

Water fleas filter water, keep it clear, and phytoplankton goes for a period, mid-June. The ponds 'clear'. When small fish grow bigger, they eat the water fleas and the phytoplankton returns. If a lake has underwater plants, the fish fry don't eat as many water fleas, and since the plants also absorb some phosphorus, water weeds grow. So where a lake still has underwater weeds, fish and fleas, water weeds may survive but in the Broads phytoplankton had taken over.

Small pens with plants were placed in Barton Broad in 1987. No fish in the pens. Lots of fleas counted inside the pens and lots of plant growth. We are nearing the end now, and David Brewster suggests that in shallower areas of the Broads it might be possible to remove fish breeding stock temporarily and/or build fish exclosures and let weeds get established.

The Anglian Authority is continuing its phosphorus removal programme!

Quite a story there, and quite a large amount of concentration needed to pick out the plot and its main points (Figure 7). It is a story about cleaning algae out, and letting the water weeds back in. The main characters are phosphorus in water, phosphorus stored in mud, water fleas and fish. And it's taken me something like four hours to read, re-read and write this out for you. Understanding people/environment relationships is hard work!

Strategies

In the short quotations given from the research about student 'D's' reading of a text, we get the impression of headings being helpful and of the student searching for points to latch on to. It is also important to skim paragraphs for their main points and try to see how the different points are connected. Then you have to read each paragraph several times, concentrating hard. In the end it is practice doing this which makes for improvement. In other words, it is a reading and comprehension skill, and the more we do it, the faster and better we become. We have of course also to be interested in the subject matter. (And just because it is tough work, don't say it is boring. That word is a great camouflage for 'I don't want to make the effort'.)

What makes the Broads story so interesting to me is that it adds to my general knowledge and impression of the Broads and their deterioration because of algae, onwards to an understanding of experiments (playing with one variable and then another). These give us an understanding of the process going on between amount of light, weed and algae growth, chemicals, fish, fleas...

In order to make my notes, I latched on to one experiment and then another as likely to be significant, because years of education had given me a hunch that experiments are important and give us facts and further ideas. The experiments give us the overall structure of the unfolding story. They are the chapters of the story with a different character/variable featuring more prominently in each chapter.

I can't say much more to try to share my process of note-taking with you. We know it isn't easy. Good luck. First skim, then look for headings and points, re-read, concentrate, get the structure, get

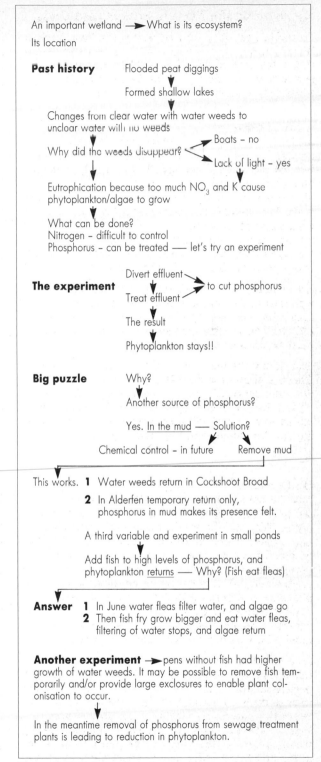

Figure 7 Norfolk Broads – notes

the detail in the structure! In time your style will develop. It won't be the same as mine, but there will be parallels.

1

Coastal management

Robert Prosser, Rosalind and Nicholas Foskett

Waves pounding the sea front at Portleven, Cornwall

Coastlines are extremely attractive to people – for homes, work and play – and so illustrate vividly the complex interactions between humans and environment. Perhaps nowhere else do human and physical energies confront each other so starkly. Along this strip where the ocean meets the land, the power of nature's forces is constantly displayed before us, for instance, waves pounding a cliff, or moving the sand beneath our feet as we walk along a beach. Humans bring all their power of technology to bear on building homes, seawalls, harbours, barrages, resorts and so on. There is growing evidence that we can be careless in our use of this precious meeting point between land and sea. There is evidence, too, that the oceans make us pay for our carelessness!

Seeds of destruction sown by clifftop developments

COASTAL developments can cause the destruction of properties up to half a mile distant, an engineering geologist said.

A study by Dr Peter Grainger and Patrick Kalaugher, of Exeter University, for district councils in Devon recommends a requirement for a geological investigation as part of the assessment of coastal planning applications.

Mr Kalaugher said that their studies had shown that if a developer stopped the movement of a stretch of cliff prone to a landslide, it could remove the source of material washed up on a beach elsewhere – and the loss of that beach could cause the cliffs there to be undermined and clifftop properties lost.

The research looked at the risk posed by the potential loss of land from clifftops, and the danger to people on the beach below, to produce 'hazard' maps for routing footpaths and the siting of warnings.

Mr Kalaugher said that even developments not requiring planning permission could pose a serious threat. Septic tanks and swimming pools were a particular risk because they could alter the groundwater regime and cliff stability.

Source: Independent, 9 January 1988

Managing the coastline

What do we mean by management? One straightforward definition of 'management' is the organised allocation of resources according to a set of rational principles and criteria. This implies that along the coastal zone, where there is intense competition, there is an acute need for management policies to establish priorities. The case studies in this chapter, taken from the USA, Scotland and Jersey, explore this process of decision-taking. They are intended to develop three fundamental understandings about environmental management:

- Policies should be based upon a thorough understanding of environmental character and processes.
- Policies are based upon a balance between conservation and development. In any individual policy, this balance will vary, according to certain identifiable priorities.
- A specific policy can be understood by examining the decision-making process, and the perceptions and values of the key decision-makers.

You could evaluate each of the following case studies on the basis of the three points listed above.

The beaches of Southern California – a special case for treatment

California has some of the most famous and beautiful stretches of coastline in the world. As this coastline becomes ever more developed, and the hazards associated with this development become better understood, the need for comprehensive management has become urgent. One result has been the setting-up, in 1981, of the *Coast of California Storm and Tidal Waves Study* (CCSTWS). The study, likely to take at least twenty years, is being carried out by the US Corps of Engineers and administered by the California Coastal Commission. The goal is to provide a comprehensive data base and understanding of coastal energies and processes along the 1700 km of the California coastline, divided into six regions. The first region to be studied has been the San Diego region in the south (Figure 1). This was given priority because of the intensity of human activity and because it has 'a long history of shoreline erosion, and suffered $116 million in damages during the severe winter storms of 1982–83 (CCSTWS, *Annual Report*, 1987, p. 7).

The study is based upon the identification of functional units along the coastline. These are called *littoral cells*, and operate as shown in Figure 2. Each cell is an open system: energy and materials enter the cell (*inputs*),

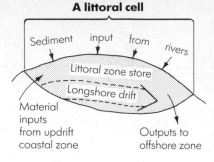

A littoral cell

Figure 2 How a littoral cell operates

move through and are stored in the cell (*stores*), and finally leave the cell (*outputs*). This is clearly a valuable framework within which coastal management policies can be developed. If these inputs, stores and outputs can be measured along a particular stretch of coast, then statements can be made about what is happening at present, and forecasts made about future characteristics. For example, if inputs of sand to a beach store exceed the outputs from the beach, that is, more sand arrives than is removed, then the beach will grow (*aggrade*). If removal of sand exceeds arrival of sand, then the beach will shrink (*degrade*). Further, ongoing measurements may reveal several rhythms in the behaviour of a cell, for instance beach store aggradation in the summer, followed by degradation during the winter, as the character of the predominant waves changes.

The essential data base for each littoral cell is the *sediment budget* (Figure 3): how much sediment enters the cell and where from (*inputs*); how much moves through the cell and how quickly (*stores* and *processes*); how much leaves the cell and where it goes to (*outputs*). If these stores and movements can be measured, then the 'bank account' or budget balance can be calculated. For Southern Californians, this is vital information, as they fear that their glorious beaches may be disappearing.

?

1 In what ways does the beach profile for Torrey Pines State Beach (Figure 4) support Californians' fears that their beaches may be disappearing?

2 Carefully read 'Are the beaches really disappearing?', the 1987 statement by the Coastal Commission, and summarise whether they feel the fears are justified.

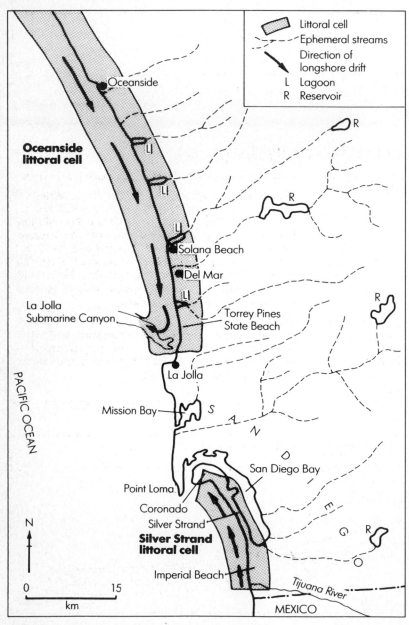

Figure 1 The San Diego region

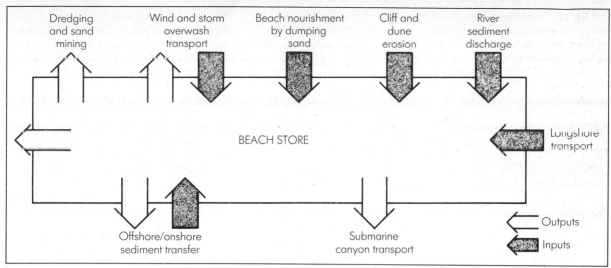

Figure 3   Sediment budget for a littoral cell: a basic model

Are the beaches really disappearing?

Recently, articles in *Time* and in *Oceans* have suggested that beach erosion has reached crisis stage in many areas. According to *Time* 82% of California's beaches are eroding at a rate of from 6 inches to 2 feet per year.

This gloomy picture is not supported by CCSTWS, at least in the San Diego region. CCSTWS Project Manager Tom Dolan: 'In southern California, the beach width has not changed significantly over the last century, except for beaches directly affected by human activity, for example, Oceanside and Coronado'.

CCSTWS' review of historic shoreline change showed that about 80% of the beaches in LA, Orange and San Diego counties have experienced accretion rather than erosion since 1875. This generally positive picture is partly the result of sound coastal engineering and beach nourishment projects. The beaches at Newport and Coronado are

good examples of stable, well-engineered beach projects.

What about the eroding beaches, such as Oceanside, Sunset Cliffs, Imperial Beach, and Sunset-Seal Beach? What about cliff erosion and failure at San Clemente and Del Mar? Here, the problem has often been development without careful consideration of coastal impacts. Over-watering of lawns on clifftops is causing much of the cliff failure in Southern California. At Oceanside, the wartime harbour construction was completed without time to thoroughly consider coastal impacts.

What does the future hold? Generally slow erosion is likely, as development inland chokes off sediment flow to the coast. But, according to Tom Dolan, 'we can probably solve this problem using CCSTWS data to develop sound coastal engineering programs'.

Source: CCSTWS, *Annual Report*, 1987, p. 13. US Army, Corps of Engineers, Coastal Resources Branch, Los Angeles

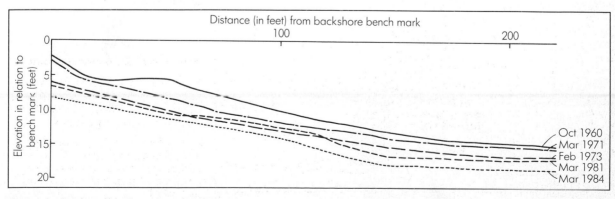

Figure 4   Beach profiles, Torrey Pines State Reserve

The Silver Strand littoral cell

This cell (Figure 5) extends northwards for 25 km from south of the US/Mexico border to the entrance to San Diego Bay (Figure 6). South of the border, the shoreline consists of a narrow beach backed by sandstone cliffs. These end at the Tijuana River delta. From this delta northwards there is an unbroken line of sandy beaches which are the front edge of a crenulate spit which has been progressively extended northwards across San Diego Bay (Figure 7).

Greater San Diego has a population of at least one and a half million, its prosperity founded upon the enormous bay sheltered by the sand spit. It is a military base, commercial port, industrial city and holiday resort. The Silver Strand spit is a mixture of homes, military installations, hotels and holiday apartments, State beaches and ecological reserves. (NB The 'Coronado' and 'Imperial Beach' mentioned in the Coastal Commission statement are both within the Silver Strand cell.)

Figure 6 San Diego Bay

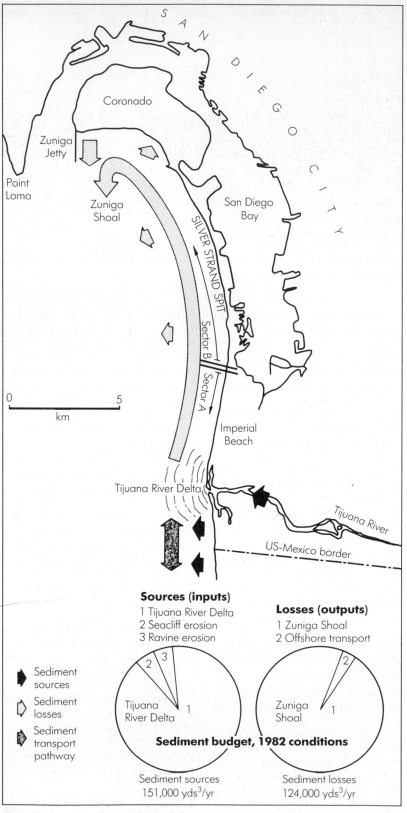

Figure 5 The Silver Strand littoral cell

Figure 7 View of San Diego Bay from Point Loma

Using historical sources (maps, photos, written accounts) and modern survey data, engineers have built up the story of the Silver Strand cell since 1851. Figure 5 shows how this cell functions. The main findings are:

1 The sand spit is slowly changing its shape. In the northern two-thirds it is aggrading and advancing (Sector B on Figure 5), while in the southern one-third it is degrading and retreating (Sector A on Figure 5). The engineers suggest that this may be caused by a minor shift in the angle of wave approach.

2 The main source of sediment is the Tijuana River. Under natural conditions, infrequent floods caused by storms over the catchment basin deposited their sediment load across the river delta. This delta accounts for at least 90% of the sediment input to the Silver Strand cell.

3 Today, there are four major dams across the Tijuana River. At least 70% of all sediment is deposited in the reservoirs behind these dams, and so no longer reaches the Tijuana delta. Net transport northwards from the delta sediment store is about 1.22 million m^3 but the sediment input from the river is only about 1.07 million m^3. Thus the delta is being overdrawn by approximately 150,000 m^3 a year. A 1988 Coastal Commission report states: 'The delta resources are sufficient to sustain such a loss for a period of only fifty years, but depreciation of this resource may lead to a long-term net loss of sediment to the cell.' (*Source*: CCSTWS, *Annual Report*, 1988, p. 18.)

4 The beaches of the northern half of San Diego Bay, for instance Silver Strand State Beach and Coronado Beach, were much narrower until the 1930s. Between 1933 and 1960, some 26.76 million m^3 of sand were dumped on the beaches, largely from dredging works inside San Diego Bay and the building of Zuniga Jetty. This artificial beach nourishment was a useful boost to tourism and acted as a storm barrier. Thus the beach at Coronado shown in Figure 6 is more than twice as broad as it was sixty years ago. (Incidentally, the beach scenes in the film 'Some Like It Hot', although supposedly in Florida, were shot on the newly widened Coronado Beach and with the Hotel del Coronado in the background.)

5 Most sediment loss from the cell is to the offshore sea-bed west of Zuniga Jetty. This jetty, when first built during the 1950s, did cause some beach aggradation to the immediate south, but it also accelerates the curving offshore drift, thereby increasing the energy for sediment removal.

6 Shoreline changes occur dramatically at infrequent intervals, energised by major winter storms. For instance, in the winter of 1982–83, at least 25% of the beach sediment store was removed from the northern beaches, that is, millions of cubic metres. At Imperial Beach, in the south, the backshore berm, the sand ridge at the top of the beach, retreated by as much as nine metres. Some of this material was redeposited offshore and has been available for transportation by waves back to the beach. In addition, major artificial nourishment schemes (1983–86) returned the beaches to almost their former size.

As an aid to writing a report for a local Californian newspaper about the Silver Strand littoral cell, answer the following questions.

1 Suggest possible reasons for the building of Zuniga Jetty.

2 Summarise how the Silver Strand cell works under natural conditions in terms of its sediment budget.

3 In what ways have human activities modified the functioning and sediment budget of the Silver Strand cell?

4 Does the research by the CCSTWS of the Silver Strand cell support or reject the fears that southern California's beaches are under threat?

Coastal erosion and property protection in San Diego County, California

Along the Oceanside littoral cell (Figure 1) the situation is different, but again based on the sediment budget. Much of the coastline is bounded by stretches of cliffs broken by marshy lagoons where non-permanent rivers reach the sea (Figure 8). These have been the main sediment source for the beaches which have protected the cliffs

from all but major storms. River controls have reduced the sediment input to the cell from 270,000 m³ a year to less than 180,000 m³. Sediment outputs via the La Jolla and Scripps submarine canyons have been measured at 200,000 m³ a year. This budget deficit is causing beaches to shrink (look again at Figure 4, for the Torrey Pines Beach is in the Oceanside cell). In turn, the cliffs are coming under increased direct wave attack, and cliff retreat is accelerating.

1 Where cliffs back the beach, and the beach store is degrading, what changes are likely in the relationship between the cliffs and the waves? Set out your answer in the form of labelled diagrams.

2 Why might this change help to increase the supply of sediment for the beach?

The problem

Del Mar is one of a series of beach communities dotting the coastline north of San Diego (Figure 1). They grew as small resorts during the 1920–40 period, but have been transformed by the

post–1960 population explosion into fashionable holiday, retirement and commuter settlements.

Seascape Chateau Condominiums are typical of this development boom. As they were built before the strengthened planning regulations of the 1976 California Coastal Act, they were set back only eight metres from the cliff top. The marvellous sea views from the top of the 25-metre cliffs helped to sell the properties, but then came the unusually strong storms of the 1982–83 winter, and the residents suddenly found themselves *too* close to the cliff edge! The severe storms and high tides resulted in the erosion of the beach sand to near bedrock levels. This removal of the sand beach allowed direct wave impact against the toe of the cliffs. As the cliff materials are poorly-consolidated gravel beds, sandstones and silts broken by joint systems, undercutting and the gouging of sea-caves take place readily, causing cliff collapse (Figure 9). As a planning report said: 'Such obvious erosion, which is the natural process of coastal cliff retreat, sparks concern among cliff-top residents, that their homes may be threatened.' (Coastal Commission, September 1983.)

The response to the hazard by the property owners

The owners of the condominiums organised themselves into the Seascape Chateau Homeowners Association. Their first action was to employ engineering consultants to assess the danger. Two reports confirmed the problem: 'The sea cave underlying the Seascape Chateau property failed in early March 1983 and since that time the coastal cliff has made a major adjustment in its profile. The setback of the building from the clifftop has decreased to as little as about four metres.' A report in September 1983 stated:

Figure 8 Southern California: coast marshes and headland

Figure 9 Unprotected cliffs at Del Mar, February 1989. Notice the weak strata, the sea caves and the cliff which shows active wave impacts. Notice too how close the buildings are to the cliff top.

The role of the Coastal Commission

The Coastal Commission has the job of approving, rejecting or modifying planning applications. They take their decisions within the framework of the laws and policies of the State of California, in particular the 1976 Coastal Act, and the County of San Diego Coastal Management regulations.

For example, the *California Coastal Act* has a basic goal to 'protect, maintain and, where feasible, enhance and restore the overall quality of the coastal zone environment and its natural and manmade resources'. However, 'seawalls and cliff-retaining walls

'Erosion at the base of the cliff is evidenced by undercutting, sea caves and block falls. Rain and surface runoff has rilled, gullied and channelled the upper cliff face. Localised slumping and human foot traffic are also evident. The collapse of the sea cave has resulted in slumping of the upper surface and encroachment of the upper cliff into the level pad area in front of the existing building. The foundations for the building are currently in danger of being undermined.'

The reports also noted that increased infiltration from regular watering of the lawns and gardens of the cliff-top properties was further weakening the cliff materials.

The Homeowners Association then asked the engineers to design a solution, based on the reports. The design was a vertical concrete seawall along the toe of the cliff, fronted by a broad pile of boulders. This boulder barrier, called *riprap*, is a common technique used to dissipate the energy of the storm waves and so reduce the impact on the seawall. It seemed a straightforward answer to their problems, so the Association submitted a planning application to the Coastal Commission (Figure 10).

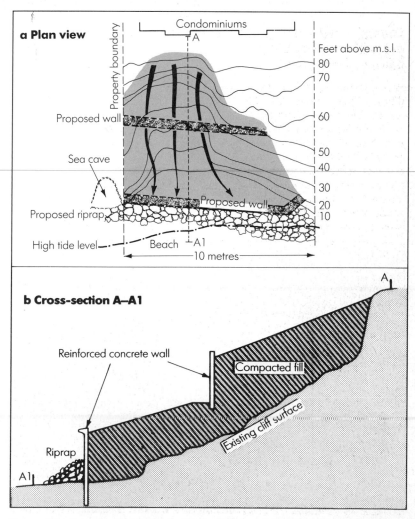

Figure 10 Seascape Chateau Condominiums. Cliff slumping and original planning proposal

shall be permitted where required to protect existing structures in danger of erosion when designed to minimise adverse impacts on local shoreline sand supplies'.

For example, *County of San Diego*: 'The County has a dual concern with reference to the coastal cliffs. On the one hand it is concerned about retention of the cliffs in their natural state for the scenic enjoyment of the public. On the other hand it is concerned about the right of property owners to protect their property against erosion.'

The response of the Coastal Commission

As they examined the planning application, the Coastal Commission officials asked three basic questions:

1 Is there really a serious hazard?

2 If the answer to **1** is **yes**, then is there an alternative to a seawall?

3 If the answer to **2** is **no**, then is the proposed seawall designed as well as possible to conform to the law and policy guidelines?

In this case, the Coastal Commission said – 'Yes, there is a hazard,' and 'No, there is no alternative to a seawall.' However, they did not like the concrete seawall with its large riprap, and so rejected the application, but with suggestions for an alternative.

Why they did not approve the first design (see Figure 10)

1 The vertical concrete wall and high riprap were visually intrusive.

2 The riprap was up to ten metres wide and six metres high, and across the beach to below mean sea level, and so would be on public-access land.

---

3 The wall and riprap would alter shoreline processes, cause waves to steepen and remove part of the beach. This would further affect the size of the public beach, and cause problems for the surrounding properties.

4 The ends of the seawall were poorly designed and would have caused increased cliff erosion on neighbouring properties.

An acceptable compromise

The engineering consultants, taking into account the advice of the Coastal Commission, designed an alternative. It was more expensive and, in the long term, may require strengthening because of the absence of riprap, but the Homeowners Association accepted it, and planning permission was granted in 1984. Figures 11 and 12 sum up the design.

1 Write a brief report to the Homeowners Association, stating why you, on behalf of the California Coastal Commission, reject the original proposal shown in Figure 10. Set out your statement in terms of the five areas of concern listed on page 22.

2 Study the revised design carefully from Figures 11 and 12, and write an article for the *San Diego Union* newspaper, under the headline – 'Latest Del Mar cliff plan gets the go-ahead'.

Figure 11 (top) The Seascape Chateau Condominiums seawall, February 1989. Notice the absence of riprap, except on the left where the entrance to the sea cave on the neighbouring property is protected.

Figure 12 (bottom) A neighbouring seawall completed a few years earlier. The landscaping is more mature and illustrates how the designers intend that the visual impact of the Seascape wall will reduce over time.

The carrying capacity of sandy coastlines

Sand dunes or flattish expanses of sand are common along coastlines with environmental conditions like those shown in Figure 14. They are an important resource, ecologically, scenically and economically, but are sensitive, fragile environments, as the Nature Conservancy Council (NCC) recognise.

'Sand dunes make an important contribution to many sand beaches. The key to successful development is to use the ecosystem sustainably, that is to alter but not destroy its natural balance.'

Source: Nature Conservancy Council, Data Support for Education Service

These beach systems are clearly the result of a long-term sediment budget surplus, where constructive processes outweigh destructive processes. The basic requirements are, firstly, strong prevailing onshore winds to provide the energy for transportation, and, secondly, an ample supply of sand across the backshore beach above the high-water mark (HWM), or across a broad foreshore where there is time between high tides for the surface layers to dry out.

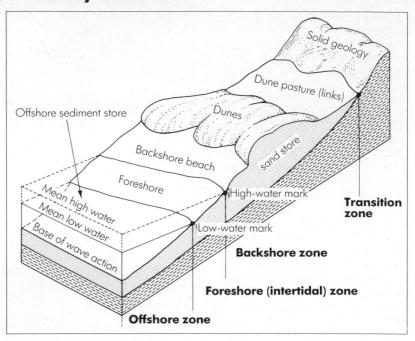

Figure 13   The coastal environment: a low coast example

Figure 14   Sand dunes on North Uist, Outer Hebrides

?

1   Why do the required environmental conditions for the creation of sand dunes help to explain that at least 60% of Britain's 56,000 hectares of sand dunes are found fringing the north and west coasts?

Breaker types

Spilling breaker

This occurs when the potential and kinetic forms of energy are moving at the same speed. Wave form is maintained and the 'head' of foam continues to move shorewards along the crest front as the wave height decreases across the *surf zone* until it becomes *swash* (water dashing against the beach). This type of wave tends to occur when long, swell waves advance over a gentle offshore slope (Figure 15a).

Plunging breaker

This occurs when kinetic energy accelerates the forward motion of the water particles to a velocity greater than the potential energy moving the wave form, that is, the water mass overtakes the wave form. The crest of the wave curls into the trough, enclosing a pocket of air, causing rebound and an 'explosion' from the pressure. It occurs most commonly when long, fairly steep waves roll across a relatively steep shoaling zone (Figure 15b).

Surging breaker

This occurs when the potential energy moves the wave form faster than the kinetic energy moving the water particles forward. The base of the wave

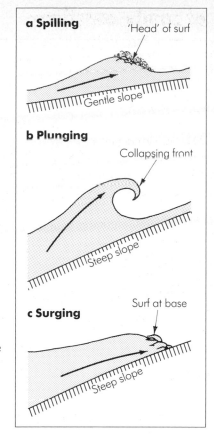

a Spilling — 'Head' of surf — Gentle slope

b Plunging — Collapsing front — Steep slope

c Surging — Surf at base — Steep slope

Figure 15   Breaker types

surges up the beach and the crest collapses and disappears. It is most common on steep beach slopes (Figure 15c).

The net sediment budget surplus is most likely to be achieved where *spilling waves* predominate, especially where long swell waves sweep up a gentle offshore slope. Yet high-energy *plunging waves*, driven destructively on to the foreshore zone, degrading the beach profile, are responsible for building storm ridges, or berms, on the backshore above the normal HWM (Figure 13). When the berm store dries out, it acts as an important source of sand for the dunes and in turn for the links or machair zone. The machair zone is the area of blown sand that is inland from the beach and dunes. It is partially or totally covered with grass and is an important source of grazing.

Adding humans to the beach system

In the case studies which follow, from Scotland and Jersey, it is useful to bear in mind these two understandings:

● Coastal environments vary widely in their ability to absorb human activity, i.e. their *carrying capacity* varies.

● Whether the environmental impacts of human activity are considered as positive or negative may depend upon the perceptions and attitudes of those making the judgements.

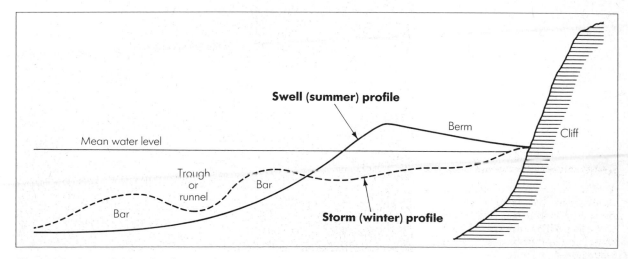

Swell (summer) profile

Mean water level

Trough or runnel

Bar

Bar

Berm

Cliff

Storm (winter) profile

Figure 16   Seasonal shifts in beach energy form
Source: P. D. Komar, *Beach Processes and Sedimentation,* © 1976, p. 289. Reprinted by permission of Prentice Hall, Inc., Englewood Cliffs, New Jersey

Achmelvich beach, near Lochinver, Sutherland

Achmelvich beach, on the Scottish mainland, faces west towards the Atlantic Ocean. It is an exposed site, in a bay between rocky headlands. Unlike in the model shown in Figure 13 there is no dune zone, for an extensive machair begins immediately above the backshore. Inland from the machair, the boundary zone of bare, rugged hills rises sharply (Figure 17).

The local crofters have for centuries used their grazing rights on the machair. At the traditional, fairly low stocking densities, the sheep and cattle played a crucial role in maintaining the machair ecosystem. Their nibbling, and the organic manure they dropped, helped to sustain a vigorous, unbroken sward of turf. This protects the existing sand, helps to trap newly-arrived sand, prevents drying out and reduces wind blow. Thus the machair surface is gradually aggraded. Up to a certain stocking density, grazing actually improves the resilience of the sward.

Beyond this limit, however, the continuous surface mat of turf may be broken and the environment suddenly looks very fragile. The animals' teeth begin to tear at the base of the plants, and their hooves loosen and then break up the surface. Despite a decline in the number of crofters, such overstocking has been encouraged by government and EC Less-Favoured Area subsidies for hill sheep and cattle.

Figure 18 shows a stretch of machair in danger of disintegration. As the surface breaks up, material is easily removed by wind and rainwash. Removal begins to exceed supply of sand and the machair store is progressively degraded. This process has been accelerated by the increase in tourism (Figure 19).

Figure 17 Western Barra, Outer Hebrides, looking south

Figure 18 The edge of a blowout in the machair

'Visitors to Achmelvich during the 1950s will recount how they arrived in summer, with caravans, to park almost alone on a magnificent open machair, overlooking white sand and blue sea. By August 1970, 150 units were counted on the same machair.'

Source: Countryside Commission for Scotland, *Highland Beach Management Project, 1977–79*, 1980, p. 8

As with animal grazing, there seems to be a critical threshold to usage, beyond which the machair system begins to break down. Note that, unlike grazing, recreation impact tends to be uneven, being particularly intense
a at access points and
b along the most direct routes to the beach.

The problem of carrying capacity summarised

'From the late 1950s onwards the combination of easy accessibility, high scenic quality and shelter attracted increasing tourist use, mainly in the form of caravanning on the machair around the beach. Little control was exercised on this caravanning, and the freedom which visitors had to drive almost at will across the machair resulted in the trampling of a number of tracks, parts of which developed into blow-outs. Almost certainly some erosional features had developed before the advent of tourism, but there is little doubt that erosion was aggravated by trampling damage caused by wheels and feet. In addition, sanitary arrangements and arrangements for the disposal of litter were inadequate, and many visitors resorted to the burial in the machair of both refuse and the contents of chemical toilets. This not only had the effect of further weakening the machair sward but also led to health hazards ... Thus the twin problems of erosion damage and health hazards emerged from the pattern of intensive and almost unmanaged use.'

Source: A. S. Mather and W. Ritchie, *The Beaches of the Highlands and Islands of Scotland*, Countryside Commission for Scotland, 1978, p. 116

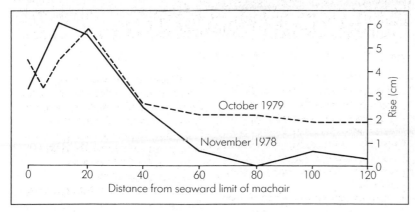

Figure 19 The impact of tourism in the machair zone, Achmelvich Bay

Figure 20 Rise in the machair surface since August 1978
Source: Countryside Commission for Scotland, *Highland Management Project 1977–79*, p. 19

1 One of the critical factors in the working of the beach environment system is the re-vegetation of eroding machair. Use Figure 20 to suggest how the management plan aims to re-establish a continuous grass cover, and how this will affect the working of the system.

2 In August 1978, a re-seeding programme was carried out on bare areas. In what ways do the graphs in Figure 20 tell us whether this has been a success?

3 As a review exercise to check your understanding, produce brief reports validating each of the following statements (systems and flow diagrams may help your reports):

- Vegetation is a sensitive indication of the functioning of the system, and the key to the maintenance of stability.

- The establishment, retention and management of vegetation is the cornerstone of conservation in this sand-based environment.

- Any conservation management strategy must permit the continued supply and movement of sand through the system.

- Relationships between the various environmental components are closest in the dune zone where plant life faces the greatest stresses from dryness and nutrient deficiency. These relationships decrease landwards across the machair as the ecosystem becomes more mature.

(Use standard textbooks as well as the materials in this chapter to help you.)

4 Use the passage 'The problem of carrying capacity summarised' and Figures 18 and 19 to suggest the ways in which recreational activity has affected the machair ecosystem.

5 Can you suggest why the machair might be able to withstand *either* the grazing *or* the tourists but is vulnerable to a combination of the two activity types?

Thus, the essential problem has been how to protect both the machair environment and the interests and livelihood of the local community. Most local people welcomed the growth of tourism as a potential source of income to supplement the meagre returns from crofting. Yet they began to realise that, under the uncontrolled situation, they made little profit from the tourists, while the machair on which their animals, and to some extent the tourism, depended, deteriorated.

As with so many environmental issues, *who* controlled the resources became a critical factor. The crofters, as tenants, were unable to carry out a management scheme, and no other body could do so while the land remained under the laws of crofting tenure. So, from 1971, Sutherland County Council negotiated with the crofters and the owner of the local estate, and in 1972, five hectares of the main stretches of deteriorating machair were taken over by the council. It then took until 1976 to produce the management scheme whose main elements are set out in Figure 21.

Les Mielles, Jersey

The west coast of Jersey and the region immediately inland has been designated as an Area of Special Interest (Figure 23). Much of it is unspoilt and wild, containing precious ecological resources. The landscape consists of a raised beach with accompanying sand dunes, backed by an impressive fossil cliffline (Figure 24). The sand dunes of Les Blanches Banques cover the southern part of Les Mielles and are among the most interesting in Western Europe. They have a rich and diverse wildlife, but in recent years they have come under increasing pressure from misuse by people.

The formation of the landscape here owes much to events which occurred during the last Ice Age. At that time much of Britain was glaciated several times and the sea level fluctuated as the ice formed and melted. At times, the ice advanced, sea levels fell and Jersey became an area of high land overlooking wide, grassy plains swept by icy winds. During the warmer inter-

Figure 22 Oyster catcher at the nest

glacials, the sea level rose, producing cliffs and beach formations which have since been abandoned. Les Mielles is an impressive example of an abandoned beach and cliffs, with the dunes of Les Blanches Banques lining the back of the raised beach.

In recent years the value of Les Mielles has been recognised and the States of Jersey (the island's parliament) has brought in legislation to allow the area to be properly managed, while the natural landscape is protected. There are many conflicting pressures on Les Mielles. In this section you will investigate what those pressures are and how the conflicts are being resolved.

Banning of casual parking

Stabilisation and reseeding programme on eroded machair

Two new caravan sites run by crofters, set back from machair frontage

Controlling of grazing and trampling by the use of fencing and agreements on stocking densities and seasons

Toilets and drainage

Car park for 60 vehicles, hidden in sand blowout

Wooden boardwalks to beach to prevent further gullying

Supervision by seasonal countryside ranger

Figure 21 Management scheme to re-vegetate the eroding machair

The background

Designation of Les Mielles as an Area of Special Interest, and a strategy for its future development, were finally agreed in 1978 by the States of Jersey. This followed nearly twenty years of study by committees and working parties (Planning Procedure p. 35). The proposed plan used the idea of land zoning. Areas of St Ouen's Bay have been set aside for different uses. Three categories of land use were chosen (recreation, conservation and agriculture) and measures are being taken to optimise the use of land within each zone.

The boundary of Les Mielles was fixed by the sea on one side and by the *view line* on the landward side. Special planning controls ensure that the view line is not broken by any building or development. Within this area the *green zone* indicates areas of particular landscape value.

?

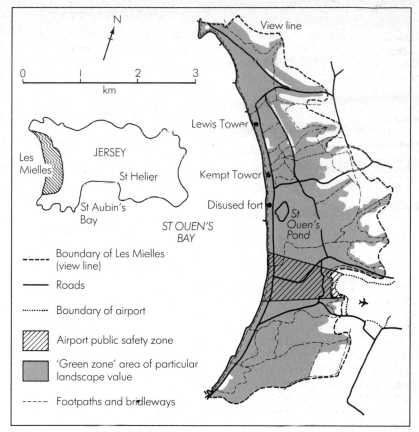

Figure 23 Location of Les Mielles
Source: Jersey States Planning Department

1 With reference to Figures 23 and 24 and the details of the planning procedure (p. 35), describe the likely reasons for designating Les Mielles as 'a special place'.

2 Explain the terms *view line* and *green zone*. What is the significance of each of these in the overall planning of Les Mielles?

The choices

It is a fact of life that in many parts of the British Isles ecological needs have come a poor second to economic development. The aim in Les Mielles is to allow multiple use of the area where possible, and to maintain a balance between recreation, economic use and conservation. The question is whether it is possible to create an environment where nearly every need is satisfied, while precious ecosystems and their rare flora and fauna are protected.

Figure 24 An aerial view of St Ouen's Bay

Activities in Les Mielles

FISHING   Fishing is available in St Ouen's Pond

SURFING   Excellent surfing from the central part of the beach

MOTORSPORT   Motorcycle scrambling occurs on the upper part of the dunes. Car and motorcycle events are held regularly on the beach in summer

ARCHAEOLOGY   Sites shown in Figure 26. **1** Les Monts Grantez – a neolithic passage grave. **2** Standing stones (menhirs) – neolithic monuments

AGRICULTURE   Some good grazing land is still available, but much of the marginal land lies neglected. Agricultural zones are areas where agriculture and horticulture will be encouraged. South and south-west facing slopes produce the earliest crops of potatoes

PICNICKING   Picnicking and sunbathing occur on the beach and in the more sheltered parts of the dunes when onshore winds are blowing

WALKING/ HORSERIDING   An extensive network of footpaths and bridleways exists. Trampling is a problem in delicate areas such as the dunes

BOTANY   The area is rich in plants, including the outstanding flora of the sand dunes (see p 31). The mild climate allows species common to the Mediterranean to grow here

FLY-TIPPING   Rubbish is often dumped in the holes left by sand excavation. This is a public nuisance, producing a visual impact and health hazard

GOLF   La Moye – eighteen-hole high-standard Par 3 course in the centre of the bay

BIRD-WATCHING   Diverse natural habitats support a variety of wild birds. Sand dunes, scrub, freshwater ponds and the shore provide rich feeding grounds and secure breeding sites. Species include:
Sand dune and scrub species: *kestrel, skylark, willow warbler, wheatear, stonechat, linnet, finches*
Beach, cliffs and inshore waters: *gulls, terns, curlew, redshank, oystercatcher, dunlin*
Freshwater ponds and reeds: *sandpipers, lapwing, moorhen, coot, brentgoose, kingfisher, reed warblers*

WATER STORAGE   Val de la Mare reservoir. Possible development of underground water supplies and St Ouen's Pond. All are safeguarded from pollution and exploitation

The dunes at Les Blanches Banques

The dunes of Les Blanches Banques are found at the southern end of St Ouen's Bay (Figure 23). They were formed by sand deposition at the back of a raised beach, adjacent to the old cliff line marking a former higher sea level. They are among some of the finest examples of sand dunes in Western Europe and are rich in wildlife and archaeological remains.

The dune ecosystem supports over four hundred different species, including thirty locally rare or scarce plants such as the dwarf pansy, upright clover and early sand grass. Seventeen species which occur in the British Red Data Book on vascular plants have been recorded at Les Mielles. The Red Data Book is a list of endangered wildlife which requires conservation activity to ensure their survival. Practical conservation here ensures that many of these species occur in healthy populations. The richness in flora is a result of the calcareous nature of the soil which has formed on the shell-rich dune sands.

Les Blanches Banques is also the habitat of numerous animal species, especially birds and insects. Stonechats, meadow pipits, goldfinches and greenfinches are all resident species and these are joined by numerous migrants and visitors in summer and winter. Butterfly species such as the Common Blue and Grayling and the Burnet Moth are also part of the dunes' wildlife heritage. Les Mielles is particularly rich in insect life. Its southerly position within the British Isles and its warmer climate attract many species more commonly found in Mediterranean regions. Estimates for the number of insect species found here are as high as five thousand, many of which are not found on the British mainland.

The dunes are very vulnerable to pressure from human activity. They are in demand by walkers, riders, motorcycle scramblers, picnickers and sunbathers – uses which are not always compatible with the aims of conservation. Some trampling and human use is beneficial as it helps maintain the dune grassland community and arrest the ecological succession into scrubland but excessive use destroys the fragile ecosystem quickly and lays the land bare.

Many archaeological finds have been made in the dunes. Excavations have revealed evidence of neolithic and Bronze Age activity. Pottery, artefacts and stone and flint tools have been found in the centre of the dunes. There is also evidence of the more recent German occupation with remnants of infantry strongpoints which surround the Second World War minefield.

Figure 25 The dwarf pansy and sea stock: typical examples of the flora of the dunes

?

For this decision-making exercise work in small groups and study the resources which have been provided. They include:

A Background information about Les Mielles

B The planning procedures leading up to the implementation of the St Ouen's Bay Development Plan

C A map to show the location and extent of the area (Figure 23)

D A list giving information about the needs for conservation, recreation, agriculture and extractive industry

E A map of the main features of the area (Figure 26)

F A base map (Figure 27)

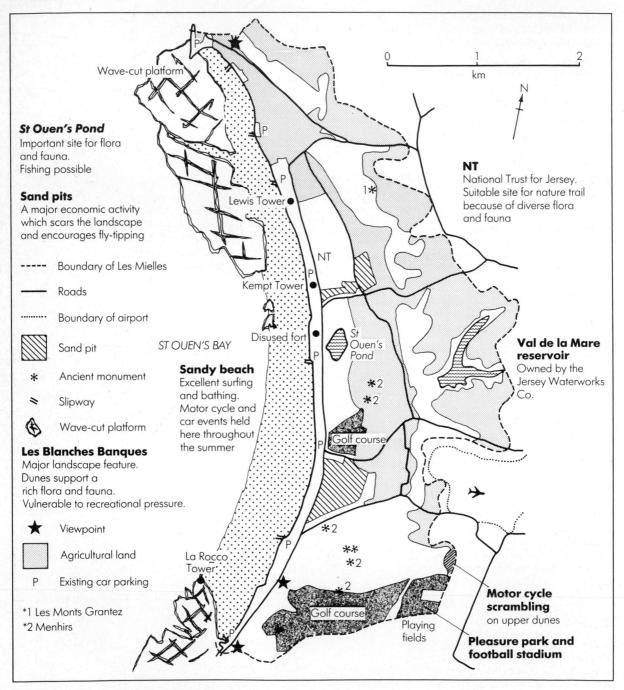

St Ouen's Pond
Important site for flora and fauna.
Fishing possible

Sand pits
A major economic activity which scars the landscape and encourages fly-tipping

- - - - - Boundary of Les Mielles

———— Roads

.... Boundary of airport

▨ Sand pit

✳ Ancient monument

≋ Slipway

◈ Wave-cut platform

Les Blanches Banques
Major landscape feature.
Dunes support a rich flora and fauna.
Vulnerable to recreational pressure.

★ Viewpoint

▦ Agricultural land

P Existing car parking

*1 Les Monts Grantez
*2 Menhirs

NT
National Trust for Jersey.
Suitable site for nature trail because of diverse flora and fauna

Val de la Mare reservoir
Owned by the Jersey Waterworks Co.

Sandy beach
Excellent surfing and bathing.
Motor cycle and car events held here throughout the summer

Motor cycle scrambling
on upper dunes

Pleasure park and football stadium

Wave-cut platform
ST OUEN'S BAY
Lewis Tower
Kempt Tower
Disused fort
St Ouen's Pond
Golf course
La Rocco Tower
Golf course
Playing fields
NT

Figure 26 Competing demands at Les Mielles   *Source*: Jersey States Planning Department

1 Discuss the best policy for the following management issues.

a **The dunes** What are the main difficulties in developing the area of dunes (Les Blanches Banques)? Which activities should be allowed and which should be discouraged here? What policies would you adopt for conserving the area?

b **Educating the public** How best can the public be informed about the use and importance of the countryside in St Ouen's Bay?

c **Sand extraction** Should sand extraction continue? What should be done with the pits which have been worked out?

d **Provision of facilities** What facilities need to be provided for visitors to the area?

e **Nature conservation** Choose two areas which should be set aside for nature conservation. Why is nature conservation an issue at Les Mielles?

2 On a copy of the base map (Figure 27):

a Choose sites for the recreational facilities you outlined in **1d**.

b Locate the conservation areas which you chose in **1e**.

c Explain your policies for recreational development and conservation in the area.

3 Make a list of all the possible uses of Les Mielles. Put a tick against the uses which are compatible with the aims of conservation, a cross against those which are incompatible, and a question mark where there is neither compatibility nor incompatibility. How realistic is it to include conservation as one of the aims of multiple use of this area?

The solution

Figure 28 is a map of the land use zones designated in the plan agreed by the States of Jersey. It shows some of the management decisions which were taken.

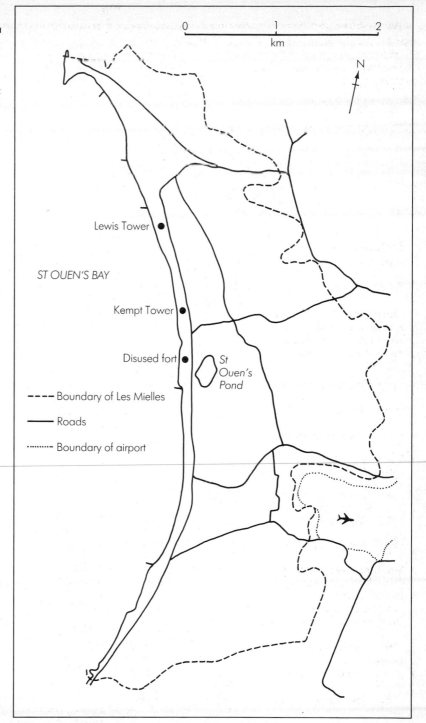

Figure 27 Base map for land planning exercise

Recreation

Most of the facilities are for use by families and individuals. Activities incompatible with the aims of Les Mielles are actively discouraged. At Le Mielle de Morville, derelict land of old refuse tips has been reclaimed and replanted to produce a dune-like landscape as an alternative to Les Blanches Banques. Horse riding and pedestrian routes are kept apart to minimise the ecological damage. Facilities are concentrated in areas with beach access and around the reservoir. No facilities will be provided at Les Blanches Banques to discourage use of this area.

Agriculture

Parts of Les Mielles are already actively farmed. Other areas which are in decline will need to be improved and restored. Dual use with recreation is to be encouraged wherever possible. Special agricultural methods may be needed in some ecologically sensitive areas, e.g. protection from herbicides or fertilisers.

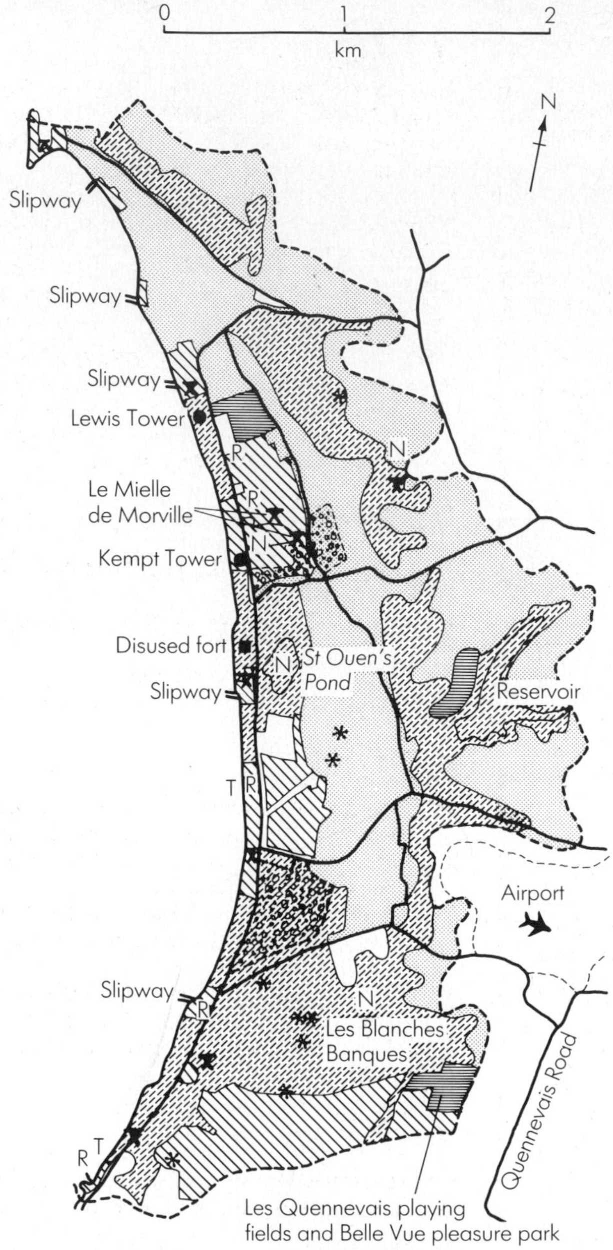

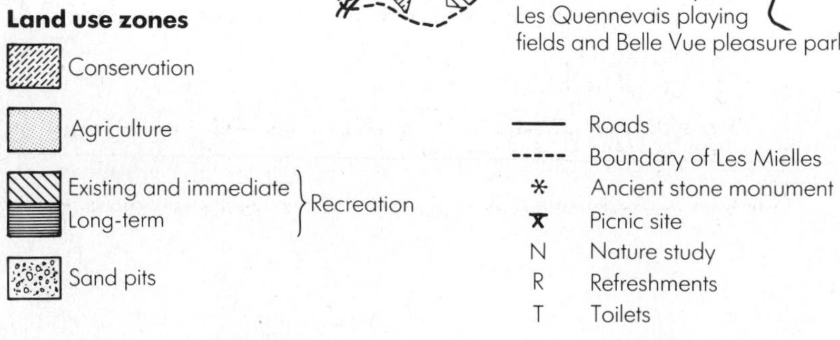

Sand excavation

Some agricultural land will be used and then restored after use. Two zones are in the north, one of which will be worked out in the early 1990s. A third area exists in the south. They will not be used for refuse disposal. Reclamation schemes will also provide recreational facilities and a new area of wetland for wildlife.

Kempt Tower

Information and interpretation centre to educate the public about the past, present and future of Les Mielles

Conservation

The most important conservation site is Les Blanches Banques. Wildlife and conservation are the main objective here, although public access is allowed. Horse riding is banned. Archaeological sites are also protected, as well as old buildings which have character and enhance the landscape. Other major areas of conservation are at St Ouen's Pond and the land surrounding the Val de la Mare reservoir. Rabbits have played an important role in maintaining the character of the sand dune vegetation. The reduction in rabbit numbers because of myxomatosis led to a serious management problem.

Map labels: Slipway, Slipway, Slipway, Lewis Tower, Le Mielle de Morville, Kempt Tower, Disused fort, Slipway, St Ouen's Pond, Reservoir, Airport, Slipway, Les Blanches Banques, Quennevais Road, Les Quennevais playing fields and Belle Vue pleasure park, N

Land use zones

- Conservation
- Agriculture
- Existing and immediate / Long-term } Recreation
- Sand pits

- —— Roads
- ----- Boundary of Les Mielles
- * Ancient stone monument
- ✗ Picnic site
- N Nature study
- R Refreshments
- T Toilets

Figure 28 The development plan for Les Mielles *Source*: Jersey States Planning Department

?

1 How successfully have the planners coped with the competing demands in the area?

2 Are there any problems which might occur as a result of the developments for the visitors at Les Mielles?

3 What opinions do you think the following people would have about the development of Les Mielles?
- a local farmer
- a local resident who uses the golf course
- a tourist with her young children
- the Conservation Officer of the Channel Islands

4 Read the following quote from Dr Michael Romeril, Conservation Officer of Jersey. Explain and illustrate the points he makes about conservation in Les Mielles. How far do you agree with him?

'... conservation seeks to achieve the planning and management of resources to secure their wise use and continuing supply.' 'The planner must ... balance compassionately, but logically, the myriad demands made on a resource where there is an obvious potential for conflict. Sensitive balance will always involve some compromise and certain sectors of the community will be disappointed. The truly unique landscape and/or wildlife habitat will usually require specific, and often rigid, controls for effective management and protection. But less valuable areas can and should be allowed to change in a sensitive and sympathetic manner in response to changing patterns of behaviour.'

Source: 'Case study: a balanced strategy for recreation, tourism and conservation – the case of Les Mielles, Jersey', *Tourist Management*, June 1983

Planning procedure

1961

Survey of the Development Plan for Jersey. The consultants gave the highest priority to the preservation of the landscape. St Ouen's Bay was described as 'a large tract of wild land ... which should be preserved at almost any cost.' It created the ideas of:
a The green zone; the area of greatest landscape value.
b The view line; the natural landward boundary following the crest of the surrounding plateau.

1963

States approval given for the Jersey Development Plan. This allowed committees and working parties to be set up to plan the development of Les Mielles in detail. The area of Les Mielles was recognised as St Ouen's Bay between the sea and the view line. Nearly all of this area was included in the green zone (Figure 23).

1966

A working party was set up to prepare a plan for the future of Les Mielles. Its aims were:
1 To preserve the scenic beauty of the area.
2 To preserve the agricultural land.
3 To allow the free use of beaches.
4 To allow careful exploitation of the natural resources.

1968

St Ouen's Bay Development Plan was published. Features included:
1 Retention of the green zone and the view line.
2 De-zoning of the area east of Le Chemin du Moulin which had been zoned for future residential use.
3 Relocation of areas for future recreation to the north of the bay thus releasing land at Les Blanches Banques for use as unobstructed open space.
4 Tree-planting to take place only where needed to screen unsightly development or to act as windbreaks.
5 Detailed proposals for car parks, toilets and cafés at four points on the coast.

1974

A sub-committee was set up. Little action had been taken to implement the 1968 plan. This sub-committee was to put the plan into operation.

1978

States of Jersey approve the designation of Les Mielles and the suggested strategy for its future use.

2

The delicate balance

Rosalind and Nicholas Foskett

Wildlife in the city: a peregrine falcon in Denver, Colorado, USA

Interaction between people and the environment

We are living in an age where people are increasingly becoming 'environmentally aware'. Issues such as the destruction of the ozone layer by chlorofluorocarbons (CFCs) produced by our use of aerosols and refrigerants, pollution of the North Sea by the dumping of hazardous waste, extinction of forest species by the destruction of the forests, and many others, are constantly brought to our attention by the media. In addition, many of these issues are being highlighted on the political stage. Green politics is big business. In the 1987 general election in Britain, all political parties were keen to outline their policies on environmental issues, and to stress that they cared. Such ideas were even introduced into the 1988 budget with the Chancellor of the Exchequer giving unleaded petrol a price advantage to encourage more people to drive suitably-adapted cars and reduce emissions of lead into the atmosphere.

But are we any further forward in protecting the 'egg-shell delicacy' of ecosystems than we were in 1972 when *Only One Earth* was written? If we were to draw up a catalogue of environmental disasters that have occurred since then – Chernobyl, ozone depletion, droughts in Africa, Bhopal, deforestation and so on – it would seem not!

In this chapter, we will look at two examples of the interaction between people and the environment. In **urban wildlife** we look at the new opportunities being given to wildlife within cities and the ways that people are managing to enrich urban ecosystems. **The Broads: wetlands under threat** considers the ecological pressures facing an endangered wildlife habitat and the management schemes which are beginning to bear fruit. In each case, the ecological issues are highlighted – keep a list as you go through the chapter, and expand on it by collecting other examples from the media during your studies.

Within our own planet (...) we know that the energy of the sun is poured out in almost limitless bounty. But we know, too, that the intermediaries and products of all this bounty – the leaves, the bacteria – are far from limitless. Remove the green cover from the soil of Central Africa and it becomes a brick-hard, everlasting laterite. Cut down the forests, overgraze the grass, and productive land turns to desert. Overload the waters with sewage or nutrients and algae consume its oxygen, fish die and produce stinking gas as they decompose.

It is because there are so many potential paths towards points of irreversible 'no return' that the self-repairing cycles underlying all living systems – we call 'ecosystems' – cannot survive indefinite over-loading or mistreatment. Admittedly, the regenerative powers of life are astonishing. Living things have survived the glaciations, the volcanic convulsions, the earthquakes, typhoons and tidal waves that have torn through our unstable planet over the billennia. But the warning is there. Like the giant reptiles of the Jurassic Age, some species have gone the 'way to dusty death.'

And this brings us to a final balance. (...) Its weakening or destruction unleashes the capacity of creatures to destroy eath other and themselves as well. There exist in nature many different patterns for ensuring to a species its food and young. Most of these patterns entail the eating of one species by another, all the way up the food chains of nature. Some animals demonstrate high though specific and limited degrees of cooperation – within the nest, the lair, the pack, the herd. Some exhibit a host-parasite relationship which can express a subtle equilibrium even though it appears unattractive to human eyes. But behind the interrelationships lies the risk of unpredictable and sometimes destructive consequences if the delicate equilibrium is overturned. A new species introduced, a chemical balance upset, an island erupting into the sky, the slow onset of the ice – all such disturbances can elicit so violent a response that the system may not be capable of returning, by itself, to a desirable and stable system.

If these are indeed the lessons learnt in piecing together the infinite history of our universe and of Planet Earth, they teach surely one thing above all – a need for extreme caution, a sense of the appalling vastness and complexity of the forces that can be unleashed and of the egg-shell delicacy of the arrangements that can be upset.

Source: Barbara Ward and René Dubos, *Only One Earth*, André Deutsch, 1972, UK. Reprinted by permission of Curtis Brown Ltd (Canadian copyright)

?

1 Read the extract from *Only One Earth*.

a Explain, in your own words, what the authors mean by the phrase 'egg-shell delicacy' in their description of ecosystems.

b What examples of this 'delicacy' do they give in the extract?

Wildfowlers shoot down reserve plan

Cowboy wildfowlers already guilty of shooting whooper swans and shelduck, have now gunned down the long-awaited plan to establish a Local Nature Reserve at Wigtown Bay.

The story is a sorry tale of petty greed and short-sighted behaviour which has destroyed a community's hope for bringing order out of chaos and may have killed off the last chance of protecting one of Scotland's most beautiful estuaries.

The small estuary of Wigtown Bay is one of the jewels of the Solway coast. In winter the mild climate and productive mudflats are a special attraction for waders and wildfowl. Local naturalists treasure memories of magical winter evenings spent on the merse waiting for the pink-feet to fly in; the night air rich with the whistling of the flocks of widgeon and the plaintive cries of the curlews.

It was all too good to last!

In recent years the tranquillity of this idyllic setting has been shattered by an enormous and unregulated increase in wildfowling.

Responsible local sportsmen have become an endangered species. In their place have come a new breed of wildfowlers, ignorant of sporting etiquette and wildfowl identification, who show scant respect for local farmers and their livestock.

In the ensuing mêlée only one proposal has offered any chance of restoring order. It was spelled out as long ago as 1977 by Dr Peter Hopkins, secretary of the SWT Dumfries & Galloway branch, and he has campaigned energetically for its adoption ever since. The proposal is that part of the estuary should be declared a Local Nature Reserve.

The proposal is a replica of the highly successful scheme operating at SWT's Montrose Basin reserve. The main points would be the introduction of bye-laws and a permit system to regulate wildfowling and the appointment of a warden to promote good conservation practice. Of prime importance would be the establishment of a special no-shooting sanctuary zone, and daily control times, so birds have a chance to feed and roost.

At Montrose, such an approach has pleased all the interested parties. Conservationists have seen a considerable increase in birds using the estuary, wildfowlers find their sport improved by proper regulation, and landowners no longer have to confront armed trespassers.

In addition to these obvious benefits, the Local Nature Reserve would pave the way for such amenities as observation hides and a possible new visitor centre which would be a great attraction for local schoolchildren and tourists. Already grant-giving bodies have indicated to SWT that they would be keen to support such projects.

So it might be expected that there would be general support for the Local Nature Reserve. Indeed, in the past the main organisations representing local wildfowlers, the Wigtown and District Wildfowling and Conservation Association and the British Association for Shooting and Conservation, have both supported such a proposal. Encouraged by their support, the staff of Dumfries & Galloway Regional Council, under the guidance of planning director, Gordon Mann, have put a great deal of effort into preparing an excellent series of proposals for the establishment and management of the reserve.

Astonishingly, at a special meeting in March, when it was anticipated that local organisations would back the Regional Council's proposals, wildfowlers' representatives effectively demolished the plan.

They proposed a daily free-for-all, with no times when shooting would be controlled, and an absurdly small sanctuary zone which could be shot over from two sides, which the birds could only fly into from the land by passing over guns, and which did not include any areas of saltmarsh where birds could feed without disturbance. These outrageous and provocative suggestions were clearly totally inappropriate for a Local Nature Reserve designation, and the meeting ended without agreement.

While reasonable wildfowlers are rightly cautious about relinquishing their right to shoot on the foreshore, at Wigtown it has long been evident that so great is the disturbance that exercising that right could no longer be termed 'sport'. It has not escaped conservationists' attention that a lucrative trade has been established by local boarding houses advertising the availability of free shooting on the foreshore.

Undoubtedly such promotion draws in shooters from all over Britain and even the Continent. Presumably these clearly commercial interests have not influenced those who have sabotaged the reserve plan in the name of sport.

Despite the frustration of this obvious setback, SWT's representatives are promoting new measures to convince responsible wildfowlers that they should stand up and be counted. In particular, new scientific evidence will be produced to support the case for a sanctuary zone and local wildfowlers have been invited to make a study tour of estuaries like Montrose and Caerlaverock where wildfowling and conservation have a successful partnership.

But conservationists fear that such measures may be too late. The reserve cannot be established without the assistance of the Regional Council which has already invested a great deal of time on this project. At worst, the Region may well take the view that their time is better spent elsewhere and abandon any idea of a reserve.

Source: John Crichton, *Scottish Wildlife*, New Series No 1, 1987

Figure 1   The SWT's Montrose Basin Reserve and its impressive standing hide – one place where wildfowlers and conservationists at work successfully hand in hand.
Source: Scottish Wildlife, New Series, No 1, 1987

1   The article 'Wildfowlers Shoot Down Reserve Plan' describes a clash of interests between wildfowlers and conservationists at Wigtown Bay, on the Solway coast.

a What is the ecological issue described in the article?

b Briefly explain the two sides of the argument in this issue.

c What solution was proposed by Dr Peter Hopkins?

d Why hasn't this solution been adopted?

e In small groups discuss the content of the article and recommend a solution to the problem.

2   In small groups draw up a list of other environmental issues where there are opposing views which seem irreconcilable.

Urban wildlife

The background

The march of the concrete jungle has been much publicised in recent years, as cities have grown and spread out over the surrounding countryside. Alongside this there has been a 'march' of a very different kind, as plants and animals have taken advantage of the new habitats that an urbanised landscape affords. The common view of cities, devoid of animal and plant life and biologi-cally unproductive, is false. Indeed, within a few metres of a house there may be as many as 50 plant and animal species. Some may be domesticated species, such as dogs and cats, but others may be wild species which have found a niche in this human landscape. Furthermore, open space covers about 20% of cities, and houses and gardens about 50%. In fact, it has been estimated that only about 2.5% of Britain's land surface is biologically sterile.

In addition, more opportunities for wildlife are occurring as factories close down and areas previously used for economic activity or housing are abandoned. In the metropolitan West Midlands, for example, there are more than 36,000 hectares of unbuilt-up land, and about a quarter of this is suitable for wildlife. These 9,000 hectares represent about 12% of the county area, which is a higher proportion of wildscape than on a modern farm. (*Source:* Chris Baines, *The Wild Side of Town*, BBC Publications/Elm Tree Books, 1986.)

Rural areas have become increasingly hostile to wildlife. The grubbing-up of hedgerows, the routine use of pesticides and herbicides, and the planting of vast areas with just one species (Figure 2) are practices which have turned some parts of Britain's countryside into wildlife deserts, just as effectively as concrete plazas and covered shopping arcades have in towns. Consequently, adaptable species have looked towards urban areas for shelter and food. Herring-gulls use skyscrapers and chimney pots as adequate alternatives to the sea cliffs which are their natural habitat. The wider spacing of nest sites in towns reduces competition between birds, and fewer chicks stray into the territory of a neighbouring nest, where they may be attacked and killed by defending adult birds. Other urban alternative habitats include rubble-strewn building sites resembling rocky screes, and bridges, which make passable

Figure 2 Monoculture: sugar beet fields in Cambridgeshire

caves for insects and bats.

The city landscape also encourages wildlife to enter right into its heart by providing easy routeways for animals to follow. Foxes live by scavenging in dustbins and on rubbish dumps (Figure 3). Railway cuttings and canals provide safe, secluded pathways. In some places urban foxes have become a nuisance, tearing open the sacks of rubbish and upsetting dustbins at night with a noisy clatter! (Figure 4)

Figure 3 *Source:* Urban Wildlife, October 1987, p. 23

Many people would be horrified to know how many species of plants and animals share their 'clean' houses. There are about 50 species which commonly live indoors. Larger animals, such as rats and mice, are usually removed quickly, but smaller animals such as silverfish, ants, furniture beetles, earwigs, clothes moths and spiders (to name but a few!) are not as easily detected. Food scraps, damp surfaces and old clothes will allow moulds to grow, and dry rot fungi may germinate if suitable conditions prevail.

In addition to the opportunist species which fill new ecological niches, towns and cities may actively encourage wildlife. Parks and ornamental gardens are particularly attractive to birds. In Regents Park in London, for example, over one hundred different species of bird have been recorded in one year. But even parks and gardens may be hostile to wildlife. Pollution may clog leaves with dust or produce acidic soils. Some poorly-managed parks may prevent species living there. One example of poor management for wildlife is the enthusiastic mowing of lawns which may turn vast areas into green deserts. Starlings are one of the few species which thrive on mown grass because they feed on leatherjackets found around the grass roots. In some cities, such as Brighton, starlings have greatly increased in numbers so that they now present a problem for the local authorities because of the noise and mess around their roosting sites.

Most people are interested in wildlife. They want a pleasant environment to live in which includes space for plants and animals. Young children, especially, should have the opportunity to learn about the wildlife in their local area and, as most people in Britain live and work in cities and towns, urban nature conservation is needed and wanted.

Figure 4 Urban fox

?

1 Parts of our towns and cities reflect aspects of the natural landscape such as the rubble screes of the building sites. Make a list of as many examples as you can and describe the types of wildlife which might take advantage of these urban habitats.

2 Count the number of species which can be found within five metres of where you live. It may be necessary to keep a log of visiting species over a period of a few days. Do you think your species count is a true reflection of the species in the area?

3 Table 3 shows some of the results of a study of the effects of urban areas on bird species undertaken in Finland. Measurements were taken in the city of Helsinki, in agricultural areas close to rural houses and in completely uninhabited forests.

a What is the difference between biological productivity and biomass?

b Which type of environment had the highest biomass and which had the lowest? Why?

c What reasons can you give for the city having a greater number of birds per square kilometre than the uninhabited forest?

d What is meant by the phrase *species diversity*?

e Which environment had the greatest species diversity? Explain why this might be so.

Table 3 Impact of urban areas on birds

	City (Helsinki)	Near rural houses	Uninhabited forest
Biomass of birds (kg/km^2)	213	30	22
Number of birds (per km^2)	1,089	371	297
Number of species (per km^2)	21	80	54
Diversity	1.13	3.40	3.19

Source: Jacobs, J, 'Diversity, stability and maturity in ecosystems influenced by human activities', in W H Van Dobben and R H Lowe-McConnell (eds), *Unifying Concepts in Ecology*, The Hague: Junk, 1975, pp. 187–207

Policies for urban wildlife conservation

A better future exists for wildlife in cities as more people become involved with urban conservation projects. Several cities have active groups working to promote urban wildlife. In Birmingham, for example, the Urban Wildlife Group works to promote conservation, environmental education and community involvement in local projects. The Nature Conservancy Council (NCC) is also active and attempts to educate the public through publications and local displays. Let us consider some of the policies which have been adopted to improve the urban landscape and provide space for plants and animals to thrive.

Re-introduction of countryside species

Many existing open spaces are ecologically sterile due to poor management. Gardening practices tend to weed out native species and to tidy up dead and rotting vegetation. These methods impoverish the urban ecosystem.

Great improvements would be made if meadow flowers were introduced into grasslands and small pockets of land were allowed to 'go wild'. New woodlands of native broadleaved trees could be established, rather than introducing exotic species, which would attract British species of birds and other animals. Dead trees provide a refuge for small mammals and may attract woodpeckers. They are also an ideal habitat for fungi and other decomposers in the ecosystem. Ponds can become rich sources of wildlife if they are managed thoughtfully. They can form an attractive centrepiece to a park if they are planted with marshland plants such as purple loosestrife, flowering rush and yellow flag (Figure 6).

Water control

The objective of most city drainage systems is to remove rainwater as quickly as possible by providing a complex network of storm drains and gutters. This can produce almost desert conditions for plants in urban areas. If

retention pools and floodplain marshes were used instead, the water flow would be slowed down. This, in turn, would reduce pollution loads in rivers, as well as providing wetland habitats. Reservoirs and sewage farms already provide rich pickings for wildlife. It has been estimated that about eighty-five million flies feed on each hectare of filter beds in sewage farms! These attract numerous bird species such as flycatchers, wagtails, warblers and starlings (Figure 5).

Figure 5 Bird life around a sewage works

Figure 6 Meadow flowers in an urban setting

Conservation awareness

Education programmes to raise people's awareness about conservation in towns can reap rewards. In recent years, developers have become more responsible when commissioning landscaping around new buildings. Landscape architects now use a greater diversity of structures and species in their schemes.

People can also be encouraged to develop their own gardens for wildlife by providing diverse habitats rather than the ubiquitous lawn (Figure 7). Small wilderness areas and attractions such as nest boxes and food tables are particularly successful.

Pocket parks

Pocket parks are small patches of previously unused land which have been established as areas of countryside for people to enjoy. The scheme was pioneered in Northamptonshire, and is backed by Schering Agriculture, the international crop protection company, and the Royal Society for Nature Conservation (RSNC). Any small area of unused land can be formed into a pocket park such as village ponds, abandoned quarries, old railway lines, and churchyards. Advice on setting up these parks is given by local Wildlife Conservation Trust officers and the RSNC.

Conservation groups

Local conservation groups are often most effective in promoting projects and involving the community. One such body is the Urban Wildlife Group, which is the Nature Conservation Trust for Birmingham and the Black Country. It works closely with the local authority and community projects, and is funded by subscriptions, grants from the Countryside Commission, the Nature Conservancy Council and the World Wide Fund for Nature, and donations from commerce and industry. Two of their schemes are described below.

Figure 7 Urban gardens as an area of wildscape

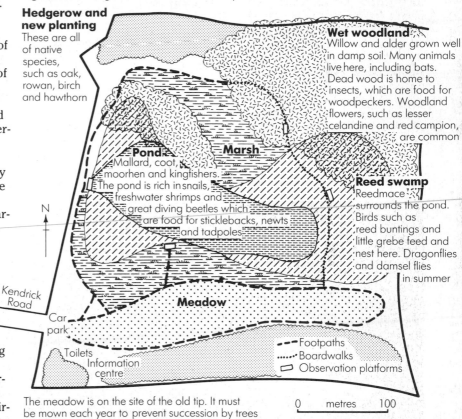

The meadow is on the site of the old tip. It must be mown each year to prevent succession by trees

Figure 8 Plants Brook Community Nature Park
Source: Urban Wildlife Group

The Plants Brook Community Nature Park

Plants Brook is a small nature reserve at Walmley, a suburb a few miles north-east of Birmingham's city centre. It was saved from becoming a tip site by a public inquiry in 1978, and was opened as a community nature park in 1985 (Figure 8). It has diverse habitats including a pond, reed swamp, wet woodland and meadow. This diversity encourages a large number of species to live in or visit the reserve.

Norman Street

The Norman Street phased project will run for four years from 1987 to 1991 and will cost approximately £156,000 at 1987 prices. Norman Street is a site in Winson Green, part of the inner city of Birmingham. The land is owned by the city council and in the past it has been used as a tip.

The Urban Wildlife Group aims to develop an urban wildlife park for the local community. Its wider aims include helping people of all ages to gain a wider understanding of environmental issues and it will demonstrate some of the ways that other inner-city sites might be developed.

Figures 9 and 11 show an artist's impression of the completed site and a site plan for the development.

Figure 9 The Norman Street Development: an artist's impression
Source: Urban Wildlife Group

The main themes to be explored in the project are:

1 It is to be a centre for Earth Education and activities based on the Sunship Earth Programme developed in the United States will be a central feature of the project. Children will be introduced to ecology by being able to feel, smell, hear and see. They will learn through play. The site will be designed to allow children to learn through experience and discovery rather than through traditional 'nature studies'.

2 Methods of alternative technology, such as wind and water power, and resource conservation will be on show to demonstrate how people can reduce their impact on ecosystems.

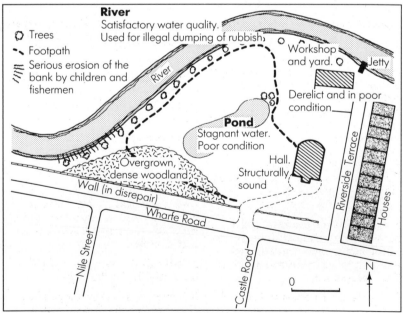

Figure 10 Site for an urban wildlife project

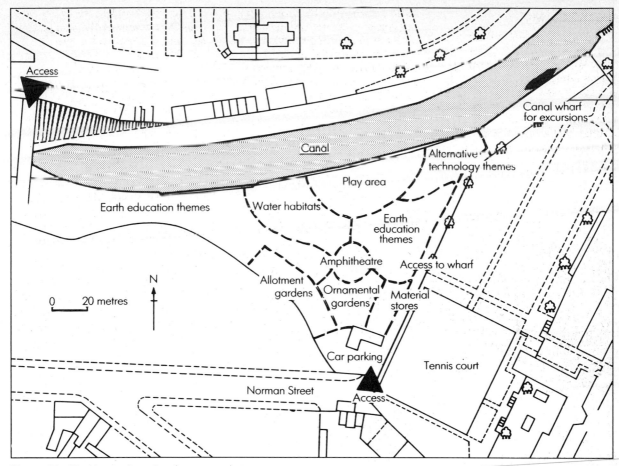

Figure 11 The Norman Street Development: a plan

1 The plan in Figure 10 shows a site in an inner-city area which is to be used to develop an urban wildlife project. Some of the features of the site are outlined on the plan. You are to be the planner. Draw up a development plan for the area which would achieve the following aims:

A The site is to be developed as an urban wildlife park with as great a range of species as possible living in a pleasant 'countryside' environment.

B Facilities will be provided for the public to raise their awareness of wildlife conservation. Environmental education for schoolchildren will be actively encouraged.

C The site will be a demonstration of methods of wildlife conservation.

Your final submission should consist of two parts:

a A plan of the proposed uses of the site showing the features of the site which will be retained and those features you would wish to develop.

b A report which describes how your planned development will achieve the aims of the project.

2 The extract 'City wildscape' from *Environment Now* by Bob Smyth on pages 46–7 outlines the current state of the urban wildlife scene. Read the extract carefully.

a What are the main urban wildlife issues described in the article?

b Bob Smyth includes examples both of schemes which will benefit urban wildlife and developments which will do harm. Identify and record these as lists.

c Why should people be concerned with urban wildlife conservation? What arguments would you use to persuade the following people to adopt measures to conserve urban wildlife?

i Your local MP.
ii The head gardener for the local authority.
iii British Rail.
iv A local resident, Celia Forsythe, who has a number of fine old oak trees in her garden which are nest sites for native birds, but which are in the way of her scheme for setting up greenhouses to grow bedding plants as part of her small nursery business.

CITY WILDSPACE

Among the objectives of the European Year of the Environment is 'the greening of towns and cities'. BOB SMYTH, author of a recently published history, surveys the urban conservation scene.

In the year and a half since the abolition of the metropolitan county councils, urban nature conservation initiatives are burgeoning countrywide. At the time of abolition there were widespread fears that concern for urban wildlife would suffer from the loss of county planning departments and their ecology sections. It now seems that the metropolitan borough councils – 33 in Greater London plus 36 elsewhere – are taking an increasing interest in wildlife issues.

In London, the summer meeting of a 'London Ecology and Nature Conservation Professional Officers Network' attracted more than 50 ecologists, planners and leisure department staff – an indication that London boroughs were taking nature conservation matters seriously. Similarly, many councils in the West Midlands, Yorkshire, Lancashire, Durham and Northumberland conurbations have demonstrated their awareness of this element of planning and leisure provision by undertaking surveys of open space in their areas as a basis for forthcoming nature conservation strategies.

Voluntary sector urban conservationists are also flourishing. The RSNC urban officer's list of urban wildlife groups (UWGs) is nowadays out of date almost as soon as he circulates each edition, with new groups springing up every month. The current tally is around 50, ranging from large organisations such as the Avon Wildlife Trust to local groups in places as unexpected as Eastbourne and Barrow-in-Furness.

The number is likely to grow as several county trusts, waking up to the importance of their urban areas both in terms of wildlife and membership potential, plan the setting up of town groups within their domains. On the south coast the Hampshire trust's urban officer is organising UWGs in Portsmouth, Southampton and the other urban districts forming Solent City. In Scotland the Scottish Wildlife Trust, after years of slight attention to its largest city, Glasgow, is turning its attention to the benefits of more active local groups in this and other cities. SWT has recently opened an urban wildlife garden adjacent to its headquarters in Edinburgh. For Peterborough, perched between Northamptonshire and Cambridgeshire, a completely new trust is in prospect.

Focus of this urban bustle and hustle is the Fairbrother Group, established a couple of years ago as the National Association of Urban Wildlife Groups. Its executive, elected by the UWGs each year, forms the RSNC's urban steering group which, as part of reorganisation following the appointment of a new chief executive, is expected to become a more important element in the Society's affairs. Fairbrother also organises three conferences during the year which provide the opportunity for delegates from groups around the country to swap technical and political (with a small 'p') expertise.

Its July conference in Manchester, attracting over 100 representatives of groups from Exeter to Aberdeen, was an ideal occasion for appraisal of conservation problems and opportunities following the general election. The government's proclaimed intention to concentrate on the regeneration of the inner cities was seen as offering possibilities for groups to contribute to urban environmental programmes. There was understandable anxiety that regeneration might be taken as an excuse to build on all and any open spaces within city limits, regardless of their natural history interest.

Former environment secretary Michael Heseltine MP who, while a minister, took a personal interest in urban affairs in Liverpool, London and elsewhere, has already responded to such fears. In a letter to me he writes: *'I appreciate your point that some wastelands are valuable nature sites and I sympathise with it. It is clear that a balance must be struck.'*

The prospect of new government agencies operating in city areas was also viewed as a mixed blessing. Urban development corporations (UDCs) and task forces might be a source of funds for UWGs wanting to manage wasteland sites, but there was also the risk that establishing relations with civil servants could be even more difficult than working with local government officers! Pioneer wildlife propagandist Chris Baines added the thought that wildlifers should consider the possibility of collaborating with commercial house builders in order to arrange for pocket wildlife parks within new schemes.

Sites at risk

Times journalist David Nicholson-Lord, author of a forthcoming book on *The Greening of the Cities* (Routledge & Kegan Paul) voiced the thought that unbridled building of factories or houses on urban vacant land might increase rather than diminish the debilitated quality of urban life. Several in the audience thought that excessive pressure on land was mainly a London problem: in other cities, following the closure and demolition of redundant factories, there was plenty of land for everyone.

Richard Robinson, chair of the London Wildlife Trust,

Camley Street Natural Park, King's Cross, London

is required. Sites of Special Scientific Interest are likely to be rare in built-up areas, while local authorities have during the past 40 years been curiously reluctant to create designated Local Nature Reserves. If there were some equivalent of environmentally sensitive areas (ESAs) as now apply in the countryside, owners of such areas of land would have to take account of this grading in managing or disposing of their landholding.

As it is, several other key London sites are at risk. The Bricklayers Arms Sidings, identified by the Greater London Ecology Unit as one of the half-dozen finest wasteland sites in the whole of Greater London, has been sold by British Rail to house-builders, with conservationists struggling to salvage a small three-acre reserve from the redevelopment. A similar site at Shakespeare Road in Lambeth was, in July, the subject of a public inquiry into a developer's plans for house-building, its future lying in the hands of the inspector and his DoE masters.

An inquiry verdict on the Shooters Hill woods, endangered by the proposed East London River Crossing road, is imminent. A further inquiry was held in August into development plans for the Crayford Marshes, despite an earlier inspector's opinion that: *'To see a heron land or take off, hear the flight call of a redshank or spot other birds among a network of water-filled ditches (intriguing to the ecologist, amateur or professional), is to appreciate the intrinsic value of the area.'* Part of an ancient woodland at Sydenham Hill Wood in south London is also a possible development site, notwithstanding an inspector's adjudication earlier this year that: *'The need to preserve areas of existing natural woodland within the urban areas is of as much importance in preserving our heritage and improving the quality of the environment as that of preserving the countryside.'*

On the positive side, local councils such as Wigan, St Helens and Leicester are this year publishing detailed 'green plans' for the protection and enhancement of wildspace within their territory. Kirklees has pioneered an interesting local equivalent to a garden festival by creating a permanent visitor centre within a former quarry at Dewsbury. Barnsley is experimenting with a scheme of environmental initiatives co-ordinated by a community advisory officer working in a cluster of parishes.

Regional ecology units continue to operate, despite met. county abolition, in Merseyside, Greater Manchester and London, and the Nature Conservancy Council is supporting the idea of an urban conservation programme to provide guidelines for city greening activities nationally. The next few years look like being a time when wildlife really does come to town.

observed that the commercial activities of British Rail and other public utilities were among the most threatening factors for conservationists. In pursuit of their obligation to maximise profit from the sale of surplus land, BR were auctioning off former sidings, some of which were not only outstanding habitats but even supported formal natural parks. Islington in north London, a borough with the least public open space in the whole capital, leased from BR land next to the Arsenal football ground to create the Gillespie Park in informal style by adding to the self-seeded vegetation features such as a pond. The site is now up for grabs with no protection for the park's continued existence. In adjacent Camden, another reserve is in jeopardy as the London Residuary Body winds up the affairs of the former Greater London Council, abolished last year. Even though the Camley Street Nature Park is possibly the finest inner city nature study centre anywhere in Britain, the LRB is talking of offering it for sale.

At the Manchester conference, several people suggested that a new classification of nature sites in cities

Source: Bob Smyth, *Environment Now*, October/November 1987, p. 11

Urban wildlife: project ideas

Aspects of urban wildlife and wildscape can make an excellent topic for an individual study or project for an examination. The following section gives some ideas for project work and some of the issues which could be studied easily within an urban context.

Ecological study of an urban pond/lake

AIM: To identify the ecological basis of the lake or pond, to investigate the environmental stresses on the ecosystem and the *human* dimension.

Possible studies:

1 To map and record aspects of the ecosystem.
- Draw up a detailed ecological map of the pond and its surrounding landuse
- Annotate with details of species, environmental factors which might affect the pond, human uses of the pond and its surroundings and so on
- Is there any evidence of the pond silting up?
- Is there any evidence of plant succession?

2 To measure the species diversity and the ecological structure.
- Use quadrats to sample the vegetation and make species diversity counts
- Investigate the structure of the community: Which species are the *producers* and *consumers*? Which species occupy different trophic levels within the ecosystem?

3 To identify the origin of the water body and its character.
- What is the origin of the pond?
- How has it changed through time?
- Take samples of water at the surface and at depth. Measure the following characteristics in the laboratory: pH, dissolved oxygen content, algae concentration, suspended solids
- Note other characteristics of the water body: transparency/colour of water, presence of pollutants, inflows/outflows, water-side/floating vegetation, animal species

4 To evaluate the human stresses on the ecosystem.
- What uses do people make of the pond?
- Is it managed in any way?
- Could it be managed any better?
- What management options would you like to see introduced?

5 To investigate the attitudes and values of people towards the lake as a landscape resource.
- Formulate a questionnaire to explore people's attitudes and values towards the pond
- Are there any differences in attitudes with age or sex?

?

Urban habitat investigation

Construct a wildlife habitat map of your local area. You will need a large-scale map as a basis for your study – the Ordnance Survey 1:10,000 (6 inch: 1 mile) or the 1:1250 maps are best, but town plans such as the A–Z Guides would be suitable. A large scale allows you to make notes directly on the map. Choose an area of approximately one kilometre square (a larger area is unmanageable).

1 Study the map carefully and mark on any habitat areas which are obvious (parks, gardens, and so on).

2 At the library, consult maps at different scales, planning documents, aerial photographs and so on for your chosen area.

3 Survey the area systematically and mark on to your map areas of wild space (railway lines, verges, graveyards, gardens, ponds), areas of green desert (mown lawns, sports pitches, 'estate' trees), and urban wildlife corridors which provide links between town and country (railway lines, canals, rivers, motorways).

4 Record details of species present, management policies and any other ecological information.

5 Write to the appropriate local authority Planning Department and the Parks and Gardens Department to find out if there is a local policy towards urban wildlife. Also get in touch with your local wildlife group to see whether there are, or have been, any local urban wildlife issues.

Figure 12 A view of the Norfolk Broads: the River Ant; (inset) Swallowtail butterfly

The Broads: wetlands under threat

What are the Broads?

Wetlands are important wildlife habitats which are under considerable pressure worldwide as the demand for land increases. Figure 12 shows the Broads, one of the major areas of wetland in the United Kingdom. The landscape is distinctive: the low-lying land is peppered by lakes (called Broads) which have reed beds and *carr woodland* at their edges. Rivers link these lakes and areas of fen, woodland and drained marshes lie between them.

This unique ecological area is protected in many parts by the Nature Conservancy Council, the Norfolk Naturalists Trust and the Suffolk Trust for Nature Conservation. A total of 3,360 hectares are designated as SSSIs (Sites of Special Scientific Interest).

Overseeing the management of the area is the Broads Authority established in 1979. Six district councils and two county councils are also involved. The Countryside Commission has three independent members and provides finance through grants for staff and administrative costs and funds project work. The Anglian Water Authority and the Great Yarmouth Port and Haven Commissioners also work in partnership with the Broads Authority. The powers of the Authority are similar to those of a National Park, and it is possible that they will soon receive this designation. The main objectives of the Broads Authority are:

1 To conserve and enhance the natural beauty and the amenity of the area as a whole, especially the wildlife.

2 To protect the economic and social interests of those who live and work in the area and to preserve its natural resources.

3 To encourage the use of the Broads for recreation and holiday purposes, both waterborne and land-based, and for the pursuit of scientific research, education and nature study.

Where are the Broads?

The Broads are found within the counties of Norfolk and Suffolk. They consist of the lower valleys of the Rivers Waveney, Yare and Bure and the two tributaries of the River Bure – the River Ant and the River Thurne (Figure 13). There are 48 Broads and 200 kilometres of navigable waterways, which are lock-free and only partly tidal.

Why are the Broads so important?

This area of wetland is home to a number of rare species. Britain's largest butterfly, the swallowtail (Figure 12), is found here, and the marsh harrier uses the reed and

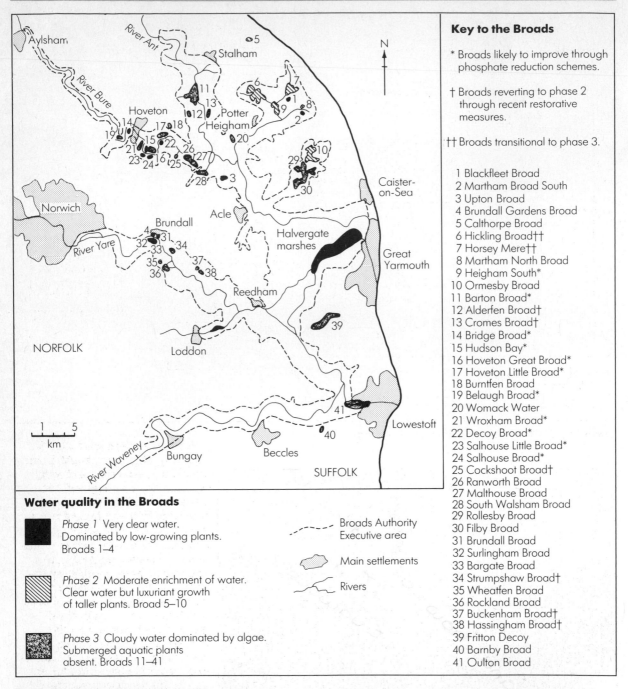

Key to the Broads

* Broads likely to improve through phosphate reduction schemes.

† Broads reverting to phase 2 through recent restorative measures.

†† Broads transitional to phase 3.

1 Blackfleet Broad
2 Martham Broad South
3 Upton Broad
4 Brundall Gardens Broad
5 Calthorpe Broad
6 Hickling Broad††
7 Horsey Mere††
8 Martham North Broad
9 Heigham South*
10 Ormesby Broad
11 Barton Broad*
12 Alderfen Broad†
13 Cromes Broad†
14 Bridge Broad*
15 Hudson Bay*
16 Hoveton Great Broad*
17 Hoveton Little Broad*
18 Burntfen Broad
19 Belaugh Broad*
20 Womack Water
21 Wroxham Broad*
22 Decoy Broad*
23 Salhouse Little Broad*
24 Salhouse Broad*
25 Cockshoot Broad†
26 Ranworth Broad
27 Malthouse Broad
28 South Walsham Broad
29 Rollesby Broad
30 Filby Broad
31 Brundall Broad
32 Surlingham Broad
33 Bargate Broad
34 Strumpshaw Broad†
35 Wheatfen Broad
36 Rockland Broad
37 Buckenham Broad†
38 Hassingham Broad†
39 Fritton Decoy
40 Barnby Broad
41 Oulton Broad

Water quality in the Broads

Phase 1 Very clear water. Dominated by low-growing plants. Broads 1–4

Phase 2 Moderate enrichment of water. Clear water but luxuriant growth of taller plants. Broad 5–10

Phase 3 Cloudy water dominated by algae. Submerged aquatic plants absent. Broads 11–41

--- Broads Authority Executive area

Main settlements

Rivers

Figure 13 The Broads and the quality of the water

fen areas for nesting and the marshes for hunting. Bure Marshes and Horsey, Hickling and Martham Broads are two of the thirteen sites in the United Kingdom listed as being of national importance for nature conservation under the 1971 Ramsar International Wetlands Convention.

The habitats (Figure 14) are under threat as traditional management techniques decline and recreation pressure increases. Boating is the main activity, with the landscape, wildlife and historic buildings playing only a secondary role in the attraction of visitors. Although this recreational pressure causes problems for the ecological management of the Broads, it also provides much-needed employment in the tourist and boat-building industries.

Historically the area was self-contained, and the local population satisfied their needs through careful resource management.

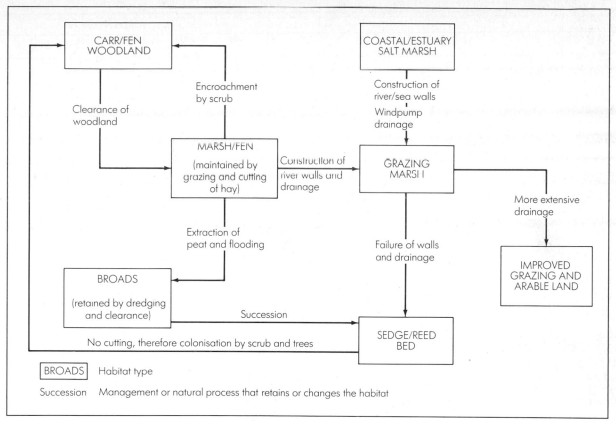

Figure 14   Broadland habitats and the processes of change

Figure 15   Reed cutters in the nineteenth century

The marshes were used to produce hay, fish were caught in the waterways, the reeds and sedge were cut for weaving and thatching (Figure 15) and the birdlife was food. With the breakdown of insularity came pressures, goods and ideas from other areas. Traditional products from fen, marsh and woods were replaced by imported materials. Therefore ecosystems such as the reed beds which need to be maintained through reed cutting and the harvesting of marsh hay have been neglected. Ecological succession by scrub vegetation, for example, is now destroying these reed beds.

Discharge of waste into the Broads causes severe local pollution. One of the principal pollutants is phosphorus from land drainage, agriculture and sewage effluent. Prior to the rapid development of the Broads in the 1800s, the level of phosphorus in the clear water was between 10 and 20 micrograms of phosphorus per litre of water (Table 4). This produced little algal growth, and the bottoms of the lakes and streams supported a wide variety of aquatic life. Today phosphorus levels are typically between 150 and 300 micrograms per litre, peaking up to 2,000 micrograms per litre. This level of pollution causes an ecological disaster as the water becomes a fertiliser and algae bloom. The waterways become choked and most other plants die. Habitats for fish decline and, as the algae die and rot, the chemical oxygen demand (COD) increases – in effect, the water is starved of oxygen. In severe cases this *eutrophication* can kill everything in the water. The loss of aquatic plants means the animals have to turn to other plants as sources of food, and the young shoots of the fringing reed beds are being grazed, increasing bank erosion.

Bank erosion is another major environmental problem (Table 5). Visitors to the Broads also bring undesirable consequences. Motor boats and cruisers produce small waves in their wake which break against the banks. People moor their boats along the banks instead of using official mooring sites. Also extensive damage has been done to the reed beds by coypus. These rodents escaped

Table 4 Changes in the mean total phosphorus concentration at Barton Broad. (Figures reconstructed from dated sediment core analyses and current phosphorus budgets.)

Date	Mean total phosphorus concentration (micrograms/litre)
1800	13
1900	52
1920	72
1940	119
1974–6	361
1981	160

Eutrophication occurs at 30–100 micrograms per litre.
Hyper-eutrophication occurs at >100 micrograms per litre.
(*Source*: **1800 – 1974–76 data**. B Moss, 'Further studies on the palaeolimnology and changes in the phosphorus budget of Barton Broads, Norfolk.' *Freshwater Biology* **10**, 1980, pp. 261–279)
(**1981 data** AWA Norfolk and Suffolk Rivers Division, *Anglian Water Annual Report and Accounts*, 1982)

from fur farms in the 1930s and have established a breeding population in the Broads. They burrow into the banks, graze on the vegetation and increase the problem of reed-bed destruction.

Recently, the incidence of disease in animal populations of the Broads has caused concern. Waterways with high salt and nutrient levels have seen an in-

crease in the alga species *Prymnesium*. This exudes a poison lethal to fish. The River Thurne fisheries have been badly affected by such fish deaths. High nutrient levels are also thought to be responsible for a type of botulism which kills birds. The disease is caused by a bacterium which lives in muds deficient in oxygen, conditions which are common in warm weather in nutrient-rich waters. Many birds have died from this botulism in recent summers.

How should the Broads be managed in future?

Landscape management requires consideration of the relative costs and benefits of any policy. Until recently, in the Broads, the environmental costs have largely been ignored and the recreational development has been allowed to go on unchecked. Policies are needed which either overcome the undesirable effects of landscape use, or future development must be halted. The Broads Authority's main concern is to conserve the local wildlife, landscape and the historic buildings. They have set up the Broads Research Advisory Committee to co-ordinate research and to advise on policies. In the Broads it is essential that the landscape is

Table 5 The state of river banks, 1980

River	Apparently undamaged (%)	Eroded (%)	Piled (%)
Thurne	43	17	39
Ant	23	54	22
Bure	10	62	28
Yare	15	56	29
Chet	16	41	42
New Cut	–	5	95
Waveney	78	9	13
Total	**30**	**43**	**27**

Source: Broads Authority, *The Ecology Group Report*, BA SMP 5, 1982

Table 6 Numbers of private and hire craft on the Broads

Date	Number of hire craft	Number of private craft	Total
1977	4,058	7,740	11,798
1978	4,041	7,718	11,759
1979	4,093	7,896	11,989
1980	4,035	8,329	12,364
1981	3,922	8,095	12,017
1982	3,640	8,234	11,874
1983	3,399	8,485	11,884
1984	3,125	9,004	12,129
1985	3,086	8,961	12,047
1986	2,931	9,346	12,277

Source: Great Yarmouth Port and Haven Commissioners, *The Broads Plan*, Broads Authority, 1987

saved, otherwise the tourist and boat industries will also perish as fishermen and holiday-makers go elsewhere.

Management policies

The Broads contain a number of ecosystems, each with their own problems and each requiring careful management. The policies being implemented are too numerous to cover in full here. We will therefore concentrate on two of the major ones: reducing the level of phosphorus in the rivers and limiting river bank erosion.

The reduction of phosphorus

Before this problem can be tackled, the first priority is to discover the nutrient balance within the waterway. This allows the authorities to establish the sources of phosphate pollution and to decide which source(s) to tackle, to bring the total phosphate in the system down to an acceptable level. Overall the level of phosphate in the Broads must be reduced. Recent research has shown that levels must decrease to well below 100 micrograms per litre of water for automatic improvement of the ecosystem. Several schemes are in operation.

1 Mud is an important source of phosphate which became trapped in the river sediments as they were deposited. This is gradually released into solution and it keeps nutrient levels and thus algal levels high. The Nature Conservancy Council and the River Commissioners have removed the nutrient-rich mud from Cockshoot Broad by suction-dredging (see page 10). They hope that this will allow higher plants to re-establish themselves. The results so far have been encouraging with lower nutrient and algae levels being recorded.

2 The Anglian Water Authority (AWA) is trying to clean up the water by removing phosphate from the sewage effluent entering

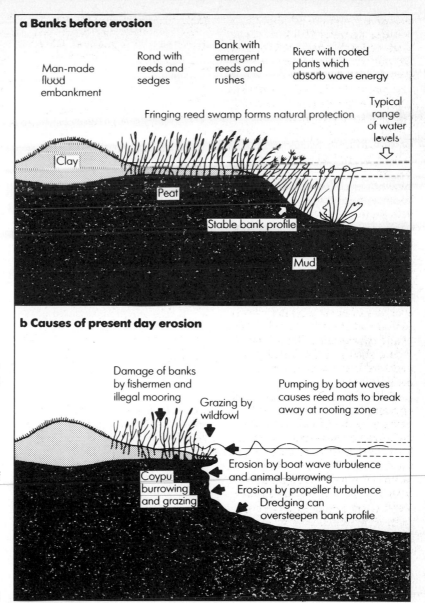

a Banks before erosion

Man-made flood embankment

Rond with reeds and sedges

Bank with emergent reeds and rushes

River with rooted plants which absorb wave energy

Fringing reed swamp forms natural protection

Typical range of water levels

Clay

Peat

Stable bank profile

Mud

b Causes of present day erosion

Damage of banks by fishermen and illegal mooring

Grazing by wildfowl

Pumping by boat waves causes reed mats to break away at rooting zone

Coypu burrowing and grazing

Erosion by boat wave turbulence and animal burrowing

Erosion by propeller turbulence

Dredging can oversteepen bank profile

Figure 16   River bank erosion

the river at North Walsham. This should have a significant effect on Barton Broad and the River Ant, which are among the most polluted waterways (see Figure 13). They started in 1977, by 1983 improvements in water quality had been noted. Phosphate levels upstream of Barton Broad were close to the 100 micrograms per litre level and water-lilies were flourishing. Downstream, at Cromes Broad, water plants had begun to

recolonise previously barren areas. The water authority has also established a phosphate removal plant at the Stalham sewage treatment works.

The erosion of banks and reed beds

Many of the waterways are suffering from erosion of their banks and the fringing reed beds (Figure 16). Attempts have been made to reduce the amount of erosion caused by boats. Bye-laws restrict their speed to eleven knots per hour (8 km/h) in the busiest stretches. Other measures include the introduction of a toll on hire craft, which will be used in bank maintenance and river dredging, and the River Commissioners have considered introducing speed-measuring devices to check boat users.

Methods of bank restoration include natural bank protection, which is the ideal solution in places where it is possible to remodel the banks to resemble their original profile. The banks are then recolonised with water plants, increasing protection. Unfortunately, in places the erosion has been too severe for this method, while in other areas boat wash makes recolonisation difficult.

In some areas artificial protection is required. The present method uses sheet steel which, although effective, is very unattractive. The Broads Authority and the Water Authority are experimenting with other techniques which control erosion and encourage reed growth. One rather expensive method, giving good results, is the use of 'Enkamat', a nylon mesh inlaid with asphalt, which protects the bank, yet allows the vegetation to grow through it (Figures 17 and 18).

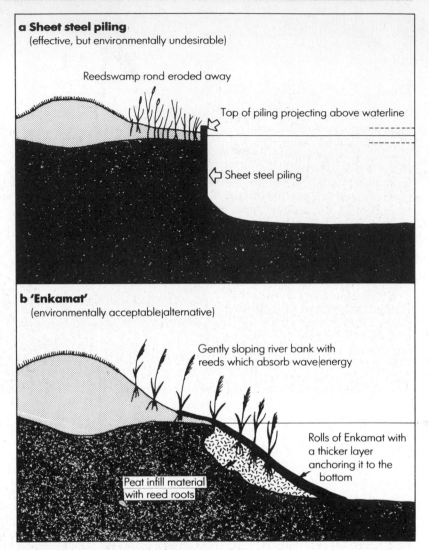

Figure 17 Two solutions to bank erosion

1 With reference to the map (Figure 13), the text and the figures for mean total phosphate concentration at Barton Broad (Table 4):

a Explain the nature of the problem of eutrophication in the Broads.

b How has the state of water quality in the Broads been classified? What is the ecological basis of this classification?

c How have the authorities tried to reduce the problems?

d What evidence is there that the measures are beginning to work?

2 Table 5 gives data on the state of the river banks in the Broads.

a Represent this data clearly using an appropriate statistical technique.

b Which waterways are suffering most from bank erosion?

c What factors contribute to the problem of bank erosion?

d What ecological impact do the following solutions have:
  i Doing nothing?
  ii Reducing boat speeds?
  iii Using sheet steel piles?
  iv Using Enkamat?

3 Table 6 shows the changes in volume of private boats and hire craft since 1986.

a Draw a graph to show the figures.

b Describe the trends shown in the graph.

c Describe some of the effects of the holiday industry on the Broads.

d Why is it important that the growth of leisure activities in the Broads is controlled?

Figure 18 Enkamat being laid (above), and the river bank some time after (below)

3

Disaster in the arid realm

Clive Agnew

Manuel Benavides on his drought-stricken ranch, Laredo, Texas, USA

Resource-rich and water-poor

The arid realm provides 82% of the world's oil production, 86% of the iron ore, 79% of the copper and 67% of the diamonds (1983). Yet our television screens and newspapers appear to be full of stories of disaster after disaster striking arid lands, from the economic hardships of 'Western farmers' through to the misery and suffering of Third World drought victims.

In fact, in many parts of the arid realm, the words *drought* and *famine* now appear almost synonymous. The worst Australian drought for two centuries ended in 1983, by which time crop production had fallen by 31% and farm income by 24%, whilst in north-east Brazil an estimated 90% of crops failed due to drought. Mexico's agricultural production fell by 12% due to the lack of rain in 1982, and in 1988 corn production in the USA was reduced by 36% (Figure 1) and soyabean by 22%. No region, it seems, can escape the ravages of drought in the 1980s.

Figure 2 clearly demonstrates the worldwide extent of this phenomenon. Using an atlas, be sure you can name the general areas of drought occurrence. These conditions parallel news reports in the 1970s, when our attention was first focused upon the plight of the inhabitants of drought-ridden areas, in particular the Sahel region of West Africa shown in Figure 3.

Of all the continents, Africa appears to have been the hardest hit. In 1983 the FAO (United Nations Food and Agriculture Organisation) reported that twenty-two countries in Africa were affected by drought and famine (*Source*: S.L. Milas, 'The years of drought', *Desertification Bulletin* **9**, 1983, pp. 10–14.) Table 1 shows that by 1987 this figure had been modified to thirteen countries, but with still 19.2 million people affected.

Figure 1 US farmer showing the damage done to his maize crop by the 1988 drought

Table 1 Population affected by drought, April 1986 (millions)

	Total	Affected	Displaced
Angola	8.6	0.6	0.5
Botswana	1.1	0.6	—
Burkina Faso	6.9	0.2	—
Cape Verde	0.3	0.1	—
Chad	5.0	0.4	0.2
Ethiopia	43.6	6.8	0.3
Lesotho	1.5	0.5	—
Mali	8.1	0.4	0.1
Mauritania	1.9	0.9	0.2
Mozambique	14.0	2.1	0.4
Niger	6.1	0.4	0.2
Somalia	4.7	0.2	0.2
Sudan	21.6	6.0	0.9
Total	**123.4**	**19.2**	**3.0**

Source: Office for Emergency Operations in Africa (OEOA), *Status Report on the Emergency Situation in Africa: as of 1 April 1986*, United Nations, New York, 1986

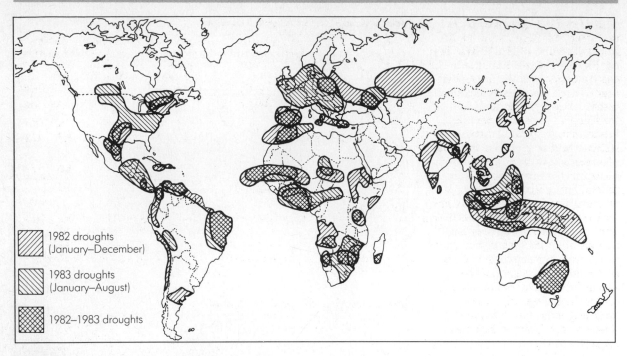

Figure 2 Occurrence of drought 1982–83
Source: D. Wilhite and M. Glantz, 'Understanding the drought phenomenon', *Water International*
10, 1985, p. 112

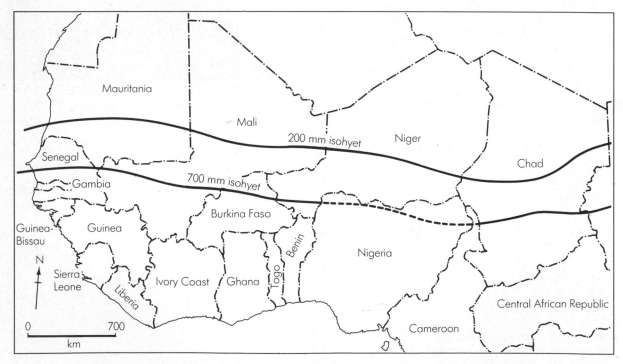

Figure 3 The Sahelian region of West Africa lies between the isohyets of 200 and
700 mm.
Source: E. G. Davy, F. Mattei and H. I. Solomon, 'An evaluation of climate and water resources for
development of agriculture in the Sudano-Sahelian zone of West Africa', *WMO Special
Environmental Report 9*, Geneva, 1976, p. 5

It is evident that over half of the drought-ridden countries of Africa lie south of the Sahara in a band ranging from Ethiopia in the east to Senegal in the west. This region has been loosely called the 'Sahel', although this term is sometimes solely used for the French-speaking West African states. The Sahel will be used as a case study in this chapter to investigate the causes of environmental and agricultural disruption in arid lands. Table 2 reveals the extent of the problem. Take the time to rank the countries for each of the variables given. Food production per capita is falling, and a large proportion of the cereals consumed are now imported. GNPs per capita are declining, and the inhabitants of this area are heavily dependent upon food aid.

?

1 Bradford Morse, director of the United Nations Development Program, said in 1987, 'drought itself is not the fundamental problem in sub-Saharan Africa … the real problem is poverty.'

What do you think he meant by these words? Is he talking about insufficient funds, lack of political power or some other deficiency? What then do you think he sees as 'the answer'?

2 Taking the data in Table 3 provided for the Sahel

a Plot rainfall and crop yields through time on a graph.

b Are any trends or changes visible? What might be causing these changes and what problems would this pose for development?

c Plot rainfalls against yields of both crops. Which one is more sensitive to drought? Is it possible to say when rainfall starts to affect yields?

d Plot crop areas through time. How does the area planted with each crop relate to rainfalls and yields?

Source: Ministère du développement rural, République du Niger, *Statistiques et Agrhymet*, Niger, 1976

Table 2 Food production in Sahelian countries

Country	Food production per capita (1969–71 = 100)		Imports as % of total cereals consumed	Food aid as % of cereals imported	GNP per capita (1979 = 100)	
	1974–6	1982–4	1984	1982	1982	1984
Burkina Faso	95	92	8	n/a	116	89
Chad	83	80	14	43	73	n/a
Ethiopia	91	93	10	64	108	85
Mali	78	83	27	47	129	100
Mauritania	69	66	89	49	147	141
Niger	89	65	2	56	115	70
Senegal	114	76	50	16	114	88
Somalia	88	60	48	44	n/a	90
Sudan	108	92	20	47	119	92

Source: after D. Curtis, M. Hubbard and A. Shepard (eds), *Preventing Famine*, Routledge, 1988, pp. 16,17,18,21

Table 3 Agroclimatic data for Niger, West Africa

Year	Niamey Rain (mm)	Yields–Niger Millet (kg/ha)	Yields–Niger Nuts (kg/ha)	Area–Niger Millet (1000 ha)	Area–Niger Nuts (1000 ha)
1978	755				
1977	543				
1976	657	402	483	2431	104
1975	668	343	130	1693	319
1974	474	395	504	2330	256
1973	371	312	212	2008	364
1972	412	390	385	2195	419
1971	570	407	650	2356	394
1970	541	377	572	2310	358
1969	645	482	647	2272	320
1968	447	387	584	1895	432
1967	813	537	836	1865	357
1966	565	483	877	1743	355
1965	662	436	810	1810	341
1964	705	570	664	1777	293
1963	558				
1962	663				
1961	695				
1960	629				
1959	653				
1958	622				
1957	608				
1956	414				
1955	560				
1954	466				
1953	689				
1952	891				
1951	566				
1950	597				

News reports of disaster in the Sahel first began to appear in the early 1970s, with the FAO (11 May 1973) reporting, 'In some areas there now appears serious risk of imminent human famine and virtual extinction of herds vital to nomad populations.' Read the telex in Figure 4 and the personal account of one herder, 'One man's experience', which reveal the misery and desolation of the time. Newspapers such as the *New York Times* and *Time* magazine estimated that some 60% of cattle perished due to drought in the early 1970s (although recent estimates now suggest losses of 30–40%), while Figure 6 indicates the substantial decrease in the yields of staple crops. The consequent economic impacts can be seen in Table 4 from Copans, who also reports drought-related human deaths of 100,000 in the period 1972–73 (*Source*: J. Copans, 'The Sahelian Drought', *Interpretations of Calamity*, K. Hewitt (ed.), Allen & Unwin, London, 1983).

Several years later the *Guardian* (10 October 1977) reported that drought had struck Sahelian crops again and noted that the

```
2000 MILE STRETCH EMBRACING ONE MILLION SQUARE KILOMETERS
MORE THAN HALF SIZE OF THE UNITED STATES
24-30 MILLION PEOPLE INVOLVED
90 PER CENT RURAL AREAS
DAKAR HAS TREBLED POPULATION IN SIX MONTHS
RUSH TO TOWNS
TENTED CAMPS SANITATION PROBLEMS TREMENDOUS
DROUGHT FOR FOUR TO FIVE YEARS
GOVERNMENTS HAVE BEEN OVERWHELMED
DESERT IS MOVING SOUTHWARD AND DRIVING THE NOMADS
INTO ARABLE AREAS AWAY FROM THE CATTLE COUNTRY
BY THE END OF OCTOBER SIX MILLION LIVES THREATENED
PROBLEM OF SURVIVAL
TUAREGS
BLUE MEN
YOUNG PEOPLE IN CITIES-A WHOLE NEW PROBLEM TO BE FACED
DROP IN REVENUE FROM CATTLE TAX-BASIS OF ECONOMY
EXPORT OF CATTLE WAS ONE OF THE MAIN SOURCES OF REVENUE
DRASTIC CHANGE IN WHOLE SAHELIAN REGION
AFFECTED REGION NEEDS 1.5 BILLION IN HELP FOR THE
DROUGHT STRICKEN REGIONS
INCLUDES WELL-DIGGING, DAMMING OF RIVERS, IRRIGATION TO
STEM THE SOUTHWARD MARCH OF DESERT
REORGANIZE RAILROAD AND RIVER TRANSPORT
INCLUDES SOME OF THE POOREST NATIONS IN THE WORLD

DESERT LINE,GAO,ZINDER,AGADEZ,TIMBUCTOO
```

Figure 4 Telex to UNICEF from the Sahel in 1973
Source: T. Clarke, *The Last Caravan*, G. P. Putnam's sons, New York, 1978, p. 103

Figure 5 Burkina Faso farmer showing the difference in crop yields of millet and sorghum between a good year and a drought year

Table 4 Changes in urban income (1969-70=100)

	Farmer income			
	1971-2	*1972-3*	*1973-4*	*1974-5*
Niger	86	69	25	82
Senegal	125	77	86	192
Burkina Faso	98	126	115	134
	Urban wages			
	1971-2	*1972-3*	*1973-4*	*1974-5*
Niger	98	90	80	111-27
Senegal	97	95	94	111-63
Burkina Faso	95	99	98	118

Source: J. Copans, 'The Sahelian Drought', *Interpretations of Calamity*, K. Hewitt (ed.), Allen & Unwin, London, 1983, p. 86

One man's experience

Q: Why did you leave the Abala region?
A: Because of the poverty.
Q: How many of your own head of cattle perished?
A: A hundred and forty.
Q: How many cattle do you have left?
A: Ten: heifers and young calves.
Q: Who is now tending the calves?
A: A younger brother in the Menaka region: we have the same father.
Q: Have you known any period when as many cattle were lost as this year?
A: I have never witnessed such distress since my birth. I suffered so much that I wondered what would become of me. I remembered that I had 50,000 francs and this enabled me to feed my family until the rain came. Then, I found myself in a difficult situation; I left for Abala where I was not given anything, even if supplies were sent there. From Abala, I came to Filingué where I found people could buy sacks of millet. I spent the rainy season there until the millet was ripe ... The President asked us to return to Abala where he told us we could be provid-

ed with food; we went back to Abala and we were given some provisions which were highly appreciated. But when the provisions stopped we had no money; nevertheless, we stayed in the hope of getting food. When we were on the point of death we returned by truck to Filingué where nothing was distributed to us. My brother and I went to our relatives living in Niamey: they gave us two sacks of millet and truck fare to Filingué ... Our mother's elder sister ... gave us some money also ... We distributed the contents of the two bags and then we came back to Niamey hungry; our aunt took us to those responsible for the distribution of foods and they gave us a sack of sorghum ... Then we were settled here. Among the ten cows I left at home, there are five animals on loan. The others which are all three years old are my personal property. How can I sell them in order to support my family? During the dry season, while I was taking cattle to the market, they died of exhaustion on the way. I lost ten of them under such conditions. These are the reasons why I am now in Niamey.

Source: A. Laya, 'Document interviews with farmers and livestock owners in the Sahel', *African Environment* **1** 2, 1975

Mauritanian government had called upon the international community to 'save human lives from a certain death'. More recently the Overseas Development Institute (ODI) (1987) announced that drought had returned to the Sahel, and the FAO estimated cattle losses of 60–70% in the early 1980s. Some now believe that drought never ceased but has continued to plague this region for the last two decades. Sir Crispen Tickell, when he was head of the Overseas Development Agency (ODA) in 1986, said of the Sahel, 'The documentary evidence for the last seventy years shows a slight decline of rainfall from 1955 and acute drought since 1968.'

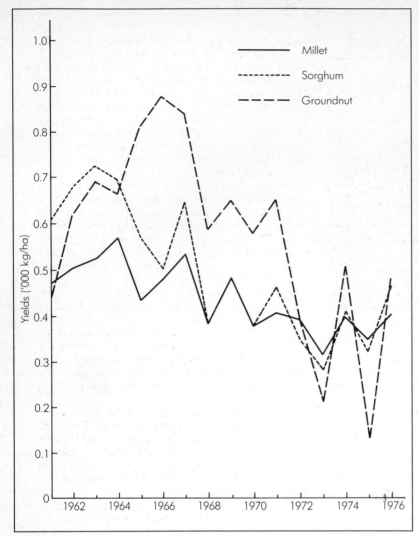

Figure 6 Agricultural yields in Niger
Source: C. T. Agnew, 'Pastoralism in the Sahel', *Third World Studies U204*, Open University, 1983, p. 11

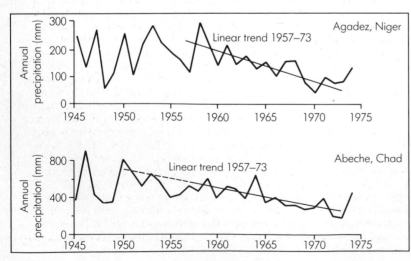

This view is supported by Flohn who commented upon:

'The Sahel drought, lasting without interruptions until (at least) 1985.'

Source: H. Flohn, 'Rainfall telecommunications in Northern and North-Eastern Africa', *Theoretical and Applied Climatology* **38**, 1987, pp. 191–97

Is the climate changing?

These reports and the marked downward trend of rainfall visible in Figure 7 suggest that the climate of this region may be changing, possibly with increasing desiccation ahead. Although the climatologist, Professor Hare, maintains there is little evidence of a worldwide pattern of increasing aridity, there is much concern for the future of the Sahel with reports suggesting that the Sahara is advancing at nine kilometres per annum.

Yet the idea of climatic change leading to increased aridity is not advocated by all. Wijkman and Timberlake, writing in the *Ecologist*, have claimed that in many areas there is no significant decline in rainfalls (*Source*: A. Wijkman and L. Timberlake, 'Is the African drought an act of God or of Man?', *Ecologist* **15**, 1985, pp. 9–18). The evidence for disaster in the Sahel appears overwhelming, with reports of livestock deaths, agricultural crops failing and even destruction of the soils in the area. However, when disasters strike arid areas of the world, drought becomes an easy scapegoat. It is all too easy to blame any environmental disaster on the climate. Increasingly, attention is being given to other non-environmental factors. Food production is being seen as a complicated system involving a highly variable environment that is being opened up to outside

Figure 7 Sahelian rainfall trends
Source: based on F. K. Hare, 'Climate drought and desertification', *Nature and Resources*, **20** 1, UNESCO, 1984, p. 4

Smiling in the Sahel

Bumper crop: Kala's millet harvest is the best for years

THE villagers of Kala in Mali are out in the bush looking for grass to weave the granaries they will need to store this year's spectacular millet harvest. It is many years since they had to build granaries of such size. But they work joyfully as the crop ripens in the field, a thick green forest of millet stalks, golden heads heavy with grain nodding as you pass.

The village of Kala, which lies some 50 miles north of the great River Niger in the Segou region of central Mali, is not alone this year in getting a good harvest. Throughout the Sahel, the dry belt that stretches along the south of the Sahara Desert, there have been three months of heavy and regular rainfall after two decades of drought. All seem to have benefited, unlike past years when some villages had the good luck to catch a storm that passed others by.

Mali's Sahelian neighbours of Mauritania, Senegal, Burkina Faso and Niger also report exceptionally good rainfall. In the grazing lands of the northern Sahel, herders are finding grass where it has not been seen for 20 or 30 years, the rains magically transforming the dry and dusty fringes of the desert itself.

The rains have also done some harm, through flooding, though nothing remotely on the same scale as that experienced by the Sudan. Damage has occurred mainly where hills and rocky soils have combined to concentrate rainwater flow into flash floods, washing away houses, people and livestock, and causing some deaths by drowning. More than a thousand people have been displaced in northern Burkina Faso and in northeast Mali following these floods. In some places, so much rain has fallen in so short a time that the sun-baked brick houses have collapsed under its force, sometimes trapping those inside. Poor urban drainage systems have meant that the water has been unable to flow away quickly, so that parts of some towns have remained in standing water for days or weeks. One of the mosques in the northern town of Niono in Mali collapsed as more than 10 centimetres of rain fell in under 48 hours.

Over the past 20 years, people have become less careful about where and how they build their homes, as dry year has succeeded dry year. They are now repairing their roofs and walls by laying a thick layer of grey mud, which provides an impermeable plaster, so rain runs off more rapidly.

Most unsurfaced roads have become impassable, even for four-wheel drive vehicles. The high-wheeled tractors used in the government rice-growing irrigation scheme around Niono are temporary kings of any road without a tarmac surface. Tractor owners are earning large sums ferrying people and goods and towing away stranded Land-Rovers and lorries whose drivers had misjudged the depth of mud.

Villagers and scientists are agreed that this year's rainfall in the Sahel is better than anything seen for 20 or more years. Not only has the total quantity been high, but since the start of the sowing rains in late June, it has seldom been dry for more than three or four days at a stretch. The 3-metre-high millet around Kala demonstrates the potential for plant growth when there is no shortage of water. But what are the implications for the longer term?

Anyone who has worked in the Sahel knows to be cautious about predicting rainfall trends. The great variability in rainfall experienced over the past 50 years gives good ground for caution; it would be risky to assume on the basis of one year, or even several years of good rain that the drought years of the past two decades are now behind us.

What these rains do mean is that people should be able to harvest more than enough to eat this year and can start to rebuild their grain reserves. The price of staple cereals is bound to slump, which will not please most farmers needing to raise cash for tax and other payments, but which should lighten the burden of buying food for the poorest social groups, such as the urban poor. It also means that builders should be in business for a good many months to come, repairing and replastering houses in preparation for next year.

One dark cloud remains on the horizon – the risk of locust swarms. Large numbers of young adult insects are maturing in dispersed colonies throughout the Sahel and will start to swarm in the next few weeks. While there is enough green grass, their preferred diet, to keep them fed and happy, the locusts should keep clear of ripening crops. But as the natural vegetation of the bush starts to dry up and the rainy season draws to an end, their attention will turn on remaining patches of greenery. At that point, the fields of millet, sorghum and rice that have done so well this year will be threatened. The farmers had better hurry up with building and filling their granaries before the locust swarms get too hungry.

Source: Camilla Toulmin, *New Scientist*, 12 November 1988, p. 69

economies and thus becoming destabilised. There are then a number of different explanations for the destruction of livestock herds and declining crop yields in the Sahel region, ranging from climatic change through to economic disruption. Let's deal with each of these alternative explanations in turn.

Climatic change

Aridity is caused by four main processes.

High pressure
Air that is heated at the equator rises, moves polewards and descends at the tropical latitudes around 20° to 30°. This descending air is compressed and warmed, leading to dry atmospheric conditions covering large areas such as the Sahara Desert.

Wind direction
Winds blowing over continents have little opportunity to absorb moisture and will be fairly stable, resulting in scarcely any precipitation and low humidities. These dry winds are seasonally constant and contribute to the aridity of south-west Asia and the Middle East.

Topography
When air is forced aloft by a mountain range, it will cool and possibly lose some moisture. On the leeward side of the mountain the same air descends and hence warms, but with a lower moisture content, leading to a dry warm wind, called the 'chinook' in the USA.

Cold ocean currents
Winds blowing across a cold ocean current close to the shore will be rapidly cooled. Mist and fog may result, as is found in the Kalahari Desert. However, as this air moves inland, it is warmed and so its humidity reduces, producing dry conditions.

In any arid area several of these processes may be operating, but their influence depends upon atmospheric conditions. When rainfall does occur, it can be a dramatic, intense and localised downpour as moist air breaks through. This is the situation in the Sahel, which is dominated from November until April by a high pressure cell, an offshore cold current and dry winds from the north-east. From May until October, moist air gradually penetrates from the south as the Intertropical Convergence Zone migrates northwards following the sun's path. Even during this period rainfall is a chancy event and extremely variable in both time and space.

The problem this creates is in discerning what is long-term climatic change as distinct from inherent short-term variability. Long records of rainfall are necessary, with a good spatial coverage, for the analysis of trends and change. Sadly, this is not the case for the Sahel region, which gives rise to a number of different opinions of what is happening to the climate in this area and why. There are three major theories: natural climatic change, air-pollution-induced climatic change and desertification-induced climatic change. As you read through the sections on each of these theories, pick out the main ideas and construct a diagram to link the ideas together.

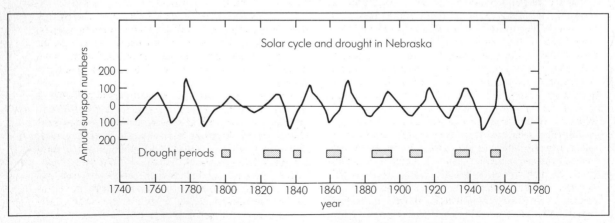

Figure 8 Occurrence of drought and sunspot activity
Source: S. Schneider, 'Is there really a food climate crisis?', *Atmospheric Quality and Climate Change*, R. Kopec (ed.), *Studies in Geography*, University of North Carolina, 1976, p. 117

Sea temperatures predict African drought

FOR THE second successive year, researchers at the Meteorological Office in Britain have successfully predicted the amount of rainfall in the drought-stricken region of Africa known as the Sahel. The technique, which they have also applied successfully to a dry region of Brazil, is based on analysis of *sea temperatures* around the world.

The researchers, led by David Parker and Chris Folland of the office's synoptic climatology branch, forecast last May another dry summer in the Sahel, a region which stretches along the borders of the Sahara from Senegal to Ethiopia. They predicted rainfall across the region at 69 per cent of the average for the previous three decades. The true figure, measured at dozens of weather stations across the region up to the middle of September, was 63 per cent.

A similar forecast made last year predicted rain in the Sahel at 75 per cent of normal. It turned out to be 70 per cent of normal. The researchers say that their technique has retrospectively predicted most droughts this century.

The technique relies on plotting anomalies in sea surface temperatures around the world. Broadly, if the seas are warmer than normal in the southern hemisphere in the spring, then the Sahel faces low rainfall during the rainy season of July and August.

So far, the forecasts have relied on the observed pattern, which Parker first spotted in 1984, without attempting to explain why it is so pronounced. The key, suggests Folland, may be the northward sea current in the Atlantic Ocean, which is the main route for the transfer of heat between the globe's northern and southern oceans.

The currents are driven largely by winds. If the south-westerly winds that blow off the Atlantic and bring rain into the Sahel are weak, then the current will be sluggish and sea-temperature anomalies will build up.

The researchers do not know what has caused the slackening in these winds and currents, which has become a frequent feature of the globe's climatic and ocean systems for almost two decades. It could be connected to global warming caused by the greenhouse effect, they say. But they have not found a mechanism.

One interesting discovery is that the sea-temperature anomalies aggregated from all three major oceans predict rainfall in the Sahel more powerfully than anomalies in any single ocean, even the Atlantic.

As part of their studies, the researchers have attempted to explore other theories about the apparent long-term drought in the Sahel. They find that El Niño, the vast switch in air pressures and ocean currents that disrupts weather across the Pacific Ocean, does not seem to be important—though it influences their drought forecasts for north-east Brazil and may be important in influencing drought in Mozambique.

Shelter against the rains. Now they will know how much to expect

The researchers' models suggest that desertification– the loss of soils and spread of desert sands into the Sahel – may make drought worse by reducing the amount of moisture present in soils that can evaporate to form clouds. But, says Parker, 'the effect of soil moisture is only a small amplification.'

In future, the forecasters hope to extend their forecasts, beginning by making separate forecasts for the east and west Sahel. They believe that they could also predict drought in eastern Africa, though complex mountain systems mean that global indicators may not be so powerful as in the Sahel.

Studies at the Meteorological Office have shown that there is a strong relationship between autumn rains in coastal Kenya and the El Niño phenomenon. And the influence of sea temperatures in the Indian Ocean seems critical in the drought lands of Sudan and northern Ethiopia.

One of the least-noticed drought regions in the world is north-east Brazil, where the rains fall between March and May. In early March this year, the Meteorological Office sent the Brazilian government a private forecast of a 'very dry' spring there. The spring proved among the driest 20 per cent of the past four decades.

March proved wet, but April and May were very dry. This 'concentration of the rainfall deficit into the latter part of the rainfall season appears to have had a particularly severe impact on agriculture in the region,' says Folland.

Source: *New Scientist*, 1 October 1987, p. 25

Natural climatic change

?

Before you read this section study
Figures 7 to 11. In pairs or groups sort
out what the graphs are showing. Then
compare your understanding with the
commentary below.

Look carefully at Figure 7. It suggests that for some locations there has been a recent downward trend in rainfalls starting in the 1950s and lasting for at least twenty years. Analysis of Sahelian rainfalls over a longer time-scale using a variety of data sources suggests that there have been several dry periods since 1600, but the twentieth century appears to be witnessing one of the most intense and protracted. Rainfalls in the Sahel correspond to general circulations and precipitation in the northern hemisphere, with one hundred- and possibly two hundred-year cycles identified. If correct, this could mean even more arid conditions in the future. However, the length of record visible in Figure 7 is much too short for such extrapolations without the causal mechanism being explained.

Climates are, of course, constantly changing and a variety of mechanisms have been suggested. Some, such as the shape and size of the Earth or the ratio of land to sea surface, change over too long a time-scale to be appropriate. Temperature gradients between the equator and the poles and vertically through the atmosphere appear important in controlling the position of the world's climatic regions.

Many climatologists favour variations in the amount of solar radiation as the likely cause for changes in these temperature gradients. Figure 8 shows a fair correlation between sunspots and the incidence of drought in Nebraska. Solar emissions have been chronicled for some time, and

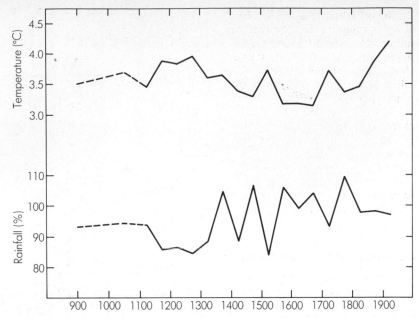

Figure 9 Reconstructed temperature and rainfalls since AD 900
Source: H. H. Lamb in T. Wigley et al., *Climate and History*, CUP, 1981

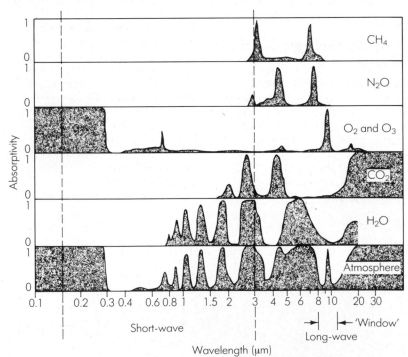

Figure 10 Absorption of solar and terrestrial radiation by atmospheric gases
Source: After Fleagle and Businger in T. Oke, *Boundary Layer Climates*, Methuen, 1978, p. 16

several cycles have been identified and related to changing circulation patterns. The amount of solar energy received is also affected by the orbit of the Earth and the turbidity of the atmosphere (dust content), and these have also been mentioned as possible causes of climatic alteration.

Nevertheless, it is still felt by several scientists that the data are incomplete and the processes involved are not sufficiently understood. In particular the association with changing sea surface temperatures has not been fully explained, while the dramatic recent increase in temperatures evident in Figure 9 cannot be accounted for solely by solar activity. This leads one to look for nineteenth- and twentieth-century changes to explain recent climatic change and droughts.

?

1 List the suggested explanations of natural climatic change in the above paragraphs. Beside each, note how strong or weak an explanation it seems to be. Continue to add to the list as you work further through the chapter.

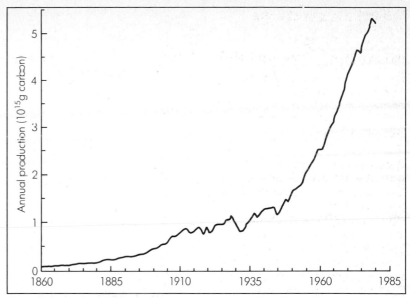

Figure 11 Annual world carbon dioxide production from fossil fuels and cement manufacture

Source: Royal Commission on Environmental Pollution, *Tackling Pollution*, 10th Report, 1984, p. 157. Reproduced with the permission of the Controller of Her Majesty's Stationery Office.

Air-pollution-induced climatic change

An alternative interpretation is that recent changes in the Sahel can be explained by atmospheric pollution. Figure 10 shows how atmospheric gases transmit short-wave solar radiation but preferentially absorb longer-wavelength terrestrial radiation. Figure 11 reveals the substantial increase in

carbon dioxide emissions since the nineteenth century (not to mention other pollutants) leading to an increase in temperatures through the 'greenhouse effect'. This could have changed the temperature gradient between the equator and the poles, so reducing Sahelian rainfall. Thus it is argued that the burning of fossil fuels could account for declining Sahelian rainfalls.

Several models have been

developed to relate carbon dioxide concentrations to temperature. These models do not fully explain changes in temperature and associated droughts over the last hundred years, while predictions of future carbon dioxide levels have been quite inaccurate, largely due to ignorance over the absorption of this gas by the world's oceans. Harrington suggests that carbon dioxide models of temperature change are only

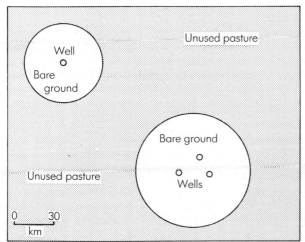
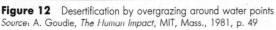
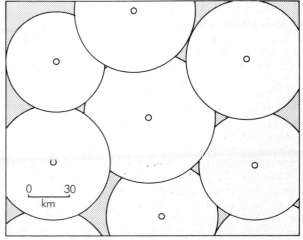

Figure 12 Desertification by overgrazing around water points
Source: A. Goudie, *The Human Impact*, MIT, Mass., 1981, p. 49

accurate when coupled with data about solar activity, air turbidity and ocean temperatures (*Source*: J. Harrington, 'Climatic change: a review of causes', *Canadian Journal of Forestry Research* **17**, 1987, pp. 1313–39). Even then predictions of rainfalls have been poor. These studies do not provide conclusive proof that either atmospheric pollution or solar acidity are to blame for drought in the Sahel. An alternative, more local, mechanism is overgrazing of vegetation.

Desertification-induced climatic change

Goudie explains how overgrazing around water points could lead to a large expanse of desertified land (Figure 12). The removal of vegetation, it is argued, results in higher surface *albedos* (short-

wave reflection) which leads to a reduction in the amount of energy absorbed by the atmosphere, producing stable air masses, so decreasing rainfall. The resulting desiccated vegetation completes the circle, producing even higher albedos and lower rainfall. Many aspects of the region's energy balance are ignored, however, and studies in the Sahel using remote sensing have suggested that there has not been any significant change in surface reflectivity. This model of change has therefore appeared invalid. However, recent studies suggest that rainfall in the region may be largely due to water that is transpired by vegetation rather than transported in by moist winds from the south. If this is the case, then removal of vegetation may well have a harmful effect upon Sahelian rainfalls.

1 Three explanations of climatic change have been offered above, but each suffers from inadequate models and data. Compare Figure 7 with Figure 13. Discuss in small groups, with reference to the graphs, my proposition that it is not altogether clear whether the climate is in fact changing. Are we just witnessing a periodic dry spell in this highly variable environment?

2 Goudie states, 'numerous studies of available meteorological data... do not allow any conclusion to be drawn to the question of systematic long-term changes in rainfall, and the case for climatic deterioration... is not proven.'
Make notes showing how you would set out evidence for and against climatic change, in preparation for writing a newspaper article.

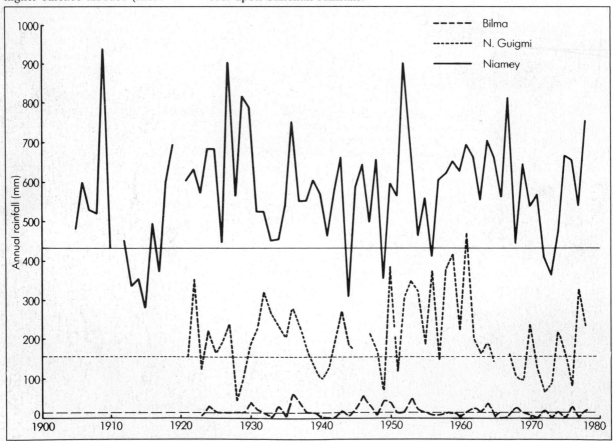

Figure 13 Rainfall figures from selected stations in Niger
Source: Ministère du développement rural, Niger

Another possible explanation

Some scientists have become more concerned with the effects of the climate upon the inhabitants of the region, leading to the question why they appear to be more susceptible to change, why they can no longer respond to fluctuations in rainfall. That is, low rainfalls are seen as the 'trigger' for disaster, not the root cause. Even more radical explanations ignore the climate altogether and place the blame fully upon economic disruption through bungled development attempts and increased economic competition.

In the next section we shall look at accounts of life in arid lands which suggest that:

1 The present difficulties are not due to drought and/or climatic change but result from contact with aspects of European culture which led to disruption of the pastoral way of life. This point of view is highlighted in passages A and B on page 71.

2 There is a second argument to be understood which concerns the pressures exerted from the growing of cash crops.

Pastoral disruption

Pastoralists herd animals in the inhospitable areas of the world where the cultivation of crops is not feasible. The essence of pastoralism is that the herd is the resource and the pastoralists survive by consuming animal products such as milk, meat and even blood. A typical diet would be 275 pounds of millet, 1,000 pounds of milk and only 33 pounds of meat. This diet is poor in vitamin A (only 68% of requirements) and vitamin C (19%) but rich in protein.

In order to combat the vagaries of the environment, several strategies are employed, of which movement is perhaps the most important. Figure 15 shows the seasonal migration patterns followed by the southern Tuareg in the Sahel region which is being used as a case study.

Figure 14 Boy of the Peuhl tribe, who keeps herds of cows and goats, Niger

There is a northwards movement during the onset of the rainy season for animals to graze upon the succulent new shoots that emerge with the first rains. Their herds of camels and goats are well adapted to the dry climate, while cattle are kept in the wetter areas to the south. By diversifying their herds they are able to exploit a variety of niches and reduce the risk of losing their total herd. Animals may also be loaned or shared and so distributed around the rangeland, ensuring some survive and prosper.

Pastoralists have thus minimised their risks through flexibility, while short-term storage of milk as yoghurt or cheese can further aid their resilience. Farmers in the wetter regions may supply cereals and pulses in exchange for animals and manure, although agricultural products and slaves may also be taken by force if necessary.

?

1 Read passages A and B which concern the perspectives of both a pastoralist and a French colonist. Write a few sentences on how the semi-arid lands should be used:

a according to the herders,

b according to the French colonists.

2 What is meant by 'market economy'? How would exporting meat affect the pastoralists either

a if it was a surplus of food above what they needed or

b if it meant selling some of what they would otherwise have eaten?

3 Using Figure 16, write a paragraph on each of the three stages indicated. In the last stage (3), the Sahel seems to be worse off than in the first (1). Can you suggest any ways in which the people could produce more food for their own use?

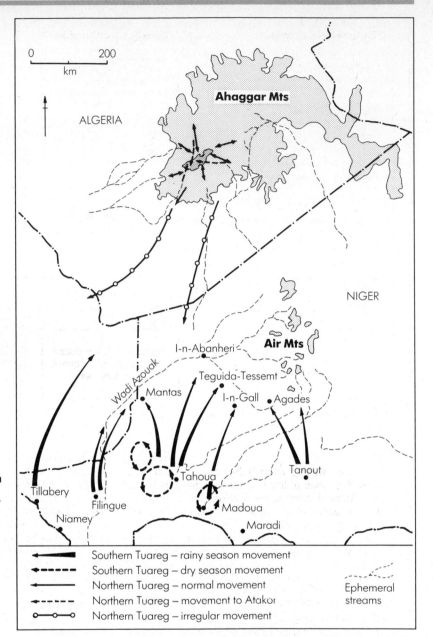

Figure 15 Seasonal migration patterns of Tuareg in Niger
Source: C. T. Agnew, 'Pastoralism in the Sahel', Third World Studies U204, Open University, 1983, p. 17

Table 5 Numbers of livestock, Niger

	1938	1961	1966	1970
Cattle	760,000	3,500,000	4,100,000	4,500,000
Sheep/goats	2,700,000	6,800,000	7,950,000	9,000,000
Camels	50,000	350,000	360,000	n/a
Donkeys	160,000	300,000	315,000	n/a

Source: R. Franke and B. Chasin, *Seeds of Famine*, Allanheld, Osman & Co., 1981, p. 100

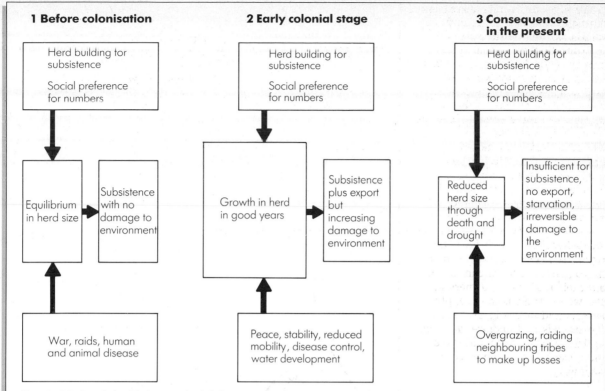

1 Before colonisation

Herd building for subsistence

Social preference for numbers

Equilibrium in herd size

Subsistence with no damage to environment

War, raids, human and animal disease

2 Early colonial stage

Herd building for subsistence

Social preference for numbers

Growth in herd in good years

Subsistence plus export but increasing damage to environment

Peace, stability, reduced mobility, disease control, water development

3 Consequences in the present

Herd building for subsistence

Social preference for numbers

Reduced herd size through death and drought

Insufficient for subsistence, no export, starvation, irreversible damage to the environment

Overgrazing, raiding neighbouring tribes to make up losses

Figure 16 People–land balance in the Sahel
Source: McKay, Sibley and Smith

Passage A

Tribal cattle-herding nomads had by trial and error evolved a method of living in the hazardous semi-arid areas without destroying the environment. Some cattle and some human beings could expect early death, and the population did not increase much.

They knew the distribution and value in different seasons of the natural grazing, and when one area had been grazed, they left it to recover, and moved along well-tried routes to another. Their wealth and prestige depended on the size of their herds, which they built up to the limits of the available fodder.

When the colonists arrived and seized some of the 'unoccupied' lands, the herders' 'drought insurance' disappeared. With their security threatened, the nomads reacted with hostility, theft and violence.

They saw the colonists as unintelligent intruders, lacking the most elementary knowledge of the Sahel environment and of its established and well-proven practices.

Passage B

Colonists saw the tribal people wandering aimlessly about with their cattle in an endless search for pasture and water. They tried, by putting down bores tapping underground water, to stop this needless movement, and establish a settled cattle-raising industry for meat export. They offered medicines against cattle diseases and were pleased when the nomads accepted these and the herds grew larger.

Then soil erosion and the destruction of vegetation set in the intensively used areas. Despite the obvious commercial necessity the tribesmen refused to reduce the size of their herds to which they seemed sentimentally attached. They showed no interest in scientific management, even when the desert seemed to be advancing. In fact, the worse the drought, the more they tried to increase their herds.

The colonists saw the herders as unintelligent savages, lacking any appreciation of modern technology and of the market economy and showing marked hostility to beneficial changes.

Source: J. McKay, J. Sibley and R. Smith, *The Third World* **3**, IDC, Adelaide

The pastoral production system is seen to offer a range of solutions to combat the arid environment in which it operates. The reports of livestock deaths listed above clearly show that this is no longer the case. What then has changed? Some researchers suggest that attempts to develop these pastoral herds led to massive increases in animal numbers prior to the reduction in rainfall commencing in 1968 (Table 5). Veterinary care, deep boreholes and the provision of water points, together with good rainfalls in the early 1960s, enabled herds to multiply, with the consequent overloading of the range. When drought occurred, livestock herds were decimated, not by lack of rainfall but through a shortage of grazing. That is, the disaster in the Sahel was due more to mismanagement of the environment than climatic change.

1 Take the last sentence and write a paragraph explaining to a twelve-year-old what is meant by it.

There are also a number of other changes taking place in Tuareg society, for instance:

- The sedentarisation (settling down) of the traditional camel-herding groups in response to economic and political pressures.

- There are increasing wage-earning opportunities from tourism through to uranium mining.

- Slavery has been abolished.

- Migration routes now cross international frontiers, which are sometimes closed.

- The constraint imposed by a lack of water is being reduced. Wells and boreholes can tap groundwater resources, while trucks can be equipped with water reservoirs and driven into the desert.

Such changes have been taking place while the demand for meat is growing, and these previously isolated societies have been opened up to Western economic influences. Figure 17 clearly reveals how rapidly manufactured goods have been adopted by pastoralists, with the consequent need to raise cash for these purchases. Such rapid, recent changes have altered the

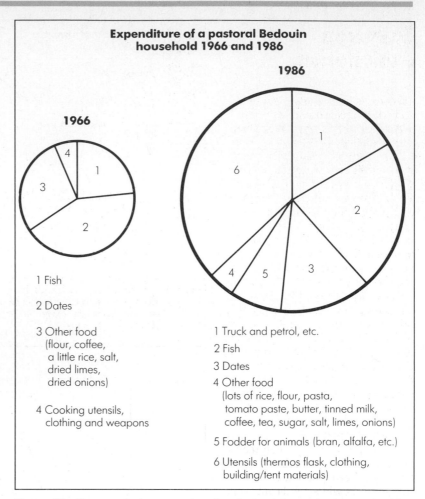

Expenditure of a pastoral Bedouin household 1966 and 1986

1966

1 Fish

2 Dates

3 Other food
   (flour, coffee,
   a little rice, salt,
   dried limes,
   dried onions)

4 Cooking utensils,
   clothing and weapons

1986

1 Truck and petrol, etc.

2 Fish

3 Dates

4 Other food
   (lots of rice, flour, pasta,
   tomato paste, butter, tinned milk,
   coffee, tea, sugar, salt, limes, onions)

5 Fodder for animals (bran, alfalfa, etc.)

6 Utensils (thermos flask, clothing,
   building/tent materials)

Figure 17 Changes in Bedouin expenditure from the Royal Geographical Society Wahiba Sands Expedition
Source: RGS, *The Wahiba Sand Sea: A Desert Resource Pack*, 1988. Reproduction by permission of the Royal Geographical Society and BP Educational Service.

labour force with the outmigration of young men and have led to an intensification of rangeland use. Inevitably, overuse has produced both land degradation and destruction of the herds. This may have been exacerbated by low rainfalls, but the cause of the disaster is seen to be inappropriate attempts to develop the pastoral economy.

Unfortunately there is very little data available to support this explanation of events. Numbers of animals are notoriously difficult to obtain, and a recent survey shown in Figure 18 suggests that the claims of decimation of livestock herds may have been exaggerated, or there has been a

rapid recovery of herd sizes. In a review of desertification, Warren and Agnew maintain that there has been an overestimate of its extent and effects, a view that is supported by studies in the Sudan (*Source*: A. Warren and C.T. Agnew, 'An assessment of desertification and land degradation in arid and semi-arid areas', *International Institute for Environment and Development Paper 2*, 1988). Clearly the pastoral production system is changing under the influence of Western intervention, but whether this has resulted in the destruction of the pastoral economy and permanent environmental damage is still uncertain.

Cash crop exploitation

Farmers in arid lands have to combat problems such as poor soils, pest and disease attack and a lack of manual labour, in addition to variable rainfall. Farmers have developed methods to work within this environmental system. The crops grown (millet, sorghum and pulses) tend to be well adapted to low and irregular rainfalls, while soil fertility can be maintained through rotations, land being left fallow and by the application of animal and human wastes. In addition, by being sown on several dates, crops are maturing at different rates and so there is less chance that pests and diseases will strike and destroy all the plants. Improved storage and developing networks that stimulate trade further minimise the risk of starvation.

Figure 19 reveals that, for one Sahelian country, Niger, crop production has generally been maintained, but with a marked variability. Comparison of Figures 6 and 19, however, indicates that production has only been kept reasonably static by generally increasing the area under cultivation, as shown in Figure 20. The reasons for this increase in cultivated area are threefold.

1 The higher rainfalls in the early 1960s encouraged a northerly migration of farmers on to the more marginal lands to the north. This increased the competition for land between the pastoralists and farmers, requiring government action to restrict the northward limit to which farmers could cultivate. There was also an attempt to prevent any damage to farmers' fields by the grazing herds through keeping animal migrations within several metres of major roads, although this then reduced the amounts of animal manure spread by the animals on to the fields.

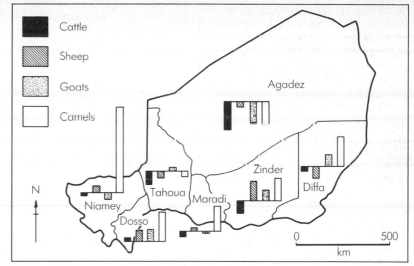

Figure 18 Changes in livestock herds. If the histogram lies above the horizontal line, then there has been an increase in those animals between 1968 and 1980.
Source: J. Swift (ed.), *Pastoral Development in Central Niger: Report of the Niger Range and Livestock Project*, Niger, 1984, p. 51

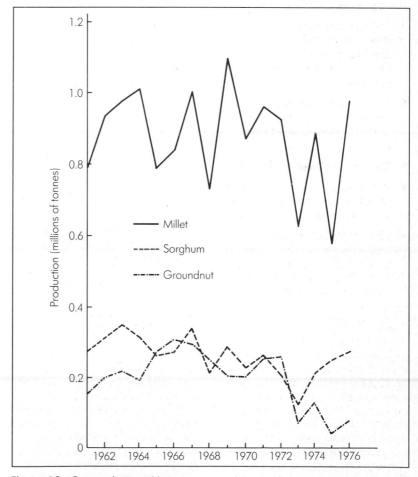

Figure 19 Crop production in Niger
Source: Ministère du développement rural, Niger

2 The growth of population through health care programmes, cessation of warfare and famine relief has created a growing demand for land. This has aided the push on to more marginal lands and led to the fallow period being reduced as land can no longer be left idle. Consequently more people are living in the drier, northern areas, while the soil fertility of much land is declining. The US Office of Technology Assessment (*Source*: *Africa Tomorrow: Issues in Technology*, Washington, 1984) reported that African cities have the highest growth rate in the world, with populations doubling every ten years. The rapid expansion of urban populations increases the demand for food, encouraging intensification of the dry-land farming system. Curtis et al. calculate that population is growing at a rate of 2.8% in African countries where famine is a risk, which is outstripping the food production growth rate of only 1.3% per annum (*Source*: D. Curtis, *Preventing Famine*, Routledge, London, 1988).

3 When each Sahelian state achieved independence, most had poorly developed economies and were consequently heavily dependent upon other nations for assistance. Following independence there was a drive to commercialise agricultural production through the introduction of cash crops in order to purchase foreign goods and also obtain some economic stability. Peanuts (groundnuts) had been introduced to West Africa in the nineteenth century, but now governments were actively encouraging the introduction of new hybrids. The United Nations (UN) yearbook shows that in 1964 peanuts accounted for 79% of Senegal's exports and 63% of Niger's. However, Table 6 reveals the declining terms of trade during the 1960s as competition with other producers increased. To maintain economic returns, more and more land had to be utilised,

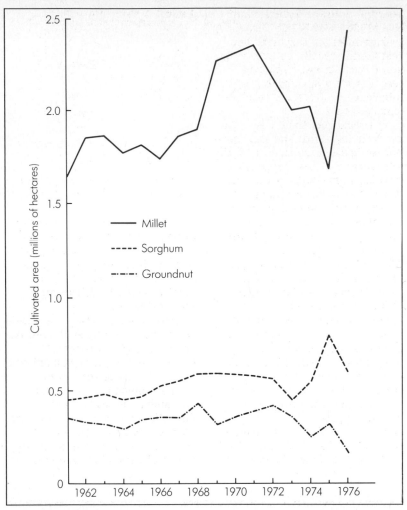

Figure 20   Crop areas in Niger
Source: Ministère du développement rural, Niger

Figure 21   A view of Nairobi, Kenya, where the population is growing by about 3% a year

resulting in lower fertilities and competition with staple cereals such as millet or sorghum. The best land is usually put into irrigation of cash crops, displacing cereal farmers and making self-sufficiency in foodstuffs an unattainable goal.

It is believed, then, that data on declining yields and static production have more to do with the introduction of cash crops and growing population pressure than drought or climatic change. Overemphasis on cash crop exploitation resulted in soil impoverishment and an expansion on to the marginal lands. Although this interpretation has great popularity, there is little hard evidence to support the claims of land-use change and soil impoverishment. Studies in the Sudan could find no evidence of increasing occupation of more marginal lands, while Figure 20 does not reveal a dramatic increase in the area under groundnuts. Perhaps the growth in groundnut production started before the 1960s and the effects were not realised until the 1970s? In fact millet shows the greatest

Table 6 Declining terms of trade

| Country | Export product | Kg produced to get 100 units of market goods | |
		1961	1970
Senegal	Peanuts	100	148
Niger	Peanuts/Cotton	100(1964)	130/135
Chad	Cotton	100(1964)	115
Mali	Peanuts/Cotton	100	174/161 (1965)
Burkina Faso	Peanuts/Cotton	100	126/118

Source: F. Franke and B. Chasin, *Seeds of Famine*, Allanheld, Osman & Co., 1981, p. 87

significant increase, which is most dramatic just after the 'drought' started in 1968. But this appears to be in response to lower rainfalls rather than reflecting a massive migration on to the marginal lands.

Interpretations, then, vary between those who believe there has been a drought (whether its causes are natural or human) and those who argue that, even though rainfall may have decreased, famine and agricultural disruption are caused by pressure on the land and economic difficulties. The debate is beset with a lack of data and unprovable

hypotheses. In order to gain any further understanding we need to examine the meaning of drought.

1 A friend of yours who does not study geography has just suggested that climate (drought) is the cause of much of Africa's problems. This is not surprising, given newspaper stories. How would you respond to the comment, having studied this chapter? Set out notes for your reply and then read the section which follows.

What is drought?

In the UK drought is defined by the Meteorological Office as fifteen consecutive days during which no more than 0.2mm of rain falls on any one day (Goudie, *Dictionary of Physical Geography*, Basil Blackwell, 1985). Such a 'meteorological' definition has the advantage of precision but means little to the inhabitants of the Sahel. Sandford suggested a more appropriate definition of drought:

'A rainfall-induced shortage of some economic good brought about by inadequate or badly timed rainfall.'

Source: S. Sandford, *Towards a Definition of Drought*. Symposium on drought in Botswana, Clark University Press, 1978

Clearly some notion of a reduction in water supplies is essential, but the variability of the climate in the Sahel suggests that the use of rainfall alone, and in particular the use of annual totals, is questionable. As the majority of the population of the Sahel are involved in subsistence agriculture, an appropriate definition of drought should focus on the deficiency of moisture for plants, for example. The US Weather Bureau definition is,

'A period of dry weather of sufficient length and severity to cause at least partial crop failure.'

To study drought and famine in Africa, it is, then, necessary to obtain an agricultural definition.

Figure 22 shows the frequency of drought years encountered by millet cultivation for the period 1967 to 1978 for the country of Niger (*Source*: C.T. Agnew, 'Sahel drought: meteorological or agricultural?', *Journal of Climatology*, 1989, vol. 9, pp. 371–82). It is meaningless to consider agricultural (millet) drought to the north of the country, as it is too dry for the cultivation of crops, but rainfalls have been abnormally low in this northern region and it would appear that pastoralists have been suffering from 'meteorological drought'. Figure 22 shows the southern half of the country to be largely free of agricultural drought for millet

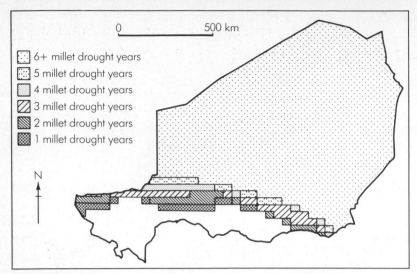

Figure 22 Frequency of millet drought years between 1967 and 1978 in Niger
Source: C. T. Agnew, 'Sahel drought, meteorological or agricultural?', *Journal of Climatology*, Royal
Meteorological Society, 1989

crops, which suggests that other factors such as declining soil fertilities may be to blame for falling yields. In between these two areas lie the marginal lands which are periodically struck by agricultural drought, but this is to be expected and should not be blamed on climatic change. If farmers do cultivate in this region of high risk, then we should be examining whether they are forced to do so or whether they are responding to an environmental opportunity.

This analysis demonstrates that life in the Sahel is precarious and much more complicated than many have believed. It appears to be undergoing both environmental and economic changes, but the significance and effects of these changes is far from clear.

Given the continuing reports of famine and disruption in arid lands, action is urgently needed, but first the cause of these disasters must be established. It appears that disaster in arid lands may be caused by a combination of factors including climatic change, economic disruption and population growth. Drought is often held to be the major constraint, but there are dangers in treating drought as a purely climatic phenomenon. The water available depends not only upon supply (rainfall, river flow and so on) but also upon demand. Changes in land use and increasing population can create drought conditions in addition to climatic change. Given this potential confusion over the occurrence of drought, the scarcity of data in these regions and the dramatic changes taking place in the 1970s and 1980s, it is understandable that there is still debate over the cause of recent disasters in arid lands. It is not possible therefore to provide once-and-for-all solutions, be they preventing air pollution or encouraging birth control.

What should be noted is that arid lands are not homogeneous regions. Also, it is difficult and dangerous to generalise over problems and solutions. In the short term there is a need to prevent famine and further deterioration of the environment. Food aid may increase reliance upon Western donors, but it can release some of the pressure on the land. Timberlake noted that, of all the billions that had been spent on the Sahel between 1975 and 1981, only 4% had gone to develop the growing of food crops and only 1.5% had gone to ecological projects such as tree-planting and soil conservation (*Source*: L. Timberlake, *Africa in Crisis*, Earthscan, London, 1985). If soils are eroded and destroyed, then there will be little worthwhile left to develop.

A sustainable future should, then, start with protection of the environment, but other measures to be taken, from population controls and land-use controls

Figure 23 A tree-planting scheme in Niger

Nicholas Woodsworth on a self-help project to reforest the Sahara
Senegal battles against the sands

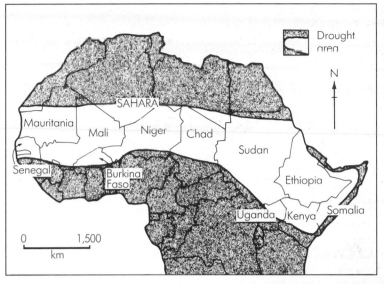

SULIMAN DIOP does not know exactly how old he is, but his memory goes further back than anyone else's in his village. A herder all his life, he now spends most of his days in conversation in the deep shade of a favourite acacia tree. In skull cap and white robe, his beard grizzled, he spends long hot afternoons recalling an Africa that no longer exists.

One of his stories is particularly hard to believe. 'Out there,' he says pointing to the sun-baked and treeless plain that stretches away from the village, 'was the forest. When my father was a young man, it was so dense and dark he didn't dare go out after dark.'

It is not surprising that the children of Louga, a district of northern Senegal forty miles from the Mauritanian border, smile in disbelief when they hear Mr Diop's story. Over the last 80 years Louga, like many communities dotting the Sahel from Senegal to Ethiopia, has been the victim of desertification.

Despite the best efforts of rock musicians and relief agencies, the two-decade-old Sahel crisis no longer looms large in the consciousness of the West. Exposed for years to the point of insensibility, Western consumers of the news have moved on to no-less-horrifying but fresher stories.

For the villagers of Louga, however, the most important part of the story is only now unfolding. There is nothing of the dramatic media event in it. There are no emotional television pledges, no relief convoys being filmed as they race to the rescue of starving children.

Instead, there is a great deal of hard work without pay and with little immediate return. No longer soliciting Western relief dollars but the energy of its villagers, Louga is striking back at the desert with one of the most evolved reforestation programmes of its type.

Launched in 1982, the Louga project is one of numerous anti-desertification programmes in Senegal bilaterally funded by Western nations and supervised by the United Nation's Food and Agriculture Organization (FAO).

Foreign involvement and the $2m provided by Sweden in 1985 for the second phase of the project is not the sole constituent of its success. Far more important is the policy of educating villagers to see their own interests in reforestation. By making them aware of the direct benefits of programmes that they themselves devise and take part in, project leaders hope that Louga is assuring itself a future long after FAO has moved away.

'The traditional attitude here can be summed up in the Muslim saying "insh'allah",' says Mr Etienne Kaisan, the Belgian supervisor of the Louga programme. 'If the desert is taking over it is the will of Allah, and there is no point in fighting it. Western agencies went some way to changing this attitude when years ago during the first Sahel projects they instituted a "food for work" policy. Villagers were motivated as long as the food arrived. Then, when it stopped coming, they quite naturally abandoned the projects.'

Today the emphasis in the Louga project is on villager participation and decision-making, a process that begins by making people aware of the role they play in the deterioration or improvement of the environment.

When Mr Diop was a small boy, the natural vegetation around Louga held the soil in place. The population was small enough to satisfy its fuel needs while allowing the natural regeneration of trees. Traditional methods of millet and sorghum cultivation meant that roots and stalks left behind after harvest not only 'fixed' the soil in the dry season but also enriched it.

That all changed after the arrival of French colonists, who made Louga the centre of Senegal's groundnut industry. The forest was over-exploited by a fast-growing population, and eventually gave way to fields.

Decades of intense cultivation impoverished the earth, and because groundnut harvesting requires that the entire plant be uprooted, the soil lay without ground cover year after year during the fallow season. Loose and dry, its richest parts were carried away by the wind, leaving an ever poorer soil.

'The answer to many of these problems, both natural and man-made, lies in reforestation,' says Mr Kaisan. 'It fixes the soil, enriches it, provides firewood, and stops desert sand from moving south. But to pay for reforestation programmes is prohibitively expensive – over $400 an acre. What we try to do is show various groups how they can benefit by undertaking the work themselves on a volunteer basis.'

Using specially trained mobile teams to cover as many of the district's 2,900 villages as possible, the project organises meetings, demonstrations, and training sessions.

Village women, for example, who are forced to walk up to 10 kilometres a day in search of firewood, obviously find a lack of fuel the most serious effect of desertification. Organising themselves into reforestation committees, they undertake to plant the kind of trees that most conveniently provide firewood. They are also shown the construction of a simple and highly economical wood-burning cooker.

Village men, on the other hand, are more concerned with farming. Forming similar committees, they are organised to plant wind-breaks to protect their fields from wind erosion.

Whether the job at hand is sand dune fixation, well digging, or the creation of living fences to protect groundcover from human and livestock depredation, self-interest has shown itself to be the best motivation in fighting the desert. But, as Mr Kaisan admits, self-interest alone cannot slow down the Sahara. What is lacking is co-operation and integrated programmes on the international level.

If some Sahelian nations achieve results while others accomplish little, none will benefit from reforestation efforts. Saharan sand, he ruefully points out, is no different from the wind that carries it. It knows no borders.

Source: Financial Times, 20 January 1988

through to the amount of cash cropping, will depend upon the political persuasion and resources of each country. You may like to consider some of these alternatives and arrive at your own long-term and short-term solutions by tackling the exercises provided below and reading through the passage 'Senegal battles against the sands'. This passage considers the problem of desertification in Senegal caused (it is believed) by the introduction of cash crops. Reforestation is seen as the solution, but with the emphasis upon self-help and training following the failure of the 'food for work' programme.

?

1 How do you react to this article, having read this chapter? Make a list of the main points the journalist is making.

2 Using Table 1 (page 57), calculate the percentage of the total population of each country that was affected by drought. For which countries would the problem appear most severe? What does the term 'displaced' mean and what does it signify in relation to the lives of those concerned?

3 Figure 24 is an attempt to show the groups involved in the food production system in the Sahel. It is not, however, complete. For instance, what about the connections between farmers and pastoralists? What are the effects of population growth on land degradation? Discuss in pairs how you can improve upon this diagram, so that all factors causing famine, loss of livestock and falling yields are represented.

4 In order to derive different solutions to the problems facing the inhabitants of arid lands, make a list of all those groups involved, for example:

Pastoralists
Dry-land cultivators
Irrigators
President of the country
USAID
World Bank
UNFAO
Oxfam
War on Want and so on.

Divide the class so that each adopts the role of one of these groups. Then consider what their aims and values would be, such as to improve security, to preserve the environment, to market animals, to increase animal numbers and so on (this really requires some research on the policies and objectives of the groups). Rank your list of aims into an order of priority and consider how these goals might be achieved. Thus a plan of action can emerge, with immediate and secondary action identified. Finally, compare the different proposals to look for common ground and conflicts. The ensuing debate and chaos may not lead to any consensus but will help to illustrate the dilemma and difficulty faced by planners and decision-makers in this arena.

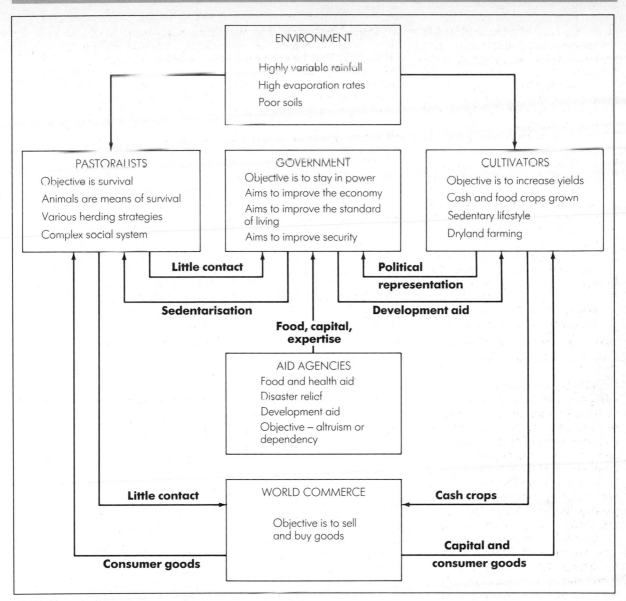

Figure 24 The Sahelian food production system
Source: C. T. Agnew, 'Checkland's soft systems approach – a method for geographers?', *Area* **16** 2, p. 172

4

Glacial environments: issues at the interface between physical processes and human activities

Colin Fenn

A graphic representation of the Wilderwurm Glacier
Source: Karl Lukan, *Alps and Alpinism*, Anton Schroll, Vienna, 1968

What are the issues?

Question: When is an issue an issue? More to the point, when is something connected with glaciers an issue?
Answer: It depends who you ask ... doesn't it?

Scene 1
An Alpine village meeting

Ask people who live in the Alps about their concern for their local environment and you are likely to be treated to a lecture about the problems associated with insensitive tourist development (Figure 1). Their concern lies as much in the intensification of the avalanche, landslip and flood hazards which have always been part of life in the mountains as it does in a desire to maintain the natural beauty and character of the environment. The clearing of slopes for ski runs, and the building of (over) expensive apartments, in zones which locals have long learned to avoid, do not only scar and intrude into the landscape: they fundamentally alter the delicate balance of the environment, increasing runoff, decreasing soil stability, and removing natural buffers and protection barriers.

Disasters can too easily follow. The massive floods and landslides which devastated parts of the Alps in the summer of 1987 (Figure 2), and the fatal avalanches in Klosters and St Anton in March 1988, attracted international attention – for a short time. Be honest, do you remember them? Time, the press and the developers may move on, but less well-publicised similar events are ever-present concerns for those who live in the mountains.

Yet tourism brings much-needed employment and income to the mountain regions. So too do the hydro-electric power schemes which, in exploiting the water reserves of glaciers and snowfields via systems of dams,

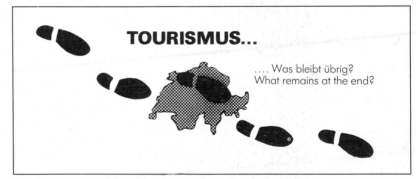

TOURISMUS...

.... Was bleibt übrig?
What remains at the end?

Figure 1 Images of the dangers of unchecked tourism in the Alps

conduits and pumping installations, bring concrete, metal and tarmacadam into the 'natural' environment. The problem, as the news clippings illustrate, revolves around how to balance the competing demands of development and conservation, how to minimise the environmental consequences of people's activities as they exploit the natural resources of the alpine zone.

?

This, of course, is not a straightforward matter. Think about this issue, for example:

1 Should ski centres be spread out thinly over a mountain area, or concentrated into large purpose-built centres (like Thyon 2000 in the Swiss Valais)? You could debate this question in class.

Figure 2 Devastation caused by mountain flood near Annecy in the French Alps, July 1987

Ski deaths as avalanches sweep Alps

AVALANCHES killed at least 21 people over the weekend as heavy blizzards continued in many of Europe's most popular ski resorts.

The most dramatic accident was in the Austrian Tyrol, where two giant avalanches 400 yards wide claimed 10 lives, including two Austrian women and five Swedish holidaymakers, shortly before 7am yesterday morning at the St Anton resort. The final death toll may well be higher.

Several houses and tourist pensions were covered by ten metres of freshly fallen snow in the avalanche, 30 miles from the Swiss resort of Klosters, where Major Hugh Lindsay, the former Queen's equerry, died while skiing on Thursday with Prince Charles.

On Saturday three people, including another Swede and two Germans, were killed in further avalanches in the Tyrol. Poor communications hampered the search for further victims and survivors. By yesterday afternoon over 200 volunteers had joined the Austrian army's special mountain rescue division, which had been sent into the area by special train. But the rescue operation was still encountering great difficulties.

Austria's western province of Voralberg remained completely cut off from the rest of the country, but the authorities in Tyrol hope to re-establish rail links with the area this morning. There was no news last night of possible victims.

The entire area of Alpine Austria remained on an alarm footing as meteorologists claimed that further avalanches could not be ruled out. People in the area have been warned not to make any journeys.

In the Italian Alps, avalanches killed at least six over the weekend – two West Germans and an Italian skier died yesterday, and two Swiss and one West German on Saturday.

In West Germany, the heaviest snowfalls in the Black Forest for six years at the weekend brought chaos to the country's most popular skiing region.

A 40-year-old man was trapped by an avalanche and killed while cross-country skiing, while in the Bavarian Alps a two-year-old boy was killed by a huge block of snow sliding down from the roof of a barn.

Source: Misha Glenny, *Guardian*, 14 March 1988, p. 20

Scene 2
A glaciological symposium

Ask glaciologists (that is, geographers, geologists, physicists, metallurgists – yes, metallurgists – mathematicians, and whomever else cares to work on snow and ice problems) what their current concerns are and they might answer: deriving realistic values for the basal boundary condition. Trust scientists to talk in jargon. In lay terms, this means trying to get a better understanding of what is going on at the bed of a glacier – that is, is the bed hard or soft, loose or consolidated, permeable or impermeable; is the subglacial drainage system stable or unstable, composed of large tunnels or small, linked cavities and pipes, operating under atmospheric pressure or water pressure? It might not immediately appear so, but finding answers to such questions is vital if we are to be able to marshal resources and reduce hazards in populated glacial areas. The two scenes converge.

French mud disaster 'could have been prevented'

TWENTY-FOUR people are missing or dead, and twelve more are wounded, after a mudslide buried a campsite last week in the French Alps. Another victim of the catastrophe was the remnant of France's former Ministry of Environmental and Technological Risk. The director of the Delegation on Major Risks resigned, saying that the disaster should have been prevented.

The meteorological office in Chamonix, in the French Alps south of Geneva, recorded 3.5 times as much rain in June than usual. On the night of 14 July, France's national holiday, a violent thunderstorm battered soils that were already saturated. A violent mudslide tore down the valley of the Borne. It formed waves a metre high before it hit the crowded riverside campground at Grand-Bornand.

The French Prime Minister, Jacques Chirac, last week announced compensation for the victims. He called the disaster 'unforeseen'. Renaud Vie le Sage, director of the Delegation on Major Risks, promptly resigned. He described Chirac's statement as 'an insult to the dead'. In 1985, says Vie le Sage, the authorities in the area asked his department, then a separate ministry, to prepare a natural risk assessment for the region.

In the assessment, says Vie le Sage, the dangers of catastrophic flooding became obvious. In July 1936, he says, a similar mudslide buried exactly the same location. The dangers at Grand-Bornand may have been raised by excavations on nearby mountain slopes to accommodate tourist facilities. This could have loosened soils.

The mayor of Grand Bornand, Pierre Pochat-Cotilloux, last week denied all knowledge of the risk assessment, saying 'we have never had precise data on such a risk (of mudslides)'. In the absence of a finalised plan for the area, says Vie le Sage, no one should have been allowed to set up a campsite on the river.

The risk assessment for the area would not have been completed until September, partly because of the reductions in the resources of Vie le Sage's department. The Ministry of Natural Risks was set up under a vulcanologist, Haroun Tazieff, by the French Socialist government in 1984. When a right-wing government came to power last year, the ministry was demoted to a 'delegation' under the Prime Minister's office. Its brief to assess risks from factories as well as fire and flood was cancelled.

At the same time, its budget for natural risk assessments was cut to £800 000 from £1.5 million. Vie le Sage estimates that it would cost £5 million a year for 10 years to assess properly the hazards run by 10 000 French communities considered at risk. A risk assessment costs £8000. Last week's disaster will cost £500 000 in compensation.

It is not clear whether the final risk assessment plan for the town would have excluded any development adequately from the riverbanks most at risk. There is strong pressure not to limit development in the depressed mountain regions of France.

Source: Debora MacKenzie, *New Scientist*, 23 July 1987, p. 19

A profile of glacier research in Norway

Norway is one of the northernmost inhabited countries in the world, situated between latitudes 58° and 72°N. In addition, the islands of Svalbard, 77–81°N, belong to Norway. Life in Norway has thus for centuries been a struggle against problems caused by snow and ice, but the struggle also created a curiosity about how best to take advantage of the snow conditions and severe climate.

In the middle of the 19th century, interest in the economic development of the mountainous areas and the Arctic and Antarctic grew remarkably. This economic interest, combined with the curiosity of explorers and scientists, was the first push to more systematic and long-lasting research on snow and glaciers.

The topics selected for snow and glacier research in modern Norway are both a heritage of the pioneering age and a reflection of our close relationship with severe winter problems. Most research projects are concentrated on improving the safety and mobility of residents, and on the economic development of mountainous and Arctic areas. Thus, the title of the Lom Symposium, 'Snow and glacier research relating to human living conditions', reflects the main objective of Norwegian research in snow science and glaciology.

There are three agencies having the main responsibility for snow and glacier research in Norway:

Norwegian Polar Research Institute (NPI)
Norwegian Water Resources and Energy Administration (NVE)
Norwegian Geotechnical Institute (NGI)

In addition, the Universities of Oslo, Bergen and Trondheim do some research, and provide the education for people later involved in research.

Norwegian Polar Research Institute (NPI)

This is the oldest of these three agencies. It was founded in 1906 to increase scientific research in Svalbard. Today, the Institute is Norway's central institute for scientific research in Svalbard, Jan Mayen, the polar seas, and the Norwegian stations in the Antarctic. The Institute is situated in Oslo, but operates a research station in Ny-Ålesund, Svalbard – at 79°N. The main sciences represented by the staff of 55 persons are biology, geophysics, geology and cartography.

The geophysical section concentrates its glaciological research on the mass balance of glaciers in Svalbard, Antarctica and Norway. The world's second long-lasting record of glacier variations is obtained from Storbreen, central Norway. In recent years, remote sensing in glaciology has been a major task. Remote sensing is used for detecting the boundaries of the snow cover and glaciers, as well as for interpreting the temperature and physical properties of the glacier surface. It is also used for regular mapping of the glaciers on Svalbard.

Another important research topic in the geophysical section is the study of sea ice. This topic has been stimulated in recent years by the oil exploitation in the Barents Sea. The section also has the responsibility for iceberg statistics in the Antarctic.

Norwegian Water Resources and Energy Administration (NVE)

This is the governmental agency responsible for energy matters and the administration of water resources. The glaciology section at NVE belongs to the Hydrology Department, and the section was founded in 1962.

Its first task was glacier mass-balance measurements, but later sediment transport investigations in glacierised river basins became important. The object of the investigations has mostly been to improve the water power production in glacierised areas. However, in recent years environmental problems have assumed an increasing importance. The areas of work are:

- the development of a national network for measuring material transport in rivers,
- glacier mass-balance investigations,
- glacier dynamics related to ice avalanches and the creation of reservoirs at glacier fronts,
- location of water divides under ice caps,
- location of subglacial river channels,
- development of snow-measuring techniques,
- setting up of a subglacial laboratory under 180 m of ice at Engabreen, northern Norway.

Norwegian Geotechnical Institute (NGI)

Snow and avalanche research at the Institute began in 1973, and the avalanche section now employs 9 scientists. NGI operates as a private consulting firm, but also receives governmental funding for the research activity. The section is responsible for both research and consulting on snow avalanches and drifting snow. The research is approximately 30% of the total workload. The section runs its own research station in Gråsdalen, western Norway, and most of the field work is done in this area. The main research projects are:

- evaluating the relationship between climatic and snow conditions and the avalanche hazard,
- measuring snow creep forces on constructions erected on slopes,
- measuring avalanche speeds and impact pressures on constructions exposed to avalanches,
- studying release mechanism for slush flows,
- release mechanism and run-out distances for debris flows,
- calculating run-out distances of avalanches based on topographical parameters.

The main agencies which consult NGI are the National Fund for National Disaster Assistance, the State Power Board, local communities, the Department of Highways and the Norwegian State Railways.

Source: H. Norem, *Ice* **86**, 2, 1988, pp. 12–13

To answer such questions as what causes glacier surges, avalanches, landslips and outburst floods we need to understand the forces and properties which control the behaviour of snow and ice masses. Does failure occur as a threshold is crossed? Is there a trigger mechanism? Can we predict, given conditions x, y and z, how a particular mass of snow, ice, rock or sediment will behave?

A similar argument applies when we wish to harness the resource potential of glaciers. To manage hydro-electric power schemes properly, we need to understand the processes which control the production and release of meltwaters and sediments in the catchment area. Nations which have glaciers within their borders have little doubt about the role and significance of glaciological research, as the autobiographical profile of work conducted in Norway makes abundantly clear. Can you think of a more sharply focused justification for an interest in snow and ice than the statement given in the third paragraph? 'Most research projects are concentrated on improving the safety and mobility of residents, and on the economic development of mountainous and Arctic areas.'

1 Read through the profile of glacier research in Norway and make a list of the 'academic topics' which qualify as legitimate areas of investigation under the 'relevance-led' theme.

2 Read through the newspaper cutting 'French mud disaster "could have been prevented".' Prepare a memo or speech for a local town meeting in which you, as an expert witness, are called upon to explain how the disaster could have been prevented.

Table 1 Glaciology hits the headlines

The *Clover Newspaper Index* provides a by-subject index of the major articles (i.e. those occupying over 3.5 column inches) appearing in the following UK newspapers: *Daily Telegraph* (DT); *Financial Times* (FT); *Guardian* (G); *Independent* (I); *Observer* (OD); *Sunday Times* (ST); *Times* (T). The index was searched for entries under the headings shown in the Table for the periods specified. Entries not relevant to the focus of this chapter are not included in the lists. The source, date, page number and title of each entry is indicated.

A Entries under **Alps**, **Antarctica**, **Arctic**, **avalanches**, **glaciers**, **ice**, **mountains** for the eighteen months from September 1986 to February 1988, inclusive.

Source	Date	Page	Title of article
Alps			
IN	16-01-88	9	Turning the Alps into a rocky desert
Antarctica			
OB	16-11-86	19	Oil magnates poised to break the ice
G	10-03-87	10	Antarctica 'waste tip'
OB	01-11-87	6	Last naming of parts as the iceman goeth
IN	30-01-88	7	Antarctica treaty will open way for exploitation
IN	13-02-88	9	Saving the great white wilderness
Arctic			
ST	09-11-86	82	Ice highway to warm up trade traffic (Over pole!)
Avalanches			
No entries			
Glaciers			
T	18-08-87	12	Chernobyl blast marks glaciers
Ice			
T	22-10-86	22	Andean ice core shows abrupt climatic change
T	22-10-87	5	Ice island goes adrift
G	07-11-87	2	Icebergs threaten bay's future
Mountains			
No entries (though many connected with blizzards, mountain rescues)			

B Entries under **skiing**, **snow** for the 1987 Christmas holiday period

DT	28-12-87	28	Skiers play tennis as Alps thaw
DT	29-12-87	24	No snow but a stiff upper lip
DT	30-12-87	2	Queues grow for ski slopes
IN	30-12-87	10	Skiers play golf on bare slopes
T	02-01-88	15	Where to go for the snow

C Entries under **France**, **floods** for two days in July 1987

DT	16-07-87	6	Twenty-one killed as freak storm wipes out French campsite
T	16-07-87	8	Toll may rise to fifty after French flood
G	16-07-87	7	Toll reaches twenty as flood engulfs French campsite
G	17-07-87	8	Experts say campsite disaster predictable
DT	17-07-87	8	French widen search for flood victims
T	17-07-87	11	Tears of grief as toll rises after French flood

D Entries under **avalanches, Austria, Switzerland** for the week of the Klosters and St Anton avalanche disasters

T	11-03-88	22	Late snow turned slope into a killer
DT	11-03-88	36	Dreaded precipice of snow
G	12-03-88	3	Alpine terror that killed Major Lindsay
IN	14-03-88	1	Avalanches kill seven at Austrian ski resort
T	14-03-88	1	Blizzard chaos in Austrian resort
DT	14-03-88	6	Seven killed as resort is swept by avalanche
G	14-03-88	20	Ski deaths as avalanches sweep Alps

E Entries under **ozone** for the eighteen months from September 1986 to February 1988 (*Note:* The list given below focuses upon those entries dealing with primary, on-site research at the Pole and in the mountains, and with the environmental effects of the ozone problem. Many entries relating to the chemistry, the meteorology and the politics of the issue are not included.)

T	06-09-86	17	Hole in ozone layer 'seasonal'
G	22-10-86	8	Mystery of polar hole
T	05-12-86	2	Space probe plan for hole in ozone
DT	15-12-86	14	Checking a hole in the ozone ... and banning a cause
T	06-01-87	15	Ozone link to dying forests
ST	18-01-87	80	Omen for ozone
G	13-03-87	22	Mystery tour by balloon through ozone hole
G	30-07-87	7	UK sends scientists to explore ozone hole
T	07-08-87	12	Growing concern at ozone layer hole
FT	05-09-87	7	Case for a freeze in the greenhouse
T	10-09-87	5	New proof of damage to ozone
DT	10-09-87	12	Chemicals 'to blame for hole in the sky'
OB	20-09-87	53	How to save the ozone layer
G	02-10-87	8	Ozone hole warning
T	02-10-87	12	Scientists alarmed by ozone finding
T	30-10-87	15	Ozone gap threatens Antarctic scientists
G	21-11-87	22	Getting a bit thin
G	06-02-88	2	European team to check Arctic ozone
IN	13-02-88	2	Survey 'proves chemical link to ozone damage'

Table 2 Applied glaciology in geographical literature

The figures refer to the total number of publications addressing the nominated topics in the period from 01-01-1980 to 21-03-1988. Where more than one topic is given, the figure quoted refers to the number of publications which address both/all topics. The data were produced from a computer search of the GEOBASE bibliographic database. The database covers over 4,000 journals and books in the fields of physical geography, human geography, geology, mineralogy, and ecology (based on entries appearing in *Geographical Abstracts, Geological Abstracts, Ecological Abstracts* and *International Development Abstracts*).

Subject combination	Number of publications
Glaciers	6,017
Glaciers, Man/Men	86
Glaciers, Hazards	38
Glaciers, Surges	54
Glaciers, Floods	121
Glaciers, Water Resources	26
Avalanches	325
Avalanches, Hazards	56
Mountains, Tourism	185
Mountains, Tourism, Damage	4
Antarctica	4,226
Antarctica, Ozone layer	1

As far as both the public and the scientific domains are concerned, then, there are pressing, common issues to be tackled in the glacierised zones of the world. (A quick aside: what do the terms *glacierised* and *glaciated* mean? Hint: the Lake District is a glaciated but not a glacierised area.) If we broaden our scope to include the permanent snow and ice regions at the poles, and to consider environmental issues of global importance, we find parallel concerns with issues such as:

- the effect of greenhouse gases on the global heat balance, thence the glacier mass balance, thence the effect upon sea level

- the depletion of the ozone layer over Antarctica and, latterly, over the Arctic

- the need to preserve Antarctica as the last unspoilt environment on the planet, in the face of growing (and competing) national designs on its mineral wealth as the Antarctic Treaty runs out in 1991.

There's also the risk of the next big ice advance. Could the impact of a giant meteorite throw up a dust jacket around the planet, triggering a cooling phase which flips us into the next Ice Age? We seem to be being pulled in opposite directions, here. On the one hand we've got the earth sweltering in a greenhouse, on the other it's shivering in a dust jacket. Maybe they'll cancel one another out, so we needn't worry? What do you think?

So, we have a set of glacier-related issues, some global, some local. Does that make them big

Table 3 Snow and Ice make it as scientific issues!

A survey of every weekly edition of *New Scientist* from January 1987 to March 1988 was conducted in order to illustrate which ice-related issues reach the scientific coffee table. Whilst the depletion of the ozone layer over the Antarctic is more the concern of the chemist and the meteorologist than the glaciologist (contrast its ever-present status in this table with its distinctly low profile in the glaciological literature summarised in Table 3), there are some *bona fide* glaciology topics in the list shown here.

Date	Page	Title
05-02-87	44	Discoveries in Antarctica's deepest bedrock drillhole
12-02-87	30	Melting glaciers pull the plug on volcanoes
19-03-87	25	Structured ozone holes
23-04-87	22	Chemical giants battle over ozone holes
30-04-87	25	Chemists unite in call for ozone protection
25-06-87	52	Siberia unfreezes its assets
23-07-87	19	French mud disaster 'could have been prevented'
13-08-87	22	Barren ski slopes blamed for Alpine disasters
03-09-87	24	High noon for ozone in Montreal
17-09-87	30	Hot air threatens ozone in Montreal
	46	Glacier surge not on the agenda
24-09-87	22	Historic ozone treaty signed – at last
08-10-87	18	Chlorine clears the ozone layer down south
12-11-87	50	What hope for the ozone layer now?
26-11-87	30	An atmosphere in convulsions
14-01-88	30	Scientists set to track ozone in the Arctic
	45	A snowball's chance
	49	Après ski le deluge
21-01-88	23	Taming the wild south
10-03-88	33	Concentrated acid on ice may explain fish kill
24-03-88	22	Ozone threat spreads from the Arctic

1 Study Table 1. What impression do you get? Is glaciology a headline grabber? What if the stories had coincided with a royal birth, or a dispute in the South Atlantic, though?

2 Study Table 3. Do you get a different impression from that which you gleaned from the newspaper survey? Are there any points of convergence?

3 Study Table 2. Same impression? What proportion of the glacier publications relate to applied issues? Does the design of the investigations into surges, floods, avalanches, and water resources necessarily matter to an objective of controlling hazards and resources?

4 Go down to the local library and conduct your own newspaper search, for a different period. They may not have the Clover Index, but they'll have back copies of the 'quality' papers.

and small, respectively? How can we assess the significance of these issues? We've already considered the concerns of the communities which live and work with glaciers. How can we get a broader opinion? One way is to consider how newsworthy our glaciers and their various issues are; what attention do our topics receive in the general press, in the popular science press and in the glaciology press? Tables 1, 2 and 3 give the results of a trawl of these various sources. The results refer to a fixed time period, but the technique of source-searching is always useful. An idea for a project, perhaps?

The material presented above has hopefully convinced you that glaciology need not be esoteric.

The 1988 Symposium of the International Glaciological Society had, for the fourth time in twelve years, an overtly applied theme, 'Snow and Glacier Research relating to Human Living Conditions'. Much of what glaciologists study is certainly applicable to the task of controlling the hazards and resources of the glacierised areas of the world. Therein lies the crux of the challenge of this particular natural environment: how can we 'use' the environment 'properly'?

The argument adopted here is that we can manage the interactions between physical processes and human activities better if we attempt to understand and work with the former. This is illustrated below in relation to a set of ap-

plied case studies, all of which demand an understanding of the climate-mass balance relationship. It is this relationship which controls glacier behaviour: how the ice waxes and wanes, how it flows, how it melts, how it erodes, transports, deposits and deforms sediments ... The flow diagram given as Figure 3 illustrates how, and provides a framework for understanding the dynamic system into which our case studies fit.

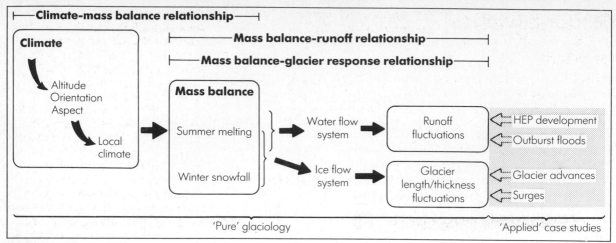

Figure 3 The links between climate and mass balance, and how they influence fluctuations in runoff in glacier position

1 Can you follow the logic of Figure 3 without too much difficulty? Make a note of any 'grey areas'. Read the commentary given in 'A guided tour of Figure 3', and compare notes. Don't worry if the picture appears sketchy at this stage – the case studies are intended to clarify and amplify matters. Make a point of seeing whether or not the case studies shed any light upon your grey areas. Come back to this diagram after you have worked through the whole chapter, and check how far your understanding of the linkages has improved.

2 Work through Figure 3, from left to right, filling in detail as you go along, and pinpointing just what it is that we need to know in order to understand:
a how the volume of water running off from a glacier varies over time, and
b how the position of the snout of a glacier fluctuates over time.

A guided tour of Figure 3

We start at the top left. The general climate is modified by altitude, orientation and aspect to produce a local climate which controls how much mass is added to the glacier by snowfall, and how much mass is lost by melting. Mass, rather than volume, must be used because a given volume of snow has a much smaller density (weight per unit volume) than the same volume of ice. Equal volumes of snow and ice thus yield very different volumes of water, when melted – as any mountaineer knows. Mass balance quantities are thus expressed in metres of water equivalent to enable proper (standardised) comparisons to be made.

The net result of a year's climate is that mass is generally gained at high elevations (where winter snows survive and become transformed into ice) and lost at low elevations (where snow and ice melt under the summer sun to form a peak of meltwater runoff which flows off across, within and under the glacier). The altitudinal gradient is thus paralleled by a mass change gradient which goes from highly positive at high elevations, through zero (mass added equals mass lost) to highly negative at low elevations. These areas of positive and negative mass balance define, respectively, the accumulation and ablation areas of the glacier. It is helpful to view this situation as a wedge of mass being added to the upper end of the glacier 'system' and a wedge of mass being taken away from the lower end. Like all well-behaved systems, the glacier responds to this imbalance by transferring mass from high to low elevations. In other words, it flows downhill.

If the glacier is in equilibrium with its climate, the mass added will balance the mass lost, and, over a period of years, the glacier will retain approximately the same dimensions; that is, it stands still by moving mass forward. If, however, more mass is added as snowfall than is lost by melting, the glacier will eventually move forward (by an amount related to the difference between accumulation and ablation, and at a time controlled by the size of the glacier, and its rate of flow). Conversely, if less mass is added than is lost, the glacier will shrink. So, climate controls how much liquid water runs off and how much solid water remains.

Glacier advances

Ice on Earth

We are living in a glacial epoch. An epoch is a time-frame measured in millions of years. Ours is simply the most recent of a succession of glacial episodes which have punctuated Earth's history. Geologists are making substantial progress in unravelling clues to the timing and causes of glaciations. The following three paragraphs are based upon Boulton's (1987) account of present thinking. (*Source*: G.S. Boulton, 'Progress in glacial geology during the last fifty years', *Journal of Glaciology*, Special Issue 1987, pp. 25–32.)

The first spate of glacial activity on Earth occurred around 2700 million years (M.y.) ago, and continued with subsequent glacial epochs in the periods 2500–2100 M.y. ago, 1000–600 M.y. ago, 470–430 M.y. ago, 300–270 M.y. ago, and from 25 M.y. ago to (and beyond) the present. Within each epoch, the global mass of glaciers fluctuates between glacial and interglacial periods which may last tens or hundreds of thousands of years. The current glacial epoch (the Cenozoic), began around 25 M.y. ago in Antarctica, expanding into mid-latitude glaciations around 2.4 M.y. and 0.9–0.6 M.y. ago. The latter, Pleistocene, Ice Age itself experienced a series of growth and decline phases (stadials and inter-stadials), as did its predecessors. The present inter-stadial developed around 18,000 to 10,000 years ago, since when there have been a series of little ice ages lasting around one or two hundred years. The last of these, from around 1500 to 1900, has become known as the Little Ice Age in much the same way as the Pleistocene has become known as the Ice Age; we have a habit of enshrining the recent. Superimposed upon these fluctuations are advance and retreat cycles which last ten to twenty years or so.

?

1 Write a brief definition of each of the following terms, as they are used to describe glaciations: epoch, period, stadial, little ice age. Draw a diagram to illustrate your definitions.

What causes glacier fluctuations?

That's an easy one – climatic change. Yes, but what causes the climate to change, and how does a glacier respond to a change in climate? The first question has been, and remains, a subject of much uncertainty and controversy. Boulton (1987) has summarised the current view as follows. It is likely that the long-term changes of climate which lead to glacial epochs are determined by continental plate distributions and plate movements. The former controlling the degree of snow and ice accumulation at the poles, and the efficiency with which ocean currents distribute (even out) temperature between the poles and the equator. The latter generating mountain-building phases which disrupt the atmospheric circulation and result in significantly colder winters.

The shorter-term fluctuations which produce glacial and interglacial periods within glacial epochs appear, in contrast, to reflect variations in incoming solar radiation, as forced by variations in the Earth's orbit, and amplified by interactions in the atmosphere/ocean/ice-sheet system. Recent research, interestingly, is tending to confirm some venerable theories. Analysis of deep sea-bed cores, for example, indicates a sequence of warm and cold phases which oscillate in sympathy with the three basic astronomical cycles recognised by Croll in 1864, and Milankovitch in 1941, as important influences upon the climate of the earth.

The first is a 100,000-year cycle related to the eccentricity of the Earth's orbit around the sun (the orbit moves from being more circular to more elliptical, and back again). The second is a 41,000 year cycle related to the tilt of the Earth's axis (which shifts between 21.8 and 24.4 degrees from the vertical). The third is a 19,000 to 23,000-year cycle associated with the shifting orientation of the Earth's axis (a phenomenon referred to as 'the precession of the equinoxes'). The Earth is like a spinning top, wobbling on its axis and orbiting, eccentrically, around the sun. It spins around on an axis that shifts its plane as it moves around in an orbit that changes its shape. The net effect is to increase/decrease the difference in insolation (quantity of solar radiation) received at the poles compared to the equator, and during winter as compared to summer, according to the concordance (harmony) of the three cycles. Glaciations occur at times and in places of low insolation receipt.

We run the risk, here, of oversimplifying an extremely complex situation. The climate of the Earth, and of particular places upon it, is affected by many factors, as depicted in the diagram shown on p. 90 (Figure 4).

Changes in one controlling variable may be sufficient to disturb a delicate balance, and the combination of many effects occurring at the same time produces a level of complexity which is difficult to unravel. Do effects *x* and *y* reinforce or buffer one another? We're getting into foreign waters here. Let's get back to the glaciology.

1 As you read through the following sections, remind yourself of your understanding of the climate–mass balance relationship introduced in the introductory section. Now's your chance to get those grey areas illuminated.

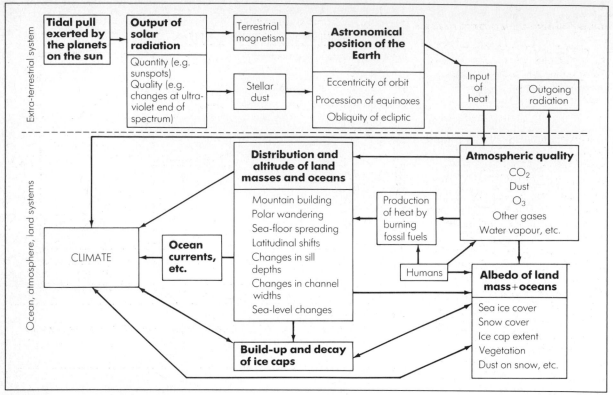

Figure 4 The web of influence upon global climate
Source: A. S. Goudie, *Environmental Change*, OUP, 1977, p. 203

Climate–mass balance links

Both the mass of a single glacier and the mass of the global glacierised area are climatically determined. Cold phases, whether as short as a winter season or as long as a glacial epoch, add mass to the glacier via snowfall. Warm phases, whether as short as a summer season or as long as a glacial epoch, remove mass from the glacier via melting. The diagram (Figure 6) shows the mass balance behaviour of a glacier over the timescale of a single year. The dashed lines show how accumulation builds up over the winter season (top line), and how ablation (melting) increases during the summer season (bottom line). The solid line, the mass balance curve, is simply the difference between the amount of accumulation and ablation over the year. In the example given, the net balance at the end of the year is positive.

Figure 5 Glacier in summer and winter. The Mer de Glace moving down the Chamonix valley

?

1 Study Figure 6, and make sure that you understand the principles involved. Sketch a diagram to show a mass balance year in which ablation exceeds accumulation.

The balance between accumulation and ablation, accounted over periods which may be as short as five years for small sensitive glaciers, or as long as thousands of years for major ice sheets, determines whether we are in a situation of positive net mass balance, in which case the glacier will grow by thickening and advancing; or negative net mass balance, in which case the glacier will decline by thinning and retreating. The climate-mass balance interaction is essentially the same whatever the order of timescale we choose, from the decade to the epoch. To express this in magnitude-frequency terms, we have a set of fluctuations of differing magnitude, duration and frequency, the shorter, less intense ones being superimposed upon their bigger brethren, with each being driven by a climatic change of corresponding order. It is thus perfectly possible to have a period of positive mass balance existing within a period of negative mass balance (or vice versa)!

Mass balance–glacier fluctuation links

Broadly speaking, the higher the elevation, the greater the mass which is added by snow accumulation in winter and the lower the mass which is lost by melting in summer. There is thus a spatial imbalance in the system, which is redressed by the flow of mass from high to low elevations. The situation can be visualised in the form of a wedge of net addition in the accumulation area being transferred to compensate for a wedge of net loss in the ablation area, as illustrated in Figure

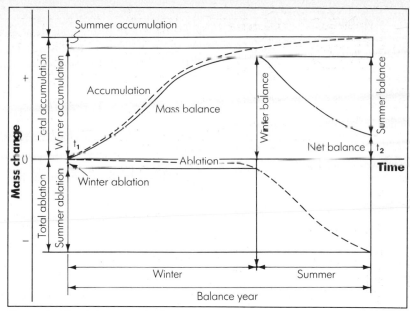

Figure 6 Mass balance terms and processes
Source: W. S. B. Paterson, *The Physics of Glaciers*, Pergamon Press, 1981, p. 45. Reprinted with permission.

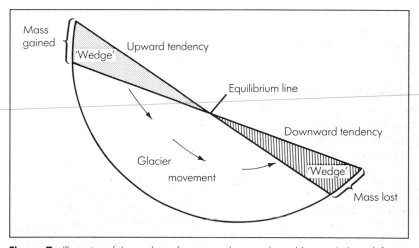

Figure 7 Illustration of the wedges of net accumulation and net ablation which result from a year's climate. The glacier flows to maintain the balance of the system.
Source: D. E. Sugden and B. S. John, *Glaciers and Landscape: a geomorphological approach*, Edward Arnold, 1976, p. 41

7. This transfer of mass is achieved by glacier flow, either in the form of movement of individual ice grains (a process known as internal deformation) and/or in the form of the glacier slipping, *en masse*, over or on its bed (a process known as basal sliding). So, climate controls mass balance, and mass balance drives glacier flow.

A glacier flows forward throughout the year, but generally more quickly in summer (when there is more water around to ease its slipping over its bed). In summer, though, the lower reaches of the glacier melt back. The forward movement is a response to a mass imbalance at some stage in the past; the point of gain is at high elevation, and it takes some years to reach the snout of the glacier (the actual number of years depending upon the size of the glacier and the rate of flow it experiences). The melt-back effect, of course, is a response to current climate. Whether a glacier advances or retreats, thickens or thins, depends upon the relative magnitudes of these opposing effects. The response time of a glacier to a change in climate thus differs for the situations of positive and negative mass balance; the locus of the former is at high elevation, and the effect takes some years to have expression as an advance of the snout, while the latter, since it acts at the snout, has rapid expression there. The response time also varies enormously from glacier to glacier, according to the size of the glacier and how quickly it flows (which depends upon how the glacier flows, how steep it is, what orientation it has ...). It is thus perfectly possible to have two neighbouring glaciers fluctuating in opposite directions, perhaps as a response to slightly different micro-climates, perhaps as a result of their different response characteristics.

Figure 8 The Glacier de Tsidjiore Nouve, Valais, Switzerland, squeezes its way down the valley between its own relict lateral lines. The glacier is small, steep and thus responsive to changes in climate. Earlier this century it was nicknamed the 'enfant terrible' of Swiss glaciers'. See Table 4 for data of its recent behaviour.

?

1 Examine the data shown in Figure 9. Which periods show general advance, and which show general decline?

2 Use the data given in Table 4 (p. 94) to answer the following questions:

a What similarities are there in the behaviour of the various glaciers? What dissimilarities are there in the behaviour of the various glaciers?

b Do the glaciers with the larger areas show a different pattern of variation from the glaciers with smaller areas?

c What other variables might exert control upon the variation in snout position? Briefly outline the nature of each variable's influence.

d Where/how would you find information relating to the variables you have mentioned above?

1 Austrian glaciers

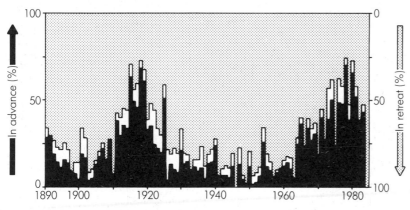

2 Swiss glaciers

3 French glaciers

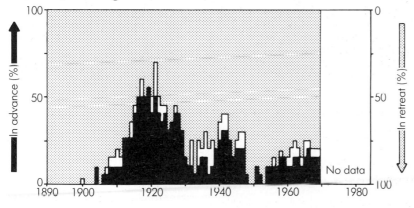

Figure 9 The behaviour of Austrian, Swiss and French glaciers since 1890. The data is expressed in terms of the percentage of observed glaciers which were advancing (black bars, reading up from the bottom axis), retreating (shaded bars, reading down from top axis) or neither advancing nor retreating, that is stationary (white areas between black and shaded bars). *Source*: J. M. Grove, *The Little Ice Age*, Methuen, 1988, p. 185

Recent fluctuations of glaciers

The response of a glacier to a change in climate is thus an individual matter. At any given time there may therefore be a good deal of difference in the behaviour of nearby glaciers. Over timescales of ten years or so, however, there is often a good degree of correspondence in glacier behaviour at regional levels (at these scales, individual tendencies tend to flatten out). You can confirm this for yourself by looking at how Austrian, Swiss and French glaciers have fluctuated during the twentieth century (Figure 9).

The human impact

The advance/retreat fluctuations discussed above sit in a context of a general retreat of glaciers from their Little Ice Age maxima (remember the point about opposites occurring at the same time?). Around half of this retreat has been attributed to the enhanced warming of the greenhouse effect, which may even have brought the Little Ice Age to a premature end. Glaciers are presently so shrunken from even their Little Ice Age positions that, in most cases, they have a good deal of ground to cover before they carry the spectre they did for eighteenth-century towns and villages. Then and before, glaciers were often seen as malevolent serpents, growing fat in their winter hideaways and advancing to threaten nearby villages with flood and ice in summer – not a bad definition of mass balance, really. The 'Wilderwurm glacier' of the chapter opening captures the image superbly. If you scan through the list of hazards experienced by the people of the Chamonix valley since 1600 (Table 5) you may perhaps be able to appreciate why this is so.

Table 4

Recent changes in the position of the termini of selected glaciers in the Valaisian Alps (Switzerland) and Mont Blanc Massif (France). Figures are in metres per year, except where denoted by the symbol ⌃, in which case the figure given relates to the *net* movement occurring since the previous measurement was made. A + denotes an advance of the snout, a − a retreat of the snout. A gap denotes the absence of available data. (*Sources*: IAHS (ICSI)-UNESCO *Fluctuations of Glaciers*, Volumes I–V 1967, 1973, 1977, 1985, 1988; *Les Alpes*, Fourth trimestre reports [produced annually]).

Glacier	Aletsch	Gorner	Findelen	Tsidjiore Nouve	Bas Arolla	Ferpecle	Trient	Argentiere	Bossons
Area (km²)	86.8	68.9	19.1	3.12	6.02	9.79	6.58	14.27	9.90
Length (km)	24.7	14.1	9.3	5.0	5.0	6.0	5.0	9.0	7.8
EXP * ACC	SE	N	NW	N	N	NW	N	NW	NW
ABL	S	NW	W	NE	N	N	N	NW	NW
Elev † max	4160	4610	4190	3800	3720	3680	3490	4122	4807
min	1510	2060	2320	2205	2135	2095	1760	1550	1230

Shift in position (metres/year)

	Aletsch	Gorner	Findelen	Tsidjiore Nouve	Bas Arolla	Ferpecle	Trient	Argentiere	Bossons
1959-60	−23.0	⌃	−19.0	−6.0	−13.0	−31.0	+17.3	⌃	⌃
1960-61	−19.1	−26.6	−20.5	−3.0	−9.0	−29.0	−26.0	⌃	⌃
1961-62	−24.8	−10.8	−32.0	−4.4	−5.9	−14.6	+31.5	⌃	⌃
1962-63	−14.8	−28.5	−15.4	−19.6	−7.4	−205.0	+21.0	−103.0	−60.0
1963-64	−26.0	−40.8	−30.0	−15.7	−10.4	⌃	+18.1	⌃	⌃
1964-65	−62.7	−22.8	−21.4	⌃	−29.2	⌃	+8.1	⌃	⌃
1965-66	−74.0	⌃	−27.2	⌃	−8.0	−23.2	+23.7	⌃	⌃
1966-67	−36.2	−54.1	−10.9	−13.6	−2.4	−4.5	+2.7	⌃	⌃
1967-68	−7.9	−40.0	−11.9	−5.8	−2.4	−2.7	+23.8	⌃	⌃
1968-69	−16.4	−33.2	+3.0	−2.0	−2.0	−2.1	+15.1	⌃	⌃
1969-70	−25.2	−18.3	−4.0	−2.0	−3.0	−0.4	+25.0	⌃	⌃
1970-71	−33.9	−19.1	−2.5	−4.0	−1.0	−0.3	+21.8	⌃	⌃
1971-72	−27.7	−16.8	+1.8	+11.0	+4.0	+1.3	+14.4	0	+14.5
1972-73	−41.6	−26.8	−17.0	+9.0	+7.0	+7.9	+22.5	⌃	⌃
1973-74	−40.5	⌃	⌃	+8.0	+7.0	⌃	+12.6	⌃	⌃
1974-75	−2.0	−31.3	−17.3	+13.0	+16.0	+0.9	+10.0	⌃	⌃
1975-76	⌃	⌃	⌃	+10.0	+6.0	+3.8	+2.8	⌃	−15.0
1976-77	⌃	⌃	⌃	+16.0	+8.0	+5.2	+4.6	⌃	−20.0
1977-78	⌃	⌃	⌃	+5.0	+8.0	+5.0	+3.2	⌃	−30.0
1978-79	⌃	⌃	⌃	+10.0	+8.5	+2.3	+9.0	+53.0	+25.0
1979-80	⌃	⌃	⌃	+10.8	+8.7	+16.6	+16.0	+12.0	+15.0
1980-81	−27.6	−55.0	+52.1	+28.0	+11.8	+10.1	+15.0	⌃	⌃
1981-82	−11.4	⌃	+48.1	+25.0	+8.4	+10.2	+15.0	⌃	⌃
1982-83	−95.0	−93.2	+18.0	+38.0	+10.6	+21.0	+9.0	⌃	⌃
1983-84	−46.3	⌃	+16.1	+26.0	+7.6	+15.0	+8.0	⌃	⌃
1984-85	−45.6	−42.7	+27.7	+21.0	+14.4	+16.0	+10.0	⌃	⌃
1985-86	−25.4	−7.0	−20.0	+12.0	+10.0	+5.2	+7.0	⌃	⌃

* Exposure of the accumulation area (ACC) and ablation area (ABL).
† Elevation (m.a.s.l.) of the highest (Max) and lowest (Min) points on the glacier.

Table 5 A record of events of glacier hazards in the Chamonix valley, France

Dates	Events
About 1600	Advancing glaciers destroy seven houses in the Argentière-La Rosière area, two at La Bonneville, twelve at Le Châtelard, and the entire hamlet of Bonnenuict. The Mer de Glace came so close to Les Bois that the village was damaged and had to be abandoned. It was also near Les Tines
1610	Water from the Argentière glacier destroys eight houses and five barns. Torrents from the Bossons glacier severely damage Le Fouilly. Three houses, seven barns, and one mill destroyed at La Bonneville. Mer de Glace still close to Les Bois and causing damage
1613/14	Glacial meltwater completes the destruction of La Bonneville
1616	Argentière glacier adjoining La Rosière. About six houses remaining at Le Châtelard, although only two inhabited. Glacier very close. At some time between 1642 and 1700 the village was finally abandoned and has never been rebuilt. Its inhabitants are thought to have settled at Les Tines
1628–30	Falls of snow and glaciers in the Chamonix valley. Flooding of the Arve due to glacial meltwater
1640s	Glaciers came close to Le Tour, Argentière, La Rosière, Les Tines, Les Bois, Les Praz and Les Bossons. 1641: Les Rosières (*not* La Rosière, but a village near Chamonix) destroyed by a flood from the Mer de Glace. 1642: avalanche of snow and ice destroyed two homes at Le Tour, and killed 4 cows and 8 sheep. 1641–43: property flooded and ruined by torrents from the Bossons glacier
1714	Several villages still threatened by glaciers
About 1730	Mer de Glace less than four hundred metres from the nearest houses at Les Bois
1818–20	Glaciers again almost at Le Tour, Montquart and Les Bois (the Mer de Glace was only twenty metres from this last village). The Argentière glacier was little more than three hundred metres from the old centre of Argentière village
1826	Mer de Glace showering debris on to the chalets below
1835	*Séracs* from the Mer de Glace threaten to fall on Les Bois
1850	Mer de Glace about fifty metres from Les Bois and causing blocks of ice to fall towards Les Tines
1852	Several glacier avalanches in the Chamonix valley due to warm winds and heavy rains
1878	*Débâcle* from the Mer de Glace. Houses evacuated as a safety measure; fields flooded. Similar outbursts had occurred in 1610 and 1716
1920	*Débâcle* from the Mer de Glace floods the cellars and ground floors of many buildings in Chamonix. Much land inundated
1949	Avalanche from the Glacier du Tour kills six people. The worst ice avalanche in the French Alps since the Glacier de Tête Rousse disaster of 1892
1977	Le Tour threatened by glacier avalanche

Source: L. Tufnell, *Glacier Hazards*, Longman Group UK Limited, 1984, p. 21–22.

Can we afford to feel confident that such hazards are confined to the past? It appears that we would be wise not to do so. Despite the greenhouse effect, there was a distinct cooling of climate in the 1950s, 1960s and 1970s. This cooling is now being expressed in the advance of many glaciers.

The data given in Table 4 reveal that many small, responsive glaciers in the Swiss Alps started to advance from 1970 onward. These glaciers are still shifting forward, year by year, and we should expect a similar effect to become apparent in the position of the larger glaciers in the near future (the precise timing being a function of their size, their rate and mode of flow, and all of the other factors which you identified in examining the data).

But surely advances of the order of ten or so metres per year do not, generally, pose much of a threat to civilisation? Maybe not, but they can, nevertheless, prove troublesome. The Linth-Limmern hydro-electric power (HEP) company has already had to convert the water intake, built to tap the waters of the Biferten glacier, from a proglacial to a subglacial structure; the ice covered it in 1982. Grande Dixence did the same with their Findelen intake; the glacier stopped its surge just short, before retreating back. (What is a 'surge'? It is explained in the next section.)

When we see annual snout movement figures of +28m, +25m, +38m ... and so on being returned for small (responsive) Alpine glaciers, perhaps we ought not to be too complacent?

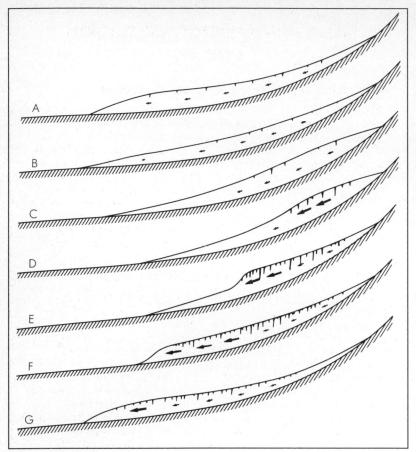

Figure 10 An idealised model of a surge cycle. Stages A to C represent the period of 'normal' transfer of ice from the accumulation to the ablation zone. Stages D to E represent the period of restricted ice transfer, the development of a reservoir of ice in the accumulation zone and the corresponding wastage in the ablation zone. Stages F to G represent the phase of accelerated ice transfer, and the surging of the ice from the accumulation zone to the ablation zone. In the example given, the surge does not lead to the advance of the glacier beyond its 'normal' position (i.e. the position in stage G is equivalent to that in stage A).
Source: J. Alean, 'Variations subites et dangereuses des glaciers', *Les Alpes*, 1st trimestre, 1987, pp. 30–41

Surges

The most dramatic of glacier advances occur in the form of surges (the term 'galloping glacier' has even been used!). What is meant by the term 'surge'? Strictly, it refers to a temporary condition of vastly increased glacier flow velocity; surge velocities may reach values 10 to 100 times greater than those normally experienced. The result of this phase of accelerated flow may be to move the front of the glacier forward by a considerable distance (relative to the length of the glacier). On the other hand, surges do not always lead to an advance of the glacier front. How come? Well, the fast flow may simply move the glacier back to a position which it would have occupied if it had not surged! Figure 10 explains this better than words can.

The hallmarks of surging: a basis for asking the right questions

Surging behaviour can be regarded as a departure from the normal pattern of steady mass transfer from the accumulation to the ablation zone. The 'surge' essentially represents a sudden, rapid transfer of mass which has built up in an upper reservoir to a lower receiving area. In this

Table 6 Some data on surging glaciers

Glacier	Location	Dates of surges	Number of years between surges	Peak velocity (metres/day)
Bruarjokull	Iceland	1625, 1720, 1810, 1890, 1963	95, 90, 80, 73	120
Variegated	Alaska	1905–6, 1911–33, 1942–8, 1964–5, 1982–3	5, 9, 16, 17	60
Carroll	Alaska	1919, 1943, 1966	24, 23	
Kolka	USSR	1834, 1902, 1969	68, 67	
Medvezhiy	USSR	1937, 1951, 1963, 1973	14, 12, 10	
Vernagt	Austria	1600, 1678, 1773, 1845	78, 95, 72	

Source: after J. Alean, 'Variations subites et dangereuses des glaciers', *Les Alpes*, First trimestre, 1987, pp. 30–41

respect, surging represents a form of unsteady response to mass balance processes. In some glaciers, a distinctly stepped long profile develops as an excess of mass builds up in the reservoir area while the unreplenished receiving area is depleted by ablation. The surge redistributes the mass, and flattens out the profile. The question which arises here is why does the imbalance in mass distribution develop?

Surge behaviour incorporates two distinct elements, a short 'active' phase when fast flow speeds are reached, and a long 'quiescent' phase when flow velocities are much slower. The duration of these components varies from glacier to glacier, but, for a single glacier, the time spans are remarkably consistent, as can be seen from the data presented in Table 6. There is thus a periodic tendency in surge behaviour, i.e. the glacier experiences a repeating cycle of slow and fast flow phases. The obvious questions here are: why is the cycle so regular? What is it that triggers the transition from the slow-flow to the fast-flow mode? What is it that causes the surge to stop, and the cycle to start anew?

So much for the pattern of surging over time. What of the spatial pattern of surging glaciers? Only about four per cent of the world's glaciers seem prone to surge behaviour, but (and this is a big but) their global distribution appears to be clustered rather than even. The question which begs an answer here is: are there any environmental factors (geological, climatic) responsible for producing the non-random distribution of surging glaciers?

Glaciologists have sought answers to these questions for many years, with limited success. Some hypotheses – notably those based on the notion that external triggers like volcanic and seismic activity can explain the temporal occurrence and spatial distribution of surging glaciers – have been rejected. The fact that single

An everyday story of surging glaciers

Tales from Trapridge: a soft bed production

Trapridge glacier has a soft bed composed of moraine, which water is able to pass through. The central area of the glacier is able to slide over its bed. The marginal rim cannot because it is frozen to its bed. The rim of the glacier thus slows down ice moving towards it. This can lead to a build-up of ice above the junction of the two zones. As the ice builds up, it exerts more pressure upon its bed and the ice just above it. This may cause the formerly cold ice at the bed of the glacier to melt, enabling the glacier to slide over its bed. Alternatively, the stress may become so great that it is able to deform the sediments resting below, causing them to carry the glacier forward on a slurry of fast-flowing sediment. The surge stops once the movement of ice results in ice pressures falling.

All change at Variegated: a loose bed production

Variegated sits on a rock bed. Water normally flows at the bed of the glacier through a system of large channels. Small tributaries feed water from other areas of the bed into the big channels. Because the bed is not perfectly flat, there are many depressions, or cavities, between the rock bed and the glacier base. Water may collect in these cavities. Some may be drained by small channels, some may not. If water reaches the bed in sufficient quantities to fill the channels and the cavities, it begins to put pressure upon the ice lying above it. In some cases, the pressure of water may be so high as to rise above the pressure exerted by the weight of the ice above, and the glacier can be pushed up from the bed (in much the same way as putting pressure upon the hydraulic fluid in a car jack can overcome the weight of the car that it lifts up). This effect buoys up the glacier, which allows water to drain across a wider area and so allows the glacier to flow faster in the affected area. The area involved can be local (resulting in mini-surges) or much more extensive (resulting in full surging). When water pressure drops, the glacier sits back down on its bed, and thus slows down.

glaciers tend to surge with a regular periodicity, together with the fact that groups of surging glaciers do not perform in phase with one another, suggest that the trigger is internal not external. This conclusion has led to a focus upon the mechanics of surge behaviour at the individual glacier level.

The mechanics of surge behaviour: the search for explanations

1968 represented a watershed in the investigation of surges. Two international meetings were held

that year, in Canada, to review current knowledge and establish future needs in relation to surging glaciers. It emerged that there were a number of inter-related theories of surge mechanics, but few detailed, quantitative surveys of surge behaviour. Evidently, more of the latter were needed to test the former (and perhaps to generate new theories). Conditions at the ice-bed interface lay at the heart of the surge theories (the basal boundary condition again):

- How does the glacier flow?
- What stresses are exerted at the bed as a result of the

weight of overlying ice and the effect of gravity acting along the slope of the bed?

● How much water is there at the bed? How does the water exist – in large channels, in a linked distributary system, or in a sheet over the whole bed?

● What is the thermal condition of the ice at the bed – is it frozen to the bed, or is it at pressure melting point (PMP)? (PMP is an important concept. It describes a condition in which an increase in either temperature or pressure will lead to ice melting. Conversely, a reduction in either pressure or temperature will lead to freezing. Glaciers whose basal ice is at PMP (temperate glaciers) can slide across their beds. Those whose basal ice is below the PMP (cold glaciers) cannot produce or maintain sufficient water at the bed to enable them to slide, and are instead frozen to their beds.)

Two important research projects have sought to provide answers to the questions posed above by studying flow, stress, temperature and hydrological conditions before, during and after a surge. The first has centred upon Trapridge glacier, in the Yukon, Canada, whilst it has been in its quiescent phase. The second is based upon Variegated glacier, in Alaska, and has encompassed the period before, during and after its 1982–3 surge. Sharp (1988) has summarised the results from both studies (*Source*: M.J. Sharp, 'Surging glaciers: behaviour and mechanisms', *Progress in Physical Geography*, **12** 3, 1988, pp. 349–370). A detailed understanding of the mechanisms involved demands a considerable grasp of the physics of ice flow, water flow and sediment deformation. The bare essentials of the processes involved in the theories proposed to explain surge behaviour, at both sites, are given in ordinary, everyday language in the box on p. 97.

?

1 Study 'An everyday story of surging glaciers' before you read the following passages. Write down the terms *build-up*, *onset* and *cessation*, and note the explanations given to account for the behaviour of the glacier in each of these phases.

Results from the Trapridge glacier study

Work designed to illuminate the process of surging at Trapridge glacier started in 1969. Since the glacier has not surged during the period of investigation, conditions during the quiescent phase have, of necessity, formed the basis for a set of theories for surge initiation which have not as yet been either confirmed or rejected by comparisons with the real thing.

Trapridge glacier last surged from 1941 to 1949. Since then, a marked bulge has developed in the ice profile, at the junction of a central zone of warm-based ice and a marginal rim of cold-based ice. The glacier has thickened considerably above the bulge, while the ice below it has slowed and stagnated. Ice-flow velocities have steadily increased in the area above the bulge, reaching levels way above those measured in the zone below the bulge. The glacier has thus developed a highly unstable profile. The explanation advanced to account for these observations is that the cold marginal zone is acting as a thermal dam upon the faster flowing ice of the warm-based zone.

The glacier has not yet surged in response to the development of this mass imbalance. It is expected that it will. The question is, by what mechanism? Two main groups of theories have been proposed. The first group of theories involves the thermal triggering of the surge. The second set of theories entertained as possible triggers of the onset of surging at Trapridge relates to

the properties of the sediments which form the bed on which the glacier lies. Refer to the box on page 97 for a brief account of the mechanisms involved.

Results from the Variegated glacier study

Work conducted at Variegated glacier since 1973 represents a global first. Detailed measurements have been made during the build-up, onset and cessation phases of the surge cycle. This has provided a unique opportunity to observe the critical events, and to develop and test explanations of those events. Our understanding of the mechanisms of surging behaviour has increased enormously as a result.

Variegated surged in 1982–3. The upper zone surged from January to June 1982, slackened off, and then surged again from October 1982 to July 1983. The lower zone surged from May to July 1983 (ending abruptly on 4 July). How do we explain this sequence of events?

The winter starts of the upper zone surges have been explained in terms of unescaped water from the summer melt season causing the jacking-up of the glacier. The jacking-up of the lower zone has been attributed to water being ponded up behind the surge front. How does it all end? As the surge propagates downglacier, it produces a redistribution of mass. Upstream of the surge front, ice thicknesses are lower than they were. At the base of the glacier, the pressure of ice normal to the bed (the normal or overburden pressure) is thus reduced. The pressure of ice acting down the slope of the bed (the basal shear stress) is also reduced (since it is a product of ice thickness and bed slope). It is the shear stress which drives the glacier forward. Let's assume that the water pressure at the bed has remained constant. Is the ice now easier or more difficult to lift than before? You may be excused for reasoning that since the ice is now thinner, it should be easier to lift. In fact, the opposite is true. As basal shear stresses fall, higher water pressures are needed to achieve bed separation. The reduction in ice thickness thus produces two opposing effects; normal pressures are lower, which makes bed separation easier, but shear stresses are also lower, which makes bed separation more difficult. The latter effect dominates the former, so once the surge passes downglacier the ice settles back down on its bed, pumping water downglacier as it does so.

Surging: unanswered questions

The current wisdom on surge behaviour is that the surge occurs because of a mass balance imbalance, and is triggered by a change in the nature of subglacial conditions. In the case of Variegated glacier, it has been demonstrated that the important change is that which occurs in the nature of the subglacial drainage system. In the case of Trapridge glacier, changes in the permeability and deformability of basal sediments are assumed to be the critical facilitating factors. There is also the thermal factor to take into account at Trapridge.

Should we be searching for an all-embracing theory to explain surge behaviour? Should we expect the same variables to be involved, whatever the site? Evidently not, as witness the lack of a thermal effect at Variegated and the presence of one at Trapridge. What of the spatial clustering of surge locations, then? How can that be explained, if not by the operation of environmental variables which determine a propensity to surge? It appears that such variables are not in the nature of external triggers, but, rather, take the form of geographical permutations of favourable basal boundary conditions. Where have you heard that before?

Figure 11 The Ferpecle valley, Valais, Switzerland, a classic example of a recently deglaciated Alpine valley. The obvious 'trim lines' separating the bare gullied slopes from the vegetated slopes mark the position of the Mont Mine and Ferpecle glaciers at the height of the Little Ice Age (around 1850 to 1870). The photograph was taken close to the present-day snout of the Ferpecle glacier. The present-day Mont Mine glacier (seen entering on the left) separated from the Ferpecle glacier towards the end of the 1940s. The edge of the lake in the middle of the photograph marks the end point of the Mont Mine glacier in 1943. Water dammed under the glacier in the basin now occupied by the lake suddenly burst out of the glacier in the summer of 1943, causing catastrophic flooding of the whole valley as far down as Sion, in the Rhône valley, some 50km downstream.

Outburst floods

Outbursts (also known as glacier floods, *débâcles* and *jokulhaups*) are high-flow events whose origin is unrelated to normal melt processes. Some outbursts involve relatively small discharges, in the order of one to three cubic metres per second (m^3/s) which last only a few hours (such as those from the Bas Glacier d'Arolla). Others involve huge flows which are sustained over a number of days (for example the peak discharge of the 1818 outburst from the Gietro glacier has been estimated to have been 8,000 m^3/s and to have involved a total water volume of twenty million cubic metres). Some outbursts occur on a periodic basis (for example that produced by the annual drainage of the Gornersee, a supraglacial lake which forms at the junction of the Gorner and Grenz glaciers, below Monte Rosa). Some are seemingly periodic (such as the *tines* of the Trient glacier, which occur once

every four to five years, or the Grimsvotn *jokulhaups*, which burst through a fifty kilometre long tunnel under the Vatnajokull ice cap once a critical level of water has accumulated in the ice depression formed by the Grimsvotn volcano. Note that *tine* and *jokulhaup* are local names for outburst events; *jokulhaup* has been adopted as a general term for a meltwater flood). Others occur repeatedly, but irregularly (for example those of the Rhone, Ferpecle and Vernagtferner glaciers), while still others have occurred, as far as we know, only once (for example, that of the Tête Rousse glacier).

A case study of outbursts in the Swiss Alps

Haeberli (1983) has documented the record of outburst floods in Switzerland. There have been over one hundred outbursts recorded in the Swiss Alps since

the start of the eighteenth century, involving forty separate glaciers. Whilst this represents less than three per cent of the total glaciers of Switzerland, they are geographically concentrated, as can be seen from the map shown below (Figure 12). These events have resulted in substantial erosion; costly damage to public and private property; and the loss of 200 lives. Moreover, it appears that they are not confined to the past: 'the rapidly advancing development of tourism in high Alpine valleys brings more and more human beings and installations into zones of potential danger that were previously avoided. The frequency of events causing damage seems to be on the increase rather than the decrease.' (*Source*: W. Haeberli, 'Frequency and characteristics of glacier floods in the Swiss Alps', *Annals of Glaciology* 4, 1983, p. 85–90)

A typology of outburst events

All outbursts involve the release of water stored in the catchment. The important questions, therefore, are
a how is the water stored and
b how is it released.

Most outbursts involve the drainage of water stored in surface lakes. These may exist on the surface of the ice (such as Gornergletscher), in front of the ice (such as Steingletscher), or trapped behind an ice barrier, either in a side valley (such as Aletschgletscher) or in the main valley (e.g. Allalingletscher). Alternatively, water may be stored in pockets within the body of the glacier (for example glacier du Trient) or in lakes held under the glacier (such as Ferpecle glacier).

Drainage of water from storage points can occur in a variety of ways:

1 by overflowing an ice dam

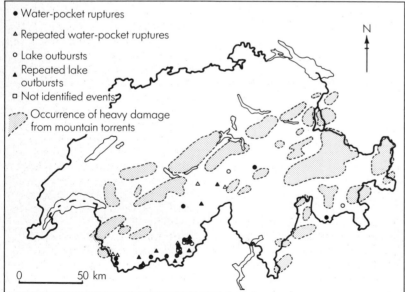

- • Water-pocket ruptures
- ▲ Repeated water-pocket ruptures
- ○ Lake outbursts
- ▲ Repeated lake outbursts
- □ Not identified events
- Occurrence of heavy damage from mountain torrents

N

0   50 km

Figure 12 The geography of outburst floods in Switzerland. Areas of extensive damage from mountain torrents, mostly in association with heavy rainstorms, are also shown.
Source: W. Haeberli, 'Frequency and characteristics of glacier floods in the Swiss Alps', *Annals of Glaciology*, **4**, 1983, pp. 85–90, published by the International Glaciological Society

2 by breaking up an ice dam
3 by floating, or jacking up, an ice dam
4 by draining out along pre-existing basal conduits
5 by draining out along enlarged basal conduits.

Most outbursts occur in the summer months, sometimes associated with the attainment of critical water pressure levels, sometimes linked to the initial development of the glacier's internal drainage system, sometimes triggered by an intense rain storm. Whatever the precise generating mechanism, the outburst tends to take one of two general forms, each having a hydrograph of characteristic shape, as shown in Figure 13.

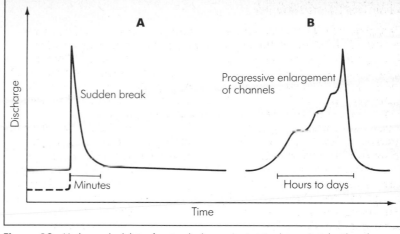

Figure 13 Hydrographs (plots of water discharge against time) associated with outbursts. Hydrograph A illustrates the 'sudden break' type flood. Hydrograph B illustrates the 'progressive enlargement of channels' type flood.
Source: W. Haeberli, 'Frequency and characteristics of glacier floods in the Swiss Alps', *Annals of Glaciology*, **4**, 1983, pp. 85–90, published by the International Glaciological Society

---

?

1 If you had to live in an area plagued by outburst events, which of these two types would you prefer them to be?

The first form of outburst is known as the 'sudden break' type, in which the rapid removal of the retaining barrier results in a flood wave with a rapid rise to peak, and a high peak relative to its total volume. These signal danger; they break suddenly, move downstream quickly and often arrive as a frontal wave. The second broad type of outburst is known as the 'progressive enlargement of channels' type, which, as the name suggests, involves the gradual release of water as the retaining barriers are sequentially removed. The flood thus rises to its peak more slowly than does the sudden break outburst, and has a smaller peak flow to total volume ratio than does the sudden break flood. The progressive release outburst is thus not as dangerous as the sudden break flood, by virtue of it yielding a longer warning time and a lower peak discharge.

Controlling outbursts: the choices

What can we do to minimise the hazards posed by outburst events? Put simply, the choice amounts to altering
a the physical processes which produce outbursts or
b the human activities which decree that the outburst constitutes a hazard.

?

1 Think about the point made in the last sentence. Debate the proposition that the physical event in itself is not a hazard, and that it becomes one only when human activities come into conflict with the 'normal' operation of the event.

Controlling the release and passage of outburst floods
Can we realistically hope to be able to control the physical circumstances which promote outburst activity? In certain cases, yes. Which cases? Lake outburst cases, where we can see what is going on. By constructing relief drainage channels, we can bleed water from the water reservoir before it reaches critical levels. We can also shore up vulnerable moraine embankments with concrete or boulder-packed gabions. (A gabion is a strong wire mesh box or cage, which is filled with large boulders to form a stable edge to a river channel.) Such a strategy has been implemented to protect the town of Saas Baden, Switzerland, from a repetition of the 1970 outburst from the Grubensee. The situation with water pocket ruptures is somewhat different of course. The structural control of water pocket outbursts is, to date, a non-starter. We simply don't have the means to drain the water pocket in a controlled fashion. Worse still, we don't in most cases know where the pocket is (though developments in radio-echo techniques offer hope of improving upon this situation).

So much for intervening at source, as it were. What about controlling the passage of the flood wave generated by an outburst? The options here are much the same as those employed to cope with ordinary floods: hold the flood before it reaches the risk zone, or route it through or

Figure 14 The Gornera, its waters held within artificial walls as it passes through Zermatt

?

1 This raises a pertinent issue: how do we know how big to make the flood channel? What if you have to make this decision for a mountain community. How would you go about doing it? Compare your thoughts with the procedures outlined in the last but one paragraph of this section.

Behavioural responses to minimising the hazard posed by outbursts

There is a limit to which people are prepared to surrender valuable land to concrete channels which are used once in a blue moon. Why can't we keep a close watch on the rate of build-up of the water reservoir, and warn those downstream when (and if) they need to take evasive action (evacuate, move upstairs and so on)? This may well be possible in the case of surface lake outbursts, where we can monitor lake levels. It clearly isn't possible, however, to measure the rate of filling of internal water pockets. Nor are there any obvious morphological hallmarks which might enable us to recognise when a water pocket rupture is likely to occur. Forewarning potential, in the case of water pocket ruptures, thus is limited to being able to recognise the event as soon as it has happened, rather than being able to predict it in advance. Improving the on-the-ground density and through-the-air/wire communications of river level gauging stations is the priority here. Nevertheless, there is a limit to what can be achieved given a few hours' warning that one's house, or school, or town is about to be engulfed by a flood wave. So how can we plan for the big one on a rational basis?

One rational strategy is to zone land use in threatened areas, along the lines of the flood hazard zoning schemes which are common in the USA and are becoming more common in the

around the risk area. No barrage has yet been built solely as an outburst protection device, but if there is spare capacity in a water supply reservoir sited below the outburst point, the flood wave can be held or reduced. The fact that most outbursts occur relatively early in the summer, before storage reservoirs are filled, is a blessing in this respect. Purpose-designed channels can be, and are, used to transmit flood waters safely through risk zones. The Gornera, for example, is strait-jacketed within concrete walls as it flows through the town of Zermatt. When the Gornersee empties in its annual flood event, the flood wave is a sight to behold, from the safety of the banks (Figure 14).

UK (for example in Shrewsbury, Bath, and Cambridge). If we can determine the areas which are likely to be affected by an outburst of a stated magnitude, we can make sensible, informed decisions about how to use that land. The choices available include vacating the land entirely (is this a real option, do you think?), building structures which are capable of withstanding the flood event, using the risk areas for functions which permit rapid evacuation (such as car parking, playgrounds). To entertain such an approach, we obviously need to be able to estimate likely outburst volumes and peak discharges. How can this be done?

Estimating outburst volumes may not be a difficult proposition in the case of surface lake outbursts, because we can measure the morphology of the stores to ascertain the maximum volume of water which they can hold. But, once again, those hidden internal water pockets pose a considerable problem. How can we estimate their capacity? Using the slightly adjusted adage that 'the past is the key to the future', the likely size of the outburst from a particular glacier can be assessed by a careful analysis of the record of its past outbursts. When have outbursts occurred? How frequently? Do we have an estimate of the maximum flow discharge? Do we know the total volume of water involved? Do we have any maps of the areas affected by the flood waters? By searching for answers to such questions, we can make informed judgements about the size of water pocket which may burst from the glacier. This method also works for surface lake outbursts.

For an outburst of specified volume, we can estimate the peak discharge using empirical formulae (the Clague–Mathews formula for progressive enlargement floods, and the Haeberli formula for sudden break floods). Having done this, we can estimate the area likely to be affected by the release of a water pocket of given volume, and thereby plan land use on a rational basis. Work being undertaken at the Hydraulics, Hydrology and Glaciology Section at the Zurich Technical Institute (ETH) is proceeding along these lines. The intention of the study is to provide the basis for positive (that is, active rather than passive) behavioural responses in outburst hazard zones.

1 You should, in reading through this section, have appreciated that outbursts from internal water pockets are much more difficult to control than those from surface lakes. Write a brief essay explaining why.

Conclusions

Tufnell (1984) in his book *Glacier Hazards* provides a neat sketch of the responses of the people of Valais to the various hazards posed by the glaciers in the region, recognising three phases of response from historical to modern times (below):

Progress would seem to amount to getting a better understanding of the physical processes, so that we can either modify them, or our own activities, to suit.

'During the earliest of these, it was thought that religious acts would induce the Almighty to quell such hazards. However, divine intervention turned out to be notoriously unreliable, so people began to look for other solutions. Inspired chiefly by Venetz, they gradually adopted a more practical attitude and this met with greater success (e.g. tunnelling through the reconstituted lobe of the Gietro glacier, to provide a release/relief conduit for the impounded lake) ... In the current, third phase, man is developing a more scientific approach to the understanding and control of glacier behaviour. New methods of surveillance are being tried, and these are producing a reorientation of the approach to glacier hazards ... Whereas formerly man responded to such hazards after they had occurred, careful scientific investigations are enabling him to predict glacier behaviour more accurately and so make it possible to take appropriate measures in the early stages of hazard development.'

Source: Lance Tufnell, *Glacier Hazards*, 1988, p. 83

PART II

USE AND MISUSE OF NATURAL RESOURCES

Ranking paragraphs

Let's go back to the Introduction to Part I. Re-read the four paragraphs at the beginning on page 4 where different beliefs and attitudes about people's use and treatment of the environment are outlined. We know people have different opinions on these matters.

Then rank each paragraph on a scale of 1 to 5 for bias. Classifying the paragraphs in this way should give rise to a lively discussion. Which paragraphs do you think are the least biased, or the most biased? What do you define as bias? The dictionary says a bias is an inclination, a predisposition towards, a prejudice; while to bias is to influence (usually unfairly), inspire with prejudice. Write out statements to justify your judgements and use them in small group or class discussion.

Finish your discussion before reading on and seeing where my thoughts led me.

After your discussion, read on

It's frustrating not to be in on your reactions to this exercise. I'd be waiting, I think, for someone to say, 'Well, I'm not going to rank the paragraphs. It all depends on what your own point of view is! The paragraph I most agree with is the least biased.' If you have a predisposition to nature and like the idea of living in a very low-technology environment, growing your own food without chemical fertilisers, taking the consequences of outbreaks of pests and so on, you will not find much bias in the second paragraph. It agrees with your values, attitudes and beliefs.

So perhaps it is not the paragraphs which display bias but our own attitudes, values and beliefs, giving us a certain point of view. Someone is 'biased' if they hold views different from our own, but they are not biased if they hold views like ours – they're good, sensible, level-headed people.

A matter of evidence

The above point won't be the only one to emerge

from the ranking exercise and it won't be the only new kind of understanding about opinion and bias to unfold. But I do hope that it's one of the points. I think some of the things we get out of an education are:

● the realisation that we all have our points of view;

● that we should look carefully at our points of view;

● that we should ask ourselves what 'evidence' we have for our opinions or points of view.

There is at least one further point. The 'evidence' may not always be a *scientific* sort of evidence. It will often be 'evidence' of a *belief* sort, a belief grounded in our values. For example, what 'evidence' is there that people can always find a way out of the difficulties we create in our environment? Have we been able to bring back an extinct bird species? (What do a few birds matter?) Have we found a way to house the homeless? (Why should we? It's their fault.) Is a belief that we can sort out the difficulties we create something based on evidence? Or something based on belief? Or is it sometimes evidence and sometimes belief?

We have then, I think, two categories to recognise when it comes to thinking about our points of view, our biases. We can either recognise our points of view and say that I have evidence of a scientific sort to uphold my view. Or we can say to ourselves that there is not much evidence of that kind around. I hold that particular view because it's a belief of mine, a value of mine, it's something I believe to be right for a human being to hold. But, for both categories or points of views, I am willing to take into account other evidence, other points of view, other arguments. It would be very difficult for me, I think, to stop believing that the parable of the Good Samaritan or the parable of the Prodigal Son were not fundamentally important points of view held in my belief/value system about how we should treat one another, but I would always want to say that I was also willing to listen to and consider another point of view. Or I would equally be prepared to consider and examine new evidence of a scientific sort about, for example, the causes of the greenhouse effect.

In geography we are never far away from controversial issues, whether these are based on beliefs/values (how to treat other people in society) or evidence of a scientific sort (what's happening to the physical environment).

A second exercise in bias

Acid rain is one of the most currently controversial issues. Perhaps one you've been exposed to once too often. Bear with me once more for a second exercise in bias as it relates to acid rain.

A geography teacher, Peter Fry, recently did some research into bias and acid rain. He believes that to be politically aware and politically educated we need to come to understand bias. He gave the following exercise to his class. It's an exercise based on two extracts about the causes of acid rain and fits into the category of having evidence of a sort of scientific kind on which to base our point of view.

?

1 Read extracts A and B one at a time and answer the questions on each one.

2 After completing the exercise and holding a debriefing discussion (Peter Fry's own account of the lesson is given in after the two extracts), consider how you would create two exercises for yourself which set out not to detect bias as in this one but
a to create bias, and
b to correct bias.

How does rain become acidified?

Extract A

Acid rain is a menacing form of air pollution. Two of the most important groups of air pollutants are the oxides of sulphur and nitrogen. Sulphur dioxide is released when fossil fuels like coal and oil are burnt, while nitrogen oxides are a by-product of almost all combustion. Though the introduction of smokeless zones and other measures have dramatically reduced some forms of air pollution in countries like Britain, sulphur and nitrogen oxide levels have not fallen the same way. Today the biggest culprit of air pollution is the coal-fired power station.

Some of the gases or particles belched from industrial and domestic chimneys fall back to earth close to their sources. This is known as 'dry deposition'. However, much is carried up into the atmosphere where, by combining with water vapour, sulphuric and nitric acid are formed. Clouds of acid vapour can then be carried hundreds of miles by the wind before reaching the ground as 'wet deposition' – mist, snow or acid rain.

Until recently, sulphur dioxide was thought to be the cause of most air pollution in Europe and North America. However, in the last few years, it is nitrogen oxide levels which have risen sharply – mainly due to exhaust emissions from the increasing numbers and use of motor vehicles.

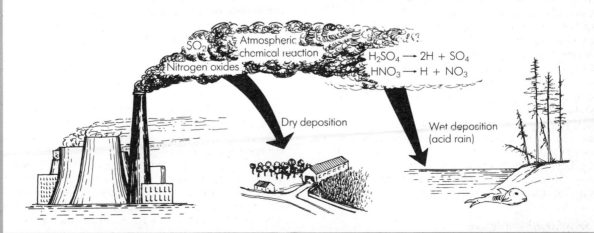

$$H_2SO_4 \longrightarrow 2H + SO_4$$
$$HNO_3 \longrightarrow H + NO_3$$

SO$_2$ · Atmospheric chemical reaction · Nitrogen oxides · Dry deposition · Wet deposition (acid rain)

Source: International Centre for Conservation Education, 1985

1 Is acid rain caused by natural or human processes? Or both of these?

2 Who or what exactly causes acid rain? (Study the diagram, it will help you.)

3a How many times is the world 'pollution' used in the passage?

b What effect does the use or non-use of the word 'pollution' have on the character of the passage?

4 What do you understand by the following phrases? What view of acid rain do these statements support?

'Acid rain is a menacing form of air pollution'.
'the biggest culprit of air pollution is the coal-fired power station'.
'particles belched from industrial and domestic chimneys'.

5 What are the interests of this author?

Extract B

The acidity of 'acid rain' is brought about both naturally and artificially. Some of it is from such unavoidable causes as the respiration of plants and animals, organic decay on land or under water, volcanic eruptions and lightening strikes. Man's contribution comes mainly from the burning of fuels and the smelting of ores.

The gases principally responsible for acidification are carbon dioxide, sulphur dioxide and nitrogen oxides. In the southern hemisphere the natural emissions of sulphur dioxide overshadow the man-made ones in their effect on rain and other deposition. In the northern hemisphere, on the other hand, man's emissions of sulphur dioxide are similar to those from natural sources. In both hemispheres the rain is acid, even in places far from industry.

Emissions from the burning of fuel, in power stations as elsewhere can make rain more acid than it would have been otherwise. Emissions are also linked with some of the substances brought down by rain. These substances can in some cases harm the environment.

Natural processes have converted ancient organisms into the 'fossil' fuels: oil, natural gas and coal. These contain the hydrogen, carbon, sulphur, nitrogen and other elements that life depends on. They were vital parts of the original living organisms.

When fuel is burnt the oxygen in the air joins the other elements to form their oxides. Emissions from chimneys and exhaust pipes therefore include these oxides. One of them is water (which is hydrogen oxide). The others – oxides of carbon, sulphur and nitrogen – are gases that can travel dry and can partly dissolve in water to form weakly acidic rain. The processes in the atmosphere are partly responsible for the higher acidity that is actually found in rain.

1 Is acid rain caused by natural or human-made processes? Or both of these?

2 Who or what exactly causes acid rain? (Study the diagram, it will help you.)

3a How many times is the word pollution used in the passage?

b What effect does the use or non-use of the word 'pollution' have on the character of the passage?

4 What do you understand by the following phrases? What view of acid rain do these statements support?

'Man's contribution . . .'
'the natural emissions of sulphur dioxide overshadow the man-made ones in the effect on rain.'
'water is hydrogen oxide'.
'Processes in the atmosphere are partly responsible for the higher acidity that is actually found in rain.'

5 What are the interests of this author?

1 Atmosphere receives oxides of carbon, sulphur and nitrogen, hydrocarbons etc. from natural and man-made sources on the ground. Some of the emissions come down and are deposited dry. → **2** Sunlight stimulates formation of photo-oxidants. These produce sulphuric and nitric acid. → **3** Sulphur and nitrogen oxides, photo-oxidants, and other gases including ammonia, dissolve in cloud droplets. The products are acids, sulphates and nitrates. → **4** Acid rain containing dissolved sulphates and nitrates. →

Peter Fry's account of the lesson on detecting bias

Having discovered how acid Acid Rain is, it was seen as the logical step to find out its cause. The extracts and question papers were issued to the class. The purpose of the lesson, detecting bias, was not overtly expressed at the beginning but it was hoped that pupils would perceive bias for themselves while doing the exercises. During the explanation of the questions the pupils became aware of the difference between 'natural' and 'man-made' processes, what 'pollution' is, and what we might mean by the 'character' of the passage: for example does the word 'pollution' make the passage distinctive in any way? For part of the exercise the author has selected value-laden phrases from the text (the pupils do this task for themselves later in the curriculum unit) and the pupils write down the meaning or what they understand by the phrases which are underlined. The term 'interests' was elaborated upon by asking why is it in the pupil's interests to come to school? It involves personal gain.

It was hoped that the pupils would perceive bias, or, rather opinions from fact, when they read the second extract. At this point many intense conversations began. The most common reaction to the extracts was, 'which one is true?' Other interesting comments were, 'surely you write down the facts', and 'the truth must be somewhere'. The atmosphere in the classroom during the exercise was mixed. Some pupils, not necessarily the most able, were confidently doing the work. Two pupils perceived bias before studying the second extract; they asked 'do I answer from the text or from what I know is right?' They were encouraged to be open to the possibility of changing their own attitudes. Other members of the class were unsure and confused by the work – an indication that studying conflicting views had not been tackled elsewhere in their schooling, and that the pupils were more confident when dealing with unconflicting reports.

At the end of the written exercises the questions were discussed by the whole class. Without exception the pupils found that the CEGB saw Acid Rain as being caused by human and natural processes, while the ICCE lay the blame with human activities only. This question was comprehension, although critical thinking was involved in the comparison between the two answers. The class saw how by omitting one cause and emphasising others a different picture of the issue might emerge. It was unclear for many pupils where the CEGB lay the blame for Acid Rain, a common answer was similar to:

'Acid Rain is caused by the respiration of plants and animals, organic decay on land or under water, volcanic eruptions and lightning strikes. It is also caused by burning fuels and smelting ores.'

The ICCE according to the pupils sees the CEGB as the main producer of Acid Rain or 'the culprit is plainly the other author.' It was agreed that the ICCE used the word 'pollution' five times while the CEGB does not mention the word, but it was cleverly added that the CEGB 'talks about pollution without mentioning it'.

During the discussion the idea of a passage having a 'character', was explained further. However, most pupils realised the effect on the passage if the same word, in this case 'pollution' was repeated frequently. The value-laden statements supported the view of Acid Rain held by the two authors, and the class were able to recognise the linking of man-made pollution and Acid Rain by the ICCE and the emphasis on natural emissions by the CEGB. While the pupils generally understood the meanings of the statements, only a few pupils analysed particular words. 'Man's contribution' for example, gave the impression to some pupils that 'others contribute more'. After discussing the terminology used, one pupil said 'if you think every word is biased you won't believe anything.' Finally the class discussed why the two groups held their views; answers varied from 'money' to 'power' and 'their view of life and the world'.

As a conclusion the class were asked to say what the general differences between the two extracts were. The question was aimed at distinguishing different types of bias. The simple discrepancies in 'facts' between the two extracts were noted. It was pointed out that each group only used the facts best suited to their cause and refused to accept other important facts. Finally, certain terms, especially adjectives, for example 'menacing' or 'belching', were seen to change the emphasis of a particular phrase.

Although it was nearly the end of the lesson a sequence of slides was shown – the class having to decide which view, the CEGB or ICCE, the slides best supported. The slide set included, without text, pictures of a working power station, erupting volcano, and car exhausts, so it formed an interesting visual summary to the lesson.

By studying two opposing views of what causes Acid Rain, the pupils gained some understanding of the dispute and, at varying degrees, learnt to adopt a critical stance towards the information given. By the use of similar questions, the class was able to dissect the views and become more aware of how a convincing argument is constructed. The pupils not only dealt with political bias, but distinguished between differing types of bias. Comparing two extracts eased the pupils into ways of dealing with political bias; it was, however, biased in itself as it limited the pupil's opportunities to deal with alternative points of view. Did the pupils have enough knowledge of the issue to know if contradictory or other relevant information was omitted? How do we know if the assertions made by the CEGB and ICCE are facts or opinions? Relevant statistical information was used to tackle these points in the following lesson.

Source: Peter Fry, 'Dealing with political bias through geographical education,' unpublished MA dissertation, University of London, Institute of Education, 1987.

5

The energy question

John Soussan

Energy conservation in Nepal: burning fuel efficiently in a mud stove

A global perspective

Energy issues are very complex. Study the following resources and work through the exercises which follow, to start to answer these key questions: Do we have an energy problem? and, if so, What is the nature of this problem?

'The oil crises of 1973–74 and 1979–80 put energy on the international agenda. Individuals faced long queues at petrol stations and paid more when they reached the pump. Governments found their economic plans ruined by huge increased in import costs and the severe recessions of the mid 1970s and early 1980s. Everyone then talked of energy gaps and worried about what to do when the oil ran out. Important reports such as the *Limits to Growth* told us with great certainty that oil and many other resources were finite and scarce. It was a gloomy picture, but at least we all knew where we stood. This certainty seems to have gone in the last few years. The dramatic events of 1986, when oil prices collapsed and Chernobyl blew up, have created an atmosphere of change and uncertainty in the world's largest industry. I'm confused. Is there an energy crisis in the modern world?'

Source: Student at seminar about the world energy picture, 1989

?

Work in pairs. Study Table 1.

1a Which countries have an energy surplus? Which have an energy deficit? Sort them into two groups.

b Explain some of the *causes* and some of the *consequences* of these differences.

2 Plot a scattergraph of per capita consumption against GNP. (Leave out the countries for which 1987 figures were not available.) Comment on your graph.

'Energy is, put most simply, the fundamental unit of the physical world. As such, we cannot conceive of development without changes in the extent or nature of energy flows. And because it is so fundamental, every one of those changes of flows has environmental implications. The implications of this are profound. It means that there is no such thing as a simple energy choice. They are all complex. And they all involve trade-offs. However, some of the choices and some of the trade-offs appear to be unequivocally better than others, in the sense that they offer more development and less environmental damage.'

Source: David Brooks (Friends of the Earth), World Commission on Environmental and Development Public Hearing, May 1986

Table 1 Production and consumption of commercial fuels for selected countries in 1987

	Production (PJ)	Consumption (PJ)	Population (millions)	Per capita consumption (GJ)	Per capita GNP (US$)
Africa	16,941	7,109	589	12	
Burkina Faso	—	6	17.3	1	150
Kenya	7	49	22.4	2	300
Libya	2,279	395	3.9	106	(not available)
Nigeria	3,183	495	102	5	640
Zimbabwe	130	169	9.4	19	620
North and Central America	75,097	79,387	412	195	
Nicaragua	2	30	3.5	9	790
USA	58,422	60,766	242.2	278	17,480
South America	11,431	8,109	279.4	30	
Argentina	1,637	1,580	31.5	51	2,350
Brazil	2,152	3,088	141.5	22	1,810
Peru	433	310	20.7	15	1,090
Asia	71,118	58,114	2,913.2	20	
Bangladesh	122	188	106.7	2	160
China	24,349	21,771	1,085	21	300
Indonesia	4,169	1,392	172.5	8	490
Kuwait	3,339	432	2	228	13,890
Sri Lanka	10	56	16.7	3	400
Vietnam	168	214	62.2	4	(not available)
Europe	41,969	64,177	494.5	130	
Czechoslovakia	1,973	2,860	15.7	183	(not available)
West Germany	4,545	10,097	60.6	166	12,080
Portugal	37	397	10.3	39	2,250
UK	10,478	8,858	56.2	157	8,870
USSR	66,197	52,671	284	187	(not available)
World total	288,367	273,201	4,997.6	56	3,000

Source: World Resources 1988–89, World Development Report, 1989, pp. 306–7

Table 2 World energy futures: two demand scenarios (M and L)

	1973		1985		2000				2020			
					M		L		M		L	
	Mtoe	toe/inhb	Mtoe	toe/inhb	Mtoe	toe/inhb	Mtoe	toe/inhb	Mtoe	toe/inhb	Mtoe	toe/inhb
Market economy industrialised countries (First World)	3,470	4.43	3,610	4.17	4,350	4.57	4,025	4.23	4,840	4.71	4,130	4.02
Centrally planned industrialised countries (Second World)	1,220	3.42	1,740	4.42	2,265	5.27	2,150	5.00	2,885	6.20	2,520	5.42
Third World (or South)	1,475	0.55	2,320	0.65	3,645	0.77	3,355	0.70	5,800	0.92	4,910	0.78
WORLD	6,165	1.61	7,670	1.59	10,260	1.67	9,530	1.55	13,525	1.73	11,560	1.48

Mtoe   = million tonnes of oil equivalent (G= giga- or thousand million)
toe/inhb = tonnes of oil equivalent per inhabitant or per capita

World per capita consumption, which remained stable at around 1.6 toe during the period 1973–1985, would rise only slightly in scenario 'M' to reach 1.7 toe by 2020, whereas in 'L' it would actually drop to 1.5 toe.

Energy intensity would continue the declining trend seen in rates between 1973 and 1985. With this fall of −1 to −1.5% p.a., demand in the industrialised North would increase only gradually, rising from 5.4 Gtoe in 1985 to 6.7/7.7 Gtoe in 2020 'L/M'.

In the South, on the other hand, the energy intensity situation, which showed no progress between 1973 and 1985, would improve considerably under 'M' with an annual average of −1% and significantly under 'L' with −0.35%.

Third World demand, therefore, would increase from 2.3 Gtoe in 1985 to 4.9/5.8 Gtoe in 2020 'L/M'. As a result of demographic pressure and relatively sustained economic development, the countries of the South would slowly catch up on the industrialised North in their share of world demand. Compared with 24% in 1960 and 1973, the South's proportion would rise from 30% in 1985 to 35% in 2000 and 43% in 2020. In the period between 2000 and 2020, the South would account for 2/3 of the increase in world consumption in 'M' and 3/4 in 'L'.

Despite this progress, considerable differences in per capita consumption would remain. In 1985, average per capita consumption in the South, including non-commercial energy sources, stood at 0.65 toe as against 4.25 toe in the North. By 2020, the corresponding figures, depending on scenario, would be 0.8/0.9 toe in the South, and 4.45/5.15 toe in the North. Thus, there is hardly any improvement in the ratio for the South in terms of consumption.

Source: World Energy Conference (1989), 'Global energy perspectives 2000–2020', WEC, London

1 Study Table 2.

a Plot a line graph of energy demand (using the Mtoe figures only) for 1973–2020. Use different colours for the three groups of countries, and dashed lines to represent projected figures for the two scenarios.

b Comment on your graph.

c Follow the text about per capita consumption under Table 2. What is the relationship between North and South?

2 Look back to the resources on pages 109 and 110. What do you think the key energy issues are:

a for people in the economically developed North?

b for people in the economically developing South?

Fossil fuels

Fossil fuels (coal, oil and gas) still supply most of the world's energy, in spite of earlier predictions to the contrary.

- Predictions in the 1950s suggested a nuclear-powered society by the year 2000.
- In the early 1980s it was predicted that oil costs would increase dramatically to reach $100 a barrel in the 1990s.

In 1987, 75 per cent of the world's energy consumption was supplied from fossil fuels (Figure 1) and proven reserves were considerable (Figure 2).

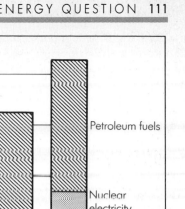

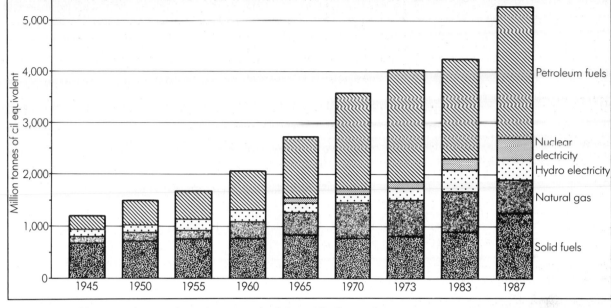

Figure 1 World commercial energy demands, 1945–87 (excluding USSR, China and Eastern Europe)
Source: Institute of Petroleum, *World Statistics*, 1988

Notes

Proved reserves are generally taken to be those quantities which geological and engineering information indicate with reasonable certainty can be recovered in the future from known reserves under existing economic and operating conditions.

Reserves/Production (R/P) ratio: If the reserves remaining at the end of any year are divided by the production in the year, the result is the length of time that those remaining reserves would last if production were to continue at the then current level.

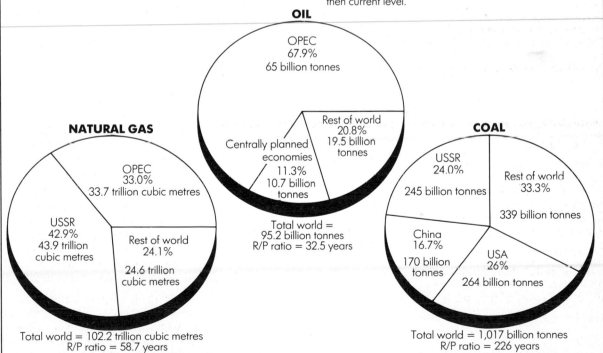

Figure 2 Proved fossil fuel reserves at the end of 1986
Source: *Statistical Review of World Energy*, 1987

A brief history of oil

As Graph A shows, the price of oil was remarkably stable and very low until 1973, since when it has moved violently a number of times. Oil prices are affected to some extent by short-term supply and demand relationships, but have little to do with long-term production capacities (Graph B) or resource availability. As the chart below shows, the main cause of both the long stability before 1973 and the volatile price since then is the political control of oil, firstly by the oil companies and then by the main oil exporting nations.

Time chart

1911
Standard Oil broken up by the US Anti-Trust Laws. Introduces real competition into oil markets.

1924-26
First oil crisis. US shortages cause a sharp rise in prices, followed by as sharp a fall as Venezuelan production expands.

1928
Achnacarry Accord signed by leading oil companies, forming a cartel to control world oil prices and divide the globe into 'spheres of influence'. Marks the start of 45 years of control by the oil companies.

1951
New Iranian government nationalises oil holdings without compensation. Oil companies refuse to buy Iranian oil, effectively isolating Iran.

1954
US-backed coup overthrows Iranian government. Marines invade, puppet regime installed. Oil facilities handed back to the oil companies, and the developing world learns a lesson.

1960
Organisation of Petroleum Exporting Countries (OPEC) formed (Table 3). Oil companies reduce oil price to $1.80 per barrel (from $2.08 in 1959). Price lasts through 1960s.

1971
Libya's new revolutionary leader Colonel Gadhaffi nationalises oil holdings. Ratified by OPEC. The battle for oil begins.

1971-73
OPEC pressure to raise oil price to $6 per barrel. Companies, supported by Western governments, refuse to discuss it.

1973
October: OPEC meeting in Geneva unilaterally raises price to $5.12 per barrel. Yom Kippur war in Middle East breaks out. Arab oil exporters boycott countries supporting Israel. Panic and shortages follow.

1974
January: OPEC raises price to $11.65 per barrel as boycott bites. Oil companies cave in, OPEC wins control of world oil market.

1974-79
Period of relative stability. Oil companies' profits increase, OPEC petrodollars flood international financial system, recession and conservation reduce demand, exploration for non-OPEC oil increases supply.

1979-80
Iranian revolution and Iran–Iraq war lead to panic in oil markets. Prices rise from $13 to $35 per barrel on spot markets. Official price rises in a series of stages to $32.50.

1981-85
OPEC loses market share to non-OPEC sources such as Alaska and the North Sea. Recession leads to falling demand and oil glut appears. OPEC maintains price by production quotas.

1970-86
Over this period three barrels of oil were found for every two used. January 1986: Oil price collapses. Reaches low of $6.90 per barrel in July before stabilising at $8–12.

1987
Price gradually recovers to $18–19 following OPEC meetings. Internal divisions and over-supply neutralise OPEC.

Since 1987
Oil prices stabilise around $15–18 per barrel, but are volatile in the short-term. Over-supply still exists, but economic boom in West leads to new shortage fears. Future uncertain. Some experts predict price falls in 1990s, others new rises. Political vacuum follows demise of OPEC, and oil companies unable to regain control. Everyone expects more crises.

Table 3 OPEC member states

Algeria	Kuwait	Saudi Arabia	Venezuela
Libya	Bahrain	Nigeria	Ecuador
Iraq	Qatar	Gabon	
Iran	United Arab Emirates	Indonesia	

Graph A Crude oil prices since 1900

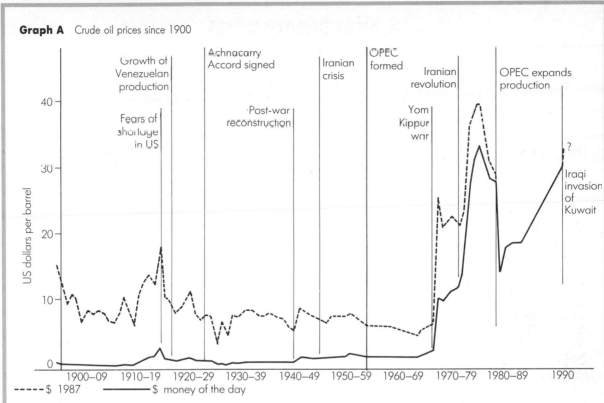

Source: Adapted from BP, *Statistical Review of World Energy*, 1988

Graph B Oil production by area

During the 1970s OPEC accounted for more than half of the world's oil production. Since then its share has declined and now stands at below one-third of the total.

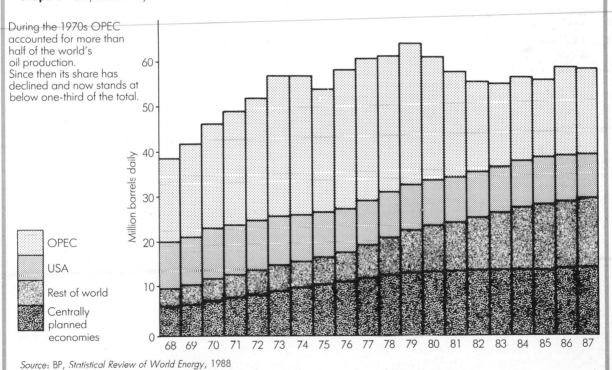

Source: BP, *Statistical Review of World Energy*, 1988

?

1 From Figure 2 we can work out (by using the Reserves/Production ratio) that if world consumption of oil increased by 2% a year the current reserves would run out in less than 25 years. In groups discuss the implications of this. (You may wish to use a computer program to calculate when the reserves of other fossil fuels will run out, if consumption grows at 2% a year, or to see what happens if consumption grows at say 5% a year.)

2 Do you think energy production will continue at the present rate? Under what circumstances might it increase/decrease?

3 From the evidence in Figures 1 and 2 and the extract 'Living in a glass house', comment on the past use of fossil fuels and how they might be used in the future.

4 In 1987 the International Energy Agency gave a figure for the recoverable oil resource of 324 billion tonnes at current consumption levels.

a How does this compare with the statistics in Figure 2?

b Can you suggest any reasons for the difference in perspective?

5 Study the box on page 112.

a Who controlled world oil prices in 1928 and for how long thereafter?

b Where are these companies likely to have their headquarters?

c What might be their priorities for oil prices?

d Why did the price of oil go up in the early 1970s?

e Why did the price of oil fall in the late 1970s and early 1980s?

6 Why do you think the predictions referred to in the text were **a** made and **b** wrong?

7 In pairs discuss when and why the next oil crisis might occur.

Are fossil fuels scarce?

Fossil fuels are not renewable and they will eventually run out. The data for the proven reserves (Figure 2) suggests, however, that in absolute terms they are not *yet* scarce. Scarcity of energy resources does exist at present, but this relates primarily to distribution, and to development and conservation strategies. There are *powerful* arguments for alternatives to fossil fuels such as wind, solar, geothermal and nuclear power. Such arguments are based on environmental and economic grounds (showing the alternatives are cleaner and/or cheaper) rather than on claims that oil wells are about to run dry.

Within this context this chapter explores some key energy issues through a study of three countries: the UK, Nepal and South Korea.

LIVING IN A GLASS HOUSE

One of the reasons that a greenhouse is warmer than its surroundings is because glass lets sunlight pass throught it, trapping infra-red heat inside. This principle helps to explain why instead of a cold, dead planet we have an environment which is kindly to life. The earth is a giant greenhouse in space, but instead of a glass roof we have a blanket of gases to keep us warm. These gases act in a similar way to glass, as they let short-wave radiation from the sun pass through them to warm the earth, but absorb long-wave radiation from the earth which would otherwise bounce back into space. Some of this heat eventually leaks out into space, and the rest is absorbed by the oceans and by the earth itself. Without the extra heat kept in by the greenhouse gases, the earth would be 30° colder: a frozen planet.

These heat-retaining gases, including water vapour, carbon dioxide CO_2, methane (CH_4), nitrous oxides (N_2O) and tropospheric ozone (O_3), have maintained a delicate balance of solar and heat radiation for thousands of years. In the last two centuries, however, human activity has begun to alter this balance by dramatically increasing the levels of these gases, and by introducing new 'super-absorbent' greenhouse gases like the CFCs and halons.

The world has already warmed by 0.5 to 0.7°C since pre-industrial times. There is now overwhelming concensus among scientists that because of the increase in greenhouse gases there will be a further rise of 0.5 to 1°C over the next few decades whatever we do, and that greater increases are inevitable unless positive action is taken to reduce emissions to a safe level, quickly. These increases may not sound like much, but even a relatively minor change in temperature can alter the climate completely: global temperature during the last ice age was only 4°C colder than today.

What are the likely consequences of further global warming? It has been predicted that without emission reductions there will be an increase in global temperature of 1.5 to 4.5°C by the year 2050, with a consequent rise in sea level of 25cm to 1.65 metres. It is likely that low-lying areas would be flooded, and responsible commentators have drawn attention to the possibility of what they call 'environmental refugees' on an unprecedented scale. Flooding would also cause widespread ecosystem and crop failure, with an increase in health problems due to sewage system damage and the spread of pests. The UK could become either much drier or wetter, depending on whether the Gulf Stream changes course as temperatures rise and on how wind patterns change. The weather may well become more extreme, with a greater frequency of major storms, intense rains and droughts.

In June 1988 over 300 world experts met in Toronto to consider the threats posed by the changing global atmosphere and how they might be addressed. Their conclusion was unequivocal: "The best predictions available indicate potentially severe economic and social dislocation for present and future generations, which will worsen international tensions and increase risk of conflicts between and within nations. It is imperative to act now."

Scientists and others who are concerned about the problem of global warming are increasingly focusing their attention on carbon dioxide (CO_2) emissions. There are two main reasons for this. The first is that CO_2 contributes as much to global warming as all the other greenhouse gases put together. The second is that CO_2 is the dominant gas in fossil fuel pollution and cannot easily be removed by filtering or other processes. It can however be reduced quickly by cutting fossil fuel consumption through measures such as energy efficiency. Most of these measures also reduce emissions of other greenhouse gases such as methane (CH_4), nitrous oxides (N_2O), and tropospheric ozone (O_3).

About four fifths of net global CO_2 emissions come from the burning of fossil fuels. The UK, with only 1% of the world's population, produces 3% of the world's carbon dioxide from fossil fuels. Western Europe as a whole produces 15%. North America 25%, Eastern Europe 26%, Japan and the Pacific countries 6%, China 11% and the other developing countries 16%.

In the UK, industrial processes, domestic buildings, transport and electricity generation are the main sources of CO_2 emission, producing 94, 90, 120 and 205 million tonnes of CO_2 per annum respectively. In the electricity generation sector, coal-fired stations account for over 90% of CO_2 emissions, with oil and gas-fired stations ac-

counting for the rest. Nuclear-generated electricity is credited by the government and the CEGB with being CO_2 free. However, many of the processes essential to nuclear generation such as uranium mining, construction and maintenance of stations, and waste disposal, require large amounts of energy and therefore produce CO_2. Though current levels are low when compared with coal-fired stations, these emissions will rise as uranium ores are depleted and become more difficult to extract.

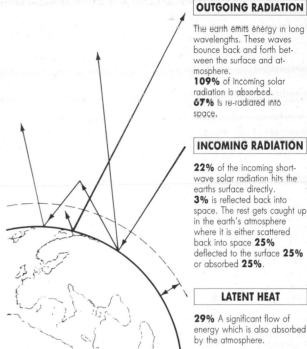

OUTGOING RADIATION

The earth emits energy in long wavelengths. These waves bounce back and forth between the surface and atmosphere.
109% of incoming solar radiation is absorbed.
67% is re-radiated into space.

INCOMING RADIATION

22% of the incoming short-wave solar radiation hits the earths surface directly.
3% is reflected back into space. The rest gets caught up in the earth's atmosphere where it is either scattered back into space **25%** deflected to the surface **25%** or absorbed **25%**.

LATENT HEAT

29% A significant flow of energy which is also absorbed by the atmosphere.

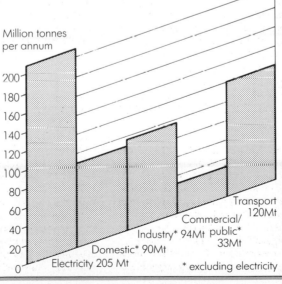

CO₂ FACTS

The generation of 1 kilowatt hour of electricity from a coal-fired power station produces 1 kilo of CO_2 (1,000 kilos = 1 tonne) (a kilowatt hour = 1,000 watts of electricity supplied for 1 hour or a 100W bulb lit for 10 hours)

The burning of 1 therm of natural gas produces 6 kilos of CO_2 (1 therm will boil a pint of water on a gas burner 160 times, or keep a burner on full for 9 hours)

The combustion of 1 litre of petrol produces around 2.5 kilos of CO_2

For the same amount of useful energy, oil emits 38 to 43% more CO_2 than natural gas, and coal emits 72 to 95% more.

Million tonnes per annum

200
180
160
140
120
100
80
60
40
20
0

Electricity 205 Mt
Domestic* 90Mt
Industry* 94Mt
Commercial/public* 33Mt
Transport 120Mt

* excluding electricity

Sources of CO_2 in the UK by sector (million tonnes per annum)

This study covers 92% of the total energy use in the UK. It does not cover the agricultural sector, nor does it take into account of some industrial processes such as coking or refining, or CO_2 produced from waste. The total is therefore lower than recent figures produced by the Energy Technology Support Unit (ETSU) and others.

Source: from *Solving the Greenhouse Dilemma*, Association for the Conservation of Energy, 1989

Energy issues in the UK

Coal

For 200 years prior to 1950 the energy picture in the UK was dominated by coal, which in the early 1950s supplied 90% of UK energy consumption. Coal production peaked at 298 million tonnes in 1913, when over a million men worked in the industry. It fuelled industry, households, transport and was used to produce gas and generate electricity. Coal was truly the fuel of the industrial revolution.

Coal is still the most important fuel used in electricity generation, but it has been an industry in decline. Production of coal has plummeted from 186 million tonnes in 1966 to 99 million tonnes in 1988. The number of miners has fallen even more dramatically, from 455,700 to 104,400 men over the same period. Pit closures announced in the early months of 1989 cut the workforce to less than 80,000, and further closures reduced the workforce to 66,000 in early 1990. Despite this, coal is still a cheap and plentiful resource. There is enough coal to last for over 200 years at the present rate of consumption, and coal is still the cheapest way to generate the large quantities of electricity needed in the UK. Advocates of coal point out that emissions of carbon dioxide from modern power stations are a fraction of those from older ones and that electricity generation is responsible for less than 10 per cent of this gas globally.

Oil and gas

Natural gas was discovered in the North Sea in 1964, and was first brought ashore in 1967. Since then it has been the most rapidly growing fuel, as it is cheap, convenient and adaptable. Gas is particularly popular in industry and households, and its price has been kept artificially high to keep the growth of demand down. Nevertheless, gas provided one quarter of all energy used in the UK in the late 1980s, with 1987 consumption at nearly 48 billion cubic metres. There are estimated to be between 2,165 and 3,632 billion cubic metres of UK gas left; between 45 and 76 years' supply at current rates of consumption.

North Sea oil was first discovered in 1969, and production started in 1974. The oil price rises of 1973–4 gave the North Sea a tremendous boost, as many fields which would have been too expensive to develop were suddenly profitable, and both the British Government and the oil companies were anxious to find oil which was not controlled by OPEC. Development was rapid, and by 1978 output had reached 80 million tonnes. Oil production levelled out at around 126 million tonnes in 1984, but was predicted to fall in the early 1990s. The fall in world oil prices from 1986 onwards has curtailed further exploration efforts in the North Sea, and a series of accidents in 1988 and 1989 led to a fall in output as capacity fell and safety in the oilfields become a matter for serious concern.

This does not mean that oil production will cease. The Department of Energy, whose figures are usually conservative, estimated the UK's recoverable oil reserves to be between 1,962 and 5,392 million tonnes in 1987, or between 15 and 45 more years' supply at current levels of production. This is compared to a total cumulative production of 952 million tonnes by the end of 1986. Some commentators believe that these official estimates are too low, however, and suggest that Britain will be a significant oil producer well into the 21st century. Whoever is believed, there is little doubt that the UK will continue to be self-sufficient in oil for some years, but the oil bonanza of the late 1970s which hid many fundamental economic problems was firmly over by the end of 1988.

Nuclear energy

A powerful coalition of industrial and political interests has for 30 years lobbied for the expansion of Britain's nuclear capability. The argument for nuclear power was

Table 4   Comparative cost of nuclear and coal-fired power electricity generation in the UK

CEGB (1988) submission to Hinkley Public Enquiry (Pence/kWh)

Discount rate (%)	5	8	10
Hinkley C (nuclear PWR)	2.24	3.09	3.80
Coastal coal plant	2.50	2.97	3.35
Inland coal plant	2.62	3.03	3.36

Coalfields community campaign (1988) submission to Hinkley Public Enquiry
(Pence/kWh)

Discount rate (%)	5	8	11	13	15
Coal	2.7	3.1	3.6	4.0	4.4
Nuclear (PWR)	3.4	4.6	6.2	7.5	9.0
Difference (PWR-coal)	0.7	1.5	2.6	3.5	4.6
Excess cost PWR (%)	26	48	72	88	104

Notes: In both cases coal stations are fitted with full flue gas desulphurisation equipment. The key importance of the discount rate used in the calculations is shown by the figures. The CEGB estimate 8% to be the best figure, but their critics claim that this is far too low. The CCC middle figure of 11% is a good estimate, and may even still be kind to nuclear power. The other differences between the two sets of figures reflect different assumptions about the capital cost of PWR reactors, the running life of different stations and other factors which influence their comparative costs.

traditionally based on cost and resource criteria (as the 'fuel of the future' when fossil fuels ran out), but recently environmental concerns such as global warming caused by the 'greenhouse effect' have also come to the fore (nuclear power stations do not emit carbon dioxide). Opponents of nuclear power argue that nuclear power is more expensive (Table 4) and presents unacceptable environmental hazards.

?

1 Read page 116 and the extract 'Oil prices soar after North Sea blast'. In pairs discuss:

a What were the factors that proved favourable to the exploitation of North Sea oil and gas in the 1970s?

b What factors are likely to limit exploitation in the future?

2 Assume that predictions that Britain's oil and gas supplies will run out early in the next century, if the present level of production is maintained, are accurate. Prepare a report from either the point of view of the Government or of an environmentalist group outlining your plans for the use of the country's oil and gas reserves.

Oil prices soar after North Sea blast

OIL PRICES soared when Britain's North Sea oil production was slashed by a quarter yesterday after an explosion which followed a gas leak at a Shell Esso oil platform shut down most of the Brent oilfield.

This disruption has probably shrunk Britain's North Sea output of crude oil to less than 1.5 million barrels a day. As Brent Blend is one of the most widely traded international crudes, the incident threatens to unravel the delicate structure of international oil prices, tighten the world oil market further and drive petrol prices up to £2 a gallon.

After the explosion on Cormorant Alpha on Tuesday night, the price of Brent Blend crude jumped about $1.50, to close last night at $21.55 a barrel. The price of oil for delivery in June closed at its highest level since August 1987. Trading in contracts for future delivery of crude oil cargoes broke records in London yesterday and there was hectic business on the New York futures market.

Cormorant Alpha is the hub for pipelines carrying some 471,975 barrels of oil daily from the Brent oilfields to Sullom Voe, Europe's biggest oil terminal, in the north Shetlands. Shell said yesterday

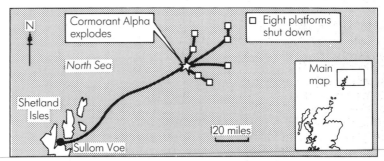

that this production was temporarily shut down, and some 40,000 barrels produced by the rig itself had ceased.

Tuesday's incident is the latest in a string of setbacks which have cut North Sea oil production, once around 2.3m barrels per day. Following the Piper Alpha disaster in 1988, oil production from the Piper field and others linked by the same pipeline to the Flotta terminal cut output of North Sea crude by about 10 per cent. Occidental, Piper's owner, hopes to bring two of the related fields, Claymore and Scapa with a daily yield of 104,000 barrels, back on stream in late May, 10 months after the disaster. Piper produced about 120,000 barrels daily.

Texaco's three linked fields – Tartan, Highlander and Petronella – begun pumping oil

again in January (after an accident), but at a reduced rate of around 36,000 barrels a day rather than the normal level of more than 60,000.

The UK's production suffered further reductions last December when the 200,000-tonne storage vessel Medora broke moorings, shutting down the Fulmar and Auk fields operated by Shell and Britoil's Clyde field, with a combined daily output of 210,000 barrels, or 10 per cent of the total. The fields came back on stream only last month.

Problems in the North Sea are part of a much wider run of accidents around the world, notably the massive oil spill in Alaska last month, which have reduced global oil production by some 80 million barrels in the past six months and tightened world oil markets considerably.

Source: Peter Torday and Ian MacKinnon, *Independent,* 20 April 1989

Falling fossil fuel prices certainly mean that nuclear fuel is more expensive than coal at present, even when the costs of waste disposal and decommissioning redundant nuclear power stations are not included. The unresolved question of waste disposal, the threat of a Chernobyl-style disaster and the demise of the fast-breeder programme have further weakened the nuclear lobby.

Figure 3 Hinkley Point nuclear power station, Somerset

Death knell tolls for nuclear power industry

THE Energy Secretary, Mr John Wakeham, yesterday sounded the death knell for Britain's nuclear power industry.

In a humiliating climbdown, the Government finally accepted that Opposition and environmental lobbyists had been saying for more than two years: atomic energy was simply too expensive to be floated off into the private sector.

Yesterday's announcement, just before 4pm in the House in Commons, signalled the end of Britain's development as a nuclear energy power.

It was a programme which started as a technical dream, a miraculous source of electricity "too cheap to meter", as it was billed during the Fifties. But the nuclear industry turned into an economic and environmental nightmare. Such are the astronomical costs of dealing with radioactive power plants at the end of their life, that the bill for dismantling them will be much more than the entire value of the electricity supply industry.

Yesterday's about-turn also threw the £20 billion electricity privatisation plans into the air. And it posed questions over the country's future energy policy at a time when North Sea oil and gas production is beginning to go into decline.

Mr Wakeham's statement was agreed with extreme reluctance by the Prime Minister and was in direct contradiction of her public support for nuclear power when she addressed the United Nations on Wednesay. The development of atomic technology was needed, she said, as a "greener" alternative to coal-burning electricity stations.

But most alarmingly, perhaps, the U-turn demonstrated the extent to which the Government was prepared to put political expediency before the practical realities of hiving-off state utilities into the private sector.

Pulling nuclear power out of the flotation will have limited short-term impact on Britain's energy policy.

Even under the original privatisation plans, nuclear stations were only expected to maintain current levels of output. At present, the United Kingdom produces just under a fifth of all its electricity from atomic plant.

But as Magnox reactors are phased out – the first of Britain's fleet of eight has already started to be decommissioned – this proportion will fall.

The eight advanced gas-cooled reactors will start to be shut down within 10 years. Now that pressurised water reactors are not going to be built, it seems Britain's nuclear power programme could be run down altogether after the turn of the century.

This will call for a radical rethink by energy planners in the long term. For even the most optimistic forecasters warn that "renewable" sources of power such as wind, wave or tide generation can only practically account for less than 5 per cent of the country's needs.

So unless the country cuts its fuel bill through more investment in energy conservation, it is inevitable Britain will step up generation from fossil-fuel sources, adding to the greenhouse effect.

Yesterday's announcement will be producing fall-out in the political arena for some time.

Source: Patrick Donovan, *Guardian*, 10 November 1989

Just how green are you about nuclear power?

ONCE UPON A TIME, green was just a colour. Now it's a universal movement. And what shade of green you are says more about you than even class or status.

To a lot of people, however, being green presents something of a dilemma:

How best to safeguard the future of mankind, *and* accept nuclear power as playing an important part in that future.

We at BNFL believe nuclear power must play a role.

By far the biggest threat to our future comes from the Greenhouse Effect.

Since the Industrial Revolution we've been burning fuels like wood, coal and oil in huge quantities. The carbon dioxide produced by this has been lingering above the earth's surface, trapping the sun's heat and causing global warming.

While the scientists argue as to what the exact consequences could be, certain facts cannot be ignored.

In 1850 there were 280 parts of CO_2 to one million parts of air in the atmosphere.

In 1984 that had increased to 340 parts per million. Unchecked it will reach 600 parts by the year 2050.

That could result in the earth being the warmest since the age of the dinosaur 65 million years ago.

A rather chilling prospect in fact.

Now, whilst the nuclear industry has never claimed to be the sole solution to the Greenhouse Effect, to say it can make no contribution to solving the problem is misleading.

Fossil-fuel power stations produce CO_2 which contributes to the Greenhouse Effect. Fact.

Nuclear power stations do not. Fact.

In France and Belgium, for example, they generate more than two-thirds of their electricity from nuclear power.

This has helped to reduce their output of carbon dioxide faster than the rest of Europe.

In Britain we could also reduce our output of carbon dioxide by increasing our investment in nuclear-power.

So sure are we of a nuclear future that BNFL is currently investing £1½ million a day at Sellafield.

Might we suggest that those people who say that you cannot possibly support a nuclear future and be green might be looking a little on the black side?

BRITISH NUCLEAR FUELS PLC.
Risley, Warrington WA3 6AS

Source: British Nuclear Fuels plc, advertisement, 1 December 1989

?

1 Using the information so far provided in this chapter, together with your own research, prepare a table listing the advantages and disadvantages of nuclear power.

2 Working in pairs prepare one speech for, and one speech against, the motion that 'This house supports the continuation of Britain's nuclear programme on the basis that global warming is far more dangerous and more likely than any number of Chernobyls.'

Renewable sources of energy

Hydro-electricity and wind power could make a significant contribution to the UK's energy needs. Sources such as solar, wave, geothermal, biomass and tidal power also have potential. The initial cost of setting up renewable projects seems to be prohibitive (but, then, the cost of developing nuclear power is also huge) and such technologies are unproved in large-scale production. The most viable is the Severn Barrage, which could supply up to 17 terawatt hours of electricity a year (6% of demand). The investment needed would be high and there could be environmental problems for a sensative estuarine ecosystem. Initial interest in alternative ways of generating electricity was based on fears of fossil fuels running out but greater urgency has been given to their consideration by the environmental damage caused by more conventional means of producing electricity.

Figure 4 Wind farm producing electricity at Tehachapi Pass, Southern California

1 Work in groups. Prepare either a wall display or a leaflet aimed at primary school children explaining what renewable sources of energy are and, as simply as possible what are their advantages and disadvantages.

2 Appoint three 'experts' who will find out as much as they can about the Severn Barrage scheme and the environmental problems associated with continued use of coal and nuclear fuel. The three experts should then be questioned at a public meeting held to protest against proposals for a new electricity generating station to be sited in the south-east of England.

Trade in energy

The tentative attitude of the British Government towards renewables is in part due to its market-orientated philosophy, but it is also influenced by the relative abundance of the UK's own energy resources, in contrast to the situation of many of its neighbours. Substantial reserves of coal, oil and gas (as well as a moderately well-developed nuclear power industry) tend to produce a more relaxed attitude compared to that of neighbours who have to import large amounts of energy. Of course such a perception is partly illusory because, on a world scale, energy is a traded commodity, so that the UK's own reserves could represent a financial asset rather than 'energy', and one that could be valued at its opportunity cost on the world market rather than a source of 'cheap' or secure energy.

Britain's emergence as a major oil producer has had a tremendous impact on its economy. The Government has received an income of, on average, about 8 billion pounds a year in the 1980s, and the turn-around from being an oil importer to an exporter has saved the Government from a series of balance of payments crises. The fall in oil prices and resultant loss of revenue was an important factor behind the worst trade deficits ever in 1988. The significance of the rapid decline of Britain as an exporter of manufactured goods, hidden by the impact of oil for a decade, will be far more apparent in the 1990s.

?

1 What advice would you give to the Chancellor of the Exchequer about the best *economic* use of Britain's energy resources into the next century?

Energy efficiency

It has been claimed that that there will be a need for larger-scale investment in new power plants in the 1990s but, just as the oil price rises of the 1970s gave impetus to a more efficient use of energy, it is possible that concern for the environment and economic necessity will lead to a better use of current sources of

Table 5 Energy efficiency in the UK — cutting carbon dioxide and making money

Energy efficiency measure	Potential saving (PJ)	Total cost (£m)	CO₂ saving (mt)	Savings on fuel (£m)
Appliances	104.24	536	25.97	1,564
Commercial space heating	337.39	415	31.63	1,687
Lighting	131.34	757	32.72	1,970
Cooking	37.69	78	4.05	188
Water heating	123.86	90	8.63	619
Domestic space heating	562.72	321	34.69	2,814
Motive power (electric motors etc.)	92.00	907	22.92	1,380
Industrial process heat	328.77	467	15.44	1,644
Industrial space heating	111.11	216	7.77	556
Total	**1,829.12 PJ**	**£3,787m**	**183.82mt**	**£12,422m**

Conclusion

Spending £3.8 billion on energy efficiency measures (at 10% discount rate) would save nearly 20% of current annual UK primary energy use, cut carbon dioxide emissions by 30% from current levels, and save consumers more than £12 billion per year in reduced fuel bills.

Source: Press release, Friends of the Earth Energy Campaign, November 1989

energy. Energy efficiency can be achieved through such things as better insulation of houses, more complete combustion of primary fuels, more energy-conscious design of automobiles, and combined heat and power installations (in which 'waste' heat from electricity generation and industrial processes is recirculated for domestic and industrial heating).

Changing patterns of use

Energy use in the UK changed between 1973 and 1987 (Figure 5 and Table 6). Such changes reflect the fall in heavy manufacturing industries, for instance.

Table 6 UK consumption of energy by major users

	1973 Mtoe	%	1983 Mtoe	%	Change %
Total energy consumption	353.5		311.7		−12.0
Conversion loss	109.5	31	94.13	30.2	−
Energy supplied to users	244.0	69	217.5	69.8	−11.1
Iron and steel industry	26.4	10.8	11.7	5.4	−55.7
Other industry	76.8	31.5	56.1	25.8	−27.0
Transport	51.6	21.1	57.4	26.4	+11.2
Domestic consumers	59.6	24.5	62.2	28.6	+ 4.3
Other consumers	29.6	12.1	29.8	13.7	+ 0.01

Source: Institute of Electrical Engineers, *Energy Supply and Demand in the UK*, 1985

Figure 5 Energy use in the UK from 1950–1987

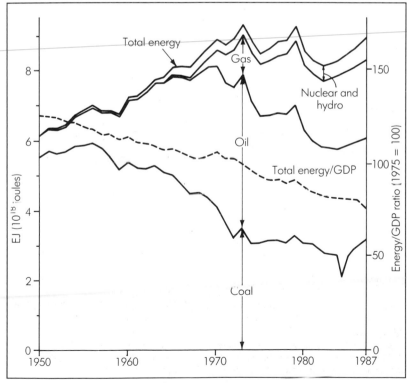

Source: Department of Energy, *Digest of UK Energy Statistics*, 1988

?

1 According to Table 5, what are the two greatest single areas of potential savings? Suggest measures that could be taken to achieve these savings.

2 Design an advertisement for one of the now privatised electricity companies which will increase public awareness of what the company is doing to improve energy efficiency.

3 Study Figure 5 and Table 6.

a What have been the main changes in energy use since 1950?

b What were the main changes in energy consumption between 1973 and 1983?

c What reasons can you give for the stabilisation of energy consumption since 1973?

Choices

Almost uniquely in the economically developed world the UK has a range of energy resources which will see it well into the twenty-first century. The impact of the oil price rises of the 1970s has led to greater energy awareness and some improvements in energy efficiency. Oil and gas should continue to make vital contributions to the national energy economy for some time, and coal reserves are sufficient for any likely level of demand for the foreseeable future. The great energy debate of the 1980s, whether to go nuclear or not, will continue for some time. A number of renewable energy options could be explored.

In this situation choices about energy use are largely political and will concern such factors as the economic situation, our attitudes to the environment, the political preferences of the government of the day, and the world trade picture.

The argument for continued use of coal as Britain's primary source of energy is summarised in Figure 6.

?

1 Make diagrams, like Figure 6, in favour of nuclear and renewable sources of energy. Include as much detail as possible on your diagrams.

2 Divide the group in to pro-coal, pro-nuclear and pro-renewable groups. Using the diagrams prepared in Question 1 and other visual material (graphs, diagrams etc.) present the case for Britain to continue or increase its investment in your chosen source of energy. Other groups should attempt to present counter arguments in the discussion that follows each presentation.

3 Ben Elton's novel *Stark* is a black comedy about the end of the world through environmental pollution. The following passage occurs towards the end of the story.

' "If only" people sighed, "if only we had *done* something. Acted when we still had time, even just ten years ago," they said, "back in the late eighties, the early nineties when there was still time. The signs were all there, why didn't we *do* something."

But they hadn't back in '89, '90 and '91, the years when the decisions needed to be taken, nothing had been done. People had listened to the politicians' empty rhetoric at election time but nothing huge, nothing drastic, nothing *real* had actually been done. Too much money had been involved, it simply wasn't economical. Nothing had been done and now the reckoning was upon us all.'

In groups discuss how you would expect politicians to maintain a balance between economic and environmental considerations (as well as short-term and long-term ones) when they make decisions about energy policy.

Energy issues in Nepal

What energy problems does Nepal face?

The energy economy of Nepal is typical of those of the world's very poor nations. Levels of energy use are very low, and wood and agricultural residues (straw, stalks and dung) provide over 90% of total energy supply (see Table 7). Consumption of commercial fuels, at 23 kilograms of oil equivalent (kgOE) per capita per year, is amongst the lowest in the world. Most energy comes

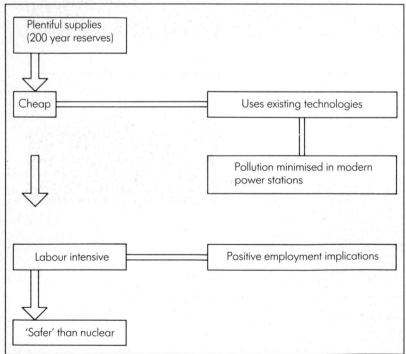

Figure 6 The case for coal

Plentiful supplies (200 year reserves) → Cheap

Cheap ⟷ Uses existing technologies

Uses existing technologies ⟷ Pollution minimised in modern power stations

Labour intensive ⟷ Positive employment implications

'Safer' than nuclear

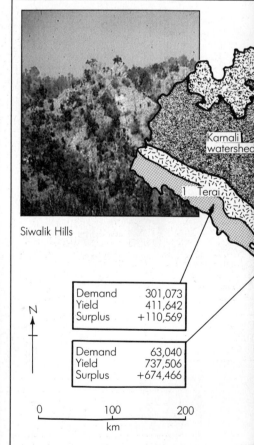

Siwalik Hills

Karnali watershed

Terai

N

Demand	301,073
Yield	411,642
Surplus	+110,569

Demand	63,040
Yield	737,506
Surplus	+674,466

0   100   200
km

from firewood used for cooking in households, and poor rural families often have problems in finding enough for their basic needs. Despite the low level of use, oil imports took up 25% of merchandise export earnings in 1986, and any growth of commercial fuel use will affect Nepal's fragile economic position. There is enormous hydro-electric potential in the mountains, but the cost of developing an electricity distribution system across one of the world's most difficult terrains and the low level of demand are likely to restrict the growth of electricity for the foreseeable future.

Table 7 Nepal: Energy consumption by sector in 1980/81 (thousand tonnes oil equivalent)

	Biomass	Petroleum	Others	Total	
Household	3089.3	30.4	6.6	3126.3	(95.1%)
Industrial	21.1	4.8	39.4	65.3	(2.0%)
Commercial	9.0	6.5	1.9	17.4	(0.5%)
Transport	–	69.1	1.2	70.3	(2.1%)
Others	–	7.8	0.9	8.7	(0.3%)
Total	**3119.4 (94.9%)**	**118.6 (3.6%)**	**50.0 (1.5%)**	**3288.0 (100%)**	

Source: J. Soussan, *Primary Resources and Energy in the Third World*, Routledge, 1988

?

1 Why might there be a 'low level of demand' for hydro-electricity in Nepal?

2 Study Figure 7.

a What patterns emerge of the relationship between altitude and fuelwood demand and supply? Draw graphs to illustrate your answer.

b Can you account for the patterns?

Figure 7 Nepal: Fuelwood demand and supply (tonnes) by ecological zones, 1983

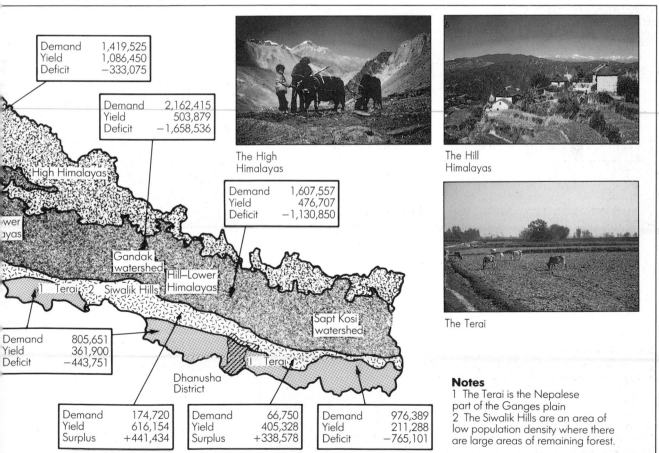

Source: J. Soussan et al, *Fuelwood Strategies and Action Programmes in Asia*, AIT, 1984.

Deforestation is being blamed for the disaster which has wrecked the lives of 30 million Bangladeshis

Doomsday view of floods nonsense, scientists say

The causes of Bangladesh's disastrous floods are the subject of fierce debate among photographers. **Nick Cohen** looks at the two schools of thought.

THE BLAME for the Bangladesh floods, which have made 30 million homeless and are threatening to bring starvation and disease, is being "stupidly and dangerously" placed on the deforestation of the Himalayas, according to leading geographers.

Scientists and foresters maintain there is no evidence to support conventional wisdom that poor mountain farmers looking for fuel have created the world's greatest ecological problem.

They say the belief that the Himalayan forests are being destroyed has been based on information which is so vague it is worse than useless. Specialists in soil erosion and water movement are demolishing the doomsday scenario of environmental collapse in the mountain region.

The orthodox theory, which has been accepted and propagated by the World Bank, governments, international aid agencies, environmentalists and the media, holds that the mountain people of Nepal, and other Himalayan areas, have been creating disaster after disaster.

The mountain population exploded after malaria was brought under control in the 1950s. Nepal now has a population of 16 million.

The pressure of the birthrate, the theory goes, has led to a desperate search for fuel and new farm land and the chopping down the forests on which the region's future depends.

Without the trees to hold back the monsoon rains, water washes into the lowlands, and clogs the great rivers of India and Bangladesh with silt.

The river beds are raised, catastrophic floods and famines follow. Meanwhile, the loss of vegetation causes changes in the climate, drought is threatened.

The Sunday Times was able to say last week: "At the present rate of cutting, the Himalayas will be bald in 25 years, topsoil will have disappeared, and the climatic effects threaten to turn the fertile plain into a new Sahel – the drought-stricken region of central Africa."

Virtually every report on the Bangladesh tragedy has accepted the deforestation analysis. The catastrophe theory dovetails neatly with Western concern about the environment. It appeals to worries about overpopulation – always stronger when the races breeding too fast do not have a white skin.

According to Himalayan geographers it has only one fault. It is complete nonsense. "The information on which agencies have been basing their policies is now seen as infamously inaccurate," Jack Ives, Professor of Geography at Colorado University, said.

"It has produced dangerous and stupid notions. In effect, a few million mountain farmers are being held responsible for the danger faced by 350 million plaindwellers – the biggest ecological threat to human life in the world.

"It's not hard to see where such ideas could lead in an area where political strife and border wars are endemic. We have already seen peasants thrown out of their valleys to make way for grandiose and pointless dam projects."

Even if there was deforestation its responsibility for the floods in the Ganges and Brahmaputra deltas would be infinitesimally small, in comparison with the natural consequences of monsoon rain and earth movements in one of the world's most geologically unstable regions.

The intellectual challenge was launched from an unlikely quarter. Michael Thompson, a quiet British anthropologist who climbed the south-west face of Everest with Chris Bonington, turned a sceptical eye on the evidence.

Mountainous Nepal was a notoriously varied and difficult country to study, Mr Thompson said. Yet, that had not deterred dozens of scientists from finding what was happening on one hill top or in the valley and extrapolating the results to cover the whole country.

Depending on which survey you wanted to believe, the Himalayas would either be stripped bare and washed down the Ganges or would be covered by everadvancing forests.

But the international lending banks, the government and the aid agencies were using these wildly uncertain figures to determine policy. Worse, they often picked the figure which best suited their interests.

Thus the UN Food and Agriculture Organisation decided to use an estimate of tree loss which was large enough to demand funds for a programme, but not so big that it made any attempted solution futile.

"There isn't a serious student now who believes in the evidence that was produced to justify the catastrophe theories," Don Gilmour, director of the Australia-Nepal Forestry project in Kathmandu, said yesterday.

"Fifty per cent of Nepal is still covered by woods. In some places the forests are advancing. Studies from the air show that private land in some regions is three to ten times more forested than 20 years ago.

"The peasants might be illiterate, but they are not stupid. They depend on wood for fuel and for food for their cattle."

The Himalayan geographers accept that they are dealing with a complex region. Deforestation can cause problems, even though, in many cases, trees are replaced by thick elephant grass or well made agricultural terraces, which retain water and soil just as effec-

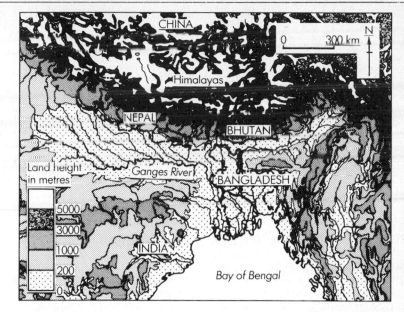

tively. They concede that forests could be advancing in one area while falling back in another.

But what it is impossible to argue, they say, is that the loss of trees can explain the floods along the Ganges and Brahmaputra.

The forests are beautifully functioning ecosystems. They must, in places, be totally protected and, in others, wisely managed. But they will not prevent floods or sedimentation on the lower reaches of major rivers.

Source: N. Cohen, *Independent*, 17 September 1988

?

1 Work in pairs. Study the extract 'Doomsday view of floods'.

a Make notes which outline the argument for the view that deforestation in the Nepal Himalayas is causing floods in Bangladesh. (Refer to p. 142.)

b Make notes of the arguments against this view.

c Consider your notes and use different colours to underline those arguments which you think are based on scientific fact, and those which are not. What are the bases of these other arguments?

How do energy problems relate to development?

Patterns of energy use both reflect and compound Nepal's development problems. In the last decade economic growth has been largely stagnant and agricultural production has failed to keep pace with population growth. Nepal is overwhelmingly rural (93% in 1985) and the bulk of its people are extremely poor. A GDP per capita of US$150 makes Nepal one of the world's poorest nations. Fuel shortages are an urgent problem for many people, and the environmental consequences of the deforestation of the Himalayas are a cause of international concern.

Deforestation is caused by: (1) clearance for agriculture, (2) commercial logging and (3) the over-exploitation of woodlands for fuel and fodder in, by and large, that order of importance. The degradation of their local resource base is having a serious impact on the ability of poor rural people to

meet their basic survival needs. As such, Nepal is faced with an acute energy crisis. It is not oil or coal, but wood, which is Nepal's main fuel, and fuelwood shortages are found throughout the country.

How do poor people cope with these problems?

This is the most important energy question for countries in the economically developing world. To answer it we must look beyond simple energy issues, as energy problems are just part of the general crisis of development found in rural areas of the developing world. Poor people in countries such as Nepal live in a biomass-based economy. Fuelwood is gathered freely from the local environment, and is just one of the many needs met with these resources (Figure 8). Peasant farmers pursue complex risk minimisation strategies based on diversity. All available environmental niches are used, including both private farm land and common resources such as forests, to produce goods for the market and a range of products for local needs (subsistence production).

This strategy traditionally gives people a guaranteed, if low, level of security. To make it work, the rural poor make decisions each day about how to best use the land, labour, cash, biomass and other resources available to them to meet their immediate needs and preserve the resource base for their future survival. *How well they cope depends on the resources they have access to. This varies greatly for different people in different places. It depends on the geographical distribution of resources and the social distribution of control of the resources.* These two together add up to the local production system.

This system works well where the geographical and social distribution of resources meet people's needs, but breaks down where the demands on the local resource base exceed it productive capacity or where inequality of control of resources (especially land) means that some people do not have access to enough resources to meet their basic needs.

Fuelwood shortages are just one of the many problems poor people face. The photograph on page 108 and Figures 9–12 show some of the ways in which people cope with fuelwood shortages. Some, such as planting more trees or managing the fire more carefully, are *benign* and *sustainable.* Others, such as spending longer gathering fuel, taking more out of the local environment than it can sustain or buying fuel, have a harmful impact on other parts of people's lives. For example, if women spend longer gathering fuel, they have less time for the many other tasks they must do. Similarly, if money must be spent on fuel, it cannot be spent on food, clothes, schooling or any of the other basic needs.

As such, the energy problem of the poor in countries such as Nepal is not just a simple matter of fuel shortages. Fuelwood shortages are part of the wider deterioration of the local resource base upon which people in Nepal depend for many basic needs. Day by day people make hard decisions about which needs will be met and which must wait.

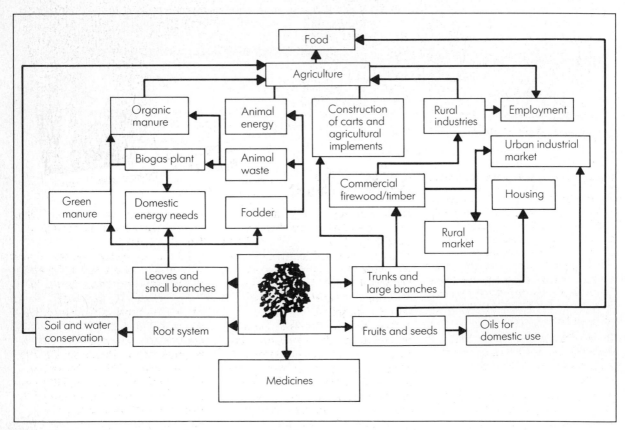

Figure 8 The contribution of traditional tree species to rural production systems
Source: V. Shira et al, 'Social Forestry: No solution within the market,' *The Ecologist*, Vol. 12, July 1982

Responses to fuelwood stress

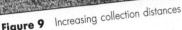

Figure 9 Increasing collection distances

Figure 11 Commodification: a wood dealer in Janakpur

Figure 10 Switching fuels: making dung sticks

Figure 12 Planting trees in rural areas

?

1 The text says that the resources to which people have access vary greatly and 'depend on the geographical distribution of resources and the social distribution of control of resources'. With a partner spend some time sorting out what you understand by the phrase quoted here. It is very important and is illustrated in the village case studies which follow.

2 In pairs discuss what you think is meant by 'benign and sustainable' ways of coping with fuelwood shortages.

3 In rural areas of the economically developing world fuelwood problems hit the poor first and hardest. Why is this?

How bad is the situation in Nepal?

Many, but not all, regions of Nepal are affected by these problems. (Look back to Figure 7.) In many areas wood shortages are so severe that agricultural wastes are widely used. Nepal's towns also use a great deal of wood, both in households and for industry, and the demands from this urban market can affect surrounding rural areas severely. These areas see what was previously a free good for local use become a commodity which is exported to the city. Where this happens it is the poor, and especially the landless or land-poor (i.e, those with little land)

who suffer and the better-off, who control the land, who benefit from the sales.

The broad picture set out above is only part of the story. To really understand energy problems in the economically developing world one must look at individual villages. This can be illustrated by considering one district in Nepal in more detail. Dhanusha District, in the eastern Terai (Figure 13), has a population of 470,000 people, over 90% of whom are rural. Densities, at 370 per square kilometre, are high and land holdings are small. Only 4% of all holdings are over 4 hectares, and

30% of rural households are landless. Remaining forest is confined to the government forest area in the Siwalik Hills across the north of the district. Much of this has degraded to semi-shrub, and is remote from many villages. Pressures on land resources are acute throughout the district, and this is reflected in a severe and deteriorating fuelwood crisis. There is little common land outside the forest, and most people depend for their fuel needs on wood from trees in fields and around the village, on crop and animals residues or, for the worst off, on leaves, small twigs and grass scavenged from roadsides, river banks and so on.

Three villages

Access to fuelwood varies by both social class and location within the district; a point which can be illustrated by a brief look at three villages (Figure 13).

Tadiya
Tadiya is in the north, adjacent to the forest area (Figure 14). Villagers here have easy access to the forest, and wood gathered is the villagers' main fuel. Despite the unequal distribution of land, there is no difference in this between social classes. Many families reported that they now need to go further into the forest to gather fuel and fodder as nearby areas have deteriorated. One of the main causes of this is the extraction of wood for the market in Janakpur, the district's main town (see Figure 13). The situation in villages like Tadiya is not serious, but could become so if the degradation of the forest is not reversed; a problem found throughout Nepal.

Sabaila
Sabaila (Figure 15) is about 12 kilometres from the forest. People can still go there to gather wood, but it needs a special journey which takes at least a day. Wood is still the main fuel, but agri-

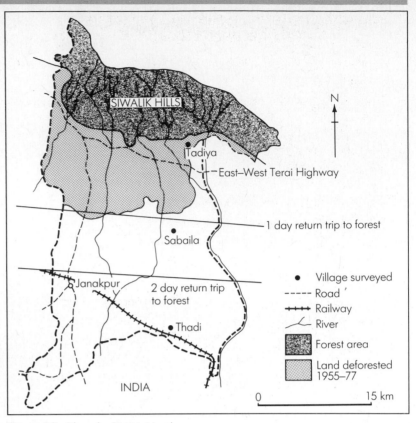

Figure 13 Dhanusha District, Nepal
Source (Figures 13–16): J. Soussan et al, *Dhanusha District Sustainable Woodfuel Strategy*, ETC, 1988

cultural residues are also important. In Sabaila, marked differences are found between social classes in their access to fuels. Better-off familes use mainly wood, which they gather from trees on their own land. For smaller farmers dung and crop residues are more important, as they do not have enough trees to meet their needs, but they still meet their needs from their own lands. Families with little or no land face greater problems. Some own a little land or livestock, but these are not enough. For the rest of their fuel they either walk to the forest to gather wood (an arduous and time-consuming journey), gather what they can from common land or, in some cases, are forced to buy wood from the market. The deforestation and settlement of the land to the north of Sabaila in the last generation has led to major fuel problems for the village's poor.

Thadi
Thadi is in the south of Dhanusha, right next to the Indian border (Figure 16). This area is at least two days' journey from the forest, and consequently no fuel is gathered from there. Population densities are greater here than in more northern parts of the district, and pressures on local resources are acute. Families with sufficient land again rely on their own resources, with the better-off using wood, and smaller farmers using more residues.

The land-poor and landless have severe difficulties in meeting their needs. Some gather animal dung or wood from larger landowners, as part payment for working on the land, but many depend on any twigs, leaves, grass and so on that they can scavenge. This takes a great deal of time, and the fuel is of very poor quality. Many poor households now cook fewer meals, use

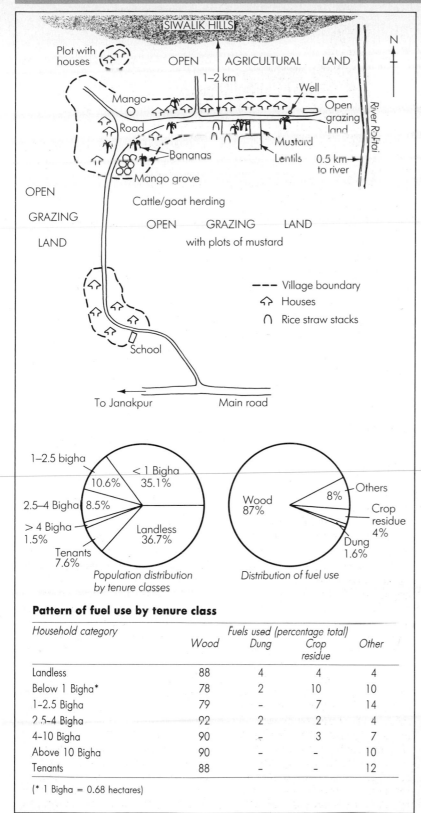

Figure 14 Tadiya

Pattern of fuel use by tenure class

Household category	Fuels used (percentage total)			
	Wood	Dung	Crop residue	Other
Landless	88	4	4	4
Below 1 Bigha*	78	2	10	10
1–2.5 Bigha	79	–	7	14
2.5–4 Bigha	92	2	2	4
4–10 Bigha	90	–	3	7
Above 10 Bigha	90	–	–	10
Tenants	88	–	–	12

(* 1 Bigha = 0.68 hectares)

quicker-cooking foods or depend on meals provided by the landowners they work for. Some, usually the poorest, are forced to buy wood in the market, leaving less money for other essential items such as food or clothing. The diet of many has deteriorated as a result of the fuel crisis in this area.

These three villages in Dhanusha District tell an important story. The fuelwood crisis in the economically developing world varies greatly according to the specific characteristics of individual localities. It is part of the wider development crisis, as the erosion of local production systems leaves the poor more vulnerable to economic and environmental stresses. For fuelwood, as for so many other development problems, it is the poor who are hit first and hardest.

?

1 Study Figures 14, 15 and 16 and decide in which village the quality of life is likely to be best for poorer people. Look carefully at the maps and statistics and give as many reasons as possible for your choice. (You will need to sort out first what factors make up people's quality of life.)

Alleviating the fuelwood crisis

Much can be done to alleviate the fuelwood crisis if a development approach which works through and supports the local production system is adopted. The summary of the 'Dhanusha District Sustainable Fuelwood Strategy' on pp. 128–9 sets out briefly the main features of an EEC-funded plan. This approach, called sustainable development, is based on harnessing local people's understanding of their environment to support the diversity of their production system. The plight of the poor is not a result

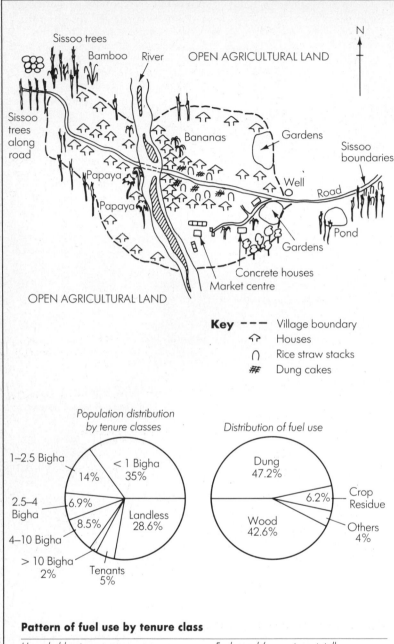

Key
- – – Village boundary
- ⌃⌃ Houses
- ∩ Rice straw stacks
- ⧣ Dung cakes

Population distribution by tenure classes

1–2.5 Bigha 14%
< 1 Bigha 35%
2.5–4 Bigha 6.9%
8.5%
Landless 28.6%
4–10 Bigha
> 10 Bigha 2%
Tenants 5%

Distribution of fuel use

Dung 47.2%
Crop Residue 6.2%
Wood 42.6%
Others 4%

Pattern of fuel use by tenure class

Household category	Fuels used (percentage total)			
	Wood	Dung	Crop residue	Other
Landless	35	46	10	9
Below 1 Bigha	37	55	5	3
1–2.5 Bigha	37	49	9	5
2.5–4 Bigha	50	42	6	1
4–10 Bigha	48	47	2	3
Above 10 Bigha	55	45	–	–
Tenants	36	46	12	6

Figure 15 Sabaila

of technological backwardness, and they are capable of building their own solutions if they are given control over their resource base and the impacts of external markets are minimised. As such, the crucial energy questions in countries such as Nepal are not only about technology, resources and economics as we understand them in the economically developed world. They are fundamentally about the survival and devel-

Dhanusha District Sustainable Fuelwood Strategy

Over a seven-month period in 1987–88 the ETC Foundation was asked by the European Commission to prepare a Sustainable Fuelwood Strategy and Action Plan for Dhanusha District. The ETC team conducted fieldwork in a number of villages (including Tadiya, Sabaila and Thadi) and, with local forestry officials, produced a plan based on principles of sustainable development. There were three main parts to the plan:

1 In rural areas the goals were to increase the biomass resource base and improve the access of the landless and land-poor to local resources. Different ideas such as encouraging small farmers to plant trees, setting up communal nurseries, making government-owned land available to landless groups and helping to make more efficient stoves were discussed with local groups. These community groups were given financial and technical assistance to set up small, local projects which they planned and controlled themselves.

2 The use of fuelwood in towns and industry was discouraged, as it led to over-exploitation of woodlands and less wood being available for the rural poor. This was done through encouraging the use of coal and kerosene, which were both

opment prospects of the world's poor. Finding solutions to these problems is the greatest energy challenge facing the world today.

?

1 Some of the difficulties with understanding fuelwood problems are finding them and assessing their impact. Design a survey to identify the effects of a severe fuelwood shortage on a village in Nepal.

cheaper and preferred, but which were often difficult to find. The aim was to lessen the impact of urban demand on rural areas whilst at the same time making sure that urban energy needs were met.

3 The forest area in the north of the district was severely degraded. Experimental plots elsewhere in Nepal had shown that the forest would regenerate quickly if the pressures on it were relieved. This would partly be achieved through the increased supplies grown in farming areas, but to make sure it worked, management of the forest was handed over to nearby villages, to ensure that they had a stake in the preservation of the woodlands, and a number of small plantations of fast-growing tree species were established at the forest's edge to provide an alternative supply for the period needed for regeneration to be successful.

Taken together, these three parts of the strategy had the potential to meet local people's needs without the further degradation of the environment. This was done through giving people direct control over the decisions which affect their lives, harnessing their understanding of the local environment and relieving the pressures on rural resources from urban demands.

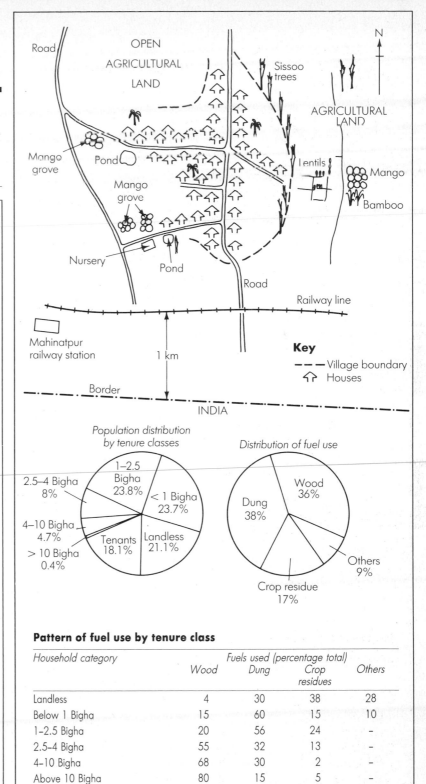

Pattern of fuel use by tenure class

Household category	Fuels used (percentage total)			
	Wood	Dung	Crop residues	Others
Landless	4	30	38	28
Below 1 Bigha	15	60	15	10
1–2.5 Bigha	20	56	24	–
2.5–4 Bigha	55	32	13	–
4–10 Bigha	68	30	2	–
Above 10 Bigha	80	15	5	–
Tenants	11	48	28	13

Figure 16 Thadi

Energy issues in South Korea

The two examples discussed above, the UK and Nepal, tell sharply contrasting stories. One is of abundant energy resources in a rich country, the other of acute scarcity for the very poor. This contrast itself reveals the most important lesson we must learn: energy resources and their use cannot be separated from the general position of different people and places in the world's economic system. Energy poverty is just one symptom of wider development and poverty problems. From this conclusion we can ask the most important question of all: *Is there a way out of the energy and development trap?*

For a few countries with small populations and huge energy resources (for example, Saudi Arabia or Brunei) energy offers a way out of the poverty trap. The rest of the economically developing world is not so fortunate, and for them the question must be asked the other way round: *Does economic development offer a solution to the energy problems of the poor?* To date the track record is not good, but a few developing countries have achieved remarkable success in the last 30 years. Our discussion now turns to one of the most successful, South Korea, to see what part energy has played in its development.

What part has energy played in South Korea's economic development?

South Korea was born out of the partition of the Korean Peninsula following the Japanese occupation and civil war which left the country's economy and environment devastated. From this problematic start South Korea experienced a transformation within a generation: from a poor, agriculturally-based economy to an industrial–urban society exporting sophisti-

cated electronic goods around the world. South Korea is a leader among what are known as the newly-industrialising countries (NICs). During the process, GNP grew from $2.3 billion in 1962 to $98 billion in 1986, a real growth rate averaging over 8% per annum. By 1987 *per capita* GDP was $2370, making Korea one of the most prosperous nations of the economically developing world.

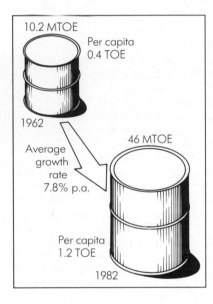

Figure 17 South Korea, total energy consumption

This economic transformation has been paralleled by the transformation of South Korea's energy economy (see Figure 17). Consumption levels (at 1408 kgOE per capita in 1986) are closer to those of the economically developed world than those of the developing world. During the 1962–82 period, energy consumption grew by 7.8% per annum. By 1984, total consumption was 53,986,000 tonnes of oil equivalent (TOE).

Has energy use changed with development?

Figure 18 shows the changing pattern of energy use in the 1962–82 period. The changing fuels used are paralleled by changes in the uses of energy. In the early 1960s the household sector dominated, but by the 1980s it was overtaken by industry and now represents just 30% of demand. In contrast, the industrialisation process was reflected in the 44% share of industry in total energy demand in 1981. The importance of energy-intensive industries such as iron, steel and shipbuilding in South Korea's early industrialisation emerges here. By the late 1980s the dominance of heavy industry was somewhat diminished, reflecting the growth of industries such as electronics, which use less

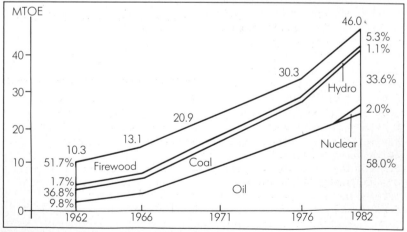

Figure 18 South Korea, energy consumption by source 1962–82
Source: (Figures 17 and 18): Ministry of Energy, Republic of Korea, 1983

energy, the growth of the service sector and increasing living standards. South Korea now has a maturing energy economy which parallels closely the continued development of the national economy as a whole.

1 Study Figures 17 and 18.

a What are the two most significant changes in the sources of energy in South Korea, between 1962 and 1982? Give reasons for your choices.

b Which energy resource remains relatively unchanged? What does this mean in absolute terms?

2 How do the changing sources of energy reflect the change in energy uses? Use graphs to illustrate your answer. (One major use of energy is not mentioned in the text. What is it? Take it into consideration in your answer!)

Has economic development eliminated energy problems?

This does not mean that South Korea has no energy worries. The development of an oil-dominated energy economy is reflected in the growth of dependence upon imported energy sources, which now total 75% of national energy consumption. These imports represented a foreign exchange bill of well over $6 billion in the mid-1980s, about 25% of total imports and in excess of one third of merchandise export earnings. This drain on foreign exchange is a problem Korea shares with many economically developing countries, and as with the others it has a negative economic impact. South Korea is one of the developing world's leading debtor nations, owing $45 billion in 1986. The cost of servicing these debts, along with energy import costs, means the economy could be vulnerable if rapid economic growth is not maintained.

What is South Korea's response to these problems?

Not surprisingly, the reduction of energy imports has emerged as the priority in South Korea's energy policy (although security of supplies is also seen as important; along with Japan, Korea is all too aware of its vulnerability to the vagaries of Middle Eastern politics). To achieve this South Korea has developed its main domestic energy resource, coal, and in 1984 produced over 21 million tonnes. Coal reserves are estimated as 1,635 million tonnes, sufficient for many years if demand does not grow too quickly. Much of Korea's coal has to be deep-mined, however, and it is frequently uncompetitive when compared to coal on the world market. The government is likely to continue to support the industry for employment and strategic reasons.

South Korea is also vigorously developing nuclear power, despite internal opposition. Korea had seven nuclear stations in 1988, with a further four under construction. Their economic viability is frequently questioned, but for the government strategic and prestige issues seem to outweigh any economic arguments. The government is also attempting to encourage conservation, with some success in industry, and has entered into a number of joint overseas ventures to develop oil resources.

1 Why is South Korea trying to develop its coal industry? What problems might this lead to for South Korea? For other countries?

2 Draw a flow diagram to illustrate the relationships between energy, industry and the economy in South Korea. Include notes on energy policy.

Is South Korea's experience relevant for the rest of the economically developing world?

These policies reflect the new energy problems of South Korea. Its industrial transformation has removed the spectre of the fuelwood crisis which haunts so many economically developing countries. In its place has emerged a set of energy problems more familiar to the economically developed world. Whether other developing countries can similarly change their energy position depends on whether they can achieve similar rapid growth in their economies. A few, such as Taiwan, undoubtedly have. Some, such as Thailand, show some signs, but have far to go, whilst others, such as Brazil, have seen early success followed by economic collapse under a mountain of debt. For the rest, and especially for the very poor countries of South Asia and sub-Saharan Africa, South Korea's economic miracle offers no hope; they must follow a different path if they are to escape their present development trap. That path must be along the sustainable development route which we talked about in the Nepal example. Perhaps in the future, when acute poverty and rapid environmental deterioration are things of the past, such countries can think of following in South Korea's footsteps. Until then survival, of the poor and their environment, is the name of the game.

1 In groups discuss whether high oil prices are a good or a bad thing for **a** the UK, **b** Nepal, **c** South Korea.

2 Imagine that a South Korean, a Nepalese and a Briton meet. Decide how they would describe the energy crisis in their respective countries and write a short script for the conversation they hold about this.

6

Forests – managing a disappearing resource

Rosalind and Nicholas Foskett

Erosion following deforestation, Acre state, Brazil

The green mantle

Forests are the natural clothing for the Earth's land surface, and, as recently as 1700, 60% of the land was forested. Today the figure is 30%, and the destruction of the world's forest resources is one of the major challenges facing mankind.

Their value is immense, for they contain 85% of the planet's biomass. In providing firewood, building materials, food, and export products, they are vital to the economic and social well-being of many economically developing countries. The use of wood for paper and construction in the wealthy states of the North, however, consumes even greater quantities in the forests. The call for forest conservation is often heard in both developed and developing nations, but is the pressure for conservation as great as the pressure for exploitation? If so, can forests be managed effectively as a permanent resource?

Table 1 Percentage of the earth's land surface covered by forests

Year	Percentage FOREST
1700	60
1925	45
1985	33

Source: Gaia Atlas of Planet Management, Pan Books, 1985

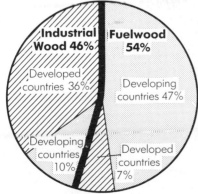

Figure 1 Global wood consumption
Source: Gaia Atlas of Planet Management, Pan Books, 1985, p. 28

Industrial Wood 46%
Fuelwood 54%
Developed countries 36%
Developing countries 47%
Developing countries 10%
Developed countries 7%

Forests and the biosphere

Majestic and diverse, the world's forests represent some of the most exuberant expressions of nature. [...] They tend to support greater stocks of biomass, produce new biomass faster, and harbour greater abundance of species (both plant and animal) than any other ecological zone.

Not only are forests powerhouses of basic biospheric processes, notably photosynthesis and biological growth, creation of fertile humus, and transfer of energy, but their exceptional contribution to the biosphere goes much further. They play major roles in the planetary recycling of carbon, nitrogen, and oxygen. They help to determine temperature, rainfall and various other climatic conditions. They are often the fountain-heads of rivers. They constitute the major gene reservoirs of our planet, and they are the main sites of emergence of new species. In short, they contribute as much to evolution as all other biomes. [...]

From a human standpoint, we can look upon forests as the great providers and protectors. They maintain ecological diversity for us, they safeguard watersheds, they protect soil from erosion, they supply fuel for about half the world's people, they provide wood for paper pulp and industrial timber.

Source: Gaia Atlas of Planet Management, (ed. N. Myers) Pan Books, 1985, p. 28. Published in the US by Doubleday and produced by Gaia Books, London

1a Sketch a graph to illustrate the data in Table 1.

b Extend (extrapolate) the line to the year 2050.

c Is the situation suggested by your graph for the year 2050 a realistic one? If not, why not?

d What are the fundamental reasons for the decline in forest cover?

2 Study Figure 1. Discuss and explain the different ways in which people exploit forests in the developed and developing countries.

3a Study the extract 'Forests and the biosphere'. Why are forests of global importance in **i** ecological and **ii** human terms?

b With reference to a textbook of meteorology (such as R.G. Barry and R.J. Chorley, *Atmosphere, Weather and Climate,* 5th edn., Methuen, 1987), explain in detail how forests are recycling carbon, nitrogen and oxygen and can determine rainfall, temperature and various other climatic conditions.

The nature of forests

The word 'forest' describes many different ecosystems. No two areas of forest are identical, and botanists have developed many classification systems. In simple terms it is possible to divide forests into three groups – the tropical broadleaf forests (Figure 2), the temperate deciduous forests (Figure 3), and the coniferous forests (Figure 4). The last of these groups is found not only at high latitudes, but also at high altitudes in lower latitudes. Figures 2–4 and Table 2 show the principal characteristics of each of the forests.

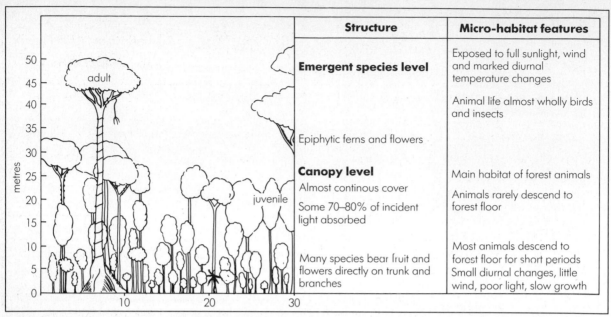

	Structure	Micro-habitat features
	Emergent species level	Exposed to full sunlight, wind and marked diurnal temperature changes
		Animal life almost wholly birds and insects
	Epiphytic ferns and flowers	
	Canopy level	Main habitat of forest animals
	Almost continous cover	Animals rarely descend to forest floor
	Some 70–80% of incident light absorbed	
		Most animals descend to forest floor for short periods
	Many species bear fruit and flowers directly on trunk and branches	Small diurnal changes, little wind, poor light, slow growth

Figure 2 Profile diagram through tropical rainforest

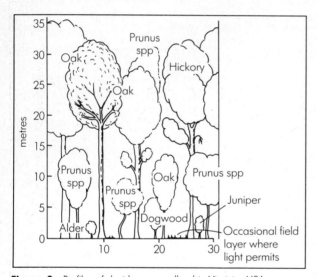

Figure 3 Profiles of deciduous woodland in Virginia, USA

Figure 4 Sketch through a boreal coniferous forest

Sources: Sketches: I. G. Simmons, *Biogeographical Processes*, George Allen & Unwin, 1982.

1a Use an atlas to provide you with the data to map the locations of the main types of forest. Make sure that the three key types are clearly distinguished, but also include on your map any sub-groups that you can.

b Does your map represent the present distribution of forest?

2a Comment on the differences between the three types of forest for each of the following categories:
i Climatic environment
ii Ecological structure
iii Ecological processes at work
iv Human challenges facing the forest

b What differences are there between the amount of biomass and nutrients in each ecosystem that are removed by logging? What impact is this likely to have on the long-term health of the ecosystem after logging?

Table 2 The world's forest ecosystems

		Tropical broadleaf	Temperate deciduous	Temperate coniferous
C L I M A T E	Sub-types	Tropical rainforest, tropical deciduous forest, monsoon forest		Also called boreal forest, taiga
	Location (° latitude)	0–25°	30–55°	55–80° and high altitudes in other latitudes
	Temperature range (°C)	25–35	10–25	−15 to +15
	Average precipitation (mm/year)	1,500–3,500	750–1,500	250–1,000
	Growing season (months)	12	4–10	3–6
E C O L O G I C A L S T R U C T U R E	Tree species/ha	30	5	2
	Typical tree species	Dipterocarps, teak, mahogany, rubber	Beech, elm, oak, maple, birch, hickory	Firs, pines, larch, aspen
	Animal species/ha	30	10	5
	Typical animal species	Apes, monkeys, snakes, rodents	Deer, fox, badger, warblers	Beaver, moose, bear, deer, lynx, owls, caribou
	Biomass (t/ha)	11,180	6,800	440
	% of global biomass	51	19	16
	Distribution of nutrients in the ecosystem	Input from rain (R); Biomass (B); Litter fall (F); Litter (L); Plant uptake (U); Decomposition (D); Soil (S); Runoff loss (RL); Leaching loss (LL); Input from weathering (W). ○ Nutrient store, ⇒ Nutrient flow	R, F, B, L, U, D, S, RL, LL, W	R, F, B, L, U, D, S, RL, LL, W
	Net primary productivity (g/m²/year)	2,000	1,250	800
	Main issues	Deforestation leading to soil erosion; species reduction; firewood shortage; hydrological effects; climatic effects	Afforestation with fast-growing conifers, pollution from industry	Deforestation, pollution

Source: Nutrient diagrams – D. Drew, *Man–Environment Processes*, George Allen and Unwin, 1983, Fig. 2.16

3a For the tropical broadleaf forest, research the differences in the structure and location of its major sub-groups.

b Find out the definitions and details of the following terms:
Dipterocarps
Leaching
Climatic climax vegetation
The greenhouse effect
Negative feedback
Positive feedback
Net primary productivity (NPP)
Biomass

Tropical broadleaved forests

The challenge

The issues of the tropical forests have made their way into the headlines and have become one of the main focuses of research by environmental scientists. The issues relate to the clearance of the forest as the climatic climax ecosystem (that is, the balanced community of plants and animals reflecting the primary influence of climate) and its replacement by a sub-climax ecosystem (the *sere*) which, as it is maintained by human interference, is called a *plagioclimax* community.

The scale of the problem

How fast are the forests being cleared? Figures are difficult to obtain, because nobody knows how much forest there is (or was) – many forested areas have never been mapped. However, about 1,600 million hectares of land would have a natural climax ecosystem of tropical broadleaved forest without human interference, of which only some 935 million hectares (equivalent in area to the size of the USA) remain today.

Figures for forest losses are less reliable still, for logging companies and governments may be unable or unwilling to provide correct data. In the late 1970s, the FAO (United Nations Food and Agriculture Organisation) estimated annual loss at 15 million hectares – slightly more than the area of England and Wales. This loss included 2 million hectares from Africa, 5 million from Asia, and 8 million from Latin America. This represents a loss of 30 hectares per minute, or the area of a football pitch every second! Since then the loss has accelerated, and in 1988 Dr Norman Myers, an eminent environmentalist, suggested that over 20 million hectares are now being cleared or severely impoverished, by logging or slash and burn agriculture, each year.

1a Using the data above, estimate the likely current extent of tropical broadleaved forest.

b Using the figures for the rate of forest depletion calculated by Myers, estimate the date at which the tropical forests would finally be cleared.

The causes of the problem

> 'It is hard to lay the blame for deforestation at the feet of any one group. The only thing we can be certain about is that the forest is disappearing and when it goes everyone will suffer.'

Source: Alan Grainger, *Ecologist*, January 1980

The clearance of forests (Figure 5) is rapid because there are so many demands for their resources. To the local tribes or farmers, it offers food, firewood and, when cleared, space. To the government, it offers space for growing food for an expanding population and a source of jobs and income when the forest is cleared and its products sold. To the people of the North, it is a source of foodstuffs, drugs and timber for construction – industry that transnational corporations can exploit and profit from. It also provides a scenic resource for exotic tourism. In the short term, exploitation of the forests appears to be in everybody's interest.

Demand for hardwood

The hardwoods of the tropical forests are a major source of timber. As Norman Myers has indicated:

> 'Hardly any of us does not lend a hand with the chainsaw. ... The reader might consider his or her own home, which may well feature a parquet floor, fine furniture, luxury panelling.'

Source: Geography Review, March 1988, p. 18

Figure 6 shows how the export of tropical logs has grown since 1950, with Japan and Europe importing 60% and 25% of this total respectively.

Figure 5 Squatter farmers claiming cleared land (Amazon basin, Brazil)

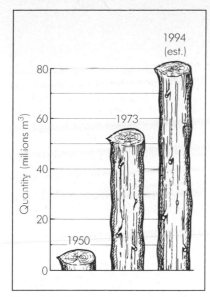

Figure 6 Expansion of tropical wood exports
Source: A. Grainger, 'The state of the world's tropical forests', *The Ecologist* **10** 1, January 1980

Table 3 Population data for developing countries with substantial areas of tropical broadleaved forest

GDP per capita ($)	Country	Population (millions)	Population density (persons/km²)	Population growth rate (%/year)	Forest area (m.ha)	Rate of forest clearance (m.ha/year)
2,021	Brazil	127	14	3.0	85	10.0
612	Cameroon	9	19	2.3	9	0.2
265	Ghana	12	51	3.4	2.5	0.05
647	Guyana	0.7	4	2.2	3	0.1
472	Indonesia	152	75	1.7	85	1.5
781	Malaysia	15	45	3.2	7	0.15
534	Nigeria	82	89	3.3	9	0.05
1,843	Panama	2	27	2.5	2	0.05
733	Philippines	51	169	2.7	6	0.26
283	Sierra Leone	4	51	2.7	2	0.05

Source: The Geographical Digest, George Philip and Son, 1987

Population pressure

Table 3 shows population data for a sample of those developing countries with major areas of tropical forest. As populations continue to grow, there is increasing pressure on land to provide food. The easiest method for poor governments to increase food supply is extensification of agriculture into previously unused land. For example, Indonesia since 1949 has had a policy of transmigration to move farmers from densely populated regions such as Java to less populated islands such as Kalimantan and Sulawesi.

Third World poverty – money from the West

Third World governments are seeking to increase their gross national product (GNP) as rapidly as possible, and one of the easiest ways of doing so is to sell primary products to the North. In 1960, exports of tropical timber were worth $500 million. Today,

their total value to economically developing countries is approximately $20,000 million per annum. It is not just timber that provides income for the South, for forest products are important as foodstuffs, drugs and raw materials. In many cases, the link between the demand for forest products in the North, the South's need/wish to earn money through foreign trade, and the destruction of the forest is clear. In other cases it is less obvious. Let us examine some examples of these links:

The pharmaceutical connection
One in five of all pharmaceuticals available in the North is produced directly or indirectly from tropical forest products. The commercial value of these commodities is about $12,000 million per annum, although only a small proportion of this value is received by the exporting countries.

The cassava connection
Demand for cheap supplies of meat in the West creates the need for inexpensive animal feed. The European Community imports large amounts of cassava from Thailand each year as feed, which has been grown on farmland specially created from tropical forest.

The hamburger link
The huge consumption of meat in North America is satisfied in part by large imports of cheap beef from cattle raised on land cleared from the rainforests of Mexico, Panama, Costa Rica and Nicaragua (Figure 8).

The firewood problem
Most of the 'forest-rich' regions covered by tropical rain forest are sparsely populated, as typified by the Amazon Basin. Where the rainfall becomes more seasonal, however, the forest changes its character to be more open, and the population density increases. It is in these zones (the 'forest-poor' regions) that the problem of firewood collection is a major challenge to the forest's existence.

Half the world's population uses wood as their main energy source (Figure 7), and half the timber cut in the world is used as firewood. Eighty per cent of this use occurs in the Third World making the fuelwood crisis a major issue in the tropical forest regions. Nearly one-quarter of tropical forest clearance can be attributed to the search for fuelwood.

A distinctive pattern of development characterises the fuelwood crisis.

Stage 1 As demand for firewood starts to exceed supply, excessive trimming of trees and removal of saplings makes forest regeneration difficult.

Stage 2 As woodlands fail to regenerate or are cleared, so the time spent and the distance travelled to collect firewood increases. Woodlands at greater distances from settlements are consumed and fuelwood becomes increasingly scarce. This is then reflected in rising costs of fuelwood in the towns.

In Nepal, in the Himalayas, half of the forested land has been cleared since the early 1950s. While this is partly due to clearance for agriculture and logging, a further cause has been firewood collection, made worse by the country's population expansion from 5 million to 15 million people since 1953. Over 90% of the country's energy needs are supplied by firewood, with each person needing an average of 600 kg of fuelwood per year. However, since regeneration of the forests only produces 80 kg per head per year, the forests have rapidly reduced in extent. In the capital, Kathmandu, fuelwood prices have increased many times, and in some rural villages the weekly supply of firewood that used to be collected in one hour now takes two days to gather.

Figure 7 Collecting firewood in Mozambique

Figure 8 Beef cattle grazing on land cleared from rainforest in Acre state, Brazil

?

1a Demand for tropical timber has increased faster than the total demand for all types of timber. Why do you think this is?

b With reference to Figure 6, what do you think the demand for tropical logs might be in the year 2000?

2 Study Table 3.
a Does population density appear to be linked closely to the rate of forest clearance?

b Do any other factors in Table 3 seem to be more closely linked to forest clearance than population density?

c How could you test the data to see which factor is linked most closely?

d Use this method to see which factor has the closest link.

3 Table 4 shows the scale of the firewood problem globally.

a Which region of the tropical world has the greatest fuelwood problem? Justify your answer.

b Choose a suitable mapping technique to display the data on a world map.

Table 4 Fuelwood in the tropics: demand versus supply

Region	Population (millions)	Fuelwood need (m.m³/year)	Fuelwood availability (m.m³/year)
Latin America (forest areas)	38	46	380
Latin America (other areas)	16	14	5
Africa (savanna areas)	132	197	118
Africa (forest areas)	37	62	73
South & East Asia (mountain areas)	29	52	9
South & East Asia (lowlands)	297	208	74

Source: Gaia Atlas of Planet Management, Pan Books, 1985, pp. 114–15

Logging Systems in Question

The process by which the highest quality logs of the relatively few commercial species are extracted is called 'creaming'. The Selective Felling System places this on a long-term basis by defining the minimum size of tree which can be cut, and the minimum number of young trees which are to be left on the site to grow into merchantable trees in the next rotation, as well as acting as sources of seed that will regenerate the forest for the future.

In Indonesia at least 25 trees over 35 cm diameter at breast height (DBH) must be left well spaced out in every hectare, and the minimum cutting limit is 50 cm DBH. The majority of trees for export will be greater than 60 cm DBH anyway. It is assumed that by this method the next crop of trees may be harvested in 35 years time [...]

An ... objection is that during and after felling a considerable number of the young trees will die as a direct result of the interference in the forest. [Several] ... surveys ... show that as much as 50 per cent of the residual stand may be damaged, and the surface soil may be destroyed when up to 30 per cent of the ground surface is exposed. According to them it will take more than 40 years for such a disturbed forest to recover, and this is longer than the desired rotation cycle.

Source: A. Grainger, 'The state of the world's tropical forests,' *Ecologist* **10 1**, January 1980, pp. 27–30

The effects of the problem

The complexity and role of the forest ecosystems is poorly understood. As a result it is difficult to persuade those groups making gains from forest clearance, or who would have to bear the economic, social or political costs of any protective steps, to change current patterns of exploitation. Figure 9 shows some of the environmental effects of forest exploitation.

The negative effects of the forest loss are not confined to the physical environment. Although there are many financial gains there are many immediate effects on people and communities that are unwelcome.

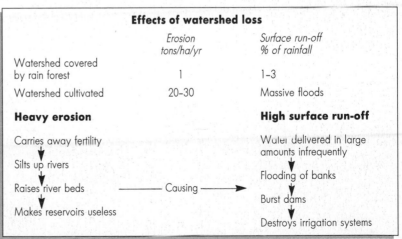

Effects of watershed loss		
	Erosion tons/ha/yr	Surface run-off % of rainfall
Watershed covered by rain forest	1	1–3
Watershed cultivated	20–30	Massive floods

Heavy erosion

Carries away fertility
↓
Silts up rivers
↓
Raises river beds ——— Causing ———→
↓
Makes reservoirs useless

High surface run-off

Water delivered in large amounts infrequently
↓
Flooding of banks
↓
Burst dams
↓
Destroys irrigation systems

Source: A. Grainger, 'The state of the world's tropical forests', *Ecologist* **10** 1, January 1980

Downstream effects

Deforestation-caused erosion means that the mountains and foothills [of the Himalayas], together with adjacent alluvial floodplains, are estimated to lose 6 billion tons of fertile topsoil every year. [...]

The Ganges Plain covers almost 1 million square kilometres. It encompasses 70 per cent of India's flood-prone lands, and an even larger proportion of Bangladesh's. Yet as a result of deforestation, monsoon rains result in floods, followed by drought conditions. River courses flowing out of forestlands on the India/Nepal border become 1.5 kilometres wide during the rainy season, before dwindling to a mere 40 metres wide at the height of the dry season.

Flood damages once totalled a 'mere' $120 million a year until 1970, when they started to soar culminating in the 1978 monsoon season, when within just a few weeks, 65,000 villages were inundated, 40,000 cattle washed away, and extensive croplands ruined. Total damage to property was estimated by the Indian Government at more than $2 billion, apart from the incalculable costs of 2,000 human lives lost through drowning.

[...] Siltation in the Ganges system has become so pronounced that a number of river beds are rising at a rate of one-sixth of a metre a year, causing worse floods. Newly-formed shoals are rendering several sectors of the main river unnavigable, while certain industrial installations in the downstream plain must suspend activities for several months of the year due to lack of water. Two main ports, Calcutta in India and Dhaka in Bangladesh, are silting up. [...]

Furthermore, deforestation-derived siltation proves a serious problem for water impoundments in several parts of the Indian sub-continent. In Pakistan, the Mangla Dam, completed in 1967, receives so much silt and debris from the Jhelum River watershed that its operational life is being reduced from more than 100 years to less than 50 years; while another Pakistan dam – the world's largest – the Tarbela on the upper reaches of the Indus, is losing its storage capacity of 12 billion cubic metres at a rate that will leave the dam useless within 40 years. In India, more than a dozen major reservoirs are silting up three times faster than engineers had expected.

Source: Earthwatch, **17**, 1984, pp. 3–4

The kill factor

IT IS just ten years ago since a maverick scientist asserted that we are not losing one species per year, as had been the conventional wisdom. He proposed we were losing one species per day. Today he believes the rate is several species per day – and that within another ten years it will rise to several species per hour.

Not that we can give a name to the species that disappeared yesterday. We have identified only 1.7 million species, out of a supposed total of at least 5 million, more likely 10 million, and possibly 30 million, conceivably 50 million. [...]

What is the evidence? Consider just three discrete areas. In the tropical forests of Madagascar, Atlantic-coast Brazil and Western Ecuador, there was originally a documented total of 26,000 vascular plant species, 12,500 of them being endemics, i.e. found nowhere else. We can realistically suppose that for every

one plant species, there were at least 20 animal species (perhaps several times more) making a minimum total of 520,000 animal species, 250,000 of them being endemics.

Forest in the three areas has either been reduced to less than 10 per cent of original extent, or will shortly become so. The findings of a scientific theory known as island biogeography indicate that when a habitat loses 90 per cent of its area, it can support only 50 per cent of its original complement of species. So recent or near-future extinctions in these three areas alone could well total more than 130,000 species, plants and animals combined. If, as is likely, the great majority of these extinctions will have occurred during the last 50 years of this century, there will have been eliminated an average of one plant species every three days, and seven animal species, possibly as many as five species every day [...]

What we are witnessing, in short is an unprecedented experiment on a global scale. We are conducting the experiment all too unwittingly: it is entirely unplanned and uncoordinated. Its workings are mostly undefined and unmeasured.

So momentous are the implications of this global experiment, and so significant would be the loss of species' 'ecosystem services,' that it should be regarded as a major threat to our biosphere. According to the Club of Earth scientists, it carries risks for the human cause that are surpassed only by those associated with nuclear war.

Source: Norman Myers, *Guardian*, 9 October 1987

Impact on global climate

Clearance of tropical forests could also have severely adverse effects on the world's climate. In Amazonia, more than half of all moisture circulating through the region's ecosystem remains within the forest: rainwater is absorbed by plants, before being 'breathed out' into the atmosphere. Were a large part of the forest to disappear, the remainder would become less able (however well protected) to retain so much moisture – and the effects could extend further, even drying out the climate for crops in southern Brazil.

Still more important, tropical forests help to stabilize the world's climate by absorbing much solar radiation: they simply 'soak up' the sunshine. When forests are cleared the 'shininess' of the planet's land surface increases, radiating more of the sun's energy back into space (the 'albedo' effect). An increase in albedo could lead to disruptions of convection patterns, wind currents, and rainfall in lands far beyond the tropics.

Although tropical forests do not significantly affect Earth's oxygen balance, they do play an important part in the carbon dioxide budget. When forests are burned, they release considerable quantities of carbon into the skies. The build-up of carbon dioxide in the atmosphere looks as if it is triggering a 'greenhouse effect', bringing on drier climates for some, especially Americans.

Source: Gaia Atlas of Planet Management, Pan Books, 1985, p. 44

Nutrient loss from tropical soils

The tropical rainforests have been described as 'forested deserts'. The regions have the greatest input of solar energy of any climatic zone; they have abundant year-round rainfall. They are the most productive terrestrial ecosystem on Earth (a productivity two or three times greater than for temperate forest) with an immensely complicated system of balances between the large number of plant and animal species. Yet the rainforests' system for cycling and storing the great quantities of energy differs from that prevailing elsewhere in the world. A very high proportion of nutrients are stored in the vegetation rather than in the soil and the recycling system is almost closed. Indeed, some of the nutrient cycling is quite independent of the soil. There are epiphytes, plants that live attached to trees, deriving their nutrients from fallen leaves and rain caught in their network of aerial roots. On the ground, nutrients are derived from the shallow litter layer by fungi which then pass nutrients directly to plant roots. The effect of these short circuits is that little leaching of chemicals occurs through the soil and hence to the rivers.

Therefore, the soils are almost barren, though the operation of the rainforest ecosystem disguises this fact very successfully. The luxuriant vegetation creates an illusion of fertility in the soil, but nowhere else on Earth is the relationship between vegetation and soil so weak. The microclimate created by the forest is also very important. Annual rainfall of 1800–3500 mm and temperatures consistently in excess of 30°C would rapidly convert the soil into a sterile laterite if the vegetation cover did not exist. Deforestation in these areas exposes the soil to direct sun over large areas and also removes the greater part of the area's nutrient store. Predictably, the results are dramatic. [...]

Extensive forest clearance in Amazonia began at the turn of the century in the Bragantina zone in eastern Brazil. Clearance along the Belem to Braganca railway provided 12,000 ha of land for new settlers to farm. Within a few years much of the land had been abandoned, the soils exhausted. Today it is an area of poverty and economic and social stagnation, covered in a scanty secondary scrub vegetation. Table 5 explains why the land was abandoned so quickly – the loss of nutrients by

Table 5 Decline in soil nutrient status (fertility) following clearance of tropical rainforest and the use of the land for agriculture. Phosphorus and organic levels increase initially due to burning, but subsequent decline in fertility is rapid. Loss of cation exchange capacity (ability to store nutrients) is immediate due to leaching.

	Soil characteristics (%)			
Land use	Organic content	Cation exchange capacity	Nitrogen	Phosphorus
virgin forest	100	100	100	100
1 year after clearance (unused)	104	82	66	120
after 2 years of cultivation	46	51	36	75

intense leaching is very rapid. Soil fertility may decline by as much as 80% within a few years of forest clearance. Soil erosion may also remove the topsoil particles, adding to river sediment and thereby affecting the fluvial system and the river ecosystem. Rates of erosion even on gentle slopes have increased thirtyfold. Increased rates of run-off from cleared areas may cause Amazon floods to increase in both magnitude and frequency, and although clear data is not yet available, flooding at Manaus is thought to have increased considerably since 1976.

Source: David Drew, *Man–Environment Processes,* George Allen & Unwin, 1983, pp. 114–17

Battle lines in the jungle

UP ON the middle reaches of the Baram River, which flows like warm treacle through the tropical rainforests of northern Sarawak, are a dozen or more logging camps – ugly agglomerations of Nissen huts and oil tanks and warehouses, and old iron cranes that lift the ten-ton mahogany trunks down and on to the barges that take them to the sea, and the waiting ships.

But during the last six months all of these camps, and a hundred more dotted around Sarawak, have fallen still. [...]

There is a small Dayak village 100 miles upriver on the Baram, a place called Uma Bawang. Six hundred people live there, growing rice and bananas and pepper, and raising chickens. There is a tiny store that sells the Dayaks their current favourites from the Great Outside – Wincarnis, ginseng extract, Arab Brand curry powder, and beer. But these days there is not much demand for fishing tackle, the shopkeeper says: the Baram has been too dirty ever since the loggers came two years ago, and all the fishable fish have now gone. He has no time for the loggers, and nor has anyone else in Uma Bawang. [...]

The track bears the scars of the tractors that until last spring ploughed into the forest, and dragged out the logs that the lumberjacks had felled – ... there is a crude barrier built across it. [...]

A dozen Dayaks – specifically these are Kayans, one of the half-dozen agriculturist tribes to be found in Sarawak – stand beside the barrier [...]

'We are here to make sure no logging continues in our forest,' says their leader, a young, well-educated, English-speaking Christian named Francis Maring. 'You see what it has done. Our jungles cut down, our rivers polluted, our animals dead, our fish gone. And these are *our* jungles, *our* rivers. They have been for many hundreds of years. Now these greedy people want them. These dirty politicians are giving our lands away. And now we are fighting back. The logging people will have to pass this blockade. We will stop them if they try.' [...]

The loss of revenue is now making the government – the highly autonomous Sarawak government, and not the Malaysian government, which has no formal say in logging and land matters and preserves an embarrassed silence in the dispute – highly exasperated. In the past few weeks it has started to take action – dismantling barricades, arresting blockaders – against the one tribal group that is both the most vulnerable, and yet has perhaps the strongest reason to object to the loggers' avarice, the Dayak tribe known as the Punan, the people who started it all. [...]

Loggers have been ranging across the Punan's lands for the last three years – ever since the Sarawak government decided on a programme of massive exploitation of the huge natural resource that was sitting up on its central mountains. At first the bewildered Punan asked for money as compensation for what they saw as the theft of their land; they petitioned the Sarawak government in Kuching; they sent a delegation over to the federal government in Kuala Lumpur. [...]

It did no good. The tractors stayed put, the chain saws continued to bring the mighty trees crashing down, the LogMan Specials hauled the timber away to the Baram. From the air the logged areas of the Punan are now huge. The forests look quite ruined: vast scars straggle across what was once whole jungle, and the rivers run with ochre mud. On the ground it was a disaster: animals scared away, rivers useless, the air heavy with the stench of diesel, the jungles echoing to the harsh whine of the saws. The Punan took it all stoically for a few months, and then, last March, they acted. [...]

Officials in the Sarawak chief minister's office have lately been pressing for a compromise, urging the Punan to wake up to the realities of twentieth century life, and urging the loggers to be more responsible in their management of the jungles. But the Punan are a proud people and get prouder by the minute: and the businessmen, urged ever onward by the commercial demands of the Japanese, who have dozens of ships hungrily awaiting wood at the lumber terminal at Jalang Baram, are eager for more and more profit – as are the many politicians who are known to be in their pay.

Source: Simon Winchester, *Guardian*, 8 August 1987

1 Compare the extract 'Downstream effects' on page 142 with the article on pages 124–5. How do they describe the role of forests in the region?

2 Study Figures 9 and 10, then read carefully each of the seven extracts on pages 141–4. Imagine yourself to be a representative of an International Environmental Consultants Group which has been invited to produce a report for the national government of a South East Asian country on 'The possible impacts of current forestry practice'. Produce a 1,000-word report suitable for presentation to the government, illustrating the problems with clear examples.

3 Which of the environmental consequences indicated in Figure 9 and the extracts are likely to have the greatest long-term effects on
a the tropical regions?
b the global ecosystem?

4 Illustrate the following ideas with examples from Figure 9 or 10 or the extracts given.
i Negative feedback.
ii Positive feedback.
iii Threshold levels in natural systems.
iv Stepwise environmental change.

5 Read the extract 'Battle lines in the jungle'.

a What objections do the Dayaks have to forestry in their region of Sarawak?
b List the other interested parties in this issue. What viewpoint does each group/individual have?
c If you were the Sarawak Chief Minister, what action would you take to resolve the issue?

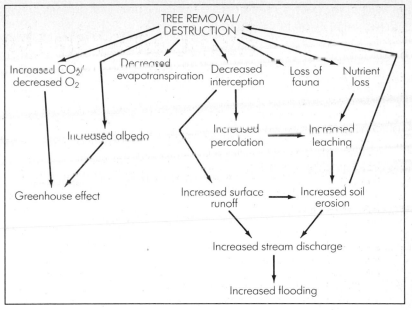

Figure 9 Environmental impacts of clearing tropical broadleaved forest

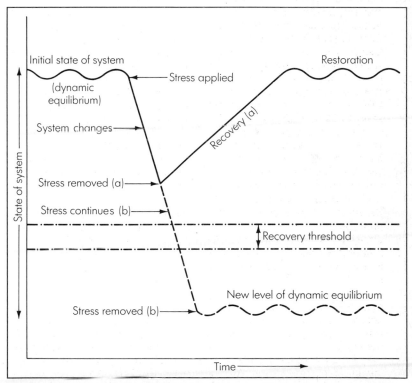

Figure 10 Response of an environmental system to imposed stress:

a with cessation of stress prior to the threshold level and therefore subsequent recovery

b with continuation of stress until the system is beyond the threshold level and cannot return to its original state. A stabilisation will occur at a new equilibrium when the stress is removed.

Source: D. Drew, *Man-Environment Processes*, George Allen & Unwin, 1983, p. 20

Management of the tropical forests – policies and practice

The problems facing the tropical forests are of global importance. The quest for suitable management solutions is vital to both North and South, as links between all parts of the Earth's ecosystem are becoming clearer. Management of the forest must provide a sustainable flow of resources, while at the same time minimising the impact of exploitation on the forest ecosystem, the hydrological cycle and atmospheric processes.

Forestry practice and management

Within the forests the process of logging (Figure 11) and the day-to-day management of the clearance has created a number of problems. The technique of 'creaming', or selective felling, works well in regions where the density of valuable trees is large, but in the tropical forests, the low density of trees that are of value means that large areas are cleared to produce small amounts of timber.

?

1 'Forestry practices in the tropical forests are nothing short of robbery with violence.' Explain carefully why this statement by a leading ecologist might be justified.

The way forward – Management strategies in the tropical forests

The adoption of management techniques to preserve and conserve the tropical forests takes many forms, and the tactics used vary according to the scale and nature of the problems. Three groups of methods can be identified:

- Forest resource conservation, where the aim is to ensure a continuing, renewable supply of timber and other forest resources
- Ecosystem conservation, where the main concern is to preserve a core area of the ecosystem and its constituent species without interference by people
- Fuel supply management, where the aim is to provide adequate supplies of firewood or alternative fuels.

?

1 Study the forest management tactics box opposite and the extracts on pages 148–51.

a Allocate each of the tactics described to one of the three groups outlined above.

b How many of the tactics might be described as 'multi-purpose'?

c For each tactic, outline the benefits and disadvantages that it might have. Think in terms of the economic, social, environmental and political implications of each scheme.

d Which tactic do you feel is likely to be the most successful? Why?

e How important in *all* the tactics, is the necessity to change policies in the North?

2 Read the description of forestry management in the Philippines.

a List the methods used in the Philippines with reference to the threefold classification of management techniques.

b For each method, explain the likely attitudes of each of the following groups:
- the government of the Philippines
- city residents in Manila
- landless farmers on Mindanao island
- an international logging company with concessions on Luzon island
- local tribesmen on Mindanao
- conservationists in the UK
- manufacturers of tropical timber products in Japan
- a group of illegal loggers on Cebu island

c What do you think the future of the forests of the Philippines is likely to be?

3a Read the description of the Korup National Park in Cameroon ('A forest of hopes', page 149).

b Why is Korup to be designated a National Park?

c Explain the nature and problems of each of the following strategies in Korup:
- the buffer zone
- hunting zones

- agricultural, forestry and fish farming advice for local people by the World Wide Fund for Nature
- road construction
- tourism development
- the Korup Research Centre

4 'Changing attitudes in the economically developed countries towards consumption are necessary to preserve the tropical broadleaved forests'. How far do you agree with this statement?

5 The article 'The Last Frontier' on pages 152–3 outlines developments in the state of Acre in Brazil. It illustrates the political and 'power' issues involved in this environmental issue. Identify the interested parties and explain their views. What do *you* believe will happen to Acre's forest over the next five years?

Forest management tactics

a Enforcement

The development of improved enforcement measures is necessary for any management tactic. This enforcement may be produced by co-operation, in the case of many of the local social forestry schemes outlined in **c**, or by coercion, in the case of containing the activities of logging companies. There is clearly a need for increased staffing levels, and the provision of trained advisory and monitoring personnel, but the major challenge here lies in finance. What sources of finance may be available to governments to improve their powers of enforcement?

b Increased wood processing

By developing wood processing industries, eg veneer production or plywood manufacture, governments can earn several times more foreign exchange from their sales than by selling logs. At present, only some 10% of tropical timber is exported by economically developing countries as processed products. While the cost of establishing wood processing factories is very high, this *could* reduce the need to clear such large areas of rainforest to provide an adequate income.

c Replanting strategies

In areas affected by deforestation and resulting firewood shortages, and/or the loss of agricultural land by the resulting soil erosion, a number of strategies for replanting land with trees have been tried.

1 Tree farms

These consist of replanting deforested areas with tree plantations, usually of a single species, which is typically fast-growing eucalyptus or pine. Such farms can provide up to ten times the harvest of a patch of untouched forest, and can overcome many of the environmental problems quickly. Difficulties arise in the acquisition of land, the provision of advice to villagers, and the ecological effects of the new species. In India, many farmers have removed eucalyptus plantations, sometimes forcibly, because their water consumption has damaged nearby crops.

2 Social or community forestry

This is the name applied to forestry schemes which involve villagers in the solution of their own wood problems. Where they are adopted they often prove highly successful, but difficulties arise in persuading villagers to join such schemes and to contribute labour and land to make them work. Typical schemes include:
i) *Fuelwood plantations and village woodlots* These take pressure off local woodlands, and can be planted with fast-growing species

ii) *Agroforestry* This involves the planting of trees on farms, and making use of small patches of marginal or peripheral land within the farm.

d Developing alternatives to fuelwood

A number of options are available to reduce the dependency on wood or fuel, as an attempt to reduce timber consumption. Clearly, alternative fuel sources must be abundant, inexpensive, preferably renewable, and within the technological capability of the local communities. Possibilities include:
i) *Mini-HEP schemes* Small scale HEP systems, supplying power for a single village or group of villages, are now available. China has built over 90,000 in the last two decades.
ii) *Windmills*
iii) *Biomass sources of energy* such as ethanol in Brazil from sugar cane
iv) *Biogas digesters* are now used in over 46 LDCs, and involve the production of methane gas by the fermentation of animal waste and sewage.

e Grassroots conservation movements

The Chipko movement.

f Replanting the forest

This is particularly difficult due to the complexity of the forest ecosystems, and the time scale they need to develop.

g Preserving the ecosystem

In 1985 some 135 million ha of tropical broadleaved forest was preserved in 1,030 protected reserves or parks. Such protected areas may be intended to preserve the whole ecosystem, or simply to provide refuge for a number of species. Typical of the former approach is the Korup National Park in Cameroon.

h Changing policies in the North

1 Provision of finance for the development of alternative fuelwood systems.

2 Reduction of consumption of exotic timber.

3 Changing domestic forestry policy to produce more home-grown wood.

4 Support for regional and international Non-Governmental Organisations (NGOs) – over 4,000 exist at present, which operate as pressure groups to influence governments.
5 The development of positive policies by existing agencies, eg the World Bank actively promotes forest conservation, and recently withdrew support for a Colombian cattle-ranching project, because the forest soils could not support the development.

The re-greening of Vietnam

Devastated by war, and one of the poorest and most densely populated countries in the world, Vietnam is determined to rehabilitate its natural environment

AT A TIME when the Earth's woodlands are disappearing at an alarming rate, one of the world's poorest, most densely populated countries has pioneered the first successful replanting of a tropical forest. After 12 years of experimentation – often fraught with failure – Vietnamese scientists have finally begun to rehabilitate the country's war-ravaged forests, devastated during 30 years of uninterrupted conflict.

Vietnam's main testing ground for tropical forest replanting is some 100 kilometres northeast of Ho Chi Minh City on the edge of a 30 000 hectare tract of land. Once covered in tropical moist forest, the Ma Da woods were a stronghold of North Vietnamese soldiers. In order to flush the soldiers out of the forest, US and South Vietnamese troops defoliated and napalmed the thickly wooded area. As a result, three-quarters of the trees died and the landscape has been reduced to kilometres of dusty bombed-out hillside and vast stretches of useless savanna, dubbed by the Vietnamese as 'American grass'.

Shortly after the war ended in 1975, Vietnamese scientists attempted to replant several species of indigenous trees destroyed during the massive defoliation raids that rained 72 million litres of herbicides over 1.7 million hectares in southern Vietnam. These initial trials failed, largely because the young saplings were burnt in grass fires ignited by the intense heat during the dry season. To protect the seedlings from the hot tropical sun, the scientists established a forest cover of exotic trees including *Indigofera tenesmani, Acacia auriculiformis* and *Cassia siamea*. When these trees gained sufficient height, they planted several species of dipterocarps. They were jubilant to discover that after more than a decade of planting trials, several species finally survived. Today, 300 hectares of acacia and eucalyptus trees give shelter to up to four different species of *Dipterocarpus*, including *D. alatus, D. dyeria, D. hopeaodorata* and *D. anisoptera*.

The experiment offers great promise for the rest of the world in replanting tropical forests, but it also demonstrates how difficult and time-consuming the process of rehabilitating tropical woodland is. It has taken the Vietnamese more than a decade to bring back only a handful of species where thousands had survived for centuries. Moreover, the recovering patch of the Ma Da woods and its adjacent nursery — representing 1 per cent of the original forest cover — stands out as a fragment of green on the edge of charred savanna and denuded hillsides. According to Vietnamese scientists, it will take decades for other plant species to regenerate, and they doubt that elephants, tigers, bears, deer and other large mammals that once inhabited the forest will ever return.

More forests have been lost in Vietnam since the US/Vietnam war ended in 1975 than during it. Because of postwar lumbering operations (the rebuilding of 10 million homes, schools, hospitals, roads and irrigation systems), the relentless collection of firewood, forest fires and centuries-old methods of slash-and-burn agriculture, Vietnam loses around 200 000 hectares of forest each year. Some 40 per cent of the country is now considered wasteland.

Last year, however, on a shoestring environmental budget, some 500 million trees were planted in Vietnam, representing 160 000 hectares. The Vietnamese give environmental recovery a high priority, despite a serious economic crisis and little foreign aid – US$4 billion from the Soviet Union and US$50 million from Sweden. Compared with a country such as Costa Rica, which receives millions of dollars in foreign environmental aid a year and which plants only 7000 hectares of trees each year to offset a loss of 50 000 hectares, Vietnam's replanting efforts are probably the most cost-effective in the world.

According to Vo Quy, dean of biology of the University of Hanoi: 'Vietnam's goal is to mobilise the planting of 200 000 hectares of trees this year and to reach 300 000 as soon as possible. The re-greening effort is the biggest challenge facing the country since reunification.'

Vietnam's Ministry of Forestry has also worked out plans for the next 10 years to reafforest 1.5 million hectares of barren hills and to rehabilitate more than 200 000 hectares of degraded forest. In addition, the Ministry of Education has made tree-planting one of its curricular activities. Every pupil must plant trees and maintain them. The Ministry of Education has allocated one tree per year for elementary schoolchildren, two trees for secondary school students, and three trees for senior secondary school students. In 1985 and 1986, Vietnamese students planted 52 million trees and built 860 000 square metres of tree nurseries.

In the Con Tien forestry school in Binh Tri Thien Province, a few kilometres from the former demilitarised zone, students have planted and maintained more than a million trees in the past six years.

Source: Elizabeth Kemf, *New Scientist*, 23 June 1988

A forest of hopes

Charlotte Howorth on an ambitious Cameroon project to save a unique rainforest that could show how a world environmental disaster can be averted.

TROPICAL rainforests are being felled, at a conservative estimate, at a rate of seven million hectares a year. If this pace of destruction continues, all rainforest will have disappeared within 50 years, with devastating effects on the world environment.

Disasters such as the Ethiopian famine are just the first warning signs.

But there is some hope. An experimental project under way in Korup, a rainforest in Cameroon, West Africa, should provide a model for the preservation of others.

The 1,250 km² Korup National Park, along the border with Nigeria, is the most species-rich rainforest studied so far in Africa. It is home for 500 species of tree and a large number of mammals and birds, some unique to Korup.

Korup is particularly suited for conservation because its land is unsuitable for plantations, it lacks valuable timber and apparently has no oil or desirable minerals. But its small, but rapidly growing, human population is a serious potential threat to the forest.

A 1982 Channel Four documentary on Korup made by Phil Agland, a dedicated young British ecologist, stimulated sufficient interest among conservation organisations to make the preservation of the forest possible.

The Cameroon Government invited Agland and Dr Stephen Gartlan, who had conducted primate research in Korup for the previous 10 years, to draw up a conservation plan for the forest. As a result, Cameroon last year decreed that Korup would become a National Park. Two more parks — both about four times Korup's size — will follow when money is available.

Impoverished farmers, especially the large numbers moving in from drought-affected areas, are the main enemy to rainforests. Four-fifths of world deforestation is thought to be caused by these people.

Once trees have been cleared, the poor soils cannot support crops for more than two or three years. This results in farmers pushing deeper and deeper into the forest.

The purpose of the Korup project is to save the forest and help the local population. Unfortunately, Cameroon law forbids people from inhabiting National Parks. This obviously presents a serious threat to the estimated 1,100 villagers living within the Korup Park.

Experts employed by the Cameroon Government and the World Wildlife Fund are exploring the possibility of allowing the native people of Korup to stay. The idea is that the villagers would be allowed to hunt for their own needs, but would be prevented from killing animals for export to Nigeria.

The Cameroon Government and the WWF are already encouraging villagers to move voluntarily to more fertile lands outside the new park, an area seen as a buffer zone. This region, consisting of similar forest, surrounds the park and is three times its size.

Here the inhabitants will be helped by aid agencies to use their intricate knowledge of Korup to grow medicinal plants and cultivate better crops.

Systems of sustainable forestry, agriculture and fish farming are to be developed, with WWF help.

In theory, this programme, along with the creation of hunting zones and establishment of livestock, will leave the park untouched, while allowing the local people to maintain their traditional way of life, but with higher standards.

A road will be built, enabling farmers to sell their produce in local markets. All these are tempting incentives for people in and around Korup.

A spokesman for the WWF Korup team says: 'The local people think the forest is infinite. They are nibbling at one side, the Nigerians are nibbling at the other.

'Soon there will be nothing left. We have to make it clear to them that it is in their own interests to preserve Korup for their children.'

The WWF maintains that the villagers hold the key to the success of the project, rather than the experts. It hopes the inhabitants will be involved in every part of it, including the policing of the park.

Restricted tourism – both local and international – will bring money into Korup and focus on its conservation. There are also plans for a research centre to screen Korup's unique organic chemicals. In time Cameroon may even be able to produce its own medicines, becoming less dependent on expensive foreign drugs.

The Korup project is the result of cooperation between the Cameroon Government, the WWF and 34 other institutes, universities and non-government organisations. Their common target is that the Korup programmes should be completed by 1991.

Britain's Overseas Development Administration has donated £444,000, which will be matched pound for pound by the WWF. A third of the £3 million needed has been raised so far.

The Korup project should serve as an example for saving other threatened rainforests. As the WWF says, 'any forest could benefit from this treatment, but it takes a lot of time and that is running out.'

Cameroon is economically balanced, politically stable and has a Government committed to conservation, planning to place 20 per cent of its land under protection. Even with all these rare advantages, preparation of the project entailed many years of confidence-building.

Source: Guardian, 21 November 1987

Forestry management in the Philippines

South-East Asia is one of the world's two heartlands of forest exploitation in the Tropics, along with the Amazon Basin, and is responsible for some 80% of the world trade in tropical hardwoods. The Philippines typifies many of the problems of management that the region faces. The Philippines was the first state in the region to start extensive logging in the 1950s, with the two islands of Mindanao (78% of production) and Luzon (15%) providing the focus for the industry (Figure 11).

Extensive logging has seriously reduced the forested area, so that it now covers only 25% of the islands compared to a cover of 75% as recently as 1940. Some of the smaller islands such as Cebu are now virtually barren, and it is estimated that soil erosion amounts to more than one million cubic metres of soil per year. This in turn results in flooding, the loss of agricultural land, the annual monsoon disasters of the loss of shanty towns around the major cities due to landslides, and the silting of irrigation canals and reservoirs. The Ambuklao Dam on the Agno River, for example, has had its sixty-year life expectancy halved due to siltation. The social, economic and environmental problems that have arisen from forest exploitation are huge, and are exacerbated by a population growing at the rate of 3.4% per annum.

Not all the problems relate to logging. Forest clearance by loggers has been extended by the movement of landless people into the rural areas, who move on to fragile land with limited knowledge of agricultural techniques. Slash and burn techniques are used for farming. This traditional system involves the clearance of plots which are farmed for a few years until their natural fertility declines. The farmers then move to a new site, and plots are left to recover and regenerate for up to 25 years. This system can support population densities of up to 30 per square kilometre, but recent migrations have produced average rural densities of 119 per square kilometre. The result has been extensive soil erosion.

Today only 70,000 square kilometres of mature forest survive, and much of this has logging concessions on it. By 1995 only some 300 square kilometres of dipterocarp forest will remain.

Below are some of the main historical developments in the management of the Philippine forests:

1960s The regime of President Marcos was eager to exploit the forest resources, and granted extensive logging permits. Timber production reached a peak of 11 million cubic metres in 1968, with 80% exported.

1974 A ban on log exports was proposed, but never introduced.

1975 Logging companies were restricted to an export quota of 25% of their cut. This was designed to stimulate the development of a domestic wood processing industry.

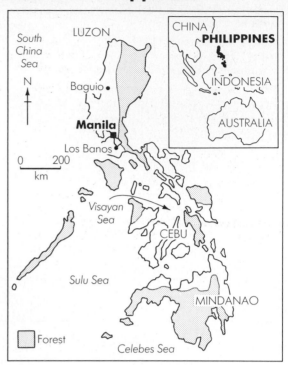

Figure 11 The Philippines

1975 President Marcos made it a legal requirement for every male over the age of ten to plant one tree per month for the next five years!

1976 Production was steady at 8.6 million cubic metres per annum, with 25% exported. Other countries in South-East Asia were showing rapid increases in production and export. The Philippines' relative decline was due to:
a Increasing domestic consumption (17% in 1971, 74% in 1976). This meant that exports of wood products (sawnwood, plywood and veneer) had expanded significantly, notably to the USA and Europe.
b Exhaustion of high-grade logs.

1978 Luzon Island experienced extensive landslides in the monsoon season, due to the exposure of slopes by deforestation. Despite the usual requirement in logging licences for the reforestation of cleared land, many licence holders had ignored the practice, and significant amounts of illegal logging were taking place. The Ministry of Natural Resources made increased efforts towards enforcement and prosecuted a number of illegal loggers together with cancelling a number of licences.

1979 The Asian Development Bank reported that the Philippines was now cutting commercial tree species faster than the rate of annual growth throughout the country.

1980s Firewood collection started to become a problem and led to forest damage on a significant scale. Logging continued at about 9 million cubic metres per annum.

1986 New President Aquino identified deforestation and soil loss as one of the country's three most pressing problems, along with poverty and international debt.

1987 The Ministry for the Environment and Natural Resources allocated 400 million pesos (£27 million) to tackle deforestation, to add to a $100 million loan from the Asian Development Bank and a $50 million loan from Japan. The money is to be used for:
a 'social forestry' schemes. The government recognises that it is unable to undertake reforestry itself on a large enough scale, and so is supporting local non-governmental organisations (NGOs) to develop schemes. These include small citizens' action groups, and groups led by the Catholic church.
b the permanent settlement of 'slash and burn' farmers, accompanied by suitable agricultural training and education.

c replanting of 1000 square kilometres per year by the Ministry.
d the establishment of tree nurseries around the country

1987 The government introduced stern measures against illegal logging. These included rewarding informers with 30% of the value of intercepted illegally-felled logs and harsher penalties for those convicted.

1988 Logging companies were required to lodge with the government a sum of money equivalent to the cost of reforesting their licence area. This is returned to them if they reforest the land themselves.

1988 The Aquino government passed a bill to reform the country's land ownership system. The aim is to stimulate food production, to make the country self-sufficient in food and to reduce the pressure for the expansion of agriculture in the forests.

Chipko – the Tree-Huggers

A voice of revolt was raised 10 years ago in one of the most backward and remote hilly regions of India – Uttarakhand region of the Uttar Pradesh Hills. It came, not from policy-makers sitting in the citadels of power, nor from scientists and academics guiding the governments and the people from their seats of learning, but from illiterate hill-women, who declared: 'The forest is our mother's home.' For the hill-women, the forest was the source of food, fodder, fuel and fertilizer and during the difficult times they looked towards the forest as to their mother's home for help.

It was these hill-women, whose husbands had left home to earn their livelihood in the plains, who felt that 'Men follow their soils'. The women were left behind to manage the family. Due to deforestation and pine-plantations, they felt scarcity of fodder and fuel, for which they had to walk long distances, sometimes 20 km a day. They condemned commercial forestry which sees the forests only as bearing resin, timber and foreign exchange, insisting that what the forests really bear are soil, water and pure air – the basis of life.

After eight years of non-violent struggle to establish this scientific truth, Chipko finally succeeded in getting a ban on felling of green trees for commercial purposes on hill slopes above 1,000 metres altitude and 30° slopes. On May 30, 1981, we set out on a foot march from Kashmir (in Western Himalaya) to Kohima (in Eastern Himalaya), walking 4,870 kms for 300 days in four stages through snow-clad passes and low valleys. Everywhere hill-people gathered to listen to the message, they repeated Chipko songs and slogans in their regional languages.

They want to restore the glory of the Himalayas which was a source of permanent peace, happiness and prosperity to them. They believe that this can only be done if trees giving food (nuts, edible seeds, oil seeds, honey), fodder, fuel, fertilizer (leaf fertilizer for organic manure) and fibre are planted. This will help to regreen the bare hill slopes and to make people self-sufficient in their basic needs of oxygen, water, food, clothing and shelter.

Source: Earthwatch **17**, 1984, p. 8

The last frontier

THE MIGHTY trunk of the Brazil nut tree, rising to the canopy of the rainforest, is a noble sight. Some are more than 500 years old and throughout Amazonia they are a protected species. Yet, when the forest is cleared, they become the sorriest of spectacles. Left alone, they stand like vast sentinels abandoned by a passing army. Too often indiscriminate slash-and-burn clearance leaves the massive trunks scorched and lifeless, the branches in petrified relief against the huge tropical skies. In Acre, the westernmost state of Brazil huddled against the frontier with Bolivia and Peru, such telling symbols of the rainforest's destruction are beginning to have some impact. Acre is the first of Brazil's Amazon states to develop at least the outward signs of a 'green conscience'.

'This is Brazil's last frontier, the least developed state, and we intend to ensure there is rational development,' says Flaviano Melo, Acre's governor since 1986. Bold words, which the 38-year-old governor emphasises in the state's new slogan – 'the green state with new ideas'. He is determined to prevent the kind of destruction wrought in neighbouring Rondonia where a combination of land-hungry peasants, cattle ranchers and fortune-hunting miners have removed as much as 20 per cent of the state's rainforest.

The state is a microcosm of every contentious issue confronting Amazonia: uncontrolled immigration, ruthless land-owners, impoverished peasants, lack of policing. Moreover, the broader issue of development versus conservation is brought into sharp focus by a controversy over plans to build the first all-weather road link across Acre, Highway 364, [...]

'So far approximately 5 per cent of the state's 152,000 square kilometres have been deforested and three-quarters of this is in a radius of some 200 km round the capital Rio Branco,' says Jorge Macedo Neves, research director of Funtac, a newly created state environmental research institute [...]

As governor, Melo finds himself caught in the cross-fire of conflicting interests. 'On one side there are the ecologists, who won't accept the removal of even a banana tree, and on the other

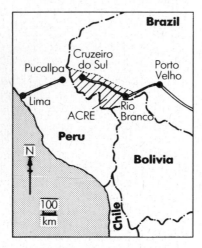

the businessmen, ranchers and timber merchants who want to knock down everything.'

The state's new-found conservationist conscience is not entirely voluntary. The ecological lobby argues that it has been forced on the authorities in the wake of the murder, last December, of Chico Mendes, head of the rubber tappers' union [...]

Acre became a key supplier of Brazilian rubber until the collapse of the boom at the onset of the First World War and, thereafter, was relegated to oblivion. The modern exploitation of Acre is a phenomenon of the Seventies, reflecting the natural expansion of the Brazilian economy and the hunger for new frontiers in an extraordinarily mobile society. Peo-

ple think little of journeying 5,000 kilometres to establish a new life. Within a decade the population increased by more than one-third to 300,000.

The impact on the land was dramatic. In 1970 only 122,000 hectares had been cleared for cattle-ranching. Five years later it had risen to 4.2m ha and now it is believed to be well over 6m ha. Put another way, almost 5 per cent of the state's virgin forest has disappeared in the last 15 years, while the population has doubled to more than 400,000.

Over 80 per cent of this clearance (currently costing $250 a hectare) has been carried out during large-scale agricultural development, and very little by small slash-and-burn settlers. The state owns relatively little land, with the majority bought up by private and corporate speculators from São Paulo. The purchase of virgin forests by such groups not only encouraged indiscriminate clearance but fomented conflict between the traditional and new users of these resources.

'You've got the large land-owners, the *fazendeiros*, and the timber merchants who want to maximise their earnings through forest clearance,' says Jorge Macedo, of Funtac. He adds: 'These people are pushing the smallholders further from populated areas or forcing them into the shanty parts of Rio Branco. At the same time the *seringueiros*, the rubber tappers, find it harder to hang on to the areas of forest where, traditionally, they have worked – each *seringueiro* operates a tapping area of 800 hectares from which he collects about 16 kilos a day of rubber.'

The situation is complicated by virtue of the large estates being run by absentee landlords through foremen – the *capataz* – who are under great pressure and strong financial incentives from the land-owners to produce results. This not only encourages the *capataz* to clear as much land as possible but, because their masters have kept the authorities sweet with money, they are allowed to hold sway over the countryside with their gunmen.

According to Mirko Soares, the *capataz* for a large *fazendeiro*: 'The ecologists are wrong when they say this land is no good for cattle – it is excellent and highly profitable.' However, he concedes that too much land has been cleared in an unplanned way and that most farming is done with minimal technological inputs. [...]

The first trial project to study the rational exploitation of the Amazonian rainforest, with help from the International Tropical Timber Organisation, has just begun. Some 67,000 hectares has been bought north of Rio Branco and, over the next three years, $3m is to be spent by Funtac studying how the forest's riches can be both preserved and utilised. 'At present only 22 species of tree are being exploited in limited ways when there are some 600 which could be used perhaps for medicines, fruits, fibres, nuts and oils,' says Jorge Macedo.

The pace of development would undoubtedly have been faster had Acre not been so remote and transport links been better. A series of strong rivers, running down from the Andes, which have traditional transport arteries, bisects the state on an east-west axis. Even today the all-weather road linking Rio Branco with Porto Velho in neighbouring Rondonia – and the rest of Brazil – has yet to be completed.

The question of roads is a broader issue which goes to the heart of the argument over the Amazonian rainforest's future. 'The population is increasing at about 6 per cent a year,' says governor Melo. 'Immigration can be limited through disincentives but the state has got to grow.' He is convinced – as is the Brazilian Government – that the key to planned growth is the cross-state Highway 364, running 600 km north-south from Cruzeiro do Sul to Rio Branco. [...]

Conservationists regard the road as a knife cutting a cake.

There is no doubt that roads throughout Amazonia have proved the precursors of deforestation. Flying over Acre, it is obvious that forest clearance on a large scale follows directly in the wake of the roads, which in turn create feeder roads. The very lack of roads has preserved Acre.

A road cutting through the Amazon rainforest

Source: Robert Graham, *Financial Times*, June 10/11 1989

The temperate forests

The temperate deciduous woodlands (Figure 12) and the coniferous (or boreal) forests, are less complex ecosystems than those in the tropics, with a smaller number of species (see Table 2). They represent, however, a major biological resource for mankind, in that they contain 35% of the Earth's biomass, and generate 14% of the new biomass each year – a total growth of 19 billion tonnes of new plant and animal material.

Temperate forest issues

Forests play an important role in the life and economy of the North. Most states have long-established forest management services (for instance, the Forestry Commission was established in Britain in 1919), and clear policies towards the exploitation and conservation of their forest resources.

The demand for temperate timber

The continuing economic expansion of the rich countries is placing significant pressures on the temperate forests. Since 1950, worldwide demand for timber for industrial purposes has risen threefold to 1,750 million cubic metres per annum, and is likely to rise to 2,100 million cubic metres per annum by the end of the century. Eight per cent of this timber is provided by temperate hardwoods (for example, oak), while 42% comes from softwoods from the *boreal* forests (for example, pine). This demand is reflected in terms of paper consumption, which at present stands at about 150 kg per head per year for the North. This figure is predicted to double by the year 2000, with 96% of pulpwood and paper coming from the coniferous forests.

Figure 12 Large beech trees, Ashridge Park, England

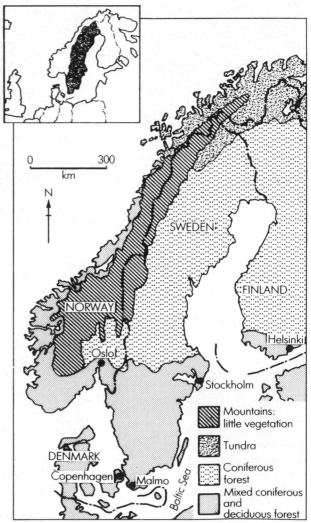

Figure 13 Types of vegetation found in Sweden

Figure 14 The European brown bear, threatened by the removal of forests

Deforestation and afforestation

The forests of Sweden

Most of Sweden lies within the boreal zone of Northern Europe, and even today, after centuries of forest use, some 57% of its land area is still forested (Figure 13). Timber provides over 50% of Sweden's export earnings (Figure 15), but the widespread exploitation of the forests is raising a number of issues. Linda Gamlin ('Sweden's factory forests', *New Scientist*, 28 January 1988, p. 41) has identified several areas of debate and dispute.

Firstly, the expansion of forestry is taking loggers into the untouched forest in Sweden's northern lands, and threatening a number of species. Research has suggested that forty species of vertebrate (for example, the brown bear Figure 14) and fifty

species of fungi, lichen and flowering plants are in serious danger due to the loss of their habitat.

Secondly, legislation to protect the forest is, in itself, destroying the ecosystem. The 1980 Forestry Act requires forest owners to replant felled areas within three years, and to produce a specified quantity of timber per hectare. This has encouraged the use of nitrogen fertilisers and the introduction of fast-growing non-native species such as lodgepole pine. The Act has also encouraged landowners to drain wetlands in the forest, to fell mixed forests and replace them with conifers. In 1982, the Swedish government removed the previous upper altitude limit (300 metres) that they had applied to forest clearance, and a number of

species including the brown bear, the wolverine and several eagles now have their habitat under threat – not only from loggers, but also from the tourists and illegal hunters who enter the forests along the newly-constructed forest roads.

Thirdly, increasing mechanisation has seen a trend towards clear felling, with resulting effects in terms of increased levels of soil erosion and flooding.

Pressure from environmental groups and scientists is widespread, and has brought some response from the Swedish government. In 1987 the government agreed to increase grants for the development of nature reserves, so that by 1990 some 350,000 ha of virgin forest will be protected in 55 new reserves. The government is also declaring a reserve in 30,000 ha of its own high altitude forest. The Swedish Society for the Conservation of Nature is pressing for the removal of government grants to clear the mixed forests, with their rich habitats.

Gamlin suggests that there are two hopes for the future conservation of Sweden's forests. The first would be an increase in the world price of paper, which would reduce demand and yet provide Sweden with a high income at the cost of felling fewer trees. Such a possibility seems unrealistic at present, but the second suggestion is more hopeful. Expansion in the re-cycling of waste paper is occurring in most economically developed countries. This has the advantage of enabling the pulp and paper mills to continue production at the same capacity, while reducing the number of trees being felled.

1a Describe the main environmental and economic issues that are raised by the development of forestry in Sweden.

b Outline the various interested parties in the debate. What are their views?

The Caithness Flow Country

Since the formation of the Forestry Commission, the British government has been encouraging afforestation – through the direct action of the commission, and through tax incentives to private landowners. The result has been an increase in the forested areas from 5% to 9%. However, this figure is still some way behind that of the average for the European Community (15–20%), and Britain still imports 90% of its timber needs.

The arguments concerning forestry expansion have recently been encapsulated in the issues surrounding forestry proposals in Northern Scotland, in the area of Caithness known as the Flow Country (Figure 15).

?

1a Outline the nature of the issues in the extracts on pages 157 and 158

b Explain and evaluate the viewpoints of the various interested parties.

c What proposals would you make concerning the use of the Flow Country? Justify your views.

The pollution problem

Figure 16 indicates the concern which has developed throughout the 1980s about what is seen as one of the major threats facing the temperate forests. Acid rain is the end product of a process that begins with the emission of pollutants into the air from industrial processes, vehicles and energy generation. Sulphur dioxide (SO_2) and various oxides of nitrogen are the main pollutants, and combine with atmospheric water to form dilute solutions of sulphuric acid (H_2SO_4) and nitric acid (HNO_3). These acids are carried back to earth in rainfall. The average pH of unpolluted rain is 5.6 but in many areas affected by acid rainfall the pH of the rainfall may be less than 4.6. The problem is most severe downwind of industrial areas, which between them produce 90 million tonnes of sulphur dioxide air pollution each year.

Figure 16 Greenpeace advertisement

Figure 15 The 'Flow Country' of Caithness

The Battle for the Wilderness

FROM where we are standing a tremendous sweep of moor lifts gently away to the first low skyline two miles off. Thirty miles beyond that, the giants of north-west Sutherland—Ben Loyal, Foinaven, Arkle, Ben Stack—are ranged on the far horizon.

Closer at hand the landscape is utterly devoid of incident: it contains no house, no man, no animal, no rock, no road, no tree. Only pools of water dot the vast expanse of rough grass, heather and moss. The air smells of fresh vegetation and water, primordially clean [...]

This is the Flow Country of Caithness and Sutherland about which furious debate is raging. Should it be preserved as a unique peat-bog wilderness, for the benefit of the plants that grow in it and the rare birds that nest there? Or should parts of it be planted with conifer forest, so that some human profit can be gained from an otherwise useless area?

Like the terrain itself, the confrontation is of elemental proportions. On one side are the Nature Conservancy Council, the Government's statutory adviser on conservation, and the Royal Society for the Protection of Birds, which in this dispute has become the NCC's voluntary spearhead. On the other, deeply entrenched, are the foresters including Fountain Forestry [...]

In the past few weeks the bird/bog lobby has made most of the running—first with the publication of the RSPB's report *Forestry in the Flows of Caithness and Sutherland*, and more recently with the NCC's own study, *Birds, Bogs and Forestry*. The NCC enraged the opposition by suddenly moving the goalposts,

increasing the area in dispute from the 470,000 acres designated Flow Country by the RSPB to a much wider area of peatlands, of nearly a million acres, and calling for a two-year moratorium on all planting [...]

The bird-men's claim that the trees will blow down before maturity is treated with particular scorn. In its report the RSPB maintained that the Flow Country

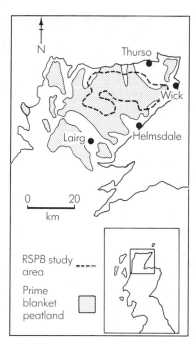

RSPB study area

Prime blanket peatland

has what is known as a wind-throw hazard class of five or six (the worst possible), rather than the class four to five claimed by Fountain. But now Fountain has exposed the fact that of the 36 sites monitored by the RSPB, only three are in forest areas [...]

The RSPB's warnings about the dangers of mass invasion by pine beauty moth are similarly damned as unrealistic scare-

mongering. It is now standard practice to mix the main crop of sitka spruce with lodgepole pine, half and half. The value of the pines is that their roots strike deep into the peat and start to drain it, thereby encouraging the spruce to root deeper. Yet they are there only as a nurse for the main crop, and are expected to die out anyway, smothered by the spruce, so that even if the moth does kill them, it will not be a great disaster.

One certain fact is that the Flow Country is no longer a virgin wilderness. At least 70,000 acres of trees have already been established. Like it or hate it, the new forest is in being.

What is more, the 300 jobs it already provides greatly benefit the human population. The tiny communities that hang on in places like Forsinard, which has five families, or at Altnabreac, where the schoolmistress teaches five children in a room of her own house, are extremely fragile: the loss of any more jobs could destroy them altogether, for out in these wilds if a man has got no work, his only hope of finding any is to move away [...]

To an outsider, there seems to be room for both the birds *and* the trees. The obvious need is for all the warring factions to meet and thrash out their disagreements as soon as possible. Also urgently needed is a long-range strategic plan, which does not now exist.

In the words of Lord Gibson-Watt, one of the Forestry Commissioners, who visited the Flow Country recently, 'this is clearly a matter to be decided by Government'; and there is every indication that the man on whose desk it will land is Mr Malcolm Rifkind, Secretary of State for Scotland.

Source: Duff Hart-Davis, *Sunday Telegraph*, 2 August 1987

SWT Says 'No' to Flow Country Forestry

Plans by forestry investment companies to afforest chunks of the mireland 'flow country' in Caithness and Sutherland – which form a rich natural home for wildlife – have come under attack from the Scottish Wildlife Trust.

The Trust has now pressed Secretary of State for Scotland, Malcolm Rifkind to call for a halt on planting grants and tax relief for forestry in the area. The flow country covers over 1,200 square kilometres and lies north of Helmsdale and east of Strathnaver.

This stretch of blanket bog provides an ideal habitat for a wide variety of water birds and waders which can breed relatively freely. For some of the rarer species such as greenshank it represents a unique refuge for a high proportion of their British population.

Britain's Serengeti

The flow country has been labelled one of the world's outstanding eco-systems, and has been called Britain's Serengeti because of its comparable importance to wildlife. A fifth of the area has been planted by conifers, mostly since 1980, and the rate of planting show no signs of diminishing.

Examining the problems of the flow country have been members of the SWT's Conservation and Science Group. In a critical new report, the Group declare: 'Ironically, just as the significance of the flows as a wildlife resource is becoming recognised, it has become all too painfully clear that, if we do not intervene effectively, this resource will not survive.'

The Group claims that: 'Timber grown on bogs cannot compete with that grown on good lowland sites such as are likely to become available in Britain when the agricultural recession really starts to bite.

'... the use of public funds to support marginal farming and recreation in Caithness and East Sutherland makes greater long-term sense than the encouragement of afforestation schemes by tax reliefs to absentee investors.

'When we contrast the hazardous prospects for forestry with the certainty of destruction of other resources the conclusion is clear enough ... logic obliges us to throw our weight behind those of our contemporaries who are actively opposing this threat.'

Trees v. Wildlife

Among the bird life found on the flows are wood sandpiper, golden plover, dunlin, red-necked phalarope, greenshank and redshank. Perennial pools on the mire lands, known as *dubh lochans*, are used as roosts by ducks. The larger stretches of water offer a home for red- and black-throated divers, red-breasted merganser, common scoter, wigeon, teal and greylag goose.

There are also breeding pairs of Arctic skua and merlin. Hen-harrier, short-eared owl and peregrine can also be found here. For trees to be grown on blanket mire, deep ploughing has to take place linked to elaborate drainage schemes followed by heavy and repeated use of fertilisers.

No one really knows just how long a new plantation will last in such adverse conditions and doubts have been raised over claims from one of the companies involved, Fountain Forestry, that their plantation can be grown for the 45-year period needed to produce crops of saw-logs. [...]

Tax Relief

More and more forestry investors, ranging from showbusiness personalities to investment houses, banks and pension funds, are buying up plots of land for planting. The preferred crop for the flow country is the North American sitka spruce which is considered by commercial foresters to be the tree best suited to the conditions and which offers the best financial return. [...]

By a number of means, the Exchequer meets about 70 percent of costs to set up new plantations by forestry companies acting mainly on behalf of wealthy investors, few of whom see the land they buy. The tax relief system itself discourages them from maintaining an interest in the plantation. [...]

Local Economy

The Group stressed that in opposing forestry developments in the flow country, the SWT was not opposing economic development – quite the contrary.

The flow country has tangible value in its attractiveness to tourists, fishermen and other sportsmen whose local spending contrasted with that of itinerant gangs of forest workers, many of them based outside the area.

'Moreover, afforestation prevents the land from being worked over for peat. In the North this is a most important resource. Exploited on a domestic scale, it provides fuel and comfort in harsh winters. On a properly organised commercial basis, it gives a sound and certain return on investment which does not rely on the idiosyncrasies of the tax system.' [...]

The Forestry Commission View

Chairman of the Forestry Commission, Sir David Montgomery, has come out against claims on the amount of damage forestry may do to the wildlife of the flow country, calling them 'exaggerated'.

Speaking on the publication of the Commission's annual report, he said: 'I don't wish to comment on any individual report or critique, but in general terms, fears have been expressed that afforestation will pose a significant threat to conservation interests.

'... the area of land which might theoretically become available for planting is limited by a wide range of practical constraints. When one realises this, some of the exaggerated claims which have been made about the flow country are put in proper perspective.'

Source: Scottish Wildlife **23** 1, January 1987

The *Gaia Atlas* suggests that damage to the West German timber industry from acid rain may amount to $800 million per year, and that the Black Forest has lost up to one-third of its trees. In the USA some 60 million tonnes of such pollutants cause $2 billion of damage to ecosystems in the USA and damage costing $550 million in Canada. The acid rain is clearly capable of damaging sensitive leaf tissue in trees, and dieback in the canopy is often seen as a major symptom. Its main impact, however, may be in its effect on soil chemistry. The increased acidity causes increased leaching of aluminium, lead, mercury and zinc from the soils, leaving behind a more acid soil.

Figure 17 Evidence of acid rain damage in the Black Forest, West Germany

Why forests fear acid drops

● EEC ministers face crucial decisions about how to stop pollution stripping Europe's woodlands. But first they must track down the real culprit. BRYAN SILCOCK reports

NEAR Liphook on the London-Portsmouth road, the Central Electricity Generating Board is plumbing a section of forest. The intention is not to keep it watered but to fumigate it.

When the installation is completed early in the new year, sulphur dioxide and ozone will be fed through the pipes, maintaining a constant recorded level of pollution round thousands of young trees.

The experiment may continue for as long as five years, and will, the CEGB hopes, finally establish

the cause of the damage to trees, first noticed in German forests, that has made acid rain the number one pollution issue of today.

Concern is such that this week, EEC environment ministers will meet to discuss far-reaching proposals from the European Commission for controlling acid rain which would require equipment costing over £1.5 billion to be fitted to existing power stations in Britain. The government opposes them on the grounds that there is not yet sufficient scientific

understanding of the acid rain problem to ensure that the controls will have the effect intended.

Paradoxically, one thing that is known with certainty about the forest damage is that it is *not* caused by acid rain. Acid rain is in fact a misnomer, which has become a blanket term for a range of atmospheric pollutants, not all of which are even acidic.

What they all have in common is that they arise from the burning of fossil fuels. Coal and oil contain sulphur which ends up as sulphur dioxide (SO_2) in the at-

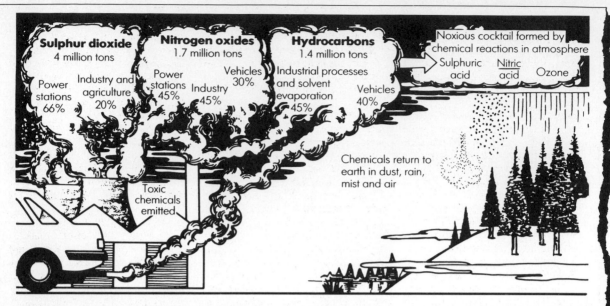

Sulphur dioxide
4 million tons

Power stations 66%

Industry and agriculture 20%

Nitrogen oxides
1.7 million tons

Power stations 45%

Industry 45%

Vehicles 30%

Hydrocarbons
1.4 million tons

Industrial processes and solvent evaporation 45%

Vehicles 40%

Noxious cocktail formed by chemical reactions in atmosphere
Sulphuric acid   Nitric acid   Ozone

Toxic chemicals emitted

Chemicals return to earth in dust, rain, mist and air

mosphere. The high temperature combustion converts some of the nitrogen in air into various oxides of nitrogen, known collectively as NO_x. SO_2 and NO_x are the precursors of most forms of acid pollution.

They can also cause direct damage. If concentrations are high enough, they erode the stonework of buildings, corrode metals, harm plants and affect human health. But these effects occur only at the high levels characteristic of big centres of population. In most of Western Europe urban levels of SO_2, at any rate, have fallen dramatically in recent years. The long-range acid pollution which is causing so much concern is a different problem.

It arises because complex chemical processes in the atmosphere convert SO_2 and NO_x into sulphuric and nitric acids. Some return to earth as acid rain, but a lot of acidity is deposited as dry particles. The toxic gas ozone can also be formed from NO_x hydrocarbons, and the oxygen of the atmosphere. All these different forms of pollution tend to be lumped together as 'acid rain'.

In the atmosphere, the pollutants may be carried great distances by the wind, so they are an international, even a global,

problem. Thus the Scandinavian countries receive most of their acid pollutants from beyond their frontiers, while Britain is a big net exporter of acid pollution.

It is, however, a myth that this is because of the high chimneys of power stations and other big plants. The proportion of the gases from a 30-foot domestic chimney and a 600-foot power station chimney that ends up hundreds of miles away is much the same. Chimney height research has been carried out as part of the European Environmental Monitoring Programme by the CEGB and others.

But because of the amount of fuel they consume, power stations are the biggest single source of acid pollution. Motor vehicles are big producers too, and their contribution is looking increasingly significant.

Acidification of lakes, streams and rivers in Scandinavia was the first effect of long-range acid pollution to be recognised. Over the years waters have become more and more acid and fish and other forms of aquatic life have died, victims of complex chemical changes. The same thing is happening in other parts of Europe and in North America. In Britain, south-western Scotland is the region worst affected.

But acid rain does not automatically lead to acidified surface waters. The geology has to be right too. If the soil has adequate neutralising capacity, acid rain does no identifiable damage.

The Scandinavians have been complaining bitterly for many years about the effects of other people's pollution on their lakes and rivers but it was damage to forests, first in Germany, then elsewhere, that turned acid rain into a major international issue.

The first signs appeared in the mid 1970s, among silver firs in south Germany: needles turned a characteristic yellow colour and then dropped off. The damage spread rapidly, particularly in the early 1980s. By 1984, 50% of forest trees in Germany were affected to some degree, though few actually died. This year the situation seems to have stabilised, though this may be a temporary respite due to the wet summer.

In the east of the country, along the borders with Poland and Czechoslovakia, the cause of the damage is clear enough. Levels of SO_2 and NO_x are so high that they are affecting the trees directly. Most of the pollution comes from the burning of brown coal in the eastern bloc, where there are few controls and trees are in an even worse state, with great tracts of forest completely dead.

Most of the afflicted German trees, however, are in regions like the Black Forest where the air is exceptionally clean. Here the damage must have a different cause from in the east.

The first theory to gain a wide following was that acidification of the soil by acid rain was responsible. This, however, has not stood up to close examination. Forests in other parts of the world are exposed to far more acid rain, yet remain healthy. And within Germany, local damage is not related to the amount of acid deposited or soil type, as would be expected if soil acidification was responsible.

With the demise of the soil acidification theory, ozone has emerged as the most likely culprit. Ozone levels have been rising in recent years, and in the affected German forests they are frequently above those known to harm plants. The ozone may well act in conjunction with other factors which cause stress, like cold and drought, disease and perhaps leaching of nutrients from needles by acid rain. The high altitude forests where the damage is most extensive are also frequently subject to mists in which acidity can reach high levels.

The one link missing in the ozone theory is that the symptoms have never been reproduced in controlled experiments. Trees exposed to ozone in greenhouses do not yellow and lose their needles in the same way. If they do not

develop the right symptoms in the more natural conditions of the CEGB's Liphook experiment either, the ozone theory may have to be reappraised.

Ozone is not acid, but it is formed in the atmosphere from NO_x and oxygen in reactions that are promoted by sunlight. Hydrocarbons also stimulate ozone formation. The effect of NO_x, hydrocarbons and sunlight is all too familiar in Los Angeles, where they combine to produce the notorious photo-chemical smogs of which ozone is an important constituent.

If ozone is indeed mainly responsible for forest damage, power stations lose their pre-eminent position as killers of trees. They are above all emitters of SO_2 but this has little to do with ozone formation. On the other hand, motor vehicles, as major producers of NO_x and hydrocarbons, begin to look increasingly important. SO_2, however, remains as the chief culprit in the acidification of surface waters.

The acid pollution problem could be solved once and for all by ending all emissions of SO_2 and NO_x. But as this is not practicable in the foreseeable future, any control strategy must aim at getting the maximum benefits from the resources available.

The EEC directive to be discussed by environment ministers this week calls for a 60% reduction in emissions of SO_2, and 40% of NO_x, from large

plants (in effect power stations and major chemical works) from 1980 levels by 1995. In Britain, meeting this larger target would require a dozen of the biggest existing coal-fired power stations to be fitted with equipment for removing SO_2 from flue gases. The equipment is available, but the initial cost would be £1.5-£2 billion, with annual running costs of over £300m. The effect of these SO_2 controls alone would be to raise electricity prices by about 5%.

Would it be money well spent? The controls might help to remove the long-standing and legitimate Scandinavian grievance over pollution of its surface waters, but it is by no means certain that they would do so. The vital question is: will reducing emissions by, say, 50% reduce acid deposition by the same amount? The evidence is far from clear. British emissions of SO_2 have fallen by 30%, the EEC's by 16%, since the early 1970s without any noticeable reduction in acid deposition.

The explanation may be that the conversion of SO_2 to sulphuric acid requires catalysts. If so, the rate of conversion could depend on the quality of catalysts available, not on the quantity of SO_2. If this bottleneck exists, investment in reducing emissions may not produce the expected payoff in terms of reduced acid pollution.

Source: *Sunday Times*, 24 November 1985

?

1 The resources 'Why forests fear acid drops', 'The browning of America begins in the mountains', 'Power plan aims to cut acid rain', 'Air pollution: International action' and Table 6 look at the issues surrounding the acid rain debate and the pollution of forests.

a What appear to be the main sources of atmospheric pollution in Western Europe? Where do they come from?

b Produce a systems/flow diagram to illustrate the process of pollution by acid rain.

c What evidence is there of the effects of atmospheric pollution on forests?

d Apart from acid rain, what alternative theories are there to explain forest dieback?

e What solutions are available for the problems, and what difficulties are faced in implementing them?

f What do you believe the outcome of this debate will be? Justify your viewpoint.

The browning of America begins in the mountains

THE ADIRONDACKS – People on the lakes where I am staying say they cannot remember when the water was so clear. [...]

No one has a single good explanation for this phenomenon. Some say it is because of the drought. In a drought, they say, nothing grows at its usual pace, even weeds under water. Others say it is because of acid rain – that deadly combination of sulphur, nitrogen and carbon in gases from the smokestacks of the industrial Mid-West that rise into rain clouds and drift to the north and east. The Adirondack mountains and lakes are early victims of these clouds. [...]

On a mountain top in North Carolina thousands of acres of red spruce have been under such stress recently from air pollution, including acids, and a series of droughts that they have simply died. As they have succumbed to the many forces of nature and man, the area looks as though it has been sprayed with the military defoliant, Agent Orange. A local plant pathologist, Robert Bruck, of North Carolina State University, says he is '90 per cent certain' that man-made air pollution coming from the Ohio and Tennessee valleys, combined with high temperatures and the droughts of recent years, have created a climate in which the spruce cannot survive. Professor Bruck thinks that the spruce, which once thrived at 6,000 ft above sea-level, may have succumbed to the kind of environmental damage that has wiped out large areas of forest land in Europe.

Here in the Adirondacks, close to the Canadian border, where the red spruce have been dying mysteriously at the 2,000-ft level for several years, they talk of 'spruce die-back'. Overall, Professor Bruck warns ominously about the 'collapse of ecological systems' along the crest of the Appalachians, from Georgia to Maine. He and other scientists suggest that the dead spruce and the brown patches on the balsams represent the 'canary in the coalmine' – an early warning that forests at low altitude are also in danger. [...]

The new formula of sulphurous and nitrogenous emissions from factories, plus ozone, has rung new alarm bells in the laboratories. The combination weakens trees to the point where they cannot resist natural fluctuations in climate, predatory insects or parasitic fungi. In human terms these trees have their own form of Aids.

Source: Peter Pringle, *Independent*, 28 July 1988

Table 6 Sulphur deposition in Europe, 1984

Country	Average annual deposits in '000 tonnes	% received from other countries
Poland	935	29
Italy	851	23
France	781	55
West Germany	781	55
East Germany	779	32
Czechoslovakia	685	41
United Kingdom	654	20
Sweden	323	84
Austria	206	81
Norway	194	93
Netherlands	152	76
Belgium	147	57
Switzerland	103	89
Denmark	94	68

Source: *Financial Times* 18 September 1986, based on United Nations/Economic Commission for Europe data

Power plan aims to cut acid rain

Drax A and B power stations in north Yorkshire, and the Fiddler's Ferry station on Merseyside, are to be fitted with equipment to cut down on acid rain, in a 10-year programme announced by the Central Electricity Generating Board yesterday.

The scheme will reduce sulphur dioxide emissions by about 360,000 tonnes a year, 15 per cent of the total emissions from British power stations, the board said.

The recently opened Drax B station will be fitted by 1993 and the older Drax A by 1995, using a process which will require more than 700,000 tonnes of limestone a year and produce more than one million tonnes of gypsum.

Fiddler's Ferry will be fitted by 1997, and use a process recycling less limestone.

Source: John Ardill, *Guardian*, 8 October 1987

Air pollution: international action

The EC is still trying to reach agreement on a Directive to cut emissions of sulphur dioxide and nitrogen oxides from all sources. In the summer of 1987, Environment Ministers discussed a draft Directive calling for a 60% reduction in total emissions of sulphur dioxide and for a 40% reduction in total emissions of nitrogen oxides, by comparison with levels in 1980.

In 1983, the United Nations set up a protocol to the 1979 Convention on Long-range Transboundary Air Pollution, which required countries to cut their sulphur emissions by 30% (from 1980 levels) by 1993. Twenty-one countries signed this protocol; 16 then ratified it and it therefore took effect on 2 September 1987. The 16 countries which ratified it were: Austria, Bulgaria, Canada, Czechoslovakia, Denmark, Finland, France, Federal Republic of Germany, Hungary, Liechtenstein, the Netherlands, Norway, Sweden, the USSR, and two Soviet republics which signed separately (*Financial Times*, 28 August 1987). Ten Western European countries have already achieved the 30% reduction called for under the protocol, which has been described as 'the world's first binding treaty to cut acid rain production' (*The Guardian*, 2 September 1987). The UK has not signed this protocol.

The UN is now seeking to establish a similar protocol to control emissions of nitrogen oxides. Talks on reducing global nitrogen oxide emissions began in September 1987, but encountered difficulties. There are many different sources of nitrogen oxide emissions ... and all would need to be controlled. Some European countries have proposed a cut of 30% in nitrogen oxide emissions from 1980 levels by 1995, others support a freeze on emissions and a third group (which includes the USA) apparently wants no controls (*The Guardian*, 5 September 1987).

Whether these proposed reductions will have any useful effect is in some doubt. Environmental groups have tried to establish the levels of pollution below which damage to the environment (by acid rain and ground-level ozone) no longer occurs; they suggest that a 90% reduction in Europe's emissions of sulphur dioxide, a 75% reduction in emissions of nitrogen oxides and a 75% reduction in emissions of hydrocarbons is needed (*New Scientist*, 11 September 1986).

Source: 'Pollution Update 1 – Air Pollution', *Geofile* **101**, Mary Glasgow Publications Ltd, London, Geofile, January 1988

Managing the forests

The management of forests in most economically developed countries is not just about the harvesting of optimum amounts of timber and ensuring that production is balanced by regeneration through replanting and growth. Modern forest management is about multiple use and ensuring that conflicts between the various forest users are minimised. A particular pressure is the growth of the use of forests for recreation and as nature reserves. In the UK the Forestry Commission sees the growth of recreational use as a valuable source of income, and by the late 1980s had constructed nearly 700 forest walks and nature trails and 21 Visitor Centres.

Furthermore, 70,000 hectares of its land (8%) are designated as 350 Sites of Special Scientific Interest (SSSIs), including the New Forest in Hampshire, which covers 27,000 hectares. Table 7 shows some of the competing demands and the compatibility between them.

1 Choose three combinations of forest use from Table 7, and explain why they are or are not compatible.

Table 7 The range of different forest uses

Uses	Direct uses			Indirect uses		
	Areas of felling	Areas of growing	Grazing	Wildlife conservation	Recreation	Slope protection
Areas of felling	—	✗	✗	✗	✗	✗
Areas of growing	✗	—	✗	✓	✓	✓
Grazing	✗	✗	—	✗	✗	✓
Wildlife conservation	✗	✓	✗	—	✗	✓
Recreation	✗	✓	✗	✗	—	✗
Slope protection	✗	✓	✓	✓	✓	—

Source: C. Hart (ed), *Worldwide Issues in Geography*, Collins Educational, 1985, p. 110   ✓= Uses are compatible   ✗ = Uses are incompatible

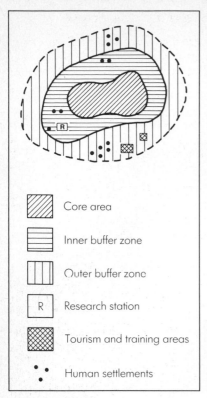

Figure 18 Model of an inland biosphere reserve

Source: University of London School Examinations Board, *Geography 16–19 A Level*, Paper 2, 1986

One method that is used for balancing competition between forest users is *zoning*. This involves the division of forests into areas with different major activities. Tourism, for example, may be directed to specific parts of the forest by locating tourist facilities at chosen points. Figure 18 is a model of the structure of such a *biosphere reserve*, and shows how the zoning works.

1 Study Figure 18.

a Copy the map and annotate it with a description of the purpose of each zone.

b Study the map in Figure 19. Explain how the management of the forest reflects, and differs from, the model of the biosphere reserve.

Designating forest nature reserves – a decision-making exercise

While it is widely recognised that there is a need to preserve areas of forest for conservation purposes, it is often difficult to decide which areas to choose. This exercise shows the way in which such a reserve might be chosen.

Nova Scotia is one of the smallest provinces in Canada, lying on the eastern coast. Eighty-four per cent of the province is forested (Figure 21), mainly with boreal forest dominated by spruce and fir, but also including mixed forest containing hardwoods such as maple, birch and hemlock. Forestry is one of the major industries, and there has been concern that a number of sites should be designated as Forest Nature Reserves to preserve typical areas.

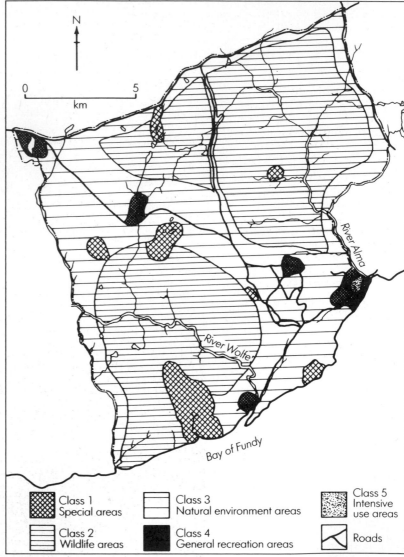

Figure 19 The proposed master plan for the Bay of Fundy National Park, New Brunswick, showing the division of the park into zones. Developed areas are kept to a minimum consistent with the use of the park for recreation. Such a plan is a public document and the subject of public hearings.

Source: I. G. Simmons, *The Ecology of Natural Resources*, Edward Arnold, 1974, p. 109

Table 8 Criteria used by nine local ecologists

Representative (including theme regions)	5
Uniqueness	4
Climax, old growth	4
Diversity, richness	3
Rarity	2
Successional stages	2
Conspicuousness	2
Threat, endangered	2
Age of trees, naturalness, stability, size of area, research potential, cultural, not representativeness, not diversity	1

Source: F.B. Goldsmith, 'Selection procedures for forest nature reserves in Nova Scotia, Canada,' *Biological Conservation* **41**, 1987, pp. 185–201

Table 9 Frequency with which criteria were mentioned in Taschereau (1974)

Mature stand, old growth	15
Finest/excellent/good example	14
Undisturbed	8
Rare plants/species rich	7
Large trees, tall	4
Research data/previous studies	4
Size of area	3
Representative	3
Regeneration, healthy, buffer zone, oldest trees, beautiful, natural, educational potential	2
Rich bryophytes, second growth, abundant wildlife, scenic, cultural, vegetation transition, fragility	1

Source: F.B. Goldsmith, *Biological Conservation* **41**, 1987, pp. 185–201

Many possible sites exist and so nine local ecologists were asked to consider what factors should be used in choosing sites. Table 8 shows their choices, while Table 9 shows the choices of an earlier survey. Table 10 indicates the criteria suggested by the Canadian Council for Ecological Areas (CCEA) for use in selecting nature reserves throughout Canada. Figure 20 and Tables 11, 12 and 13 show the results of data surveys for a number of possible sites in Nova Scotia, together with a map of their locations.

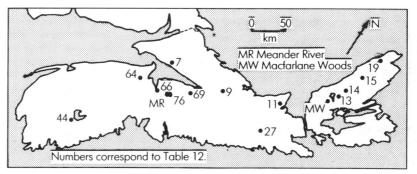

Figure 20 Location of potential forest nature reserves
Source: F. B. Goldsmith, *Biological Conservation* **41**, 1987, pp. 185–201

Table 10 Criteria recommended by the Canadian Council for Ecological Areas

1 Diversity
2 Rarity
3 Size
4 Condition
5 Endangerment
6 Fragility
7 Replication
8 Significance

Source: F.B. Goldsmith, *Biological Conservation* **41**, 1987, pp. 185–201

Figure 21 Forested land in Nova Scotia, Canada

Table 11 Rare and uncommon species recorded at each site
(* Species referred to in Maher et al.'s (1978) publication on provincial rarities.)

Species	Meander River	Kemptown	S. Maitland	Grand Anse	Lake O'Law	Pipers Glen	Sixth Lake	Kentville Ravine	Ste Croix	Macfarlane Woods	Moose River	Clydesdale	Smileys	*
Allium tricoccum		1												*
Arisaema stewardsonii	1	1	1					1					1	
Caulophyllum thalictoides	1	1	1										1	*
Claytonia caroliniana						1								
Clematis virginiana			1											
Cypripedium arietinum			1											*
C. calceolus			1											*
C. reginae													1	*
Cystopteris bulbifera	1								1					
Dicentra cucullaria		1		1										
Dryopteris felix-mas				1	1									
D. marginalis	1				1				1					
Equisetum scirpoides	1							1						
Erigeron hyssopifolius			1											*
Erythronium americanum		1	1											
Goodyera repens										1				*
Hystrix patula	1													*
Ilex glabra							1							
Lilium canadense	1	1												*
Poa alsodes			1						1		1		1	*
Polystichum braunii					1							1		
Sanguinaria canadensis	1	1	1										1	
Shepherdia canadensis			1											
Trillium erectum								1				1		
Triosteum auranticum	1	1												*
Number of rarities	9	9	10	2	3	1	1	3	3	1	1	2	5	

Source: F.B. Goldsmith, *Biological Conservation* **41**, 1987, pp. 185–201

Table 12 Values for each criterion for twenty sites (Tree diameters in brackets are not typical of the area.)

Site	Number of species	Number of rarities	Area (ha)	Largest tree girth (m)	Other features	Status	Ref. no. of site
South Maitland	99	10	147	2.09	Cave, river	Proposed Nat. Env. Park	69
Meander River	99	9			River		
Kentville Ravine	94	3	39	3.00	Research	Fed. Res. Station	64
Pipers Glen	92	1	27	2.57	Waterfall		13
Lake O'Law	89	3	35	2.50			14
Ste Croix	87	3	121	(3.40)			66
Clydesdale	84	2	78	2.27	Stream		11
Macfarlane Woods	83	1	78	2.33			
Smileys	66	5	12	(3.50)	River	Prov. camp & park	76
Moose River	66					Clear-cut	7
Sixth Lake	59	1	81	2.60	Lake		44
Grand Anse	(89)	2	1616	3.05		National Park	19
Kemptown		9	0.4				9

Source: F.B. Goldsmith, *Biological Conservation* **41**, 1987, pp. 185–201

?

1a Decide on the order of importance of the criteria for designating a forest nature reserve in Tables 8, 9 and 10. Bear in mind the views of the scientists who drew up the tables, but, in the end, make your own judgement, choose five important criteria and rank the factors in order.

b Allocate a weighting to each factor to give a more accurate measure of its relative importance in your opinion. Do this by allocating 50 'weighting points' between the criteria. All criteria must score at least one point, and the order of allocation must follow the ranking you produced in **a**.

c For each of the factors chosen as criteria above, use the data in Figure 24 and Tables 11, 12 and 13:
i to place the sites in order of value as nature reserves, giving 13 points to the highest-ranked site, and one point to the lowest.
ii Then multiply the score for each site by the weighting allocated in **b** for the factor under consideration.
iii Finally, add up the total score for each of the 13 sites.

Table 13 Ranking of the top five sites for each criterion (Sites are listed in order of overall priority.)

Site	Number of species	Number of rarities	Area	Largest girth	Other features
South Maitland	1	1	1		Cave
Kentville Ravine	3	5		3	Research
Meander River	1	2			
Hemlock Ravine				1	History
Ste Croix		5	2		
Lake O'law	5	5			
Pipers Glen	4				Waterfall
Kemptown		2			
Grand Anse				2	(National Park)
Clydesdale			3		
Macfarlane Woods			3		
Smileys		4			
Moose River					
Sixth Lake					

Source: F.B. Goldsmith, *Biological Conservation* **41**, 1987, pp. 185–201

d Draft a brief report for the Provincial Government, nominating four sites for designation as nature reserves on ecological grounds. Give full justification for your choices. Include in your report a summary of non-ecological factors that would need to be considered in making any final decision on designating your chosen sites as nature reserves.

The necessity for management

Forests are one of the principal resources that humankind possesses. It is clear that they are a resource under pressure, and that the loss of the forests will almost certainly have extensive repercussions for the global ecosystem and for the very survival of people. Despite a lack of understanding of the detailed functioning of forest ecosystems, the necessity for management is now understood.

A number of key issues need careful consideration in conservation and management planning.

● How much do we know about the working of forest ecosystems and their relationships with the rest of the global system?

● How far is the loss of forest attributable to each of the following:

a Demand from the North?
b Poverty in the South?
c Population growth and pressure?
d A lack of global co-operation in economic development?

● What management methods are available, and what limits their use?

● What impact does forest clearance have on the quality of life and living standards in:
a the short term and
b the long term?

● What similarities and differences are there between the problems and issues in tropical forests and temperate forests?

● What role can/should the individual and the governments of the economically developed countries play in the tropical and temperate forest issues?

?

1 In a small group, discuss your views on the issues raised?

2 'Forestry management in the South is about the issue of deforestation: in the North it is about re-afforestation.' How true do you think this statement is?

3 In 1980 the International Union for the Conservation of Nature (IUCN), the World Wildlife Fund (WWF), and the United Nations Environment Programme (UNEP) jointly developed what they called a 'World Conservation Strategy'. Its aim is '... to help advance the achievement of sustainable development through the conservation of living resources ... the maintenance of essential ecological processes and life support systems, the preservation of genetic diversity, and the sustainable utilization of species and ecosystems...'

Are management strategies in the world's forests moving towards the achievement of these aims?

7

Oceans and seas

Hance Smith

Gunboats and a frigate escorting an oil tanker through the Persian Gulf, 1987

This chapter contains much information on the oceans and seas. We suggest that you use the main section headings to divide up your use of the chapter. Read a section through quite quickly to get an overall impression, and then go back and construct notes for each section as we have done for the Norfolk Broads (see pp. 12–13). This will help you get a sense of the main parts of each section. Then, in class, you can go through some of the group activities. You may wish to add to your notes after the groupwork.

Development and management of the seas

The starting point for the study of the seas is, as always, observation. For most of us this has to be done from the coast: the world ocean covers as much as 71 per cent of the Earth's surface, but most of it is out of sight of land, far from centres of population. This can easily lead people to think that the seas as a whole are hardly used or affected by human activity. In fact, nothing could be further from the truth. Coastal waters are obviously associated with much activity, readily observable from the land; but so too are the seas covering the continental shelves beyond, and even the deep oceans far from land.

Patterns of marine use

The uses of the sea (see Figure 1) are the geographical manifestations of the processes of development which provide the driving force that directs human activities in the marine environment. It has been so since the voyages of early peoples, through the voyages of the great explorers, down to the present. These processes of development are complex, but several strands are recognisable. It is necessary to be aware of these strands in order to understand the geographical patterns of uses, and interactions among uses, in the marine and coastal environment.

The processes result from the need for food, mineral and energy resources, communications, and the development of technology and scientific knowledge. These in turn generate the need for management of the marine environment, including the allocation of sea space and resources, and the political and legal processes which govern sea use management generally.

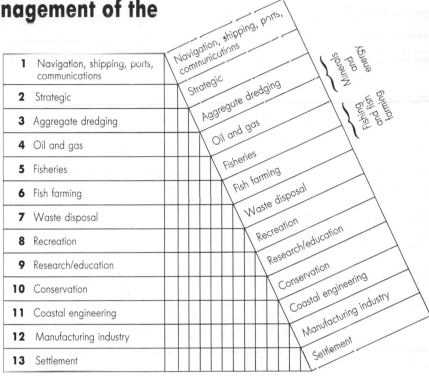

1	Navigation, shipping, ports, communications
2	Strategic
3	Aggregate dredging
4	Oil and gas
5	Fisheries
6	Fish farming
7	Waste disposal
8	Recreation
9	Research/education
10	Conservation
11	Coastal engineering
12	Manufacturing industry
13	Settlement

Figure 1   The uses of the sea: conflict analysis matrix

1   Make a large copy of Figure 1. Then, using extracts A–F, fill in as many of the boxes as you can. Fill in any other boxes if you can think of more examples of conflicts of use. Compare your matrices in class and write a paragraph to summarise your findings.

2a   For your own local sea area or one that you have studied, list and classify the area uses.

b   Using Figure 1, identify possible conflicts of sea use and briefly describe them.

c   What kinds of environmental impacts are likely to be associated with each sea use?

3   In small groups, discuss what you think would count as a marine resource. Draft a short definition to describe the term 'marine resources'.

A

Clean-beach resort fights sewage plan

PLANS to pipe millions of gallons of raw sewage away from the already-polluted beaches of south Cornwall and discharge it off the north Cornish coast are expected to be approved by Mr Chris Patten, the Environment Secretary, within a month.

The £63 million plan has angered the people of St Ives, which has just gained a blue flag for bathing beach excellence from the European Community. They feel that the tourist industry on the north coast is threatened.

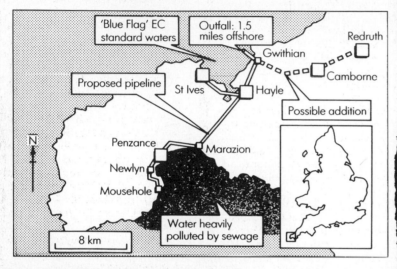

Source: Paul Brown, *Guardian*, 29 December 1989

B

Cornish fishing under threat from 'pirates'

IN THE EARLY hours, in weather bad enough to discourage daylight from putting in an appearance until an hour after its allotted time, the Cornish port of Newlyn comes alive as a fishing centre.

But the industry, which provides jobs for 500 locals, is under threat from a Spanish "pirate" fishing fleet, taking fish allocated to British trawlermen by exploiting a loophole in the rules.

In general, the fishermen are slow to complain, but they have been angered by the Government's capitulation this week to a European Commission directive which declared illegal recent British attempts to keep the Spanish boats out of British waters using crew nationality rules.

Spanish fishermen have been registering their boats as British, entitling them to fish in British waters, but Britain had insisted that the crew of such a trawler must be 75 per cent British.

Michael Townsend, chief executive of the Cornish Fish Producer's Organisation which represents boat owners, said the ED decision "drove a coach and horses" through the national quota system and the attempts to conserve fish stocks which lay behind the quotas. "Foreign boats can set up under any nationality and, like pirates, take that country's fish."

Source: Mike Prestage, *Independent*, 28 October 1989

C

Fight to save dock from marina plan

MORE THAN 4,000 signed objections to a developer's plans to close Exmouth Dock in Devon were delivered to the Department of Transport in London yesterday by supporters of the KEW (Keep Exmouth Working) campaign.

The campaign is fighting a proposal to banish almost all commercial traffic from the busy dock and create a 150-berth leisure marina with 443 associated homes on the site.

The local planning authority, East Devon district council, wants the change because of alleged nuisance caused by cargo handling over several years and a desire to improve Exmouth's tourist image.

The dock employs 50 people directly and is said to affect the livelihood of another 200 in the area. Each cargo unloaded brings in an average of £8,000, and KEW claims about 500 ships a year use the dock.

Planning officials claimed that the dock, surrounded by houses, had created an increasing nuisance, with bad smells and clouds of dust.

◄ *Source*: Dennis Johnson, *Guardian*, 8 September 1989

D

Scientists to study role of sea in global warming

SCIENTISTS will sail from South Wales today on a voyage to understand the impact of the oceans on the greenhouse effect.

The research ship Discovery, with 20 scientists on board, will go to the North Atlantic to examine how carbon dioxide, said to be the main cause of global warming, is absorbed into, and then given up by, the oceans.

Scientists believe that every year the oceans absorb 105 billion tonnes of carbon and release 102 billion tonnes, but the danger is that as the atmosphere gets warmer the oceans may put more carbon into the atmosphere rather than taking it out.

Most models predicting changes in the climate do not take the oceans into account, largely because not enough is known about the complex biological physical and chemical processes involved.

Tiny plants, called phytoplankton, take up the atmospheric carbon during photosynthesis. It may be returned in a matter of days or weeks as the plants decompose, but about one tenth of the carbon will eventually sink to the deep ocean as particles, where it may remain for hundreds or thousands of years. If the carbon becomes part of the sediment, it may be there for many millions of years.

Although the phytoplankton are too small to sink they may be eaten by small sea animals known as zooplankton or aggregate into larger clumps.

These larger particles, and the faeces of zooplankton form a "marine snow" and are big enough to sink at rates of 100 metres per day. The UK scientists will take samples and measurements to assess the flux of the carbon from the surface regions to the deep waters, and they will examine how phytoplankton is formed and how zooplankton capture and feed on the plants.

Source: Mary Fagan, *Independent*, 8 May 1989

E

Ash blamed for 'marine desert'

THE dumping of ash from coal-fired power stations is smothering part of the seabed off Northumbria, turning it into a "marine desert" according to fishermen and divers.

Each day, two ships leave port for a 20-mile square dumping area three miles offshore carrying thousands of tons of "fly ash" from burnt pulverised coal. One of the ships, the MVA, was the target of yesterday's action by Greenpeace.

Dumping at depths of 90 to 140 feet has gone on for years, and the seabed in some areas looks as if it has been concreted over, according to Mr Steve Drury, a spokesman for 13 boats which run angling trips from the Tyne.

A spokesman for the National Power division of the Central Electricity Generating Board said it was carrying out a legally-approved operation.

It tried to sell as much ash as possible, but it was not possible to dispose of all the waste this way. Disposal on land as an alternative to dumping would create different environmental problems.

Fishermen are also worried about pollution from sewage. Mr Drury says they have found sanitary towels and bags of syringes in their nets.

Source: Stephen Cook, *Guardian*, 17 January 1990

F

Fishermen want action as America's worst spill covers 100 square miles

AS an ever-widening patch of spilled oil expands steadily across Prince William Sound, Alaska, experts seem divided over how to cope with this threat to one of the world's most fertile fishing areas.

Prince William Sound contains millions of fish: herring, salmon, crab, and other crustacea. Seabirds proliferate, and the area is home to such wildlife as sea otters, seals, sea lions, and killer whales.

An oil-coated otter being kennelled so that it can be flown to a cleaning centre

Source: Christopher Reed, *Guardian*, 28 March 1989

Classifying by purpose

The uses of the sea can be classified in terms of fundamental purposes. There are three sets of these namely, communication, resource extraction, and the general use of the marine environment:

1   The communication set includes navigation, shipping, ports and submarine cables; and strategic use of the sea.

2   The resource extraction set includes mineral and energy resources, which are best considered together as these are run by large corporations managing large-scale capital-intensive projects, while the principal offshore energy resource, petroleum, is a mineral; and fisheries and aquaculture which, worldwide, are mainly organised in the form of numerous small businesses.

3   The environmental uses consist of four groups: waste disposal, marine recreation, science and conservation.

4   Additional fundamental-use groups of the coastal zone also have to be borne in mind: manufacturing industry, settlement and coastal engineering (land reclamation, coast protection, harbour construction).

The sea-use groups proper also have their land counterparts, for example fisheries/agriculture and forestry; and land transport/ shipping.

Old and new groups

The development of sea uses also has distinctive temporal (time) patterns dating mainly from the 'industrial revolution' of the late eighteenth century. Four of the groups in the above list may be thought of as 'old', that is, the major groups which were well developed by the middle of the twentieth century. These are: navigation and communication, strategic uses, fisheries and marine sciences. Since then these have all greatly expanded.

Meanwhile, the other four groups (mineral and energy extraction, waste disposal, marine recreation and conservation, which were also present earlier) have now also become major use groups since World War 2.

All these use groups have largely developed and been managed sectorally, that is, with separate industrial and management organisations for each major use. One example is the ports and shipping industries, where the management of navigation includes coastguard, lifesaving, pilotage and other navigational and management organisations.

Spatial organisation: core and periphery

The development processes already discussed above also give rise to well-known land-based patterns of spatial organisation. What is less well known is that this spatial organisation pattern extends to the marine environment, although the oceans and seas are not settled in a conventional sense. The basic form of spatial organisation is the *core* of settlement and economic activity (usually urban) and the rural or sparsely populated *periphery* which acts as a source of raw materials and environmental resources generally for the core:

These core/periphery patterns exist at three major scales:

1   the local scale of the port town or city and its hinterland;

2   the regional scale of major concentrations of population and industry, such as the central part of western Europe, and;

3   the global scale of the North Atlantic core of the global economy and its developing peripheral cores – notably around the Pacific rim – which have become the leading edge of world economic development as a whole.

?

1   Using Figure 2 and an atlas, name the development core areas. Which of them lie on the 'Pacific rim'?

2   Write a paragraph to comment on the pattern of fisheries development in Figure 2.

3   Which area has fewest ports on major sea routes? Suggest reasons for this.

Spatial patterns lead to management systems

These core/periphery patterns are reflected in the intensity of sea uses and the corresponding sophistication of sea use management systems. At the *global* scale this is most clearly shown in the dense pattern of shipping routes, strategic activities and fishing activity in the North Atlantic. *Regionally* there are similar concentrations of navigation, fisheries, mineral resource extraction, waste disposal and marine recreation, especially in Western Europe, eastern North America, California, Japan, and eastern Australia, as well as the other small centres illustrated in Figure 2. *Locally* there are many port-related areas with the most intensive coastal use patterns of all. Beyond the cores are the peripheries, used mostly for fisheries, marine recreation, scientific research and conservation.

Overall there are four groups of sea use management systems which have developed in response to these patterns:

● the urban port system;

● the rural coast and shelf sea system;

● the 'wilderness' system, which covers most of the sparsely populated coasts and deep ocean areas;

● the global system, used for some navigation, whale conservation and other purposes.

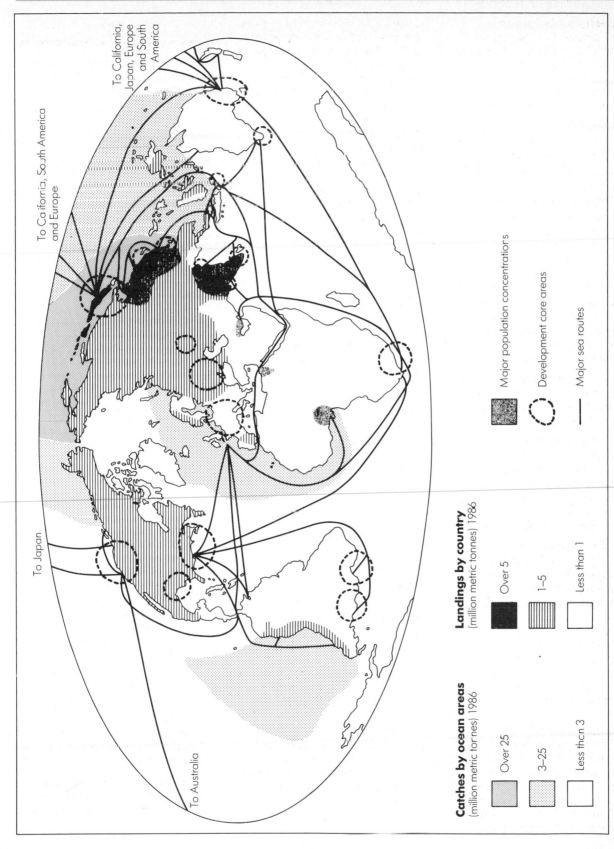

To California, Japan, Europe and South America

To California, South America and Europe

To Japan

To Australia

Catches by ocean areas
(million metric tonnes) 1986

Over 25

3–25

Less than 3

Landings by country
(million metric tonnes) 1986

Over 5

1–5

Less than 1

Major population concentrations

Development core areas

Major sea routes

Figure 2　Global development patterns

Conflicts among uses

Sea use management means dealing with conflicts between uses on the one hand, and the environmental impacts of those uses on the other. There are a number of management *objective groups* which apply in varying extents to all the groups of uses, even though there are separate use-based management organisations. The objective groups include:

- safety of life and property, for example in shipping;

- the allocation of resources, such as sea space defining maritime boundaries between states, and fish stocks by means of quotas;

- environmental control, including pollution control and conservation of ecosystems and commercial fish stocks;

- scientific research as a knowledge basis, both for its own sake and as a basis for all development and management decision making;

- regional development, concerned with the influence of marine industries upon employment, population movement, income and regional industrial structure.

1 Read the article about fishing quotas.

a Who is in conflict with whom? Draw the conflict using a suitable diagram.

b Explain how the conflict relates to the five objective groups listed above.

The law of the sea

One of the most important starting points for the resolution of conflicts among uses and adverse environmental impacts has been the law of the sea. The evolution of the modern law of the sea can be traced back to seventeenth-century Anglo–Dutch conflicts over maritime trade and fisheries – especially the North Sea herring fishery. Since then it has evolved by means of dispute settlement in the courts to build up what is known as customary international law. This, together with a series of international treaties, relates to certain activities such as navigation management, fisheries and pollution control. Beginning in the 1950s, a more concerted approach towards the law of the sea has been developed, resulting in the 1982 Law of the Sea Convention which will probably officially come into force in the early 1990s, although many of its provisions were gradually adopted in the 1970s and 1980s.

P = physical impacts E = ecosystem impacts	Sea surface Water column Rivers		Seabed zone		Intertidal zone		Beach/cliff		Land	
	P	E	P	E	P	E	p	E	P	E
1 Navigation, shipping, ports communications	O	O	O		O	O	O	O	O	
2 Strategic	O		O		O	O	O	O	O	
3 Aggregate dredging	O	O	O	O	O		O			
4 Oil and gas	O	O	O		O		O		O	
5 Fisheries		O	O	O						
6 Fish farming	O	O	O	O	O	O	O			
7 Waste disposal	O	O	O	O	O	O	O	O	O	O
8 Recreation	O	O	O	O	O	O	O	O	O	O
9 Research/education										
10 Conservation		O		O		O		O		O
11 Coastal engineering	O	O	O		O	O	O	O	O	
12 Manufacturing industry		O		O	O	O	O	O	O	O
13 Settlement		O		O		O	O	O	O	O

Figure 3 The environmental impact of sea and coastal uses

Fishing quotas 'may halve Scottish fleet'

AN AGREEMENT on fishing quotas reached by EC ministers yesterday could push half of Scotland's fleet to bankruptcy, Scottish Fishermen's Federation chief executive, Mr Bob Allan, said.

The Agriculture Minister, Mr John Gummer, and the Scottish Secretary, Mr Malcolm Rifkind, celebrated the small gains they had been able to negotiate, but admitted that the industry in Britain faced a tough time in the coming year.

The agreement, reached after 26 hours of talk in Brussels, will reduce British quotas for haddock and cod in the North Sea. The result will be drastic cutbacks for East Coast fishermen, most of them in Scotland.

The industry would seek compensation from the Government for the effects of the quota cuts, Mr Allan said. In Scotland about half of the 600 boats currently operating could be severely affected.

"The figures don't constitute more than about six months of real and viable fishing for our fleet," he said. "What has happened is that we have been clawed back from the disastrous level of whitefish we started at to a position in line with the top end of scientific advice."

The haddock quota for 1990 was set at 36,280 tonnes compared with 51,400 tonnes this year. The final result is better than the 32,000 tonnes originally proposed by the Commission and is the maximum catch recommended by scientists to stop fish stocks disappearing.

Mr Gummer's determination to win the highest figures advised by the scientists failed for the North Sea cod quota. Britain will have 46,180 tonnes in 1990, compared to 55,600 this year. Scientists had recommended a maximum of 47,400 tonnes.

Source: Alan Hope, *Guardian*, 20 December 1989

Table 1 List of parts: United Nations Convention on the Law of the Sea 1982

I	Introduction (1)
II	Straits used for international navigation (2–33)
III	Archipelagic states (46–54)
IV	Exclusive economic zones (55–75)
V	Continental shelf (76–85)
VI	High seas (86–120)
VII	Regime of islands (121)
VIII	Enclosed or semi-enclosed seas (122–3)
IX	Right of access of land-locked states to and from the sea and freedom of transit (124–32)
X	The Area (133–91)
XI	Protection and preservation of the marine environment (192–237)
XII	Marine scientific research (238–65)
XIII	Development and transfer of marine technology (266–78)
XIV	Settlement of disputes (279–99)
XV	General provisions (300–4)
XVI	Formal provisions (305–20)

ANNEXES

I	Highly migratory species
II	Commission of the limits of the continental shelf
III	Basic conditions of prospecting, exploration and exploitation
IV	Statute of the Enterprise
V	Conciliation
VI	Statute of the International Tribunal of the Law of the Sea
VII	Arbitration
VIII	Special arbitration
IX	Participation by international organisations

FINAL ACT

(numbers of articles in brackets)

Jurisdictional zones

A key feature of this legal evolution has been the development of a series of zones of jurisdiction based on distance from the coast and relating separately to the sea itself and the seabed (see Figure 4). The principal zonal groups are:

- Internal waters and the territorial sea in which the coastal state has nearly complete jurisdiction;

- The exclusive economic zone (EEZ) and the continental shelf in which the coastal state has rights and obligations relating to resources and environment but in which certain international freedoms are maintained, such as rights of navigation.

- The high seas and Area which broadly coincide with the deep ocean beyond coastal state jurisdiction, and in which the rules of public international law are paramount.

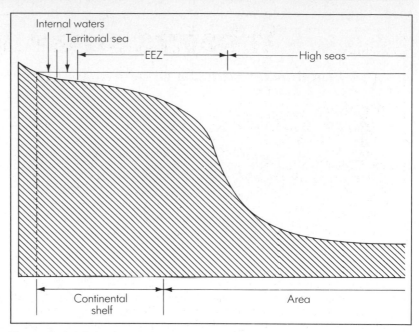

Figure 4   Jurisdictional zones

1   Study the article 'Scale of fishing increases' and use an atlas to locate the places named in it.

a   Describe in two sentences what the conflict is about.

b   What jurisdictional zones are involved?

c   What might happen in this conflict if the jurisdictional zones did not exist?

2   Study the article 'Whalers strike again'.

a   Describe what the conflict is about.

b   What jurisdictional zones are involved?

c   List a range of ways in which conflicts such as this can be resolved. How many of these ways relate to the law of the sea?

Scale of fishing increases

JAPAN and Taiwan have refused to halt or reduce the use of drift gill nets in the South Pacific. The 16 nations of the South Pacific Forum say that drift nets threaten to wipe out the albacore fishery in the region within two years (This Week, 17 June). The nets—which environmentalists call the "wall of death"—also snare many other marine animals.

Next week in Kiribati, the heads of government of the forum nations will discuss ways to prevent Japan and Taiwan from sending large fishing fleets to the region. One plan is to ban boats with drift nets from entering the Exclusive Economic Zones of nations in the Pacific, which each extend 200 miles from the coast.

New Zealand, which is in the process of passing legislation to ban gill-netting vessels from its own territorial waters, is likely to propose the plan. New Zealand will also ban the boats from its ports and refuse to allow the catches to be moved from the fishing boats to larger storage vessels.

If all the nations took similar measures, the boats would have to go east of French Polynesia before they could legally move north-south across the Pacific, according to Talbot Murray from the New Zealand Ministry of Agriculture and Fisheries. "This would make it difficult and costly for them to operate in the Pacific," said Murray.

Last week in Fiji, at a meeting of the Forum Fisheries Agency, Japan and Taiwan rejected claims that fishing stocks in the South Pacific are threatened by the nets. The Pacific nations say that the boats caught more than 40,000 tonnes last fishing season, about four times as much as the fish stock can withstand, according to the agency.

Murray says that the catch could well be an underestimate. Last week, Japan revealed that it had 60 vessels with drift nets in the South Pacific, twice the number that it had acknowledged.

Source: New Scientist, 8 July 1989

Whalers strike again

Paul Brown on the Japanese hunters beyond international opinion

THE Japanese whaling fleet began killing 300 minke whales this week in Antarctic waters despite international condemnation and the threat of a United States trade embargo.

Whale meat, once a cheap form of protein for a hungry country, is now a luxury. Last year's catch is selling in Tokyo's fashionable department stores at £70 a pound.

There is an international moratorium on commercial whaling imposed by the International Whaling Commission. A loophole in the IWC rules allowing taking whales for scientific purposes was immediately exploited by Japan, Iceland and Norway which said they were killing whales in order to assess stocks.

This year Iceland, facing an in-creasingly successful international boycott of its fish exports organis-ed by Greenpeace, decided to stop its scientific programme. Norway has now pledged to cut its kill to five whales in 1990. The Japanese have decided to kill 300.

The Japanese fleet left Tokyo in mid-November and began killing whales this week. For two years they have limited their catch to 300 minke whales and this year said they intended to increase this to 825 minkes and 50 sperm whales. However, in the face of many international requests to stop the programme, the govern-ment announced, before the fleet sailed, that they would again only take 300 minkes.

United States pressure on Japan to stop the whaling has so far been limited to excluding the Japanese fishing fleet from its territorial waters. A second, much more damaging sanction, which would have to be imposed by President Bush, would mean banning Japanese fish imports to the United States. Last year Green-peace harried the Japanese fleet of four ships, a 23,000 ton factory ship and three catchers, for nine days in Antarctic waters. Mr An-dy Ottoway, the British whale campaigner said: "Up to 99 per cent of blue, fin, hump-back and sperm whales have been wiped out and still the Japanese plan to kill more whales. They do not need the meat, it cannot be economic, it makes no sense to kill these mammals – it must be stopped. We want people to voice their pro-test to the Japanese embassy."

Source: Guardian, 8 December 1989

Limits

The end result of the legal pro-cess has been the geographic divi-sion of the sea in relation to a series of limits drawn from the coast. The key divisions relate to:

- the territorial seas (usually ex-tended over the years from 3 to 12 nautical miles) and en-compassing what may truly be termed coastal waters;

- the offshore seas, roughly coterminous with the extent of the continental shelves, with an outer limit of 200 nautical miles;

- and the deep oceans beyond which cover approximately 56 per cent of the total area of the world ocean.

At first sight this division ap-pears to correspond fairly well with patterns of use intensity – greatest in coastal waters and progressively declining towards the deep ocean. In fact this is quite misleading, as it cuts across the true pattern of use intensity, which is related more to the core –periphery pattern at local and regional scales (see above).

Technical management

Also arising from the law of the sea is the mistaken idea that law is the same as management. The law is a necessary condition for most effective management measures, but it is only *one* of a whole range of technical manage-ment functions, which are the real work of sea use development and management (Figure 5).

These include:

- Environmental monitoring, surveillance of uses, and management of this data using information technology. This type of work is done by, for example, fisheries laboratories and the coastguard services respectively.

- Technology assessment which might be involved in, for ex-ample the design of new fishing gear or offshore oil platforms, and project develop-ment carried out by profes-sional firms such as surveyors and engineers.

- Environmental assessment, in-cluding economic assessment of the value of resources, assessment of both physical and economic risk involved in sea uses such as shipwrecks, and environmental impact assessment such as estimating the effects of major coastal engineering works on beach erosion.

- Social assessment, including the law of the sea and coastal zone already discussed; sea use planning involving allocation or sea space among conflicting uses to provide for example navigation routes and conservation zones, and social impact assessment concerned with, for example, the influence of offshore oil development upon industry and employment in adjacent coastal regions.

1 Using Figure 5, think of examples of technical management jobs for about ten of the spaces in the matrix.

2 What would you say to someone who thinks that law is the same as management?

General management

Beyond the *technical* management level lies a *general* management level. This involves both co-ordination of technical management and policy making as a whole. It is here that the organisation of sea use management becomes important. Sea use management is divided into private, public and voluntary sectors; and into local, national, international and supra-national (European Community) scales of operation and spheres of responsibility (Figure 6).

Each sea use group needs different combinations of sectoral management inputs at different geographical scales. Perhaps the greatest challenge in the effective management of the marine environment lies in how the numerous groups can be co-ordinated in relation to the pressing issues involved. Due attention must also be paid to overall objectives and the technical management tools available to accomplish the necessary tasks. We shall return to this challenge in the simulation exercise at the end of the chapter. But, first, it is necessary to look more closely at

Technical management categories \ Sea use groups	Navigation and communication	Strategic uses	Mineral and energy resources	Biological resources	Waste disposal	Recreation	Research	Conservation
Monitoring								
Surveillance								
Information technology								
Technology assessment								
Project development								
Resource assessment								
Risk assessment								
Environmental impact assessment								
Law: coast and sea								
Sea use planning								
Social impact assessment								

Figure 5 Technical management of sea uses

the three major divisions of use intensity and people-environment interaction in order to more fully appreciate the geographical patterns, issues and decisions involved.

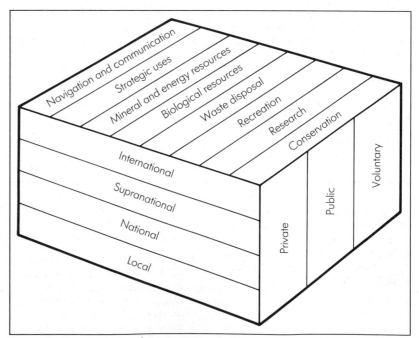

Figure 6 The organisation of sea use management

The urban seas and coasts

In the economically *developed* world (which contains about one-third of the world's population) most people live in cities and towns, and many of these are on the coasts. In the economically *developing* world, most people still live in rural areas, but urbanisation is increasing rapidly. Thus the perception and experience of most people about the marine environment is that of the urban sea and coast (where they live) and perhaps of rural coasts if they pursue a marine recreational activity such as sailing).

Characteristics

The nature of the urban sea and coast in both the economically developed and developing worlds has distinctive characteristics as regards development and resource management (see Figure 7). On the development side, there is enormous pressure on land resources for industrial, commercial and residential use. Many cities are on estuaries or bays, with a high level of coastal engineering works for harbours, coast protection and land reclamation. Most of the waste which enters the marine environment originates in the urban sea – industrial outfalls, warm water from power stations, sewage outfalls and adjacent solid-waste dumping grounds. Many urban areas are ports (indeed, the port function may have been the reason for the establishment of a town in the first place) so that there may be considerable shipping traffic. If inshore aggregates are available, there may be sand and gravel dredging to supply local building materials. There is also an enormous demand for marine recreation of all kinds – especially that based on the day trip.

Recreation

Urban land use

Waste disposal

Coastal engineering

Navigation, shipping, ports communications

Aggregate dredging

Figure 7 The urban sea and coast: New York cruise ship terminal

Management problems

The management problems which arise from this are legion. Perhaps the dominant ones are:

● the need for sea use planning to allocate conflicting uses such as navigation, recreation and waste disposal;

● the continuous monitoring of water quality and regulation of waste disposal and pollution control;

● provision of comprehensive navigation management services including radar-based vessel traffic control systems, pilotage, dredging and emergency services;

● the redevelopment of redundant ports. This latter function may include conservation of a historic core, with provision of maritime heritage facilities such as maritime museums and marine developments to attract visitors; and development of large areas of dockland for non-port uses such as light industry, housing and associated yacht harbours or marinas.

Liverpool

Some of the best examples of the urban sea and coast are to be found in Britain. This is hardly surprising, considering Britain's primary role in the industrial revolution and the growth of global maritime trade. The enormous problems presented by pollution control and inner-city redevelopment are amply demonstrated by the Mersey estuary. The Sandon Dock is now the site of a huge sewage works which processes effluent from the Liverpool and Manchester conurbations, and there are plans to build a barrage across the estuary. Dockland redevelopment initially took place around the

Albert Dock complex adjacent to Liverpool city centre (Figures 9 and 10), and was supplemented later by conversion of part of the upstream docks to parkland, on the site of the 1984 Garden Festival. Further redevelopments are also taking place on the opposite Wirral shore. We can appreciate the scale of the adjustment necessary when we realise that Liverpool was once Britain's leading export port. Now major changes have posed new challenges to managing this urban sea environment.

1 Using Figure 8 and any other available sources in this chapter, identify coastal and marine uses. Suggest where the urban/rural sea boundary might lie.

2 What are the major management objectives and organisations involved?

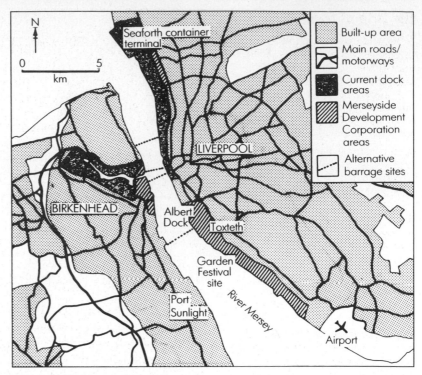

Figure 8 The Mersey estuary

Figure 9 Albert Dock, Liverpool during its heyday in the 1930s and **Figure 10** (inset) Albert Dock today. In 1988 it was Britain's third most popular tourist attraction with 3.5 million visitors

The Firth of Forth

A second good example of managing urban sea areas is the inlet of the Firth of Forth. The settlement pattern here is dominated by Edinburgh, capital city of Scotland, as well as numerous historic fishing villages and small former ports. The coast therefore has high urban and rural amenity value. There are strong pressures for amenities to be maintained for residential and recreational purposes, and for parts of the environment to be conserved, such as the Bass Rock bird sanctuary. However, the Forth also has major industrial and port facilities in the form of Grangemouth refinery and Longannet Power Station, with a nuclear power station at nearby Tor Ness. Perhaps the most significant recent developments have been associated with the North Sea oil industry, with the crude oil export terminal at Hound Point and the liquified natural gas plant (LNG) at Moss Morran and its associated terminal at Braefoot Bay. There is a full-scale marine traffic control system operated by the Forth Ports Authority based at Leith, with stringent pollution control, and planning constraints on land to maintain the characteristics of the coast.

Figure 11   An aerial view of the Firth of Forth

?

1   Study Figure 12. What are the conflicts of use in the Firth of Forth?

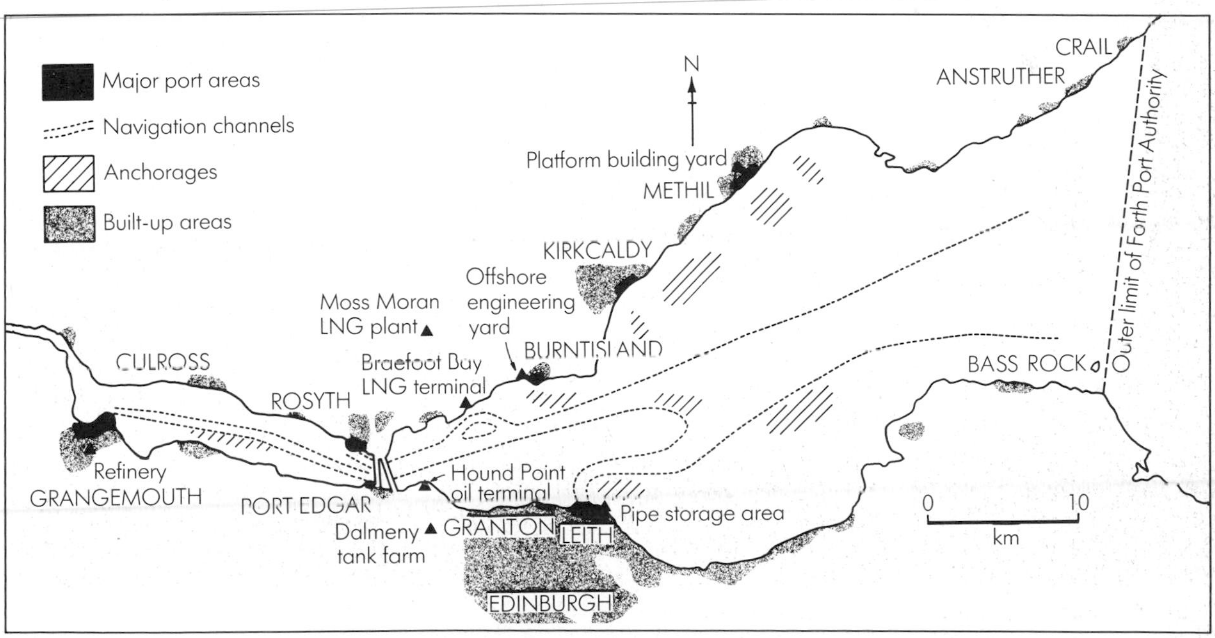

Figure 12   The Firth of Forth

The shelf seas and rural coasts

Characteristics

The rural sea often begins where port limits and associated high multiple-use intensity ends. Like rural land, the shelf seas are rich in resources and fairly intensely used. Their landward extent is roughly coterminous with what may be termed 'settled' coasts, characterised by small towns, villages and farmland. However, the patterns of use are quite different from those of the urban sea. Predominant is resource extraction – especially fisheries and fish farming, offshore oil and gas extraction, and aggregate dredging, together with marine recreation and conservation along the coasts. These often possess very high amenity and conservation value, especially in relation to the nearest major urban concentrations. Major deep-sea and short-sea (ferry) routes also exist in this area. Waste disposal is limited. Shipping or offshore oil accidents are often perceived as the greatest risk in this environment – for example, disasters such as the *Amoco Cadiz*, *Torrey Canyon* and Piper Alpha, which can cause enormous environmental damage as well as loss of life.

Figure 13 The rural sea and coast: Bacton gas terminal, Norfolk

Management problems

The technical management tasks in these seas are those of:

1 monitoring and surveillance, especially of resource extraction;

2 valuation of resources, and

3 environmental and social impact analysis of industrial developments on adjacent coasts.

Here too are to be found the problems of delimiting international maritime boundaries. The general management challenge of integrated management also exists – for example, in coping with the impact of the offshore oil industry as it affects the land and sea;

fisheries planning; and international scientific monitoring of resource use and the environment.

The North Sea

In temperate waters the North Sea provides a good example of the issues involved (see Figures 14 to 18).

Fishing
Fisheries management is the oldest strand in the pattern. The North Sea has been intensively fished since the sixteenth century. In the 1970s the herring stock collapsed and herring fishing was banned for six years.

Oil and gas
The advent of the oil and gas industry in the 1960s provided the impetus for a relatively amicable settlement of maritime boundaries among the states. It also created large environmental and social impacts, especially in Scotland and south-western Norway as well as in East Anglia.

Pollution
More recently, in the 1980s, the problems of coastal water pollution arising from the several urban seas in the south have led to the convening of North Sea ministerial conferences. This may yet lead to the political basis for

a permanent, comprehensive management approach.

Scientific research

On the science side, much of the early history of the International Council for the Exploration of the Sea (ICES) based in Copenhagen had to do with monitoring the North Sea environment and commercial fish stocks.

1 Using Figures 14 to 18 list what problems are likely to be posed for rural communities as a result of offshore industrial developments. Suggest how these may be solved.

2 It has been decided to produce a fisheries plan for a Scottish island fishing community, with major decisions being taken by fishermen, fish processors, the local authority, national government and fisheries scientists. Use Figure 15 and other material in this chapter to identify the main responsibilities of each decision-making group. The data about the fishing community is provided below.

Catches 10,000 tonnes per year (5,000 tonnes of herring caught between June and September; 2,000 tonnes of cod; 2,000 tonnes of haddock, 1,000 tonnes of other species including 500 tonnes of shellfish caught all year round).

Landings All herring and shellfish, and 80–90% of other stocks.

Boats 14 large boats, including 4 herring fishing only. 10 small boats which catch all the shellfish and 1,200 tonnes of the remainder (excluding herring).

Market Herring exported frozen; all shellfish exported by air; 1,000 tonnes of cod and haddock processed locally for export; the remainder exported frozen.

Employment 120 fishermen; 50 processors part-time; 200 ancillary jobs.

Source: Figures 14–18. Bliss, P. A. and Keckes, S. 'The regional seas programme of UNEP', *Environmental Conservation*, vol. 9, no. 1, pp. 43–49, 1982

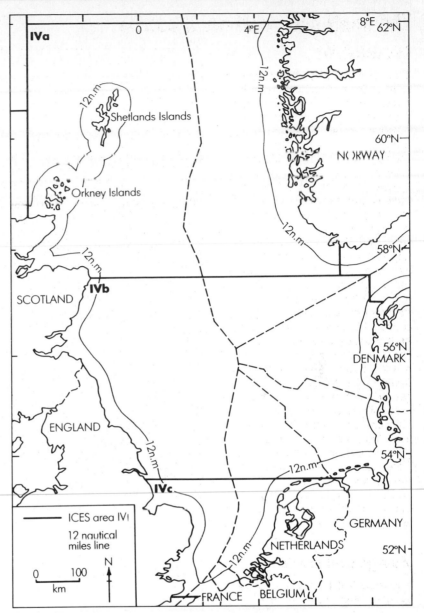

Figure 14 The North Sea, showing the maritime boundaries

The Great Barrier Reef

A good tropical example of shelf seas and rural coasts is parts of the Great Barrier Reef. The primary value of the Reef lies in recreation and conservation of a fragile ecosystem, although there are important localised fishing and navigation interests, for example in the Capricornia section (Figures 19 and 20). Here exists perhaps the most comprehensive sea-use planning system devised to date. It is based on the Great Barrier Reef Marine Park Authority. The whole of the Reef is designated as a marine park, with controlled use combinations ranging from virtually exclusive conservation or scientific use to various degrees of 'general use' areas. These contain recreational and commercial fishing, tourism and navigation. Such areas are less restricted.

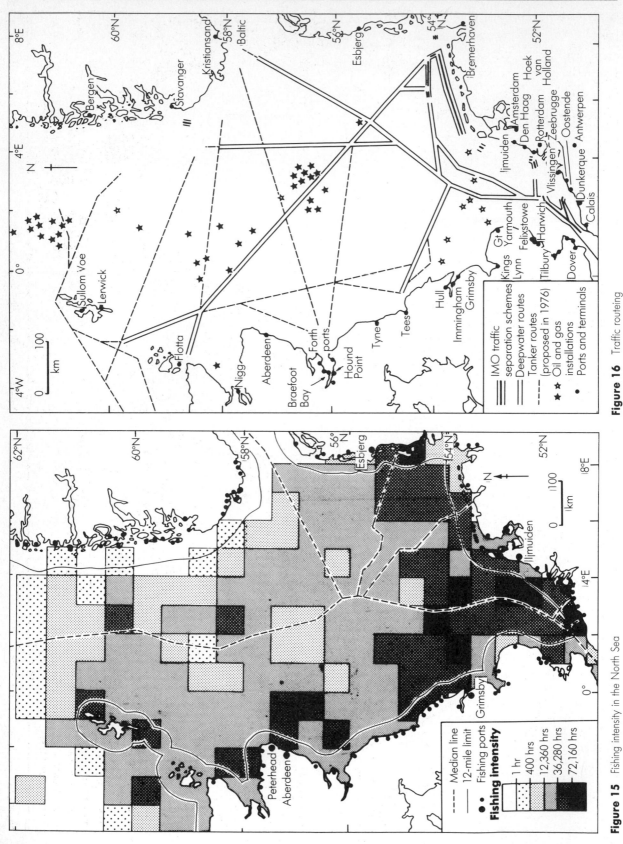

Figure 16 Traffic routeing

Figure 15 Fishing intensity in the North Sea

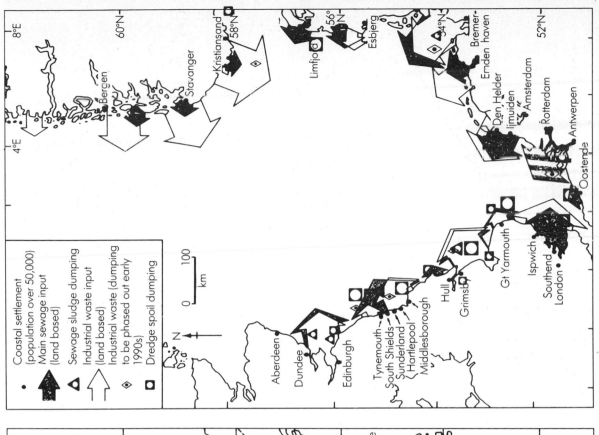

Figure 18 Sewage and waste inputs

Legend:
- Coastal settlement (population over 50,000)
- Main sewage input (land based)
- Sewage sludge dumping
- Industrial waste input (land based)
- Industrial waste (dumping to be phased out early 1990s)
- Dredge spoil dumping

Figure 17 Petroleum production systems

Legend:
- ★ Oil fields
- ★ Gas fields
- Oil pipelines
- Gas pipelines
- ● Oil terminals
- ○ Gas terminals
- - - - Median lines

EAST SHETLAND BASIN

NORTHERN NORTH SEA BASIN

EKOFISK GROUP

SOUTHERN NORTH SEA BASIN

Sullom Voe
Flotta
Nigg
St Fergus
Braefoot Bay
Hound Point
Seal Sands
Easington
Theddlethorpe
Bacton
Kårstø
Kaergarde
Emden
Uith Jizen
Callantsoog
Iimuiden

Bergen
Stavanger
Kristiansand
Limfjord
Esbjerg
Bremer-haven
Emden haven
Den Helder
Iimuiden
Amsterdam
Rotterdam
Antwerpen
Oostende
Aberdeen
Dundee
Edinburgh
Tynemouth
South Shields
Sunderland
Hartlepool
Middlesbrough
Hull
Grimsby
Gt Yarmouth
Ispwich
Southend
London

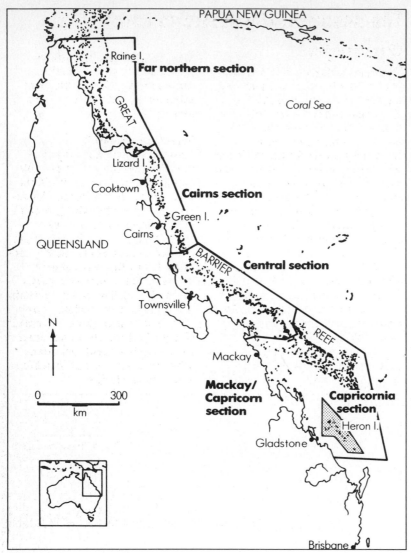

The Capricornia Section

The Capricornia Section is the first section to be developed and implemented (1 July 1981). Within this area zones are established, each with different objectives, as follows:

GENERAL USE 'A' ZONE

Objectives of the Zone

The objectives of the General Use 'A' Zone are:

a to provide opportunities for reasonable use consistent with the conservation of the Great Barrier Reef;

b to provide areas for trawling; and

c to provide for Replenishment Areas where fishing and collecting are prohibited for limited periods to enable resource stocks to regenerate.

GENERAL USE 'B' ZONE

Objectives of the Zone

The objectives of the General Use 'B' Zone are:

a to provide opportunities for reasonable use consistent with the conservation of the Great Barrier Reef;

b to protect reefs from the potential effects of trawling and commercial shipping;

c to provide for Replenishment Areas where fishing and collecting are prohibited for limited periods to enable resource stocks to regenerate; and

d to provide for Seasonal Closure Areas to protect from human intrusion some important bird and turtles.

Figure 19 The Great Barrier Reef and Marine Park Authority

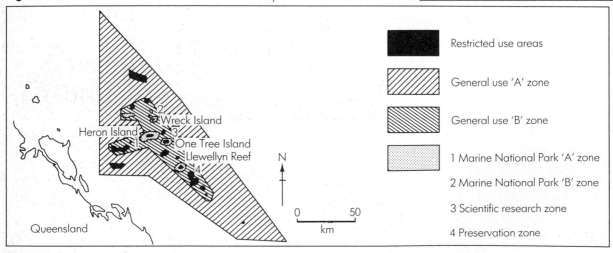

Figure 20 The Capricornia Section

The ocean wilderness and coast

Characteristics

The term 'wilderness' strictly applied refers to areas without any human habitation or influence. The oceans may be free of human habitation but they are not free from human influence. Even the remote Southern Ocean has been denuded of whales, and suffers from persistent atmospheric pollution (witness the emergence of ozone destruction at high latitudes). Rather, the ocean wilderness and coasts are those areas which are uninhabited or sparsely inhabited, and which are relatively unaffected by human activities. It is these areas which bestow Earth's primary characteristics as a 'water planet'.

The principal activities in these regions (Figure 23) are scientific research, distant water fisheries, deep-sea navigation routes and strategic activities (such as navigation of nuclear submarines, and missile-testing ranges).

Scientific research

These areas are the subject of modern international large-scale monitoring and research efforts, such as the World Ocean Circulation Experiment (WOCE), a detailed long-term study of ocean circulation, and the Biogeochemical Ocean Flux Study (BOFS) concerned with the geochemical cycles in the oceans (see pages 171 and 188). The oceans contain much of the key to global environmental change (such as climatic change) and long-term pollution risks associated with persistent substances such as radionuclides and organochlorines.

Strategic

Research/Education

Navigation, shipping, ports communications

Fisheries

Conservation

Figure 21 The ocean wilderness and coast: a research ship from the British Antarctic Survey

Ocean survey to investigate impact of climate change

THE biggest global study to chart the effects of climate change has been launched from an international head-quarters in Surrey. The World Ocean Circulation Experiment (WOCE) will gather data needed to build climate models on the needs of the next century.

Dr Peter Koltermann, director of the international project office at the Institute of Oceanographic Sciences at Wormley, near Guildford, explained: "The key to understanding climate change lies in the ocean but no one knows how it acts as a memory for activity in the atmosphere.

The project, planned since 1985, was approved by the World Climate Programme in Paris two years ago. Scientists from more than 40 countries will gather information for five years. Satellites will record global sea-surface temperatures, winds and currents. Surface and deep-water measurements from ship-based surveys covering hundreds of thousands of miles are also planned. The first vessel leaves Argentina for the South Atlantic this month.

Source: Nigel Williams, *Guardian*, 6 January 1990

Fishing

The most important distant-water fisheries are the tropical tuna fisheries (Figure 22 and 23). Commercial whaling began in the North Atlantic on a large scale in the seventeenth century and continued for much of the present century mainly in the Southern Ocean. It has now been banned by the International Whaling Commission (IWC), although controversy remains over the catching of whales for 'scientific purposes', including monitoring stocks.

Navigation and shipping

The really important deep ocean sea routes are relatively few, crossing the North Atlantic and North Pacific linking the major core regions of the global economy (refer back to Figure 2).

Figure 23 Deep-sea vessel fishing for tuna

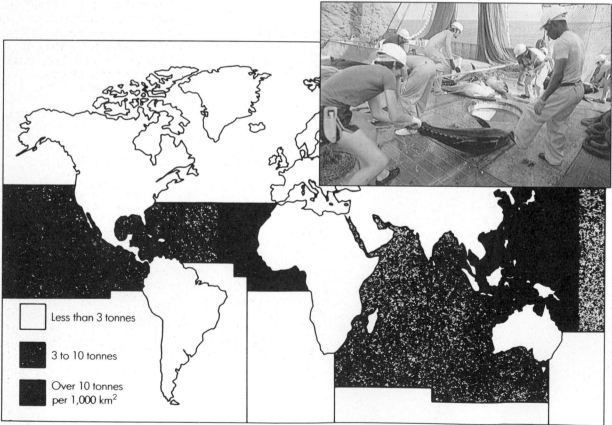

Figure 22 Major tuna fishing areas

Less than 3 tonnes

3 to 10 tonnes

Over 10 tonnes per 1,000 km²

Other important routes are those through the Mediterranean Sea and northern Indian Ocean, with links southward along both the American and African coasts and across to southern Australia.

Strategic uses

The modern strategic use of the ocean as a means of long-distance communication for surface fleets, and constant patrol by nuclear submarines, is well known. The North Atlantic and Pacific approaches to North America have been 'wired' with listening devices for detection of submarines. The oceans, particularly the enormous Pacific, have also been used as rocket ranges for testing intercontinental ballistic missiles, and of course for testing atomic bombs – first on the surface in the 1940s and 1950s, and later underground, on the coral atolls of French Polynesia (Figure 24).

Figure 24   US atom bomb explosion on Bikini Atoll in 1946

?

1   Using the four principal activities of the ocean wilderness and coasts, list the effects of human actions on these environments

Management problems

The management of ocean wildernesses poses a particularly complex challenge. These are the traditional high seas; they remain so for navigational and strategic use and for scientific research.

Fisheries are regulated by international commissions. A fledgling environmental protection programme is taking shape for a number of areas in the form of the United Nations Environmental Programme's (UNEP) Regional Seas Programme (Figure 25).

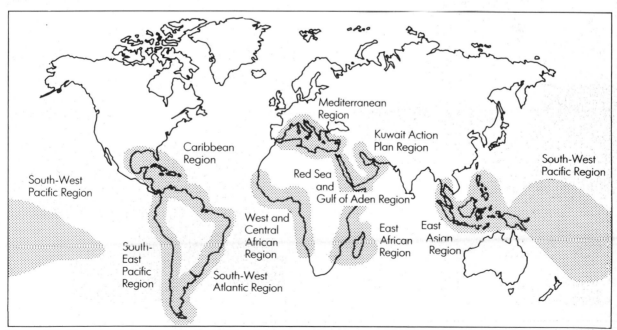

Figure 25   Management of ocean areas: the UNEP regional seas programme

The management issues involved in the oceans were brought to a head during the UNCLOS III negotiations over the considerable resource potential of parts of the deep-sea bed for polymetallic nodules (Figure 26). These are rich in certain metals likely to be in short supply in the foreseeable future, such as manganese, cobalt, nickel, and tungsten.

This circumstance led to a proposal for the creation of the Area (in other words the deep-sea bed beyond the exclusive economic zones) as the common heritage of humanity, to be administered for the good of all by the International Seabed Authority as an agency of the United Nations. This proposal was strongly supported by the Group of 77 (the economically developing countries – far more than 77 in all) at the negotiations. It led to a potential serious weakening of the 1982 Convention, as a small number of key states possessing deep-sea mining technology (USA, UK,

West Germany and Italy) refused to sign the treaty on account of these provisions. Nonetheless, a Preparatory Commission has been set up to make all necessary arrangements on the assumption that the 1982 Convention will come into force in the 1990s.

A second major challenge in deep-ocean management is to maintain the large marine ecosystems of which it is composed. As already noted, the most notable of these – the Southern Ocean – has been fundamentally altered by the decimation of the whale population in the course of the twentieth century. It is particularly appropriate, therefore, that the first international convention to make explicit provision for the conservation of an oceanic ecosystem is the Convention for the Conservation of Antarctic Marine Living Resources (CCAMLR) (Figure 27). This is administered from Hobart in Tasmania, on the edge of the world's greatest wilderness, the Southern Ocean, and Antarctica

beyond. It is worth noting that Antarctica itself is, of course, administered by a small number of nations primarily for scientific purposes under the Antarctic Treaty System.

?

1 A UK mining consortium wishes to establish a deep ocean mining venture in the Pacific Ocean. The water depth at the site is 5,000 metres and is 300 km from the nearest deep-water port (which has no processing facilities). The consortium hopes to extract 10 million tonnes of ore per year. The value of the raw ore equals £50,000 per tonne of metal content. Research is needed on weather conditions, disposal of dredge spoil and the effects of ocean life.

Identify the environmental, political and economic considerations involved, together with the major decision makers. What roles might the UK government, the United Nations and the consortium play in the enterprise?

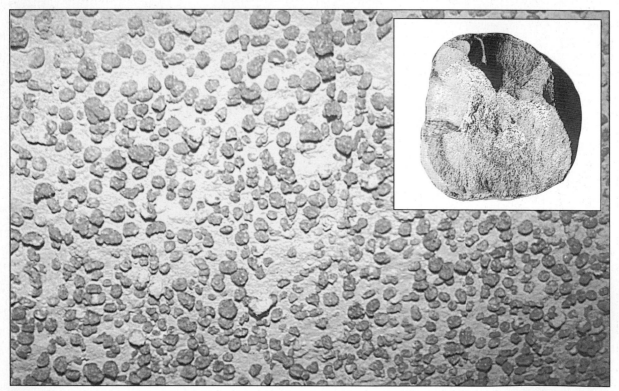

Figure 26 Manganese nodules on the sea bed and a section through a nodule

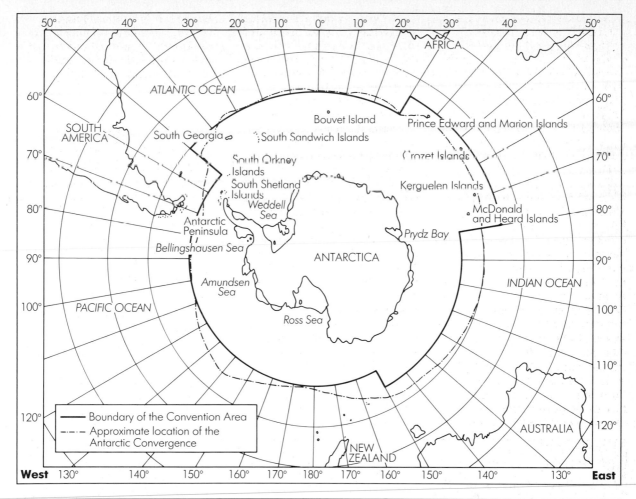

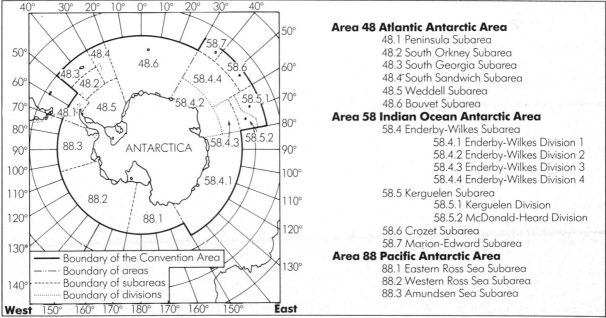

Area 48 Atlantic Antarctic Area
48.1 Peninsula Subarea
48.2 South Orkney Subarea
48.3 South Georgia Subarea
48.4 South Sandwich Subarea
48.5 Weddell Subarea
48.6 Bouvet Subarea

Area 58 Indian Ocean Antarctic Area
58.4 Enderby-Wilkes Subarea
    58.4.1 Enderby-Wilkes Division 1
    58.4.2 Enderby-Wilkes Division 2
    58.4.3 Enderby-Wilkes Division 3
    58.4.4 Enderby-Wilkes Division 4
58.5 Kerguelen Subarea
    58.5.1 Kerguelen Division
    58.5.2 McDonald-Heard Division
58.6 Crozet Subarea
58.7 Marion-Edward Subarea

Area 88 Pacific Antarctic Area
88.1 Eastern Ross Sea Subarea
88.2 Western Ross Sea Subarea
88.3 Amundsen Sea Subarea

Figure 27 The CCAMLR Area

Development and management: present and future

The development and management of the world ocean is one of the key challenges facing humankind as we move into the twenty-first century. Indeed the 1982 Convention on the Law of the Sea is unique in the wide measure of agreement reached among all nations – perhaps second only to the formation of the United Nations itself. The management of the oceans assumes special significance because the oceans are so important in influencing global climate and humans are dependent on ocean resources.

There are four points to be emphasised in the overall approach to ocean development and management:

1　the decision-making groups;

2　the technical development and management tasks;

3　the general management approach; and

4　the regional frameworks involved.

Decision-makers

Development and management is carried out by groups of people organised in various ways and for different purposes. A primary responsibility obviously lies with government and, especially with the specialist agencies set up to manage particular aspects (such as fisheries, marine science or environmental protection).

The second set of groups is the private sector – the sea users with primary responsibilities for development, ranging from individuals (especially in marine recreation) through small businesses (especially fisheries) to giant corporations such as the offshore oil industry and shipping companies.

The third set is the voluntary sector, which is particularly active in conservation, and includes well-known names such as Greenpeace and Friends of the Earth. Their principal function is to focus the considerable public interest in the sea, for education and recreation, and to bring political pressure to bear on both government and developers as specific issues emerge. These issues range from nuclear weapons testing in the South Pacific to polluted beaches in urban industrial areas.

Development and management

The first level of development and management is the practical, technical level already outlined, which is where day-to-day decisions are taken. For example, management of the fisheries involves gear regulation, quotas, closed seasons and areas, and vessel licensing. The application of these tools in various combinations to achieve both effective conservation of stocks and stable employment is a complex, specialised business. Much of the technical management workload begins with specific project development, such as introduction of new fishing gear or building an offshore oil platform.

Technical management operates within a general management framework which involves co-ordination of technical management inputs – such as the fishing example noted above – and development of policy. This in turn brings in what may be termed second-order management objectives, such as political motives and economic circumstances which influence the sea uses in question. These can be among the most difficult decisions to take.

Regional framework

Finally is the regional dimension within which all the decision-making takes place. The most pressure is undoubtedly on the urban seas and coasts, and the shelf seas and rural coasts. In particular, these pose problems of conflict among uses, excessive extraction of resources, and enormous environmental impacts (Figure 28). As it happens, most of these areas are in temperate or sub-tropical waters with a dynamic, relatively resilient marine environment.

By contrast, the relatively little used deep ocean wildernesses are often ecologically fragile, tropical or polar regions, many bordered by less developed countries and regions possessing limited scientific and administrative resources for effective management. It is here, in the deep ocean basins, that a conflict over resource use has occurred. This conflict has partly focused on industrial versus developing countries. The oceans remain a primary theatre for resolution of conflicts: people versus the environment, and rich versus poor. It is to be hoped that the Law of the Sea Convention of 1982 will prove a promising technical management response to these general management challenges.

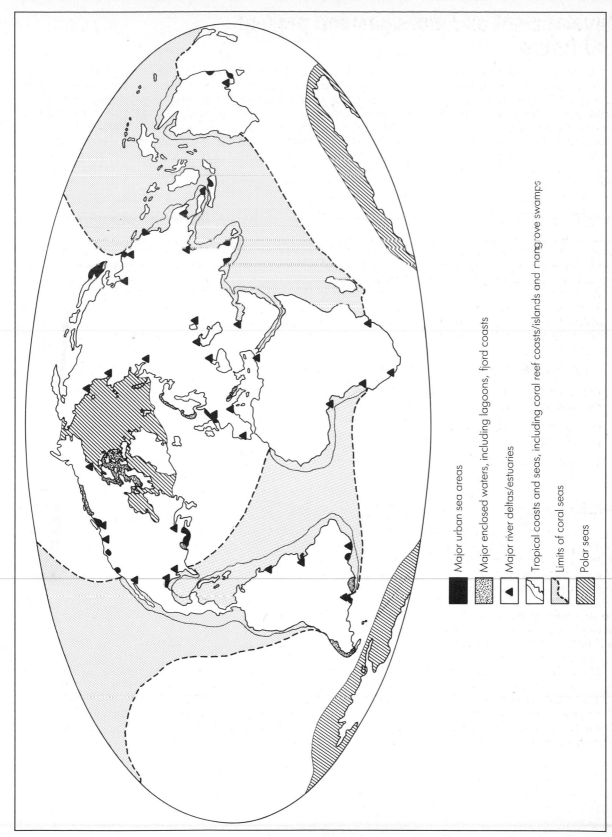

Figure 28 Sea use management problem areas

Major urban sea areas

Major enclosed waters, including lagoons, fjord coasts

Major river deltas/estuaries

Tropical coasts and seas, including coral reef coasts/islands and mangrove swamps

Limits of coral seas

Polar seas

The Seychelles: data sheet

The Seychelles is a group of about 92 islands in the Indian Ocean, about 1,200 km from the coasts of East Africa, Madagascar and India (Figures 29 and 30). The country achieved independence from Britain in 1976.

Area: Total land area of 453 sq. km, although the islands are scattered over an area of 1,035,995 sq.km.

Population: 70,000 (85% live on the main island, Mahé).

Capital: Victoria, on the island of Mahé.

Climate: Temperature averages between 24° and 30°C; average annual rainfall varies between 132cm and 234cm.

Economy: Tourism is the main economic activity (see pages 242–3). Tuna fishing is being promoted to lessen dependence on tourism.

Politics: The government pursues a non-aligned foreign policy. The islands are strategically important, as they lie on major shipping routes for oil tankers from the Gulf. The Seychelles is part of the Indian Ocean Commission, set up in 1982 and comprising the Seychelles, Madagascar, the Comoros, Mauritius and Réunion. The IOC promotes co-operation in the region, including maritime surveillance. The Seychelles has a US Air Force tracking base on Mahé and a BBC transmitting station, but also receives assistance from North Korea and the USSR. Soviet, French, British and US military ships use the dock facilities.

Main islands

Mahé: This is the largest and most inhabited island. It is a granite island with lush tropical vegetation and some agriculture. The capital, Victoria, is a port with a harbour serving the fishing industry. The island is also the most developed for tourism, with opportunities for swimming, boating, snorkelling and fishing.

Praslin: This is the second largest island in the Seychelles. It is a granite island with lush vegetation. It is popular with tourists, but development has been kept small-scale. It contains the Vallée de Mai National Park which protects the unique 'Coco de mer' double coconut palm and the rare black parrot.

La Digue: This is a granite island, similar to Praslin, but much smaller.

Fregate: This is a granite island, sparsely inhabited and remote but visited by tourists. It contains several unique and rare species, including birds and giant tortoises.

Bird Island: This is a privately-owned coral island, with one hotel. As its name suggests, it is home to thousands of birds, many of them of rare species. This island has a barrier reef offshore, ideal for snorkelling and swimming.

Desroches Island: This is a coral island in the Amirantes group, a long way from the main group of islands. There is extensive scope for water sports, including windsurfing, waterskiing and diving.

Aldabra Islands: A group of very remote coral atolls, the Aldabras are undeveloped, but are a United Nations world heritage site because of the 150,000 giant land tortoises present on the islands.

1 Work in small groups. Assume that the Seychelles wishes to produce a sea use plan for its exclusive economic zone.

a Trace the map (Figure 30). Illustrate the marine and coastal environment and its uses. Label the EEZ (refer back to Figure 4) and add major sea routes (Figure 2).

b Read p. 194 and pp. 196–7. Identify the major decision-making interests and allocate roles and responsibilities in the planning process to each.

c Construct the sea use plan. (Refer to the Capricornia section in Figures 19 and 20.)

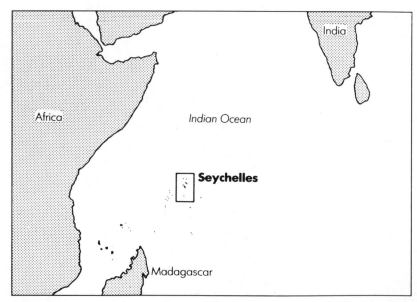

Figure 29   Location of the Seychelles

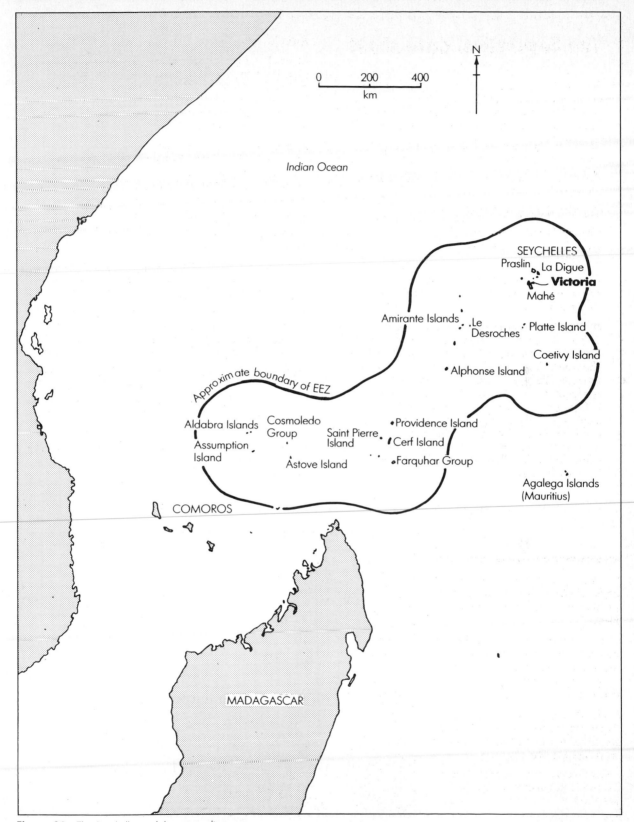

Figure 30 The Seychelles and the surrounding area

Fishing for the money-spinners in waters close to home

The commercial harbour at Victoria, Mahé

TOURISTS are a fickle lot and the Seychelles has been trying to overcome its dependence on the industry and exploit other resources, few though they may be.

So far, only fishing has emerged in recent years to rival the vital role tourism plays in the economy, but a growing deficit has forced the Seychellois to look elsewhere for needed revenue.

The country's distance from other markets and steep freight costs as well as a tiny population rule out many forms of enterprise. High wage rates mean that Seychellois are not attractive to multinationals seeking cheap sources of labour. And a brain drain of about 1,000 migrants a year has serious depleted the already small pool or skilled labour.

"The end result is that almost anything we manufacture here we can import it cheaper," said Mr Jacques Hodoul, the Minister for National Economic Development. It is still a government priority, however, to become less dependent on imports of food and other basics to save on foreign exchange.

Although the French settlers who arrived two centuries ago were attracted to the Seychelles by the prospects of farming copra, cinnamon bark, vanilla and patchoulli plantations, the prices of these commodities have fallen too low because of stiff competition on the world market to be exported at a profit.

Nearly half the country's land has been designated nature reserves and little of the remainder is suitable for cultivation.

Fishing of the rich tuna stocks in the western Indian Ocean was seized on in the early 1980s as a potentially valuable sources of income.

Licensing of foreign fishing vessels in the 300-mile Seychelles economic zone offered the first revenue opportunity.

Last year, the country earned about $4.9 million from granting monthly fishing licences to the 48 foreign purse-seiners – including 20 from Spain and 20 from France. There were also licences sold to more than 150 longliner vessels, mostly registered in Japan and South Korea.

Between them they caught about 220,000 tonnes of the yellowfin and skipjack tuna, nearly all of which was transhipped from the port at Victoria.

In addition to licence fees, the

government's Seychelles Fishing Authority (SFA) has been able to profit from a newly expanded port by increasing the servicing offered to the foreign vessels, including refuelling and minor electrical repairs.

Servicing of vessels has not been as profitable as the fishing authority would like mainly because high labour costs have prompted some foreign fleets to go as far as Madagascar for repairs. The lack of a dry dock in the Seychelles mean that major operations must be undertaken elsewhere.

But the industry has received great encouragement from the start-up last year of a tuna canning factory, 70 per cent state-owned and 30 per cent belonging to a French company.

According to Philip Michaud, the managing director of the SFA, there are plans in the coming months to commission the first Seychellois purse-seiner in what will eventually become an indigenous industrial fishing fleet of 10 vessels. But while industrial fishing has been going ahead at full steam, the government is becoming concerned about the lack of progress in fishing for the local market and the prospect of over-fishing.

Seychellois consume more fish than anywhere else in the world. However, over the past five years, graduates of the maritime college have overwhelmingly migrated to other fields and youngsters are reluctant to consider fishing or even farming as a career.

Despite a rise in the number of fish caught by smaller fishermen and shipped on ice to France and Britain, the government is finding it hard going to promote other sea resources including giant clams, sea crabs and prawns.

Outside the fishing industry, the future is even less certain.

Over the past few years, the country has become painfully aware of the growing reluctance of donor countries to extend concessional loans. The Seychelles was given quite a shock when the grace period on earlier loans begun to lapse in 1985–1987 and this year confronts debt servicing and repaying costs that will acount for nearly 30 per cent of the budget.

The rise in the current accounts deficit has meant that spending on housing and education, for 10 years the priority of the government, cannot continue unless more wealth is generated.

The economic squeeze has in part promoted the new investment policy announced this year which lowered the rates of duty on imported technology, cut import tax and reduced the interest rate by two points to 17 per cent to encourage entrepreneurs. The government is also actively seeking foreign investment.

Some of the Seychelles' unique wildlife: a giant tortoise

Source: Suzanne Goldenberg, *Guardian*, 9 June 1989

PART III

ISSUES OF GLOBAL CONCERN: DEVELOPMENT

What are our attitudes to the Third World?

In the previous introductory pieces, I raised the question of attitudes, values, beliefs, opinions, bias, preference and prejudice in relation to the environment. In this piece let us concentrate on our attitude, opinions, biases, etc. about other people. I can make my opening statement because each chapter in this section tells us in depth something about how we treat other countries – through aid and tourism and how we treat people – women and refugees.

Our treatment, I think it is fair to say, is closely related to our attitudes and values. If our attitudes and values were different. I think our treatment would change too.

Read the article on the attitudes of Swiss children to the Third World. Use it to stimulate a small group or class discussion. Perhaps you could as a geography class carry out a similar survey in your school and get a local journalist sufficiently interested to publish it in a newspaper. After all, do we differ from the Swiss?

THE WORLD WE LIVE IN

A study of the attitudes to the Third World of Swiss school children in Years 7, 8 and 9

Why this study?
The school children who took part in the study were given the chance to comment and criticise on it at the end of the questionnaire. A large number of the pupils made use of the opportunity. Many expressed very positive views about the study, writing for example 'I am glad that for once we are also asked our opinions...'

Others, in contrast, were more sceptical. One of the main criticisms was 'You would have been better off sending the money which the study cost direct to the Third World.' This reproach demands the following comment: As far as cost goes, compared with other studies, this one is a great bargain. But it is one in which the return on investment seems very important.

Actually, a good many people in Switzerland express indifference to Third World problems. Now, one of the aims of the study was to see how we might be able to promote in young people, in those responsible for the future, an open and responsible attitude towards the Third World. This involves school, the family, TV, radio and newspapers. In the long term, developing such openness of mind would be worth more in the long run to deprived people than giving aid equivalent to the cost of the study.

Results
261 classes of Years 7–9 in Switzerland received and filled out questionnaires. The classes were chosen by means of a long and com-plicated method (the list of all classes was kindly put at our disposal by the Federal Office of Statistics). We ensured that the three linguistic regions (German, French and Italian) and the different school types and school levels were pro-portionately represented. The choice of each class was random, like the lottery. We assured the pupils of the anonymity of their responses; consequently, it is im-possible to know which student in which class gave which response.

World problems
We first wanted to know what im-ages and ideas Swiss youth have of the world, generally. From a list citing fourteen problems we asked them to choose the three which ap-peared greatest.

It is evident from Figure 1 that nearly three in four students identified hunger as the No. 1 world problem, followed by the environment and then militarism and war.

Girls more frequently named hunger (74% against 65% for boys) whilst the latter mentioned militarism and war a bit more often. We are tempted to see here a reflection of the difference in education between boys and girls.

The youngest students, those fourteen and under, mentioned hunger more often whilst older students volunteered militarism and war.

We see then that students tend to quote problems which are familiar to them from their own construction of the world. This seems especially so where unemployment is concerned. Unemployment is more often mentioned by those who attend 'lower status' schools and are, therefore, close to their working life (38%) than by students from 'higher status' schools (29%).

Whilst the 'trinity' of hunger, environment and war predominated in German-speaking Switzerland (which is 75% of all Switzerland), in Francophone Switzerland, hunger, war, and racism were predominant. In Italian speaking (Ticinoese) Switzerland it is hunger, drugs and war. Differences in feelings about ecology in our country are enormous. German Swiss are the most responsive. French Swiss are self-reportedly more preoccupied with racism and xenophobia, whilst the Ticinoese (Italian Swiss) are more concerned about drug problems.

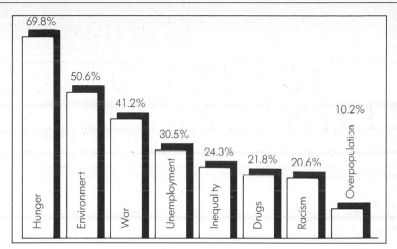

Figure 1 World problems

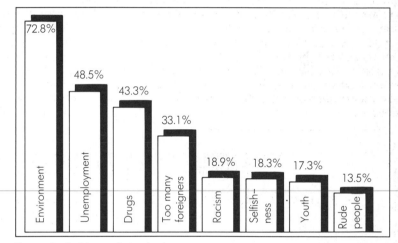

Figure 2 Problems in Switzerland

Problems in Switzerland

Whilst the main global problems identified deal with basic survival (e.g. hunger), Figure 2 shows that those relating to Switzerland refer more to the quality of life: environment, unemployment and drugs.

Girls were more sensitive than boys about drugs (though in terms of the level of drug-taking there are much fewer of them hooked on drugs). Girls were less concerned about the number of immigrants here.

The youngest students felt more concerned about the environment, unemployment and drugs than their older peers. The latter more often cited the fact that there are too many immigrants; they also mentioned racism and selfishness. So, the younger still seemed receptive to the general problems of society whilst the older students seemed more preoccupied with individual problems.

For French Swiss students, 'too many immigrants' ranked third as a national problem. There is no doubt that the immigration issue is 'hotter' in French Switzerland than in other parts of the country; the results of recent elections in some cantons demonstrate that. The Italian Swiss reported very different concerns from their compatriots. The main one was unemployment, followed by drugs, with the environment coming in only third place.

Third world Images

'An impoverished and starving Africa' – that very broadly is the image that young Swiss school children have of the Third World. Initially, we asked students to shade on a map the parts of the world that they thought make up the Third World. A majority (51%) of all students totally ignored the location of the Third World and so didn't reply to the question.

It was the girls, the youngest pupils and those in the 'low status' groups who equated Africa with the Third World. In contrast, it was especially the boys, the older students and those attending higher social status schools who had an impression closer to reality (they shaded three continents: Asia, Africa, Latin America).

The French-speaking and Italian-speaking pupils (the latter, especially) had a more exact impression of the regions making up the Third World than their German-speaking peers.

Age and school type played a role here given that most of this kind of knowledge is only acquired in higher grades. Differences between the genders are worth noting. Girls seemed less conscious than boys of the extent of the Third World. It seems in effect that, already at this age, boys are demonstrably more knowledgeable than girls on this topic.

What is the Third World?

To be more precise about the meaning of this phrase and concept we asked students to pick out from 20 key words the three which they thought best described the Third World. A large majority chose hunger, poverty, sickness and drought (overpopulation ranked fifth).

We can see that young Swiss people have an image of the Third World which is very negative. For them it is mainly external reasons (climate, natural disasters) which are the causes of the circumstances in the Third World. Some students chose, from the list of negative causes, inferred characteristics of the people themselves such as 'lack of hygiene' or 'ignorance'.

After students had completed their images of the Third World, we asked them what recently occurring events in the Third World they remembered. More than a quarter (27%) remembered no events at all, with recall varying considerably with linguistic region.

51% of pupils mentioned famine, either in general, in the Sahel or in Ethiopia. Other events mentioned were almost insignificant compared with the predominance of famine.

We should quote, nonetheless, industrial disasters were named by 14% of pupils (Bhopal in India, the oil refinery fire in Mexico) and natural disasters such as the tidal wave in Bangladesh. Finally, 10% of students mentioned wars, especially the Iran–Iraq war.

Having said this, however, 24% of German-speakers, 33% of French speakers and 34% of Italian-speakers remembered no event at all.

In terms of acquiring knowledge about the Third World, it's interesting to note that:

- French and Italian-speaking pupils seemed more receptive to school learning and that

- German speakers seemed more receptive to the incidental learning through sources other than school (TV, radio, papers, home discussions).

Sources of Information

But where precisely does this information come from? What, for Swiss children, are the principal sources of information about the Third World? As Figure 3 shows – and as we expected – mass media played a major role, especially TV and radio. For 91% of students. TV and radio are the principal sources of information followed by newspapers (66%). School comes in only third place (48%) followed by discussions at home (41%).

Opinions about the Third World

We presented students with a list of frequently heard comments about the Third World. Each comment reflected a particular point of view. Table 1 contains these comments and a regional analysis of the percentage of students who agreed with them.

Table 1 Percentage of students from the three Swiss language groups who agree with statements

Comments presented to students	German Swiss	French Swiss	Italian Swiss
Switzerland and the Swiss must do all they can to help the Third World.	73.4%	75.5%	82.3%
We must give Third World producers a fair price even if it costs us more.	32.5%	30.9%	32.6%
Many Third World people are not very bright. That's why they will never go it alone.	18.4%	13.6%	17.6%

Figure 3 Sources of information about the Third World

Three out of four students favoured our country giving aid to Third World countries. Girls were more inclined to give aid than boys (80% against 68%) as were the youngest students (76% of the under 14's compared with 71% of the over 15's).

In contrast with what has been said previously, boys approve more than girls of the suggestion to pay more to Third World producers (34% against 30%). Students who attended a 'higher status' school, and who claimed that religion was important to them, espoused this idea more readily than the others.

Only a minority (17%) replied negatively to this question which, by the way, was presented in the study in an indirect way. 21% of the boys, compared with 14% of the girls thought this way.

French-speaking students stood out as responding more positively to this question (63% against 53% for Switzerland as a whole). The oldest French-speakers were the most clearly positive (67% of the over 15's against 57% of the younger students).

Foreigners in our country

Being open-minded isn't only about having a positive attitude towards distant peoples and places. It is also about accepting other people in one's own country. We tried to gauge the level of tolerance and intolerance towards immigrants by suggesting to students three situations they might be confronted with:

- Accepting, or not, a refugee into their home.

- Finding oneself in competition to secure an apprenticeship.

- Being able to imagine marrying a black person one day.

The results hint at two tendencies.
- Girls were less xenophobic than boys (if we regroup the three situations 10.4% of the girls were xenophobic against 17% of the boys).

- The young working class students were generally more xenophobic than the students of the higher social classes, although the differences were not very great.

In the first two situations, the French and Italian Swiss were the most xenophobic. Maybe they felt threatened by immigrants because they are, themselves, a minority in Switzerland. On the other hand, the situation was reversed for the marriage question. German Swiss found it much more difficult than their compatriots to imagine that one day they might marry a black person.

Inclination to take action for the Third World

We asked the students whether they would be prepared to set aside a bit of pocket money for a Third World project they knew of and, if yes, for how many months. Once again it was the girls and youngest students who stood out as being inclined to give aid: 40% of girls against 25% of boys were ready to donate pocket money for three months or longer. In terms of age, 39% of the under 14's and 27% of the over 15's would give the equivalent of three months or more.

Readiness to act was influenced by two factors:

- The more family and friends indicate that they are disposed to act positively, the greater the chance that the young will be equally ready to take action for the Third World.

- Students who claim that religion occupies a relatively big place in their life or in their family are more disposed to act than those for whom religion is not important.

Considerable regional differences exist. German Swiss students were less inclined than French and Italian-speakers to take action and give a significant part of their pocket money. French-speakers came out on top as far as action is concerned. 29% German Swiss, 37.% French Swiss and 51.7% Italian Swiss were prepared to give three or more months pocket money.

Conclusions

This study has shown that knowledge acquired about the Third World does not necessarily influence, in a positive way, opinions, attitudes and readiness to take action.

It was the girls and the youngest students in particular who were ready to do something for the poorest. But, as we have seen, it was not they who were the most knowledgeable about the Third World. They are motivated by their values, especially religious values, and by what one might call a feeling of justice.

We must take account of another factor in taking action for the Third World: the attitude of the immediate social network (family and friends). This ought to give cause for thought to adults, especially parents, and make them attentive to their importance as role models for the young. It is important to emphasise that the values for justice have a tendency to evaporate with age (especially with boys).

Older boys who attend higher status schools were the most knowledgeable about the Third World. But they showed little inclination to do something for it. Are they waiting for a political shift or have they succumbed to the gravity of real world problems?

But it was the boys from the working class who were the least open to the world that surrounds them. They had little knowledge of the Third World. They were anti-immigrant and were, in fact, scornful of them. It is these students, especially, who exhibit a feeling of powerlessness towards life in general. What's necessary for them, first of all, is a supportive schooling which enables them to acquire the required knowledge but which should also help them to overcome their feeling of dependence and powerlessness. They need to learn that they can change their own situation and that of the world in which we live.

Source: Monique Hirsch-Cahannes, Ueli Techlenburg, *Geographical Education*, vol. 5 no. 3, 1987

8

The aid business

John Tanner

US aid being unloaded for disaster relief in the Philippines, 1981

This chapter examines the $44 billion business of aid from rich countries to poor countries. It should help you to understand why people and governments give aid and how far that aid actually works. The chapter also puts overseas aid in context. It leaves it up to you to decide whether aid is a good or a bad thing.

Aid givers and receivers

Aid conjures up pictures of Oxfam volunteers rattling collecting tins or of hungry emaciated Africans lining up for food handouts. Both images are true but they do not represent the main business of aid.

For a start, aid is mainly about one government giving money to another government. Secondly, most aid is not spent on famine relief but on paying for imports or financing development projects, such as irrigation schemes or railways.

Most aid is given by the richer donor countries of the North, sometimes called industrial or developed nations. It is received by the poor countries of the South, also termed Third World, developing or underdeveloped.

Note: The divide shown in Figure 1 was first used in the Brandt Report (*North-South, A Programme for Survival*, Pan, London, 1980), but notice that Australia and New Zealand are part of the 'North'.

Note: 'Third World' was coined at Bandung in Indonesia in 1955 by the leaders of newly independent countries. They wanted to denote their opposition to both the First World of the United States and the West and the Second World of the Soviet Union and its allies.

?

To obtain some notion of the scale of the divide in living standards between North and South, your group or class should carry out this exercise:

1 Ask a quarter of your group to stand up; they represent the people of the North. Now ask the other three-quarters, the people of the South, to stand up instead.

2 Now ask one-third of those standing up to put their hands up. They represent the 730 million people on our planet who in 1980 did not get enough to eat. By now their numbers will have increased (Figure 2).

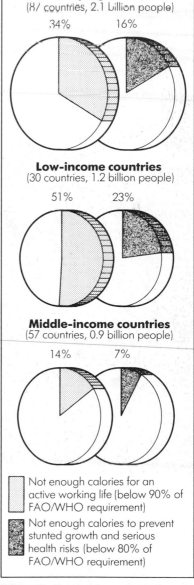

Developing countries
(87 countries, 2.1 billion people)

34%   16%

Low-income countries
(30 countries, 1.2 billion people)

51%   23%

Middle-income countries
(57 countries, 0.9 billion people)

14%   7%

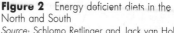

Not enough calories for an active working life (below 90% of FAO/WHO requirement)

Not enough calories to prevent stunted growth and serious health risks (below 80% of FAO/WHO requirement)

Figure 2 Energy deficient diets in the North and South
Source: Schlomo Retlinger and Jack van Holst Pellekann, *Poverty and Hunger*, World Bank, 1986

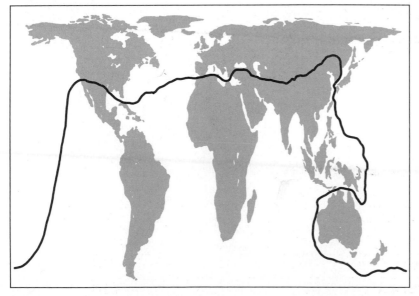

Figure 1 Peters projection of the world, showing the North–South divide

In 1986 richer countries spent $44.1 billion ($44,100,000,000) on official development assistance (ODA) to poorer nations (Figure 3). Over three-quarters of all ODA comes from the West: from members of the Organisation for Economic Co-operation and Development (OECD).

OECD nations contributed $37 billion in 1986. Members of OPEC (Organisation of Petroleum Exporting Countries), actually part of the South, gave $4.54 billion. The Soviet Union and Eastern Europe spent $4.2 billion according to OECD estimates.

The figures add up to more than $44.1 billion because money given to multilateral organisations, such as the World Bank or UNICEF (United Nations (International) Children's (Emergency) Fund), is not necessarily spent that year.

Either way, these figures sound and are enormous and have been spent on aid since 1945. But compared to the gulf in living standards between North and South, the amounts of ODA are not so great.

Whereas Britain's GDP (gross domestic product) in 1985 was $8,460 per person and, in Australia, $10,830, in Bangladesh the GDP per person was only $150 and in Zimbabwe, $680. The gap between North and South is still widening, despite the aid.

On average, OECD countries spend only 0.33% of their GNP (gross national product) on overseas aid. Few rich countries have managed to meet the target of 0.7% GNP for aid set by the United Nations in 1971. Saudi Arabia spends 4.5%, but the Soviet Union only 0.33% of GNP.

Note: GNP and GDP both measure the total wealth produced by a country in one year. Gross *national* product includes money moving in and out of the country. Gross *domestic* product does not.

1 Look at Figure 4 showing the amount of aid given by OECD countries in 1986. Make a list, in order, of countries spending the largest and smallest amounts on aid. Do you find the pattern surprising or not?

2 Why do you think some of the richest countries spend a smaller proportion of their GNP on aid?

3 Do the countries which spend a higher share of GNP on aid have anything in common?

Figure 3 Aid from the major donor countries
Source: OECD, 1988

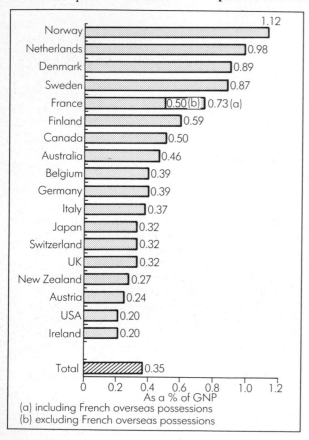

(a) including French overseas possessions
(b) excluding French overseas possessions

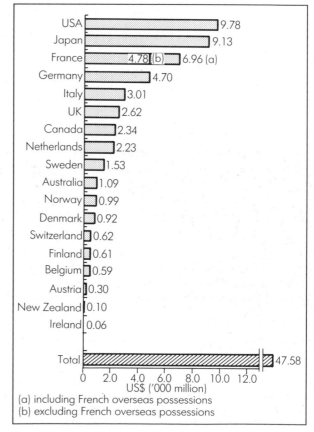

(a) including French overseas possessions
(b) excluding French overseas possessions

The biggest recipients of aid in the South are, in descending order, India, Israel, Egypt, Bangladesh and China. While the poorest countries received 61% of aid in 1986, the slightly better-off (middle-income) nations were given 39% of financial help.

Sub-Saharan Africa received nearly twice as much aid as South Asia, where there are three times as many hungry people. Amounts of aid vary greatly from $15 per person in Ethiopia in 1986, to $3 for each Mexican and $2.70 for every Indian.

The uneven distribution of aid to the South reflects the wide differences in living standards between those countries. It is also a product of the various motivations for donors to spend their aid in different countries.

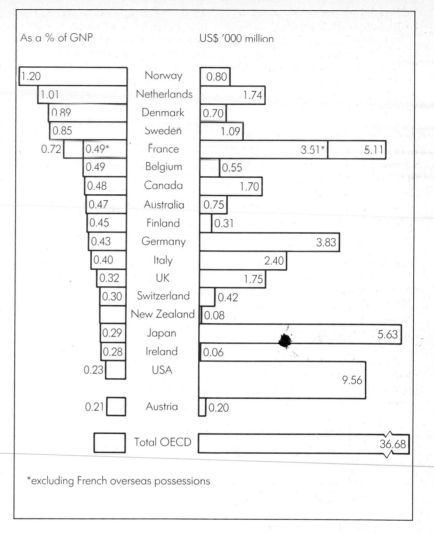

Figure 4 Aid from OECD countries in 1986
Source: OECD, 1988

As a % of GNP		Country	US$ '000 million	
1.20		Norway	0.80	
1.01		Netherlands		1.74
0.89		Denmark	0.70	
0.85		Sweden		1.09
0.72	0.49*	France		3.51* 5.11
	0.49	Belgium	0.55	
	0.48	Canada		1.70
	0.47	Australia	0.75	
	0.45	Finland	0.31	
	0.43	Germany		3.83
	0.40	Italy		2.40
	0.32	UK		1.75
	0.30	Switzerland	0.42	
		New Zealand	0.08	
	0.29	Japan		5.63
	0.28	Ireland	0.06	
0.23		USA		9.56
0.21		Austria	0.20	
		Total OECD		36.68

*excluding French overseas possessions

The motivations for aid

People and governments give aid to poor people and poor countries for all kinds of reasons.

Sometimes they give aid for straightforward humanitarian reasons, sometimes out of political motivation and sometimes for commercial advantage.

Charity for the hungry

When famine struck many of the countries on the southern fringes of the Sahara Desert in 1985, millions of people in the West gave money to help the hungry.

Ghastly television pictures of skeletal babies dying in their mothers' arms made a deep impact.

Voluntary aid agencies, such as Oxfam and World Vision, gave $3 billion to the poor of the South in 1986. But this was still only a fraction of the $37 billion spent on aid by OECD governments that year using taxpayers' money.

Irish pop singer, Bob Geldof, organised fund-raising concerts in London and Philadelphia which were watched on television by millions of people all over the world, raising their awareness of poor countries' needs. Giving to overseas aid charities in Britain, for example, almost doubled in two years.

The public responded to appeals to help the hungry out of compassion for fellow human beings. By 1986 the British public were giving £130 million a year to voluntary aid agencies, such as War on Want and Save the Children; this sounds quite generous.

Looked at another way, British people were each donating £2.30 a year (4p a week) to aid agencies.

But through their taxes they were contributing £1,193 million, which worked out at £21 per person a year (41p a week) – nine times as much – which was significantly more.

In 1987 the British Government declared that the basic purpose of aid is 'to promote sustainable economic and social progress and alleviate poverty in developing countries'. One of the main motives of any aid programme is the humanitarian one of fighting poverty.

A Marplan opinion poll, conducted for Action Aid in Britain in 1987, suggested taxpayers want aid used to help those most in need. 62% of those asked were prepared to pay a penny more in tax if they knew it was going to help the very poorest people in the Third World.

Figure 5 Bob Geldof visits an emergency feeding centre for drought victims in Ethiopia, 1985

Geldof raps Howe speech

BOB GELDOF has made a new attack on the British Government for not doing enough to help Africa tackle its famine and debt problems. He described Foreign Secretary Sir Geoffrey Howe's speech to the United Nations special session on Africa as 'crap'.

Britain and other Western donors have refused to commit themselves to helping African governments raise the £80 billion they believe is needed to put their countries back on the road to economic recovery. Western governments have instead stressed the importance of self-reliance.

The Band Aid founder, waving a copy of Sir Geoffrey's speech, marched up to British ambassador to the UN, Sir John Thomson, in New York, and said bluntly: 'This is crap.'

In a reference to last Sunday's Sport Aid race, he said: 'Sir Geoffrey Howe's speech did not represent the compassion of the British people. The million-plus people who ran in Britain last Sunday are going to be very dissatisfied that governments have not followed the public lead and that this session has produced so little.'

Sport Aid was deliberately timed to precede the UN special session and draw attention to the problems facing Africa.

Organisers of Sport Aid say 'millions' of pounds have been raised from last Sunday's races around the world, although precise sums will not be available until tomorrow. They add that it is unlikely that the total figure will top the £60 million raised by Band Aid.

Half the money from the race will be used in Band Aid projects in Africa and the other half has been pledged to an emergency appeal by Unicef to meet urgent needs in African countries.

Meanwhile, Overseas Development Minister Timothy Raison said in New York that the British Government does not intend to contribute to a new £200 million fund set up by the International Fund for Agricultural Development to help the very poorest African farmers to grow more food. Britain is one of only four Western countries that is not contributing.

Mr Raison said that, while the British Government was 'actively looking' for projects to help small farmers, it was already giving a lot to multilateral aid funds and supported an enlarged World Bank fund.

Source: Shyam Bhatia and John Madeley, *Observer*, 1 June 1986

Oxfam income at £51m as public responds to famine in Africa

Public response in Britain to the famine in Africa has more than doubled Oxfam's income in the past 12 months. The charity's annual review, published today, shows a record income of more than £51 million in 1984–85, compared with less than £24 million the year before.

But the nature of the famine, particularly in Ethiopia and Sudan, means that an unprecedented proportion of the aid budget – almost 70 per cent – has had to be spent on disaster relief. Even so, the overall increase in income made more money available for long-term development projects.

Today's annual meeting sees the end of Mr Guy Stringer's 16 years with the organisation. He leaves as director, a post he has held for the past two years, and is succeeded by Mr Frank Judd, formerly director of Voluntary Service Overseas and a former Labour minister.

Other leading charities also report hugely increased donations during the last financial year as a result of the campaigns to relieve famine in Africa.

War on Want reports donations up from £1.6 million in 1983–84 to £9.25 million in the year to April. 'Our general donations are increasing because of the Ethiopian crisis heading the news,' a spokesman said.

Christian Aid figures show that the charity's income between April 1 and the end of May this year was £2,610,000, more than double the £1,292,000 in the same period last year.

Christian Aid is one of five leading charities which have collectively raised £9 million to relieve famine in Africa and £5 million specifically for Ethiopia.

● Aid statistics released by the Government yesterday show that aid from Britain last year, as a proportion of the gross national product, was one of the lowest in the developed world and lower than at any time in the past 10 years.

The United Nations General Assembly set a target figure of at least 0.7 per cent of GNP at the start of the Second Development Decade in 1971.

Britain's highest recorded percentage, according to yesterday's figures from the Government Statistical Services, was 0.52 per cent in 1979. Last year's figure was 0.33 per cent.

Among the OECD countries, the highest proportion is recorded for Holland where the total aid was £949 million, or just over 1 per cent of GNP. Britain comes 12th out of 17 countries, between Japan and Italy. Norway, Denmark and Sweden are the next highest after Holland. The United States comes last with a proportion of 0.24 per cent of GNP.

The report costs £5.50 from the Overseas Development Administration.

30m tuned into Live Aid

More than half the population of Britain – 30 million people – tuned into television coverage of the Live Aid concerts last Saturday, according to figures released yesterday by the Broadcasting Audience Research Bureau (BARB). It was the biggest-ever figure for a single BBC broadcast.

At the same time, the Band Aid Trust said that the global figure for donations had reached £34 · million, largely boosted by a surprisingly high figure from Britain.

Hundreds of BBC staff worked overtime for the event and donated their overtime pay to Live Aid.

Soviet state television said yesterday that about an hour of the concert will probably be shown to Russian viewers next month after an international youth festival in Moscow.

Source: Michael Simmons, *Guardian*, 20 July 1985

?

In small groups say what you think are the answers to the following questions:

1 Why do people in the North give to overseas aid charities?

2 Which charities in your country and overseas do you think are most deserving of support? Why?

?

Study the results of the Marplan opinion poll (Tables 1 and 2). Now try to answer these questions:

1 What percentages of people were against and in favour of helping poorer countries? Does this surprise you?

2 What differences in attitudes to aid were there among men and women, the young and the old and in different regions of the country?

3 Why do you think so many people said they would be prepared to pay a penny more in tax to help the very poorest?

4 Why do you think women and Scottish people were more likely to say 'yes' to the question about a penny on tax?

5 With a partner, discuss the attitudes portrayed in the article on page 209.

Figure 6 A training workshop at an Oxfam-supported agricultural co-operative in Rwanda

Table 1 Which of these statements best describes how you feel about Britain giving help to poorer countries?

| | | Sex | | Age (years) | | | | Region | |
	Total	Male	Female	15–24	25–44	45+	Wales	Scotland	England
Unweighted base	1492	744	748	300	516	676	75	135	1,282
Weighted base	1492	715	777	278	496	718	75	135	1,283
I am in favour of the idea	695	338	357	145	240	310	35	77	583
	47%	47%	46%	52%	48%	43%	47%	57%	45%
I am against the idea	277	149	128	35	90	152	12	11	254
	19%	21%	16%	13%	18%	21%	16%	8%	20%
I don't feel strongly either way	507	221	286	94	164	249	28	47	432
	34%	31%	37%	34%	33%	35%	37%	35%	34%

Source: Marplan opinion poll, 11–15 September 1987

Table 2 Would you be prepared to pay a penny more in tax if you knew it was going to the very poorest people in the Third World?

| | | Sex | | Age (years) | | | | Region | |
	Total	Male	Female	15–24	25–44	45+	Wales	Scotland	England
Unweighted base	1492	744	748	300	516	676	75	135	1,282
Weighted base	1492	715	777	278	496	718	75	135	1,283
Yes	926	417	510	185	297	444	57	97	772
	62%	58%	66%	67%	60%	62%	76%	72%	60%
No	530	284	245	87	190	253	16	36	478
	36%	40%	32%	31%	38%	35%	22%	27%	37%

Source: Marplan opinion poll, 11–15 September 1987

How Europeans feel about aid to the Third World

The findings of a survey of public opinion in Europe towards development aid, carried out at the end of 1983, have recently been published in The Courier, the Community's magazine devoted to Third World issues.

The survey, based on interviews with 9,719 individuals, was conducted under the auspices of ten associated national institutes forming the European Omnibus Survey, co-ordinated in Paris, and conforming to the professional standards laid down by the European Society for Opinion and Research (ESOMAR). The results were weighted, so as to ensure that each country was represented in proportion to its population.

There is no doubt, says The Courier's report, that Europeans are aware of the severity of problems of Third World countries: two out of three Europeans believe that it is important or very important to help these countries.

However, in the autumn of 1983, Europeans believed that they had their own serious problems and difficulties to deal with: unemployment, terrorism, pollution, uncertain energy supplies, tension between the major powers, regional problems. Among all these preoccupations, the necessity of helping Third World countries was in only eighth place [...]

Europeans believe that the world regions which need help are above all Africa, followed by India and Pakistan; South America and South East Asia to a much lesser degree.

A study of images and prejudices concerning Third World countries reveals a high degree of perception concerning the problems posed by a rapid increase in the population, instability of the political systems, the disorder caused by the appropriation of resources by privileged minorities.

On the other hand, Europeans do not accuse the populations of not wanting work. At the same time, they admit that these countries are confronted with problems of underdevelopment that Europe lived through, and took centuries to overcome, while favouring, in principle, a model of development which is not based on the model of industrialised countries.

Overall, only one-quarter of Europeans expressed points of view determinedly critical or negative concerning the Third World countries.

The principle of helping Third World countries is widely accepted: eight out of ten Europeans are favourable or very favourable, and believe it should be maintained at a current level at least; even given the hypothesis of the worsening of the recession, which would decrease the standard of living in Europe, four out of ten say that the aid programme must be continued.

An underlying reason for these favourable intentions to aid is the feeling that the industrialised countries in Europe have a moral duty in relation to the Third World – this often results, says the report, from a certain feeling of guilt from the colonial era. But, at the same time, there is a clear conscience due to the fact that development aid provides a reciprocal interest for Europe.

Europeans who have personally visited or lived in a Third World country seem to be the most motivated in favour of aid to development; those who only have contacts with nationals from Third World countries living in Europe are just as favourable, though slightly less motivated. Therefore, the presence of immigrants in Europe does not result in a rejection of aid. Indeed, even people who show a certain hostility towards the presence of immigrants in their country (hostility measured by the fact that they consider their country 'does too much' for immigrants) are to a large degree favourable to aid to Third World countries.

As to what forms this aid to Third World countries should take, the public clearly favours all those which tend to encourage independence, in particular training and equipment, and are much less interested in assistance (for example, food assistance or sending experts). The promotion of small concrete projects at a local level is regarded three times more favourably than financing large projects which may encourage classical industrialisation. More generally, the type of actions which appear the most appropriate are those which have a short-term effect and which directly involve the population.

In terms of usefulness, aid provided by private associations and international organisations such as the United Nations, is preferred by the public to aid provided by governments or the European Community. The action of the Community was clearly underestimated by the public at the time of the survey, no doubt through lack of information.

Aid should not be seen as a primarily commercial interest; in fact, 53 per cent of Europeans feel that, in the coming ten to fifteen years, the events in the Third World countries, their political, economic and demographic situation, can have an effect on the lives of Europeans in their own countries. There is undoubtedly a feeling of interdependence between Europe and the poor countries of the Third World.

Just how far are Europeans ready to go? Many of them (one in ten) say that they would accept one per cent taken from their income to provide better aid to Third World countries. This is doubtless a slightly premature reply, though at least it confirms the sincerity of the positions taken in favour of aid.

Source: *Europe 85*, March 1985, pp. 14–15

Motives for aid

Humanitarian motives alone cannot explain why governments in the North give money to governments in the South. The House of Commons Foreign Affairs Committee in Britain said there was a need for the Government to spell out its aid priorities.

There was a 'conflict of priorities which we consider (to) arise from the overt introduction into Britain's aid programme of commercial interests alongside development and political ones', said the all-party Committee in 1987.

Because of the African famine the British Government increased the amount of money spent on famine relief. But the Foreign Affairs Committee complained that the extra famine relief was at the expense of aid for long-term development projects, such as improving irrigation or roads.

'We cannot agree that less money should be available for development just because more is needed for humanitarian assistance', said the MPs. 'What is required is that the development budget should not be raided to provide funds for humanitarian assistance', the Committee added.

In its official reply to the Committee the British Government claimed there was no conflict of interest between the various motives for aid. Separate budgets for famine relief and long-term development would be unnecessarily inflexible.

'Give a person a fish and you feed them for a day; teach them to fish and you feed them for life', runs the saying. So both famine relief and aid for development can be seen as humanitarian and aimed at fighting hunger and poverty.

Most people would agree that the aim of aid is to promote development and relieve poverty. But 'alongside that fundamental objective, political and commercial considerations are also taken into account', said the British

Figure 7 A small-scale appropriate technology project: Neemgachi fish culture project, Bangladesh

Government in their reply.

'The business of the aid programme is aid', said the official response to the Committee. 'There is one objective, which is the promotion of development. This is entirely compatible with also serving our political, industrial and commercial interests.'

What matters to the poor people on the receiving end is not so much the motivation as what kind of aid they receive and how much. But aid, which often grew out of old colonial links, is the result of a confused mish-mash of motivations and aims.

Discuss in your class or group the following questions. You could give yourselves different roles to bring out the contrasting views and conflicts of opinion.

1 Why do you think wealthy governments spend money to help poor countries?

2 Is there a conflict between humanitarian, political and commercial motives for aid?

3 Do governments ever act out of humanitarian concern? Give some examples.

Figure 8 Large-scale aid-backed development: a power station in Banjangara, Indonesia

ers of the Falklands/Malvinas, who were much wealthier, received £10 million or about £5,000 each.

British colonies have always received special help from the overseas aid budget, and in 1982 Britain fought a war with Argentina over the South Atlantic islands. Clearly the British Foreign Office felt it was in Britain's interests to support the islands' economy.

Other examples are less dramatic. Zambia and Bolivia both had very similar populations (6 million plus) and gross national products ($3 billion) in 1984. But Britain's aid to its ex-colony, Zambia, was £31 million in 1986, compared with only £2 million for Bolivia.

Table 3 Aid from selected donors to Nicaragua, 1986

	$ million
Australia	0.1
Canada	4.3
France	14.1
Italy	13.7
Japan	0.2
New Zealand	nil
Soviet Union and Eastern Europe	169.4
United Kingdom	0.1
United States	nil

Source: OECD, *Geographical Distribution of Financial Flows to Developing Countries*, Paris, 1988

In 1986 the United States financed and trained 'Contras', rebels who were fighting the left-wing Sandinista Government in Nicaragua. Examine Table 3 then discuss these questions:

1 Why did the United States give no aid to the Nicaragua Government?

2 Why did the Soviet Union and the countries of Eastern Europe allocate so much aid to Nicaragua?

3 Why did France and Italy give some aid to Nicaragua and the United Kingdom hardly any?

Looking after your friends

It seems natural for rich governments to concentrate their aid on poor governments with which they are familiar and of which they approve. But the dividing line between helping a friendly country and financing a client state can be a thin one.

Patterns of aid-giving tend to reflect historical and cultural ties as much as the distribution of poverty and need in the South. For example, Australia concentrates much of its aid on the Pacific, and Saudi Arabia on other Islamic nations.

The French allocate large sums to their ex-colonies in Africa, while the British tend to favour the Indian sub-contintent, which was once British India. The most blatant examples are the aid budgets of the United States and the Soviet Union, heavily targeted on their political allies.

There is so much poverty in the South and so many people, that political allocation need not damage the usefulness of an aid programme. But the temptation for donors to use their aid budgets to win friends and influence people is very strong.

In 1986 Britain allocated £37 million to Bangladesh, the poorest country in the world after Ethiopia. That worked out at 39p for each Bangladeshi. But the island-

Andrew Whitley on Israel's plea to Washington to maintain financial support

Shamir moves to head off US aid cuts

MR YITZHAK SHAMIR, the Israeli Prime Minister, pleaded apparently successfully this month with President Ronald Reagan that Israel should be treated as a special case when the US Government comes to review its foreign aid programme in the coming weeks.

As the largest recipient of US aid, in absolute terms at least, Israel has most to lose from the impending budget deficit cuts. Whether it is the most deserving is another matter.

Mr Shamir's appeal to spare Israel from the cuts – delivered during a visit to Washington – comes at a time when most indicators show the Israeli economy in better shape than for at least 15 years and apparently less in need of external support.

The country's foreign exchange reserves have swelled to unprecedented levels – more than $5.7bn (£3.1bn) – following last month's payment of the $1.2bn civilian portion of the aid for the current US fiscal year. Military grants of $1.8bn are still to come.

The dark days of summer 1985, when the country was rapidly running out of hard currency to pay for essential imports and an emergency injection of $1.5bn from the US became vital, now seem light years away.

Inflation, down to an annual level of just over 15 per cent, is at its lowest since 1972 – the start of its big upward spiral. Monthly price rises may be showing a stubborn resistance to further big falls, but at least there is a gentle downward trend.

Economic growth and investment, the traditional weak spots of the Israeli economy for the past

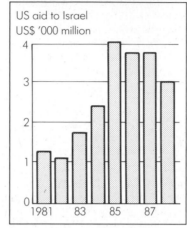

US aid to Israel
US$ '000 million

two decades, appear to be responding to improved conditions. Preliminary forecasts suggest that GDP could rise by as much as 3.5 to 4 per cent in 1987, the best performance for a long time.

Even defence spending – always cited by Israel's supporters in justification of the country's unquenchable appetite for foreign aid – is nowhere near as onerous a burden as it was. Buried away in the Bank of Israel's 1986 report is the remarkable conclusion that, as a percentage of national income, defence spending is now lower than at any time since the 1967 Middle East war.

Much of the improvement can be attributed to sound economic management under Mr Moshe Nissim, Israel's Finance Minister, and Professor Michael Bruno, governor of the central bank. During his 19–month tenure, the mild-mannered Finance Minister has astounded his early critics with an unexpected display of toughness towards an array of powerful vested interest groups: from the defence establishment to the Histadrut labour federation.

His stand against the expensive Lavi combat aircraft project this summer led Mr Nissim to break ranks with his own Likud party and a large, vocal section of the populace. Far from rebounding against him, it ended up enhancing his already high popularity.

It is against this background of a resurgent economy and a general feeling in the country of economic well-being, that the Shamir Government has dug its heels in to resist any cuts in its US aid. There is to be no repetition of the gesture made by then Prime Minister Shimon Peres in January 1986, when Israel magnanimously volunteered to return $51.6m (1.4 per cent) from the $3.75bn it received that year from the US taxpayer.

Instead, the US budget deficit-cutting exercise notwithstanding, ingenious ways are being sought to squeeze yet more money out of the US. Reductions in debt interest payments and an increase in military offset purchases in Israel are among current ploys. When Mr Yitzhak Rabin, the Defence Minister, follows Mr Shamir to Washington next month he is expected to argue hard that the termination costs the Reagan Administration has agreed to pay on the Lavi (a project financed by the US in the first place) should not come out of the pledged $1.8bn aid.

To put the generosity being heaped on Israel into perspective, it is only necessary to look at the aid appropriations Congress approved last year for the poorest parts of the world – not to mention the amounts Israel used to receive before its economy went off the rails. Latin America and

Source: *Financial Times,* 3 December 1987

the Caribbean received $410m in financial year 1987, while near-destitute Africa was given $323m – both figures down on the previous year's allocation.

In glaring contrast, aid to Israel tripled over the five years from 1981 to 1986, climbing from $1.29bn to $3.75bn.

The usual justification for this disproportionate sharing out of the cake is that Israel is an invaluable strategic asset for the US, solid and reliable in an unstable region. Many Israelis go further, arguing that they and their crack armed forces are an under-valued asset. The US gets Israel on the cheap, they seem to be saying.

Maybe. But the question can legitimately be asked whether Israel's not-so-secret support for Iran throughout the Gulf war, while the US has increasingly favoured Iraq, can be said to constitute the action of a loyal ally using its weight in furtherance of US interests in the Middle East.

And what about the filching of US intelligence which enabled the Israeli airforce to bomb the Palestine Liberation Organisation's headquarters outside Tunis in 1985, severely embarrassing the US in its relations with a friendly, moderate Arab state?

The refusal of Mr Shamir to contemplate seriously any other formula for resolving the Arab-Israeli dispute than his own narrow, sectarian interpretation of the 1978 Camp David agreements has done little to advance the US-sponsored 'peace process'.

In the eyes of the Arab world, the US is left looking foolish and impotent in the face of its ally's recalcitrance – while Jordan's frustrated King Hussein looks like nothing other than a bridegroom jilted on the steps of the church.

In the world of foreign aid it might appear that nothing succeeds like failure, if it were not for the fact that now Israel's own economy is in much sounder condition.

Nicaragua, a small country of three and a half million people in Central America, is certainly not one of the poorest nations in the South. In 1985 its GNP per person was $770, two and a half times that of India and its living standards were broadly similar to those in Nigeria.

The number of babies who died before reaching their first birthday was about 7 in every 100. In India, for comparison, infant mortality was 9 in every 100 but in Britain and the USA it was 1 in every 100 live births.

The average Nicaraguan was officially about thirteen times poorer than the average French person or Australian. But factors other than need or underdevelopment have influenced governments over the amount of aid they have donated to Nicaragua.

Seventy per cent of aid from the Soviet Union is said by the OECD to be allocated to Cuba, Mongolia and Vietnam. The major recipients of OPEC aid in 1986 were believed to be Syria, Jordan, Sudan, Bahrain and Yemen – all Islamic and Middle Eastern.

United States aid, says the OECD, is concentrated on 'countries of high security interest in the Middle East and Central America'. The top recipients are Israel, and the newspaper clipping opposite goes into more detail, with $1.9 billion in 1986 and Egypt with $1.7 billion.

The United States' total aid budget that year was $9.8 billion, so about one-third went to Israel and Egypt, neither of them particularly poor countries. The World Bank places Egypt in the lower-middle income bracket and Israel is termed upper-middle income.

But there is a strong lobby of support in the United States for the Jewish state, and Egypt has received large quantities of US aid since the Camp David peace accord in 1979. The United States encouraged Egypt to make a separate peace with Israel.

'Free' offers

It is said there is no such thing as a free lunch. Aid apparently freely given can have all kinds of commercial strings attached. Indeed one of the arguments for aid to the South is that it helps to create markets for donors' products.

'If we help to build up the economies of poorer countries, we create potential markets for

Figure 9 A modern tractor lies abandoned because of the shortage of spare parts for repairs

our own trade', said Britain's Minister for Overseas Development, Chris Patten MP, in 1987. It is said that a wealthier South is in everyone's interests.

But aid can have the effect of tying recipients into long-term commercial arrangements that are of most benefit to the donor country. The United States' Public Law 40 (PL40) on food aid has helped to create a taste for imported US flour in many poor countries.

Irrigation pumps, tractors or medical equipment supplied, for instance, by the Soviet Union or Japan, can lead to a dependency on those suppliers for spare parts (Figure 9). Aid donors often insist that most of the aid money must be spent in the donor country.

In 1986, for example, 79% of British bilateral (country-to-country) aid was spent on British goods and services. For every £1 contributed by Britain to multilateral agencies, such as the World Bank, it is claimed that £1.20 comes to Britain in company orders.

Sometimes aid funds are used to help firms in donor nations to

UK aid buys India £65m Westland helicopters

THE UK has agreed to make a virtual gift to India of 21 Westland helicopters costing £65m for use on offshore oil wells.

After facing stiff competition from Aerospatiale of France, the British Government is to provide £65m of aid in the form of outright grants to cover the full cost of the Westland 30 helicopters with Rolls-Royce engines and basic spares to be used by India's Oil and Natural Gas Commission.

Contract arrangements are being completed in New Delhi and on a parallel sale of six VIP Westland 30 helicopters for use by senior government personnel, bringing the total business for Westland to about £85m. Aid is not being provided for the VIP aircraft nor for extra spares on the offshore wells helicopter order.

The decision to use aid to cover the full price of the £65m order was referred to Mrs Thatcher for approval and is likely to be controversial.

Three months ago there was public criticism in the UK of the British Government's decision to provide aid of £131m to cover all the import costs, and some local costs, of a power station being supplied by GEC Turbine Generators for Bharat Aluminium of India.

Together, the orders for the helicopters and the power station will be taking up a large part of Britain's annual £120m in aid grants to India and may prevent tenders for other projects receiving aid support.

Westland's first major success in India came early last year when it won a £200m navy order for Sea King helicopters equipped with British Sea Eagle missiles. Since then it has been seeking orders for its series 30 model because of a shortage of work in its factories.

Source: John Elliott, *Financial Times*, 12 October 1984

Helicopter deal will not be underwritten

THE GOVERNMENT yesterday refused demands to underwrite a potential order for 21 Westland WG/30 helicopters from the Indian Government that would guarantee the Yeovil company's future for two to three years.

Mr Norman Lamont, the minister for defence procurement, told the Commons yesterday during defence questions that the Indian Prime Minister, Mr Rajiv Gandhi, had made it clear during his visit last week that he had not come on a purchasing trip.

He hoped that the Indian Government would take a decision on the order shortly. The British Government was still willing to make a £65 million aid package available to the Indians if

they place the helicopter order in Britain.

Mr Ken Eastham (Lab, Manchester Blackley) said that 6,000 jobs would depend on the contract and would provide two to three years' work for Westland's, but to secure its long-term future the company needed the confidence of the British Government. This could only be shown by placing orders for its products.

Mr Kevin McNamara, Labour's defence spokesman, asked how the Government could justify a policy of seeking to maintain the defence industries at the expense of the overseas aid budget. He said the only answer was to face up to the problems caused for the defence budget by the decision to

buy Trident and cancel the missile system.

Mr Paddy Ashdown (Lib, Yeovil) supported demands for the Government to underwrite the order for the few weeks until it was firmed up. 'Westland's have shown courage in carrying the considerable risks in pursuit of the Indian order. They deserve better. A minister's shillying and shallying is itself threatening jobs.'

Mr Lamont said the Government had shown it was prepared to go a long way to support Westland's and wanted to see the company prosperous but they could not underwrite the order. The use of the aid budget was perfectly proper as the WG/30 was not a defence helicopter.

Source: Alan Travis, *Guardian*, 23 October 1984

win contracts in the South, even where the projects have questionable development value. In 1985 Britain allocated £65 million in aid to India for 21 British helicopters that India did not really want.

Westland, Britain's only helicopter company, was desperately short of orders and 2,000 jobs at the company were threatened. India was the UK's largest single recipient of aid and was in the market for helicopters for its oil and gas industry.

Helicopters were wanted by India's Oil and Natural Gas Commission to service off-shore oil and gas rigs. But Prime Minister Rajiv Gandhi, a former pilot, told British premier Margaret Thatcher that India did not want the Westland machines.

Gandhi reportedly told the British that the Westland 30s had technical drawbacks and were too costly. Britain replied that if the deal did not go ahead, India could lose some of the aid it expected to receive from Britain.

In the end India accepted the free gift of 21 W30 helicopters and Westland's order book was secured. Whether the poor and hungry in India wanted 42% of British aid to their country that year spent on helicopters is another question.

Most aid-giving governments use some of the aid money to enable companies in their own countries to win contracts overseas. For large projects, donor nations may try to outbid each other with offers of aid in order to capture the contract for their company.

The Aid-Trade Provision (ATP) is the part of Britain's overseas aid programme which assists British exporters 'to win sound investment projects in developing countries'. In 1986 £78.2 million was spent on the ATP (13% of the UK's bilateral aid).

Critics argue that in practice subsidising UK companies is the main aim of the ATP and the value of the projects in combating poverty comes second. They say that the ATP should not count as part of Britain's aid to the South.

In 1986 the biggest ATP grant, for £59 million, was made to Biwater International for laying on water supplies to villages in Malaysia (Figure 10). Providing clean water to poor villagers, which will improve their health and help women especially, seems very worthwhile. But Malaysia is another middle-income country which might be expected to pay the full cost of such a project itself. Because of the Biwater grant, Malaysia was the second largest recipient of UK aid that year, receiving far more than poverty-stricken Bangladesh.

So aid is not simply a matter of poor countries being helped by rich countries. Aid is supplied for a variety of reasons: humanitarian, political and commercial. Sometimes the aid helps the donor country more than it helps the recipient.

?

1 Conduct a role play into the Westland affair. You will need the following people to be represented: a trade union leader at Westland, a British Government minister, an Indian Government minister, the head of India's Oil and Natural Gas Commission and a poor farmer from an Indian village.

Each character must decide how they want £65 million of British aid to India spent. Discuss in small groups the arguments in favour of the position each character has adopted. Now give each character five minutes to put their case. The class or larger group can ask them questions if they wish.

2 Take a vote on whether Westland should or should not have received the order for 21 W30 helicopters. What do you think the British aid should have been used for?

Figure 10 Construction of Jementah reservoir, Malaysia. The reservoir has a capacity of 4,500 m³ and forms part of Biwater's Malaysian Rural Water Supply Schemes contract

The effectiveness of aid

Aid to the South is used for many purposes: to build power stations, start peasant farmers' credit unions or pay for imports of food and equipment. But does aid really work? Does it create wealth and diminish poverty? This section attempts to answer these questions.

Aid for the rich

For some people aid is about poor people in rich countries giving money to rich people in poor countries. Very often aid projects seem to end up assisting the better-off in the South while very little of the money trickles down to the poor and hungry.

> 'Large-scale development occurs in many places without foreign aid, and did so long before foreign aid was invented.'

Source: P. Bauer, *Reality and Rhetoric*, Weidenfeld and Nicolson, London, 1984

Professor Peter Bauer believes that aid reinforces the power of Third World governments and makes poor nations dependent.

'It diminishes the people of the Third World to suggest that, although they crave for material progress, unlike the West they cannot achieve it without external doles'. Bauer points to the economic success of South Korea and other South-East Asian countries.

But aid critics such as Bauer tend to underplay the huge and widening gulf in living standards between rich and poor countries. They also tend to disregard the large quantities of military and humanitarian aid supplied to South Korea and Taiwan in the past.

Figure 11 Comparisons of GDP in the North and the South
Source: World Bank, *World Development Report*, OUP, 1987

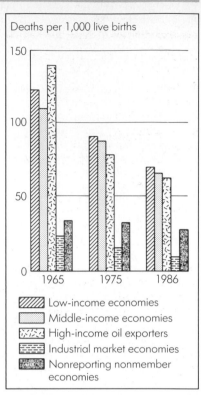

Deaths per 1,000 live births

| Low-income economies |
| Middle-income economies |
| High-income oil exporters |
| Industrial market economies |
| Nonreporting nonmember economies |

Figure 12 Comparisons of infant mortality in the North and South
Source: World Bank, *World Development Report*, OUP, 1988

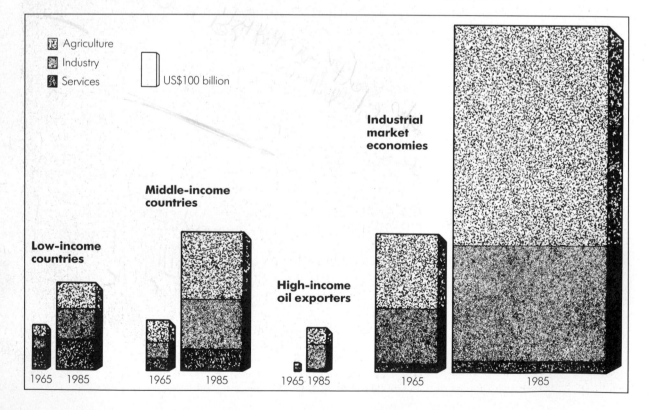

Agriculture
Industry
Services
US$100 billion

Low-income countries
Middle-income countries
High-income oil exporters
Industrial market economies

1965 1985   1965 1985   1965 1985   1965   1985

?

Study Figures 11 and 12 and then answer the following questions:

1 Which countries are recording the sharpest increases in living standards, those of the North or the South?

2 Was the gap in living standards between the North and the South greater or smaller in 1985 than it was 20 years earlier?

3 Have the biggest improvements in infant mortality (babies who die before their first birthday) happened in the South or the North?

But Professor Bauer is not the only critic of aid. Aid has also been criticised for being wasted on 'white elephants' or 'cathedrals in the sand' – large and expensive prestige projects, such as new capital cities, which have not helped the poor.

An all-party group in the British Parliament in 1985 attacked its Government's aid to Africa for failing to target agriculture. They claimed aid was wasted on power stations and roads, which provided contracts for British companies, while peasant farming was ignored. 'There appear to be substantial areas of inconsistency between what the Government says it is doing and what it actually does', the group of MPs concluded. Construction projects and help for commercial farming were valuable but not the priority.

Against the background of the 1984–5 famine, the MPs wanted more resources to support peasant farmers to grow more food. They were critical of aid projects like the Songea–Makambako road in Tanzania (Figure 13) and the Khartoum North electricity power station. Such large-scale construction projects took the lion's share of what British aid funds were available. They also tended to benefit the better-off in Sudan who could afford electric light and the traders in Tanzania who could afford lorries.

In poor countries, as in rich ones, it is often easier to target help on the slightly better-off than on the poorest of the poor. Hungry peasants in isolated villages, families living on the streets, or unskilled workers, can slip through the aid net.

Taking risks

Whenever there is a disaster in the Third World, such as a flood, an earthquake or a famine, there are always stories in the press and media about aid not getting through to the people who need it most. Sometimes they are true.

There are corrupt merchants and governments who will take their share of any international aid. But most emergency aid does get through to the needy. What is surprising, given the disruption that any disaster creates, is that more aid does not go astray.

In the 1984–5 famine in Ethiopia some newspapers were outraged that sacks marked US AID were appearing in Ethiopian markets. But in very poor countries nothing is wasted, not even the sacks in which food aid is delivered. Everything is re-cycled.

Figure 13 The Songea–Makambako road project in Tanzania cost £73 million. In 1983 it was the largest project funded by the UK

Most aid, of course, is not emergency relief but aid for longer-term development projects or to pay for essential imports. This aid is rarely put under the media spotlight, but it is probably less successful at reaching the poor than relief aid.

The fact is that development, trying to improve people's living conditions, is a risky business. Even the best-researched projects may not work out in practice for instance if there are years of drought, if world prices fall or the developing country's government runs out of money.

A study for the World Bank found that one-third of aid projects failed to achieve their stated objectives, 'but a safety-conscious aid programme would promise little for the poorest people in the poorest countries'. (*Source*: Robert Cassen, *Does Aid Work?* Clarendon Press, Oxford, 1986) 'If the recipient government is not concerned with the relief of poverty, even the best aid efforts can founder', the study also concluded. Many governments in the South do want to help their own poor but the interests of the élite and the needy are not necessarily the same.

Even when the givers and receivers of aid are determined to make the aid work, there can be all kinds of problems. Take the real-life examples of sugar production in Kenya, providing land for peasants in Brazil and drilling wells in India.

In the 1970s when world sugar prices were quite high, development experts advised a number of Third World nations to grow more sugar. In Kenya the Mumias sugar complex was created by Booker McConnell, British aid and the World Bank.

The aim of the project was to create employment, supply Kenya's sugar needs and boost exports. By 1988 28,000 people were employed, Mumias was making Kenya self-sufficient in sugar, but the collapse of world prices meant exporting was out of the question.

In Brazil in the 1980s foreign debts and the emphasis on cash crops for export created thousands of landless peasants. To provide land for these rural poor the Government set up the Polonoreste project in the Amazon, one-third financed with World Bank aid.

The rural poor were offered flights to the Amazon and given plots of land on condition they cleared it of forest. At first the land produced good crops, even if it was a hard life for the settlers. But soon soil fertility declined and crops failed (Figure 14).

In India an aid agency was drilling wells for drinking and irrigation. In one village, after discussion with the village elders, a well was dug. Some time later the aid workers returned to find everyone happy except the harijans or untouchables.

The well had been dug on land belonging to one of the wealthy village elders, who was happy to allow higher-caste villagers to draw water. But he stopped low-caste harijans using 'his' well and so they continued to take water from a stagnant pond.

These are three examples of aid projects that went wrong. Discuss each project and then answer the following questions:

1 Choose one project and explain why it went wrong. Whose fault do you think it was?

2 Which group of people do you think benefited most from this project: the Government, the aid donor, the poor or some other group?

3 Could action have been taken to make the project a success? If 'yes', say what action and if 'no', say why not.

Figure 14 Erosion caused by rainforest clearance in the Amazon basin

Aid that works

Aid frequently achieves what the donor intends but helping the poorest rise out of their poverty may not be the donor's main aim. The idea of success may be very different for the taxpayer, the donor, the recipient and the poor.

After the Second World War, Western Europe received millions of dollars in loans from the United States under the Marshall Plan. The plan hastened economic recovery in war-devastated Europe and also restored an important market for US exporters.

In Bangladesh, reconstruction aid helped restore the economy after the devastation of 1971, when the country fought for independence from Pakistan. Everyone, rich and poor, benefited from the rebuilding of bridges blown up during the civil war, for example.

The primary purpose of the aid to Western Europe and Bangladesh was to restore the economy and in both cases it worked. The poorest people would undoubtedly have suffered most if the economies had remained shattered.

India's 'Green Revolution'

The report for the World Bank noted that aid for India 'has never exceeded two or three per cent of its GNP'. But India, unlike many poor countries, has a capable administration, developed industry and an advanced education system.

In the 1960s and 1970s India was able to take advantage of the aid it received to carry out a 'Green Revolution'. New high-yielding strains of wheat and rice, needing inputs of fertiliser and pesticide, were introduced.

> 'Before this happened, the Indian economy was grinding to a halt whenever there was a bad harvest,' the study concluded. 'It can truly be said that the high-yielding grain varieties have helped to transform the Indian economy.'

Source: Robert Cassen, *Does Aid Work?* Clarendon Press, Oxford, 1986

India no longer has to spend huge sums of foreign exchange (dollars, pounds and yen) on food imports. At the end of 1987 India had built up cereal stock of 15 million tons, equivalent to 10% of annual production by India's farmers, largely thanks to aid. But the Green Revolution, while creating some rich farmers in the Punjab, also increased the numbers of landless people. Poor peasant farmers, with only a few hectares of land, could not compete with the large-scale farmers who were using the new methods.

Food production per person in India increased by 20% between 1979 and 1984, which is a tremendous achievement. But there are still millions of poor, hungry Indians, and even *average* calorie intake is still way below the minimum required for proper nutrition.

Table 4 India's improved food situation

	1974	1985
Cereal imports (million tonnes)	5.3	0.01
Food aid (cereals, million tonnes)	1.6	0.3
Fertiliser input (kg per hectare)	11	39

	1965	1985
Daily calorie supply per capita	2,100	2,189

Source: World Bank, *World Development Report*, OUP, 1987

Note: The Food & Agriculture Organisation (FAO) says 2,300 calories per day are necessary for proper adult nutrition. In the United States daily supply per capita was 3,663 calories in 1985. US farmers used 104 kilograms of fertiliser per hectare that year.

?

Examine Table 4 and answer the following questions:

1 What successes did aid for the Green Revolution in India have?

2 What failures were there for the aid-financed Green Revolution in India?

3 In your view was the aid to India for the Green Revolution a success or a failure overall?

The International Fund for Agricultural Development (IFAD) was set up in 1977 by the United Nations to help the world's poorest people. IFAD has had remarkable success in aiding poor people in rural areas with incomes of less than $100 a year.

IFAD pursues a grassroots approach to development, working with village groups and encouraging small-scale farmers. With only two hundred staff and a relatively small budget IFAD claims to be helping 9 million families in the South.

One of IFAD's success stories is the Grameen Bank in Bangladesh which provides low-interest credit to poor farmers. If a peasant wants to borrow $50 or less, often he or she can only turn to money-lenders, who charge very high interest rates. The Grameen Bank makes small loans to farmers, to buy tools, fertilisers or perhaps a bullock for ploughing. The farmer then repays the loan from the higher productivity of the farm, and IFAD says 99% of loans are repaid.

On the face of it aid from IFAD, jointly funded by OPEC nations and OECD countries, seems ideal. But for donors nearly all the money goes in local costs, so there are very few export opportunities for companies in donor countries. From the viewpoint of the receiving government, helping poor farmers is not very likely to boost the developing country's exports. For both donor and recipient, IFAD projects are not the kind of high-profile schemes which grab the headlines.

Most aid does what it is intended to do but that may not be helping the poorest people. Aid for development is always risky and certainly can help the very poorest people. But only two-thirds of aid projects achieve their own objectives.

Putting aid in context

Aid is, of course, only part of the relationship between North and South. Whatever you now think about aid, it is important to remember there are also banking, trading and political links between rich nations and economically developing countries.

Banking on debt

After 1973, Western banks were full of money deposited by OPEC nations, which had just quadrupled oil prices. The banks were anxious to lend the petro-dollars and persuaded a large number of countries in the South to borrow.

Interest rates around the world were low and bank loans seemed an obvious way for the South, especially Latin America, to finance its development and pay for oil imports. Everything was fine until the 1980s, when interest rates shot up.

The world economy was in recession and poor nations found it more and more difficult to pay interest on their loans. The banks became reluctant to lend new money to the South, and in 1982 Mexico effectively defaulted on (refused to repay) its loans.

By 1987 the South owed a huge one trillion dollars ($1,120,000 million) mainly to

> Like thousands of other poor people in Jamaica, Maria had been crushed by the international economic forces, by debt and recession. Jamaica's debt consumes about 40% of her entire export earnings. The government, to satisfy IMF conditions, has drastically cut public spending and subsidies. As a result, food prices went up 60% in just one year, unemployment has soared and health services have evaporated. In the area of Kingston where Maria lived, the number of health workers was cut from 200 to 25. For the want of a decent diet and a few pence worth of medicine, two-fifths of pregnant women suffer from anaemia. Maria was just one casualty. There are thousands more. And she leaves behind two orphans who bear the scars.

Source: Oxfam White Paper on Aid, October 1987, p. 6

banks in the United States and Western Europe. The banks had by then stopped lending to most of the South, but they still demanded their interest and the repayment of loans.

The effect of all this was that the net flow of finance (new loans, interest and repayments) from North to South became negative. Instead of money moving from the rich North to the poor South, the flow of finance actually went from South to North.

In 1987 the South paid $119 billion in interest and repayments to the banks and aid agencies. As new bank loans dried up and aid did not increase, there was a net flow of finance from the poor South to the rich North of $29 billion.

Clearly the South could not go on being bled dry by the debt crisis, but by 1988 the haemorrhage was in its fifth year. Living standards in the biggest debtor nations of South America had fallen by one-seventh since 1980 and in sub-Saharan Africa by a quarter.

Most debt is owed by better-off Latin American countries. But for other countries the outlook is grim, 'the poorest and most heavily indebted countries of sub-Saharan Africa have no chance whatever of returning to viability by their own efforts', said UK finance minister, Nigel Lawson, in 1987.

In 1986 the World Bank, the largest of the aid agencies, actually received $201 million more from poor countries in Africa than it lent. It seems that the South may be aiding the North more than the North is assisting the South.

In the face of the one-trillion-dollar debt mountain, the aid efforts of the North look like small change. The $44 billion in aid to the South is only about one-third of the money paid in repayments and interest by the South to the North.

How a debt crisis happens

a A bank lends a Third World president $1,000,000 at 5% interest a year. Only half the development projects succeed producing an annual income of $25,000.

b For the first five years the president pays the $25,000 to the bank and borrows again to pay the rest of the interest. At the end of five years the debt totals $1,245,894.

c Then interest rates rise to 15%, export prices fall and the development projects stop producing an income. The first $100,000 repayment of the loan is also due.

d At the end of six years the loan has grown to $1,432,778 and the president has no money to pay the bank. Meanwhile the bank has received $250,000 in interest payments.

Prior to the debt crisis, Florence Tembo of Chawama Compound, Lusaka would have been regarded as one of the better off. Now she is one of a new stratum – the 'nouveaux pauvres' – and at the time that John Clark met her, she was close to breaking point. For four years prices of basic foods had been rising rapidly and it had become more and more difficult to survive on her husband's salary – he is a junior clerk in a government office...

At about this time Florence discovered that she was pregnant. The couple wanted a third baby, but she could not stop worrying about how the family was going to survive. A week later her husband came home with the news that due to the IMF austerity programme, introduced to rescue the economy, the price of maize meal, the staple food, was going to double. 'When my husband told me I just couldn't believe it,' she said. 'Then I looked into his eyes and saw it was true. Suddenly it occurred to me that we just wouldn't survive – we would all go hungry! And then I just burst into tears.'

Florence Tembo is the human face of the international debt crisis.

Source: Oxfam White Paper on Aid, October 1987, p. 7

Table 5 Net financial flows to the South

	US $ billion
1981	35.2
1982	17.8
1983	7.1
1984	−7.3
1985	−20.8
1986	−30.7
1987	−29

Source: World Bank, *World Debt Tables*, Washington, 1988

1 Re-read the box on page 220, 'How a debt crisis happens'. Consider that someone has just expressed the opinion that developing countries have been given too much help. Write notes on the points you might use to counter that opinion.

2 Would *you* want to counter that opinion?

Bankers see need for Third World debt relief

PARTIAL DEBT forgiveness for Third World nations, coupled with additional new lending, may be essential in any permanent resolution of the world debt problem, a group which included many top US commercial bankers said for the first time yesterday.

This conclusion, underlining the growing impatience of US bankers with present approaches to Third World debt, was reached by a panel of senior financiers and developing country representatives.

The group was co-chaired by Mr Anthony Solomon, former president of the New York Federal Reserve, and Mr Rodney Wagner, vice-chairman of Morgan Guaranty Trust. It included Mr William Rhodes, Citicorp's chief debt negotiator.

Significantly, indicating the emerging divergence of opinion in the previously unified US banking community on the debt issue, Mr Rhodes – since 1982 the dominant figure in the biggest debt rescheduling deals – endorsed the report's general conclusions.

Other top international lenders, including Mr Wagner of Morgan and Mr Thomas Johnson, president of Chemical Bank, gave the report their unqualified support.

However, Ms Susan Segal, representing Manufacturers Hanover Trust, the US bank considered most vulnerable to further write-offs of Third World debt, refused to sign the document and rejected any 'broad application' of debt service reductions 'even on a co-operative and negotiated basis.'

The panel, which met under the auspices of the US United Nations Association, said 'voluntary debt service reduction should be pursued as a serious alternative and complement to more lending', because it would help the debtors and could have 'considerable benefits to creditor banks, despite the losses entailed'.

The report specifically rejected the argument that debt relief would discourage future lending to developing countries. This argument has been a major element in debt policies promoted in the past by US banks and government officials.

Source: Anatole Kaletsky, *Financial Times*, September 1988

Fair trade – not aid

Another important link between North and South is trade. The South sells everything from orange juice to coffee and television sets. In return the North sells, among other products, motor cars, high-technology equipment and wheat.

The problem for developing countries is that most of them depend on exporting commodities. Only a handful of nations, such as South Korea and Hong Kong, export large quantities of manufactured goods, such as televisions.

The price of these commodities, such as sugar, cotton or tin, has tended to fall in recent years. However, the prices of exports from industrial countries, except for grain, have tended to rise with inflation.

In 1986, for example, the 'terms of trade' (e.g. how many motor cars the South could buy from the North for a boat-load of coffee) fell by 20%. In terms of what the South could buy from the North, the South lost $80 billion that year because of the adverse terms of trade.

In other words in 1986 the fall in the prices of the South's exports and the rise in the prices of exports from the North, more than wiped out the aid given to the South by the North. At best aid compensated to some extent for the South's trade loss.

Note: Special Drawing Rights (SDRs) is international paper money measured against a basket of currencies. 'Real Prices' are measured against the rise in prices of the North's manufactured exports.

One reason that more developing countries do not export manufactured goods is that the North restricts their import. The United States, Western Europe and Japan impose trade barriers against items such as steel, textiles and TVs from the South.

Earnings from trade provide the South with about 20% of its gross domestic product (GDP) or wealth in any one year, whereas foreign aid provides less than 2% of the South's wealth in any one year. Trade, then, is much more important than aid.

But for particular countries, very often the poorest countries in Africa, aid can play a much bigger role. 'In sub-Saharan Africa, aid accounts for some 50 per cent of investment and 40 per cent of imports', a World Bank study noted. (*Source*: Robert Cassen, *Does Aid Work?* Clarendon Press, Oxford, 1986)

In 1985, for example, Bangladesh obtained as much wealth from trade as from aid, 6–7%. In the same year Mali, in sub-Saharan Africa, obtained 21% of its income from exports but as much as 35% from foreign aid.

So how important aid is depends to some extent on the particular developing country. For very poor nations aid is often the main source of revenue for the government because most of its people are simply too poor to pay taxes.

But for most economically developing countries a fall or a rise in the prices of copper, coffee

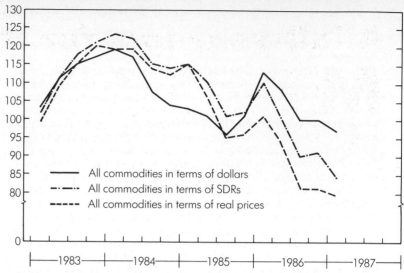

Figure 15 The prices of commodities exported by the South (excluding oil) 1983–87
Source: United Nations, *Trade and Development Report*, 1987

or cotton, or a raising or lowering of import barriers by the North against manufactures, is far more significant than the level of aid.

The politics of aid

Until the middle of the twentieth century most of the nations of Africa and South Asia were colonies. Although these countries are now independent, international companies and banks, based in the North, still have a huge impact on the lives of people in the South.

The former colonies are politically independent, but economically the South is still in many ways dependent on the North. This dependent relationship is sometimes called 'neo-colonialism' or new colonialism.

Britain no longer rules the Indian sub-continent, and France no longer rules large areas of Africa. But Japan still concentrates its economic ties with Asia, France with its ex-colonies in Francophone Africa, and the United States with countries in Latin America.

The International Monetary Fund

It is strange to arrive in the capital of some developing countries and find a representative of the International Monetary Fund (IMF) sitting in the Ministry of Finance. He or she knows as much about the finances of the country as the government.

The IMF is not an aid agency but is intended to help countries (rich and poor) who get into difficulties with their balance of trade. Since the Third World debt crisis the IMF has been intervening in the affairs of more and more developing countries.

The IMF, which is effectively controlled by the United States, Japan and Western Europe, is a kind of financial police officer. Poor countries can only obtain fresh loans from the banks, if they follow IMF-approved economic policies.

When a country in the South cannot service its foreign debts it will turn to the IMF for help. The IMF then suggests austere policy adjustments, including devaluing the currency, cutting government spending and boosting exports.

Increasingly foreign aid is being used to support IMF policy reforms. Developing countries are told they will receive more aid if they carry out the IMF changes and that aid will be cut if they refuse to implement the new policies.

A full-year loss for the Midland

MIDLAND BANK yesterday became the first major clearing bank in a century to announce a full-year loss, when chairman Sir Kit McMahon reported that the group had gone £505 million into the red before tax in 1987 compared with a £434 million profit a year earlier.

The blame was put on the £1.1 billion cost last year of dud loans made years ago to the Third World, and especially Latin America, which may never be fully repaid because of continuing economic crisis.

On top of a £1.06 billion one-off provision for suspect Third World debts Midland profits were hit by a £71 million loss of interest payments which Brazil owed but failed to pay last year and £21 million as the share of Third World losses at Ubaf, a consortium bank in which Midland has a 25 per cent stake.

But Midland set a pattern which is expected to be followed by NatWest, Barclays and Lloyds next week, in revealing bumper profits from the United Kingdom where the high streets have been helping to fill some of the Latin American black hole. UK profits surged 35 per cent to £394 million.

If it had not been for the losses of £1 billion in the international business the group would have made £511 million before tax.

Sir Kit threw into the pot £46 million of losses and closure costs at Midland Bank's equity market-making subsidiary in London, which has been shut. The investment banking activities as a whole had weathered the October crash 'very well indeed.' There was also a £60 million profit from the sale of Midland's Irish and Scottish banks.

As a recently appointed chairman Sir Kit is seen in the City as grasping the opportunity to sweep out as much old rubbish as possible in order to rebuild the bank from a firm base, helped by a partnership announced last year with Hongkong & Shanghai Bank, and a big injection of new capital from shareholders during 1987.

He said the results reflected a 'substantial start' to a three-year programme of strengthening and modernising the group. He is maintaining the dividend unchanged but the shares dropped 10p to 398p, because the losses were near the top end of City predictions.

There is a warning sign for staff in the domestic business, who face a three-year cost-cutting drive to raise profits which will involve redundancies, especially in back-office support jobs.

Hopes of cutting the high costs of running the domestic business were dashed last year, partly by the size of pay increases.

Sir Kit warned of radical changes in the bank over the next three years. These will bring their own investment and redundancy costs but he would not say how many jobs may be lost.

Midland's foreign bad debt provisions are now 29 per cent of its loans to countries in payment difficulty, though Sir Kit said the figure was 34 per cent calculated on the basis used by US banks.

Helped by the fall in the dollar, in which most of the business is denominated, the sterling value of Third World loans has fallen from £5.1 billion to £4.1 billion in a year, of which £1.2 billion is to Brazil, £1 billion to Mexico and £600 million to Argentina.

Source: Peter Rodgers, *Guardian*, 19 February 1988

The IMF medicine is controversial because it is often the poorest people who suffer most from the austerity or adjustment. Devaluation puts up the price of imported food, and cuts in government spending hit jobs (Figure 16), schools and health clinics, for example.

Figure 16 Unemployed women graduates in India: a consequence of austerity measures

UK minister in interest rate plea for Africa

A FRESH plea for concessionary interest rates to be made available to the poorest countries in sub-Saharan Africa when their official debts are rescheduled by the Paris Club was made yesterday by Mr Christopher Patten, UK Overseas Aid Minister.

'As things stand at present, the poorest countries won't be able to pay their debts in full,' he told a round table organised by the Council of Europe North/South Campaign.

'Sooner or later, losses will have to be taken. It makes sense to do this in an orderly manner which ensures equitable burden-sharing among creditors.'

Advances had been made in providing fresh money to the poorest countries through the International Monetary Fund and World Bank, but progress in providing debt relief on export credits had been less good.

Mr Jean de Rosen, a French of-ficial who acts as vice-president of the Paris Club, injected a note of caution when he said most industrial countries rejected the concept of concessionary rescheduling for official debts.

There were two main fears, the first that such a move would impair the creditworthiness of the countries concerned and render them ineligible for further commercial credits. Second, it would reduce the money available for other forms of aid.

Mr Patten said the UK Treasury had accepted clearly that the cost of concessionary rescheduling should not be taken out of the existing aid budget. He welcomed a move taken by the Paris Club to reschedule debt over 20 years rather than 10.

Without actual debt relief, however, many African countries 'are likely to face an inexorable growth in their debt burden.'

Mr Peter Mountfield, the UK Treasury official responsible for aid and export finance, said countries accepting concessionary reschedulings need not worry about a loss of creditworthiness provided they also accepted that new debt took precedence over old debt. The UK's Export Credits Guarantee Department had been willing to offer fresh money on this basis in selected cases.

Mr Patten said the Overseas Development Administration was giving priority to non-project aid in Africa with the aim of increasing imports and helping to resume growth so that both redevelopment prospects and debt servicing capacity would be enhanced.

Though the Paris Club should be prepared to offer concessionary interest rates on rescheduled export credits, it would be inappropriate for the IMF and World Bank to reschedule debts.

Source: Peter Montagnon, *Financial Times*, 16 February 1988

Third World debt warning

THE RECENT 'quantum leap' in Third World debt provision by international banks is unlikely to need to be repeated, said Midland chairman, Sir Kit McMahon.

He made it clear he believed those provisions should not be seen as the banks' surrendering the principle of being able to reclaim all the capital they had lent to the developing countries.

In a speech to a group of senior London-based international bankers last night, Sir Kit said the dangers of 'macho' provisions – where banks with a strong capital base pushed up provisions to put pressure on weaker rivals – were now more clearly understood. So too were the tactical disadvantages they created in negotiations with the debtor countries.

He went on to argue that although some countries could abrogate their obligations and run the risk of being cut off from the international financial community, 'for the major countries it is explicitly not an option'.

From the banks' point of view 'it is certainly without precedent in dealing with a going concern debtor to acknowledge that anything less than 100 per cent collection of principal is appropriate,' he said.

Provisions made against lending to individual countries would change in time but he argued that 'short of something like a cataclysm, it is unlikely to be appropriate for major banks with substantial exposure to the main rescheduling countries to make another quantum leap in their average levels of provisions.'

His view of provisions, he said, suggested strongly 'that present levels should not be regarded as only one step on a long progression to 100 per cent.'

Sir Kit dismissed as 'oversimplified' the view of some major governments that the issue of developing country debt could be left to banks and debtor countries to sort out.

Source: Mark Milner, *Guardian*, 14 April 1988

The IMF argues that there is no alternative and that no country can go on importing more than it exports for long. By boosting exports a Third World country will be able to repay its debts to the banks and borrow new money for development.

The World Bank will only offer aid to a country in the South if that country has received the IMF seal of approval. About one-fifth of British overseas aid is now only given on condition that the recipient has accepted IMF adjustment.

'It is ludicrous to see structural adjustment as being imposed on unwilling aid recipients by bloated Western capitalists', said Chris Patten MP in 1987. He wants 'to help aid recipients make the painful adjustments which are sometimes necessary'.

But writer Susan George sees things differently. 'Because debt allows the rich to maintain and reinforce their control over the poor, it will not be readily relinquished.' Aid can help to maintain that control. (*Source*: Susan George, *A Fate Worse Than Debt*, Penguin, 1988)

Third World radicals argue that, far from being there to help the poor, aid is primarily intended to help the donors. Certainly aid tends to reinforce the political links between countries of the North and their regions of influence in the South.

Aid *to* the South is swamped by the finance flowing *from* the South because of the debt crisis. Earnings from trade are ten times as important to the South as aid, which can be used to maintain the South's economic dependency.

?

1 Read the newspaper articles on pages 223 and 224. In pairs, discuss the role of banks and the IMF in the aid business. List the costs and benefits of aid to **a** banks and **b** countries that receive loans.

Role play

Conduct a roleplay about the aid business. Assign the following roles to members of your group or class: banker, Third World president, Aid Minister, director of a multinational company, peasant leader.

1 Invite each character to explain why they want to see aid going to the South.

2 Then ask each character to say what kind of aid they want to see.

3 As a group discuss which kind of aid is really in the best interests of the poor and hungry in the South.

Conclusion

This chapter has looked at the phenomenon of aid from rich countries to the Third World. It has looked at who gives aid and who gets it. It has asked why countries spend money on aid and if aid really works. Finally it has examined the significance of aid and of trade.

Aid agencies like Oxfam, Christian Aid and Cafod market games and simulations which further illustrate the points raised in this chapter. It is worthwhile to play *The Trading Game* (Christian Aid) and *The Grain Drain* (Oxfam). Check with the agencies for any new games on the market.

9

Is tourism good for development?

Roger Millman

Tourist photographing a Masai woman, Kenya

The background

Sun, Sea and Sand

'Tourist' most often means those who come from Western Europe, North America, Japan, Australia and New Zealand. Those who stay in resort hotels and travel on package tours are most prevalent and most victim to the structure and marketing-style of the industry.

Tourism attracts both tourists and 'hosts'; where tourism exists in a situation of justice, both groups will benefit. But the expectations of one group often conflict with those of the other. This conflict creates a tension between the tourist and the host which makes relating one to one as fellow human beings almost impossible.

For the host people, traditional values and lifestyles are challenged by the motivation behind the tourist visit and by tourist behaviour in the host country. Host and 'guest' rarely meet on equal ground where they can truly come to know each other.

Much of this conflict is due to the way in which the tourist industry is structured. Its priority is its own profit. As long as its first concern is for money, the relation between tourist and host will reflect that concern; the tourist will want the most for the dollar and the host will want the most dollars for the 'hospitality' given. The poor host is always being defeated by his hunger for money. If tourist and host are to meet as human beings, this priority of money over people must change. The industry's structure must change.

Changing the industry's structure will not happen easily. We can, however, look at places where people together are seeking to overcome the 'principalities and powers' of tourism which control their communities and are trying to reclaim much of the independence they have lost.

Source: Cynthia Z. Biddlecomb, *Pacific Tourism: Contrasts in Values and Expectations*, Lotu Pasifika Productions, 1981, p. 9

In this chapter tourism and the development of tourism are examined from several points of view.

?

1 Before reading on, brainstorm in your class what is meant by the terms tourist and tourism. What is a tourist? Who is a tourist? What is tourism? Why does it exist?

2 After the brainstorm read the article 'Sun, Sea and Sand'. List the points which came up in your brainstorm and which are also in the article. Make a second list of points in the article which did not come up during your brainstorm. This chapter will examine and expand upon the points made in the article.

Tourism is now a booming world industry. Between 1961 and 1976, international tourist traffic more than trebled. Income from tourists in the same period increased more than five-fold. By the late 1970s overseas travellers spent something like one thousand million US dollars every day. The number of international tourists doubles every four years. In the late 1980s, over 400 million people from economically developed countries (including Australia and Japan) took holidays abroad each year, making tourism one of the world's largest industries, larger than the arms trade.

Table 1 Who goes where

Geographical location, language and historical connections all play their part in directing Western tourists to Third World countries. Here we show the nationalities of visitors to some of the popular destinations in 1982.

Tourists' nationality	Destination			
	Haiti	Kenya	Indonesia	India
USA	45%	9%	9%	4%
France	12%	4%	n.a.	5%
Canada	9%	2%	1%	2%
W. Germany	3%	19%	n.a.	4%
Italy	2%	6%	n.a.	n.a.
UK	1%	13%	9%	9%
Netherlands	1%	n.a.	n.a.	n.a.
Switzerland	8%	n.a.	n.a.	n.a.

Source: after *New Internationalist*, December 1984, pp. 10–11

Developing countries are now the destination of 17% of international tourists.

Peters projection

Low-income countries	Visits
India	1,288,162
China	764,497
Pakistan	313,600
Sri Lanka	407,230

	Visits
Indonesia	592,046
Peru	403,000
Costa Rica	371,582
Kenya	361,801
Dominican Republic	341,166

Lower middle-income	Visits
Thailand	2,218,429
Jordan	2,075,416
Morocco	1,815,408
Egypt	1,423,133
Turkey	1,390,522
Tunisia	1,355,129
Colombia	1,127,662
Philippines	1,109,870
Syria	745,855
Jamaica	467,763

Upper middle-income	Visits
Mexico	3,767,600
Singapore	2,956,690
Malaysia	2,095,121
Iraq	2,020,109
Brazil	1,146,881
South Korea	1,145,044
Argentina	1,039,674
Algeria	970,000
Uruguay	621,732

Figure 1 Developing countries attracting more than 300,000 tourists in 1982
Source: after *New Internationalist*, December 1984, pp. 10–11

International tourism expenditure per head of population (US$)

		US$
1	Norway	447
2	Austria	366
3	Switzerland	346
4	W. Germany	264
5	Denmark	260
6	Holland	237
7	Sweden	228
8	New Zealand	168
9	Israel	163
10	Finland	131
11	Canada	130
12	Australia	121
13	UK	106
14	France	95
15	USA	53
16	Japan	34

The graph shows international tourist expenditure for major Western countries. But as the table indicates some of the smaller countries are spending more per head of population.

US$ (billion) — Total tourist expenditure

W.Germany
USA
UK
Japan
Canada
Australia

1978 1979 1980 1981 1982

In economic terms alone tourism is a startling phenomenon. However, tourism is not just concerned with money. It is mainly concerned with *people*, as consumers and employees. So tourism development raises basic questions of economic justice and of human integrity. Thus:

● What is the economic impact of the global tourism industry, particularly on the Third/Two Thirds World 'host' countries which now attract a large share of world tourism (currently about one-fifth of all international travel, and growing)?

● How are the people of host countries and their visitors changed by the sudden confrontation of different values, expectations and styles of living?

?

1 Figures 1 and 2 and Tables 1 and 2 set out some basic facts. Select ten facts from the sheet which seem to you to be interesting and briefly explain why they seem interesting to you.

2 Imagine that you are:

a the photographer

b the Masai woman in the photograph on page 226. Try to imagine the thoughts of each person. What message does this photograph bring to us?

3 How accurate are tourism statistics? Consider some of the problems in making accurate surveys of international tourists and of collecting, collating and comparing sets of figures between different countries or groups of countries.

4 Study Figures 4 and 5 and the poem 'When the tourists flew in'.

Figure 2 The big spenders
Source: after *New Internationalist*, December 1984, pp. 10–11

Table 2 Estimates for total world travel in 1983

	Arrivals		Receipts $ m	
Africa	6,700,000	2.3%	2,000	2.1%
East	1,200,000		435	
Middle	160,000		65	
North	4,150,000		1,175	
South	390,000		47	
West	800,000		278	
Americas	50,928,000	17.6%	23,261	24.2%
North	33,978,000		13,661	
Central & S.	10,200,000		5,700	
Caribbean	6,750,000		4,000	
E. Asia & *Pacific*	23,250,000	8.1%	9,300	9.7%
Europe	196,150,000	68.5%	57,000	59.2%
East	30,500,000		1,250	
North	22,450,000		9,750	
South	64,200,000		20,000	
West	78,000,000		25,000	
Middle East	7,000,000	2.4%	3,300	3.4%
South Asia	2,450,000	0.9%	1,250	1.3%
World totals	**286,478,000**	**100.0%**	**96,211**	**100.0%**

Source: after *New Internationalist*, December 1984, pp. 10-11 (WTO Regional Economic Statistics)

**Note: World tourism has grown dramatically over
the last 30 years. It slowed during the recession of
the late 1970s but started to pick up again in
1983/84.**

Figure 3 A private beach for tourists in Panama

Who controls global tourism?

As tourism has grown, control of the industry has become more and more centralised, with the big airline companies in particular playing a dominant role. The airlines have moved into the hotel industry and control the largest tourist agencies. International cruise ship operations (also linked to airlines through fly/cruise deals) are booming, especially in warm regions of the world. The total money flow in all the transnational businesses concerned is unknown, but must now amount to hundreds, if not thousands, of billions of dollars annually.

World tourism is controlled mainly by transnational companies (TNCs) based in the economically developed countries, so the tourism business is part of the larger pattern of economic controls which characterises the unequal relations between North and South. There may be short-term costs or benefits from tourism for economically developing countries but tourism's overall effect is (a) to bolster the dominance of rich countries in the international economy and (b) to make the poorer states on the 'periphery' of that richer economic system ever more dependent on it.

Money talks

The rich tourist has power, in the form of money. That money 'talks': it enables hotels to be built, beaches to be reserved (Figure 3) and developing countries' economies to be adapted to suit tourists' needs. By contrast, many ordinary people in the economically developing world are powerless. Often they are not consulted about plans for their localities which may ruin their livelihoods.

During the 1960s, many poor countries looked on tourism as one of their *passports* to development. They had sun, sea and sand, and the wildlife, archaeology and culture that are so much in demand. Tourism was seen as a way of realising these assets, to bring in more foreign exchange and to help create local jobs.

For many developing countries reality has turned out very differently (Figures 4 and 5). Although much more reserach needs to be done, there is already a good deal of evidence that the costs of tourism to people in these countries far outweigh the benefits and that some of the poorest, least powerful people are suffering most. The gulf between rich and poor countries is being widened still further by tourism. Scarce resources are being diverted to costly projects like airports, roads and hotels, in practice, mainly benefiting the tourists. Only a fraction of the tourist dollar goes to the poorly-paid hotel workers, restaurant staff, guides, 'hospitality girls' and others in tourist services. In some cases as much as 80% of what tourists pay for their holiday goes to the transnationals who control world tourism, or to their client companies.

Of the foreign currency that remains in a developing country, much never reaches the poorest people: some of the money may be diverted to expanding and supporting the holiday industry and services – money that could have been spent improving food production systems, better health and education, or better housing. In reality, much scarce foreign exchange earned by tourism goes to repay interest on the loans needed to set up and run tourism to Western standards. Often design and construction expertise, fittings, furnishings, tour buses and even food are imported, together with senior tourism management and consultancy.

When the tourists flew in

The Finance Minister said
'It will boost the Economy
The dollars will flow in.'

The Minister of Interior said
'It will provide full
and varied employment
for all the indigenes.'

The Minister of Culture said
'It will enrich our life ...
contacts with other cultures
must surely
improve the texture of living.'

The man from the Hilton said
'We will make you a second Paradise;
for you it is the dawn
of a glorious new beginning!'

When the tourists flew in
our island people
metamorphosed into
a grotesque carnival
– a two-week sideshow

When the tourists flew in
our men put aside
their fishing nets
to become waiters
our women became whores

When the tourists flew in
what culture we had went out the window
we traded our customs
for sunglasses and pop
we turned sacred ceremonies
into ten-cent peep shows

When the tourists flew in
local food became scarce
prices went up
but our wages stayed low

When the tourists flew in
we could no longer
go down to our beaches
the hotel manager said
'Natives defile the sea-shore'

When the tourists flew in
the hunger and the squalor
were preserved
as a passing pageant
for clicking cameras
– a chic eye-sore!

When the tourists flew in
we were asked
to be 'side-walk ambassadors'
to stay smiling and polite
to always guide
the 'lost' visitor ...
Hell, if we could only tell them
where we really want them to go!

C. Rajendra

Source: Ron O'Grady, *Third World Stopover*, Risk Books/World Council of Churches, Geneva, 1981, p. 9

?

1 How much of the international tourism expenditure reaches the local people in economically developing countries? Discuss what processes inhibit the distribution of tourists' spending to local people – especially in poor countries.

2 As you read through the rest of this section draw a diagram to show the possible impact of choosing to develop tourism on the host economy and society.

Then on pages 232–3 you will find a case study on tourism in Orissa. Read the case study through and compare what it says with your 'impact' diagram. If you feel it is necessary, add extra points to your diagram.

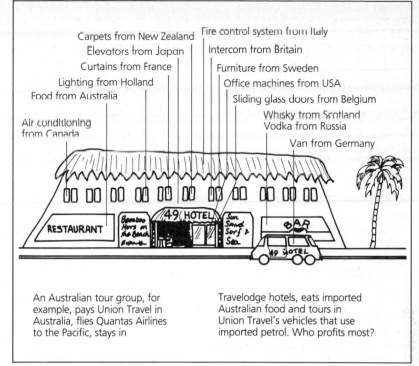

Carpets from New Zealand
Elevators from Japan
Curtains from France
Lighting from Holland
Food from Australia
Air conditioning from Canada

Fire control system from Italy
Intercom from Britain
Furniture from Sweden
Office machines from USA
Sliding glass doors from Belgium
Whisky from Scotland
Vodka from Russia
Van from Germany

An Australian tour group, for example, pays Union Travel in Australia, flies Quantas Airlines to the Pacific, stays in Travelodge hotels, eats imported Australian food and tours in Union Travel's vehicles that use imported petrol. Who profits most?

Figure 5 Does tourism actually bring in foreign exchange?
Source: *Contours*, 2nd quarter, 1987

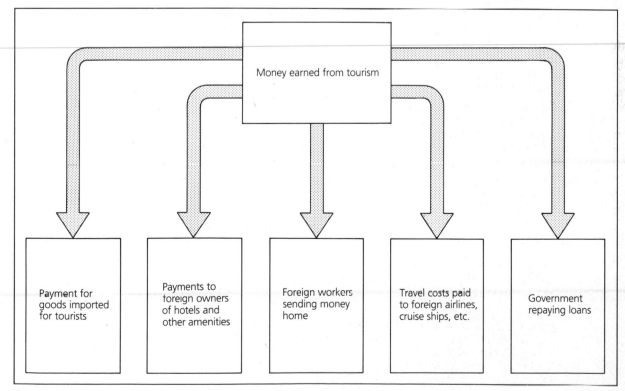

Money earned from tourism

| Payment for goods imported for tourists | Payments to foreign owners of hotels and other amenities | Foreign workers sending money home | Travel costs paid to foreign airlines, cruise ships, etc. | Government repaying loans |

Figure 4 Some of the ways that money leaks out of a country
Source: R. Prosser, *Tourism*, Thomas Nelson, 1982, p. 18

The environmental cost of tourism

Tourism, wrongly handled, may be very exploitative (Figure 6). For example, a meal in a first-class hotel in Jakarta or Manila may cost more than the monthly salary of the waiter who serves it. In countries with hundreds of thousands, or millions, of squatters and homeless people, governments – even some that claim to be socialist – invest in hotels and convention centres rather than in housing or basic services. The resulting debt charges and the foreign tourists' ability to pay for luxury goods and services help to fuel inflation (price increases) beyond levels that many poor people can afford. Natural resources and the environment become commodities to be exploited by the tourist industry with too little attention given to the needs of local people.

Aw, come on darlings – say cheese…

Figure 6 Exploitative tourism
Source: *Third Way*, January 1988, p. 9

TOURISM DEVELOPMENT
FOR WHOM? AT WHOSE COST?

Tourism is an industry in Orissa in the North East of India. In order to develop tourism, the Government has taken much care to promote the local hotel and transport industries.

Hotel Industry in Orissa

The Orissa Government declared hotels an industry. It started with the inauguration of a luxury hotel, *'Kalinga Asheka'* last year. Later new hotels came up at Paradeep, Puri, Bhubaneswar and Cuttack. The New Taj, Oberoi, Sheraton, Apize groups are interested to have a chain of hotels in Orissa to cater to the needs of Western tourists. The state Government has already spent Rs 15 million for construction of hotels at different places, through Orissa State Financial Corporation and Orissa Tourism Development Corporation. Seventeen hotels have been sanctioned during 1982, with a total of 697 rooms of which 96 rooms have been constructed so far.

The hotel industry is coupled with slum eviction. Especially at Bhubaneswar (the state capital) and at Puri; both are Hindu religious centres, known as temple cities. Since 37 years ago the construction workers do not have particular places to stay and are always pushed away from the central part of the cities. The city is kept clean and beautifully decorated to present a good image to the tourists. No effort has been made to organise the slum dwellers and construction workers.

Similarly, at Puri, part of the sea beach is occupied by the fishermen. There are nearly 25 thousand people there distributed in three slums. All are from the neighbouring state of Andhra and are Telugu-speaking. Some families came to Puri during the British regime nearly a hundred years ago: there are about 10,000 of these people there now. The other 15,000 came to Puri between 1947 and 1962. Only a floating population of 4–5 thousand come occasionally for fishing: they do not stay there permanently. On average they catch 15,000 million tons of different kinds of fish per year using traditional methods.

This gives a lot of profit to the Government, but in return the people cannot own land for housing, they stay in mud huts; no electricity or water facilities are provided for them; they do not have ration cards nor can they obtain rations at a fair price from the shops. But they are enrolled on the voters' list and there is a police station inside the slum *'to protect the citizens!'* They are threatened by police and the revenue officials to be evicted. There is a plan to evict the fishermen to a place 12 kms away from Puri. There is no doubt that the people will be disadvantaged in fishing, preservation and transportation.

Beach Tourism

Beach tourism is developing fast in Orissa today. Where there is lodging and bathing facilities, tourists like to go there both for swimming and sun-bathing. The coast line in Orissa is more than 500 kms from Golapur to Chandipur. The Government has a plan to utilise the maximum area of beach for the purpose of tourism. By the same act of the Government, it is not only the fishermen of Puri but many more villages which will be evicted. What will be the alternative for them?

Wild Life Tourism

Orissa is full of forests and wild animals and, of course, wild human beings, who have not experienced the so-called civilisation of the rulers. According to Government statistics in 1980–1981, the forest occupied 38% of the land. Now it is around 11%. In the 1979 census it was found that there were 173 tigers and 2,044 elephants alive. The Orissa Government has declared 2,500 sq kms at Simlipal as a tiger reserve. This will also be declared as a National Park soon. There are nine declared sanctuaries for tigers, elephants, crocodiles, lions, deers, birds and other animals. Now the Government is planning to declare 12 more places as sanctuaries. The total population of Orissa is 26,370,217 people in an area of 156,000 sq.kms (approximately), the total rural population is 23,259,984 and the total tribal population is 5,915,067 (based on the 1981 census). The total forest area is 66,000 hectares. It is not difficult to see how many people will become homeless to create the 21 sanctuaries. From Simlipal alone, 550 villages have been evicted and not received any land yet. The tribal economy and culture has been totally shattered. The tribal people are rooted up from their homelands and are working as bonded labourers in other parts of Northern India.

Tribal Tourism

There is another aspect of tourism which encourages the tourists to see the tribal life and culture. The Government is using small pockets of tribal areas as a human zoo. By encouraging this kind of tourism, the tribal community is again exploited in many ways. They are not allowed to enter the forests or use any of the forest products; most of the forest products are taken over by the contractors or the forestry department. Even the minor forest products are not theirs any more. Moreover the tribal women are sexually exploited, many young women have no alternative but prostitution. There is, however, an awakening among the tribal people.

Action

Our organisation is responding to the situation I have described above by trying to take action in the following ways:

* Educating and organising the fishermen and tribal people to struggle against eviction.

* Educating the tourists as far as possible towards an understanding of the local situation and the price paid by local people for their tourism.

* Educating the middle class through periodical publications with facts and figures in the regional languages.

* Putting pressure through people's organisations on the Government to change its tourism policy.

* Helping the church to relate its ministry with the suffering population and to be an instrument in social transformation.

Hotel developments in Orissa, India

Source: Purna Chandra Jena, *Contours*, 2nd Quarter, 1986, pp. 10–11

?

1   A few days after reading the article 'Tourist Development – for Whom? At Whose Cost?', you meet a person who insists on telling you all about their wonderful holiday in Orissa. How do you respond? Discuss this situation in small groups.

2   Governments choose:
a to develop,
b not to develop,
c *how* to develop their tourist potential.

3   Read the comic strip 'Raising the money for a tourist industry' (Figure 8). Again in groups discuss what your decision would be. Write a report of your decision in the form of a memorandum to the President or Prime Minister.

Homes or hotels?

Beach hotels, for example, are rarely built on wholly unused land. In Orissa state, India, many poor people were made homeless because seaside hotels were built on the land on which their homes used to stand. (See pages 232–3.)

Impacts of tourism on people and the land

Again in India, when a large tourist company wanted to build a five-star tourist resort in Goa, it purchased land that was farmed by local rice-growers. They were supposed to have been consulted, but a local official was bribed to say that no one objected. It was suggested to the people whose families had farmed the land for generations that they might in future produce handicrafts for visiting tourists.

In the economically developing countries fishing areas are very vulnerable to development as hotels are often built on the beaches from which local fishermen have traditionally made

a living. They may be cleared away, often with no compensation. In one area of the Philippines local men were forbidden to fish within forty kilometres of a new hotel zone.

Moreover, in such sites, and many other tourist developments, excessive water demands may cause serious problems, especially in times of drought. Tourists expect unlimited water on holiday (Figure 7): a hotel guest might use up to 500 litres of water a day and this may be ten times more than the local people. In fact, many developing countries have water supply problems, hence the one hidden cost of the tourists' demands is that local people, including farmers, may go short of water. Then, if crops do badly as a result, local people may be hungry as well as short of water. There may be similar problems with electricity. Also, inadequate sewerage arrangements in beach hotels, as well as tourism damage to the fish-rich coral reefs, may further jeopardise coastal fishing communities.

Figure 7 Use of water by tourists in a hotel complex in Goa, India

Figure 8 Raising money for a tourism industry
Source: R. Prosser, *Tourism*, Thomas Nelson and The Schools Council, 1982, p. 19

?

1 Study the cartoon in Figure 9 and list the environmental impacts it portrays.

Figure 9 The impact of tourism
Source: Contours, Vol. 2, No. 8

The human costs of tourism

Images of wealth and poverty

The most visible cultural confrontation provoked by tourism in the poor countries is the gross disparity between the tourist's wealth – or apparent affluence – and local poverty, as this is seen by indigenous peoples.

Tourists as a group can also project, often unwittingly, a distorted image of themselves which can have detrimental effects on the self-image of local people who are obliged to serve them to earn a living (Figure 10). Moreover, in societies already divided

'Local people look on with amazement; the tourists seem to have the power to act like gods. The jobs created are jobs in which Third World people serve the rich. There may be nothing wrong with being a servant. But in tourism, all the serving is one way.'

Source: Third World People and Tourism, ECTWT, Bangkok, 1986

by wealth and class, free-spending or insensitive tourists can reinforce such decisions. The world of high-rise, luxury accommodation, air-conditioned cars and con-

spicuous consumption is brought into sharp relief against the facts of local poverty and deprivation. The indulgent consumer lifestyle provided for the visitor may also be adopted by local élites, The contrast between the two lifestyles can undermine the cultural integrity of the host people, especially in the big cities.

?

1 Study the photograph in Figure 10. What image of themselves might the tourists be projecting?

Figure 10 A group of cruise-boat tourists in Grenada, an island in the Caribbean

Impact on local culture

Anthropologists and sociologists may identify conflicting details of the impact of tourism in different countries and communities, but certain trends are clear. People in tourist destination areas may be used as objects, presented in tourist literature as 'warm', 'hospitable', 'exotic' attractions to be viewed. They risk becoming poseurs for voyeurs, especially if the tourists use cameras insensitively (Figure 11). Local traditional arts and crafts may be packaged and their production streamlined to entertain visitors (Figure 12). Some people may argue that, on balance, this helps to preserve local culture; others see tourism as an indignity and a subtle threat to traditional lifestyles.

Change of some kind is inevitable, yet problems may arise through the nature, scale and speed of the change which occurs. Mass tourism often causes subtle

Figure 11 Display of Masai dancing for the benefit of tourists

Figure 12 Tourism can disturb or destroy traditional culture and crafts which may be commercialised (or even adapted) to make them more acceptable to tourists

damage to local cultures. In particular, family life often comes under pressure. For example, a thirteen-year-old boy in Sri Lanka (before island terrorism saw tourism fall off) found that he could make twenty pounds a month by sponging off tourists – twice as much as his father earned. He stopped going to school, and the ensuing tension between father and son caused the boy to leave home.

One of the more disturbing, and increasingly publicised, ways in which mass tourism has affected local cultures is by increasing prostitution. This is especially evident in countries such as Thailand and the Philippines. The spread of AIDS has been well publicised in economically developed countries but in some tourist areas there are still attempts at a 'cover-up'. What the tourist brochures coyly call local 'night life' is a well-organised business involving international travel agencies and hotel chains, as well as local pimps, businessmen and police. Marxist countries earning tourist currencies are by no means immune. In Bulgaria at least, the police run, or at least connive at, prostitution rackets. In Thailand, rural girls under ten may be sold into prostitution by impoverished parents. In recent years three out of every five Japanese tourists to the Philippines have been men on package tours with open opportunities for taking advantage of prostitution.

1 Study Figure 13.

a Describe how the people are being 'sold' to tourists.
b What aspects of local culture are not likely to be shown in tourist advertisements?

2 Collect a range of tourist brochures and colour magazines. Cut out photographs that show local people. Classify them according to whether or not you think they show the people as 'objects'. In small groups, discuss your classifications.

3 A friend argues that tourism can be 'an indignity and subtle threat to individual lifestyles'. What arguments would you use against this point of view?

Figure 13 Selling the people as a tourist attraction: Ireland, Wales and Texas

TO TOUR - OR NOT TO TOUR?

The 'luxurious' lifestyle of tourists contrasts with the comparative poverty of many 'hosts'. Despite differences of income and occupation at home, all tourists seem equally rich and leisured to their hosts overseas.

When people meet on an equal footing, the encounter with different lifestyles and cultures can encourage the sense of being 'one world family'.

Frequently tourists meet their 'hosts' only as 'servants' – cleaners, waiters, etc.

———

Tourism may bring better roads, transport, power supplies – but only to the tourist areas. Elsewhere in the country, people may be crying out for education, elementary health care or sanitation.

Local people often have very little say in whether or not they become 'hosts' to tourists. Such decisions are made at national level and influenced by the wishes of the 'consumer'.

———

Often, the profits do not stay in the country visited by tourists. They are paid back to multi-national travel or hotel chains or as wages to specially-recruited expatriate staff.

Tourism can give time for rest, reflection and the receiving of new ideas.

Tourists 'getting away from it all' may behave quite differently from normal – e.g. indulging in topless bathing or sexual freedom, wearing skimpy clothing.

Tourism can bring in its wake prostitution, drug abuse, alcoholism, an addiction to gambling and an unhealthy worship of money.

———

Traditional customs may become no more than sideshows for the rich. On the other hand, tourism may lead to the preservation of local history and wildlife as a valuable (saleable) commodity.

———

Travel brochures play on fantasies of a 'sun-soaked paradise'. Tourists must not be disillusioned. Normally, care is taken to protect guests from the realities of poverty and injustice which may exist side by side with the newly-built hotels.

Source: The Methodist Church Division of Social Responsibility, 'Focusing on international tourism', *Bulletin*, 1986, p 7

The tourist

Whether aware of it or not, a tourist is usually isolated, that is, physically present in a host culture but emotionally and imaginatively separated from it. Such isolation tends to confirm rather than challenge the preconceptions and fantasies gained by reading tourist literature. Also, the tourists' experience of heightened luxury, and remoteness from a strange and perhaps poor local environment, can encourage them to feel a curious mixture of guilt and a superiority which is less than a fully human response to their hosts. Both security and prejudice may be reinforced in packaged group tours.

'Tourists from the West bring to the Third World a totally different set of values. "Have money – demand attention" is the unspoken message from the tourist, who ignores local customs – visiting sacred temples "half-naked", for example, and snapping people in prayer, despite requests not to do so.'

Source: *Third World People and Tourism*, ECTWT, Bangkok, 1986

?

1 From the six examples given in 'To tour or not to tour', choose four and write provocative headlines for each to give the reader a taste of the conflict.

More than one kind of tourist

While there is much truth in the stereotype of the affluent tourist on the package tour, there are more and more kinds of tourists as tourism enters a new phase. Specialist services, for instance venture tourism and personalised itineraries, are being provided for a growing number of travellers who want to escape the programmed hotel-resort circuit. More people, especially those under forty, are travelling alone or in small groups, though they may, often unwittingly, take a great deal of Western cultural baggage uncritically with them. Despite their aims, backpackers may suffer from this syndrome; they may, in innocence, initiate mass tourism in marginal areas.

A world of difference

Our eyes met
And for a few seconds
... two worlds apart
Faced each other.

Standing with a pick in her hand,
A sleeping baby on her back,
She stopped work for a few minutes.

Headscarf of faded cloth,
Tied back dusty, uncombed hair.
Hands and feet leathered
From the constant work on
the mountain road.

Snow lay around the shacks ...
A child playing, no nappy, no shoes.
Icicles hanging on bamboo walls.
A group crouched around a wood fire
Turn ...
And met our gaze too.

What do you really think of us?
Foreigners?
Strangers?
From another planet ...
Called 'Affluence';
As we pass by over your handiwork,
Your toil and sweat.

She stared back at me,
– How could I understand?
Not just a car window
Between us
... A world of difference.

Source: Anonymous (Bhutan) *Contours*, 2nd Quarter, 1986, p. 11

Figure 14 Tourist stereotypes
Source: *Contours*, Vol. 1, No. 4, 1983

But travellers who accept the packaged experience offered by mass tourism may themselves be manipulated and cheated of the kind of experiences which attracts many people to travel in the first place. Rather than escaping from the materialism and conformity of life at home, tourists are guided (not always involuntarily) into a pattern of behaviour which is a product of materialist and consumer values with which they feel secure in an unfamiliar environment.

On an organised tour, visitors are separated from local people as if by a one-way mirror. If the purpose of travel is to interact and learn with people of another culture on equal terms, then the package tour makes this almost impossible. So, strange as it may seem, much in modern tourism cheats both tourists and their host communities. If badly managed, tourism is economically unjust, degrades the environment and is dehumanising.

?

1 Read the poem 'A world of difference'. Whose viewpoint does it show? What values are embedded in it?

2 What stereotypes are represented in Figure 14? Do you think their use is justified? Give your reasons.

A dilemma

Tourism in the Seychelles: a counterfeit paradise?

Newly independent and socialist, the Seychelles are striving for social reform and nationalized industries. Yet tourism, the Seychelles' major industry, threatens nationalist ideology and socialist ambitions. It has spawned an array of economic, social and cultural contradictions.

An archipelago of 92 islands, with 67,000 inhabitants, the Seychelles lie east of Nairobi and southwest of Sri Lanka over 400,000 square miles in the Indian Ocean. With their median temperature of 74°F (24°C), surfeit of beaches and natural beauty, the islands attract tourists year-round. Brochures depict the Seychelles as 'far removed from the march of civilization,' 'a home of sea, birds, trees, peace, beauty, quiet and hospitality,' 'an oasis of sun-drenched cays, lapped by the Indian Ocean.'

SEA, LAND AND SOCIALISM

As Western tourists paddle in the cays, the state-controlled radio stations and party newspaper expound the government's criticism and resentment of capitalism and imperialism. Such contradictory messages are not merely cosmetic paradoxes, indigenous to the task of nation-building. In the Seychelles, they indicate deeper inconsistencies.

Tourism was first initiated by the British to help the Seychelles to meet its balance of payments. In 1969, a British Economic Aid Mission visited the Seychelles and concluded that 'the possibilities of tourism would enable the Seychelles to become economically self-sufficient within ten to fifteen years.'

Before the construction of an international airport on Mahé in 1971, the few stray adventurers who arrived by steamer were housed as honorary guests at colonial clubs or in one of Mahé's small hotels. In 1966, 529 tourists visited the islands. By 1972, tourist numbers swelled to 3,100. By the mid-seventies visitors numbered 37,000, and in 1980, 79,000.

The completion of the airport was followed immediately by road and hotel construction, mainly on Mahé. Job opportunities led to heavy migration from the outer islands, resulting in food and housing shortages and reduced labor supplies for agricultural production. While 80% of the population had been employed in agriculture and forestry in 1947, by 1977 these sectors accounted for only 17% of total employment. Hotel competition for produce led to food imports and increasing dependency on tourism.

From 1961 to 1979 the value of food imports from South Africa increased by 200%, those from West Germany by 500% and from France by 700%. These increases reflect attempts to cater to the increasing number of foreign tastes as well as an increase in local demands.

The need for imported food is also reflected in the market for fish. Coastal waters have been fished out because of tourist demand for seafood. Now the best fishing areas are accessible only by motorboats or bigger fishing vessels. From 1978 to 1979, fish imports nearly doubled.

Four-fifths of the tourists who visit the Seychelles book

their holidays through foreign tour operators. Even more stay in foreign-owned hotels Thus, the bulk of tourist revenues do not benefit the country. While job opportunities increased during the initial period of infrastructural growth required for tourism, employment has now fallen off. Construction opportunities in 1979 were half of what they were in 1977 The bulk of jobs now available go to women in the service sector.

Tourism in the Seychelles is characterized by heavy private investment with ownership in the hands of foreigners and local élites. Socialist leader Albert René brought to power by a coup in 1977, has attempted to control more of the profits from tourism, yet nationalization of local tourist-related industries – such as boating, fishing and crafts – will discourage local initiative.

SOCIAL REFORM?

Seychellois society has long been divided between a relatively small élite of 'Grands Blancs,' white descendants of European colonizers; a large mulatto and black class, the descendants of African slaves who were dumped on the islands; and Chinese and Indian immigrants. In the past, Grands Blancs have prided themselves on their European association and values and have looked down on the Creole population. Now a middle class, composed of government bureaucrats and managers in tourist and related industries, aspire to upper class, Westernized lifestyles.

While René seeks to equalize economic opportunity, tourism undermines his efforts. The hotel industry exemplifies the subtle process by which class inequalities are in fact reinforced.

Any employment that requires interaction with tourists demands personal qualities usually associated with élites. The ability to understand, communicate, act like and entertain tourists, to foresee and manage their needs are valuable skills in service industries – skills which Western-oriented élites most often have. The more adept workers are at 'impression management' and cross-cultural communication, the more they are rewarded. In this way élites are culled into the highest-paid positions, while the lower classes, indifferent to tourists' cultural concerns, remain in the poorest-paid positions.

In hotels, Creole maids and waitresses have separate changing and eating facilities from the management team of expatriates and élites, an arrangement which reinforces class distinctions. While Creole individuals with the incentive to acquire management skills may ascend to better-paying jobs, they often reject their Creole background in the process.

One vehicle for upward mobility is the hotel training school. Here students learn foreign languages and how to type tourists through courses in 'Visitor Psychology,' 'Courtesy,' 'Beauty Care' and European history. Yet the school only attracts those with relative financial security who do not need to start work at a young age and can afford to postpone employment. Students at the hotel school do internships in hotels where, as one manager put it, 'they are taught to smile, be nice, and love tourists.' Hotel management teams make it a custom to instil workers with manners and communication skills by occasionally asking them to lunch in management facilities where they must converse in English or French. The end result is the creation of an upwardly mobile population seeking Western identification and rejecting its Creole roots.

Waiters covet tourist addresses in pocket notebooks, enhancing their status with allusions to overseas acquaintances. Women quit their jobs to frequent hotel discotheques in hopes of embracing, however temporarily, tourist affluence.

This affluence whets local appetite for foreign commodities – clothes, personal accessories, and other consumer goods. From 1977 to 1979, clothing and personal accessory imports doubled. Nearly nine out of ten Seychellois now have radios.

INFLUENCE FROM THE WEST

As is the case in other developing areas, tourism cannot be separated from other Western influences. The Seychelles house an American tracking station and U.S. personnel have influenced local values and priorities, as have foreign movies and videotapes. Americans also paved the way for tourists as prime catches for local women. As one Seychelloise grandmother put it: 'If a Seychellois asked me to marry him, I wouldn't; but if an American asked me, I'd jump at his neck.'

Foreign media create false stereotypes of Westerners that are reinforced by tourists and feed a host society with illusions. Contrary to the impression often made by tourists, Europeans are not accustomed to lengthy periods of leisure, to being served day and night, to spending amounts for goods that are several times more expensive than what everyone else pays. They do not publicly fulfil their fantasies, sexual or otherwise, or usually parade along public streets in string bikinis.

Tourism is a capricious industry, founded on the fashion trends of a Western bourgeoisie. In its present state, international tourism offers escapism and fulfilment of romantic notions, only rarely a sincere experience of another culture. At best, tourism allows an economy to run in place. A story in the Seychelles captures this irony:

In the Seychelles, it is the custom for fishermen to go to sea very early in the morning and return with their catch by 9:00 or 10:00 a.m. They can spend the rest of their day as they choose. A tourist watched for several days as the fishermen returned from sea and spent the rest of the day idle, gazing at the ocean. Amazed, the tourist finally approached one of the fishermen and asked: 'Why do you sit here all day long? Why don't you fish all day? You could sell more fish and make a lot more money.'

The fisherman then asked the tourist, 'What would I do with the money?' Whereupon the tourist replied, 'Well you could afford to do just as you wanted. You could sit on the beach all day long.'

Source: From Cultural Survival Quarterly, vol. 6, no. 3 (1982). Reprinted with permission

Governments of economically developing countries, many now desperate for foreign exchange, tend to keep quiet about tourism's disadvantages. Tourists do not see the way in which tourism competes for local resources, and that can mean local people are denied access to them. The problems of world tourism are unlikely to be overcome until there is a more just international order that allows poor countries to earn more in other ways and so have the power to stand up to the global tourism industry.

Indeed, there are signs that 'host' governments in economically developing countries have increasing misgivings, but it is difficult to see what effective controls on tourism are possible. If a country's tourism controls are too strict (or fashions change, or there is a political crisis, for example) in the very competitive world travel market, tourists will take their money elsewhere. If exploitation and consumerism within a host country, and the commercialisation and trivialisation of its local culture, are to be countered, a change of values among tourists is required, together with a more critical understanding of tourism's impact on host countries and local communities. In turn, this needs more sensitive governmental controls.

?

1 Read the extract 'Tourism in the Seychelles: a counterfeit paradise?'. In small groups discuss what the dilemma is for the Seychelles. Give examples of the conflicts involved.

2 Read 'Tips for the tourist' and 'Just travel'. Make your own list of specific tips (e.g. learing a few words in the host country's language) that tourists could consider.

Humanising tourism

Today, nearly 150 years after Thomas Cook launched his pioneer humanitarian vision for popular travel, we can see tourism's potential as well as its dangers. Travel could overcome the ignorance and prejudice which separates people in the rich and poor countries. As long-haul air travel becomes more available and less expensive, millions of people from wealthy countries could travel in a few hours to societies struggling with all the problems of under-developed economies. The opportunity is there to see, to listen and to share as between people of very different backgrounds. That way, Westerners may start to see just how underdeveloped their own societies are, in human terms. The tragedy of mass tourism is that rather than encouraging authentic interaction and the discovery of solidarity, it has reinforced false and sentimental preconceptions among tourists and their hosts.

'The faces looking through the tinted windows of the tourist bus see without understanding. The farmers in the paddy field are seen through a camera, an illustration in a glossy magazine.'

Source: *Third World People and Tourism*, ECTWT, Bangkok, 1986

The challenge to humanise tourism

Tips for the tourist

- Travel in small groups rather than in large parties. That way you will have more chance of meeting the local people in a natural way.

- Stay in a few places longer rather than hurry through as many countries as possible.

- Read up on the place of destination – its history, culture and present political situation – before leaving.

- Make contact with someone in the host country before leaving and so avoid the tourist treadmill.

- Make an effort to eat local food, visit local markets rather than tourist shops and travel by local transport used by the local people.

- Spend time outside the big cities and experience life in the rural areas.

Source: Christian Council of Asia, Manila, 1984

JUST TRAVEL – AN EXPERIMENT IN ALTERNATIVE TOURISM

In an article especially written for CONTOURS, Ms. Julie Wenham, an Australian lawyer, speaks of an experiment being made by an Australian co-operative who are concerned to respond to Third World people with regard to Alternative Tourism.

More and more Australians are travelling every year. With our guaranteed four weeks paid annual holiday leave and our relatively high wages an overseas holiday is within the reach of many Australians. In fact, it can be cheaper for us to spend a week in a Third World country than to spend a week on the Gold Coast in Queensland.

Australia has the Pacific Islands right next door and countries such as Bali, the Philippines, Hong Kong, and Singapore within temptation's reach. Travel agencies lure thousands of Australians with glossy brochures on package holidays to these countries every year. The type of experiences they offer, however, leave much to be desired. Many tourists come back from three weeks in a new country without any experience of life in that country. Groups are ferried by airconditioned buses on a compulsory tour of the tourist sights and returned to their glorious five-star hotels to 'get on with their holiday' – relaxing, lazing in the sun around a swimming pool with fellow Australians. A totally incubated experience.

A few Australians, however, are searching for more meaningful experiences. We realize we are relatively wealthy and will continue to travel because we have a thirst for new experiences and cultures. We are asking, however, can we utilize our desire to travel while recognizing the dignity and right to self-determination of our neighbours in the host countries?

In 1980 Just Travel was formed. Just Travel seeks to offer Australians an alternative form of travel to Third World countries primarily by offering group package tours. With the encouragement of Just Travel members all tours are initiated, planned and organized by local people in Third World countries and great emphasis is placed on meaningful cultural experiences and the opportunity to develop deep relationships with local people. We are attempting to return the control of our Third World experiences to the Third World people themselves. Any profits that are made from the tour are in turn returned to the Third World people to further alternative tours and ventures. Pretour preparation is a vital part of any Just Travel experience with several days of learning about the country, the culture, its problems and achievements. Post-tour reflection is also important and participants are encouraged to continue to foster international solidarity with new-found friends.

We believe that the tours that have been organized to date have been very successful. We have been hosted by the people of the Philippines, Indonesia, Hong Kong, China and India. The Australian participants have received the tours with mixed reactions. For many the new experience was a life-changing one which for the first time challenged them to question social justice issues and their own comfortable lifestyle. For others their experience was a frustrating one because they were not ready to question their own comfortable existence and have become angry when challenged to do so.

A small minority have indicated that they could have spent their valuable four weeks' holiday leave in a more relaxing, less traumatic manner. Australians still believe if they work hard for forty-eight weeks of the year they deserve at least four weeks to lay in the sun and recuperate.

The members of Just Travel have reflected carefully on the varying responses to our tours and are determined to continue to challenge Australians to question tourism. We recognize, however, that education is a long process and there are still many Australians who would not even consider joining us on a Just Travel tour. However, our Third World hosts have been excited and inspired by the thought of offering their own form of tourism and we wish to support them in whatever way possible in their venture.

Source: Contours, 2nd Quarter, 1986, p. 6

How can we humanise tourism

Firstly, this means confronting the transnational interests which control the tourist industry and the streamlined consumerism that TNCs find very profitable. Secondly, tourists themselves must become more sensitive to their hosts and more aware of attitudes and behaviour which might exploit or degrade local people and their culture. Some tourists seem to be becoming more aware of the ambiguous nature and impact of mass tourism. In many economically developed countries, pressure groups concerned for the environment, world development and human enrichment produce a growing volume of literature to promote more sensitive travel. Also the growing awareness of the risks from AIDS and from skin cancer is likely to have a sizeable impact on international sex tourism and 'sun lust' package tours.

Nevertheless, despite the best intentions, even the free-ranging lone tourist or venture trek group visiting remoter communities risk bringing with them miniaturised imports of mass tour culture more visible in popular, well-established tourist centres elsewhere. Thus tribal hill villages in the Himalayas or remote island beach communities in the South Pacific may be very vulnerable to cultural disruption which inappropriately introduced tourism can bring. Ideally, in any locality, tourism development should be a partnership of interests, in which the community or country is in control of its own destiny. The reality, however, may be many shattered illusions and some painful experiences for local people, tourists and tour operators. Recently, through a concern to redeem past mistakes and to advance wholeness and life fulfilment in tourism, the World Council of Churches, through the Ecumenical Coalition on Third World Tourism, have been encouraging responsive travel.

For anyone planning a visit to an economically developing country, there are a number of dos and don'ts. Be very sensitive that you are in another culture; think carefully about what you are doing; listen, look carefully, ask questions; scrupulously observe local customs and never jump to conclusions! Due heed to such things will not only offer the traveller a richer experience, but also greatly improve relations between tourists and hosts around the world. In future years many of the new travel and tourism courses in schools and colleges will be taught by world studies specialists, to increase the awareness of all people involved in tourism of the truly recreational opportunities open to responsive, sensitive travellers.

Role play
The tourism development game

Scenario 1
A consortium of international commercial leisure interests is proposing a conspicuous, popular, state-of-the art, winter ski-ing complex, doubling in summer as a multi-activity-based time-share development in a remote in a remote, scenic and ethnic rural district in north-west Europe.

Scenario 2
A consortium of international commercial leisure interests is proposing a large, popular multi-activity-based hotel and time-share development, and nearby separate exclusive beach paradise complex, in a beautiful coastal area of a poor tropical country.

Scenario 3
A group of prominent international venture-trek agencies have negotiated rights with airlines, government officials and with local concessionaries to bring Western, urban tourists into a remote, game-rich area of tropical forest and savanna inhabited sparsely by traditional river and hill-tribe people within a developing country.

In each case, identify the main actors involved and compile an appropriate script to include the main arguments likely to be voiced and the likely course of events. How, in each case, would the conscious full involvement, from the outset, of the local people stand to alter the stances of the actors and the possible course of events in tourism development?

The very significant International Workshop on Tourism, sponsored by the Christian Conference of Asia and attended by 30 participants from 18 countries, was held in Manila, the Philippines, September 12–25, 1980. One of its statements concerned the politics of tourism.

THE POLITICS OF TOURISM

The growth of tourism should be seen within the political context of the struggle between the North and South, the developed and the underdeveloped, in which the powerful dominate the powerless. In this global perspective, the poorer nations are urged to promote tourism in the interests of strengthening their economy and removing inequalities, but in the process are placed in the subservient role of obeying the dictates of the powerful.

Through tourism, developed nations export their politics, trade and lifestyle to give them both economic and political gain. Materialistic and money-oriented political systems are reinforced, thus undermining the heritage and destroying the human dignity of the indigenous people and leading to the violation of human rights.

Tourism as a global industry enables the First World to look for markets for their products and investment for their profits. The medium used is the Transnational Corporations (TNCs) which have developed sophisticated operations to control many activities in the tourist industry. Airline companies, tour operators, hotels, restaurants, credit cards and similar come under the care of TNCs.

Because the TNCs benefit so much from tourism, they continue to exploit the resources of the Third World and make use of cheap labour to increase their own growth. Compliant Third World governments give their blessing to this activity.

TNCs have used their economic leverage through state governments and financial lending institutions to influence and impose tourism as a priority programme of Third World governments. Many Third World countries have accepted this pressure without protest and without consideration of whether it reflects the real needs and aspirations of their people.

Those Third World governments which adopt repressive measures to retain power have found in tourism an effective political weapon to build up their international image. Government bureaucracies, business élites and sometimes the military have joined forces to promote tourism despite the high investment cost. Such governments have been more than willing to make extravagant concessions to TNCs to enable them to begin operations. Once the tourist industry is established, the country can obtain overseas aid and support in order to maintain 'peace and order' so that its tourist industry may not suffer. Tourism thus becomes another instrument of political repression.

The legal system is often party to this pretence. Laws which benefit foreign investment are common, and are imposed without proper participation by the people affected. Martial law in many Third World countries has accelerated this trend and led to many unjust laws. Examples are the minimum wage laws, bans on strikes and union activity, anti-subversion laws, laws prohibiting rumour-mongering and squatting. Each of these laws is used to preserve power for the élites rather than protect the rights of the people.

When legitimate laws run counter to the prevailing mood, then they are quietly ignored or by-passed. Examples are the laws against prostitution, soliciting, gambling and laws which protect the rights of workers. For the sake of tourism development, laws are made or ignored according to the dictates of the market. An oppressive or authoritarian government can justify many of its actions against its own people by arguing the need for tourists.

To the poor, whose voice is seldom heard, there is little solace or help coming from the tourist industry. They have to accept whatever benefit trickles down to them from the overflow of tourism. They must not make any objection to being dispossessed or victimised in the name of tourism development or they will be treated as subversives. As it exists at present, the tourist industry offers little hope to the poor.

Source: Contours **1** 2, 1984, p. 13

?

1 Read 'The Politics of Tourism'. To what extent do you agree or disagree with what is being said? *Either*

a write to the editor of *Contours* setting out your understanding of the politics of tourism, *or*

b pretend that a friend has just read the article and believes it to be too farfetched. Write down your considered response.

10

Women and development

Kate Harris and Caroline Moser

A census counts a man's cows, but not the hours his wife spends tending them

What is development?

Development can be defined as the process of making people's lives better. To some extent it can be measured by economic growth and rising per capita incomes, but these only reveal part of the picture. In many countries average per capita incomes and a high rate of economic growth hide great inequalities in the way in which wealth is distributed, so many people's lives are not necessarily getting any better. It is therefore helpful to take account of improvements in such things as health care, education, diet and water supply when thinking about development. Less tangible factors like the length of a working day and people's status within their community also contribute to the quality of life. In all these areas there may be great disparities between different groups within a single country or region, as well as between different countries and regions.

This chapter looks at women and the quality of their lives in a range of different contexts. It invites you to consider to what extent and why their position is different from that of men; and whether there are particular ways in which women contribute to development.

Women and agriculture

'The world must aim to abolish hunger and malnutrition by the end of the century' declared the *Brandt Report on International Development Issues* in 1980. Agriculture and food production are clearly key factors in any consideration of development. To what extent do women contribute to agricultural productivity? How much influence do they have in this area?

The overwhelming majority of people in almost any economically developing country live in rural areas and practise subsistence agriculture. The extract 'Invisible farmers' (pages 250–1) and the interview in Bori Arab (page 252) looks at women's role in such areas. The article ' "It's the crops that are seasonal" ' on page 253, which deals with women agricultural workers in the UK, provides points of both comparison and contrast.

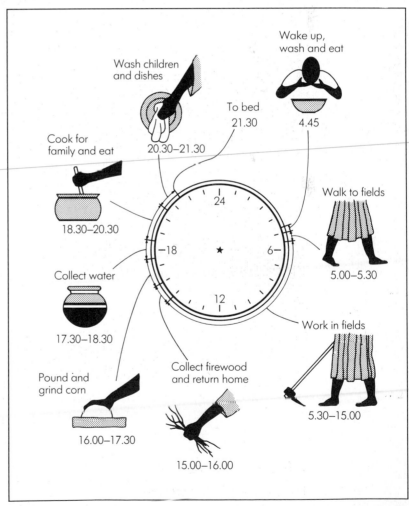

Figure 1 A woman's work is never done: time chart of work performed by women in rural Africa
Source: Maggie Murray and Buchi Emecheta, *Our Own Freedom*, Sheba Feminist Publishers

INVISIBLE FARMERS

WOMEN have always known who weeds the sorghum, transplants the rice seedlings, picks the beans, tends the chickens. In fact, it has been estimated that their labour produces half of the world's food.

But it has taken a long time of the rest of the world to discover these facts. In Africa, for example, three-quarters of agricultural work is done by women. They are half of the agricultural force in Asia. And even in Latin America and the Middle East (where men tend to deny that their mothers, wives, daughters do any work outside the home) detailed questioning reveals that women are doing a substantial amount of the farming there too.

As with their domesetic work, much of women's agricultural work tends to be overlooked because it is unpaid. In Malawi and Botswana, for example, over three quarters of women work unpaid on the land. Even when unpaid work is taken into account, however, women's agricultural workload still tends to be underestimated. This is largely because so much of it takes place away from the fields and the pastures. One study in Pakistan, for example, found that women's 'invisible' agricultural activities – like their vegetable garden beside the house – took just as much times as the 'visible' ones, like weeding and hoeing, usually counted as agricultural work.

It is not only in developing countries that women's farm work is underestimated. The traditional European 'farmer's wife' – who just bakes bread, churns butter, feeds a few hens, and clears up after her mud-spattered menfolk – may be no more than a myth. Surveys in Turkey and Spain found farmers' wives working up to 70 hours a week out on the farm itself.

Modernisation for men

That women farmers in the developing world have been made invisible is only too evident from the statistics for agricultural innovations and projects. Information collected from 46 African countries showed that only 3.4 per cent of trained government workers providing agricultural advice to people in rural areas were women. In other parts of the world the situation is the same. In Nepal, for instance, studies show that women provide between 66 and 100 per cent of the labour in many agricultural activities and make 42 per cent of agricultural decisions – choosing which seeds to plant, deciding how much and what kind of fertilizer to apply. But a review of government projects in 1983 discovered that, of all the agricultural advisers trained to help villagers, only one was a woman – and she had been trained in 'home economics', not agriculture.

This tendency – to help women farmers only with those skills that are associated with their domestic role – has been found in many other countries too. In Ghana, where women grow half the food, around a third of cash crops like cocoa, rice, sugar and cotton, and manage two-fifths of the coffee farms, over 70 per cent of agricultural workers assigned to help women were only trained to teach about nutrition and the preparation and storage of food.

But it is not only training and advice about agriculture that has been directed more at men. When new technology is introduced it usually helps men with their traditional tasks of ploughing, irrigation and harvesting, but leaves women to continue their back-breaking work of weeding, thinning, transplanting, by hand or with primitive knives and hoes.

The rain-watered rice grown by women in Gambia, for example – which makes up 84 per cent of the country's entire rice harvest – covers 26 times as much land as the irrigated rice grown by men, but receives only one twenty-sixth of government spending on rice projects. In Sierra Leone the tractors and tillers introduced to help with swamp rice cultivation made men's working day shorter, but increased women's workload by 50 per cent because they allowed more land to be cultivated.

FAO [the United Nations Food and Agriculture Organisation] sums up the situation: 'In all regions the introduction of modern agricultural technology is primarily aimed at male tasks and used almost exclusively by men ... Agricultural productivity cannot be substantially increased, nor can rural poverty be alleviated, unless women's access to key productive resources and services is substantially improved. The consequences of patriarchy for agricultural productivity are very expensive. Developing countries cannot bear their heavy cost.'

Famine in Africa

The heaviest of the costs to which FAO is referring is famine. It is now becoming clear that the acute food shortages in Africa, while dramatically and tragically exacerbated by drought and war, may be due in large part to the way women have been systematically excluded from access to land and from control of modern agriculture in that region.

Part of the problem is the sheer amount of work African women are expected to do. In Malawi, for example, women do twice as much work as men on the staple maize crop and an equal amount in the cotton fields, *plus* their domestic chores at home. And in Zambia, Ghana, Botswana and Gambia, studies found that the amount that was havested depended, not on what the land could yield, but on the amount of work women could fit into the daylight hours.

Source: Adapted from *New Internationalist*, July 1985

A Kikuyu woman in the Highlands of Kenya. Her husband has gone to work in a factory. Because she is supporting a bundle of firewood – using a traditional Kikuyu headstrap – she carries her baby in front. Collecting wood for fuel is mainly a woman's task. It can take hours every day. This woman also runs the family farm, does all the household chores and brings up six children

Another reason for declining food production in Africa is the introduction of cash crops to men. In the Ivory Coast, for instance, a shortage of food staples resulted when the government encouraged men to grow cash crops, because some of the best land (where women had previously been growing food) was claimed by their husbands for the new cash crop and because wives had to spend so much of their time working on their husbands' fields.

The combined results of factors like these is a gradual reduction in *per capita* food production in Africa over the last two decades. AS FAO points out: 'Despite the well-documented, crucial role that women play in food production in this region, agricultural modernisation efforts have excluded them, leading to negative consequences for food production and the perpetuation of rural poverty'.

Passive resistance

Women have not submitted lightly to their loss of land and livelihood. Some are objecting in the only way they can. They dare not actually go on strike: married women risk divorce and loss of their access to land if they defy their husbands, and mothers are prevented from withdrawing their labour completely through fear for the welfare of their children. But they are refusing to co-operate.

When government pricing policies sent men's maize profits soaring in Zambia and led to more land being put under maize, women kept working doggedly in their own groundnut fields and refused to turn them over to the more lucrative maize: because they – and not their husbands – kept the money from sales of groundnuts.

Investing in women

It is a tragedy that women are forced into conflicts like this, because the evidence points to the fact that, given the same kind of help, encouragement and incentives as men, women are actually better farmers. In Kenya, for instance, where 38 per cent of the farms are run by women, those women manage to havest the same amount per hectare as men, despite men's greater access to loans, advice, fertilizers, hybrid seeds, insecticide. And when women were given the same level of help, they were found to be more efficient than men and produced bigger harvests.

The key, according to FAO, is to ensure that women can acquire and hold on to independent access to land and loans – independent, that is, of men. All-women co-operative farms and rural credit schemes appear to be the most promising way forward. And these have been tried with some success in countries such as Vietnam, Bangladesh and India. But, laments FAO, 'Policy-makers and international experts have persistently resisted the idea of all-women's co-operatives' – even in West Africa where such co-operatives are traditional.

Yet when women are able to profict directly from their work in the fields, they are not the only ones to benefit. Studies in Burkina Faso, Bangladesh, Nepal, the Philippines and Swaziland have indicated that when women do have time or money to spare they use it to improve the health and well-being of their children.

From an interview in Bori Arab

Bori Arab is a village in central India. The interviewer is an American Gail Omvedt. Bhimrao is a young (male) union organiser whose home village is Bori Arab. Kaminiban is a middle-aged female agricultural worker from the 'scheduled' (or 'untouchable' caste).

Bhimrao feels the need to intervene ... 'Yes there is male supremacy ... in the work they do in the fields, men get more daily wages and [women] get less, and the reason for that is that men's work is heavier, more toilsome. Women's work is different –'

'– but women –' I begin.

And then Kaminibai burst in:

'– have to do *double* work!' 'We have to do the housework and when the housework is finished we have to do the field work and when the field work is finished we have to take care of the children, we have to do all the work! What do men do? They get up, take a bath, they eat some bread and go to the fields. But understand what their duty is: they only do the work that is allotted to them in the fields. They only do one sort of work–'

She pauses for breath and I say that, in the US also, women who work outside the home get less pay than men and also have to work in the house without pay.

'Oho! That is the case here too. We remain without pay. If it would have been paid we would get *double* pay! If housework were paid it would go to the women! Are you men listening? Admit it! If there is competition about housework we would defeat them completely.'

The second shift, the unpaid shift, the double burden of women. And wages for housework! Did anyone say there weren't some universal issues of the women's movement?

Source: Ed. Hazel Johnson and Henry Bernstein, *Third World Lives of Struggle*, Heinnemann, 1982

?

Refer to the notemaking exercise on pages 12–13. Read (or re-read) it if necessary then apply the 'formula' used there to the article 'Invisible farmers'. Produce a diagram which shows the main points and links in the article. Then answer the following questions.

1a Why according to the article 'Invisible farmers' is much of women's agricultural work overlooked?

b Which other work is ignored for the same reason?

2 In small groups discuss why you think there has been a tendency 'to help women farmers only with skills associated with their domestic role'. List as many reasons as you can.

3 In your groups discuss what is meant by 'key productive resources and services' (paragraph 9, line 6).

4 Prepare a timechart like the one in Figure 1 for:

a yourself;

b a female adult (e.g. your mother);

c a male adult.

Compare your results with those of the rest of your group. What conclusions can you draw about the division of work in this country?

?

1 Read the Bori Arab interview. Explain the 'double burden' of women referred to in it.

2a From the evidence in 'Invisible Farmers', Figure 1, and the interview list four measures which might improve the quality of life for women living in a rural area in the economically developing world. Include as much detail as you can about who would be responsible for carrying out such measures.

b Rank your measures in terms of which you think should be given most urgent priority.

3 According to the article 'It's the crops that are seasonal' how do farmers in the UK discriminate against women agricultural workers?

4 What attitude does the author suggest underlies this discrimination?

5 Draw up a table of similarities and differences between the position of women part-time agricultural workers in the UK and women farmers in economically developing countries. (You do not necessarily need to restrict your answer to the information in this chapter.)

6 The interviewer in Bori Arab implied a direct connection between the position of women in economically developing countries and that of women in countries like the USA and the UK. In small groups discuss to what extent you feel this comparison is valid.

'It's the crops that are seasonal'

Semantics, it is claimed, is being used by farmers to get round the 1976 Sex Discrimination Act which obliges them to pay men and women doing similar work the same wages.

Ann's day is spent planting lettuces in the featureless landscape of East Kent. Sitting with a team of women at the back of a tractor, in a wind that's bitingly cold, she's bent double picking seedlings from a tray and transferring them to the planter. When the lettuces are finished, it'll be time for another crop, and so it goes on, week in week out, throughout the year, with only a break at Christmas.

Ann is one of 40,000 women in Britain employed as seasonal or casual labour in agriculture. But she says: 'It's the crops that are seasonal, not the women, but that's how they class us'. For the past seven years she's worked a 30-hour week for the same employer – part of a guaranteed workforce that he relies on. She therefore finds it hard to accept that he does not regard her as a regular part-timer entitled to holiday pay and with a degree of security, but as a seasonal worker with no entitlements at all. During the Christmas break, when she's laid off, she receives no standby payment and has no guarantee that she will get her job back next year. If she were recognised as a regular part-timer, her employer would be required to increase her pay: the minimum statutory wage which can be paid to a regular part-time worker is nearly 20% higher than Ann's minimum as a seasonal worker.

Margaret Holmes, an official of the Agricultural and Allied Workers' Union (a branch of the TGWU) who represents horticultural workers in Kent, believes farmers use the label 'seasonal' to get round the 1976 Sex Discrimination Act which affords men and women workers equal pay. She claims that women get a particularly raw deal out of agriculture. They work in conditions that would shock the average factory worker: out all day in fields where there are no toilet or washing facilities, in an industry that, after construction work, is the second most hazardous in Britain. They are treated, she claims, as second-class citizens doing the job just for pin-money; yet many of them are single women or divorced women with children to support, who rely entirely on what they can earn.

In the Fens of Lincolnshire, where 80 per cent of the land is farmed, agricultural work is about all that is available locally for the school leaver. Here a system of working persists that seems more appropriate to the 1880s than the 1980s. A body of men called gangmasters range the countryside in vans, gathering workforces, mainly women, for the farmers who need them. It is the gangmasters who agree the rate for a job and pay the workers; and they're not always fussy about statutory wage minimums.

Women, bent double, picking calabrese

Although there are some reputable gangmasters, there are others, according to Conservative MP Sir Richard Body (Holland with Boston), who abuse their workers' trust by not paying their tax and national insurance contributions. It's disgraceful, he says, that people with enough self-respect to want to work rather than live on the dole should be cheated in this way. Sir Richard has long campaigned for a register of gangmasters and stricter controls.

Mavis Carpenter had worked 21 years for the same bulb-packing firm in Spalding. Then one day last year the all-female workforce was laid off – no notice, no redundancy pay. Although Mavis had originally been a full-time worker, in 1982 her employer cut her hours and handed over her P.45. He clearly now regarded her as another disposable seasonal worker.

Less than one per cent of agricultural seasonal workers are union members, so it was hardly surprising that the union's demands for a substantial wage rise made little impact on the body which sets the minimum hourly pay, the Agricultural Wages Board. Seasonal workers' wages, like the brussels sprouts they picked, were frozen. The National Farmers' Union, pleading another bad harvest, claimed it couldn't afford a bigger wage bill, and it's true that some small-scale farmers have a struggle to make ends meet. But only 22 per cent of landowners employ Britain's agricultural workforce and, as one union official put it, somewhat wryly, this year and next they'll still be riding round in their Range Rovers and Mercedes, because they always do.

Source: Adapted from Jenny Cuffe, *The Listener*, 19 June 1986

Women and recession: Guayaquil, Ecuador

Caroline Moser

The second section of this chapter looks at recent changes in the lives of women in the Indio Guayas *barrio* (neighbourhood) of Guayaquil, Ecuador (Figure 2). The material is based on field research carried out in Indio Guayas over the period 1978 to 1988.

Ecuador - the background

Ecuador is a middle-income country and its economic development has been oil-led. In terms of social progress 'much of the oil income was well spent' (World Bank, 1985). Between 1960 and 1980 more than ten years were added to life expectancy; death and infant mortality rates dropped by 40%, and by 1980 virtually all children attended primary school.

Over the past 25 years Ecuador had an average annual GDP growth rate of 6.7%, although from 1982 to 1988 the rate was only 2.2% per annum. The fluctuating rates reflect the development and decline of the petroleum and oil industry. Oil exports rose from 0% to 70% of total exports between 1970 and 1983 although with the subsequent decline in oil prices its share has dropped to about 42% of total exports, below agriculture at 52%.

Public sector revenues and expenditures became heavily dependent on oil receipts and external borrowing during the 1970s when public expenditure grew by 9.6% per year in real terms. High oil prices and the availability of cheap international credit for oil exporting nations meant that large public sector deficits could be covered, leading however to a thirteen-fold increase of the public external debt. While manufacturing industry contributed to growth during the oil boom years, mainly because it was highly protected and catered

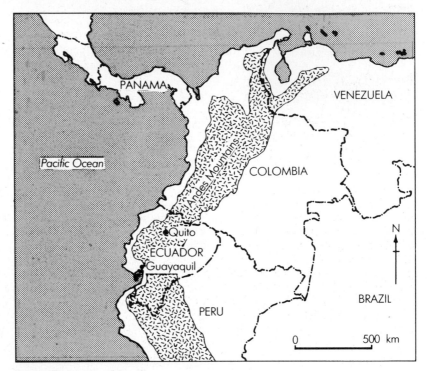

Figure 2 Location of Ecuador

essentially for the home market; it was neither able to compete in foreign markets nor to cope with the depression associated with the post oil boom. Oil income had been spent on current consumption rather than on longer term productive investments. A strong and appreciating *sucre*, Ecuador's currency, further undermined export-oriented manufacturing as well as agriculture.

Since 1982 Ecuador has faced a fundamentally changed world economic environment in which new commercial lending has dried up, real interest rates have risen and oil prices have declined.

The Ecuadorian government have taken a series of economic measures to *adjust* to the fall in their revenues. (Such measures are referred to as structural adjustment measures.) In 1982 in order to control demand, the *sucre* was devalued and controls placed on imports, current expenditure and public investment,

while the debt payment was revised. The aim was to reduce real incomes and thus demand for imports and potential exports.

In 1984 the *sucre* was devalued again and subsidies reduced on food, energy, and fuel. Incentives were offered to exporters. Further measures were taken in 1985 and 1986. However, despite the government's declared intention to restrict spending, the public sector deficit continued to increase, rising from 5.1% of GDP in 1986 to 12% of GDP in 1988. The rapid expansion in public expenditure was not, however, only intended to satisfy basic priorities but rather also to meet the political demands of powerful interest groups.

The combined effect of the adjustment measures brought a profound recession in the economy. By 1988 Ecuador's economic situation was critical. The main problems were identified as the size of the foreign debt and the acute recession in internal economic activities. Agricultural production for the internal market stagnated together with food processing and textiles as the real incomes of salary – and wage – earners alike fell.

Barrio Indio Guayas, Guayaquil, 1978

Within the Ecuadorian economy, Guayaquil is the country's largest city, chief port, and the major centre of trade and industry. Its population growth has reflected the agricultural sector's declining capacity to retain its population as much as the city's potential to create industrial employment. It expanded rapidly during the 1970s at the time of the oil boom because of very high rates of immigration, mainly from the surrounding rural areas. This helped to swell the population from 500,000 in 1960 to 1.2 million in 1982 and an estimated 2 million in 1988.

Indio Guayas is the name given to an area of swampland (near the edge of the city) which has no clear physical limits but in 1978 had some 3000 residents. Indio Guayas was then a pioneer settlement of young upwardly mobile families, who had moved out from rented inner city accommodation, becoming the *de facto* owners of their 10-by-30 metre plots. They built their first houses of split bamboo and wood on catwalks (Figure 3), relying on irregular visits by water tankers and pirated electricity. During the late 1970s and early 1980s the residents mobilised and petitioned local politicians and the government to provide infill (which makes dry land from the swamp), drinking water and electricity for their community.

In 1978 the average age for both men and women was 30. Most households were headed by men and the average household size was 5.8 persons. The men were employed as mechanics, construction workers, tailoring outworkers, unskilled factory workers or labourers, while the women were employed as domestic servants, washerwomen, cooks, sellers and dressmakers. However, far from being society's casualties, the residents of Indio Guayas were an upwardly aspiring community, struggling through hard work and initiative to improve their standard of living and to improve employment prospects for their children, if not for themselves, through health and education.

?

1a Briefly outline what has happened to the economy of Ecuador since 1982.

b What does this mean for the people of Ecuador?

2 Use these headings to make notes about Indio Guayas in 1978: Housing; Employment; Services.

Figure 3 Indio Guayas in 1978. Houses of split bamboo and wood were built on catwalks in the tidal swampland

Recession and *barrio* Indio Guayas

Table 1 shows the changing employment for men and women in Indio Guayas between 1978 and 1988.

Changing employment for men in Indio Guayas

The decline in oil revenue and attempts to cut back public-sector spending have reduced private investment, particularly in the construction sector, resulting in an important change for men. The number of men in construction remains very much the same: 11% in 1988 compared to 13% in 1978. However, with a downturn in demand for labour on large infrastructure and office building projects, most of the men are now employed in the *suburbios* on local house upgrading for extensions. The consequences are that real wages in the construction sector have declined and are now only worth half to two-thirds for their 1979 value.

Changes in work conditions have also occurred. Fewer skilled men work on contracts with social security benefits and, increasingly, like their unskilled colleagues they are employed on a daily basis, which means unemployment for long periods, sometimes up to six months of the year. The number of artisans has also remained stable, although more shoemakers and tailors were found in 1978 than in 1988, and in 1988 there were slightly more mechanics and carpenters. A breakdown of the statistics for factory and labouring work shows that the only real area of expansion for male employment has been in sea products, particularly the shrimp industry. In 1988 around 7% of the male heads of households had jobs in this well-paid sector. With shrimp farms covering an extensive area along the Pacific coast, this has resulted in a small-scale but increasingly significant pattern of circulatory male migration from Indio Guayas, in which only

Table 1 Employment in Indio Guayas by occupational categories, 1978–88 (in %)

Census occupational category	Women 1978	Women 1988	Men 1978	Men 1988
Professional				
Teacher	1	2.9	1.4	.8
Nursing auxiliary	–	2.9	–	–
Others	–	2.9	–	1.7
Managers	–	–	1.4	.8
Office workers	1	1.4	4.6	4.0
Sellers	36	33.8	10.7	21.0
Agricultural labour	2	–	1.8	.8
Transport	–	–	8.4	9.0
Artisan/machine operator				
Shoes	–	–	2.3	–
Dressmakers	14	17.6	–	–
Tailors	–	–	6.6	2.5
Mechanics	–	–	4.7	6.0
Skilled construction	–	–	13.0	11.0
Carpentry/laquer	–	–	6.0	9.0
Other artisan	–	–	–	2.5
Other factory workers	–	2.9	9.8	8.0
Labourers	–	–	9.8	6.0
Personal services	39	35.2	6.1	6.1
Other	7	–	4.6	4.0
Total	**100**	**99.7**	**99.5**	**99.1**
Number	(230)	(131)	(213)	(118)

one weekend in three is spend at home.

Women's employment and the impact of men's problems

With fewer men now generating a reliable income, and the value of their wage packet lower, what has been the impact on households in Indio Guayas? First and foremost, *more women have to take paid work*, with female participation rates increasing from 40% in 1978 to 52% in 1988.

Although more women are working, the majority have not been able to take up new opportunities in the labour market, but are forced to remain in the traditional areas of domestic service and street selling in which women have always worked. In 1978 39% of economically active women were domestic servants, cooks or washerwomen (Figure 4), while by 1988 35% were in these occupations. The wages of an average worker had fallen to two-thirds of their 1979 value. The same is true of street and front-room selling, which is probably the most flexible part of the informal sector, capable of absorbing additional labour but without increased productivity. In 1978 36% of women were street sellers, compared to 33.8% in 1988. The proportion of dressmakers (14%) remained the same.

The biggest change has been the increase of those in professional occupations (such as teachers and nursing auxiliaries) and office jobs. These categories have risen from 2% in 1978 to 10.1% in 1988. This change, which involves mainly young women, reflects the slowly increasing differentiation in the socio-economic composition of

Indio Guayas as the city's spatial expansion makes it more attractive to higher-income groups.

Data from the 1988 survey shows that, in those households with working daughters, the highest proportion were employed as shop workers (36%). Although the majority had completed secondary school, they were either on short-term, insecure contracts or selling on commission. A further 15% were in professional and office jobs, and over 20% were in domestic service. Employment opportunities are not commensurate with women's increased educational qualifications, and the likelihood is that the majority, once they have their own dependants, will retreat into the residual female occupations of selling and domestic service.

?

1 The above is an account of the impact of the recession on men and women in Indio Guayas. In physical geography we often use systems diagrams to show relationships, inter relationships and impacts from one variable to another. In pairs, sketch a systems diagram of the above information to illustrate variables and impacts. Start with a circle broken by the word 'RECESSION'. You can add to the system as you read further in the case study. You will probably eventually find it necessary to look at three systems dealing with women's reproductive, productive and community-managing work.

Changes in households

A second fundamental change resulting from the fall in incomes has been the increase in the number of economically active people in the households. (See Table 2.)

There have also been changes in the composition of the household, with the number of female-headed households increasing from 12% to 19% in the past

Figure 4 Carmelina washed other people's clothes to earn a living. She was helped by one or more of her eight children

Table 2 Economically active people in households in Indio Guayas, 1978 and 1988 (in %)

Number working	1978	1988
1	49	34
2	32	32
3 or more	19	32

?

1 Study Table 2. In which two categories have there been changes in the numbers of people working in a household? Why have these changes occurred?

2 In pairs discuss who the extra people working are likely to be, and what the effects of more people working in a household might be for that household.

decade. While there are certainly more older women in the community than there were ten years ago, who have been either widowed or deserted, there is also an increasing number of *de facto* female-headed households. In some of these cases men have temporarily migrated to the rural areas to work in agriculture or the shrimp industry, leaving their families in Indio Guayas because of better opportunities for female employment and children's education in the city. Frequently, however, men soon set up other households in the rural areas, resulting in a decline in their responsibility for their urban households.

Changes in patterns of consumption

During the past decade the cost of living has increased for low-income households. One of the principal long-term root causes is the agricultural development policy adopted during the petrol boom period when changes from the production of basic grains for subsistence to export-oriented cash crops provided a decline in the production of food for the home market. Since 1982, inflationary rises in food prices have been caused not only by supply problems but also because subsidies on basic staples have been removed and the *sucre's* devaluations have increased the prices of imported foods. With wages frozen while food prices, and other essential items such as energy and petrol, have risen (with knock-on effects for transport costs) real incomes have fallen. It has been estimated that in 1984 the minimum salary for those with stable wage employment was meeting only 65% of the costs of the family shopping basket. Furthermore it has also been calculated that the purchasing power of informal sector earnings covered only 35% of the value of the family food basket. Price increases in staple food items in Guayaquil during the one-year period June 1987/88 ranged from a 50% increase on milk to 194% on potatoes. Other important changes included 79% on eggs, 55% on fish, 117% on tomatoes, 25% on plantain and 93% on rice.

This has resulted in changes in household diet. In 42% of households milk is no longer drunk, *at all*, while in those where milk is still drunk, the average consumption has decreased sharply from 4.6 litres per household per week to 1.4 litres. Similarly the average

number of times fish is eaten per week has declined from nearly three to under two, for eggs from an average of 4.9 per week to 2.6. There has been a shift from potatoes to plantain, and from drinking fresh fruit juice to powdered fruit drink or water. There is a tendency to eat less per meal and thereby stretch the food previously eaten at one meal to cover both the midday and evening meals; secondly to eat fewer meals, with first supper and then breakfast being cut out. In July 1988 one-quarter of households were eating one meal a day, with the cutting out of breakfast being justified at times by the mistaken assumption that 'the children get free milk at school'.

Changes in dietary patterns have resulted in a deterioration in the nutritional status of whole households, but particularly of children. A two-week survey of all children under 12 attending a local health centre revealed that 79% were suffering some level of malnutrition. It was also evident that women feed themselves last, and eat least, with anaemia a common complaint.

Changes in government spending

During the oil boom, government spending in the social sector (education, health, social welfare) increased considerably. One of the government responses to the economic crisis has been to cut this spending. The real *per capita* value of, for example, the health budget declined by 18% between 1981 and 1985.

In an Ecuadorian urban low-income community such as Indio Guayas, the main problems in basic health, education and community services relate not so much to lack of provision as to their *quality*, and the extent to which they are free or must be paid for.

In Indio Guayas deteriorating government provision of health care has resulted in increasing

privatisation, with increased costs being borne by the low-income population.

The state primary school suffers from inadequate equipment and low-quality teaching. Despite these limitations, increasing competition to enter the labour market has led to an expansion of demand for education. There is widespread concern to educate both sons and daughters for as long as possible, despite a very high failure rate. Low-income families invest considerable proportions of their income and savings to educate their children. In 1988 36% of families sent their children to private, fee-paying schools.

Although state education is technically free, in reality numerous charges are transferred to the parents. Over the past decade the annual school enrolment fee, particularly at the secondary level, has become a crippling expense for families who are unable to save during the year. Enrolment fees can cost the same as a domestic servant's monthly salary. When additional costs such as uniform, school books and transportation are included, the annual cost of attending secondary school per year can be between one and two minimum monthly salaries.

The impact of recession on women in Indio Guayas

The productive role of women

The combined effect of the fall in real income due to cuts in wages, inflationary food prices and increased expenses on education and health means that the majority of households in Indio Guayas are poorer in real terms than they were ten years ago. With men contributing less or at times no cash to the household budget, women have had to find more resources. This change has had a number of important implications for them in terms of their productive role.

1 *More women are working*
In many cases they have become the primary or only reliable income earner, because both domestic service and selling, although badly paid, provide relatively stable employment opportunities in comparison with the increasingly irregular day labour available for men.

The particular stage in the household life cycle affects which women work. The few women not working tend to be in either extended or female-headed households where *daughters, sons or their partners* are now contributing to household income, and the woman's duties are entirely confined to reproductive work to meet their needs. This option also suggests that the size of household can affect its level of income.

When women go out to work depends on factors both external and internal to the household. All the women stated that they had started paid work because their household income was not sufficient to cover family needs. Inflationary food prices in 1987–8 were seen by women as the direct cause of their going out to work. Within the household, the other most important cost identified as pushing women out to work is that of secondary level schooling, again exacerbated by the inflationary increases in enrolment fees over the past two years. Households with one or more children in secondary school are therefore under additional financial pressure.

Where women work depends not only on their skills but also on their level of mobility. Least mobile are those who work from home (Figure 6) because of young children or their husbands' opposition to their going out to work. The less skilled run highly competitive front-room shops, while the more skilled work as dressmakers. Slightly more mobile are those selling cooked food on the corner of nearby main roads, leaving their children for short

The triple role of women

Figure 5 A local community leader, dressmaker and mother

In most low-income households in developing countries, women have three roles. 'Women's work' includes not only *reproductive* work (the childbearing and childbearing responsibilities) required to guarantee the maintenance and reproduction of the labour force, but also *productive* work in income-generating activities. In addition, women are involved in *community-managing* work undertaken at a local settlement level. With the increasingly inadequate state provision of housing and basic services such as water and health, it is women who not only suffer most, but also who are forced to take responsibility for the allocation of limited resources to ensure the survival of their households.

Although men are involved in productive work, they do not generally have a clearly identified reproductive role, and although they are involved in community-level activities, they do so in markedly different ways from women. While women have a community-managing role based on the provision of items of collective consumption, men have a community leadership role in which they organise at the formal political level, generally within the framework of national politics.

That women and men have different roles has important implications for policymakers. Because the triple role of women is not recognised, the fact that women, unlike men, are severely constrained by the burden of simultaneously *balancing* these roles of reproductive, productive and community-managing work is ignored. In addition only productive work is valued as work, because it is paid. Reproductive and community-managing work, because they are both seen as 'natural' and non-productive, are not valued. This has serious consequences for women. It means that the majority, if not all, of the work that they do is made invisible and fails to be recognised as work either by men in the community or by those planners whose job it is to assess different needs within low-income communities.

Figure 6 Learning to cook jam (to try to earn money while based at home) as part of a community non-formal education programme

periods. Laundry women must be able to travel for periods of the day, while the most mobile are domestic servants, many of whom leave the house at 6 a.m. in order to cross the city, returning at 8 or 9 p.m. Evidence suggests that among unskilled women there is a correlation between mobility and the amount earned.

2 *Longer hours*
Women are working longer hours in income-earning activities than before. The fact that women are earning less in real terms than they were ten years ago means that many are working longer hours. This is most evident in the case of the poorer, less skilled women, particularly heads of households, who have always worked in laundary or domestic services. Whereas ten years ago they 'did' for one family or possibly two, the majority are now fitting in two to three families, working as long as 60 hours a week, including Saturdays, in order to earn, in real terms, the same amount as before.

3 *Younger children*
Women are going out to work when their children are younger than before. Even the poorest women are reluctant to go out to work until their children reach at least primary school age, while among higher-income families entry into secondary school is preferred. Preliminary evidence suggests not only that most women work once their children are in primary school but that they increasingly enter the labour force as soon as possible after their last (intended) child is born. Of those in the subsample entering the labour market since 1978, all began to work prior to their youngest child's tenth birthday, and nearly 80% before its sixth birthday. An equally important determinant would seem to be the age of the eldest daughter or the presence of other women able to assist in reproductive activities.

4 *The effect on daughters*
The potential productive role of daughters is increasingly constrained by their present reproductive activities. The composition of the household in terms of the number of other females involved in reproductive work affects which women go out to work, when they go out to work and where. However, it is the number of daughters and their age which directly determines the strategies followed. With a greater number of women both working, and working longer hours, their daughters are increasingly forced to dovetail their schooling to their mothers' working hours. Although, the half-day school shift makes it possible for daughters to continue at school while taking on reproductive responsibilities, it nevertheless means that daughters have less time to do homework than their brothers. Girls, therefore, can be disadvantaged in terms of academic achievement, causing them to fail in school and this in turn may affect their future educational potential.

The reproductive role of women
In their reproductive roles as wives and mothers women have been affected by the recession and the government's response to it directly through changes in income, and indirectly through changes in consumption patterns (poorer diets, more expensive education and health-care).

1 *Less time for reproductive responsibilities*
Despite the fact that more women are working than in 1978, the cultural norm in Indio Guayas (that reproductive work is women's work) has not changed. Increasing pressure for women to earn an income has resulted in less time than before to dedicate to childcare and domestic responsibilities. The capacity of women to balance productive and reproductive work depends both on the composition of the household in terms of other females, and on the particular stage in the household life cycle. In fact the number of women in the household can be identified as one of the most critical factors affecting a household's ability to cope in a crisis.

When women with only very young children are forced out to

work they have no alternative to locking the children up while they are away, which is obviously the gravest of all solutions. The eldest daughter very rapidly assumes responsibility for her siblings, but is not given cooking responsibilities until the age of ten or eleven. In this situation women start their day at 4 or 5 a.m. cooking food and leaving it ready for their children to eat during the day, and doing additional domestic tasks on their return. Once daughters are able to undertake cooking, as well as childcare responsibilities, women do not get more rest; instead, they work longer hours outside the home. Those households with more than two daughters make maximum use of the half-day school shift system by sending out different daughters to different shifts, thus freeing the mother for full-time work.

There were a small but growing number of households effectively headed by daughters who undertook not only all reproductive activities but also attended community meetings on Saturdays and Sundays, thus also fulfilling their mothers' community management role. Despite the fact that the women may still have a number of young children, their only role now is a productive one. Ten years ago this phenomenon was not apparent, suggesting that women were balancing their reproductive and productive activities better. The problem is obviously exacerbated in those households headed by women.

Preliminary analysis shows that women's reduced time for reproductive activities has the following implications:

a) *Young children are receiving less care than before.* When young children are locked up unattended, or attended by elder sisters, they often receive less care. They are more likely to play truant from school, and to become street children – although they are not necessarily identified as such – roaming locally, running errands in return for food, and protected by sympathetic neighbours only as long as they remain in the street.

b) *Young children are suffering additional nutritional problems when not fed by their mothers.* Food left for division amongst children is often not fairly divided, and there are often nutritional problems in food cooked by elder siblings.

c) *Elder daughters forced into reproductive activities at an early age are themselves suffering from less parental care and guidance.* Although socialised to assist their mothers with domestic tasks, daughters do not automatically accept the responsibilities thrust on them. Resistance causes conflict with their mothers, and leads them to become irresponsible, neglecting their siblings; it can also lead to early promiscuity and even prostitution.

d) *Less parental control is detrimental for sons.* One of the greatest concerns expressed by women forced out to work was the fact that it reduced their capacity to control teenage sons who were often tempted to drop out of school, become involved in street gangs and be exposed to drugs. This problem was exacerbated when the parental responsibility of the father also disappeared, as a result of migration.

2 *Smaller families*
The pressure to earn an income is making it increasingly important for women to effectively control their fertility. While a quarter of women were not using any form of contraception, and a further quarter were using the coil, 42% had undergone an operation to have their tubes tied at the birth of their youngest child, in order to try and ensure that they could afford to bring up their existing children.

The community managing role of women
During the late 1970s and early 1980s women played an important community managing role in struggling to acquire infrastructural resources such as infill, water and electricity for the area (Figures 7 and 8). This centred around popular mobilisation, linked to particular political patronage, with intensive activity at election time. Cutbacks in public spending since 1983 have meant that patronage of this type has

Figure 7 Before: In 1978, Indio Guayas families relied on irregular visits by water tankers to provide them with water for drinking, cooking, washing and cleaning

virtually ceased. In this context non-governmental organisations (such as aid agencies) are playing an increasingly important role in providing services.

Women are spending more time on community managing activities than before in order to negotiate systems for the delivery of NGO services. NGO programmes, such as Plan International, are based on the voluntary unpaid involvement of women on a regular long-term basis. Women community leaders are expected to provide access to the community, and, along with paid community development workers, to supervise the allocation of resources for development programmes. In order to get access to resources, families are required to attend weekly meetings (Figure 9) and undertake community-level voluntary activities. Other than in leadership positions participation is almost entirely by women. As an extension of their domestic role, women take primary responsibility for the success of community-level projects.

Figure 8 And after: In 1988 women had successfully lobbied politicians to get a piped water supply to Indio Guayas

The decreasing provision of services by the state has led women to recognise the importance of encouraging the establishment, and ensuring the long-term survival, of community-based programmes. At the community level above all, it is lack of commitment or the necessary time which results in failure. In order to ensure that NGOs continue working with them, women are forced to find the time. In August 1988, for instance, up to 200 women were

Figure 9 In their community-managing role, women organise and attend local-level meetings

Figure 10 A typical woman who is just about 'hanging on'. Aracelli has four children (two daughters and two sons). She works as a dressmaker and in 1978 was involved in a community programme to improve the structure of her house

meeting for three hours every Sunday afternoon in order to get access to Plan International's community-level housing improvement programme; women with constantly sick children make it their business to attend the Saturday afternoon health talks run by the NGO health clinic. Even men are gradually beginning to recognise this role. A local carpenter summed it up when he said, 'I earn the money, and my wife looks after the children and attends the meetings.'

?

---

1 What third role played by women does the author add to the 'double burden' identified in the first section of this chapter?

2 Why do you think women (rather than men) have taken on this role in Indio Guayas?

3 In small groups discuss whether you think that NGOs (such as aid agencies) should deal particularly with women. What are the advantages and disadvantages of their doing this:
a for women?
b for the community?

Women, time and the triple role

Policymakers have become preoccupied that recession and adjustment have resulted in an extension of the working day of low-income women. The evidence from Indio Guayas shows that the real problem is not the length of time women work, but the way in which they balance their time between their reproductive, productive and community-managing roles.

Over the past decade low-income women in Indio Guayas have always worked between 12 and 18 hours per day, depending on such factors as the composition of their households, the time of year, their skills etc. The hours they work have not therefore changed fundamentally. What has changed is the time allocated to the different activities they undertake. The need to get access to resources has forced women to allocate increasing time to productive and community management activities, at the expense of reproductive activities, which in many cases have become a secondary priority. This has a significant impact on children, on

women themselves, and increases the likelihood of disintegration in the household.

Not all women can cope under crisis, and it is vital that the romantic myth of their infinite capacity to do so be debunked. They do not form a heterogeneous group, but fall into three rough groups, in terms of their capacity to balance their three roles in these changing conditions. Provisional estimates as to the size of each group have been made.

1 *Women who are coping*
These are the women balancing their three roles. They are more likely to be in stable relationships, with partners who have reliable sources of income. The household income is likely to be supplemented by other working members, and there may be other females also involved in reproductive work. About 30% of women are coping.

2 *Women who are burnt out*
These are women no longer balancing their three roles, and where the productive role has become predominant. They are most likely to be women who head households or are primary income earners working in domestic service, with partners who make no financial contribution to the household. They are often older women at the end of their reproductive cycle, physically and mentally exhausted after years of responsibility for a large number of dependants. Their inability to balance their roles results in a tendency to hand over all reproductive responsibilities to older daughters who cannot or will not fully assume these responsibilities. The consequence is that their younger still-dependent children drop out of school and roam the streets. About 15% of women are no longer coping, already casualties and burnt out.

3 *Women who are hanging on*
These women are under pressure but still trying to balance their

three roles, making choices depending on the composition of the household and the extent to which other household members are providing a reliable income. Some are women without partners, who, if they are the main income earners, have sufficient support from other females. Others are women with partners who have been forced out to work to help pay for the increased household expenses. These women are using up future resources in order to survive today, sending their sons out to work, or keeping their daughters at home to take over domestic responsibilities. About 55% of women are invisibly at risk, only just hanging on (Figure 10).

The priority group
A report to UNICEF recommended that the priority group for assistance in Indio Guayas should be those women who are 'hanging on'.

1 In small groups think of as many reasons as possible why this recommendation was made.

2 Discuss what could be done for women who are 'burnt out'.

Policy recommendations

The policy recommendations on the right were put forward as provisional recommendations at UNICEF's request.

1 Ecuadorian government measures

a The Ministry of Education should develop a more equitable enrolment policy and exercise greater control over the financial demands made by individual headteachers on low-income parents.

b The Ministry of Education should develop a far more comprehensive policy over school books than is currently the case, in order to prevent their sale at prohibitive prices, the profiteering practices of schools, publishing houses and school book suppliers, all of which have a particularly severe impact on the low-income population.

c The Ministry of Education should make information about school costs, curricula and essential and non-essential materials available at the community level. This would help to demystify education and allow parents to make better decisions in choosing the most appropriate type of education.

d The Ministry of Education should ensure that childcare/nutrition is adequately included in the curricula of both boys and girls in primary and secondary school.

2 NGO projects

a External and local non-governmental organisations should ensure that future health programmes and projects prioritise primary health care.
  Such projects should be managed by the community and employ local women as much as possible, and outside professionals as little as possible.

b Programmes should ensure that information about previous health projects remains in the community and is recorded at the regional level, to better assist those intending to design and implement future projects.

c Non-governmental organisations wishing to assist in the development of local-level income-generating activities for women should consult with local women in the prioritisation of skill training.

d Non-governmental organisations should develop appropriate projects for community-level skill training for local teenagers, to dovetail with their formal schooling. This would help to keep boys off the street and provide more appropriate intermediate-level skill training than is currently available in the formal school system. This should employ the maximum number of local men and women possible. The provision of a crèche or play area would ensure that teenage girls are not excluded from such facilities.

1 Study the 'Guidelines for implementing development projects'. They suggest that women are under-utilised in terms of their productive role. Explain why this is the case.

2 Study the lists of recommendations to the Ecuadorian government and to the NGOs. Think about why each

recommendation is made, and briefly note your thoughts.

3 In small groups design a project which would fulfill a need for women in the Indio Guayas community. Make sure that it fits in with the policy recommendations and follows the guidelines for implementing projects.

Describe what prior research you would do and how you would implement your project.

Get another group to evaluate your work. Make any modifications which will improve the project.

Guidelines for implementing development projects

Programmes and projects which contribute to the production and delivery of services needed are more likely to succeed when they are planned in collaboration with, and implemented by, community-level organisations, especially those led and organised by women.

- Although women are the victims of adjustment, they are also a largely untapped resource, with their community-managing role unrecognised. Yet they are prepared to invest commitment and time in those interventions directly or indirectly likely to benefit their families and children.

- One of the greatest problems experienced by aid agencies is the survival and development of programmes which prioritise the needs of low-income communities. Therefore, when agencies plan and implement such programmes and projects, they should consult directly with local women who, in their community-managing role, know community needs and can identify the particular constraints, rather than rely on professionals who often neither know the communities, nor have the same level of commitment to project success.

- When agencies plan and implement such programmes and projects they should work directly with local women who are under-utilised in terms of their productive role. In communities such as Indio Guayas many women have academic qualifications, or have undertaken numerous courses that equip them for a diversity of skilled and semi-skilled, as well as unskilled, activities in community-level projects. These projects should generate maximum employment for women in the community, rather than being seen as a means to generate employment for professionals, even when public-sector cuts create pressure to provide such employment.

Migrant women workers

The first two sections of this chapter have looked at women in specific national contexts. Clearly their positions are affected by the world economy and decisions taken in other parts of the world. For some women the complex interdependence of economic and social developments on a global scale is more explicit and personal. The article 'Maid for export' on pages 266–7 looks at the lives of migrant women workers who do duty in the homes of the rich from Turin to Riyadh, and assesses the economic importance of their labour.

The article was introduced with these words: 'The "debt crisis" is providing many middle-class women in Britain, Italy, Singapore, Canada, Kuwait and the USA with a new generation of domestic servants. When a woman from Mexico, Jamaica, or the Philippines decides to emigrate in order to make money as a domestic servant, she is designing her own international debt politics. She is trying to cope with the loss of earning power and rise in the cost of living at home by cleaning bathrooms in the country of the bankers.'

?

1 Design a leaflet of use to women coming to Britain as migrant, domestic workers. Include information about language classes, helplines, etc.

2 Using information from the article, prepare a report for the government or national trade union organisation of a country from which many women migrate as domestic workers. The aim of the report is to convince the recipients that these women have a vital economic importance, and that help should be available for them. Use graphs where appropriate to present the information. Include a list of recommendations for measures which could be taken to help the women migrants.

Figure 11 Domestic workers have begun to create informal networks among themselves and campaign for better conditions

MAID FOR EXPORT

In 1986, money sent back home by citizens working abroad – "remittances" – comprised 78 per cent of the money that Pakistan earned from exports. For Bangladesh, the figure was 56 per cent; Sri Lanka, 27 per cent; India, 25 per cent; Philippines, 18 per cent; Thailand, 10 per cent.

The women and men who send this money home go abroad to do quite different sorts of jobs. The men emigrate to work as seamen and construction workers. Tankers bombed in the Persian Gulf during the recent Iran–Iraq war were owned by Kuwait, Norway, the United States, Japan, Greece; but they were manned by Indian, Pakistani and Filipino crewmen. The women whose home governments rely on them for remittances go abroad to work as nurses, maids, entertainers and prostitutes.

Sri Lanka and the Philippines are the two countries to-day whose economic stability is most dependent on female migrant labour. Sri Lankan and Filipino women who leave home to work abroad have become economically more important than their male counterparts. Some of the Filipino women are recruited to work as nurses, some as entertainers. But the greatest number work as domestic servants. Their governments have relied on feminised labour at home – on plantations, in tourist resorts, in Export Processing Zones – to stay financially afloat. Now they also depend on women's overseas earnings to keep foreign creditors and their financial policeman, the International Monetary Fund, content.

Turin is one of Italy's booming industrial centres. Its economic success has also made it a centre for foreign domestic workers, especially women from Ethiopia and the Philippines. Italian families want household help at low wages. Filipino maids – many of whom are college graduates and have worked as teachers or nurses back home – often arrive in Italy with tourist visas, which prohibit paid work.

But there is an informal network of Filipino women already working in Turin who help the new arrival to make her way through the bureaucratic labyrinths of the Italian immigration department. To convert her tourist visa into a longer-term "guest" visa, a Filipino woman becomes a "guest" of her employer, often the adult man in the household. He then becomes her emissary to the Italian government. For a Filipino woman who has been in Italy for only six months and knows little Italian, this arrangement is attractive because it protects her from bureaucratic intimidation.

In the process, however, the domestic worker's place of employment becomes a prison as well as a sanctuary. The Filipino is only a legal resident of Turin so long as her employer will vouch for her as a guest. Though many Italians stereotype Filipinos as docile and hard-working, with no social life of their own, domestic workers have tried to create, with the help of Catholic nuns, informal networks among friends, sisters and cousins. Here they share news from home and discuss ways of improving their working conditions.

Elsa arrived in Italy in 1982 on a tourist visa and started her job as a domestic servant three days after her arrival. Elsa begins work at 6.45a.m. She makes breakfast for the husband and wife and their two children. After they leave she makes her own breakfast and begins household chores. At 11a.m. Elsa goes to the market to buy food. This is one of her few opportunities for social contact, but since she knows little Italian, she keeps to herself. She prepares a five-course midday meal for the family, using recipes she has had to learn since arriving in Italy. After an hour's rest, Elsa returns to household chores. She must complete them by five or six in the evening so she can start preparing the family's evening meal. She eats alone in the kitchen. Between 9.30p.m. and 10p.m. she finishes the dishes. Then she is free to go out. Usually she is too tired. She is also afraid of getting lost. Besides, she may be harassed by men at night, who will presume that she is a prostitute. So most nights she chooses to finish any cleaning that must be done and then go to bed.

Back home, under President Corazon Aquino, the Philippines is as dependent on income from domestic servants such as Elsa as was the previous regime of Ferdinand Marcos, but it is more sensitive to the contradictions between national dignity and sexist development. By 1988, an estimated 175,000 Filipino women were working overseas, 40 per cent of them as contract workers. As many as 89,000 of the 152,000 Filipino nurses were working overseas, leaving the country with a shortage of medical staff. An estimated 81,000 women were working abroad as domestic workers.

The government requires that overseas workers send home a minimum percentage of their pay; if they do not, the government can withdraw their permission to travel abroad. They were sending home $60 million–$100 million in foreign exchange each year, outstripping the contributions made by either sugar or minerals. Each overseas worker is believed to be supporting at least five dependants back home. Remittances from Filipino men and women together amounted to 18 per cent of the country's $5.7 billion in foreign exchange.

In Singapore, the government requires Filipino domestic servants to take a pregnancy test every six months. If a woman is found to be pregnant she forfeits her work permit and must return home. Women working in Asia, the Middle East and Europe tell stories of being sexually assaulted by the men of the households they worked for. In Hong Kong, Filipino women and domestic service have become so merged in the popular culture that a doll sold widely is called "Filipino maid".

Source: Adapted from Cynthia Enloe, *New Statesman and Society*, 1 December 1989

Sri Lankan, Padmini Palliyaguruge

Padmini Palliyaguruge had been an elementary-school teacher in Sri Lanka. She had also been an activist in local women's organisations. After taking part in a strike to better low-paid teachers' conditions, she found herself locked out of employment. Desperate for work, she decided she had no choice but to sign up with one of the 450 Sri Lankan agencies recruiting Sri Lankan women to work as domestic servants in Saudi Arabia. A woman working as a domestic servant in the Middle East received thirty times the wages she would in Sri Lanka. Even with agency fees of $500–$1,000, and despite the fact that male recruiters have a reputation for abusing women, the opportunity seemed worth taking.

In 1984, an estimated 18,000 Sri Lankan women migrated to take paid jobs overseas, most on short-term contracts. This was the first time that Sri Lankan women outnumbered Sri Lankan men in foreign employment. Of the 200,000 Sri Lankans working on contract in the Middle East in 1987, 70 per cent were women working as maids. Most of them were married. Most came from the country's Singhalese ethnic community, whose men dominate government offices. The repatriated earnings of women working abroad made foreign remittances Sri Lanka's second-largest foreign exchange earner, after tea.

Once in Saudi Arabia, Padmini, like other Sri Lankan maids, had to provide her employer with around-the-clock service.

For some maids the price of the isolation has been excruciatingly high. They are victims of abuse or physical assault by irate employers impatient with their inability to operate electrical appliances, their unwillingness to work long hours or their resistance to sexual advances. Despite these experiences, some women, faced with family bankruptcy, return to the recruiting agency, pay the fee and sign up for another tour of cleaning and cooking abroad. Thus the flow of remittances to Sri Lanka continues, allowing the government to continue paying interest on outstanding foreign loans.

Improving conditions

Padmini Palliyaguruge spoke at the 1985 United Nations Decade for women conference in Nairobi. She spoke not as victim but as an organiser. She was one of the participants in a non-governmental panel intended to make the special problems of migrant women workers visible. The panel's organisers recalled how difficult it has been, even among internationally conscious feminists, to keep migrant women's political issues on the agenda. They seemed to slip out of sight so easily. Thus, organising a separate panel at Nairobi was a deliberate effort to make their conditions visible to other women and to governments. It was also designed to give women organisers a chance to exchange analyses and strategies with each other.

Padmini Palliyaguruge was in Nairobi representing Sri Lanka's Progressive Women's Front. She was exchanging ideas with women who had been migrant workers or were helping to organise women working abroad. It had been almost impossible to get local trade unions to take their issues seriously. Many trade union men didn't see domestic workers as genuine workers. Their work looked too much like what their wives did without pay. Furthermore, these domestic servants' employers were themselves women, hardly challenging adversaries for male union bargainers!

The experiences of domestic workers serves to underscore how simplistic the First-World/Third-World split is, and how inadequate it is to make sense of today's international politics. Literally hundreds of thousands of women from Third-World countries are cleaning the homes and minding the children of *other*, more affluent Third-World women. In China today, the government and the Communist Party's own Women's Federation are officially encouraging urban households to hire maids as a way of reducing the housework responsibilities of other women. As in Britain and the United States, maids are being seen as the solution to the career woman's "double burden". In Latin America "domestic worker" is the single largest job category for women. Most of those women are working for other women. Furthermore, most Sri Lankan women working in the Gulf States and Filipino women in Singapore and Hong Kong are employed in what we still refer to as "Third-World" societies.

The creation of networks and institutions to empower women working as domestic servants has called for activists to rethink how changing power relations both within and between countries depend on ideas about "home", "motherhood" and "job". Politically active maids have not always found feminists in the host countries to be reliable allies. Too often, local feminist groups in countries importing maids were led by women of precisely the social class that hired domestic workers. Combined with the differences of language and race that often accompany the domestic politics of paid housework, the barriers proved hard to surmount.

Finally, some politically active women seemed to have trouble even seeing a domestic servant as a "worker". She didn't capture activists' imagination the way a garment worker or a prostitute did. The dangers and struggles involved in washing another woman's kitchen floor were less apparent than those in sewing blue jeans in a hot and dusty factory.

One of the conclusions domestic workers have drawn from these experiences is that they need to build their own organisations. Their principal alliances may be with working women back home, not with either host-country trade unions or host-country feminists. In making these connections, domestic workers throw into sharp relief the connections between their governments' policies of feminising low-paid factory work, relying on women as mothers and wives to carry the burden of cutbacks in public service imposed by the IMF and women's own internalised notions of familial duty.

11

Refugees: problems and prospects in the late twentieth century

John Rogge

Vietnamese refugees arriving in Hong Kong, 1988

A Christmas of death for Sudan's refugees

CHRISTMAS came early to Hilat Shok this year, leaving seven dead and many injured. Hilat Shok is a rubbish dump in the flat desert on the southern fringes of Khartoum. It is littered with broken, rusting things, heaps of smouldering refuse and about 20,000 people. The sun glares down ferociously as if the earth were closer to it here than anywhere else, intensifying the heat and stench.

It is only a few minutes' drive from the centre of Khartoum – destitution always seems worse when it is close to comfort. The people who exist here – live is too strong a word – have crawled hundreds of miles from the civil war in southern Sudan, seeking the safety of the capital. Mostly Dinka and Nuer people, they have lost their homes, their cattle and in many cases their children, who have been kidnapped or just died of hunger on the way. They are only a few of the million and a half displaced people who hang on to the fringes of Khartoum.

Hilat Shok has improved since I visited it two years ago. There is a makeshift school of reeds, and the local Catholic school has given it some books. Oxfam has provided donkeys and water carts to bypass the local merchants who were charging exorbitant prices for water.

But the main improvements have been made by the people themselves. They have reproduced their beehive homes – which would have been made of grass in their villages in the southern savannah – but here they have made them with cardboard boxes, neatly stiched together with strips of rubber. The quality of cardboard is high; I found walls of Pampers nappies and Heineken

Dinka people who have fled the war in the South find refuge in Hilat Shok Camp, Khartoum, Sudan

boxes, and one hut made of Highland Spring Water boxes. How they will stand up to rain is not yet known. They were made after the August flooding which turned the whole camp into a putrid lake for a week.

Not even after the floods did the camp receive a visit from a government official, and not a penny has been given by the government to the displaced people here. But journalists from Danish radio, in Khartoum to cover the floods, went home and launched a campaign to collect blankets for Hilat Shok. They collected 7,000 and sent them to Sudan with a request to the Sudan Red Crescent to distribute them. Sudan Red Crescent officials had never been to the camp before, and new nothing of the clan structures and tribal rivalries which still dominate the government of the camp. The officials simply lined everyone up and gave out the

blankets. Within a day there was a riot and seven people were dead. All the Nuer people from Hilat Shok had to flee with whatever they had to hand.

I found about 50 Nuer families a few miles away on another rubbish dump. Within sight of the Khartoum skyline, with the occasional airliner passing overhead, they had absolutely nothing except the rags they stood in. They had slept on the ground since they had arrived, and there was no sign of food or water. Women and children were huddled under scraps of plastic draped across thorn twigs to escape the blazing heat. Some had already cleared little patches of rubbish, and the men were planting sticks in the ground, but there was nothing to cover them with, not even cardboard. We gave the chief what money we had, and said we would tell one of the aid agencies about them.

Source: Richard Dowden, *Independent*, 24 December 1988

Cold comfort for refugee Kurds

Tim Kelsey reports from Mus, south-eastern Turkey

AT THE top of the field, thick with snow just behind the barbed wire, a Kurdish mother made her way towards a small makeshift cemetery. She bent down, her bright and flimsy dress blowing in a lashing wind, and laid a handful of twigs on one of the clay headstones.

'That was her son,' said Hassan, who had been an electronics engineer in Iraqi Kurdistan before joining the *peshmerga* fighters. 'But she's not the only one. The cold is terrible for the children.' With temperatures dipping below −10°C during the night and with constant snow falls, the weather in the refugee camp near Mus in south-eastern Turkey could hardly be worse for the 8,000 Iraqi Kurds sheltering in dozens of tiny, cramped bungalows originally built for local earthquake victims.

Christmas Day, for the very small Christian minority among the generally Muslim Kurds who will mark it, will be a solemn occasion. Nobody here can forget that five months ago the Iraqi President, Saddam Hussein, started his campaign against the Kurds of northern Iraq – an offensive which involved the use of at least three different kinds of chemical weapons against the population. Tens of thousands fled into Turkey with little money and few clothes. They remain officially as 'guests' because the Turkish government is reluctant to offend Iraq by granting them refugee status.

Despite the barbed wire, the Kurds are philosophical. There are shortages of essentials – for instance, no baby-food or fresh milk – but conditions, most agree, are preferable to those in the temporary tent camps they inhabited immediately after crossing the border in September. 'We are very grateful to the Turks for all their assistance,' an elderly Kurdish man said. 'They are not a rich people and they have done as much as they can, although we worry it is not enough to ensure all our children will live.'

There is increasing optimism that conditions will improve in the new year because the Turks, now desperately short of resources, have asked the United Nations to provide assistance. But the sense of impotence, the lack of control over their immediate destiny and a desperate concern for friends and relatives still fighting in Iraq have created an atmosphere of listlessness and pessimism in Mus.

In the other two refugee camps in Turkey, near the towns of Diyarbakir and Mardin, where conditions and the climate are marginally better, the Kurds have been quick to arrange sporting activities, to elect governing committees and even, in Mardin, to establish a Kurdish choir. But not Mus. 'Nobody does anything here,' said a mother washing clothes in one of the communal water troughs. 'We aren't dying, but not quite living either.'

Source: Independent, 24 December 1988

1 Read through the newspaper articles. Locate in an atlas the places and towns mentioned.

2 You may be reading this chapter in 1990, 1991, 1992 ... What similar articles can you find in newspapers? Has the refugee problem gone away? Why, or why not? In class, brainstorm to make a list of the events which make people refugees.

3 This is a detailed chapter. However, it is not intended that you learn all the details, but rather that you grasp the overall issues. As you work through the chapter note down the problems that are common to refugees and those that are common to asylum countries.

Changing migration patterns

The *involuntary* migration of people, either as individuals or in groups, is the oldest form of migration. Throughout history, the *push* factors that have produced migrations have ranged from environmental deterioration – often as a consequence of over-population – to a wide array of natural catastrophes and to the consequences of people's inhumanity to fellow beings, expressed in wars, the persecution by the state of individuals or groups, or by intolerance of one part of society towards another. Migrations undertaken primarily for economic gain, or the mass migration from the countryside to the city are, in comparison, relatively recent phenomena.

During the nineteenth century and in the earlier part of this century, the opening-up of the New World, together with the accelerating pace of urbanisation that paralleled the spread of the Industrial Revolution, resulted in the greatest economic migration that has ever taken place.

Today, the process of urbanisation in the industrialised world has run its course; most of its population is now urban, and traditional European source areas for New World immigrants are no longer producing many migrants. Instead, it is in the developing nations that there exists an ever-growing process of emigration to regions of better opportunity. The economic and social *push* factors in the Third World, and the economic *pull* factors of the industrialised world, intensify as disparities between rich and poor nations grow. The number of potential migrants is far greater today than was ever the case in nineteenth- or early twentieth-century Europe. However, with the exception of immigration into the US, Canada, and to a lesser extent, Australia, and some limited possibilities for temporary labour migration to Western Europe, the Middle East oil-producing states, and some other areas, there are few opportunities for permanent emigration from the Third World.

?

---

1 Study Figure 1 and try to take in the detail. Rank the number of refugees for each country listed from highest to lowest. What are the worst spots in terms of numbers? Compare your list with Figure 3.

As we approach the end of the twentieth century, involuntary migration is once again becoming a major form of population movement. Political conflicts, racial and religious intolerance, and natural catastrophes are, between them, producing an ever-growing proportion of the world's total

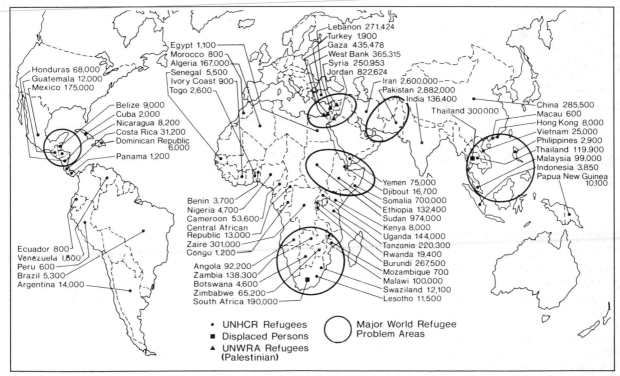

Figure 1 Number of UNHCR and other refugees in countries of asylum
Source: Refugees, No. 48, UNHCR, December 1987

Figure 2 Somali refugee camps, 1979

migrants. There are currently over twelve million officially-recognised political refugees – most of them originating from the Third World.

In addition, there are probably as many, if not more, involuntary migrants displaced *within* their own countries by political conditions or natural disasters, for example in the Sudan. And, as economically disadvantaged or oppressed people in the Third World find doors to economic opportunity in industrialised countries closing ever tighter, an increasing number of them are choosing to claim refugee status in desperate attempts to gain permanent access to a better life. Consequently, basic questions such as:

a Who really is a refugee?

b What sort of solutions need to be adopted in dealing with real or bogus refugees? and

c Why is there such a widespread and general deterioration in public and government sympathy and tolerance towards refugees?

are being asked with increasing frequency, yet are becoming ever more complex to answer.

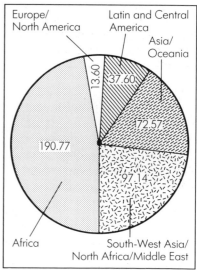

Figure 3 UNHCR expenditure by region (US$m) 1986
Source: Refugees, No. 48, UNHCR, December 1987

Who is a refugee?

This section relates to definitions and dilemmas to do with refugees. Read through the resources carefully. Before we look in detail at our case studies of Africa, South-East Asia and Canada, it is necessary to reflect upon the question of *who* is a refugee. The problem of determining who is a *bona fide* refugee has become very complex; many people claim to be refugees, but many of these claims are not accepted by asylum states or the international community. Hence the term *economic refugee* has been coined to refer to migrants who claim refugee status, but are in reality migrating primarily for economic reasons.

Most international response to refugees is based upon statutes laid down after World War 2 by the International Refugee Organisation and its successor, in 1951, the United Nations High Commission for Refugees (UNHCR). The 1951 United Nations Convention on Refugees adopted a very specific definition of a refugee. A refugee has to demonstrate that he/she has fled their normal country of residence for reasons of persecution or fear of persecution. The cause has to be *political* and the migration has to be across an *international* border.

Rules for determining refugee status

In 1967, the United Nations Protocol Relating to the Status of Refugees further refined 'rules' governing refugees. It removed, in recognition of growing Third World refugee problems, the 1951 dateline and European focus of the Convention, and specified two fundamental rights for refugees, namely, the *right to asylum*, and the *right to non-refoulement* (forcible repatriation). Most UN members have become signa-

tories to both these statutes, although there are some notable exceptions, especially major refugee asylum states such as Mexico, Pakistan and Thailand. Most countries have adhered to these 'rules', even those who are not signatories. However, as the burden of refugee support continues to grow in some regions, there are indications that these rights may not always remain acceptable to potential asylum states; the spectre of forcible repatriation is threatening in several places. This will be discussed later in the chapter.

It is evident that these international statutes have some serious shortcomings, and that contem-

porary refugee migrations cannot be dealt with as readily as were earlier post-war refugee migrants from Eastern and Central Europe. Today, many refugees do not meet all criteria spelled out in the Convention, yet they face danger or threat to their lives: severe economic oppression usually has political roots. Food is increasingly being used as a weapon. A consequence of this is a growing grey area of definition between clearly identifiable Convention refugees and purely economic migrants who masquerade as refugees in desperate attempts to secure a better future in wealthier countries.

The 1951 UN Convention definition of a refugee

'An individual who as a result of events occurring before January 1951 and owing to well-founded fear of being persecuted for reasons of race, religion, nationality, membership of a particular social group or political opinion, is outside the country of his nationality and is unable, or owing to such fears, unwilling to avail himself of the protection of that country; or, who, not having a nationality and being outside the country of his habitual residence as a result of such events, is unable or, owing to such fear, is unwilling to return to it.'

List of state parties to the 1951 UN Convention and the 1967 protocol relating to the status of refugees

Algeria, Angola, Argentina, Australia, Austria, Belgium, Benin, Bolivia, Botswana, Brazil, Burkina Faso, Burundi, Canada, Central African Rep., Cameroon, Chad, Chile, China, Colombia, Congo, Costa Rica, Cyprus, Denmark, Djibouti, Dominican Republic, Ecuador, Egypt, El Salvador, Ethiopia, Equatorial Guinea, Fiji, Finland, France, Gabon, Gambia, Germany (FRG), Ghana, Greece, Guatemala, Guinea, Guinea-Bissau, Haiti, Holy See, Iceland, Iran, Ireland, Israel, Italy, Ivory Coast, Jamaica, Japan, Kenya, Lesotho, Liberia, Liechtenstein, Luxembourg, Malawi, Mali, Malta, Mauritania, Morocco, Netherlands, New Zealand, Nicaragua, Niger, Nigeria, Norway, Panama, Papua New Guinea, Paraguay, Peru, Philippines, Portugal, Rwanda, Sao Tome and Principe, Senegal, Seychelles, Sierra Leone, Somalia, Spain, Sudan, Suriname, Sweden, Switzerland, Togo, Tunisia, Turkey, Tuvalu, Uganda, United Kingdom, United Republic of Tanzania, Uruguay, Yemen (Arab Republic), Yugoslavia, Zaire, Zambia, Zimbabwe.

Signatories to the *Convention Only*: Madagascar, Monaco, Mozambique.
Signatories to the *Protocol Only*: Swaziland, United States, Venezuela.

Source: World Refugee Survey, 1987

Comments on the UN Convention

A refugee in the strict sense of the Convention must meet the persecution test, but persecution is not defined. Article 33, which refers to a threat to life and freedom for the reasons stated, comes close, but other serious human rights violations would also constitute persecution. Persecution may stem from action by State authorities, or from sections of the population. In the latter case, persecution would come within the Convention only if it were knowingly tolerated by the authorities, or if the authorities refused, or were unable, to offer effective protection.

In different regions of the world it is now argued that many of today's asylum seekers do not qualify as refugees under these criteria. Asylum seekers may indeed face danger of a threat to their lives, safety or freedom, but it is claimed that these do not arise for 'Convention reasons'. Other dangers or threats, for example, from sustained generalized violence, foreign aggression and internal conflicts or massive violations of human rights, do not amount to persecution in the sense of the Convention and thus cannot form the basis for a claim to refugee status. At the same time, some receiving States claim that many asylum seekers do not leave their countries of origin because of danger or threat to their lives or freedom, but for economic reasons or other reasons of personal convenience.

Source: Refugees No. 50, February 1988

TAMIL ASYLUM SEEKERS

Tamil asylum seekers in Switzerland

Twenty thousand Tamils chose to settle in the Federal Republic of Germany, 20,000 in France, 4,500 in Switzerland and as many again in the Netherlands and Denmark. After lengthy procedures, a large number – around 85 per cent – of the asylum applications submitted to the competent authorities were refused. The governments concerned were generally reluctant to send Tamils back to Sri Lanka. Many took notice of strong appeals by UNHCR and the fact that the situation in Sri Lanka remained unstable, and allowed the Tamils to remain on their territory, although not always in acceptable conditions. Legislative provisions allow some States to grant residence permits for humanitarian reasons. In the majority of cases, however, remaining in host countries means a shadowy existence – no residence permit, no work permit, no social security. This absence of any firm legal status or rights puts the Tamil asylum seeker in a highly precarious situation, making him entirely dependent on his more fortunate compatriots, living from day to day in anxiety and uncertainty. The treatment of Tamils in India is hardly more enviable: 30,000 people have been settled in camps in extremely precarious conditions.

Source: Refugees No. 48, December 1987

Refugees in orbit

An Eritrean being interrogated by the Ethiopian police for political reasons managed to escape from his country of origin. He went directly to Italy and asked for asylum. He thought that his reasons were strong and expected no problem in being granted asylum. The Italian authorities refused him asylum, however, despite the fact that the Italian Constitution prescribes the granting of asylum to political refugees. He came from Africa; Italy still upholds geographical limitations to the 1951 Refugee Convention and the 1967 Refugee Protocol. Our refugee was not discouraged; he travelled farther north and entered Switzerland. Once again his application for asylum was rejected: a prerequisite for asylum in Switzerland is that application be made within twenty days of the escape from the country of origin, and he had now been *en route* for longer than that. He had to go on, and entered the Federal Republic of Germany. He went to the 'Aliens Police', only to find that there was no possibility of his remaining in that country. They felt his fear of persecution was not well founded: so far he had not been persecuted, and he had voluntarily left Ethiopia. His case was not even referred to federal authorities responsible for refugee status determination. He decided to seek asylum in Sweden, but made the mistake of travelling to Sweden via Denmark. The Swedish Immigration Board decided that our refugee, who had by now spend a few weeks in detention should be returned to Denmark, the nordic state he had first entered. The Swedish authorities could invoke a provision in the Nordic Convention concerning the Waiver of Passport Control at Intra-Nordic Frontiers.

Denmark also rejected his application for asylum, invoking a bilateral agreement with Germany to return him to that country. As he realized that asylum in Germany was out of the question, he continued immediately on to the Netherlands. The Dutch authorities accepted that he was a *bona fide* refugee, but could find no reason why the Netherlands should grant him asylum. He had, after all, escaped several months earlier from his country of origin and had passed through a number of other countries, each of which could have granted him asylum. The Netherlands could not be considered the country of first asylum, and his having been refused a residence permit in a number of countries was no reason for him to be allowed to remain there.

In Belgium his application for asylum was also rejected, since he had been *en route* too long. Not even in France was his application taken seriously. As Italy, according to the French authorities, should be considered the country of first asylum, he was returned to that country. Here he did not even bother to make a new application, but continued to Switzerland, and then to Germany, Austria, and Sweden. He may still be floating around Europe, constantly afraid of discovery and forced to continue his odyssey. He is a refugee in orbit, and he is not a unique case.

Source: G. Melander, 'Refugees with no country of asylum: strategies for third country resettlement', J. R. Rogge (ed.), *Refugees: A Third World Dilemma*, Totowa: Rowman and Littlefield, 1987, pp. 37–38. Reprinted by permission of the publisher

The case of Sri Lankan Tamils in Europe illustrates this problem of status determination. Sri Lanka is clearly a country experiencing serious internal political confrontation, yet, are all Tamils fleeing the country necessarily fearing persecution, or are some simply seeking to emigrate to an industrialised country?

There are many other groups like the Tamils. While politicians and bureaucrats grapple with the problem of status determination, refugees live in a protracted state of uncertainty and precariousness. Unable or unwilling to return home, and denied refugee status in their country of first asylum, they migrate elsewhere to begin the refugee-claimant process again. The term *refugees in orbit* has been used aptly to describe this type of refugee migrant. There are many thousands of them in Europe and increasingly also in North America.

1 In groups or as a class discuss the limitations of the definition of a refugee. What would you want to do with the definition – expand it or narrow it? Why?

2 List the overall consequences of any changes you make to the definition.

3 What countries do not appear on the list of parties to the convention and protocol relating to the status of refugees? What arguments would you put forward to try to persuade someone to join?

4 In groups discuss your reaction to 'Refugees in orbit'. Hypothesise about possible solutions to this problem. Write a scenario suggesting the whereabouts and living conditions of the refugees today.

Africa's refugees

Africa is the first of our case studies. It contains about one-third of refugees recognised by UNHCR, but, in addition, there are many more involuntary migrants displaced within their countries. Over half of Africa's states are currently hosting refugees, and many have accepted refugees from more than one neighbouring country. Tanzania, for example, has refugees from six of its eight neighbours, as well as from South Africa and Namibia. Ten countries have over 100,000 refugees, and one, Sudan, has very close to one million. Many African states are both recipients and sources of refugees; this is a feature unique to Africa.

Figures 4 and 5 show the distribution of Africa's refugees over time. The first contemporary refugees were displaced as Africa's independence era was

dawning in the mid-1950s; the war for independence in Algeria, and the civil war that erupted in southern Sudan on the eve of Sudan's independence in 1956, were the first major refugee crises on the continent. By the mid-1960s, some half a million refugees had been created, and, in 1971, the one million mark was passed.

1 Look closely at Figures 4 and 5. List countries which did not have a refugee problem in 1972 but did in 1986.

2 Make a list of countries with refugee problems, and beside each country note the reason why.

3 Examine Figure 6. Make sure you understand the terms used before reading the commentary that follows.

Durable solutions

In any refugee situation, three desirable solutions are normally sought. These are referred to as *durable solutions*: ones that are lasting and benefit refugees. Both first-asylum states and the international community usually strive together to achieve such solutions. They are not always successful, as the growing number of *refugees in orbit* in Europe, the long-term confinement of Palestinian refugees to *holding camps*, and the *refoulement* of Cambodians from Thailand in 1979, all clearly testify. Africa, however, has achieved considerable success in implementing two of the three common durable solutions: *local integration and settlement* and *repatriation*.

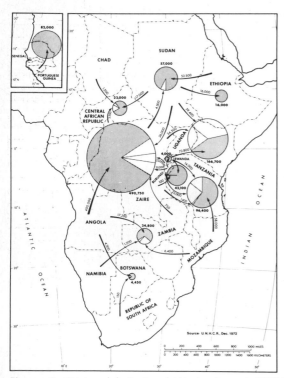

Figure 4 Origin and destination of Africa's refugees in 1972
Source: UNHCR, December 1972

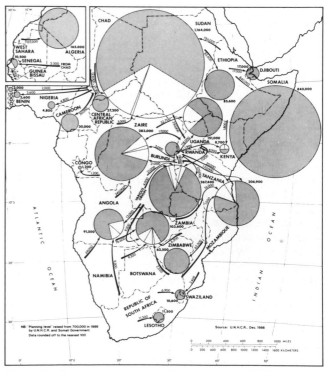

Figure 5 Origin and destination of Africa's refugees in 1986
Source: UNHCR, December 1986

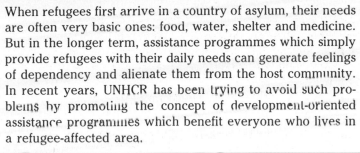

When refugees first arrive in a country of asylum, their needs are often very basic ones: food, water, shelter and medicine. But in the longer term, assistance programmes which simply provide refugees with their daily needs can generate feelings of dependency and alienate them from the host community. In recent years, UNHCR has been trying to avoid such problems by promoting the concept of development-oriented assistance programmes which benefit everyone who lives in a refugee-affected area.

Source: *Refugees* No. 48, December 1987

Local integration of refugees

By far the most commonly adopted solution to refugee crises in Africa has been local integration and settlement. African asylum states are among the world's poorest nations, and, consequently, few resources are available for diversion to refugees. The sooner refugees become self-reliant, the less the burden imposed upon an asylum state. Given prevailing levels of poverty, the support provided to refugees by African asylum states has been exceptionally generous. This is especially the case in countries that have had very large and long-term influxes such as Sudan and Tanzania.

In most cases, African asylum states have tried to introduce development-oriented assistance programmes for refugees. Land has been provided, either through government grants for organised agricultural settlements, or by local chiefs for spontaneously settled refugees. Refugees have been encouraged to produce food and take care of their other needs as quickly as possible, as well as contribute to local economies through sale of surplus produce or labour.

Some countries have incorporated refugees into regional development strategies.

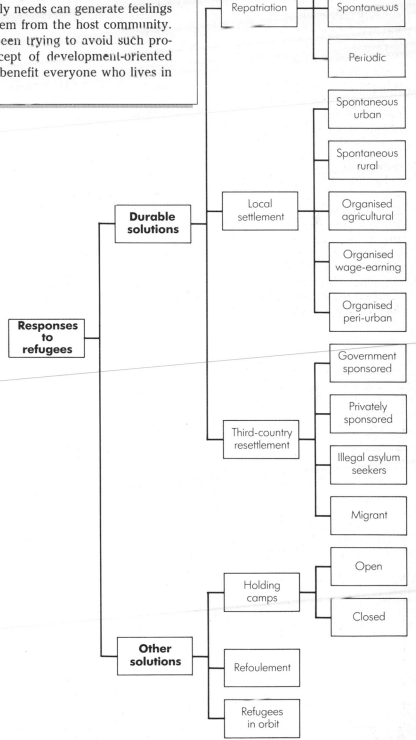

Figure 6   Durable and other solutions to refugees

Figure 7 Tanzanian settlement scheme for refugees from Burundi

Tanzania

Tanzania, for example, resettled Burundi refugees into hitherto underdeveloped areas and has succeeded in developing these areas into productive agricultural zones. The three Burundi settlement schemes at Katumba, Mishamo and Ulyankulu (Figures 7 and 8), which between them accommodate some 175,000 settlers, are now virtually self-sufficient and are major contributors to their regional economies. Moreover, Tanzania is almost alone among African asylum states in offering citizenship to locally-integrated refugees.

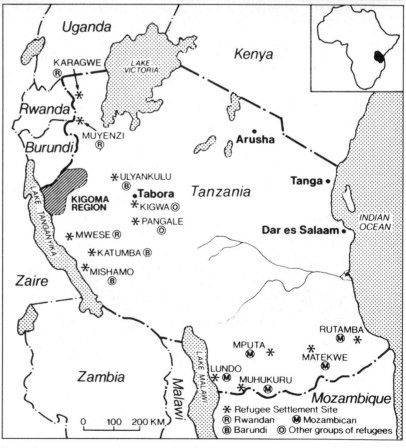

Figure 8 Location of refugee settlements in Tanzania

A synopsis of Sudan's Regulation of Asylum Act 1974

1 The granting of asylum by Sudan is a peaceful and humanitarian act and should not be seen by the government of the country of origin of refugees as sympathy by Sudan for the cause of the refugee exodus.

2 The optimum solution to any refugee dilemma is the voluntary repatriation of refugees.

3 In the absence of repatriation or alternative solutions such as third country resettlement, refugees should be discouraged from spontaneously settling in either rural or urban areas and instead be relocated on government-organised settlement schemes located away from sensitive border areas, with the aim of becoming self-sufficient either through agriculture or by selling their labour.

4 The level of support and infrastructure made available to refugees by government agencies and the international community should not be greater than that available to local Sudanese communities; whenever possible, installations on refugee schemes should also be available to local Sudanese.

5 To provide solutions to the problem of urban refugees, especially students who require continuing education and vocational training.

6 To provide for the needs of the growing number of orphans, aged, widowed, and handicapped refugees who are unable to fully support themselves.

7 To launch long-term programmes that will integrate as far as is possible the settlement schemes into the overall development strategies for the areas in which they are situated.

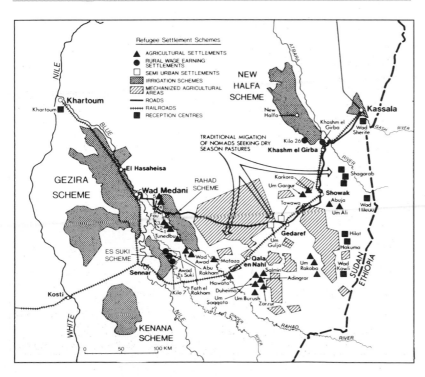

Sudan: progressive refugee legislation

Africa's largest refugee host, Sudan, must be cited for its progressive refugee legislation. The Regulation of Asylum Act 1974 entrenches the rights of refugees in Sudan. It emphasises the importance of self-reliance through organised agricultural settlement and integration into regional development strategies. Also, it recognises that assistance to refugees should never appear to make them a privileged group by providing infrastructural facilities superior to those available to locals; whenever possible, installations on refugee settlements by UNHCR, or its implementing voluntary agencies, must be available to local populations.

Since the first wave of Eritrean refugees from Ethiopia started arriving in Sudan in the late 1960s, large tracts of land have been set aside for refugees by presidential decree. Indeed, the first six agricultural settlements south of Qala en Nahal (Figure 9) were established on a land grant of over 100,000 acres in an area with sufficient rainfall for sorghum and sesame seed production. However, as more and more refugees arrived, later organised settlements, such as those near Showak, were located in areas much too dry to support reliable cultivation. The little progress made in this area was wiped out during the drought years of 1984–5. Also, because of land scarcity, authorities established rural and sub-urban wage-earning settlements, where refugees were to become self-reliant solely through the sale of labour. They proved to be the least successful of Sudan's settlement schemes. Land scarcity and lack of rural economic opportunity have contributed to a large and illegal migration to urban

Figure 9 Organised settlements in eastern Sudan

areas. Sudan contains Africa's largest urban refugee population, most of it living in abject poverty at the very margins of society.

Eastern Sudan illustrates a problem common to many refugee situations. Initially, indigenous residents were sympathetic and supportive of refugees, according them traditional African hospitality. However, as numbers grew, and competition for resources and access to services and essential commodities became acute, this hospitality soured and outright hostility ensued. Refugees now outnumber locals in some areas of eastern Sudan, and the locals complain that the refugees are 'too many and have been around too long'. Figure 10 illustrates the tremendous growth of Sudan's refugee population from the mid-1970s onwards; most of this growth is concentrated in eastern Sudan.

Today, the finite and fragile land resource of this region is competed for by large irrigation schemes which produce Sudan's principal crop – cotton, by extensive mechanised dry-farms which produce Sudan's other two primary crops – sorghum and sesame seed, by traditional semi-nomadic herdsmen who use the land for dry season pasture, by local shifting cultivators, and by refugees who now constitute nearly 50% of the rural population. All the ingredients for confrontation have clearly been assembled, and demonstrations against refugees, some of which lead to fatalities, are increasing in frequency. Similar problems are occurring in urban areas like Khartoum, Port Sudan, or Kassala, where refugees are blamed for the rising cost of food and housing, for depressed wages, for taking jobs from locals, and for anti-social activities and crime. Several refugee shanty towns have been torched.

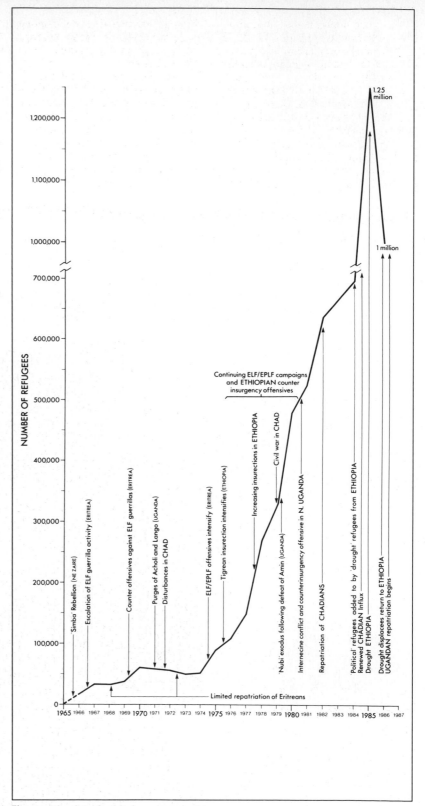

Figure 10 Growth of Sudan refugee problem
Source: UNHCR

The saloon bar notion that immigrants take the jobs of the indigenous population and thereby create unemployment is simply wrong. It involves the remarkably persistent fallacy that there is only a given amount of work to do in the economy — and if a foreigner or a machine takes it over, unemployment will surely result.

While there continue to be unmet wants in any society, this theory is demonstrably wrong-headed. An increase in the factors of production – land, labour, capital – is an opportunity for a rise in output.

Imagine the implications if this 'lump of output' fallacy were true. There would have been no rise in the output of the British economy since the industrial revolution, and the increase in the size of population from 11 million at the time of the Napoleonic wars to 58 million today would inexorably have been accompanied by an equivalent and equal rise in unemployment to a total of 47 million.

In the real world removed from private paranoia, market economies are flexible and people's demands for goods and services are hard to sate. Economies are able to absorb large increases in labour extremely rapidly, with generally only short term transitional or 'frictional' costs.

Source: Christopher Huhne, *Guardian*, 14 June 1989

?

1 You are to write a memorandum to a charity or aid organisation in another country with the purpose of giving ideas on how to cope with refugees. Use Tanzania and Sudan as examples. Do not neglect to suggest how possible difficulties might be overcome.

Figure 11 Refugees in Senegal packing their belongings to return home to Guinea-Bissau

Repatriation of refugees

The ideal solution to any refugee situation is repatriation. What is more natural than refugees returning home? Certainly, African asylum states, the refugees, the Organisation for African Unity (OAU), and much of the international community, all assume that most African refugee migrations are only temporary phenomena and that, sooner or later, all will repatriate. This view is to some extent understandable when one compares the causes of many of the continent's refugee migrations with causes in other world regions. It was inevitable that anti-colonial wars would be won and that refugees would, therefore, return. Most early post-independence civil wars were also regarded as passing phases in the adjustment process to self-rule. Many repatriations have taken place over the past two decades as shown in Table 1.

Voluntary repatriation?

Another issue is that of the *voluntariness* of repatriation. Even though African states are signatories to the UN Protocol that guarantees the right of non-refoulement, there is growing concern that some African states, in responding to rising hostility among their own people towards refugees, may begin to use force in repatriating them. Sudan, for example, made an unequivocal statement in February 1988 that it will no longer permit refugees to enter eastern Sudan. While it has yet to enforce this threat, the growing pressure on government to do something about refugee numbers could conceivably result in such drastic actions.

Table 1 Repatriation of refugees in Africa

	Scale and direction of major repatriations 1971–88		
Year	Total repatriating throughout Africa	Major groups of repatriates	Size of group
1971–2	19,271	Zairans from Burundi	7,000
		Zairans from Sudan	1,068
		Zairans from Zambia	9,250
1972–3	92,015	Zairans from Burundi	20,000
		Sudanese from CAR	17,000
		Sudanese from Ethiopia	7,400
		Sudanese from Uganda	25,600
		Sudanese from Zaire	21,000
1973–4	87,826	Sudanese from Ethiopia	14,216
		Sudanese from CAR	16,000
		Sudanese from Uganda	53,000
		Barundi from Rwanda	4,000
1974–5	47,969	Guinea Bissauans from Senegal	40,000
		Mozambiquans from Tanzania	2,000
		Zairans from Tanzania	4,700
1975–6	112,583	Guinea Bissauans from Senegal	74,000
		Mozambiquans from Tanzania	37,000
1976–7	12,510	Guinea Bissauans from Senegal	10,000
1977–8	22,049	Barundi from Zaire	6,000
		Comorians from various states	16,000
1978–9	190,045	Zairans from Angola	150,000
		Zairans from Burundi	36,000
		Angolans from Zambia	3,000
		Angolans from Portugal	1,000
1979–80	130,757	Zairans from Angola	2,000
		Zairans from Burundi	35,000
		Zimbabweans from Botswana	19,900
		Zimbabweans from Mozambique	11,000
		Zimbabweans from Zambia	20,000
		Equatorial Guineans from Cameroon	20,000
		Equatorial Guineans from Gabon	15,000
		Ugandans from Tanzania	4,000
1980–1	166,740	Zimbabweans from Botswana	22,000
		Zimbabweans from Mozambique	72,000
		Zimbabweans from Zambia	21,000
		Angolans from Zaire	50,000
1981–2	327,281	Zairans from Burundi	20,650
		Chadians from Cameroon	67,500
		Chadians from Sudan	13,000
		Chadians from other states	69,500
		Angolans from Zaire	46,000
		Ethiopians from various states	110,000
1982–3	146,963	Chadians from Nigeria	3,500
		Chadians from Sudan	2,000
		Ugandans from Zaire	15,000
		Ethiopians from various states	126,000
1983–4	238,612	Zairans from Burundi	2,062
		Ethiopians from Djibouti	35,000
		Chadians from Sudan	1,000
		Ugandans from Zaire/Sudan	200,000
1984–5	206,880	Zairans from Angola	6,800
		Ethiopians from Djibouti	6,200
		Ethiopians from Sudan	170,000
		Ugandans from Sudan	5,833
		Ugandans from Zaire	14,800

Year	Total repatriating throughout Africa	Major groups of repatriates	Size of group
1985–6	158,117	Zairans from Angola	6,800
		Ethiopians from Djibouti	7,475
		Ethiopians from Sudan	121,000
		Rwandans from Tanzania	2,000
		Ugandans from Sudan	3,353
		Ugandans from Zaire	14,798
1986–7	253,798	Chadians from CAR	19,775
		Ethiopians from Sudan	150,000
		Ugandans from Kenya	2,600
		Ugandans from Rwanda	30,400
		Ugandans from Sudan	33,000
		Ugandans from Zaire	16,740
1987–8	288,757	Chadians from CAR	16,932
		Chadians from Sudan	15,000
		Ethiopians from Djibouti	3,223
		Ethiopians from Somalia	80,000
		Ethiopians from Sudan	65,000
		Sudanese from Kenya	1,400
		Ugandans from Sudan	100,000
		Ugandans from Zaire	6,000
Total	**2,502,173**		

Source: UNHCR

Djibouti has reacted. Since 1983, it has pressured Ethiopian refugees to repatriate, even though many refugees continue to fear for their safety on returning. Essentially, refugees have been given no choice but to return, as this small and impoverished country rids itself of the burden of refugee support.

1 Using Table 1, an atlas and two outline maps of Africa, trace the direction of repatriation during:
a 1970–80,
b 1980–8.

2 Note the size of the largest groups of repatriates on each map.

3 Comment on any patterns you have found.

Figure 12 Ethiopian refugees in Djibouti, 1977

The Indochinese refugees

The end of the Vietnam War in 1975 unleashed a massive outpouring of refugees from three of the countries that make up Indochina – Vietnam, Laos and Cambodia (Kampuchea). It also set in motion ever greater involuntary migrations within the region (Figure 13). However, we will examine only the refugees who sought asylum in other countries of the region, either as *boat people* or, in the case of Thailand and China, who fled overland into exile – the so-called *land people*.

?

1 Examine Figure 13 and write an account of what it tells us.

Between 1975 and 1977 refugees continued to flee overland to Thailand, albeit on a reduced scale, but in 1978, departures by boat from Vietnam, to any country in the region that would permit them to land, began in earnest (Figure 13). The exodus hit crisis proportions in 1979, when around 200,000 boat people dispersed throughout the region. The consequence of this refugee crisis was that asylum states in the region became very resistant, if not openly hostile, to accepting more refugees. Malaysian authorities pushed overloaded boats back out to sea, some of which never reached another landfall, and Thailand forcibly repatriated some 42,000 Khmer Rouge to an uncertain fate in Vietnamese-controlled Cambodia. Pirates added to the suffering of boat people. It was only after a UNHCR-sponsored conference produced a commitment from industrialised countries to resettle refugees that first-asylum countries reluctantly agreed to accept more.

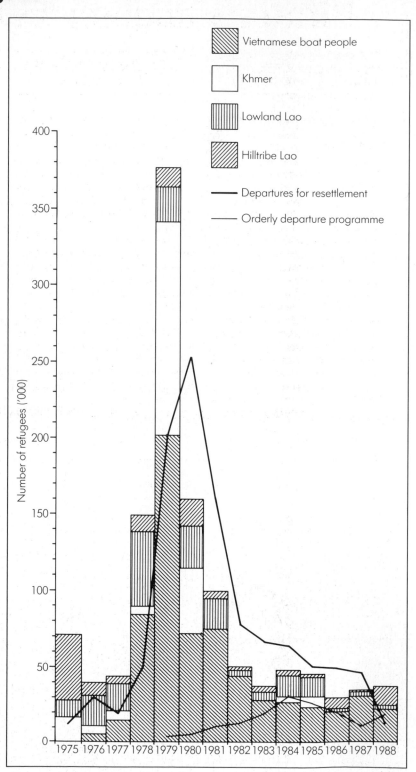

Figure 13 Indochinese refugees, 1975–88
Source: Compiled from UNHCR data

Pirates slaughter boat people

PIRATES attacked a boat carrying 84 Vietnamese refugees in the South China Sea, killing most of the men on board and kidnapping the women and children.

UN officials in Malaysia said yesterday that only 13 survivors had been found.

The boat left Vietnam early last Thursday. By Sunday evening the 84 had reached the Malaysian coast, one step away from a refugee camp and possible resettlement in the West. Instead, they were intercepted by two fishing boats and dragged out to sea.

After robbing them and transferring the women and children to their two boats, the supposed fishermen started killing the men, who had been put in the hold, with sticks, iron rods and axes. "In the panic that followed [refugees] tried to storm the hold but were contained by the pirates, who tied fishing nets over the opening," a statement from the

From Terry McCarthy
in Bangkok

UN High Commissioner for Refugees in Kuala Lumpur said.

As the men tried to cut their way through the net, the pirates returned to their vessels and rammed the Vietnamese boat until it sank. The pirates then "systematically killed" those who tried to swim to safety.

Three survivors were found the next morning by oil workers close to an Esso rig, and 10 more were later picked up in boats and a helicopter sent out by the oil company.

This is only the latest in a series of increasingly violent attacks on Vietnamese boat people off the Malaysian coast. If the 71 missing are in fact dead, it brings to 271 the total of known killings by pirates this year.

Most of the attacks on the Vietnamese are carried out by Thai fishermen. Since 1982, the UN has funded an anti-piracy programme in Thailand, and so far has given the Thai government $20m for distribution among the navy, police and public prosecution department. The programme appeared to be having some success but last year attacks again increased, and refugee officials privately linked this to the decision by the Thai government to prevent boat people from landing.

It was thought at the time that the pirates had been earning more money from transporting Vietnamese refugees from Cambodia to islands off the Thai coast, and smuggling Thai goods into Cambodia on the return trip, than from engaging in piracy.

But when the Thai navy stepped in to stop the inflow of refugees, the pirates started attacking the boat people again.

Source: Independent, 10 August 1989

Piracy and the boat people

In 1981, the reported attack rate on refugee boats landing in Thailand was no less than 80 per cent. In the first six months of 1987, the attack rate was down to 9 per cent. In that period, only seven refugees had been reported missing as a result of piracy, all of them victims of a single attack.

Source: Refugees No. 45, September 1987

Figure 14 Vietnamese boat people being rescued at sea, 1985

The resettlement solution

Whereas the durable solutions implemented in Africa are either *local integration* or *repatriation*, in South-East Asia, with few exceptions, only a single durable solution is acceptable to first-asylum states – *permanent resettlement in third countries* outside the region.

1 Why do you think the only acceptable solution to first-asylum states in South-East Asia is permanent resettlement of refugees in third countries outside the region?

2 Look back at the list of parties to the 1951 UN Convention and the 1967 Protocol relating to the status of refugees on page 273. Compare this list with Figure 15. What factors might influence the ultimate resettlement region for a group of refugees?

Table 2 shows the exceptionally heavy burden that Thailand has had to bear because of its geographical location. Most refugees have been resettled; by the end of 1988 some 1.1 million had been accepted by Western industrialised nations.

In addition to refugees resettled from first-asylum countries, there have been others who have been resettled directly from Vietnam under the *Orderly Departure Programme* (ODP). The ODP was first negotiated between UNHCR, the US and Vietnam in 1979, in an attempt to curb the boat-people exodus by allowing potential refugees to migrate directly to a country of permanent asylum. Since the programme's inception, close to 150,000 have left Vietnam for numerous Western countries (Table 3). The success of the programme is illustrated by the US which increased its quota for ODP refugees from 8,000 to 25,000 per annum for 1989.

Figure 15 Resettlement destinations, 1975–88
Source: Compiled from UNHCR data

Table 2 Cumulative arrivals and departures, 1976 to April 1988

Country of asylum	Total arrivals	Total departures	Residual caseload
Thailand – boat people	98,873	86,810	13,013
Thailand – land people	596,780	500,237	105,296
Malaysia	227,995	218,513	11,456
Hong Kong	118,008	113,774	10,976
Indonesia	100,398	99,717	1,675
Philippines	40,221	38,237	2,829
Singapore	30,091	30,098	46
Macao	7,060	8,043	494
Japan	8,652	8,613	440
Total – boat people[1]	**631,889**	**606,254**	**40,994**
Total – inc. land people[2]	**1,228,671**	**1,106,491**	**146,290**[3]

[1] Includes other areas not listed above.
[2] Excludes Vietnamese evacuated to the US in 1975, Vietnamese who fled to China in 1978, and Khmer currently in UNBRO border camps.
[3] Includes natural increase.

Source: UNHCR data

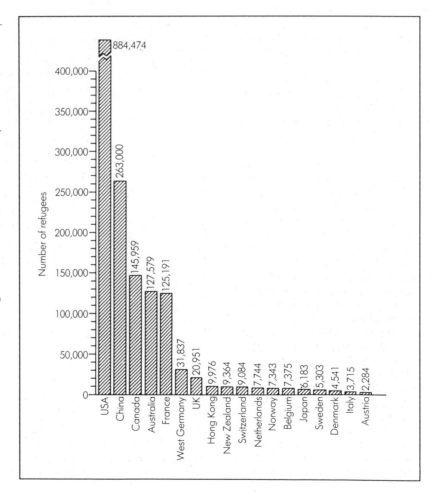

Table 3 Orderly departure programme

Receiving countries (June 1979 – July 1988)

USA	69,165
Canada	24,862
France	13,645
Australia	11,206
West Germany	8,247
UK	3,076
Belgium	2,616
Sweden	1,719
Norway	1,233
Netherlands	1,042
Others	4,447
Total	**141,258**

Source: Refugees No. 56, September 1988

Although most refugees are now permanently resettled, and only 160,000 UNHCR-recognised refugees remain in first-asylum countries, the refugee problem in South-East Asia is far from over. All remaining refugees are expected to be resettled, but potential resettlement countries have cut back or even discontinued their Indochinese resettlement programmes. Most residual refugees have been rejected by resettlement countries. Many have been rejected by more than one country. The reasons vary: some are rejected because of factors concerning their age, health, lack of any education or skills, while others cannot meet security clearances (such as suspected former Khmer Rouge collaborators). More recently, an additional variable has been injected – namely, newly arriving refugees are being seen as economic migrants rather than as persons having 'a well-founded fear of persecution'.

Figure 16 shows the distribution of residual refugees at the end of 1988. The majority are in Thailand. Moreover, in addition to the UNHCR-recognised refugees, Thailand also hosts some 300,000 *displaced persons* from Cambodia, who entered Thailand after 1985 and live in border camps controlled by the three political factions that make up a loose coalition

fighting to topple the Vietnamese-installed government in Phnom Penh. A special UN agency, the United Nations Border Relief Operation (UNBRO), has been created to provide assistance to these Khmer displacees. None of them are eligible for resettlement: Thai policy is unequivocal on their future – all must repatriate as soon as it is safe for them to do so.

Thailand's refugee policy

Long before the Vietnam War created the contemporary refugee dilemma in the region, Thailand had been accommodating refugees from all its neighbours.

Vietnamese have been seeking refuge in Thailand since the late eighteenth century, and, as anti-colonial wars with France intensified throughout Indochina from the late nineteenth century, Thailand received several waves of refugees. This was added to after World War 2 by refugees from China, including remnants of the defeated Kuomintang army, as well as Malay and Burmese refugees (Figure 17). No international assistance was received by Thailand in coping with any of these migrants and most have remained permanently in Thailand. Much of the insurgency that Thailand faced during the 1960s along its northern and southern borders was blamed on refugees.

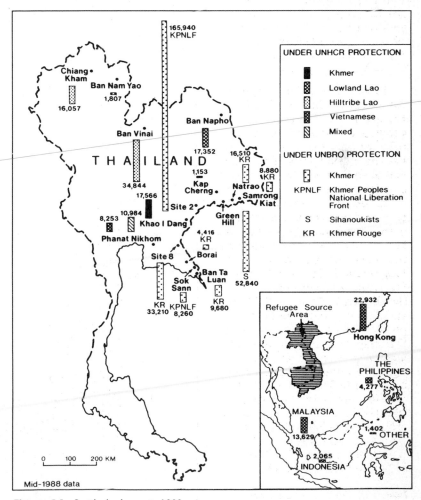

Figure 16 Residual refugees in 1988
Source: Compiled from UNHCR and UNBRO data

It is not surprising, therefore, that Thailand has adopted a defensive posture towards refugees. Moreover, the Thai, Vietnamese and Cambodians have a long history of distrust and hostility towards each other. Consequently, when the post-Vietnam War deluge began, Thailand reacted firmly to the spectre of having yet again to become a permanent host to refugees. Its policy was emphatic: under no condition would Thailand permit any local integration and settlement of refugees from Indochina. In the absence of a repatriation solution, Thailand would only permit refugees to enter Thailand if there was a guarantee that they would be subsequently resettled elsewhere. Western countries provided that guarantee at the height of the 1979 crisis.

Why has Thailand remained so firm in its policy? Several reasons can be cited, some of which are more easily acceptable than others. They are:

- existing population pressure
- competition for limited resources
- security considerations
- animosity towards refugees, especially in border areas
- a general compassion fatigue
- recent indications that refugees are primarily economic migrants
- a belief that the refugee problem was created by the US and hence it should shoulder the consequences.

To emphasise its point, Thailand introduced in 1981 a policy of *humane deterrence*; newly arriving refugees would be placed in austere, minimally serviced camps with no eligibility for resettlement until all the back-log of refugees had been resettled. Thai authorities hoped that word would get out to potential refugees that Thailand was not an attractive place to seek refuge in. It is debatable whether the policy had any great effect in reducing the overall flow to Thailand, or

The situation at the Thai–Cambodian border

Handicrafts at the Khaol Dang Camp, Thailand

At the end of August 1988, there were nearly 300,000 displaced Khmer living in camps just on the Thai side of the border with Cambodia. They were assisted by the UN Border Relief Operation (UNBRO). The International Committee of the Red Cross (ICRC) and 12 voluntary agencies also operate in the border area under UNBRO's overall co-ordination. Because of hostilities in many areas adjacent to this border, access is controlled by the Thai military.

One new development in 1988 is that UNHCR has begun to assist Vietnamese boat people whom the Thai Government has been sending for temporary asylum to a new camp near Site 2, known as Ban That. Site 2, the largest camp in Thailand, accommodates some 170,000 displaced Khmer.

The Khmer live in bamboo and thatch huts which they fashion from materials provided by UNBRO, which also supplies basic food ration items including rice, tinned fish, beans, some fresh vegetables and cooking oil. In an attempt to minimize the 'dependency syndrome', UNBRO has been encouraging as much self-management of in-camp activities as possible, to prepare the Khmer for returning to Cambodia. Primary education has been expanded this year as well, along with vocational training and the teaching of life skills.

While some observers note that, in terms of relief supplies, the Khmer in Thailand benefit from a relatively high level of assistance, it is also recognised that the psychological toll of prolonged stay in camps has been heavy. Thus, it is hoped that recent diplomatic efforts to resolve the Cambodian political problem will succeed so that these Khmer, some of whom have been living as displaced people along the border since 1979, will be able to return home soon.

Source: *Refugees* No. 56, September 1988

whether it had any impact upon increasing the pace of resettlement admissions to the West. In 1987 it was abandoned. (Hong Kong continues to maintain a humane deterrence policy.)

?

1 What will become of the residual refugee problem in Thailand?

2 Thailand has often been criticised for its hardline response to Indochinese refugees. In your opinion is such criticism justified?

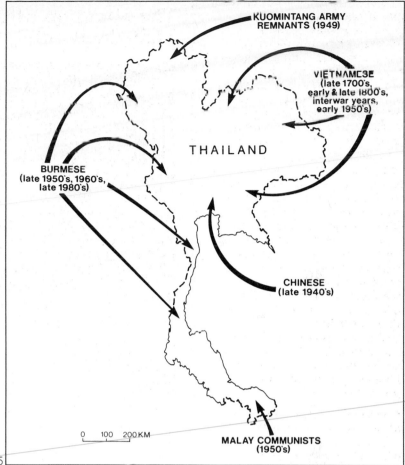

Figure 17 Refugees in Thailand before 1975

Refugees in Canada

> Professor Hawkins points out that both Canada and Australia have doubled their populations in fifty years due in large part to an immigration respectively of more than 5 and 4 million people. Both countries' governments have liberalised their immigration policies in recent years because they have been convinced of its economic and social benefits.

Source: Christopher Huhne, *Guardian*, 14 June 1989

Canada is a nation of immigrants. Only 1.7% of its population are native Indian or Inuit, yet some 16% are foreign-born (compared to less than 6% in the US). Since the end of World War 2, Canada has absorbed over five million immigrants, many of them refugees. Current population policy continues to stress immigration, especially since Canada's birthrate is following the pattern of decline below replacement level already experienced by most European countries. Therefore, sustained population growth, which is widely regarded as desirable by Canadians, can be achieved only through increased immigration.

Most of Canada's immigrants now come from Third World countries. Herein lies the problem – of the many thousands of potential Third World migrants who would like to emigrate to Canada, who is it prepared to admit?

The annual refugee plan

Refugees have featured prominently in immigration to Canada since World War 2. Table 4 lists some of the major groups of refugees that have been resettled. Before 1970, refugees accepted by Canada came from Europe, as did almost all its other immigrants. However, this

Minister's statement on 1989 plan

OTTAWA Employment and Immigration Minister Barbara McDougall today announced plans to accept between 150,000 and 160,000 immigrants to Canada in 1989. 25,000 more than the 1988 target.

The Minister said, 'This year's *Annual Report to Parliament on Immigration Levels* reflects the government's policy of continued growth through sound management, consistent with Canada's economic, social and humanitarian goals'.

The *Annual Refugee Plan* forms part of this yearly announcement. The projected level for refugees admitted from abroad in 1989 under government sponsorship is 13,000 and 10,000 for private sponsorships. There is a preliminary estimate that some 7,000 refugees will be accepted under our new domestic determination process which will be administered by the recently established Immigration and Refugee Board. Such individuals will be eligible for the same settlement services as the government-assisted refugees.

Overall, there will be a significant increase in the number of refugees needing Canada's protection to whom the government will provide direct assistance. Between 3,000 to 6,000 people will also be admitted for humanitarian reasons which could bring the total intake of humanitarian applicants up to the 33,000 to 36,000 range. During the next year, the government will be carefully monitoring the results of the new determination system for refugee claimants already in Canada. It will also be giving more attention to the selection of government-assisted refugees from abroad.

Source: Employment and Immigration Canada, Press Release, 23 December 1988

Table 5 Planning levels by class

Family class	57,000
Government-assisted refugees and members of designated classes	13,000
Privately-sponsored refugees	10,000
Refugees landed in Canada	7,000*
Humanitarian (special measures)	3,000–6,000
Selected workers:	
Principal applicants	21,000–24,000
Spouses and other dependants	24,000–28,000
Business immigrants:	
Principal applicants	4,000
Spouses and other dependants	9,000
Retirees	2,000
Total	**150,000–160,000**

* Preliminary estimate based on expected landings under the new refugee determination system to be administered by the recently established Immigration and Refugee Board.

Source: Employment and Immigration Canada, *Annual Report to Parliament on Future Immigration Levels*, December, 1988

situation has changed dramatically since the early 1970s, and especially following a new immigration policy in 1978. For the first time, the resettlement of refugees became part of the overall immigration plan: the government was required to set planning levels annually for all classes of immigrants, including refugees.

?

1 Read the news release reporting the minister's statement on the 1989 Plan, and look at Tables 4–7, to obtain a view of Canada's immigration policy. Make a list of its major features.

Tables 5 and 6 illustrate how these planning levels were set in late 1988 for implementation in 1989. In addition to targets for *government-* and *privately-sponsored* refugees, there are now two additional categories, one for *asylum seekers* (persons who arrive in Canada and declare that they are refugees) who succeed in having their claim for refugee status upheld, and secondly, for *humanitarian* cases, most of whom are asylum seekers who fail to gain refugee status but are not deported for various humanitarian reasons. In all, some 22% of immigrants targeted for 1989 will be refugees or asylum seekers.

Table 6 shows the major source areas of government-sponsored refugees: refugees who are selected in first-asylum countries for permanent resettlement Canada. The government does not set regional targets for privately-sponsored refugees, but recent trends in private-sector

Table 4 Canadian response to refugee crisis since World War 2

Refugee group	Number accepted	Period of arrival
European displaced persons	186,150	1947–57
Hungarians	37,149	1956–7
Czechoslovakians	11,943	1968–9
Tibetan	228	1970
Ugandan Asians	7,069	1972
Chileans	5,608	1975–7
Lebanese	11,321	1976–9
Indochinese	69,113	1979–81

Source: G. Neuwirth and J. Rogge, 'Canada and the Indochinese refugees', B. Reynolds and S. Chantavanich (eds), *Indochinese Refugees: Asylum and Resettlement*, Chulalongkorn University Press, Bangkok, 1988

Table 6 Planning levels by region

Government-assisted refugee allocations by world area, 1988 and 1989

Area	Number
Eastern Europe	3,400
South-East Asia	3,000
Latin America	3,400
Africa	1,000
The Middle East and West Asia	1,800
Other world areas	100
Funded management reserve	300
Total	**13,000**

Source: Employment and Immigration Canada, *Annual Report to Parliament on Future Immigration Levels*, December 1988

Figure 18 The Oriental quarter in Toronto, Canada

sponsorship have seen a shift away from the sponsorship of South-East Asians in favour of Central Americans.

Since the Indochinese crisis years of the late 1970s, Canada's refugee intake has been dominated by refugees from Third World countries (Table 7), and especially by Indochinese. Between 1979 and 1987, 10% of *all* immigrants were Indochinese refugees, resulting in Indochinese now constituting one of the largest Third World immigrant groups in Canada. In Australia, with its almost complete restriction on non-European immigration prior to the mid-1970s, Indochinese have made an even more pronounced impact: they are easily the largest Third World immigrant community. As more and more Indochinese become Canadian citizens (they become eligible after three years), they have begun to sponsor family members under *family class* immigration provisions. This is more than compensating for any reductions in government-sponsored refugee intake from South-East Asia.

Table 7 Canadian response to refugees by world region and total immigration, 1979–87

Region of origin	1979	1980	1981	1982	1983	1984	1985	1986	1987	Total	% of refugee intake 79/87
South-East Asia	24,828	35,274	8,873	5,293	4,660	5,839	6,109	5,708	5,696	102,280	54.66
Eastern Europe	2,225	4,116	5,325	9,312	4,207	3,550	3,805	5,105	6,644	44,289	23.67
Latin America	432	437	137	779	2,303	2,786	3,380	4,159	4,711	19,124	10.22
Africa	0	138	151	372	823	1,038	957	1,217	1,377	6,073	3.25
Middle East	0	0	0	257	684	952	723	1,028	3,803	7,447	3.98
Others	155	396	510	895	966	1,235	1,576	1,139	1,048	7,920	4.23
Total refugees	27,640	40,361	14,996	16,908	13,643	15,400	16,550	18,356	23,279	187,133	100.00
Other immigrants	84,456	102,756	113,622	104,239	75,514	72,839	67,752	80,860	126,105	828,143	
Total	**112,096**	**143,117**	**128,618**	**121,147**	**89,157**	**88,239**	**84,302**	**99,216**	**149,384**	**1,015,276**	
Refugees as % of total immigration	24.66	28.20	11.66	13.96	15.30	17.45	19.63	18.50	15.58	18.43	
South-East Asians as % of total immigration	22.15	24.65	6.90	4.37	5.23	6.62	7.25	5.75	3.81	10.07	

Source: Employment and Immigration Canada data

Asylum seekers

Canada's liberal refugee policy has, however, begun to run into serious difficulty since the mid-1980s. Instead of being able to completely control its selection of refugees through recruitment in first-asylum countries, as was the case up to the mid-1980s, Canada has since faced a mounting tide of refugee-claimants who arrive directly at its borders. As a signatory of the UN Convention and Protocol on Refugees, Canada is required to admit all such claimants until such time as their claims are proven false. This process has often taken as long as five years.

At the beginning of 1989, there was a backlog of some 85,000 asylum seekers whose claims to refugee status had still to be judged. A new, and much-criticised, law came into effect in January 1989. Its aims are to streamline the refugee-determination process and to reduce the number of arrivals whose claims to refugee status are, essentially, bogus. It is widely believed that as many as three-quarters of asylum seekers are really *economic* migrants claiming refugee status in order to become landed immigrants. Portuguese, Turks, Brazilians and Trinidadians were among the most questionable claimants during 1987 and 1988.

One of the impacts of this crisis is that public sympathy for refugees has become jaded and government is under growing pressure to reduce the influx. On the other hand, refugee advocacy groups, including many church groups actively involved in private sponsorship of refugees, fear that the new legislation will discriminate against *bona fide* refugee claimants. The impact of the new legislation, however, has been clear: refugee claimants who entered Canada after 1 January 1989 were screened within days of arrival and the first deportations were effected by the middle of the month.

Canada: passage of two bills

Two bills before the Canadian Parliament relating to refugees received Royal Assent on 21 July. Bill C-84 takes effect this year and introduces fines for transportation companies bringing in undocumented passengers, interdiction at sea provisions for a limited period, and, *inter alia*, gives increased powers to detain persons deemed to be security risks.

Bill C-55 is expected to come into force in January 1989 and will affect determination procedures for asylum seekers. Under the present system, asylum seekers are initially interviewed at the entry point and then proceed to an inquiry. Subsequently their case is referred to the Refugee Status Advisory Committee in Ottawa for a recommendation on eligibility, made to the Minister of Employment and Immigration. Under the new system, asylum seekers will go through a pre-screening at various entry points by an access tribunal. If found to have a credible basis for their claim, they will then be referred to the Immigration and Refugee Board, represented in the major provincial cities of Canada. As part of the new procedures under this bill, asylum seekers who come to Canada through a so-called safe third country will be removed to that country provided they are allowed to return there.

Source: Refugees No. 56 September 1988

Minister's statement on Bill C-55

Canada has one of the most generous refugee systems in the world. Anyone, regardless of what country they come from, is entitled under our laws to make a refugee claim. Such persons are afforded due process of law and also enjoy the protection of the Canadian Charter of Rights and Freedoms.

Our current system is vulnerable to abuse. Many people come here making refugee claims in order to circumvent our immigration laws. Many are aided and abetted by unscrupulous agents and racketeers who, for money, hold out the promise that Canada will not send people home, even if they are not found to be refugees.

In the recent past there have been thousands of people arriving in this manner. Many have arrived without any documents or have destroyed their documents *en route*.

The new refugee determination system which comes into effect on January 1, 1989 introduces a much faster system for both determining genuine refugee claims and for screening out obviously non-credible cases. The rationale is clear – genuine refugees will get our protection but the non-genuine claimant will be sent home.

The same rationale will be used for dealing with the people who are now in Canada whose claims have not as yet been heard. *There will be no amnesty.*

Source: Statement made by Barbara McDougall, Minister for Employment and Immigration, Toronto, 28 December 1988

?

1 How does the Canadian response to asylum seekers compare to the British policy in Hong Kong towards Vietnamese refugees?

Adaptation of refugees

Before the mid 1970s, economic and social adaptation of refugees was not problematic since most refugees came from Europe, were usually educated and had transferable skills, and, on arrival in Canada, were readily absorbed into established ethnic communities such as the Polish, Czech or Hungarian. But such easy processes of absorption have not been the case for Chileans, Salvadoreans, Ethiopians, Somalis, Vietnamese, Cambodians or Lao, since Canada had never previously received immigrants from these areas. Linguistic and cultural gaps are often very wide, and many lack the necessary qualifications that facilitate rapid economic adaptation. Despite such disadvantages, however, many refugee groups are successfully integrating.

The problem of resettlement

'All refugees have to learn the hard way that appearances are against them. Nothing a man learns, no disguise, can change his features or the colour of his skin; perhaps not even his accent. Even love for his new country, growing as homesickness fades, is not enough. The disappointment that he cannot melt into the new background is, however, only one of the things which an exile has to bear. When times are bad, when there are economic difficulties, refugees, less firmly established than others, often find themselves thrown back as scapegoats into the insecurity of the early days of flight.'

Source: Yefime Zarjevski, *Refugees* No. 53, May 1988

Downward occupational mobility is widespread among refugees that come from the skilled and professional classes of their home countries. Many fail to have their qualifications recognised by Canadian institutions (or they cannot provide evidence of their qualifications since they fled without their documents). For the majority of Third World refugees, however, the problem is one of obtaining basic skills applicable in an industrialised country. Until this is achieved, refugees normally find their first employment in unskilled jobs paying very low wages, and where few Canadians actively seek permanent employment.

Of the Indochinese who entered Canada during the crisis years of 1978–81, only 3% found jobs in professional occupations and 4% in other white-collar occupations; the remainder became blue-collar or unskilled workers. However, their *labour force participation* rate (the ratio of persons working or actively seeking work to the population) was 90%, considerably higher than that of Canadians. Indeed, such labour force participation rates are common not only to refugee migrants to Canada, but are also widespread among most other recent immigrants from Third World countries, and are a positive indication of prevailing desires to become fully economically adapted into the mainstream of society.

1   Read the extract 'The problem of resettlement'. In small groups, discuss whether what the writer says is true. Refer to any data on pages 289–93 and add examples from your own knowledge.

2   If development means the process of making life better, discuss how this relates to the issue of refugees.

3   Use the example of Canada, and the rest of this chapter, to make notes about the differences and similarities in the way First World and Third World countries have responded to refugees.

Conclusion

The issues which cause the problem of refugees are at heart very human problems. This chapter has outlined some of the characteristics and concepts associated with the refugee problem. The case studies provide a more detailed knowledge of actual examples. You could have a class discussion in which you raise your thoughts and feelings about what is in the chapter. Your teacher or a chairperson could keep a record of the main points that are raised and you could ask yourselves after examining the record, 'What points did our discussion hinge around? What did we leave out?'

PART IV

ISSUES OF GLOBAL CONCERN:URBANISATION

Each summer term, students training to be geography teachers at the Institute of Education, University of London prepare a Geography 16–19 fieldwork investigation. The investigation is planned and prepared for sixth formers in the London area who then join the students for a day's field work.

Recently, Spitalfields was chosen as the area to be investigated. In previous years, we had examined issues embedded in the redevelopment of Covent Garden, Coin Street, Docklands (various areas, including Canary Wharf, St Katherine's Dock, the Royal Docks, etc.) and King's Cross. It's not difficult in a large metropolis to find some area being redeveloped. Redevelopment actually only really means an area is changing or being changed, with one function being replaced by another.

Any change in the land use or function of an area – urban or rural – makes it ripe (to use the developers' language) for a 16–19 style enquiry.

The group of us working together had a hunch something was happening in Spitalfields and so we followed the 16–19 Route for Enquiry to find out more. What follows is intended to be a guided walk along the route for enquiry. It may be of help to you when you come to undertake an investigation for yourself.

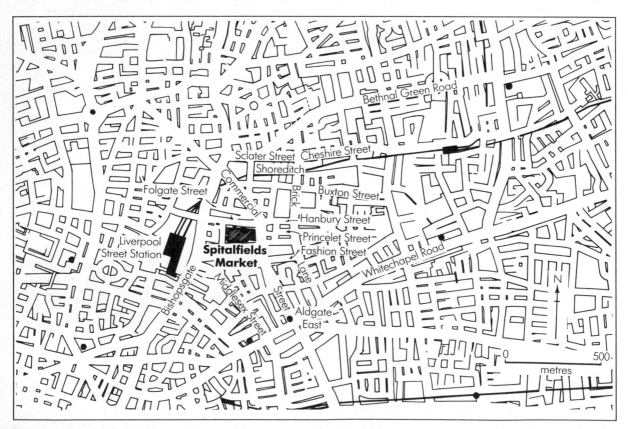

Figure 1 Plan of the Spitalfields area

Stage 1 Observation and perception (what and where?)

We first had to achieve some understanding of the area by going down looking around, talking to people informally, setting up more formal interviews, contacting people whom we thought might know more and interviewing different kinds of organisations in the area. We also started collecting any mentions of Spitalfields in the newspapers or on TV. At the end of our first morning's exploration we had a very pleasant Bengali meal in Brick Lane. So far, so good.

The new East Enders

Some parts of the city are solid, some are grand, or elegant, or slick, talking and smelling of money. Others are animated, flimsy like a set, stages for the shifting, shabby-bright, talking and smelling of elsewhere.

Welcome to Brick Lane, London E1. Home to Huguenots, Jews and now Bangladeshis. Where deals are done and machines still whirr in upstairs rooms and basements, where paint is but a memory and the head-lease a marvel and mystery. Where English has been the second language for several centuries, where British notions such as order and regulation and the book are nodded at with smiles, where sites gape from long-gone bombs and midnight torches, where nothing is neat, or simple, or straightforward. And where everybody seems always to be on the move.

And now, after the Huguenots, and the Jews, and the Bangladeshis, the City is coming. The search for space has seen it march and creep through great new developments and past Liverpool Street up to Commercial Street, where the Spitalfields Market waits to feed its maw. And the Bishopsgate site, and the brewery site in Brick Lane itself; about £1,000 million and 30 acres of ripe development, spanking shiny buildings, temperature-controlled homes for smooth-running systems ready to rise around and among all that mess and squalor and life. Can Brick Lane survive? Should it?

Abbas Uddin is the Labour councillor who has the sari shop on the corner of Brick Lane and Princelet Street. Abbas was a community worker before he opened the shop a year ago. He enjoys it: 'I had a bit of criticism. Some people thought it was capitalist. Is it capitalist to own a car? It is capitalist to wear pinstripe suits? I'm employing people. If I hadn't taken it, they would have made it into an estate agents.' Bryan Gould would be proud.

Abbas is 39. His father has returned home to Bangladesh, disenchanted with Britain, but Abbas is an optimist. He thinks the Bangladeshi community settled and stable around Brick Lane. He wants to turn Brick Lane into 'Banglatown', like Chinatown, restaurants and shops, pedestrianisation, bilingual signs. He wants more money.

So does Mr Kadir. Mr Kadir runs the newsagent's and the sports shop further up Brick Lane and he wants more money spent on things like car parks. Mr Kadir is the chairman of the Stepney and Bethnal Green Conservatives. He supports the Tories because they don't interfere with religion or promote homosexuality, and because, unlike Mr Kinnock, they don't dance in the streets, something offensive to Moslems, to win votes.

Mr Kadir used to be secretary to the Brick Lane mosque; he felt the attackers of Rushdie were helping to sell the book, and he had firm doubts about the Ayatollah's sanity.

Mr Kadir paused to sell a father some trainers for his son. The father said he was a Pakistani film producer and paid with plastic bags filled with pound coins. He left. Mr Kadir said that, really, he ran a gambling place round the corner. Mr Kadir had been in the rag trade, in leather. Foreign imports were ruining it. That was why the workers in the sweat shops round Brick Lane were paid so badly: stop the imports and the wages would rise. It was one view of the market economy.

Money is going into the area. The local Task Force, set up by central government to fund inner-city projects and improvements, has spent £1.8 million since autumn 1987 on start-ups for small businesses, on training in office skills, English as a second language, training in the clothing industry. Business in the Community (President: Prince Charles, 'visibly shaken' by conditions when he toured in 1987) has paid £1.5 million since July 1987 in pursuit of 'enlightened self-interest', job creation and small business development.

Since 1980, Tower Hamlets, the local authority, has invested over £2 million, matched by £5m from the private sector, in job creation and preservation. The Spitalfields Small Business Association (SSBA) says more is needed.

Ayub Ebrahim, known as Chey, rents one of the SSBA's workshops in Brick Lane. Chey International, leather garment manufacturers, turnover around £1 million a year, turns out about 250 jackets in a week in peak season. Chey pays £100 a week rent; he used to pay £300 a week for worse accommodation around the corner in Bethnal Green Road.

Chey is confident there is a market for the Brick Lane leather businesses; but only if they lead demand rather than just follow West

▶

End and wholesaler wants. Chey is a Gujerati; he might stay in business here, or he might go to Mauritius, or Los Angeles. Right now, he has to go and get some more leather.

Tariq Qayyum, one of his machinists, is a Punjabi and, with Chey, part of the 20 per cent round here who are not Bangladeshi. He has worked for Chey for three years, in the leather trade for 12. A 50-hour week will bring him £250. The worst place he ever worked paid him £70 a week. He lives in Il-ford. Does he like Brick Lane? 'The streets are dirty, the shops are dirty. It's just the money, otherwise I wouldn't bother coming.'

Go to Princelet Street to see the worst sweat shop, says Tariq. Down in a basement, Tunu Miah is overseeing about six other workers under strip lighting. 'I grew up here,' says Tunu. 'I like the area, but everything should be cleaned.' Tunu earns £80 to £100 a week for 40 hours: 'I'm not educated. What else am I going to do?'

Across and up, paintless and cramped, with windows covered against the light, Abdul Khalique is earning £100 for 60 hours. What did he like about Brick Lane? 'Nothing at all.'

Mr Ghazi-ul Hasan Khan, formerly President of the All Pakistan Students' Union, formerly of Fleet Street, makes a point: 'The first generation of Bangladeshis didn't have any skills, any technical know-how. The vast majority went into catering as waiters or chefs, or into the rag trade. But now the new technologies are here, their sons and daughters should take advantage of them, avail themselves of the op-portunities. *They must come up to*

the mark!'

Mr Khan has another SSBA workshop, where he produces his weekly Bengali newspaper with English supplement, and prints for other people to fund it. Mr Khan wants to produce an English news-paper for all British Asians, a newspaper which would remain true to their traditions and culture, but would take in Kylie Minogue and Frank Bruno, too.

Meanwhile, press day is looming, and Mr Khan has another dream, that one day his people will not only come up to the mark, that they will become 'a vital force in every walk of life, every walk of British life.'

Yes, said Akaddas Ali, with the happiest of beams, it *was* easy to make money in Britain. Mr Ali came here in 1963, started working in steel, moved on to handbags, and then opened his own grocery shop in Fashion Street in 1970 with £250 stock. Restauranteurs began to come to him for his fish and vegetables, his rohi and kadu, and his spices, his tukmaria, haldi and masala mix.

Mr Ali moved into property. Now he owns six shops in Fashion Street, 15 properties all told. Mr Ali has five daughters and one son. No, the daughters would not be joining the company. 'It is our religion that they should not work,' said Mr Ali.

Still beaming and wearing his white grocer's coat and brimless Bangladeshi cap, Mr Ali gave a guided tour of his Fashion Street empire. Mr Ali is converting it bit by bit, basement by cellar, accor-ding to a master plan he keeps in his head; one day, a few judicious blows will reveal an integrated, mighty emporium half the length of

Fashion Street.

Now he lives in Forest Hill, and might move further, into the coun-try. He is looking for more proper-ty. 'I will buy for £2 million'. Money is not a problem: 'I can get it. When you've got a good busi-ness, anybody will give you any amount.' Mr Ali gave his broadest beam of all.

At the City end of Brick Lane, in Osborn Street, Mr Ahmed the banker was sitting in the spanking, shiny new headquarters of the Sonali Bank, of Bangladesh, recent-ly arrived from the Square Mile. It was his view that the Bangladeshi community, and the Asian com-munity as a whole, had reached a turning point, of which the Rushdie affair was a symptom and example. They had to make vital decisions about their part in the community.

He thought that the Bangladeshis had patience, cohesion, energy, and a will to succeed. He thought their culture would enrich ours. Mr Ahmed the banker spoke gently of the harmony that plants of different colour and shape can achieve in a garden.

On Friday, more than 2,000 of the faithful filed out into Brick Lane, down the steps of the mos-que, which was the synagogue, which was the protestant church before that, before they – and the President of Bangladesh – raised £350,000. Outside they were pre-sented with a Ramadan fasting timetable, sponsored by New Taj stores, a message of support for the Ayatollah over Rushdie, and an in-vitation to the grand opening of the Docklands light railway.

Source: Sunday Telegraph, 9 April 1989

Spitalfields has an interesting location between the City of London and the redeveloping Docklands. Like Covent Garden it has outgrown its location as changes in transport, the coming of big trucks, brought traffic congestion. The attractive nature of the old market, as with Covent Garden, made it easy to see why property developers had decided on a chic future for the area.

Literature from the developers and our walk around left us in no doubt that the process of redevelopment was beginning. We were quickly into Stage 2.

Stage 2 Definition and description (what?)

We were into the second stage of a 16–19 enquiry, the definition and description of the issue. We could define it as an issue of redevelopment and set out our initial thoughts like this.

What is the process of redevelopment in Spitalfields?

Figure 2 Part of the Bengali community in East London

Introduction

Spitalfields is a close-knit community in East London which is under pressure from major redevelopment. It is a traditional centre of the rag trade, based especially around Brick Lane, the Watney and Truman brewing sites, and also the Spitalfields fruit and flower market. The population is largely Bengali, with some Pakistanis too. The Jewish community are retiring, although they still own much of the property. Much of the property is in a bad state of repair, leases are expiring and not being renewed, and thus the area is becoming identified by various developers as a potential site for redevelopment.

The City of London faces major problems of congestion, partly due to the presence of some traditional markets and other retailing systems in the area which necessitate the entry of many large vehicles into the centre of London. The congestion, noise and other pollution associated with the infrastructure necessary for these outlets not only contradicts the ethos of elite office and shopping complexes, but also creates a real practical problem of access. Several such sites in London have been redeveloped recently – examples include Covent Garden and Docklands (notably Canary Wharf and St Katharine's Dock). For broadly the same reasons as the Covent Garden market was moved to Nine Elms, it has been decided to move the Spitalfields market to Hackney Marsh, and inevitably there is now much interest in developing the site and surrounding area. Spitalfields's location between the city and the new redevelopment in Docklands means that it is especially sought after.

To gain a fuller understanding of the process of redevelopment, we need to understand the positions of the various groups involved. After the introductory talk, we will split up into groups and consider in broad terms the positions of the following groups from various angles:

● The external developers (for example big insurance companies seeking to build a new office).

● The internal developers from within the community.

● The local small businesses.

● The local tenants.

● The local property owners and gentrifiers.

Each group will then concentrate on one of these groups in particular, and consider them under the broad headings of:

● What problems they face?

● What do they need?

● What are their options in practice?

● What are the likely effects of the new proposed developments on this group?

With this introduction, we will then go out into the area and see at first hand the impact the various factors have had on land use and the area generally.

After lunch, we'll try to put what we've found in a broader context by trying to develop a model of the process of redevelopment. All the time we hope you will see that there is a *process* of redevelopment going on, an active interplay between the various groups and constraining factors involved, which we should try to understand and explain, as opposed to just describing a pattern.

So in summary, various key questions emerge which we will aim to answer:

● Where and what is Spitalfields?

● What is going on there, and where?

● How and why is the process operating?

● What is the likely future for Spitalfields?

● What ought to happen if the process of redevelopment is to take place as fairly as possible?

Compiled by Duncan Heaster

A brief account of the five groups involved in the development of Spitalfields

Internal developers

Internal developers are people from the local Spitalfields community who are taking part in the medium to large-scale redevelopment of the area. Their close links with the community, for example via friends and family, as well as their intimate knowledge of the area, place them in a unique position among developers. Internal developers may use their links with the community to buy into the area, or they may own sites ripe for development already.

External developers

The Spitalfields Development Group represents those interested in developing areas as outsiders, having evaluated the land potential. Their power is strengthened by joining up with other developers to use their combined financial backing to reap the profits associated with large-scale redevelopment. The SDG are planning to develop the area currently occupied by Spitalfields market into shopping malls, offices and luxury residential apartments, focusing essentially on restaurants and quality stores.

Renters

This group includes council tenants, housing association tenants, and those renting privately from landlords. Those renting privately from landlords may well be forced to leave the area if rents go up too high. The housing association aims to keep rents at 'fair prices', but fears this may become impossible. People in this group are relatively powerless and their future (whether or not they can continue to live and work in this area) will largely depend on decisions made by their landlords.

Landlords and gentrifiers

Some people, foreseeing that property prices would increase in Spitalfields, have bought property while prices were relatively low. These gentrifiers either live in their property themselves, or rent it out. Most of them are likely to sell it in a few years and make a good profit. Landlords will also do well – many are able to charge more rent; others will sell their properties for financial profit.

Small businesses

These are mostly comprised of one rag trade, with a largely Bengali workforce. They are poorly organised, and under pressure from foreign imports. However, with better marketing structures, increased specialisation and modernised workshops they could become more attractive to buyers, be competitive and also provide better working conditions for the workers. However, little help is being offered by the potential developers, whose job opportunities in services are mismatched to the local manufacturing workforce.

Compiled by Alison Gillett

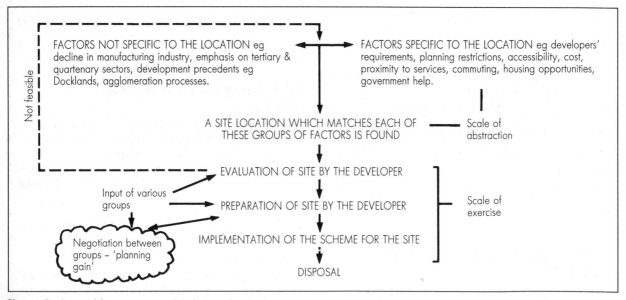

Figure 3   Proposal for a process model of physical redevelopment

Source: Jane Herrington, 1989

Stage 3 Analysis and explanation (how and why?)

This third stage of developing the study concentrated on analysis and explanation by finding out more about the different groups involved in Spitalfields and setting up exercises for the sixth formers.

We found out much more than can be included here. On the day with our sixth formers we split into groups and guided them through the area.

Each group of people in Spitalfields is experiencing redevelopment in a different way and to understand this is to begin to understand what redevelopment means. The relevant sheets and exercises for just one of the five identified Spitalfields groups are included here.

As we worked together to answer the key question 'What is the process of redevelopment in Spitalfields?' we realised a number of things. Spitalfields is made up of different groups of people making decisions in the area according to their perceptions and needs, their economic resources and aspirations, their power, knowledge and influence. This led us to analyse:

- What groups are operating?
- What decisions are they able to make?
- What impact does this have on land use in the area?

The exercise for one of the five groups follows:

Information sheet: Internal developers

Who are they?
Inside developers are people from the local Spitalfields community who are taking part in the medium to large-scale redevelopment of the area. Their close links with the community, for example via friends and family, as well as their intimate knowledge of the area, places them in a unique position amongst developers. Internal developers may use their links to buy into the area, or they may already own sites ripe for redevelopment.

What do they want?
It is worth remembering that the internal developers are not a homogeneous group. Different developers want different things. The list shows the sorts of things that internal developers might want:

- to expand their businesses by buying and developing adjoining land or property;
- to refurbish their property in order to accommodate their businesses more suitably;
- to refurbish property in order to sell it off;
- to expand and to provide local employment;
- to convert a building to a different use or function;
- to improve the local environment;
- to make use of the derelict or empty properties;
- to provide new workplace units to provide services to existing firms.

What help is there for the internal developers?
The local authority, Tower Hamlets, has designated certain parts of Spitalfields as 'industrial improvement areas'. These areas are particularly rundown and require improvement. The authority offers help to some developers with plans for developments within these areas. They particularly favour 'local initiatives'. This help can include:

- Improvements to the local roads by the local authority;
- grants towards the cost of converting or extending premises;
- grants towards rents;
- loans to carry out work on premises;
- loans to acquire property;
- grants for landscaping and improving the appearance of the local area;
- grants for clearing land, building access roads, etc.

The unique position of internal developers

Internal developers are in a unique position because of their links with and knowledge of the local community and area. For example, they might have:

- an intimate knowledge of the local area, the condition of its buildings, local sites with potential for redevelopment;
- an intimate knowledge of who owns which properties;
- informal as well as formal links with members of the community;
- the support of elements of the local community;
- the support and backing of local authority initiatives such as the those found in the 'industrial improvement areas'.

Problems faced by the internal developers

The position of the internal developers has its disadvantages as well as its advantages. Possible disadvantages include:

- the opposition of groups within the local community to certain developments;
- the internal developers might not have the financial clout of the large-scale external developers;
- their lack of financial backing may mean a lack of power, opportunity and choice.

What options are there for internal developers?

There may be a number of options open to internal developers, such as:

- not improving properties, letting them decay and then selling them off to property developers;

- working in co-operation with other internal developers on local projects;
- developing property and selling it off to external developers or business interests.

The timetable

The processes of redevelopment are under way in Spitalfields. The planned redevelopment of the fruit and flower market is well under way, and will provide an important precedent for further developments in the area. Thus the redevelopment issue is an important and vital one. What will be the role of the internal developers within this process of redevelopment in Spitalfields?

Compiled by Jane Herrington

Activity sheet: Internal developers

This sheet sets out the activities and questions we will be tackling on the field walk and in the report back. Key questions you will need to keep in mind all day include:

- where are the sites for redevelopment?
- which sites are
  a ripe for development
  b are being developed
  c have already been developed?
- what are the sites being developed into?
- what do you think are going to be the effects of the redevelopment processes in the area?
- who gains? who loses?

The activities will be divided in the following way:

The field exercise

- For the first part of the exercise we will be looking at the overall process of redevelopment in Spitalfields. We will be asking:
  What kinds of redevelopment are taking place?
  Who is doing the redevelopment?
- For the second part of the exercise we will be looking at the contribution of the internal developers to the redevelopment process in Spitalfields. To do this you will

need to:
  a complete the site and land use base map;
  b fill in the site analysis table.

You will need the map and table for the report back exercise.

The report-back exercise

- In this exercise the aim is to identify the *processes* taking place in Spitalfields and involving the internal developers. To do this you will need to refer back to your data collected on the field exercise and the key questions. Using the data can you answer the key questions.

- Site X is a potential site for redevelopment. You are an internal developer and you are looking for a suitable site for relocating your garment factory. Can you come up with the processes you would go through in identifying and redeveloping a site?

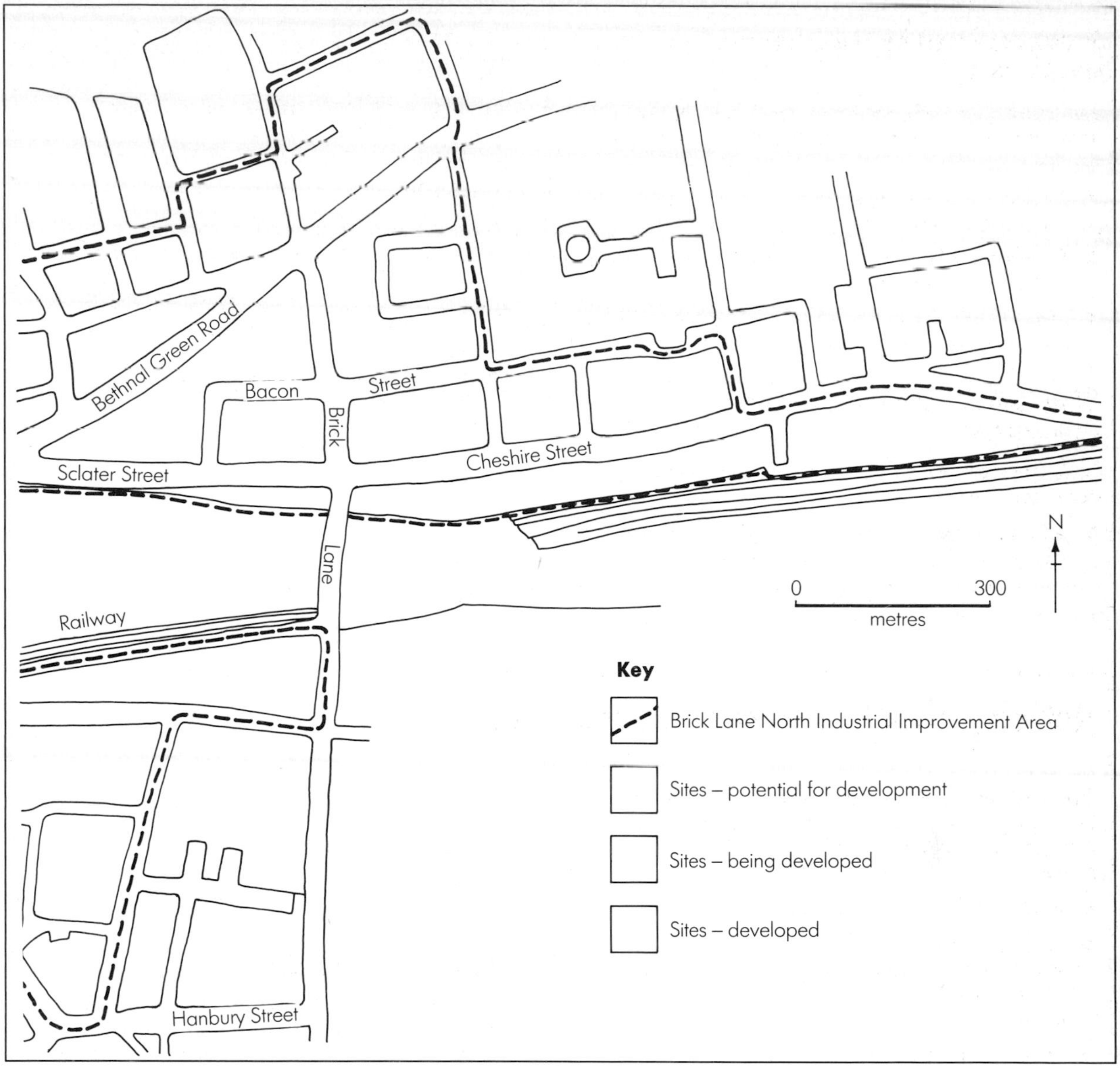

Figure 4 Development sites

Table 1 *Redevelopment in Spitalfields. Part of the process: internal developers*

Site number	Site name and description	Stage of development*	What kind of development is taking place?	Who by?	Possible disadvantages possible advantages

* Stages of development: undeveloped
 developing
 developed

Case study: An internal developer

Yes, said Akaddas Ali, with the happiest of beams, it *was* easy to make money in Britain. Mr Ali came here in 1963, started working in steel, moved on to handbags, and then opened his own grocery shop in Fashion Street in 1970 with £250 stock. Restauranteurs began to come to him for his fish and vegetables, his rohi and kadu, and his spices, is tukmaria, haldi and masala mix.

Mr Ali moved into property. Now he owns six shops in Fashion Street, 15 properties all told. Mr Ali has five daughters and one son. No, the daughters would not be joining the company. 'It is our religion that they should not work,' said Mr Ali.

Still beaming and wearing his white grocer's coat and brimless Bangladeshi cap, Mr Ali gave a guided tour of his Fashion Street empire. Mr Ali is converting it bit by bit, basement by cellar, according to a master plan he keeps in his head; one day, a few judicious blows will reveal an integrated, mighty emporium half the length of Fashion Street.

Now he lives in Forest Hill, and might move further, into the country. He is looking for more property. 'I will buy for £2 million.' Money is not a problem: 'I can get it. When you've got a good business, anybody will give you any amount.' Mr Ali gave his broadest beam of all.

Source: Sunday Telegraph, 9 April 1989

Stage 4 Prediction, evaluation, theory construction (what might?)

After taking the sixth formers into Spitalfields, dividing them into the five groups and having them go through the exercise designed for each group, we adjourned to a classroom and went through a model building or theory construction exercise based on the form below.

In this way, each group of sixth formers, like the different groups in Spitalfields, came to have an understanding specific to their groups and an understanding of other groups and possibilities concerning redevelopment in the area.

Title of group: _____

What is happening?

Where is it happening?

What are the reasons?

What are the gains for your group?

What are the losses for your group?

What power and resources has your group got?

Stage 5 Decision making
(what decision?)

The final exercise of the day after the model building was a decision-making one, in true 16–19 fashion. A personal evaluation and judgement on a hypothetical situation was brought into play. Taking into consideration the points raised in other section introductions, can you predict what evidence or what beliefs, values, ideologies, priorities, your decisions would be grounded in if you went through the Spitalfields enquiry?

We all knew, at the end of the day, a little bit more about power and influence and decisions affecting changes in a small part of London. We were all conscious too of the questions 'Who gains?' and 'who loses?' by such changes.

These two questions are always present in any geographical study and you will find you can ask them and find answers to them in the chapters in this section.

Griffiths Property Developers
Sawyer House
City Road
LONDON
N1 2JR

Mr J. Clements
Tower Hamlets Industrial
   Development Office
Bethnal Green Town Hall
LONDON

Dear Sir

My company has received information referring to the vacancy of Truman's Brewery site on Hanbury Street, Spitalfields. Being a business person with the interests of local people, as well as of the business world at heart, I believe if I were to be given planning permission to develop the site it would be advantageous to the area as a whole.

My plan for the site is made up of a mixture of offices and luxury apartments. There will be landscaped gardens - something this area desperately needs. The buildings will be modern and attractive, which should improve the general look of the area.

I have been informed that there are other possible plans for the site including new council housing, housing association flats and a small business centre. I think you will agree that my plan (full details are enclosed) will help the area become alive again. It would no doubt attract other businesses, thus providing jobs and contributing to the general development of Spitalfields.

I do hope you will consider my application for planning permission and I look forward to meeting you soon to discuss the mater.

Yours faithfully

C. F. Griffiths

Mr C. F. Griffiths

12

Britain's housing environment

Paul Machon

Housing: a basic need with special characteristics

Housing: the key questions

These two newspaper articles ('Noel's £2½m Mansion' and 'New plan to aid homeless') appeared on the same day in November 1988. Both deal with housing, but they could not have been more different from one another, with homelessness in one and lavish expenditure in the other. Housing is a very unusual basic need! What makes it so unusual? Why is it that housing choice is open for some, but only homelessness available to others? How does the housing market work? Why is Britain's housing now being described as 'in crisis'? This chapter looks at some of the housing issues in Britain today – and some approaches to enquiry – so that we may begin to answer questions like these.

NOEL'S £2½m MANSION

ROOMS WITH A VIEW ... a Victorian mansion which will become the Edmonds home.

Noel and wife Helen ... to the manor drawn

Telly star wants the Good Life

TV STAR Noel Edmonds has forked out £2.5 MILLION for a taste of the Good Life — by buying a huge country estate.

Noel, 39, plans to get away from it all on the isolated 855-acre spread near Okehampton in Devon — and commute the 210 miles to London in his helicopter.

For his cash, loadsamoney Noel gets historic 36-room Broomford Manor, three farms, two lodges, stables, a cottage — and a herd of wild deer.

He said yesterday: 'I hope this will change my lifestyle.

'This estate has barely changed over the years. It is like a time warp — it has never been extensively farmed or modernised.'

His rural retreat is well off the beaten track. The nearest village, Jacobstowe, is so small it has NO pub and NO shops.

Source: Rob Skellon, *The Sun*, 17 November 1988

NEW PLAN TO AID HOMELESS

MOBILE homes could be brought into the Harborough area in a bid to solve the desperate housing crisis.

Harborough District Council's housing waiting list is at a record 1,213 people and most of those people may never get a home.

And this year the council expects to give bed and breakfast accommodation to a record 45 people and that figure could rise still further.

Booming house prices coupled with fewer council houses and private homes for rent have forced dozens of families and individuals on to the streets.

In the past few weeks more people than ever before have appealed to the council to give them a roof over their heads.

Now the crisis is to be tackled by the council's health and housing committee.

And among the options to be considered by the committee tonight (Thursday) are:

● Importing mobile homes — similar to the static homes at seaside resorts.

● Buying small terraced houses.

● Converting homes into accommodation for homeless families.

The homeless crisis is worst in Harborough, Lutterworth and Broughton Astley and some people have been put up in bed and breakfast accommodation in Leicester because of a shortage of space in the Harborough area.

Committee chairman John Shaw said: "The problem is increasing and we must do something. But the Government must help. It is cutting back our cash but saying we must help the homeless."

The radical mobile homes idea was suggested by committee member Phil Knowles who said: "The homeless problem is going from bad to worse. Every possible option must be explored."

But fellow committee member Mrs Carol Lo Galbo said: "I am not happy with mobile homes. There is no privacy but it may be a short term answer. But something must be done."

Councillors are likely to call for a full report on all the options in a bid to solve the crisis at tonight's meeting.

Source: *The Harborough Mail*, 17 November 1988

?

1 Below are eight statements which are important to an understanding of housing's special charcteristics. Take each in turn and, *before* you read what follows, discuss in pairs what you think is the significance of each statement with regard to British housing. Ask yourself each time: Is this true or false? And explain your decision.

a Housing is a basic need.
b Housing is an important influence on health and welfare.
c Housing occupies space.
d Housing as a commodity is expensive.
e Housing is too important to be free from political intervention.
f Housing reflects social divisions.
g Houses have long lives.
h Houses tell the world about us.

Then consider the information in the newspaper extracts about Noel Edmonds and the homeless people of Harborough. What would they feel about each of the eight statements? Keep a note of your conclusions.

Housing's special characteristics

1 Housing is a basic need
Like food and clothing, housing is an essential human requirement. However, what people find acceptable in terms of the quality and availability of housing provision depends on the expectations and values of a particular society. These expectations and values may change. Many people in Britain today tolerate 'modern' homelessness (living, for example, in bed and breakfast accommodation) in a way which they might not have done a decade ago.

2 Housing is an important influence upon health and welfare
Houses are where families are raised and the social pattern of the future is set. This is sometimes called *social reproduction*. We may see social reproduction in two ways. Firstly, if the physical condition of the housing is poor, then illness increases, perhaps bronchial in the cold damp winters, and intestinal or nutritional in the summers because of poor food storage. Secondly, if social attitudes are formed in conditions marked by squalor and deprivation, so parental experience, habits and expectations will be made and remade in their children.

3 Housing occupies space
Housing is the majority land use in urban areas. This use of space by housing inhibits, and can even halt, other use of the land and the use to which the neighbouring sites are put. It is a most important geography. The irony of this simple statement is that this built form resulted from growth in the first instance, but then impedes subsequent growth. Further development must find new sites (perhaps even in the Green Belts) or become involved in cycles of urban clearance and redevelopment. In either event, the

presence of a competitive land market is a reminder of the relationship that limited supply and increasing demand has a price. Housing is therefore expensive.

4 Housing as a commodity is expensive

Houses require substantial capital to build, and for the majority of people a house is the most costly thing they ever purchase. These substantial costs for both builders and buyers have led to the formation of institutions specifically to provide capital for construction and purchase, such as the building societies. The importance and independent power of these institutions in the very special housing market should not be obscured by the consistent financial returns investors and borrowers have historically enjoyed, (for example by the end of 1988 many house owners in the South-East found their earnings over the previous three years had been exceeded by their housing capital gains). This characteristic of Britain's housing market has now assumed such importance that housing is often thought of as an *investment good* (i.e. something acquired because it will increase in value) rather than a consumption good (i.e. something acquired to be 'consumed' or used) and the financial institutions as neutral, even benevolent agencies. This conceals other repercussions of their activities which, it can be argued, are less beneficial.

Many argue, and certainly it is a central theme of this chapter, that money is *the startpoint* in any study of housing.

5 Housing is too important to be free from political intervention

Earlier points should remind us that housing has important social implications. Accordingly, governments have long intervened in the standard of houses built to ensure at least minimum levels of provision with respect to health, and between 1919 and 1979 built

more than 6.6 million local authority houses. More recently governments have taken steps to maintain the investment value of houses, because some types of housing *tenure*, especially owner-occupation, have been seen to be politically desirable in their own right.

6 Housing also reflects social divisions

There are considerable differences in the houses in which people live, both in terms of their quality and location. Both attributes are reflected in the price of houses. We return to housing as a consumption good. Who 'consumes' what – and where – reflects and re-makes socio-economic class distinctions within society at large. These distinctions

Figure 1 An enclosed court with a view of the Thames and the *Cutty Sark* – some of the new owner-occupied housing available (at a price) in London's Docklands

Figure 2 Within a mile of the flats in Figure 1 are balconied local authority flats of the pre-war period

exist at different spatial scales. Locally we know the 'good' and the 'bad' districts in our cities; recently the 'gentrification' of traditionally working-class areas means that there can be very stark housing contrasts even in a small area of a city; while at a larger scale the 'prosperous South' constrasts sharply with the 'declining North' on many indicators of housing quality.

7 Houses also have long lives

Houses usually last far longer than the particular relationships of home, work, markets and social life that existed when they were first built. It is also comparatively easy for alterations in the buildings, changes in the occupying density or the lifestyle of the occupants to extend the continued usefulness of the building. Consequently who occupies houses changes over time and place. For example, in many inner cities grand Victorian houses have been sub-divided into flats or, when the demand for houses has risen more rapidly than their supply in 'desirable' sites, so terraced cottages originally built for the labouring classes have been occupied by the professional classes. Changes in the pattern of the journey to work have been especially important in severing earlier relationships of home and work and opening up previously inaccessible areas to urban workers. However, it would be false to imply that these factors open housing choices to all.

8 Houses project many signals of a personal kind

Houses have many symbolic and status associations of place, taste and class in much the same way that the ownership of particular cars projects the owner's personality to the world at large. A majority of people within a society share an understanding of these associations, consequently their transmission is powerful, often consciously performed and consciously understood (Figure 3).

Figure 3 The symbolism of housing is so important that it is reflected in architectural styles

However, in one important way houses differ from cars, for houses are *wealth* and as such can be used as collateral against capital borrowing. It will, however, be easier to borrow against some houses than others and thus credit-worthiness is locked into symbolic meaning.

In evaluating housing's special characteristics, opinions and personal viewpoints are as important as hard facts. This inevitably leads to disagreement and debate when people consider housing issues.

?

1 Look back at your answers to the first task in this chapter. In the light of what you have read about housing's special characteristics, assess your answers. How often was the range of your answers broadly right? What sort of things did you miss?

2 Which statements would have most effect on how decisions are taken about housing? Decide on an order of importance for the eight points:
a for an individual,
b for a government.

3 As a class, share your answers to question **2** and come up with an order of importance for **a** an individual and **b** a government.

4 Close to the rear of the High Street of a rapidly expanding southern market town (Figure 4) is a long-established residential area. Half the houses are privately owned and, although small and terraced, are much sought after as 'first homes'. They present a well-maintained, pleasing late-Victorian townscape (Figure 5). The other houses are dispersed groups of local-authority rented dwellings, many indistinguishable from their privately-owned neighbours (Figure 6). In two small estates, however, the authority has been housing tenants with a poor housing record (shifting tenancies, sub-letting, public disturbance and rent arrears).

Mindful of the need to promote the town's continuing expansion, the local authority Planning Department is anxious to develop back from the High Street – a chance now presented because of the expiry of leases on shops they own on the High Street, which, if demolished would give access to the area behind. The Planning Department prepares a plan in conjunction with a property developer. The plan calls for the demolition of the two 'difficult' estates, so allowing a throughway from the gap that now exists in the High Street to a new mall development that would substantially upgrade the town's retail facilities.

The authority is not surprised by opposition to the scheme from local owner-occupiers worried by threats of

Figure 4 The High Street

Figure 5 Small Victorian terrace houses

Figure 6 Local-authority rented dwellings

____?____

increased traffic to their environment and property values. They *are* surprised to find dismay from their own Housing Department, worried by how this would worsen long waiting lists and a concern about the rehousing of these particular 'difficult' tenants.

a Draw a sketch map of the area under discussion. Use the information to suggest sensible locations for the features mentioned. Mark on your map the proposed changes.

b In pairs, and bearing in mind housing's eight 'special characteristics', identify all those with an interest in this issue. What are the crucial problems which face each of them? What access might each group have to the decisions that will be made with respect to this development?

5a In groups of eight students, each pair should take on the role of *one* of the major interest groups:
• the Planning Department
• the Housing Department
• the Local Residents' Association (include the views of residents from the 'difficult' estates as well as the owner occupiers and their local-authority-tenant neighbours)
• the property developers.

b Each interest group defines its aims and identifies who else might support its case.

c The interest groups then identify what problems they may face and assess how powerful the opposing groups may be.

d In the light of **b** and **c**, each group prepares an A4 'brief' to state its case. (Likely problems of your own position should, of course, be omitted but you may wish to highlight the shortcomings of opposing viewpoints.)

6 Each group of eight students should now swap all briefs with another group and as a whole group review the briefs. How were the strengths of each case made out? Were the problems seen by others? Whose needs and wants were being served by each group? Finally, what would be the likely outcome of such a proposal – who wins, who loses?

Housing tenure: Who owns the roof over your head?

Tenure is the term given to the distinctive legal right a person has to occupy a dwelling. This right is usually purchased and so involves financial responsibilities for the seller or owner of the property as well as for the purchaser or hirer. Money can be seen as the basis of *all* housing issues. In Britain there are two types of tenure that divide the housing market: *owner-occupation* and *renting*. Each tenure type has powerful class distinctions and has been subject to very different government policies. Each of these tenure types also has distinctive relationships between the *supply-side agencies* (builders, building societies, banks, local authority landlords, private landlords and housing associations) and the *demand-side agencies* (owners, mortgagees and tenants)

Table 1 Leicester's housing tenure

Ward	Owner-occupied		Local auth. rented		Hsg. assoc.		Private rent	
	Number	%	Number	%	Number	%	Number	%
Abbey	2,643	88.3	21	1.0	31	1.0	195	6.5
Aylestone	3,019	71.8	559	13.3	151	3.6	391	1.8
Beaumont Leys	1,312	30.5	2,152	50.1	747	17.4	76	1.8
Belgrave	2,601	65.1	464	11.6	420	10.5	464	11.6
Castle	2,134	39.5	270	5.0	345	6.4	1,450	26.8
Charnwood	2,793	67.8	464	11.3	370	9.0	289	7.0
Coleman	1,130	33.7	1,901	56.7	238	7.1	63	1.8
Crown Hills	2,503	83.8	157	5.3	44	1.5	195	6.5
East Knighton	2,465	59.2	94	2.3	126	3.0	1,374	33.0
Evington	2,259	62.8	854	23.7	19	0.5	401	11.2
Eyres Monsell	759	19.9	3,051	79.8	6	0.2	0	0.0
Humberstone	1,958	48.4	1,519	37.5	282	7.0	245	6.0
Latimer	1,524	67.6	270	12.0	69	3.1	339	15.1
Mownacre	678	23.8	1,989	70.0	6	0.2	157	5.6
New Parks	766	18.1	3,353	79.0	50	1.2	56	1.3
North Braunstone	264	8.5	2,812	91.1	0	0.0	6	0.2
Rowley Fields	1,618	50.7	1,337	41.9	13	0.4	194	6.0
Rushey Mead	3,364	86.0	358	9.2	6	0.2	132	3.4
Saffron	1,117	29.8	2,485	66.3	38	1.0	88	2.4
St Augustines	2,830	72.0	496	12.6	100	2.5	471	12.0
Spinney Hill	2,051	69.4	138	4.7	308	10.4	427	14.4
Stoneygate	2,191	59.9	251	6.9	163	4.5	621	17.4
Thurncourt	1,926	45.7	2,198	52.2	56	1.3	19	0.4
Westcotes	2,893	70.5	289	7.0	19	0.5	891	21.7
Western Park	2,586	61.8	1,243	29.7	94	2.2	213	5.0
West Humberside	1,983	61.1	992	30.6	0	0.0	220	6.8
West Knighton	2,938	75.1	276	7.1	389	9.9	301	7.7
Wycliffe	923	21.5	2,523	58.7	420	9.8	402	9.3
Total	**55,228**		**32,516**		**4,510**		**9,680**	
Average		**53.3**		**31.3**		**4.1**		**8.7**

Percentages may not sum to 100%

Source: Ward Tables 1983, Leicester City Council, 1988

of the housing. These relationships are determined by the self-interest of each: for example, the banks seek to maximise their interest from lending, or tenants seek dwelling improvements without rent increases. Into this conflict-ridden world other influences intrude, such as estate agents (who govern access to sales), surveyors (who authorise sales) and, last but not least, central government (which drafts the laws that govern the conduct of these relationships).

These distinctive relationships produce distinctive spatial forms. An example is shown in by relating Table 1 to the map that follows (Figure 7).

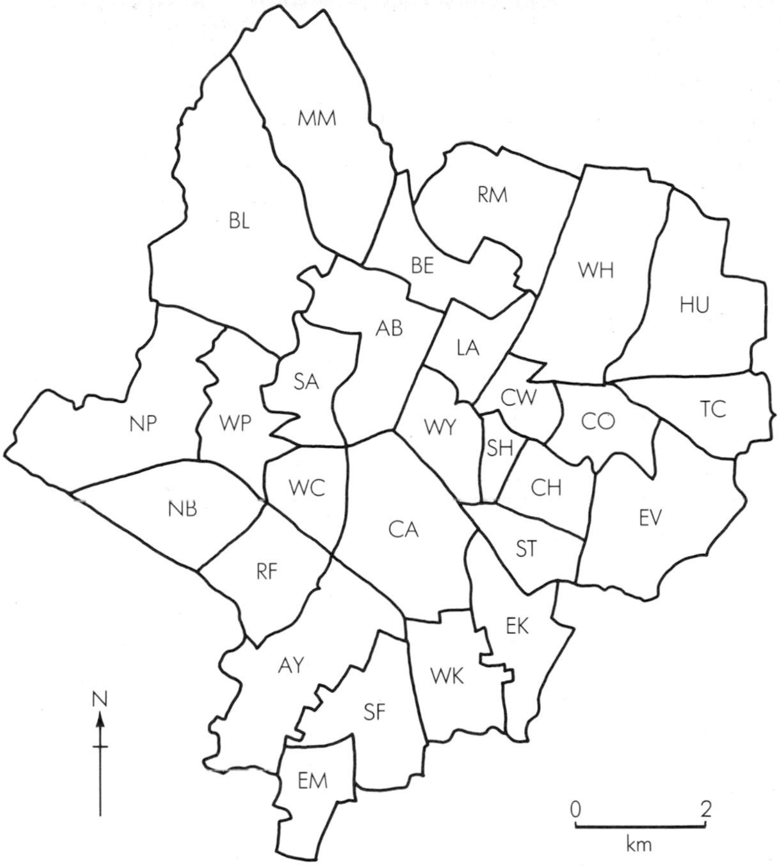

This data is for Leicester, a free-standing Midlands city of some 276,000 people, typical in the ordinariness of the development of its housing. A first examination of Table 1 underlines just how rarely the 'average balance' between tenure types actually occurs ward by ward (owner-occupation 53.3%, local authority 31.3%; Housing associations 4.1% and private renting 8.7%) and how more frequently single wards are dominated by the one tenure type. This observation ought to be borne in mind in the following sections where the tenure types are dealt with.

1a Trace the ward map of Leicester (Figure 7) three times.

b On your first map shade in the distribution of owner-occupation by using this key:

0–20%	61–80%
21–40%	81–100%
41–60%	

c On your second map repeat the exercise for local authority renting.

d On your third map shade in the distribution of housing associations and private renting by using this key: 0–20%; 21–40%.

2 In groups of three, taking a tenure type each, identify where the greatest deviations exist between the average for all wards and the figures for particular wards. Are the wards with figures well above the average, or well below the average, in particular parts of the city?

Owner-occupation

Owner-occupation is the purchase of a dwelling usually with a specially designed hire purchase agreement (the mortgage) from a building society. This loan is supported by tax concessions. Mortgagees do not pay tax on the interest they pay in respect of the first £30,000 of their loans. The societies dominate this market

Figure 7 Leicester's city wards

AB Abbey	EM Eyres Monsell	SH Spinney Hill
AY Aylestone	HU Humberstone	ST Stoneygate
BL Beaumont Leys	LA Latimer	TC Thurncourt
BE Belgrave	MM Mowmacre	WC Westcotes
CA Castle	NP New Parks	WH West
CW Charnwood	NB North Braunstone	Humberstone
CO Coleman	RF Rowley Fields	WP Western Park
CH Crown Hills	RM Rushey Mead	WK West Knighton
EK East Knighton	SA St Augustine	WY Wycliffe
EV Evington	SF Saffron	

(with a 71% share in 1988), with the clearing banks accounting for most of the remainder.

An important feature of the building society industry is its ability to fix *interest rates*. *Deposits* (the source of subsequent mortgages) are attracted by high interest rates, while the mortgagee pays an interest rate higher than the rate paid to savers; but there is a dilemma at the heart of their operation – for, while deposits may be made in the short term, perhaps only for hours, borrowers have their loans over longer terms, usually as

much as 25 years. In addition, most deposits are small, while loans are large (at the end of 1988 the average mortgage exceeded £37,000). This dilemma is managed by driving the interest rates as far apart as possible (see Figure 8) and lending conservatively. This conservatism consists of carefully vetting mortgage applicants and the properties (especially their location) for which mortgages are being sought. This behaviour explains much of the disinvestment in Britain's inner cities and investment in suburban estates – both

familiar urban geographies. To see that this behaviour has been successful: consider the assets of the building societies (Table 2); think about their 'High Street presence' (how many branches are there in your local High Streets? check in the telephone book if you need to); look also at Figure 9 which shows how they have managed to keep a substantial difference between the interest rates on deposits and interest rates on lending, and hence increased the amount of money they have available (their liquidity).

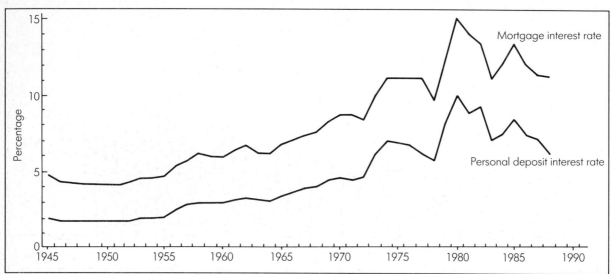

Note: After April 1982 deposit interest rates were Building Societies Association 'advised' rates, calculated from the Share Rate Index.

Figure 8 Building society interest rates, 1945–88

Table 2 The building societies: the big twelve: 1986

	Name	Assets (£m)	Shareholders	Borrowers	Branches
1	Halifax	28,694	7,980,380	1,490,800	729
2	Abbey National	23,041	7,705,900	1,109,396	676
3	Nationwide	12,202	3,492,662	565,375	530
4	Alliance & Leicester	8,101	2,140,934	417,428	421
5	Woolwich Equitable	7,827	2,101,230	362,885	412
6	Leeds Permanent	7,775	2,670,214	413,755	480
7	National & Provincial	6,048	1,047,045	314,474	338
8	Anglia	5,368	1,818,608	297,333	400
9	Bradford & Bingley	4,417	1,684,713	208,744	253
10	Britannia	4,212	1,052,666	213,748	245
11	Cheltenham & Gloucester	3,854	760,386	156,347	165
12	Bristol & West	2,540	689,347	105,690	168

Shareholders: ordinary deposit (short term and liquid) share accounts.
Borrowers: essentially the number of mortgagees.

Source: Building Societies Association, 1987

1 Show your understanding of the mechanics of building society finance by logically working out what would happen to mortgage supply and the mortgage interest rate if deposits were to fall – for example as they did at the time of the British Telecom share sale. (Use Figure 8 and 9 here.)

2 The basis of the humour in Figure 10 exists in the differences between the purpose and manner of the original societies and their modern image. Collect a number of current advertisements from the societies and analyse their content. Discuss what image they are now projecting. How has this changed from the original image portrayed in Figure 10?

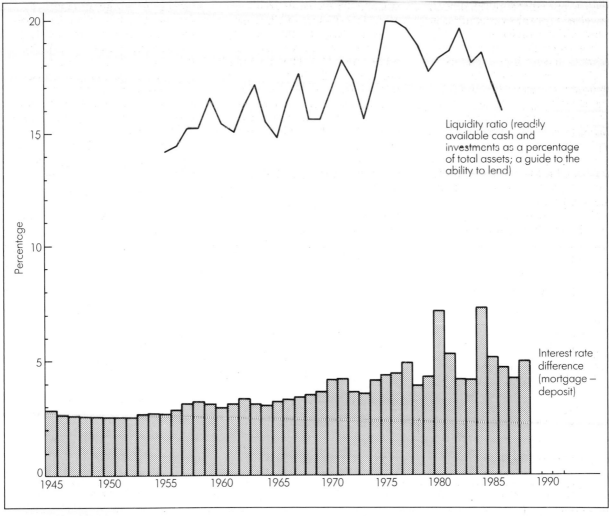

Figure 9 The building societies, the liquidity ratio and the interest rate gap, 1945–88

Figure 10 The changing building societies

Renting

Renting is the hiring of property from a *landlord* by a *tenant*. A distinction is usually made between local authorities, private landlords and the housing associations.

Local authority

Local authority renting in its modern form dates from the Housing Act 1919. This was intended to make a 'decent' landlord of local government and to supply housing of a good standard where the private market did not. This Act established the relationship between central and local government methods of subsidy and marked the emergence of housing professionals. Subsequent Acts tinkered with these ground rules, but it was not until the Housing Act 1980 that the first principles of local authority housing were re-examined.

Table 3 summarises the number of local authority houses built between 1919 and 1980. World War 2 had an obvious impact, but other changes can be accounted for by variations in Britain's economic well-being, changes in public policy (and governments) and the introduction of new building techniques. Where these factors worked together, for example in the high-rise rehousing from slum clearance schemes in the 1950s and 1960s, the total number of new dwellings built was huge. However, this tenure sector never shook off associations of low status, especially on larger pre-war estates, and the high-rise flats and their crises were often dramatic and even sometimes fatal (see 'Ronan Point' extract). Local management's need to eke out financial resources too often led to unsympathetic behaviour towards tenants, reflecting the tension that has always existed in this sector between housing's social role and its substantial cost.

Table 3 The construction of local authority housing 1920–87

Year	Completions	Year	Completion	Year	Completion
1920	576	1921	16,786	1922	86,579
1923	67,062	1924	19,586	1925	23,862
1926	49,508	1927	83,948	1928	120,492
1929	69,677	1930	73,268	1931	63,996
1932	79,013	1934	68,156	1935	57,326
1936	70,486	1937	87,423	1938	92,047
1939	121,653	1940	60,926	1941	20,122
1942	5,985	1943	4,095	1944	4,922
1945	3,364	1946	25,013	1947	97,340
1948	190,368	1949	165,946	1950	163,670
1951	162,584	1952	186,920	1953	229,305
1954	223,731	1955	181,331	1956	154,971
1957	154,137	1958	131,164	1959	114,324
1960	116,358	1961	105,529	1962	116,424
1963	112,780	1964	141,132	1965	151,305
1966	161,435	1967	181,467	1968	170,214
1969	162,910	1970	157,067	1971	134,000
1972	104,553	1973	88,148	1974	104,279
1975	129,883	1976	129,202	1977	163,000
1978	131,000	1979	104,000	1980	107,000
1981	85,000	1982	50,000	1983	51,000
1984	50,000	1985	39,000	1986	21,320
1987	18,880	1988	18,604e		

e : estimate

Sources: State Housing in Britain, S. Merrett, Routledge and Kegan Paul, 1979 and *Housing and Construction Statistics*, HMSO, 1988

Ronan Point

In 1968 five people were killed when a gas explosion caused the partial collapse of Ronan Point, a 21-storey tower block in Newham, East London. In 1984 an official structural report confirmed allegations by architect Sam Webb that the block was unsound and could collapse. It was decided to demolish the block in 1986. During his investigations, Webb disclosed through *The Times* that files from the public enquiry held after the disaster had gone missing from the library at the Department of the Environment. As a result of the Great British Housing Disaster of the post-war years, scores of other tower blocks are likely to be demolished for structural or social reasons over the next few years.

1 Local authority housing has been subject to many influences. Identify these by drawing a simple line graph from Table 3, and then annotating the graph to account for the numbers of houses constructed, giving details of social, political and economic factors. You may find it helpful to refer to a social history textbook to accurately locate the dates of elections and other details.

Private renting

Private renting exists when there is a sufficient profit to be made from the invested capital that the ownership of property represents. The introduction of controlled rents in the 1940s reduced the potential for profit and the sector has substantially contracted. Even so it is an important sector where densities can be raised and accommodation standards are not of the first importance. Young people saving up to buy a house, recently arrived immigrants and students often live in privately rented accommodation.

Housing associations

Housing associations were formed to provide decent housing at affordable rents long before the local authorities started to do so. The capital to do this was originally charitable, for example the Peabody Trust in London, but most associations now receive government funding directed through the Housing Corporation. Associations often target particular groups, such as the disabled or the elderly. They have a good record of rehabilitating older properties in the inner cities; these are frequently converted into hostels or 'sheltered' accommodation.

Changes in tenure

Historical changes in tenure have been of dramatic proportions in the very recent past and are the best evidence we have of the changing balance of advantage and disadvantage the different tenure types have. These changes are summarised in Figure 11.

In the space of a lifetime the importance of the private rented sector and owner-occupation has been reversed, and two 'new' tenure types have been created, one of them containing nearly one-third of Britain's households. In the last decade change has continued to be of significant proportions: owner-occupation has risen by nearly 10% and the local authority rented sector has contracted for the first time in its history.

These changes occur when a dwelling is transferred from one tenure type to another or new dwellings are constructed. Changes only take place when the supply-side and demand-side agencies in the housing market see that change is rational, i.e. when the gains involved in the transfer outweigh the losses. It has been comparatively easy at some times to find an answer to equations such as these, for example if private landlords find that rent acts are driving down their profits, but that the price of houses being sold is rising, it becomes rational to sell property, especially if there are no long-term prospects of those trends being reversed. Sometimes the causes of change are harder to find, for although often financial these 'gains and losses' may also reflect the way an individual perceives their housing needs. They may, for example, be bothered by the image they present to others – the 'symbolic content' of their dwelling that is determined by cultural norms and expectations. Tenure choice is rarely a neat answer to a simple question.

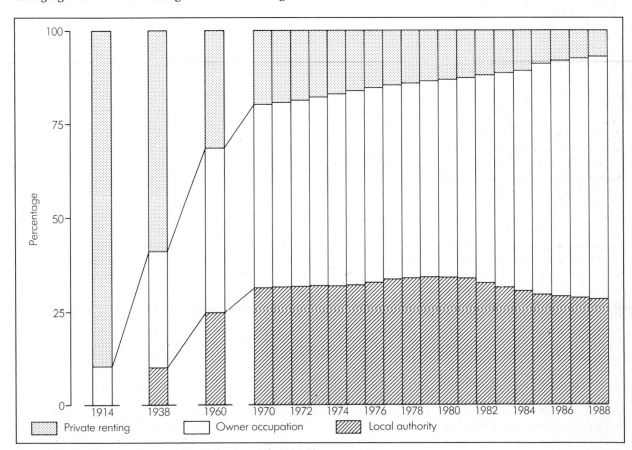

Figure 11 Changes in the tenure of Britain's housing stock, 1914–88

?

Look back to the maps and data about Leicester.

1 Social welfare has been described as 'access to goods, proximity to bads'. Do you think that tenure type and therefore city location determine 'access' and 'proximity'? If so, how?

2 A well-known model of urban structure is that of E. Burgess. (If you are not familiar with this, find it in a text or reference book.) Compare his model with the approach we have used for Leicester. Have they anything in common? Which represents the real world best?

3 Does your nearest town, city or urban district show the same sort of complexity as Leicester? Do some research. Find the data about housing tenure and begin to look for explanations of the distribution of housing in an area you know well.

Changes on the housing scene

The geography of housing is always changing. The processes that drive these changes are many, varied and complicated and have rarely been more so than in the 1980s. To keep in touch with these changes, to learn for oneself, requires constant attention to current articles and programmes from the media set against the sort of background that has already been sketched out. Figure 12 summarises the cross-tenure changes that have occurred – or are likely to occur – as a result of structural changes in the workings of the housing market since 1979. From this diagram perhaps the most important pair of issues are rising house prices and the dismantling of the local authority 'empires'. These are now dealt with in more detail.

House prices

On 13 January 1988 a nurse in Bromley, Kent, paid £18,950 for a bedsit created out of a converted broom cupboard. In 1970 the same sum would have bought nearly four new houses. Inflation notwithstanding, the real price of houses increased very dramatically in recent years (Figure 13)!

Superficially the cause of house price increase seems simple. Their number is limited and their supply inelastic; meanwhile demand increases because of the growth of population. It seems like a simple case of supply and

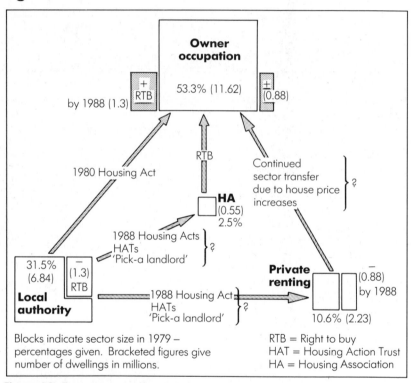

Figure 12 Tenure sector transfers, 1979–88

Blocks indicate sector size in 1979 – percentages given. Bracketed figures give number of dwellings in millions.

RTB = Right to buy
HAT = Housing Action Trust
HA = Housing Association

demand. However, the reality is more complex.

Firstly, there are enough houses (if we ignore the standard of many of them – the National Federation of Housing Associations considered that 1.2 million were '*unfit*' in 1985). They're simply in the wrong places (the North, the inner cities) and their location is fixed. Consequently big differences exist between Britain's regions. Figure 14 shows the

average prices regionally in the first half of 1988, showing that Britain's housing market is really a mosaic of regional markets, containing within them even more local markets. Mobility between markets is easy if an owner 'trades down'; indeed capital can be released in such a move. On the other hand, 'trading up' may be financially impossible, a fact which is already restricting the mobility of labour.

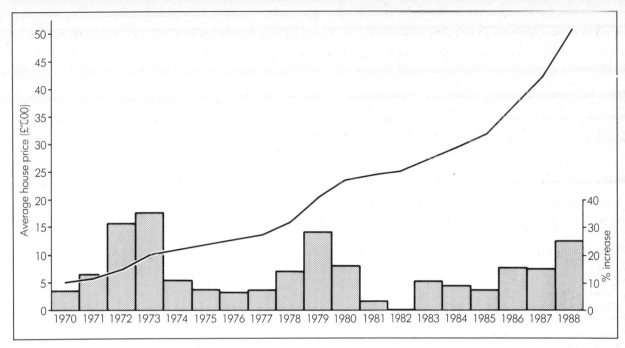

Figure 13 Changes in house prices, 1970–88
Source: Building Societies Association and DOE *Housing and Construction Statistics*, 1988

Secondly, demand is stimulated by very generous tax concessions (on the interest paid on the first £30,000 of the loan) and exemption from tax on any capital gains that accrue if a house sale produces a 'profit'. These combine to make the other tenure sectors very unattractive when compared with owner-occupation. Why pay rents that are higher than mortgage payments? Buying houses as an investment is further fuelled when the financial institutions have plentiful funds (for example when after the Crash of October 1987 investors switched heavily to the building societies), as this hastens sales and further reduces supply. To summarise, this is not a 'free' market where simple supply and demand could operate, but one rigged to achieve specific policy goals.

As house prices rise, first-time buyers are gradually squeezed from the market, the *Guardian* calling them 'an endangered species' in 1988! But everyone has to borrow more, and the institutions are pushed to modify

Figures in £
Upper: 1979
Lower: 1988

Figure 14 Regional house prices in Great Britain, 1979–88
Source: Building Societies Association, 1988

their rules for lending. (As a rule of thumb, lending was at three times an applicant's salary in 1986. It is now commonly four times.) As salaries rise, even modestly, this further increases prices. An example will make this point. In 1985 a £10,000 earner could raise a mortgage of £30,000. A wage increase of only 10%, but coupled with the change in the societies' own lending rule, lifts this to £49,500 or an increase of 65%. Increased lending closely follows income rises, further exacerbating regional differences. More cautiously it can also be argued that these price increases have underwritten huge increases in consumer spending (especially on credit), are inflationary, drive up wage levels and are related to Britain's poor industrial investment record.

However, all investment markets have risks – house prices can fall (although that's rare; Britain, as we've seen, has no other viable tenure sector to transfer to) as well as rise, especially if governments use interest rates to control inflation. The larger the mortgage, the greater any increase in interest will be, and defaulting on mortgage payments, as Figure 15 shows, is a growing trend with unpleasant consequences. Equally as house prices rise (and, as we've seen, this can be ahead of wage increases), so the entry point for purchase is raised, increasing family pressures (newly-marrieds living with in-laws for long periods, for example) and increasing homelessness.

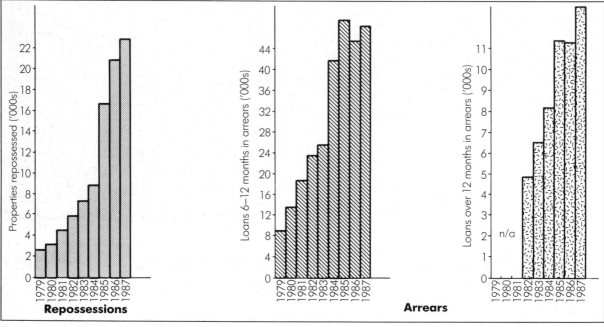

Figure 15 Mortgage repossessions and arrears, 1979–87   *Source*: Building Societies Association

?

1 House purchasing decisions are usually a private affair, a mix of financial and other factors. In threes take one each of the scenarios that follow and:
a calculate the financial implications of the proposed move, and,
b identify what non-financial considerations might be taken into account.

Tom Brown. Tom bought his house in Leeds in 1979 for £3,000 and its value has increased tenfold (although he still owes the building society £1,000). His employer is moving to Brighton and, although Tom has found a house his wife and fourteen-year-old daughter like (at £70,000), his monthly salary will remain at £800 after tax. (You can estimate approximate monthly mortgage repayments by multiplying the total loan by 0.012.)

Jake Hake. Although 24 and married with two baby boys, Jake is still living with his parents and finding the cramped conditions difficult and explosive. His London job earns him £14,000 after tax, a figure that makes the purchase of a home nearby difficult. He's tempted to move right away but is uncertain about work elsewhere.

Myra White. Myra bought her house in Camden, Central London, in 1979 for £7,000 and its value has increased fifteenfold (although she owes the building society £2,000). Myra's journalism now only needs a fax link to London, and she's seen a cottage near her family in the Yorkshire Dales for £31,000 that she intends to buy.

Outline the implications, both financial and non-financial of the proposed moves to the others in your group. Collectively then summarise the housing needs and wants in each case, and identify the extent to which they were likely to be met or thwarted.

Government policy and house prices

In 1988 and 1989 the government began to use higher interest rates as a method of controlling inflation. (The idea is that, if it is more expensive to borrow money, people will still borrow less and there will be less money available to purchase goods; sellers will therefore not be able to increase their prices sharply.) House price inflation has responded to these measures (see the extract 'House prices start falling as interest rates bite') and there has also been some evening-out of the North–South house-price divide. These may seem desirable trends in the light of what you have learned in the preceding section, but they may bring their own problems.

House prices start falling as high interest rates bite

HOUSE prices fell in the first quarter of the year south of a line from the Wash to the Severn Estuary, the Halifax building society said yesterday.

In the three months to March, prices in East Anglia, Greater London, the South-east and South-west fell by 1.3 per cent, the Midlands and Wales rose by up to 4 per cent, and the North-west, North, Yorkshire and Humberside rose by 6.8 per cent to 8.5 per cent.

The figures reflect the change in the market since last summer when the Government began pushing up base rates from their 10-year low of 7.5 per cent and abolished multiple tax relief. House builders are now having to fight for every sale, while architects report that waiting lists for materials have disappeared.

House price changes

Percentage changes based on regional indices of house prices compared with previous quarter and same quarter a year ago

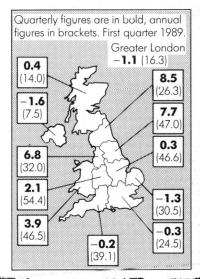

Quarterly figures are in bold, annual figures in brackets. First quarter 1989.

Greater London −**1.1** (16.3)

0.4 (14.0)
−1.6 (7.5)
6.8 (32.0)
2.1 (54.4)
3.9 (46.5)
−0.2 (39.1)
8.5 (26.3)
7.7 (47.0)
0.3 (46.6)
−1.3 (30.5)
−0.3 (24.5)

Source: Larry Elliott, *Guardian*, 12 April 1989

?

1 Read the extract from Brian Gould's interview with Brian Walden on page 320.

a What, according to Brian Gould, are the psychological implications of a buoyant housing market?

b What effect are these likely to have on inflation?

2 Read the extracts 'House prices start falling as high interest rates bite' and 'Interest rates increase mortgage repossessions'. List the consequences in the housing market of higher interest rates.

3 Clearly government policies affect the housing market. With reference to all three extracts, and thinking about what you have already read in this chapter, discuss in groups the ways in which house prices are affected by government measures.

Interest rate rises increase mortgage repossessions

The Labour Party yesterday published the results of a survey of regional mortgage increases which showed that by March this year the average first-time buyer was paying £386.42 a month, rising to £745.80 in Greater London — an increase of £29.11 a month since January.

Mr Clive Soley, Labour's housing spokesman, said another half per cent rise in mortgage interest rates would add a further £15.05 a month to the average family's repayments — £26.53 in Greater London — and exacerbate the country's homelessness situation.

He said a survey of private sector rents since the Housing Act came into force on April 1 had also shown they were now beyond the income of many tenants.

In the first two weeks of April, he said a typical two-bedroom furnished flat in London would cost £640 a month to rent, £220 in the West Midlands, £425 in Glasgow and £275 in Wales. Mr Soley said that many people are now spending half their income on housing, against the ideal of no more than 20 per cent of their take-home pay, and first-time buyers were paying £60 a month more than a year ago.

Although one in 10 of the 118,000 families which presented themselves as homeless in the past 12 months already cited mortgage repossession as the reason, he believed a further interest rate rise would exacerbate the problem.

Source: Larry Elliott and Alan Travis, *Guardian*, 20 April 1989

Labour plan to curb home loans

Text from Brian Gould's interview with Brian Walden

Gould: The purposes for which mortgages are made have not been closely enough controlled; everyone knows this, I have done it myself; on switching houses they have deliberately gone for a larger mortgage than they need in order to produce extra spending.

Second, the effect of that has been to create a degree of asset inflation through house prices in the South-east and then in the rest of the country, which has induced a psychological mood that without doing anything, they can sit at home and watch their wealth grow, and that has induced a willingness to go out and take on other forms of borrowing. That is where the problem has arisen.

Walden: So you are going to restrict mortgages?

Gould: What we have to be clear about and the Chancellor is clear about this — that 85 per cent of personal borrowing takes the form of mortgage advances . . .

Walden: You are saying something very interesting indeed. You are saying we are going to attack the problem where the problem really is, which is the 85 per cent of borrowing for mortgages?

Gould: That's right.

Walden: No new mortgages?

Gould: No, we are not saying no new mortgages . . . What we are saying is stricter conditions.

There are conditions — 25 years is generally thought to be the permissible term for a mortgage.

Three times gross salary might be regarded by many building societies as about the maximum that they would lend.

These are controls, limits, which can be adjusted — which we believe ought to be adjusted — if that form of lending or borrowing is growing too fast . . .

Walden: Some people will say it will inevitably hit young couples.

Gould: That is a real worry. That is why I make it clear we would provide special conditions for first-time buyers. We want to see them having easy access to that ladder of home ownership.

Source: Independent, 16 October, 1989

Dismantling the local authority empires

The second major routeway shown on Figure 12 is the transfer of local authority dwellings to other tenure sectors. This may be looked at in two parts. Firstly there is the transfer of individual properties to their tenants who become owner-occupiers. This 'right to buy' (RTB) was introduced in the Housing Act 1980 and is therefore a well-established policy. Secondly there are the more sweeping changes of the Housing Act 1988. As this chapter was written immediately following its implementation, calculating the consequences of this legislation is difficult – however, *you* should now be able to gauge its results more fully!

The Housing Act 1980 and 'the right to buy'

The sale of local authority housing is not new (see Figure 16) but the creation of a *right* to purchase was, and turned out to be an electorally powerful piece of policy. Since the Act, more than 1.3 million dwellings have been bought by their tenants. And no wonder, for the Act provided for generous discounts on the house price (averaging some 48%, according to David Trippier, an Environment Minister, in November 1988), with 83% of all sales sampled by the Department of the Environment producing a final valuation of less than £14,000 per dwelling! RTB has stripped the local authorities of their 'best' properties and consolidated their holdings into the largest estates and the high-rise flats. Authorities have also lost their 'best' tenants, the two factors combining to make the contemporary management of local authority stock very arduous indeed. Rent arrears are one symptom of the problems.

The Housing Act 1988

This is a complex Act, with the promise that its various parts combining together will produce fundamental changes in the geography of housing.

A key element is the continued relaxation of controls on the level of rents and security of tenure, with the hope that, as rents rise, so private-sector renting will be encouraged. Local authority rent levels would also continue to rise, again making RTB an attractive option.

Perhaps the most important element for local authority tenants is the ability to 'opt out' by introducing in the Act a 'tenants' choice' of landlord clause. Sometimes sarcastically called the 'Pick a Tenant' scheme (because of the power of many of the prospective landlords), transfer to a new landlord is to be negotiated by a curious voting system (non-voting is to count as a vote for transfer!) while the 'social responsibility' of the new landlord is to be ensured by the Housing Corporation.

It is expected that existing housing associations will be the 'new' landlords, but so far they have been less enthusiastic about this new role than the government hoped. The reason for this is partly the increase in the extent of their activities – in Leicester, for example, wholesale transfer would increase the association's stock by more than seven times! Transfer would also threaten their traditional role in providing special-needs housing, and there's little that is attractive in presiding over residualised housing in the face of rising rent levels.

Existing Associations would not, however, be the only new

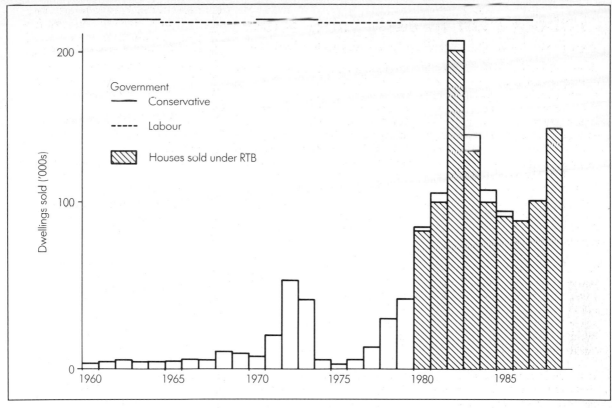

Figure 16 The sale of local authority houses, 1960–88

Source: DOE, *Housing and Construction Statistics*

landlords possible. At Rochford in Essex the local authority registered a new association to which its housing stock would be transferred – only to have the proposal overwhelmingly rejected 2,224 to 180 by the existing tenants. In Torbay the transfer 'succeeded', but only because 42% (2,186) tenants did not vote, so overturning the actual voting of 2,210 against and 787 for – a final balance of 2,210 against 2,973, a result so daft that the Secretary of State asked the Torbay Council to think again. Finally, private landlords could take over housing stock, a desirable proposition If its capital valuation were low enough and its rent yield high enough. This is most likely to occur in the South-East as a consequence of high house prices. For example, in Hertsmere, St Albans and Three Rivers, three Hertfordshire authorities within commuting distance of London, financial consultants have been employed to consider the implications of such a transfer.

The Act further encourages such transfers by establishing the possibility of Housing Action Trusts (HATs), non-elected bodies charged with the task of rehabilitating run-down local authority estates. These Trusts make transfer from local authority control or exercise of the RTB more likely, the former because of the estate's improvements (most of the HATs nominated so far have been in London) and the latter because rent levels will rise substantially to reflect the improvements, again bringing rent levels and mortgage payments together.

Whatever the outcome of the 1988 Act, there is little doubt that its impact on Britain's housing will be substantial, accelerating the already dramatic changes of the last decade. The geographer's task is to monitor these changes and to know the forces which drive them. In this way it should be possible to have an understanding of the forms and processes that is as subtle as the forms and processes themselves.

Read the newspaper article on page 322 'The foundations start to crumble.'

1 As a group similar to the Midland Area Improvement Housing Association:

a List the aims of your association.

b Prepare a letter to a group who wish to set up a housing association on an estate in Sunderland. Give them as much helpful advice as you can and outline what you see as the significance of the changes brought about by the Housing Act 1988.

The foundations start to crumble

Midland Area Improvement Housing Association Ltd, to give its full title, is neither a democratically-controlled housing authority nor a profit-making company, but a charitable outfit that sits rather uneasily between the two.

Tenants agree that a housing association is preferable to the alternatives. Midland Area is now a well-established feature of Handsworth having been set up by local volunteers 21 years ago. It is regarded as being less ruthless than a private owner, and more accessible than the local authority, which has 120,000 properties compared to Midland Area's 2,600.

But the special position enjoyed by Midland Area may now be under threat. New government regulations could undermine its charitable objectives and force it to abandon the middle ground between public and private sectors.

The aim of the 1988 Housing Act is to give housing associations like Midland Area a more prominent role within British housing. By doing so the Government hopes to expand them whilst cutting back on council housing.

But there is a stick behind the carrot. Before they can take over from local authorities, housing associations must be exposed to market forces. The Housing Act requires individual associations to set their own rent levels, and borrow money from city financiers rather than rely entirely on government grants.

The impact of these radical changes is only just being felt in Handsworth. On January 15 fair rents, which previously had been set independently by rent officers, were abolished overnight for all new housing association lettings and replaced with "assured tenancies". Midland Area must now set its own charges when any flat becomes vacant.

At the top of the association's list of charitable objectives is the duty to provide housing for people in need and "on terms appropriate to their needs".

In the absence of official guidelines, Midland Area has followed the advice of its own national body, the National Federation of Housing Associations, that rents should not take more than 20 per cent of tenants' average incomes.

Midland Area made its first offer of a new assured tenancy last Tuesday — a two-bedroom flat in Handsworth which would have cost £14.25 a week under fair rents. The new rent is £20.89 — an increase of nearly 50 per cent.

The second assured tenancy was a self-contained flat offered to a single working woman on a weekly income of less than £100. She was stunned when she heard that the old rent of £19 had jumped overnight to £24.35. She took the flat out of desperation, even though the combined rent and rates will bite almost a third out of her salary.

The bulk of Midland Area's work, as its full name implies, involves buying and renovating run-down properties, of which Handsworth has more than its fair share. Under the new private funding system, tenants in improved housing of this sort could pay anything up to £50 in rent.

"We do have to ask ourselves who is going to be prepared to pay that amount," the director Mike Ager said. "It will be very difficult for us to do what has always been our main purpose in Handsworth — improving old houses. I am not sure we can convince ourselves that we can carry on with it."

The association's very reason for being — housing those in need — is under test. Rent increases could have a crippling effect on its tenants, 70 per cent of whom are unemployed and living off benefits, and a total of 93 per cent who have weekly incomes of less than £90.

The people who are most immediately threatened are ironically not the unemployed, because they can still get all their rent paid for them, but those in the middle — single people or families who are struggling to make ends meet on very low incomes.

Tenants paying the new rents of say £40, will be forced into a poverty trap. They would have to earn in excess of £130 a week before their standard of living rises above dole levels.

At the worst scenario, the housing association could be left having to house only the unemployed or up-market households who could afford higher rents. But that the association is loath to do.

The association's traditional client group — the unemployed and people on very low wages — will continue seeking its help because, after all, they have no other option.

Source: Edward Pilkington, *Guardian*, 25 January 1989

?

It was suggested that rent arrears in the local authority sector were a measure of the increasing concentration of tenants with financial housing difficulties in the sector. This is, however, open to differing political interpretations. Table 4 and Figure 17 provide some evidence relating to this issue – but do they allow you to draw political conclusions?

1 Initially work in pairs to make a comparison between the political party and the level of rent arrears in reach of the London boroughs. Is there a connection between the two variables, or does some other factor, such as nearness to the centre seem to contribute to the arrears level? Equally, does being near the centre of the city influence voting patterns?

2 What reservations do you have about drawing political conclusions from this data?

3a Now individually – but using the same information – prepare two draft political speeches, the first from a Conservative member advocating reform of the local authority sector, and the second from a Labour member proposing greater financial support for the sector. In each case evidence should be drawn from the results of question **1**.

b What does this tell us about the political debate concerning housing?

Table 4 London's local authority housing: rent arrears

Borough	Rent arrears (£) 31.3.88
Barking	751,729
Barnet	800,760
Bexley	281,909
Brent	16,668,415
Bromley	391,185
City of London	68,124
Camden	4,660,402
Croydon	1,322,118
Ealing	2,195,819
Enfield	1,177,386
Greenwich	4,784,538
Hackney	8,417,497
Hammersmith and Fulham	2,152,938
Haringey	4,119,000
Harrow	404,366
Havering	480,962
Hillingdon	468,128
Hounslow	900,746
Islington	9,764,151
Kensington and Chelsea	1,059,328
Kingston-on-Thames	133,310
Lambeth	12,553,466
Lewisham	4,700,000
Merton	1,132,312
Newham	3,626,000
Redbridge	801,831
Richmond	431,885
Southwark	19,019,317
Sutton	436,622
Tower Hamlets	2,218,411
Waltham Forest	3,140,577
Wandsworth	2,408,547
Westminster	1,779,000

Source: Parliamentary Answers (Written)

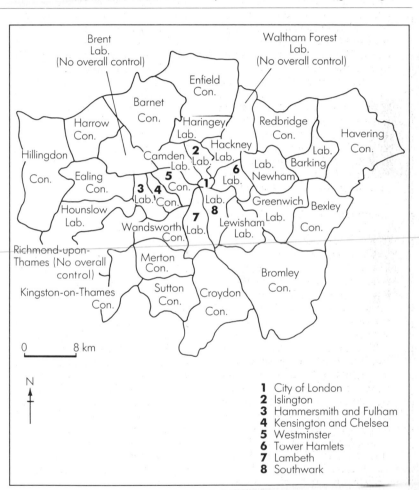

1 City of London
2 Islington
3 Hammersmith and Fulham
4 Kensington and Chelsea
5 Westminster
6 Tower Hamlets
7 Lambeth
8 Southwark

Figure 17 Political control of the London boroughs in 1988

Homelessness

Although in absolute terms there may be enough houses for households in the UK, a growing number of people find themselves without a home. The article 'The Forgotten Army' looks at the reasons for increasing homelessness and its implications for individuals.

The forgotten army

All the homeless people: where do they all come from?
Steve Platt gives some startling answers and talks to the
faces behind the numbers.

Who are the homeless? Increasingly, they're people just like us

Homelessness is, by and large, too boring to merit much of a mention in the media. The occasional incident brings it back to public attention. A death in a bed and breakfast hotel, the shooting of a dosser tackling armed raiders on London's South Bank, and an article in the *Sunday Times* slagging off Shelter are among the few to have done so this year. But for the most part horizons are limited by the simple news value formulae:

Housing = House Prices;
Housing Problems = Mortgage
                    Rate Rises.

There are signs, however, that this year may be slightly different. The interest rate crisis has hit home-buyers so hard that is has suddenly dawned on even unfaltering devotees of the property-owning democracy in the pro-Tory media that homelessness is not just something that hits the feckless and

irresponsible, but that it can happen to anyone.

Seven per cent of all households accepted as homeless by English local authorities in 1988 became so because of mortgage arrears: twice as many as for rent arrears.

The sudden recognition that home ownership may bring its own problems and that not everyone can afford (or should be encouraged) to buy may bring some genuine assistance to the homeless in general for the first time since the 1977 Housing (Homeless Persons) Act gave local councils a statutory duty to house certain categories of homeless. But even the £100 million promised by the government will not make up for the extra costs to current housing programmes resulting from the government's high interest policy. In relation to the cuts in housing investment made during the past ten years, it is tantamount to stealing a cake and returning some crumbs.

In 1980–81, for example, the English local authorities' housing investment programmes amounted to almost £3,400 million. In 1988–89, they had fallen to just over £1,100 million. The number of council houses built fell from 94,000 in 1980 (already down from 140,000 in 1977) to under 25,000 in 1988. Central government housing subsidies to local authorities showed an even more dramatic fall — from £2,200 million in 1979–80 to £470 million in 1987–88. The total number of new homes, including those in the private sector, fell from about 250,000 each year in the 1970s to 176,000 by 1987.

Nor did housing associations, now being projected by the government as the vanguard of social housing provision, pick up the difference. Housing association new builds fell from 19,000 a decade ago to 9,000 last year. Altogether (mainly because of right-to-buy sales to sitting tenants and the continuing decline of private renting), the rented sector has shrunk by 1.2 million homes since 1981.

It should be no surprise, then, that homelessness has grown — from 57,000 households accepted by English local authorities in 1979 to 116,000 accepted in 1988. In Wales it has increased from 3,204 in 1978–79 to 6,818 in 1988; in Scotland from 16,037 to 24,335. The total number of homeless applications in England in 1988, including those refused assistance by their local council, was 242,470. That represents about 700,000 people, or 14 in every thousand. For the first time, councils in 1988 rejected more households than they accepted.

The number of homeless in temporary accommodation has also grown — from 9,450 in 1981 (1,620 of them in bed and breakfast) to 33,750 in 1989 (11,720 in bed and breakfast). You can't stop building social housing and expect the private sector to provide instead. Private provision works only when the customers have the means to pay the market price.

It's not that government ministers don't know this. The social history of the past ten years has been littered with reports warning of the consequences of cuts in housing on the scale carried out by the Conservatives. Indeed, one of the most remarkable features of the housing debate during the past decade has been the degree of consensus, almost unanimity, among non-government organisations about the extent of the problem and the nature of the solution. From the churches to the building societies, from charities to big business, the conclusions fly in the face of the government's bald assertion, made most recently in its expenditure white paper, that: "In most parts of the country there is now an adequate supply of housing."

There clearly isn't. While a crude surplus of homes over households may exist, it disappears as soon as any account is taken of their condition or location, of the number of concealed households living with friends or relatives, or of the rate of growth of households needing housing during the next ten years. The National Housing Forum, which represents virtually all the major housing bodies in the country, estimates that there is an immediate need for two million new homes and for an additional 3.2 million by 2001.

Nor is it simply the case that the government is not prepared to spend money on housing. Mortgage interest tax relief is projected to cost the exchequer £6,750 million in 1989–1990 — almost five times as much as ten years ago. Discounts on council house sales to sitting tenants and the absence of any form of taxation on house owners' profits from price inflation cost thousands of millions of pounds more.

The human cost of the housing shortfall has now begun to bubble up on to the streets. The appearance of burgeoning numbers of increasingly young homeless on the streets of London has presented ministers with a spectre at the post-socialist feast.

A Salvation Army survey, published this summer estimated that when people in hostels, bed and breakfast hotels and squats were taken into account, there were 75,000 overtly homeless people in the capital — "a shanty town as large as might be expected in any Latin American city but it is hidden".

Figures from the DSS and other sources suggest that nationally there could be as many as 250,000 people who fall into these categories.

It isn't just London that is affected. In fact, while in absolute terms it remains the area with by far the worst problem, during the ten years since 1978 it has one of the *smallest* percentage increases in homelessness — up 93 per cent in the inner boroughs, 113 per cent in the outer boroughs. This is less than the Midlands, the North, the North-West, the North-East and East Anglia. In Tyne and Wear, for example, homelessness was up by 194 per cent, in South Yorkshire by 228 per cent, and in Manchester by 325 per cent.

Nor is homelessness limited to the big cities. In 1988, 43 per cent of homeless households were in small towns and rural areas. And many of those who become homeless in larger towns and cities are actually people who moved there in search of work and accommodation from less urban areas.

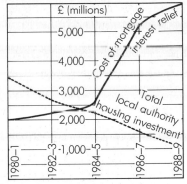

Local-authority housing investments and mortgage tax relief

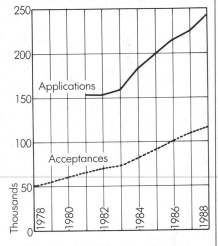

Applications and acceptances of homeless people by English local authorities

It's easy to get immersed in the statistical arguments, to lose sight of the real individuals they represent. But they provide a rational basis for a righteous anger. Back in the 1960s when *Cathy Come Home* tugged at the nation's heartstrings, there were a few thousand homeless families. Last year the total accepted by English, Scottish and Welsh authorities was more than 156,000. Nearly 35,000 are currently stuck in temporary accommodation, including almost 12,000 in bed and breakfast.

Among them is Glenn, the son of Caroline who tells her story here. Born in bed and breakfast, this two-year-old has been homeless all his life. We hear a great deal from the government about how there is too little concern for the victims of crime, while criminals walk free. If Glenn is the victim, who is the criminal?

One room in Bayswater

Caroline has been in bed and breakfast hotels with her son since 1986

"Before I became homeless I was living with my mum. At that time I had my daughter with me. I was on Westminster's housing list but I wasn't given anywhere.

Then I went to a friend's in Yorkshire, where I became pregnant. I'd lived in Westminster all my life but I went to Leeds because I'd had problems and I went to get away from them. I would have stayed but the Yorkshire housing officer told me London was my home town and they weren't going to rehouse me. So they more or less sent me back to Westminster.

I couldn't get a place of my own. I'd been on Westminster's list for eight years when I was living with my mum, so I went to them. This was in 1986.

They said they had nothing to offer me. The only alternative was to put me in B&B, which they told me was for nine months, then another two months, then another five. It went up and up and gradually the homelessness problem got worse and it took them years before I could get somewhere.

I stayed in Earls Court for a year and a bit, then they moved me out because it was too expensive. Now I'm in one room in a hotel in Bayswater. There's a kitchen in the basement—two cookers for a hundred and odd families, and even they've broken down.

I was pregnant when I was put in bed and breakfast. My son, Glenn, was born while I was in the Earls Court hotel. At the time I felt really depressed, but I decided I've just got to help myself, keep occupied—take him out, go round my mum's at weekends. If I don't keep myself occupied I can see myself having a nervous breakdown in here. I've already seen one person have a nervous breakdown in my hotel.

Because Glenn was brought up in a hotel I've seen him grow up to be a very aggressive boy—throwing things around, shouting, kicking. What can I do? I can tell him off but

it doesn't seem to be working because the pressure of living in one room is what's really doing it.

After this interview I've got to go up to the council because they're no longer using this hotel for homeless families. God knows where I'm going to be put. I've had no help from officials, none at all. They just tell you to wait your turn. They say wait another two months, and another five months . . . I'm not asking for much, just a flat where I can settle down and live a proper life.

I just think that something should be done soon, especially when there are children locked up in rooms for

so long. Thank God mine's at the age where he doesn't understand. At least I haven't got the difficulty of getting proper schooling for him as well.

I tried to get a housing association place when the council couldn't help. They ask you, 'Why do you want a housing association flat?' and look at your background to see if you are a problem family. I don't think that's right.

Some people look at homeless people as problem families. We're not problem families. We just haven't got anywhere to live."

Source: Steve Platt, *New Statesman and Society*, 3 November 1989

?

1 'In most parts of the country there is now an adequate supply of housing', Government White Paper, 1989. Discuss this statement in the light of the evidence in the extract 'The Forgotten Army'.

2 In the UK all mothers of young children are visited by a Health Visitor who checks on the welfare of the mother and child. Caroline's Health Visitor is concerned about her accommodation problem and its effects on Glenn and Caroline. She decides to make an enquiry at the Housing Department about the possibility of Caroline being re-housed soon. In pairs, role-play a conversation between the Health Visitor and the housing officer in which each states their case.

3 In groups of three or four prepare a brief outline for a TV documentary about homelessness. You will need to give it a title and consider the following questions:

- What will the *focus* be?
- What images will you show? You may find it helpful to use sketches, or photographs cut from newspapers and magazines.
- What statistics will you use? Do you need to research additional statistics? How will you present the figures to be interesting and accessible to viewers?
- Would you include interviews with, or profiles of, homeless people? Describe some of the people you would wish to feature.
- Who would present the programme? A neutral male/female voice-over? An investigative reporter speaking to camera? A well-known personality? (Explain your choice.)

Alternatively, your programme could be a drama-documentary in which actors present a fictionalised narrative about homelessness. Outline the narrative and explain what issues to do with homelessness you are highlighting.

4 With reference to all the information in this chapter, work in pairs and choose one or more aims from the following list which seem to you to be desirable:

a to help first-time buyers to enter the housing market

b to maintain the property values for people who already own houses

c to increase mobility between different parts of the country

d to increase owner occupation

e to provide decent housing for all

f to prevent the escalation of house prices

What advice would you give to the Chancellor of the Exchequer to help him/her achieve the aim(s) you have chosen?

Postscript: An approach for fieldwork

Geography begins at home *by Alice Coleman*

It is possible to compare two major housing models: planned and unplanned.

Unplanned housing evolved by a process of natural selection: discovery by trial and error. From the cave shelter to the earth-floored hut, to the use of brick and the development of windows from flush to bow to bay, it was an advance consisting of millions of individual choices and adjustments, progressively improving. It evolved by doing rather than rationalising, and was implicit rather than explicit, so it was easily, if wrongly, dismissed as haphazard and inferior.

Planned housing, by contrast, was born of words and ideas rather than practical experience. It was supported by vocal and organised exponents led by the Swiss architect-planner, Le Corbusier, who was a legend in his own lifetime with enormously infectious appeal as an advocate of social engineering. He was convinced that he knew what kind of lifestyle would be best for everyone and what kind of architecture would steer them into it. He believed that communities could be created by throwing people together. Individuals would be thrown together in open-plan dwellings. Dwellings would be thrown together in tower blocks, and tower blocks would be thrown together in 'Radiant Cities', raised aloft on colonnades of pillars amid communal green spaces. The problem with this alluring picture was that Le Corbusier never tested it. He did not produce a single scrap of evidence that it would actually work, but it was nevertheless welcomed by housing planners, who needed to justify their role by means of something radically different from the unplanned semi-detached design.

Factual testing of the models

An attempt was made to provide the evidence that would link building design to human behaviour by Oscar Newman. He argued that the built environment had a part to play in *determining* behaviour by evaluating design feature in New York with the levels of crime associated with them (*Defensible Space*, 1972). He identified eight harmful designs, all of which had been officially advocated in Britain by housing research staff in the Department of the Environment. Unfortunately the Directorate did not respond by withdrawing the indicated designs but chose to protect the record by disparaging Newman's work.

In 1979 the Land Use Research Unit at King's College, London was funded by the Joseph Rowntree Memorial Trust to undertake a 'design-disadvantagement survey' of over 4,000 blocks of flats and 4,000 houses (*Utopia on Trial*, published by Hilary Shipman, 1985). The results not only vindicated Oscar Newman, but also produced much additional information. The number of culpable designs was extended from eight to fifteen, and they were shown to encourage other kinds of social breakdown besides crime: litter, graffiti, excrement, vandalism and the placing of children in care.

New methods of analysis have been devised: trend lines, disadvantagement thresholds, disadvantagement scores and abuse scores. Both types of score can easily be adapted for A level fieldwork, but trend lines and thresholds cannot, because they are derived from a very large number of blocks. They are, however, needed as background to make the scoring methods more understandable.

Trend lines

Trend-line graphs can be drawn for each of the design variables. Figure 18 shows that, as building height increases from 2 to 27 storeys, there is also a rise in the proportion of blocks having the various categories of crime and social breakdown. Trend lines show only the presence or absence of a particular test measure in each block, but if actual numbers of crimes, children in care, etc., are analysed, they are seen to increase much faster than the number of dwellings as block height grows. High-rise is definitely deleterious, but it is not the only harmful design, or even the worst of the fifteen.

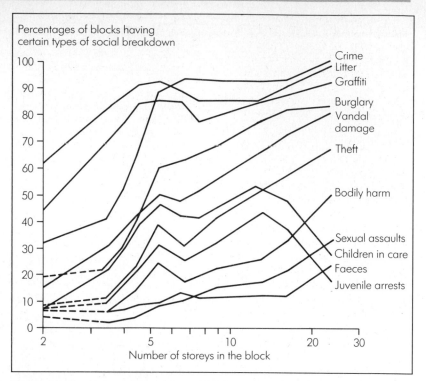

Figure 18 Types of social breakdown and building height.
This trend line graph for number of storeys has four clear characteristics:
1 There is an increasing percentage of blocks with crime and social breakdown as building height becomes greater
2 There is a check in the rise of the trend lines after five storeys, attributable to the reduction in child densities of storeys by lifts
3 There is a sharp drop in the incidence of juvenile arrests and children in care in blocks of over 12–13 storeys, where families with children have been more assiduously transferred
4 Crime rates rise faster than social breakdown rates, probably because the profitability of burglary and theft causes them to be deliberately maximised

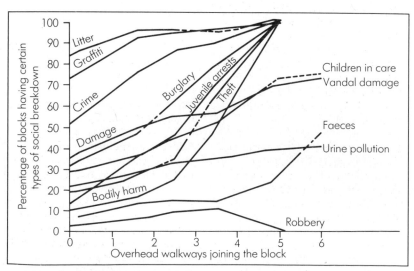

Figure 19 Types of social breakdown and overhead walkways linked together
The trend lines for number of overhead walkways linking blocks together show that crime rises noticeably more rapidly than the social breakdown measures, except for robbery, which may not be fully representative as there were only 29 cases

The trend lines have been slightly smoothed by plotting running means of three values to eliminate random fluctuations. The irregularities that remain, therefore, have a real meaning. Most conspicuous are the sudden descents in the curves for children in care and juvenile arrests in blocks of over 12 to 13 storeys. These appear to reflect efforts made by social workers to transfer the worst problem families out of the tallest tower blocks. A lesser effect (either a flattening of the curve or a temporary dip) begins at about 5 or 6 storeys. This results from reducing child densities on storeys where lifts are needed. However, child density is only a contributory factor, and the trend lines continue to rise thereafter.

Figure 19 shows trend lines for the number of overhead walkways leading off each block. This is the most powerful design for spreading crime from building to building. Theft, for example, occurs in 18 per cent of blocks without walkways, but in 100 per cent of those with four or more. Local authorities do not reduce child densities on the basis of walkways: quite the reverse. Such blocks may become the reception areas for families transferred from the towers, and as a result the curves for juvenile arrests and children in care can go on rising instead of dropping dramatically. Walkways are clearly detrimental to children and should be demolished, to leave each block free-standing.

Disadvantagement thresholds
If all the harmful designs were modified down to the optimum value appearing on their respective trend lines, each block would almost certainly be converted into a house – which would be prohibitive. A more practical goal is the divide between design values with better-than-chance and worse-than-chance frequencies of each test measure. This is the disadvantagement threshold, and

Table 5 Check-list of deleterious designs

Design	Standard threshold	Spaces for surveying Block A	Sample survey of Block B
Size variables			
Dwellings per block	12	_____	48*
Dwellings per entrance	6	_____	24*
Storeys per block	3	_____	6*
Storeys per dwelling	1	_____	2*
Circulation variables			
Overhead walkways	0	_____	0
Interconnecting exits	1	_____	1
Interconnecting lifts and staircases	1	_____	3*
Dwellings per corridor	4	_____	4
Entrance characteristics			
Position	Facing street	_____	Facing
Type	Communal only or individual ground floor doors with front gardens	_____	_____
Stilts of garages under the block	0	_____	0
Features of the grounds			
Gates/gaps into the site	1	_____	2*
Blocks per site	2	_____	3*
Play areas	0	_____	0
Spatial organisation	Semi-public	_____	Confused*
Disadvantagement score		_____	8
Test measures			
Litter		_____	2
Graffiti		_____	1
Damage		_____	1
Faeces		_____	0
Abuse score		_____	4

its value for each design variable is given in Table 5.

Disadvantagement score
Table 5 can be used as a field check-list for recording the design disadvantagement of any block of flats. The block is examined for each of the 15 designs consecutively, and the values observed are entered in the spaces provided. An example is given under the heading, *Block B* and each design that exceeds its threshold level is marked with an asterisk. The asterisks are then totalled and entered as the disadvantagement score; the score of 8 for Block B, is average for 4,099 blocks included in the study.

Figure 20 on page 330 shows trend lines drawn for disadvantagement scores instead of individual designs. Zero-scoring blocks were crime-free in the survey year and also had the lowest probability of the social breakdown measures. The worst-scoring blocks have the highest probabilities; those with scores of 13, 14 and 15 averaged one crime for every five dwellings.

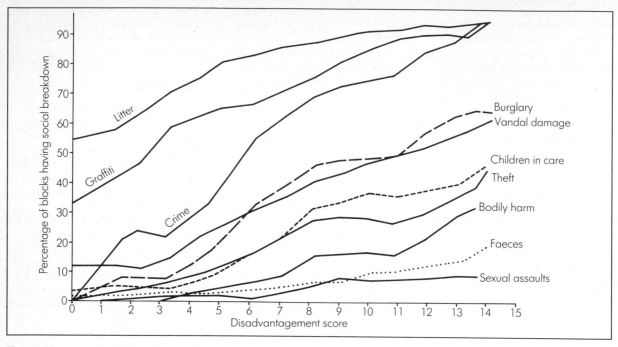

Figure 20 Types of social breakdown and disadvantagement scores
Trend lines for disadvantagement scores show all 15 design variables combined. Purpose-built flats show a clear rise for ten test measures, with crime tending to rise more rapidly than social breakdown

Abuse score

How can a class check whether worse designs attract worse values of the test measures? Crime and children in care cannot be observed directly, and urine pollution is rather erratic, depending on where alcoholics congregate. We therefore use an abuse score based on the four remaining measures (Table 5).

In either of these cases the abuse scores of groups of houses may rise to an average of 1 or more, but usually they are of the order of 0.2 to 0.3. Houses that have been converted into flats score worse than single-family homes but better than purpose-built blocks.

In areas with few flats it may be rewarding to study houses in three age groups. We found that 17–25% of pre-1914 houses had litter, as compared with 8–12% for the more highly evolved inter-war group. Post-war houses, the product of planning, tended to range from 20% up. Those of the 1950s, which are more like tradi-

tional dwellings, tend to be better than very recent ones, but as the latter are usually only small infill sites in the Inner London area, they are unlikely to show such high scores as large out-of-town estates.

Certain design features have been found to score well irrespective of age: front gardens over 3 metres deep with waist-high walls and gates; bay windows with an unobstructed view up and down the street; front-facing doors in recessed porches; and back-to-back gardens behind the house without rear alleys or roads.

Unfortunately there is not sufficient space to define all the features to look for in houses or flats. There are other features, such as spatial organisation (which is important as the most powerful design affecting the sheer volume of crime), that could be considered.

Design improvement

Housing improvement usually consists of repairs, refurbishing

and relandscaping (RI), which restores the fabric of buildings and grounds but leaves all the disadvantaging designs intact. Security improvement (SI) attempts to control crime by means of tougher materials, locks, entry-phones, etc., but does not affect basic causes and, according to the Home Office, is not a great success.

Management improvement (MI) speeds up litter collection, minor repairs, etc., but again does not affect the causes of antisocial behaviour, and Anne Power, its originator, points out that any relaxation of effort leads to relapses. Design improvement (DI) has proved capable of reducing crime rates in the USA, and has also been successful in Britain, although not often tried because of DOE discouragement. Design changes are permanent and do not relapse; they also seem to reach basic causes and *prevent* a great deal of antisocial behaviour, instead of merely clearing up after it.

The aim of DI is to study the defective designs in each block and modify them so that each one is brought down to its threshold level, thus reducing the disadvantagement score. We have carried out a design-disadvantagement survey of an estate in Westminster and recommended a DI programme that would reduce its average disadvantagement score for 29 blocks from 12.8 to 4.8. Similar recommendations for two estates in Cheshire would reduce their scores from 8.1 to 2.7 on average. In both cases the implementation of the DI will cost less per dwelling than is currently being spend on many RIs and SIs, and the improvement should be vastly greater. In practice, there is no guarantee that RIs and SIs will effect any improvement at all; we have monitored 17 such schemes which proved to have nearly three times as much vandal damage afterwards as before.

A DI programme would start with the removal of overhead walkways to leave each block free-standing. The second step is the division of the grounds, to enclose each block in its own walled territory with only one gateway. Thirdly, attention is turned to the block itself, to see how far it can be partitioned into smaller self-contained sections, each with its own separate grounds. And, finally, an attempt is made to replace confused estatescape with something more like the traditional streetscape that was not beset with social problems. This involves continuous building facades, with new houses in the gaps between blocks, and also more continuous frontages with waist-high walls and gates.

Conclusion

Approaches to fieldwork like those outlined here are useful because they begin to quantify features of the landscape that can otherwise only be interpreted in a more subjective way. Equally it should not be overlooked that much of the chapter's earlier content would be difficult to convert into fieldwork, in part because this material is not *determinist* in character but *structural* – arguing that humans make their environment – and to understand what *that* is like we need to understand how that is done.

13

Changes in West European cities

Paul White

Petticoat Lane market, East London

What are the forces producing change?

The 1970s saw a number of changes in the fundamental processes influencing urban growth and change in Western Europe.

1 Zero population growth became characteristic of the subcontinent as death rates and birth rates came into balance. In some countries, such as West Germany and Denmark, the size of the population began to fall.

2 For the first time ever traditional migration movements from the countryside to the towns were reversed, producing a phenomenon that has been labelled *counterurbanisation*, meaning population movement away from cities.

3 The large-scale international flows of low-skilled workers into Western European countries were halted, although family members continued to immigrate in many cases.

Post-industrial economies

Many people have claimed that these changes are part of the evolution of Western European countries into what is called a *post-industrial* (after the industrial revolution) phase. This means that the major growth areas of the economy are no longer traditional manufacturing industries. Instead an increasing proportion of wealth is today being created through:
- new types of productive industry, often in much smaller factories than used to be the case,
- the service industries.

The industries from which employment has been shed fastest are those that were associated with industrial growth in previous phases of economic growth, such as textiles, steel, heavy engineering, chemicals, ship-building and even, in some countries, certain more recent consumer goods industries (such as car manufacture). The large scale of the manufacturing plant normally involved meant that these industries were inevitably urban in location, because they needed:
- a large labour force,
- close connections with suppliers and markets, and
- good transport links.

The new growing industries often involve relatively small plant and are generally of a high technology nature, requiring

Figure 1 Relocation advertisement for a small city, Peterborough, stressing the availability of skilled labour

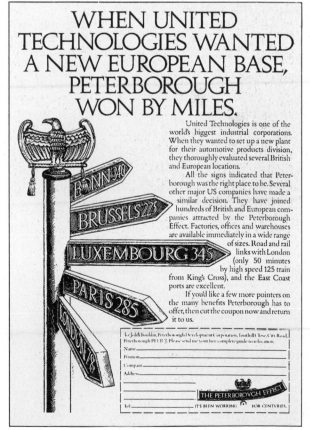

Figure 2 Relocation advertisement stressing Peterborough's good transport links

skilled labour inputs, unlike the semi-skilled or unskilled labour needed by many of the declining industries. Much of this new industry is not orientated to the big cities, but instead to the smaller market towns and accessible rural areas. The creation of such new industry has been part of the cause of counterurbanisation. The industrial geography of Western Europe is undergoing a dramatic 'greening' – a transformation from industrial locations based in big urban centres to a new more decentralised pattern in more rural areas.

Employment changes

One of the most significant results of this process of industrial change in the biggest cities is to be seen in the derelict industrial sites and in the nearby areas where the classic problems of inner-city decay and high rates of unemployment have been highlighted in recent years, especially in Britain.

In many smaller cities the decline of traditional industry has not been matched by the creation of major new employment possibilities. However, in the biggest urban areas (the capital cities of Western Europe and some of the biggest provincial cities) there has been a rapid growth of employment in service activities, both those serving the general public (for instance, retailing) and, more especially, those serving national or multinational business organisations. Such organisations locate their national or regional head offices in the big cities, and those offices then require the assistance of other firms such as accountants, lawyers, merchant banks, and advertising agencies.

Offices

In the biggest cities the rapid growth of the office sector has resulted in the creation of new office parks and in the expansion of existing central business districts (CBDs) through changes or conversions of land use on the fringes of the CBD. Three ex-

amples help to illustrate these developments.

1 In Paris the creation of the office development pole at La Défense to the west of the city centre has given the city its first real Central Business District: previously business functions were located in a chaotic confusion alongside a whole variety of other functions including the fashion industry and diplomatic and governmental activities in the western part of the inner city.

2 In Düsseldorf one of the most notable recent developments has been the progressive dominance of a specific sector of the inner city by Japanese companies, a sector now designated as the 'Japan Center'. The largest Japanese holding companies have selected Düsseldorf as the base for their operations in West Germany and surrounding countries. They have created their own inner-city business district in the area around Immermannstrasse as an eastward extension to the old CBD.

Figure 3 A recent advertisement set apparently in Dallas, but really photographed in the new office complex at La Défense in Paris: an American-style development in a European city

3 The case of Vienna shows the effects of international organisations. Here a 'UNO-City' for United Nations agencies has recently been constructed. The location chosen was a previously unbuilt (green-field) site in the Danube flood plain, just across the river from the main city. The site is massive, over 10 hectares, impossible to obtain within the existing built-up area. The site chosen was the nearest possible to the city core, and was linked to it by a new underground railway.

Schemes for office development in London's Docklands are similar in type to these three examples: new office parks are being created with a new rapid transit link to the old CBD (the Docklands Light Railway).

The problems of change

The deindustrialisation of the big city and the growth of the service and office sectors creates the problem of incompatibility between the two employment trends. On the one hand there is a decline in manual employment, generally male employment. On the other hand, the rapidly growing office sector is creating jobs for skilled white-collar personnel, often with advanced training in the new technologies (such as computing). In part there is also a problem of gender: the male, semi-skilled, industrial worker finds that the new jobs on offer at a similar skill level are clerical and office jobs – traditionally seen as 'women's' work.

A shift is occurring in big-city employment structures towards more non-manual, white-collar and middle-class employment sectors. The coexistence of these two branches of the labour market, with little mobility between them, explains why many of the biggest European cities today have both high unemployment rates (of ex-manual workers) and large numbers of job vacancies (for skilled office staff).

Figure 4 Part of the Japan centre in Düsseldorf

Figure 5 The United Nations office complex in Vienna, across the River Danube from the old city centre

Figure 6 Job changes in East and West London
Source: Department of Employment

?

Examine the graph in Figure 6 on page 335 showing recent employment changes in East and West London.

1 Name the employment sectors that are declining throughout the city. Are these sectors in productive industry or in services?

2 Name the employment sectors that are increasing everywhere. Are these in productive industry or services?

3 Write a brief 'newspaper article' about London's changing jobmarket using Figure 6 and any other information you may have. Highlight the differences between changes in West and East London.

4 In this introduction I have discussed changes relating to:
a economies (post-industrial economies),
b employment, and
c problems arising from change.

If you had to set up a series of newspaper headlines and sub-headings for this introduction, what would you write? Two or three headlines with several sub-headings should be enough. Do this as a group activity and present your ideas on a poster. Compare your group's headlines with those of other groups – note similarities and differences in emphasis.

Housing

Recent years have seen the start of some particularly interesting developments in housing in Western European cities. The urban housing market in England and Wales has been traditionally different from that in countries of mainland Europe in two respects. (Scotland has been closer to the general pattern of the mainland.)

1 In the cities of England and Wales there has been a much higher level of owner-occupation than elsewhere. The reason for this is the existence there of building societies which, until recently, could only lend money for house purchase or improvement. Similar financial institutions have not been so well developed on the European mainland, where the money to buy a house has more often been available only from a bank, on shorter repayment periods and at higher rates of interest than in England and Wales, or by borrowing from relatives.

2 A much higher proportion of the urban population in England and Wales compared with that in Western Europe lives in single-family houses. In the cities of the rest of Western Europe apartment life has been the norm. This phenomenon has a long history – the typical working-class dwelling in many nineteenth century English cities was a house in a terrace, whereas in Scottish, German or French cities it was a tenement flat (Figure 7).

In recent years both these points of distinction between England and Wales and the rest of Western Europe have started to erode, producing a convergence in housing characteristics. Owner-occupier levels are now rising rapidly throughout Western Europe. At the same time the proportion of single-family properties in the housing stock of mainland European cities is also rising. Note that in certain British cities the rehabilitation of old industrial areas (such as the Docklands in London, the Albert Dock in Liverpool, the canalside near the Parish Church in Leeds) is increasing the number of luxury, inner-city apartments available.

The post-war problem

To understand these contemporary changes in housing structures in Western Europe it is worth examining the post-war evolution of urban housing. Throughout Western Europe the first twenty years after the Second World War saw a massive urban housing crisis brought about by a combination of three processes:

1 Wartime housing destruction.

2 A legacy of poor housing (slums) in need of clearance. Much of it dated from the early years of industrial urban growth and was neglected during the depression years of the inter-war period.

3 Continued urban population growth occurring through:
a high levels of migration to the cities accompanying rapid economic growth (such migration was both domestic and international in character), and
b the renewal of higher levels of natural population increase after the low birth rates of the 1930s.

The general solution in Western Europe was the construction of social or council housing. On the European mainland such property was invariably flats. England and Wales, with their rather different traditions of vernacular working-class architecture (such as the terraced rows of nineteenth century industrial housing) built estates of flats and also of single-family housing, as occurred in the New Towns planned and constructed during this period.

John Tuppen finds cross-Channel parallels
with Britain's fight against urban decay

Squalor of the inner cité

The depressing spectacle of half-empty and vandalised blocks of flats, set against the back-cloth of a rundown urban environment is today a new and unwelcome feature of French cities, just as it is in Britain. The issue has become so pressing that over the last four years the French government has spent more than 4 billion francs (about £400 million) on rehabilitation programmes. But unlike Britain, where the problem is seen to stem mainly from the 19th century, in France it is a consequence of the huge, seemingly interminable apartment complexes (often called *grands ensembles*) which formed such a significant feature of the country's rapid post-war suburbanisation.

The *grands ensembles* were built in response to the severe housing crisis in the 1950s and 1960s produced by the combined effects of a high birthrate, a substantial inflow of immigrants and returning colonial expatriates and a large-scale movement from rural to urban areas. In these huge estates, the largest housing more than 20,000 people, shortcomings were soon apparent: a high-rise, high-density living environment, poor construction, lack of shops and services, few local jobs. But at the time they were regarded as a success simply because they provided homes.

Twenty years later many of these vast, anonymous 'cités' are rejected. The more affluent have moved to new houses which have mushroomed on the outskirts of the cities, leaving behind empty flats in deteriorating areas no longer respected by their inhabitants.

The *grands ensembles* were increasingly the refuge of families with low incomes, the unemployed and a large and diverse immigrant population often resented or misunderstood by the French and with a high proportion of adolescents, an inevitable consequence of the arrival 20 years ago of a large number of young families. Members of this group now face particular problems in getting jobs, especially when, as is often the case, their educational standards are low. Not surprisingly, many of these youngsters feel rejected and frustrated.

In the early 1980s their resentment exploded with a series of violent outbursts, notably in the huge complexes of Les Minguettes at Lyon and 'Les 4000' at La Courneuve in the northern suburbs of Paris. It was clear that a major programme of remedial action was needed.

The government commission appointed to look into the problem put the emphasis on improving educational and vocational training and promoting racial harmony. Local bodies were given greater administrative responsibility to end the delays caused by the previous need to get the agreement of several ministries for rehabilitation measures.

The most obvious improvement since then has been to the physical environment. Tower blocks have been demolished, despite their recent construction, and an increasing number of the remaining apartments substantially remodelled. Balconies have been added, kitchens enlarged and the buildings' previously austere and uniform façades brightened up in the hope that residents will take greater pride in their surroundings; usually they are consulted on improvements in advance.

To improve conditions generally, health centres, post offices, computer centres, and recreation halls were built and evening classes started. More social workers now operate in these areas; and advice is available on managing the family budget. Young people are helped to find jobs. Foreign housewives can learn about French cuisine, and considerable information and guidance are available to try to assist young people to find their first job. More ambitiously, employers have been urged to provide work in the immediate neighbourhood and some rehabilitation jobs are available for the local residents.

There has been a significant change of attitude among the housing bodies responsible for the estates. Their role in the past was simply to manage the property, often from a distance. Now some have established a local presence to resolve daily problems, such as the need for repairs, which were previously left unattended. Similarly, allocation procedures have been revised to ensure a wider assortment of occupants in any one block.

More than 120 suburbs have now been designated for priority rehabilitation; and in the last four years 40,000 flats have been modernised and vacancy rates have fallen; the unrest of the early 1980s has largely evaporated.

But, in spite of the obvious progress, problems remain. Few new jobs have been created. Moreover, as the number of areas qualifying for government assistance has grown, expenditure in any one district has diminished, leading to the disappearance of some new services and a dissipation of the initial enthusiasm.

Source: The Times, 26 November 1986.

Figure 7 (top) Apartments in Paris; (middle) Victorian terrace housing in North London; (bottom) turn of the century tenements in Glasgow

?

1 It has become common in all Western European countries to blame the housing design for the present difficulties in such estates. Read the newspaper article on page 337. In pairs, list arguments for and against this idea.

2 Imagine you are a local authority housing manager. You have to decide which tenants should be allocated to high-rise flats and which should be offered single-family housing. Which type of tenants would you put where, and why?

Change since 1970

The 1970s witnessed much reduced, or even reversed, levels of urban population growth. In some countries, for example West Germany, with its very low rate of population increase, the urban housing crisis in certain cities was much reduced in scale. No longer was there a general housing shortage: the shortfall now affected only certain types of housing demand, such as that for cheap housing or housing for young, single adults. At the same time, the world economic recession and the progressive move of govern-

ments away from *neo-Keynesian* (involving state intervention in the free market) economic policies resulted in a reduction in the involvement of local and national governments in new housing. The outcome of these combined demographic, economic and political forces has been a slowing down in new housing completions with an increased proportion of housing being constructed by private developers for sale rather than rent.

Governments in various countries have acted to make house purchase easier, often by the creation of special government-funded housing credit agencies (moving towards the British building society in style, if not in the origin of funds). Sales of council housing have also been encouraged by governments, for example in the United Kingdom and France.

At the same time, an increasing number of older, privately-rented apartments have been sold by their landlords into the co-proprietorship of their tenants. In many countries this is a response to the existence of rent control legislation and other measures giving security of tenure to tenants or measures pegging rent levels. Often such changes in ownership have been accompanied by improvement or redevelopment of the property involved, bringing it up to a higher standard.

The growing power of the consumer

There is also strong evidence that in the new climate of private construction in mainland Europe, consumer tastes are asserting themselves clearly in favour of single-family houses on the English model – indeed the English example is often held up as a marketing point by developers who give their estates English names or advertise the properties as 'English style'. Apparent changes in the types of housing demanded are in part a reflection of changes in the characteristics of the consumers – now that the large-scale slum clearance programmes are largely complete in many cities (or at least much reduced in scale from the 1960s) the market for new housing is no longer a 'captive' working-class market but the growing ranks of the urban middle class. This is not to say that the consumer is king: in London, for example, where the growth of the middle class interest has manifested itself in a rapidly spiralling inflation of house prices, the element of choice is scarcely present for the vast majority. However, the developers' interests now lie in providing housing for the middle class – a fact that is also in accord with governmental views in countries such as the United Kingdom or West Germany, with right-of-centre administrations.

Post-war housing in Paris

The evolution of new housing schemes in post-war Paris admirably illustrates the changes that have occurred recently in the nature of the housing market, and of housing demand, in Western European cities.

Housing conditions in the early post-war years were nothing short of scandalous. The census of 1954 showed that 29% of young married couples were having to live with their parents because of a lack of alternative accommodation; over a quarter of a million families were listed by the municipal authorities as in need of rehousing from slum conditions. Over 50% of households had to share a lavatory with another household, and only 19% of households had their own bath or shower.

The worst housed of all were the immigrant workers and their families, many of whom inhabited the *bidonvilles* or shanty towns of the Paris suburbs. By 1966 eighty-nine such *bidonvilles* housed 40,000 people, who were foreigners almost without exception.

During this early post-war period the population of Paris was increasing more rapidly than at any other time before or after. French men and women were flocking from the provinces to the capital, joined by thousands of immigrants from Spain, Italy and North Africa.

The major solution to the growing housing problem was to build new housing in the suburbs, in order to permit slum clearance in the inner city and to house the influx of migrants to the city region. Low-cost, subsidised social housing (the equivalent of British council housing) was built in a number of large estates (*grands ensembles*) around the city. Each *grand ensemble* contained an average of 8–10,000 dwellings designed for a population of 30–40,000, living in tower blocks and other arrangements of apartments (Figure 8). The speed of construction of these estates meant that by 1969 one person in six in the Paris region was living in one of these estates.

However, these estates provided a housing solution only. There were from the start major problems associated with them. Many of the estates were built without any real consideration of the lifestyle of the people rehoused there. Sometimes schools and shopping facilities were provided only some years after the estates had been occupied. The populations of the estates tended to lack variety, almost everyone offered this housing belonged to the poorer sections of society and had young children. Many of the estates were inaccessible to employment opportunities or to other facilities elsewhere in the urban region. The massive scale of the developments led to people feeling anonymous and a new

Figure 8 Part of a *grand ensemble* at La Corneuve in the northern suburbs of Paris

depressive illness was recognised named 'Sarcellite' after Sarcelles, the biggest of the estates. The new housing was well provided with modern internal amenities, but the external environment was lacking in inspiration.

In the 1970s, to cope with the continuing population influx into Paris, the planners turned from the *grand ensemble* solution to the housing problem to a *New Town* policy. New housing growth, instead of being spread around the edge of the urban area, would be concentrated in eight specific locations (later reduced to six when the population growth rate began to decrease). These locations would overcome the disadvantages of the *grands ensembles* by providing employment opportunities, shops, schools, leisure facilities

Figure 9   The 'Pyramids' housing development at Evry New Town, Paris

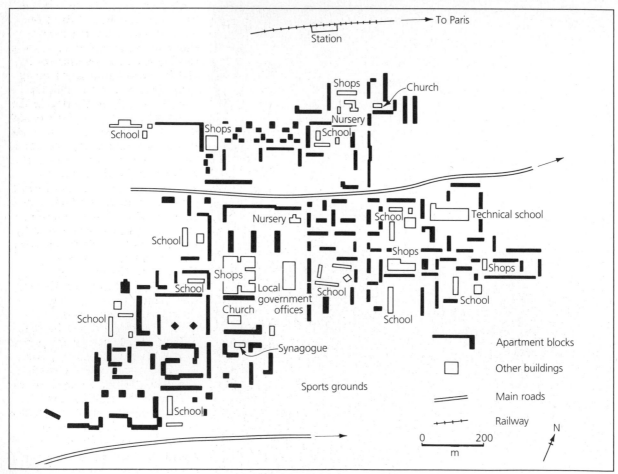

Figure 10   The *grand ensemble* of Massy-Antony (population 40,000)

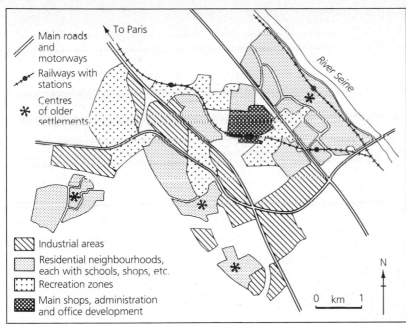

Figure 11 Evry New Town

and other amenities that the great apartment estates had lacked. Also, housing was to be grouped in neighbourhood units to reduce the problems of anonymity. Significantly, the housing units were still apartments – 70% of early New Town housing was of this type. The architects were permitted to use a great deal of imagination and many of the housing constructions were revolutionary, such as the 'Pyramids' at Evry (Figure 9) or the 'Arenas of Picasso' at Marne-la-Vallée (Figure 12).

Since 1975 there has been another change in housing policy in Paris, but one reflecting long-established desires. As early as 1945 a survey found that over half of all Parisians would prefer to live in their own house instead of in a flat, even if it meant living further out from the city centre. By 1964 two-thirds of Parisians felt that way. Until the housing shortage of the region as a whole was lessened all government initiatives went towards providing more flats. It was not until the mid 1970s and the slowing of the population influx into Paris (coupled with increased out-movement) that construction companies could build for the private consumer rather than for the municipal authorities. The result has been a massive creation of estates consisting of single-family housing, often recognisable as inspired by the standards of British suburban life, and advertised as such (Figure 13). The planning authorities had to recognise this trend, and even in the New Towns, restrictions on the number of properties to be built as individual houses or for private ownership have been set aside.

Thus, from a housing stock dominated by rented flats, Paris, at least in the suburbs, has recently moved rapidly towards a new structure dominated by owner-occupied houses.

Figure 12 Part of the 'Arenas of Picasso' housing development at Marne-la-Vallée New Town, Paris

Figure 13 The 'in' thing now for
suburban middle-class living in Paris is a
detached house, preferably in a
development with an Anglo-American name.
A recent advertisement in *Le Figaro*, a French
newspaper

SUNSET VALLEY GRANDE OUVERTURE

UN NOUVEAU VILLAGE KAUFMAN & BROAD
EN VALLÉE DE MONTMORENCY.

Au Plessis-Bouchard, d'un accès direct à
Paris-La Défense par l'autoroute A15, découvrez des
maisons de 5 et 6 pièces d'un rare niveau de qualité.

Bureau de vente sur place ouvert tous les jours,
dimanche compris, de 11 h à 20 h, avenue de Siegfried,
95130 Plessis-Bouchard, Tél. : 34 15 68 68
Prendre autoroute A15 sortie Ermont-Plessis-Bouchard

Kaufman & Broad

Ethnic minorities

In looking at ethnic minorities as a second theme, we must be clear that we should generally no longer be talking about 'immigrants'. In many Western European cities groups of people who are still sometimes referred to by that term are increasingly composed of individuals born in the countries concerned. Ethnic minority populations of many Western European cities are moving towards a situation in which there are equal numbers of people with direct experience of immigration, and those of the second or third generations.

The halting of the low-skilled labour flow

One very important point for any discussion of recent change in the size of ethnic minority populations in European cities is the general halting of labour movement that occurred in 1973–5. Many commentators believe the cause of that halt was the economic recession brought on by the 1973 oil crisis, but others have argued that the stopping of labour movement was likely at that time for other political and social reasons, for example, the growing racial tensions in France caused Algeria to stop its workers migrating there. Britain was the exception to this trend, having moved to control international labour inflow during the 1960s.

But bans on labour inflow did not curb migration of family members and dependants. It is arguable that once the male labour migrant could no longer enter and leave his country of employment at will, the inevitable result would be family reunification there – be it in West Germany, France, the United Kingdom or Switzerland.

Residential concentration

To the urban geographer the crucial question about ethnic minorities in Western European cities concerns their residential distribution. We are accustomed to looking to the USA for many of our models of urban change: are such American models of any use in analysing the new ethnic minority communities in Western Europe? Keep this question in mind as you read through the next section.

Who are the ethnic minorities?

The urban ethnic minorities of Western Europe present a great deal of complexity. Three basic groups can be identified:

1 Single, male guestworkers of any nationality. In West Germany, Austria and Switzerland the original labour inflow was only of this kind, predominantly men from Turkey, Yugoslavia, Greece and Italy.

2 Family groups from other European countries where the distinction between incomers and host populations is not great (for instance in the case of Spaniards and Italians in France, Irish in the United Kingdom, or Finns in Sweden).

3 Family groups whose ethnic origins are non-European. In Western Europe as a whole many such groups are Islamic, from North Africa, Turkey or Pakistan. Others in this non-European category include Indians, West Indians, West Africans and Chinese.

The urban circumstances of these three groups differ quite markedly.

Single, male guestworkers

Often single, male guestworkers were housed initially by their employers in hostels at their industrial sites, many of which were on the edges of large cities. Later, more general hostels were constructed, often in locations nearer to city centres, whilst many immigrant workers moved into the ordinary housing market living in poor-quality, run-down, inner-city properties. Today the number of single, male guestworkers is diminishing as family reunification takes place, whilst the urban areas that have become associated with their residence are often subject to redevelopment or urban renewal programmes.

European ethnic minority families

Ethnic minority families of European origin have been quite rapidly assimilated into their urban places of residence. Although the starting point of these minority communities may have been single, male, labour migration, followed by family reunification, their residential locations today are widely dispersed and there are few real areas of concentration. Certain inner-city facilities such as restaurants, clubs or community centres, may retain a social centrality for the group as a whole, but the significance of such facilities is often low for the second generation, children born and brought up in the country their parents migrated to, and who may hold the citizenship of their birthplace.

Non-European ethnic minority families

The picture is rather different for the families of non-European origin. Often, their arrival in Europe has been more recent than for the European minorities. They have, in many countries, been subject to societal prejudices and have stayed in low-status employment, with high levels of unemployment amongst the second generation. In addition to these *external* factors limiting their circumstances, there may be *internal* desires to stay together for cultural solidarity in an alien and sometimes hostile environment. For all these reasons the general assimilation of the European minority groups has not occurred as easily for these non-Europeans.

The location and importance of non-European migrants within the urban community structure however, differs from country to country and from city to city. Generally there are high levels of migrants in inner-city locations as well as in the inner-suburban areas containing late nineteenth century property, typical of Chapeltown in Leeds and Brixton in London to name two British examples. Kreuzberg in Berlin is another case, where a high concentration of Turkish families live in an impoverished area of the city.

However, these are not the only locations of such non-European minority communities. Others are also present:

1 In many cities there are particular concentrations in industrial suburbs where the immigrants have taken over the housing as well as the jobs associated with certain activities, for example, in many mining suburbs in the German Ruhr (Figure 14).

2 In some countries, such as France and the Netherlands, ethnic minorities of non-European origin have been given access to council or social housing, often on the large, suburban, post-war estates referred to earlier in this chapter (page 339). This produces concentrations of ethnic minority families in selected locations, usually at the edges of built-up areas, often with poor access to employment and to urban amenities, thus isolating them further from the urban mainstream.

Where ethnic minority groups are concentrated in inner-city locations, either as single males or as family groups, there are indications that the model of settlement being followed is not the same as that of North American cities, for two reasons:

1 Even in districts with the highest levels of ethnic minority presence there are always substantial numbers of the indigenous population present, unlike, for example, Harlem in New York or Watts in Los Angeles where almost 100% of the population is black. Such figures of ethnic minorities are only found at house-plot level in Western European cities and are rarely found at the level of industrial streets: they are unheard of at neighbourhood level.

2 The long-term stability of inner-city, ethnic minority concentration areas in Western Europe is being threatened by renewal and redevelopment pressures, including gentrification, associated with the changing economic and social structures of cities (see pages 333–5). Several cities, Paris and Amsterdam among them, have already in the post-war period seen the rise and fall of particular ethnic minority areas as a wave of in-movement into a poor neighbourhood is followed by large-scale demolition and rebuilding of better properties, or by piecemeal housing improvement.

Figure 14 Industrial housing in Duisburg in the Ruhr. In this block over 90% of the residents are Turks, employed in low-skill jobs in the steelworks next door

Ethnic minorities in Vienna

The Austrian capital provides an interesting illustration of the complexities of the creation of ethnic minority groups and their evolution in Western European cities. Vienna has two distinctly different types of minority community:

1 A community made up of largely unskilled 'guestworkers' and their families, from countries with a lower level of economic development than Austria.

2 An immigrant population made up of the households of highly skilled employees in international organisations and international businesses. These migrants are generally from countries with levels of economic development similar to or greater than that of Austria.

Of the guestworkers in 1981 the Yugoslavs were the biggest group, comprising 59,000 Viennese residents. It is clear that the number of guestworkers increased very rapidly during the period from 1961 to 1981, especially during the years from 1961 to the oil crisis of 1973/74. Over this period economic growth was rapid in Austria, creating a labour shortage for factory work and in particular for short-term casual work (for example in construction). The first migrant arrivals were men, their families followed later after a few years. In 1971, for example, amongst the Turkish population of Vienna there were two males to every female.

With the oil crisis of the mid-1970s new unskilled labour immigration was halted by governmental action, but family reunification continued so that by the 1980s, what had originally been an immigrant population dominated by men was rapidly becoming a balanced community of resident foreigners which included males and females, whole families and young children (Figure 15). The 1981 census showed that females made up 47% of the Viennese residents who originated from the guestworker countries; similarly 30% of the total population with such origins were aged under twenty. This guestworker community has considerable potential for rapid growth: Viennese families now average only 1.31 children, but guestworker families average 2.56 – nearly twice as many. However, many of the guestworkers have not yet put down roots in Vienna. A survey carried out in 1981 found that only 7% were almost certain to settle permanently, 30% were likely

Table 1 Foreign population of Vienna

	1961	1981
Total population of Vienna	1 627 566	1 531 346
Total foreigners	24 058	113 417
Of which 'guestworkers' (chiefly unskilled workers from Turkey and Yugoslavia)	3 014	80 374
Other foreigners (chiefly skilled employees and their families)	21 044	33 043

Source: *Mitteilungen aus Statistik und Verwaltung der Stadt Wien*, No. 4, 1984, p. 4

to return 'home', but the vast majority were undecided or felt at home neither in Vienna nor in their country of origin – they were 'living in two societies' in the words of the Austrian geographer Elisabeth Lichtenberger.

The foreigners in highly skilled employment are a very different group, coming from a large variety of countries. They have come to the city to work for organisations such as the International Atomic Energy Agency (IAEA), the Organisation of Petroleum Exporting Countries (OPEC), the United Nations (UN), or various private companies. Most have come on short-term contracts and will later move on to other world cities in career moves: they will not settle to become Viennese (Figure 16). Most have brought their families with them from the start, such that for every ten foreign employees there are fifteen dependants.

Figure 15 The decaying environment associated with the presence of guestworkers in Vienna

?

One of the strongest contrasts between the two foreigner minority groups concerns their place of residence.

1 Trace the blank map (Figure 17) twice and then, using the data for 1982 given in the table, shade in one map to show districts with above average proportions of Turks and Yugoslavs, and shade the other map to show above average proportions of high-status foreigners.

2 Then, using the information below the map, write a commentary on factors influencing the location of ethnic minority groups in Vienna.

In the medium term it seems that the guestworker groups will continue to die out, that ethnic minorities of European origin will continue to assimilate into the community, but that the position of the minority groups of non-European origin will remain fragile. Indeed, their plight may well worsen as poor-quality,

Figure 16 Recently renovated old housing in the inner city of Vienna, attractive to short-stay, high-status migrants

inner-city housing is progressively barred from them through urban renewal schemes which result in higher rent and property prices. The alternatives available are then **a** movement back and forth between short-term blight areas or **b** removal to the poor environment of the suburban, social housing estates.

Table 2 Foreigners in Vienna as a percentage of the total population

District number	Turks and Yugoslavs	High-status foreigners
1	2.8	5.9
2	6.5	4.1
3	5.0	3.3
4	3.6	4.8
5	8.0	3.8
6	5.7	3.3
7	6.5	3.9
8	5.1	4.0
9	5.1	3.9
10	4.1	1.4
11	2.1	1.1
12	3.8	1.5
13	1.6	3.0
14	3.9	1.7
15	9.1	2.6
16	8.2	1.8
17	9.1	3.5
18	6.6	5.2
19	2.2	5.3
20	5.8	2.1
21	1.5	1.1
22	1.5	0.9
23	2.9	1.6
Total	**4.6**	**2.6**

Source: Mitteilungen aus Statistik und Verwaltung der Stadt Wien, No. 1, 1984, p. 10

District 1 consists of the conservation area of the historic inner city

Districts 2, 3, 4, 5, 6, 7, 8, 9, 10, 12, 15, 16 and **20** have the greatest concentrations of poor-quality housing, although districts **2, 3, 9, 10, 12, 16** and **20** also have some better properties.

Districts 10, 11, 13, 14, 21, 22 and **23** all contain newer social (council) housing and/or owner-occupied properties. Foreigners are not eligible for social housing. Guestworkers cannot afford to buy a house, while skilled foreigners are not in Vienna long enough for it to be worth their while .

Districts 14, 17, 18 and **19** have the best access to the beautiful districts of the Vienna Woods.

Districts 16, 17 and **18** contain a mix of property: that nearest the city centre is old and dilapidated, that furthest out is of good quality surburban villas.

District 19 contains several international schools for the children of employees of international organisations.

Figure 17 Vienna

The pattern of the city

What is changing?

Changes in the economic base of big cities and in the operation of the housing market are reflected in new changes, potentially of high significance, now starting to make themselves felt in the distribution of different social groups within the city. To summarise, there is now an increasing trend within the *inner city* towards gentrification (with an increase in the proportion of its residents who are drawn from the middle classes) and a polarisation phenomenon whereby these gentrifiers are increasingly contrasted with other groups who are impoverished and/or seen as undesirable neighbours.

Changes in the *outer areas of cities* are less marked, but the tendency, at least in mainland Europe, is for the increasing interest in single-family housing on the English model to lead to suburbanisation and the overall growth of the built-up area, despite the general decrease in urban populations that has occurred in the 1970s and 1980s. At the same time, aspects of social segregation within the suburbs are maintained and strengthened.

These processes, or aspects of them, appear to be operating in a large number of Western European capitals and large cities in the mid 1980s, and to be a function of some of the factors discussed earlier in this chapter – decreased family sizes, de-industrialising economies, growing service employment and so on.

Gentrification

Gentrification is occurring in almost all major cities. It is well documented as a relatively recent phenomenon in, for example, both London and Amsterdam, whilst the inner city of Paris has followed this trend for some time. In London the specific areas of

the city most affected are Islington, Clapham, Fulham and, increasingly, Wandsworth, Acton and Battersea, all areas of older property where the incoming middle class is replacing a more working-class population.

Inner city locations are attractive to the highly educated or wealthy who wish to maximise their access to the amenities of the city centre. The existence of such a group is not new – what is new is its rapid growth in size and importance. This results from the employment transformation that the inner cities are undergoing, taking place alongside other changes in the overall demographic structure, in marriage rates, in childbearing and in female employment levels. The popular press may focus on the Sloanes, Dinkies and Yuppies, but the general phenomenon of social and economic change in the inner city is far wider than can be described simply by these labels.

Marginalisation

Gentrification is, however, only half the process of social change in the city centres, and anyway it only significantly affects the biggest cities with their wide range of office sector employment possibilities. The other side of the coin to gentrification is that at the same time as attracting the young wealthy middle class, the city centre also attracts or retains the function of housing the poorest people in society – low status ethnic minorities, the very poor (including families on or below the poverty-line and the elderly poor), students (who may become in the future part of the middle-class group) and those on the fringes of society; squatters, punks, the homeless and other marginalised social groups.

As the status of the inner city rises the position of these marginalised groups becomes ever

more threatened, particularly in terms of their access to housing. At the same time, the escape to social housing in the suburbs, traditionally of importance for the poor (and, in some countries such as France, for ethnic minorities) is being cut off by reductions in the construction of such property and the re-orientation of the housing market towards the private (and dominantly owner-occupied) sector. The result is that these marginalised groups inhabit the areas of planning blight, zones awaiting reconstruction and so on – the 'inner city problem areas'. The whip hand in this evolving social polarisation is held by the interests promoting gentrification (property developers, financial institutions and, often, local government) for it is through the conversion of housing and neighbourhoods to middle-class use that the returns on investment can be maximised. One inevitable result is the creation of conflicts of interests between the two polarised groups – the 'haves' and the 'have-nots' – seen recently in London over the various plans for the Docklands Redevelopment Area with its provision of expensive middle-class housing for incomers in an area of poor housing standards and high unemployment levels for the indigenous working-class population.

It is also possible to detect elements of change in both the inner and outer suburbs. In many ways it is the inner suburbs now that are the seat of the greatest social problems in contemporary Western European cities. Gentrification processes and suburbanisation increase the middle-class interest in the inner city and the outer suburbs: it is the old inner suburbs (generally dating from the late nineteenth century and containing an obsolete housing stock) that form the areas of the greatest and most uniform

Nimbies v Aids centre

What is happening in Kensington today could happen all over England. MAX PRANGNELL visited a borough divided

PLANS by a London charity to establish the first British residential care centre for Aids sufferers have been met by a virulent attack of the Nimby syndrome from local residents. Nimby, or 'Not In My Back Yard', as it is known to the people at Nirex, is known in its primary stages to cause petitions and letters to the council. Rowdy public meetings can follow, and, in its advanced stages, it has been known to erupt in bitter recrimination among normally amicable neighbours. Recent goings-on in the staunchly Tory royal borough of Kensington and Chelsea have proved no exception. Rows and vicious innuendos are rife.

It began in May, when Christopher Spence, the former director of Life Story, a counselling service catering especially for the bereaved and disabled, had the idea of setting up a residential centre (he doesn't like the word 'hospice') for those who have been diagnosed as carriers of the human immuno-deficiency virus. It would provide 'a continuum of care, guiding people safely home, possibly over a period of years'. Through his newly registered charity, London Lighthouse, he and his fellow directors applied for, and got, a much-publicised grant of £50,000 and a further interest-free loan of £750,000 from John Paul Getty Junior. Spence then applied to his local council for permission to convert a disused school opposite his house into the centre. It all seemed so easy.

But that was when Anna Hooper, a local housewife and mother of two pre-school children, found out about it. In mid-July the council wrote to her asking if she had any objections to the proposed centre. So miffed was she at the prospect of having it in her street that she sent out an unsigned circular to another 150 residents telling them of the proposals. Support wasn't long in coming; by the end of the month Mr E A Sanders, director of planning and transportation for the borough, had received a petition of 839 signatures objecting to the proposals and by August 9, she and Bonny Milner, another local resident, had formed a fighting committee, the Kensington and Chelsea Community Concerned, to organise a more coherent opposition.

Three days later, London Lighthouse sent out a leaflet that prompted over 3,500 signatures in favour of the scheme, and the biggest petition in the history of the borough. The committee wasn't taking it lying down either. The very evening that the names of the 'favourables' were delivered to the town hall, committee members were out on the streets with a swift rearguard action. One resident of a newly built square adjacent to the proposed site commented: 'It was absurd, you'd answer the door to one lot, and then as soon as you'd sat down again, the other lot were ringing the bell. I'm sure they were following one another.'

On September 9, Kensington and Chelsea's town planning committee agreed by a majority decision to grant planning permission for the project. The chairman, Councillor Simon Orr-Ewing, said: 'We are a compassionate and responsible local authority, but for us this has probably been one of the most difficult decisions the town planning committee has ever made.'

So, that was that. Christopher Spence was over the moon, Bonny Milner said she'd never take her two-year-old to the local swimming pool again, and West 11 gets the first residential care centre for Aids sufferers in Europe. If all goes according to plan, it will have 26 beds and will be a counselling centre for up to 300 sufferers on an outpatient basis. Spence says he hopes to open a vegetarian restaurant and gym once they get the funding sorted out.

Bonny Milner is still angry: 'It's an amateur attempt to deal with the problem, slap bang in the middle of a residential area. I mean, wouldn't it be better if these people were out in the country, at least they could look at a bit of greenery in their final days.'

Martin Weaver of the Terrence Higgins Trust says this reaction is typical: 'People's fears are based on nothing more than ignorance and bigotry, caused by disinformation from the press and lack of information from the government.'

Anna Hooper was a bit more guarded than Bonny Milner: 'I'm not in the slightest bit worried about the prospect of catching Aids, I know it doesn't float on the wind. I just feel that building is completely unsuitable, it's far too big. It was going to be a school for dyslexic children. That would have been far better.'

Source: The Sunday Times, 28 September 1986

Aids hospice opens after a struggle

Shyama Perera on Hackney's reaction to victims of 'a self-inflicted illness'

MR HENRY Jones of Pam's pet shop on the Hackney Road, East London, looked out to where Europe's first Aids hospice opened this week.

He said: 'They knock on our door and ask the way to the hospice. They're all suited and booted. They're the ones who make the decisions – whether they're right or wrong and whether or not we want it.

'The people round here have got the hump about it. I've lived here all of my 47 years, but Aids patients can get treatment there and I can't.

'That can't be right – it's a self-inflicted illness. It used to be a general hospital and the standards were blinding.' Mr Frank Drea, drinking in The Axe pub, added: 'I'm not worried about catching anything from Aids patients, but we have lost a hospital. We were conned.'

The Mildmay Mission Hospital, an independent Christian hospital run on donations and grants, this week opened its doors in the heart of London's East End to the first of nine carriers of the virus. The hospital will be officially opened by Princess Alexandra on May 19.

Over the next year or so it hopes to expand to 17 beds, but its efforts have come up against threats and local ignorance about the real nature of the disease.

Mrs Helen Taylor-Thompson, the chairwoman of the board of governors, said last night: 'We did have trouble locally when the idea was first mooted, but that has now stopped. We are providing a service for those who need it most, just as we dealt with the local cholera epidemic when the hospital was set up over 100 years ago.'

She added: 'Although our patients may return home if they have remissions, most of them will be just near the end. They are terminal from day one, really, but we have experts and facilities on hand to make it all easier.'

The hospice initially caused much hostility in Hackney, where it sits at the head of a road filled with tower blocks and industrial premises. The property was attacked a few times, but last night there was little anger.

Mr David Connor, a taxi driver, aged 29, said: 'I bet half the people around here don't even know about it. I get passengers from there sometimes and people say to me, "Didn't you hose your cab down after?" I say, "What for?" '

There had been talk of house prices falling, he said. But prices have been untouched by the hospice. It will still cost £100,000 for a two-bedroom house half a mile down the road.

Mr John Ward, the acting manager of The Axe, said: 'It really doesn't bother me. It must be a relief for them to have somewhere to go and it is no real threat to us.'

But Mrs Frances King, of the Tower Galleries, across the road from the hospital, said: 'I think they should build these hospitals on the Outer Hebrides. I don't see any point in them hanging on for a tragic and painful death. If it was me, I'd put a gun to my head.'

Source: Guardian, 25 February 1988

poverty and highest levels of deprivation. It is these inner suburbs that now provide the housing for the economically marginal groups squeezed out of the inner city.

In the outer suburbs of many cities sectors of great social homogeneity occur, but with great contrast between sectors. There are the peripheral, social housing estates of the early post-war period with high proportions of unemployed people, a concentration of young second generation members of ethnic minorities (something found much less in suburban areas in the United Kingdom than in, for example, France because of the smaller numbers of immigrants permitted social housing in the United Kingdom), and the social malaise that has been ever-present since their construction.

In contrast, in sectors close to new transport links (roads and railways have attracted considerable investment in many cities) and in environmentally attractive, peripheral areas, there are new estates of single-family dwellings again occupied by the middle classes. Although the evidence is fragmentary and partly anecdotal, it is likely that the life cycle for many of the new middle class will take in a period of up to fifteen years of single or early married life in the inner city followed by a residential move to the outer suburbs to bring up a family.

These changes in the outer areas of cities are far less significant in the United Kingdom than in the rest of Western Europe because of the long tradition in England and Wales of middle-class, single-family housing in the periphery.

The gentrification of Amsterdam

Twenty years ago the inner city of Amsterdam presented a classic example of youth culture and marginal activities. It was the residence of large numbers of recently-arrived immigrants, many from the then-Dutch colony of Surinam in South America, but with important numbers from Morocco, Turkey and other places in the Mediterranean Basin. There were also large numbers of young people, Dutch, Northern European or North American, living in squats. A major element of the local culture was anti-establishment, led by the *provotariaat* ('provos'). Drugs were easy to obtain, and part of the inner city was an international centre for prostitution.

Today much has changed. The prostitution and the drugs market are still present, although they are kept under the watchful eye of the city authorities who tolerate a certain level of both activities to prevent them going 'underground' and becoming uncontrollable. But the squats are now being eliminated, and the immigrant population removed elsewhere in the city.

- 63 injured as building is taken over
- Streets and pavements ripped up

Squatters in police fights

From Brendan Boyle in Amsterdam

A simmering conflict between the homeless in Amsterdam and the Socialist city council developed over the weekend and yesterday into fierce clashes between squatters and police.

At least 63 injuries have been reported since the first clash on Friday evening and the mood here late yesterday remained tense.

The fighting began on Friday when demonstrators against the city's housing policy took over an empty building from which squatters had been evicted a week before. A 100-man police unit, which tried to evict the squatters a second time, was driven from the area by about 400 of the squatters and their supporters.

While the mayor, Mr Willem Polak, tried to negotiate through the local radio station, Stad Radio Amsterdam, squatters and hundreds of supporters ripped up streets and pavements and used building equipment and parked cars to barricade the street approaching their squat.

The negotiations broke down yesterday when the squatters rejected an offer of a meeting if the council was allowed to clear the barricades without opposition.

Two hours later, helicopters dropped pamphlets warning families to stay indoors and a convoy, including six tanks and a number of armoured vehicles, rolled into the quiet Vondel Street residential area. Road scrapers attached to the tanks were used to clear the barricades while squatters looked on, but fighting broke out later when supporters attacked police at some blocked crossings.

Twenty-five policemen had been injured on Friday. Monday's clashes led to 25 civilian injuries and a further 10 to policemen.

Crowds converged on the Dam Square in the centre of the city about 10 a.m. and there were further clashes. Some demonstrators who fled into the New Church were evicted by police.

Police reported that calm had returned by the afternoon, but there were fears that a demonstration planned to begin last night could cause fresh violence.

The confrontations over the past three days stem from growing bitterness in Amsterdam about the city's housing policy. A city hall official said on Monday that there were 300,000 houses and flats in the city and 52,000 applications for municipally controlled homes.

This figure represented applications rather than individuals and did not include the 'tens of thousands' of people who do not qualify for the official home seekers' list.

Building of low-rent homes was at a standstill, he said, and there was no way to solve the housing problem without building new homes. Only 80,000 homes had been added to the supply since 1945, he said. Officials estimate that between 6,000 and 7,000 buildings in Amsterdam are controlled by squatters.

Source: Guardian, 4 March 1980

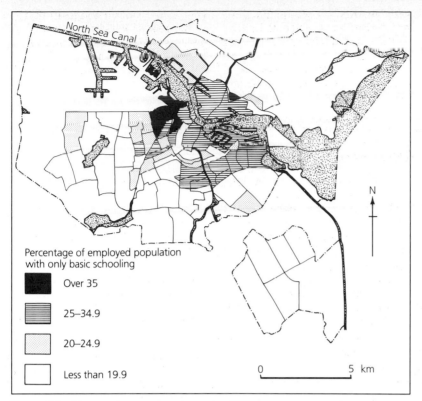

Percentage of employed population
with only basic schooling

▉	Over 35
▤	25–34.9
▦	20–24.9
☐	Less than 19.9

0   5 km

N

Figure 18   Educational attainment in Amsterdam 1971

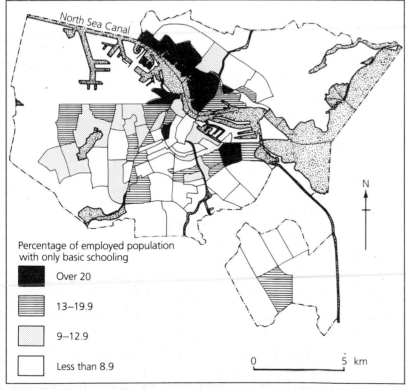

Percentage of employed population
with only basic schooling

▉	Over 20
▤	13–19.9
▦	9–12.9
☐	Less than 8.9

0   5 km

N

Figure 19   Educational attainment in Amsterdam 1977

RIOT police in Amsterdam yesterday evicted squatters from an Amsterdam building, which had become a symbol for their movement after minor clashes. The squatters had threatened fierce resistance. About 500 officers in riot gear cordoned off the house, Singel 114 on one of the city's central canals. They made baton charges and used a water cannon to push back squatters and their supporters. Wearing gas-masks, they sawed a hole through the roof to reach the top floor of the building. Squatters left voluntarily. Singel 114 was cleared out last December but squatters re-occupied it and fought eviction in the courts. It became a focal point of protests against buildings being left empty or knocked down to make way for hotels. Previous evictions have caused disturbances, including riots in 1982 which left a trail of destruction. Earlier yesterday, protesters set up barricades of paving stones and burning tyres across streets in the city centre and police arrested a total of 17 people in brief clashes. Squatters occupy hundreds of run-down buildings in Amsterdam, which has a serious shortage of cheap accommodation. The problem is worsened by the large numbers of young people who come to the city because of its liberal policies, especially towards drugs.

Source: Reuters Ltd., 24 October 1984

The pressures that have led to these changes may be summarised as follows:

1 The creation of major, new, office parks around the edge of Amsterdam, resulting in the removal of certain offices from the congested inner city.

2 The resultant vacancies in attractive, older property enabled conservation schemes to be created, which further enhanced the attractions of the housing stock.

3 As a result of a general increase in employment possibilities in the tertiary economic sector (service and high technology industries), coupled with a reduction or stagnation in employment in industry and the port, in-migration to Amsterdam progressively changed from low-skill to high-skill migrants.

4 Many of the incomers were young and childless, with high earnings, and they wanted an inner-city residence.

5 Competition for housing between these gentrifiers and the original, poorer inhabitants resulted in victory for the gentrifying interests (supported by property developers), bringing higher housing costs and an increase in home-ownership in the inner city.

The changes were quite remarkable during the 1970s. Look at the series of maps (Figures 18, 19, 20 and 21). The first pair (Figures 18 and 19) show by district the concentrations of the employed population with the lowest educational attainments. Note the changes in the individual districts that make up the inner city.

The second pair of maps (Figures 20 and 21) show the distribution of owner-occupation in Amsterdam in 1971 and 1982. Again, note the changes in specific inner city areas.

What happened in Amsterdam was that the poor residents of the inner city (many of them foreign-

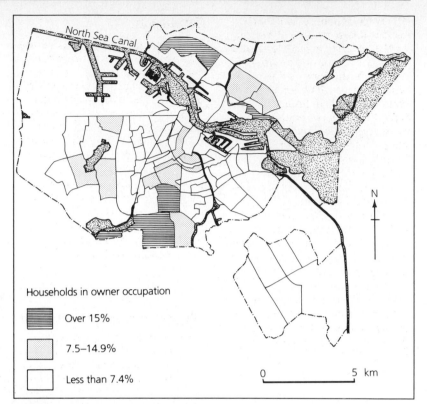

Figure 20 Owner-occupiers in Amsterdam 1971

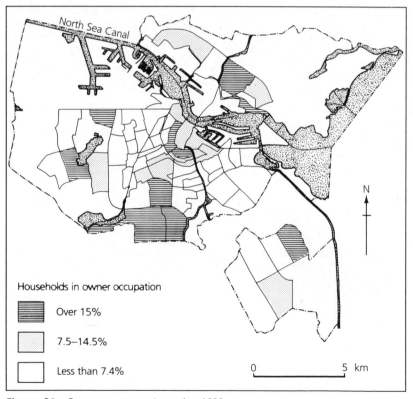

Figure 21 Owner-occupiers in Amsterdam 1982

ers) were rehoused in suburban estates (often municipal housing) or they found themselves rented accommodation on the open market in the inner suburbs, from which the previous lower-middle-class tenants had departed. Where have these people gone? The answer is that many of them have chosen to leave Amsterdam entirely to live in expanding, commuter settlements within the wider urban region, often to the north of the North Sea Canal.

Will the wealthy new residents of inner Amsterdam stay there for ever? The answer is probably 'no'. As these residents age and start families their needs change and there is evidence that they start to move out to wealthy, suburban estates, to be replaced in the inner city by the next generation of the high-earning young.

Imagine you are a high-earning employee of a major bank located in the inner city of Amsterdam.

1 List the facilities of the city that you might want access to if you were under twenty-five and single.

2 List the facilities that you might want access to if you were thirty-five, married, with two children.

3 What sort of locations might you start looking at for accommodation in these two cases?

Conclusion

The cities of Western Europe are displaying an interesting set of changes which are part of the evolution towards a post-industrial economy and society. This has brought a new series of social realities, enhancing the size of the middle classes, destabilising traditional working-class occupations and communities and thereby producing a new employment structure and a new series of structural connections between an individual's or a group's social position and the significance of their location within the city.

The two paragraphs above are my way of summing up some of the trends that I see operating in Western Europe today. Throughout the chapter I have described and given examples of what is happening. You may not reach the same conclusions. Here's your chance.

1 Starting with the phrase, 'In this chapter I have learned...', state what you think you have learned. (You may find it easier to do this exercise in groups.) Then go back to my conclusion and say what you think is meant by such phrases as:

a 'a new series of social realities.'

b 'a new series of structural connections between an individual's or a group's social position and the significance of their location within the city.'

It can be argued that these processes contribute to a convergence between different Western European urban societies, for example with the replication of an 'English' model of suburban housing, both in type and in tenure. Another indicator of convergence is gentrification where Britain is starting to follow the traditional continental interest in inner-city locations for higher-status living. Underlying these trends is a common evolution of the economic base, occurring in a similar way in the large cities of different countries.

c 'these processes contribute to a convergence between different Western European urban societies, for example with the replication of an 'English' model of suburban housing, both in type and in tenure.'

d 'a common evolution of the economic base.'

In other words what do these four phrases mean in relation to, and in the context of, the chapter?

14

Asian cities

Raymond Pask and Nick Devas

The contrast between the traditional *kampung* housing and the hotels of central Jakarta

China's urban challenge

Urban challenges exist not only for China's 450 million urban dwellers (in a total population of 1.2 billion), but also for its administrators and policy makers. Urban, as well as rural, living standards need to rise; the problems of urbanisation so obvious in other developing countries (see pages 365 to 377 need to be avoided; economic development must continue without increasing existing environmental and social problems.

China's urban places vary tremendously. They range in size from Shanghai, one of the world's biggest cities with over 12 million people, to the hundreds of urban places with fewer than 50,000 people. As Figure 1 shows, China's urban places vary significantly in their location.

Figures 2, 3, 4 and 5 illustrate some of this variety. Look at the photographs and read their captions. This should add to your understanding of China's urban variety.

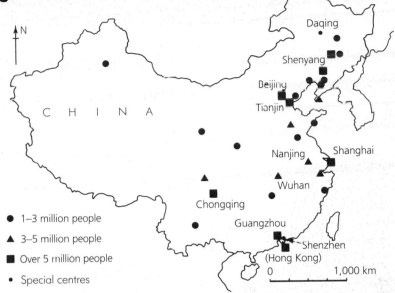

● 1–3 million people
▲ 3–5 million people
■ Over 5 million people
• Special centres

Figure 1 China's largest urban places

Figure 2 'I am old now, but I have seen so much in Beijing. My parents used to talk in whispers about the Forbidden City, now I go often go there with my grandson and his parents. Sometimes we climb Coal Hill (above left) to look over the city. Beijing has changed; mostly for the better. Before Liberation in 1949 there were beggars in the streets. The open drains have gone, along with the flies and most of the old city walls. The worst slums have been cleaned up. We have electricity and water now too. I think my grandson will see even more changes to Beijing in his lifetime.'

Figure 3 'I love Shanghai. It's an exciting place. Everyone in China wants to come here. The buildings are big and very modern looking. Lots of these places were built when Shanghai was run by foreign traders and governments. I think the city is something of a trendsetter for the rest of China. There is always something new happening in films, theatre, sport or fashion. I suppose it has a darker side too. Some of my brother's friends are still unemployed three years after leaving school. And the place is so big – China's biggest city in fact. That makes it hard to get around and even harder finding a bigger place to live.' (right)

?

1 Use Figure 1 to describe the distribution of China's largest urban places. Is this pattern similar to a pattern in other parts of the world, such as Europe or North America?

2 Name two differences you can see between the appearance of the Chinese cities shown in Figures 2 and 3 as well as 4 and 5 on page 356. Use the captions to the photographs to put forward some reasons that could explain why differences between Chinese cities exist.

What is the significance of China's urbanisation?

China is a country in transition. It still has many of the characteristics of economically developing countries, such as India or Indonesia. Yet, by the end of the twentieth century its planners, rulers and most of its population hope China will be more like a developed country. Its population should be better fed, housed, clothed and educated than at present. Its increased wealth should be reflected in more leisure time, higher levels of consumption and, hopefully, greater happiness amongst all its people. An economically developed society has come to mean an urban society. By the year 2000, more than half of China's population (or over 500 million people) will probably be living in or near cities and towns.

Such changes for so many people involve huge challenges. China already has some of the world's biggest cities. Shanghai, Beijing and Tianjin each have more than 8 million people. The 14 largest cities hold 5% of China's 1.2 billion people. Any large increases in the populations of these cities will strain their infrastructures even further and impair their ability to produce goods and services and provide a decent lifestyle for their inhabitants. Directing people and economic development away from such centres is no easy job as governments throughout the world have found.

Since 1979 the Chinese government has sought to develop a limited market economy with less price fixing and with greater profit incentives. China's planners want to use these mechanisms to move people out of farming into the more productive and lucrative areas of providing goods and services. Many of these activities will be urban-based. As a consequence important issues are arising. Should individuals and private companies be allowed to build privately, to own and trade in housing or other urban services? Will such measures create greater divisions in wealth distribution rather than less? Should individuals with enterprise and initiative be allowed to accumulate personal wealth? In short, many of the basic ideas of traditional Marxism-socialism are being questioned by such developments.

Figure 4 'I was sent to Daqing after graduating as an engineer in Nanjing. Like hundreds of others before me, I had no choice. But I am slowly accepting it. It is very different from my home town. Daqing is just a series of separate large villages and towns, with each one involved in some aspect of oil extraction and processing. It has grown quickly since oil was discovered in 1959. Now 70,000 people live here. Living conditions are tough, especially during the long northern winters. Some of the apartments are alright, but a lot of us are still living in mud-covered dormitories.'

Figure 5 'I'm lucky. I've got a job in Shenzhen, one of China's Special Economic Zones. Shenzhen is near Hong Kong and when it grows to about 500,000 people it will be as modern as anywhere in the world. It is all part of the government's plan to change China into an advanced manufacturing and trading nation. This place is so different from Guangzhou where my family lives. My wages are high and I can buy Western style clothes and other goods. There are even condominiums for retired Chinese from overseas. I live in a new Western style apartment with two other girls I work with.'

What is the quality of life in China's urban areas?

This section allows you to evaluate important aspects about the environment, day-to-day living, housing, movement and employment. You can also compare the quality of life in China's urban areas with that in other countries. In addition, how these living standards have changed and are likely to go on changing is looked at.

The environment

Table 1 Sulphur dioxide levels in East Asian cities

City centre commercial areas, 1982–5

City	Daily mean (mg/m^2)	Peak levels (mg/m^2)
World Health Organisation recommended maxima	40–60	100–150
Beijing	167	459
Guangzhou	81	206
Shanghai	54	217
Hong Kong	62	121
Tokyo	25	58
Osaka	29	57

Source: Far Eastern Economic Review, 8 June 1989

High population density, improving and changing lifestyles, increased industrialisation and more motor vehicles on the roads are combining to make China's urban environments problem ones. In particular, rapid industrialisation, largely using coal as fuel, has often been pursued without sufficient environmental safeguards. As a result, appallingly high levels of sulphur dioxide were recorded in China's main cities in the 1980s (see Table 1).

Natural pollution involving dust storms from the country's arid and semi-arid regions continue to plague many towns and cities, even those in the eastern part of the nation.

Urban pollution threat grows

Environmental sanitation in urban districts has long been neglected, and this has caused serious environmental problems. Beijing households, factories and shops use coal for cooking and heating. When coal is burned, smog is created, and the air becomes seriously polluted. Visibility can drop to less than 4 kilometres in Beijing and the smoke-laden air has, in recent times, hung over the city for more than 100 days a year.

Incomes have risen and the standard of living has improved in recent years. People eat more pork, eggs and vegetables and less rice and grain. With increased consumption, more waste is discarded and there has been an increase in dumped paper, metal, plastics, wine bottles and rags. This organic waste will certainly increase annually. The amount of equipment and space required for collection, removal and disposal will grow.

Over the last 35 years, Beijing has built 48 million square metres of living and work space. But city planners have paid little attention to the addition of sanitary facilities, storage space, refuse container baths, space for maintenance personnel, and so on. What is more serious is that city planners have not yet considered any additional funding for improving these facilities.

There is a serious shortage of professionals and experts in city cleaning. There are currently only 2.1 sanitation workers per thousand of population. The business of city planning is a comprehensive science. The key to proper management is adequate, qualified manpower. With the raising of living standards, the city should have 5–6 sanitation workers for each thousand of population.

Source: China Daily, 27 August 1985

Figure 6 Coal burning is responsible for much of the pollution of Beijing's skies.

Improving urban environments

There have been some notable achievements in environmental control. Increases in gas consumption will help reduce coal burning in cities. The planting of 200,000 hectares of new forest has helped reduce Beijing's notorious dust storms to the point where environmentalists predict only 'harmless winds by 2000'.

Yet the work remaining is huge: polluted streams, untreated wastes (especially from industries on urban fringes), increasing noise levels in central areas dominate official reports and personal complaints about environmental quality.

Official government policies enshrine environmental principles in the new constitution and in recent Five-Year Plans. Increasingly factories are located more sensitively with regard to their operation and disposal of wastes. But the gaps between official policies and desirable environmental practices and qualities are still substantial. Future increases in living standards will involve more cars, household goods and heating – all of which will place further demands on existing problem environments.

Chinese cities hit by sharp price increases

China's major cities have been hit by a sharp rise in retail prices, with the *China Daily* reporting a year-on-year, first-quarter rise of 13.4% for 32 large and medium-sized cities. Food prices in these cities rose 17.9%, with vegetables alone rising 48.7%. The overall first-quarter inflation rate was an annualised 11%, up from an average of 7.3% last year, the State Statistical Bureau reported.

Vice-Premier Yao Yilin recently said that the government would try to keep inflation at 10% this year, but that it might be difficult, in light of concurrent efforts to revive the economy.

Source: Far Eastern Economic Review, 20 April 1988

?

1 In what ways has increased industrialisation lowered the environmental standards in Chinese cities?

2 Outline some actions that individuals, enterprises and government authorities could do to reduce pollution levels to those of other East Asian cities. Which groups of people in China could find these measures hard to accept?

Day-to-day living

Day-to-day living in China's urban environments have many features familiar to urban dwellers in richer countries. For example, the basic facilities of shops, schools and health centres exist within all

Table 2 Major complaints, 1986

1 Using power to seek private gains.
2 High commodity prices.
3 Nepotism.
4 Lack of job mobility.
5 Unreliable legal system.
6 Frequent policy changes.
7 Few opportunities to earn money.
8 Inequality in pay.
9 Low salaries.
10 Uncertainty of income.

neighbourhoods throughout urban areas.

The freer price mechanisms operating since 1979 have contributed to inflation and genuine fears about falls in living standards (see the article and Table 2). Household budgets, such as the one in Figure 7, reflect heavily subsidised rents and transport facilities as well as limited supplies of consumer goods.

Food dominates household budgets, as Figure 7 shows. Supplies are organised from nearby communes through state and private contracts. Over 75 per cent of vegetables and 50 per cent of meats and fish are bought from free markets like the one in Figure 9. These free markets, often run by enterprising peasants from suburban and country communes, supply food more efficiently but more expensively than state-run stores. The greater variety of food has contributed to rising urban dietary standards. Nevertheless in the late 1980s rationing of key food items still existed in many cities.

Large Chinese cities, like their Western counterparts, are trend-setters in consumption habits and social behaviour. Advertising, like that in Figure 8, has encouraged people to save for the current

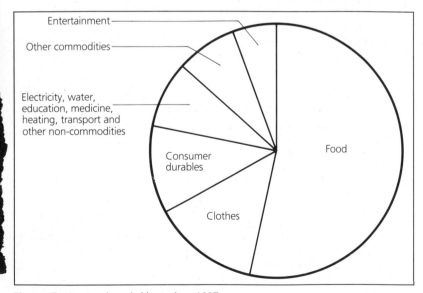

Entertainment
Other commodities
Electricity, water, education, medicine, heating, transport and other non-commodities
Consumer durables
Clothes
Food

Figure 7 Average household spending, 1987

Figure 8 Street advertisements in Beijing encouraging consumerism

Figure 9 A free market in Guangzhou

'big five' status symbols – television sets, sewing machines, tape decks, refrigerators and washing machines. As in developed countries, such advertising holds out the promise of a better future, courtesy of the manufacturer and retailer.

Future trends

Income levels are both increasing and becoming more varied in urban environments. Such differences have the potential to create moderately rich groups with preferred lifestyles and locations within a city. At the same time average incomes and living conditions for urban dwellers remain ahead of most of the rural population. Such trends run counter to orthodox socialism and may create their own problems in the future.

?

1 Name two features of day-to-day living in Chinese cities that are

- also found in cities in your country,
- not found in cities in your country.

2 In what ways is day-to-day living in Chinese cities becoming more like living in a Western city?

Housing

Table 3 Urban living space

	sq. m per person
China	6.3
USA	18.0
France	13.0

In the 1950s shanty towns similar to those found in the cities of today's economically developing countries dominated Chinese cities. Community self-help schemes improved drainage, water supply and shelter. As China's manufacturing enterprises developed, bricks, concrete, glass and pipes could be used to produce low-cost housing, such as that shown in Figure 13. Kitchens and bathrooms were included on a shared basis between families.

By the late 1970s urban authorities were building with pre-stressed concrete, aluminium and lifts. Apartments built in recent years have larger private kitchens and more have private bathrooms than previously. Figures 10 and 11 show this change.

Housing units were frequently

Figure 10 Housing in Nanjing

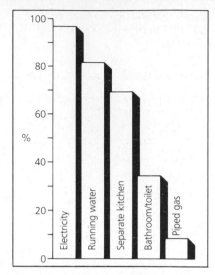

Figure 12 Average urban facilities, 1985

built next to work places and arranged as neighbourhood units.
Social facilities were important
but minimal and included meeting
halls, crêches and small shops like
the one in Figure 15.

In the 1960s in the semi-rural
suburban zones of cities, satellite
towns were built to relocate people and factories from the crowded inner districts. Like Meishan in
Figure 14, housing units were not
only functional but remarkably
equal in quality. Access to basic
services of education, shops and
entertainment was provided
within each satellite town.

Despite all of the above developments, the Chinese authorities
consider their country's urban living standards as 'relatively low'.

Figure 11 The interior of Mrs Fan's
flat in Beijing

A 1984 survey found that between 30 and 50 per cent of all
urban housing was in need of
demolition or substantial renova-
tion. Figures 10, 12 and Table 3
illustrate these 'low' aspects.

Living space is particularly
critical. The amount given in
Table 3 is, however, only an
average. More than half of
China's urban dwellers have less
than 6.0 sq. metres each while
another 26% have less than 4.0
sq. metres each. Nearly a third of
urban households share all their
rooms with other households.
This latter group would include
newly-weds living with parents
and in-laws. Inevitably such living
spaces create high population
densities. In central Shanghai

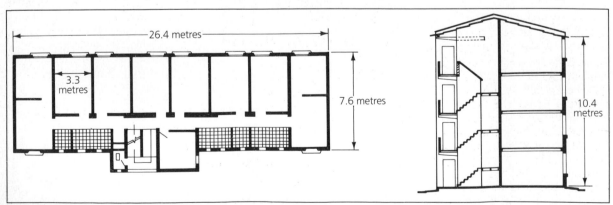

Figure 13 Lost-cost housing built in Chongqing in the 1950s

these densities can reach over 100,000 people per square kilometre.

?

1a In your classroom measure out the average living space for a Chinese urban dweller.

b Decide how you would arrange the internal space of this area.

c How would this arrangement change if two or five people were in the one household?

d Compare your home living space with those of urban dwellers in China. Make reference to Figure 10 in a concluding statement.

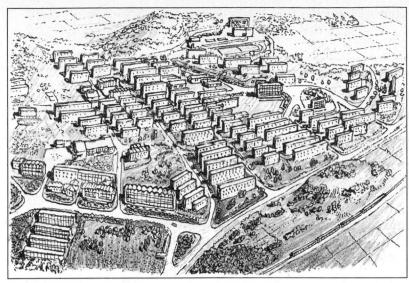

Figure 14 Meishan, a satellite town in the rural suburbs of Nanjing.

Figure 15 A neighbourhood unit shop

Future housing

Only 17% of all urban housing is privately owned in China's cities. To date most housing has been built, owned and maintained by state and local authorities or organisations such as factories. Rents have been very low, averaging between 1 and 4 per cent of total family income (see Figure 7). This low-rent policy has provided insufficient funds for maintenance of existing housing or the development of new housing stock.

Who gets the 'Early Harvest' apartments?

The 'Early Harvest' Food Processing factory in Shanghai has three apartments to be allocated to its workers. Use the point system (below) that will decide who gets the apartments. Points are allocated to ensure that the 'most desirable' people (politically, socially and economically) are rewarded.

Alternatively, devise your own point system so that people you consider to be deserving are rewarded. Be sure to justify your decisions.

Name	Marital status	Age	Number of children	Years of Party membership	Worker status	Years with factory	Number of work bonuses
Mr Wu	married	29	3	0	skilled	14	2
Mr Lin	married	23	1	5	ordinary	4	0
Mrs Chen	married	28	1	11	technician	6	16
Mr Teng	single	21	0	0	ordinary	3	1
Mr Chunyang	married	45	2	22	manager	20	7
Mrs Zhou	married	34	3	12	sub-manager	18	10
Mrs Li	widow	60	2	0	skilled	38	15
Mr Hua	married	54	3	32	ordinary	38	11
Mrs Cheng	married	34	2	0	ordinary	17	3
Mr Fei	married	49	5	5	sub-manager	32	6
Mr Gan	married	51	4	28	manager	30	13
Mrs Chen	single	27	0	7	technician	6	12

Points for housing allocation

No. of points	Reason
+2	One child family
1	For each child above the one-child limit if the worker is under 30 years
+1	For every five years of party membership
+1	For every five years with the factory
+1	For every three bonuses earned
−1	If single
−1	If under 25 years of age

In future, the market forces of private investment for profit are likely to dominate home construction. Sales of apartments by the authorities to individuals started in 1982. To encourage further sales, rental subsidies are being reduced as wages rise. The full impact of these policies is yet to be felt in China's cities. It may well be that pockets of moderate to significant affluence could appear amidst areas of basic housing.

Movement

High population densities within cities (see above) generate high population densities of movement. Staggered work hours and working days together with thousands of visitors from the countryside (Shanghai and Beijing had respectively 1.8 and 1.2 million additional 'visitors' each day in 1988) help swell the numbers of people and vehicles using the streets.

1 Read the reactions below to a suggestion to change China's 'low-rent policy' in cities. Which groups in society would you expect to support such a change? Which groups would you expect to be against changing it? Where would you stand and why?

- 'We're working hard and doing well. I'd like to leave my children their own apartments when I die. Why shouldn't I?' (*Private restaurant owner*)

- 'I have relatives in Hong Kong and elsewhere who would back me in building private apartments here in Shanghai. We could build them to attract retiring overseas Chinese.' (*Retired government factory manager*)

- 'Our wages are fixed and we're unskilled. If the state stops subsidising our rent our living standard drops.' (*Factory worker*)

- 'The system at present is fair. No one is exploited like our grandparents and their parents were. Change the system and we run the risk of developing a landlord class again.' (*Primary school teacher and Communist Party member*)

- 'Rents from this apartment block barely cover day-to-day repair costs. There's no money for new electrical wiring, improving bathrooms and kitchens unless rents go up or the state pays.' (*Maintenance manager of housing estate*)

- 'Many families have two or three members working. They can afford higher rents and could move out so less well-off families could have their places.' (*General manager of housing estate*)

Road works ahead

Antiquated transport networks in China's big cities are struggling with more people and vehicles on the move. The numbers of passengers using public transport have grown so fast in recent years that congestion is acute.

China's urban planners have promised to alleviate the transport crush. Subways are being planned, built or expanded, and officials are planning ways to move jobs nearer where people live. Still, the traffic grows, propelled by a wealthier and more mobile population than in the past.

More cars, buses, trucks and bicycles are coming onto the streets each year. Urban motor-vehicle growth rates in China are among the highest in the world – 16% a year for Beijing and 20% for Canton. Since 1949, Beijing's motorised traffic has increased 100 times to 380,000 vehicles, and 13-fold in Shanghai, while each city's roads have expanded only 12- and five-fold respectively.

Changes in modes of transport are compounding the congestion problem. Bicycles and buses were once the only available and affordable way of getting around. Urban Chinese now want more speed and comfort, and more goods are being moved around inner-urban areas as well. For this reason, motor-vehicles will become increasingly important.

Most of the 270,000 cars in use are imported, but domestic car production is planned to rise from last year's level of 20,000 to more than 150,000 by 1995. Production of mini and light trucks is also to expand, from 143,000 last year to 350,000 in 1990.

China has 20 times more buses on the road than it did in the early 1950s, but passenger numbers have increased 68-fold. An estimated 200,000 more buses will be needed nationwide before the end of the century just to keep pace with demand.

Other efforts to relieve pressure include moving workers' residences nearer to their places of employment, encouraging more companies and institutions to move from central areas to the suburbs, developing local consumer and business centres, staggering workdays to spread traffic movement over longer periods of the day, and controlling bicycles by centralised traffic monitoring systems and tighter road regulations. Shanghai's authorities have banned motor-vehicles registered elsewhere and all trucks over eight tonnes from using the city roads between 7 a.m. and 7 p.m.

However, these measures do not address the fundamental problem of adapting old cities to the traffic demands of an expanding and modernising economy. The costs of congestion are high: time is lost in commuting, goods are delayed and industrial productivity undermined. Even with planned improvements, moving about will remain a headache for China's urban dwellers.

Source: Far East Economic Review, 7 July 1988

Figure 16 *An everyday scene on Nanjing Road, Shanghai*

Urban transport is congested by pedestrians, buses, trucks and, since the mid-1980s, taxis and private cars – all moving at different speeds. In smaller cities and towns, mules, tractors and people pulling and pushing carts complicate the mixture. Bicycles dominate, with ownership rates equivalent to car ownership rates in the most affluent societies on earth. Beijing alone had nearly 7 million bicycles on its roads in 1988.

China's cities inherited an inadequate road system that had developed in some cases over several hundreds of years. Despite extensions and improvements to road networks together with the expansion of bus and train lines, the transport systems today barely cope with the huge volume of available passengers. In all but the smaller towns, huge investments of scarce funds are needed to make noticeable improvements to traffic flows.

1 What similarities and differences exist between the situation outlined in the article 'Road works ahead' and:

a Jakarta (see pages 370–2),
b one city in the richer part of the world?

2 How might China's growing urban affluence make the problems of movement:

a worse,
b better?

Work

Around 85 per cent of China's working urban population are employed in state-run enterprises such as factories, offices and shops. Most of these 100 million people were allocated their jobs by government planning agencies. Job allocation has traditionally brought with it residence permits, grain ration coupons and a wide range of work-based social and welfare benefits.

Despite recently introduced short-term contracts, most workers in state-run enterprises see their jobs as an 'iron rice bowl' (in other words, guaranteed life employment). Overstaffing, combined with a lack of motivation and initiative, dominate reports about state-employed workers' attitudes.

Collective, private and self-employment account for another 40 million workers in Chinese towns and cities. Increasingly their employment conditions and wage structures have become more flexible than those of state employees during the 1980s.

Since 1979 street traders, such as the one in Figure 17, have been allowed to operate in all Chinese cities and towns. Most traders operate under licence from larger enterprises such as factories or nearby farming communes. The decision to license street traders, like that of encouraging private employment in service industries, has done much to mop up urban unemployment.

1 Breaking the 'iron rice bowl' is advocated by many Chinese officials.

a Suggest what this change in policy could mean.

b Why might officials support breaking the 'bowl' while many workers want to retain it?

Figure 17 *A self-employed shoe repairer at work on a busy Shenyang street*

Conclusion

The urban systems that existed before 1949 provided very unequal lives for the inhabitants. China's new government was determined to change its urban environments. The cities were no longer to be consumers of people, food and other resources from the countryside. They were to become producers of goods and ideas that could be used in the countryside. For people living in cities, life would become more equal and for the majority, far better than in the past.

Transforming the cities has, however, been hindered by a lack of investment in urban redevelopment and new development. Nevertheless, important changes creating greater spatial justice than in the past have taken place.

Cities are still the 'bright lights' for millions of rural Chinese. Government programmes eliminating food shortages, poor housing, exploitation and lack of social opportunities have been implemented to improve not only the lives of rural people but to dampen their enthusiasm for moving to cities. Urban facilities are both overstrained and often inadequate for millions of urban people. Allowing free movement of people into urban areas from the countryside would inevitably further overload urban environments.

Small and medium-sized urban centres of between 50,000 and 300,000 people are the preferred focus of expansion and development. Larger centres should only develop where necessary, as at Daqing (Figure 4), the site of the nation's largest oil reserves, and at Shenzhen (Figure 5).

1 Suggest why China's urban planners have opted for growth in small and medium-sized centres rather than larger ones.

2 What advantages does a totalitarian government have for solving urban problems? Can you suggest any disadvantages it may have?

Dilemmas facing Beijing's future: to grow, slow or decline?

Beijing, the nation's capital, has grown rapidly in the last 40 years despite restrictions on people moving to the city from the countryside and other cities. By 1990 Beijing's permanent population had reached 10 million. This exceeded its planned target for 2000. The urban core's population of over 6 million, including 1.2 million non-permanent residents, was some 2 million greater than the level of the Master Plan of 2000. As a consequence municipal services, for example, may only reach half their planned level.

A number of proposals are being considered by city planning authorities. However, such proposals have their drawbacks in terms of implementation as well as undesirable consequences.

Proposal A
Continue to enforce one-child family policies to hold down natural population growth. Natural population growth adds 50,000 to 60,000 more to the city's population every year.

BUT: One-child families are now the norm in Beijing and an extension of such measures is limited. Some local districts have early signs of an ageing population that requires different services to those currently provided.

Proposal B
Develop an out-migration policy, especially from the overcrowded urban core to satellite towns, the relatively neglected smaller cities and to the semi-rural suburban areas near to Beijing.

BUT: Such a policy requires government decentralisation of departments in a very centralised political system. Many industries and services may find locations away from the urban core undesirable.

Proposal C
Prohibit further non-permanent residents coming to Beijing and progressively relocate the 1.2 million who are already there.

BUT: These people often work under contract on building projects and sell food and offer personal services for urban residents.

Proposal D
Tighten movements of peasants moving from rural areas outside of Beijing to rural areas under Beijing's jurisdiction. Since the 1960s this movement has increased the so-called 'suburban' population of Beijing and acts as a reserve for future movement into the urban core as either permanent or non-permanent residents.

BUT: Most of the newer arrivals are young and could help offset any ageing of the resident population.

Proposal E
Consider Beijing and Tianjin in a regional context to avoid unnecessary duplication of services and manufacturing enterprises and promote the integration of infrastructures such as transport, water supplies and new growth towns.

BUT: The rapid development of the cities, especially Beijing's heavy manufacturing sector, has proceeded almost independently of each other for 40 years making new arrangements difficult. The region's urban centres would function more effectively and serve to attract more people and enterprises from other parts of China.

?

a Which of the above proposals do you think would place the greatest demands on government spending? Why?

b Suggest why the population control proposals should be applied together rather than separately. Which of the population control measures do you think would be the least easy to enforce? Why?

c Government policy is to promote the development of smaller cities and larger towns as opposed to the further growth of large cities. What advantages and disadvantages could this create for
● the smaller cities and larger towns,
● the large cities,
● rural areas near both large and small cities?

d In the short-term period of about 5–10 years, which proposal (or combination of proposals) do you think would be most effective in controlling Beijing's growth? Which proposal(s) would be most effective in a longer term period of about 10–50 years? Be sure to say why.

e Argue for and against a policy that allows a further growth of large cities such as Beijing. In your argument try to use the experience of other large cities in developing countries (for example, Jakarta, pages 365–77) and in developed countries (for example, Amsterdam, pages 347–53).

Urban services in Jakarta

Jakarta – your view

Jakarta, the capital of Indonesia, is 11,700 km from London, 16,200 km from New York and 5,500 km from Sydney. Write down all the words and images which come into your mind when Jakarta is mentioned. How many times in the last three months can you recall it being mentioned in the news? Now check its position on an atlas; note its precise latitude and longitude. The short description which follows gives you one person's images of Jakarta.

Jakarta – one person's view

Jalan Thamrin – a ten-lane highway of fast-moving traffic, and the main street of Jakarta – on either side high-rise office blocks, banks, hotels and shopping plazas. The very image of a dynamic, modern city. Step back one block from this road, behind these impressive buildings – quite a different picture: the *kampungs*, densely packed, small houses, some no bigger than a shed – hardly space for a motor-bike, let alone a car, to pass between the houses. Everywhere people spilling out onto the pavement, thousands of people, all crammed together, walking, talking, eating, washing, sleeping, buying, selling; perpetual, vibrant activity.

The noise is constant noise. Cars hooting, children crying, the screech of scooter-cabs, street vendors banging their gongs to advertise their wares, the sound of prayers being called from the mosque ... and the smells: a mixture of exotic flowers and fruit, *kretek* (clove) cigarettes, spicy fried rice being cooked, and the stench from the canals which run through the *kampungs* and which serve as the city's sewers. Yes, this is Jakarta, one of the world's largest and fastest growing cities, and capital of the world's fifth largest nation.

Jakarta's rapid growth

Jakarta is situated on the northern coast of the island of Java, the most populous of the 13,000 islands which make up Indonesia. It is built on the swampy land of the coastal plain, and has a hot and humid climate. The history of Jakarta goes back nearly 500 years when it became the centre of the Kingdom of Jayakarta. When the Dutch arrived in the early seventeenth century, they made it their headquarters, renaming it Batavia. Since the end of the Second World War, Jakarta has been the capital of the Republic of Indonesia.

Like many cities in the economically developing world, Jakarta is growing at a phenomenal rate. In the 40 years since the Second World War, the population has increased more than tenfold. It is currently increasing at a rate of about 4% per year, which means an additional quarter of a million people have to be accommodated annually. This rapid growth has been largely due to the pressure of population on the island of Java: with over 100 million people in an area roughly the size of England, Java is one of the most densely populated regions of the world, and has a serious problem of rural landlessness.

Table 4 Population of the city of Jakarta (DKI)

1945	623,000	1970	4,437,000
1950	1,432,000	1975	5,404,000
1955	1,885,000	1980	6,503,000
1960	2,911,000	1985	7,756,000
1965	3,463,000		

Source: Jakarta Dalam Angka, 1986

The government of Jakarta

The city of Jakarta is administered by a provincial government, the Special Capital Region (DKI) of Jakarta. This administration is headed by a Governor, appointed by the President. There is an elected Assembly, in which the Government party, GOLKAR, is the dominant group. The Indonesian regime is generally pro-Western.

Since nearly all the land area of the city is already built up, much of the recent population growth has taken place outside the city boundaries, in the adjoining districts of Bogor, Tangerang and Bekasi, within the province of West Java. The population of the Greater Jakarta region (JABOTABEK) is estimated to be roughly twice that of the city itself.

What are the implications of such rapid growth?

Such rapid growth places a great strain on basic urban infrastructure and services, many of which were already totally inadequate when the city was only a fraction of its present size. For example, the city has no sewerage system, and much of the disposal of human waste takes place through open canals which run through the city, as happened in medieval European settlements; the municipal water supply only serves about one-third of the city's population; and the city suffers from regular floods because of the inadequate drainage system. The government (at both

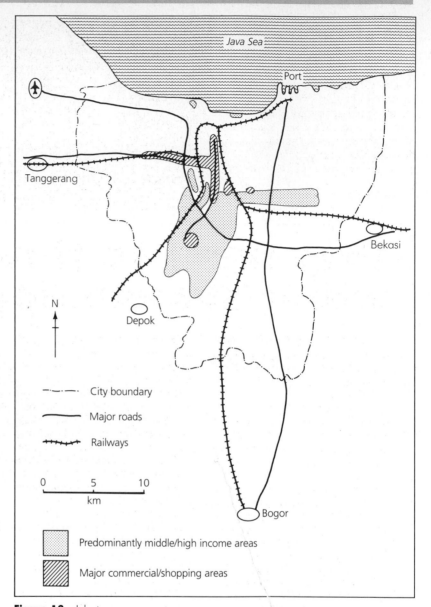

Figure 18 Jakarta

national and city levels) has invested massive resources in improving the city's infrastructure and services, yet enormous problems remain.

This chapter will look at the problems which this rapid growth presents for three particular aspects of the city:

● the water supply

● public transport

● the 'informal' housing areas or *kampungs*.

?

1 How would you set about making an estimate of the population of the city of Jakarta in the year 2000?

2 Would you expect there to be any change in the relative distribution of population between the city and the surrounding districts over this period?

3 Attempt to make a rough estimate of the population of the city, and of the city-region (JABOTABEK), in the year 2000.

Water supply

Clean water for drinking, cooking and washing is vital. The World Health Organisation (WHO) recommends that everyone should have access to at least 60 litres of clean water per day. But many of those living in Third World cities, in particular the poor, are deprived of clean water.

Figure 19 Using canal water for family washing

Drip turns to flow in city water system upgrading

JAKARTA (JP): It may take some time, but there's hope for North Jakarta residents that their water problems will be over before very long.

An official of the City Water Service (*PAM*) told reporters Tuesday the pipe system which carries the water from the city plant to consumers in the area will undergo a complete overhaul in the next few months.

A citizen's delegation from North Jakarta in July visited the Jakarta City Legislature to complain about the city water service in their area.

In response, *PAM* has decided to entirely replace the ten-year-old system with a new system in order to better serve its 1,200 clients in North Jakarta, according to Mr. Tri Harsono, *PAM* Director for the Jakarta Metropolitan area.

According to the citizens' complaints, only a small fraction of the 1,200 *PAM* clients have in the past year or so enjoyed tap water from the City Water Service, and then only in trickles.

The problem, according to officials, was that most of the area's old metal pipes had been corroded by salt water seepages from the sea.

PAM is now planning to replace those with PVC pipes. A beginning was made in late August and the work is to be expanded this month.

North Jakarta in the past received its tap water supply from the Pejompongan plant. After complaints, the new Pulogadung plant was connected to the system, but apparently with little result because of the many leaks.

Similar complaints, meanwhile, have been received from consumers in the Depok area to the south of the city where *PAM* officials said the leakage was estimated to about 50 per cent of the water supplied in two major areas of the township.

PAM officials have estimated that approximately 40 per cent of the city water supply is at present lost by leakages in the distribution system, either because of natural damages or stealing.

The service has recently offered residents a present of three months free water supply from the *PAM* system for those who report such "leakages".

Only a very small fraction of Jakarta's population of six million at present enjoys clean tap water from the City Water Service.

To add to the present supply, the Government recently signed a 11,646 billion yen loan agreement with Japan for the expansion of the Pulogadung plant, which by 1987 is hoped to supply another 3,000 litres of water a second.

The City Water Service was meanwhile reported to be studying the feasibility of building a new plant for West Jakarta, the area most in need of a clean water supply.

Jakarta's water problems are a clear reflection of the country's rising need for dependable clean water supplies.

In all of Indonesia, the number of people enjoying clean tap water from the various city water services are estimated to amount to about 40 per cent of the total Indonesian urban population of about 30 million.

The Government's development plans are aimed at raising this number to about 60 per cent by 1985 and to 75 per cent by 1990. For the current third Five Year Development Plan (*Pelita-3*) ending in March next year, the target is to provide clean water to 200 towns and cities throughout Indonesia.

Up to now, 399 towns and cities have installed tap water systems – well in excess of the target.

Source: Jakarta Post, 2 September 1983

?

1 Study the article about the water supply system of Jakarta; list the main problems identified in it. Check these with the problems identified below.

The City of Jakarta operates a municipal water undertaking, *Perusahaan Air Minum* (PAM), which provides drinking water to the citizens. However, the PAM system is unable to cope with the demands, for four main reasons.

1 It does not have sufficient raw water or treatment capacity to provide water to all consumers on the scale required.

2 PAM's distribution network is inadequate, so that many households cannot have a connection to their own house.

3 The water treatment system is not able to deal with the highly polluted raw water coming into its treatment plants, with the result that the water which PAM supplies is still very impure.

4 The substantial amount of 'leakage' from the system, arising not only from old and corroded pipes, but also from illegal connections to the system. Because of the high rate of 'leakage', water pressure in certain areas is minimal, and this means that polluted water can enter the pipes.

In fact, PAM is currently able to serve only a relatively small proportion of the city's population directly. As a result, most people depend either on obtaining water from wells, rivers and canals, or on buying water from private vendors. Many people have their own well or borehole, but the quality of the water from these is often unsatisfactory. In particular, in the north of the city, there is a serious problem of seepage of sea water, making the ground water saline. Water from the rivers and canals is highly polluted.

Figure 20 Water vendors queuing to fill their tins at the stand-pipe

Water vendors operate in many areas where the PAM supply is inadequate. These vendors purchase their water from a public stand-pipe, or from a private borehole, and then transport the water on barrows or shoulder-yokes to their customers (Figures 20 and 21). Inevitably, the cost of water from such vendors is substantially higher than that of water from PAM.

Table 5 PAM water supply, 1986

Number of connections	
Residential	128,900
Public stand-pipes	1,200
Government facilities	2,800
Offices and shops	20,300
Industry and port	800
Total number of connections	**154,000**
Average production of water	6,490 litres per second
Total amount of water sold in 1985 (million m³)	
Residential	44.2
Public stand-pipes	5.4
Government facilities	27.0
Offices and shops	13.0
Industry and port	7.4
Total water sold	**97.0 million m³**

Note: 1,000 litres = 1 cubic metre (m³)
Source: *Jakarta Dalam Angka*, 1986

Figure 21 Water vendor carrying his supplies on a shoulder-yoke

?

1 Using Table 5 calculate approximately what proportion of the city's population is supplied with water by PAM? (Assume that a house connection serves around 10 people, and that a public stand-pipe serves around 400 people.)

2 What are the average consumption levels per person per day for those with house connections, and for those using public stand-pipes? (Use the data in Table 5 and the same assumptions as in Question 1). How does this compare with the WHO recommendation (p. 367)?

3 What is the proportion of leakage within the system (i.e. the difference between the amount of water produced and the amount sold)?

4 How much does the production capacity need to be increased in order for everyone to receive at least the WHO minimum level of water? (Assume that the amount of water required for government facilities, shops, offices, industry and port remain unchanged.)

5 Write a short report for the World Health Organisation which:

a Explains what changes are required to the water supply system to ensure that everyone receives at least the minimum amount of water?

b Identifies some of the problems which result from the relatively high level of pollution of water supplies, even those provided by PAM?

Charging for water supplies

The Jakarta water undertaking (PAM) charges its customers for the water they consume (the amount consumed is recorded on a meter). There is quite a complicated tariff, which differentiates according to the type of consumer (residential, business, industry, and so on), and according to the level of consumption (those who consume only a relatively small amount of water are charged at a lower tariff rate than those consuming large quantities).

Water from public stand-pipes is also charged for. The stand-pipe is leased to a concessionaire who sells the water and then pays PAM. Although these concessionaires are supposed to charge only the official price, in practice they often charge considerably more (anything up to *Rupiah* 50 for a 20-litre tin). It is generally the poor who use the stand-pipes, since the rich can afford to pay for their own private connection or borehole.

Table 6 PAM tariffs, 1986

Rates quoted in Rupiah (Rp) per m³ (£1 = approx. Rp 3,000)	
Public stand-pipes	125
Residential consumers	40 for less than 15 m³/month
	80 for between 15 and 30 m³/month
	300 for more than 30 m³/month
Government facilities*	210
Offices and shops*	460
Industry and port*	470

* There are variations according to the particular type of facility and levels of consumption; these are average rates.

?

1a Make an estimate of the amount of water which you and your family consume per month. (You may need to calculate the volume of water used each time someone has a bath, fills the basin or sink, flushes the toilet, and so on to calculate the amount of water consumed by your household in a typical day.)

b How much would you have to pay for that amount of water if you lived in Jakarta and received your water from PAM? How does that compare with what your family pays for water here? (*Note*: £1 = approx. *Rupiah* 3,000.)

2 Set out in two columns the advantages and disadvantages of paying for water through direct charges, as in Jakarta, compared to the system of paying through property taxation or water rates, as has been the practice in this country?

3a Ask yourself: do you think it is a good policy to charge different categories of consumer different prices, as they do in Jakarta? Why should those who only consume a small amount of water pay less than those who consume more?

b Imagine the sort of discussion which might take place within the city's elected assembly over this matter, between a representative for an industrial area, who objects to industries in his ward having to pay a higher rate for their water, and a representative for a low-income housing area. Write out the possible dialogue.

4a What level of profit do you estimate that stand-pipe concessionaires are making each month, if the average price they charge is *Rupiah* 25 for a 20-litre tin? Why are stand-pipe concessionaires able to charge so much more than the official price? What could be done to try to curb this overcharging?

b In addition, for those who have to buy water from private vendors (who carry the water from door-to-door) the price can vary from *Rupiah* 100 to *Rupiah* 300 for a 20-litre tin, depending on location. Is this fair?

c Think about these questions and then write a letter to the Editor of the *Jakarta Post*, giving your views.

Public transport in an overcrowded city

Jakarta boasts an amazing variety of types of public transport, as indicated in Table 7.

Table 7 Types of public transport in Jakarta

	Indonesian name	Length of journey	Number of passengers	Fare system
General passenger transport				
Large buses	*Bis Kota*	Long/medium	50–100	Flat fare (Rp 200)
Small buses	*Metro Mini*	Medium/long	30–40	Flat fare (Rp 200)
Minibuses	*Mikrolet*	Medium/short	8–15	2–3 stage fares (Rp 200–300)
Pickups	*Bemo*	Short/medium	6–12	2–3 stage fares (Rp 200–300)
Individual hire transport				
Taxis	*Taksi*	Medium/long	3–5	By meter: Rp 500–3,000 according to distance
Scooter-cabs	*Bajaj*	Short/medium	2–3	Negotiable: Rp 300–1,000/trip
Cycle rickshaw	*Becak*	Local	1–2	Negotiable: Rp 200–1,000/trip

Table 8 Motor vehicles in Jakarta

	1980	1985
Private cars	222,345	339,812
Trucks/commercial vehicles	77,781	149,785
Motor-cycles	428,144	696,389
Public transport	26,338	32,547
Large buses	*2,967*	*3,393*
Small buses	*1,518*	*2,935*
Mikrolets	*1,960*	*3,633*
Bemo	*1,085*	*1,096*
Taxis	*6,165*	*7,949*
Bajaj	*12,643*	*13,541*
	754,608	**1,218,533**

Source: Jakarta Dalam Angka, 1986

Table 9 Public transport passengers, 1985

	Average number of passengers transported within Jakarta per day	
Rail	57,000	
Bus	4,129,000	Large buses only
	Other n.a.	

In addition, there is a suburban train network, although this carries only a relatively small share of passengers. There is no underground.

The two main problems of public transport in Jakarta are:

1 The lack of capacity, especially of the bus services, leading to severe overcrowding, particularly at peak periods.

2 The generally overcrowded state of the city's streets, resulting in serious traffic delays for all road users.

The proportion of roadspace to land area in the city is very low by international standards, and this limited roadspace has to be shared not only by public transport vehicles and a rapidly growing number of private cars, lorries and motor-cycles, but also by pedestrians and a huge number of street traders. As Table 8, shows the number of motorised vehicles on the roads of Jakarta increased by 60% between 1980 and 1985. However, it is very difficult to increase road space, not only because of the cost but also because many people would be displaced.

Figure 22 Public and private transport: traders and pedestrians competing for the same road space

Public transport in Jakarta is relatively cheap: the fare on buses, *Rupiah* 200, is only about 7 pence for any distance; *mikrolets* and *bemos* normally charge the same amount for short distances, but somewhat more for longer distances. At least until the recent increase in fares the government-owned bus company (PPD), which provides the bulk of the large bus services in the city, was making heavy losses, and received substantial subsidies from the government. Fares for *bajajs* and *becaks* have to be negotiated with the driver at the start of the journey, and are typically between *Rupiah* 200 and *Rupiah* 1,000, depending on distance.

Figure 23 *Bajaj and mikrolet*

1 The article below refers to some of the ways in which the city government is trying to reduce traffic congestion. Do you think these are good ways? Which groups would gain, and which would lose, from these proposals? What other policies might the city consider? Discuss these questions in groups and then write your own short report.

Figure 24 *Bemos, each can carry 7 people*

City moves to unravel traffic snarls

JAKARTA (JP): Disorderly parking has been identified as the main cause of traffic jams in the downtown area, and the authorities are doing something about it.

New regulations are expected to come into force later this month to limit public parking along Jalan Gajah Mada and Jalan Hayam Wuruk – the twin roads alongside the canal which runs from the Harmoni intersection behind the palace of Glodok and Pancoran – to certain hours of the day.

To alleviate the problem, the authorities are also considering other measures, such as tightening restrictions on construction of new buildings in the central downtown business area and spreading business activity to other areas of the city.

Governor Soeprapto, in an earlier statement said the city government would look into turning the former Chinese embassy building near Pancoran into a multi-level car garage, for which purpose the Foreign Ministry would be contacted. Another car park maybe built over the Ciliwung canal.

Public buildings and offices would be required to reserve adequate parking space, the Governor said. The city government, he said was also studying the possibility of limiting private cars in certain zones during peak times.

There are at present about 2,500 city parking attendants in Jakarta. The city derives an average monthly income of about Rp 180 million from parking fees.

Source: Jakarta Post, 3 September 1983

The end of the becak?

Another policy which the city authorities have adopted in order to try to reduce traffic congestion is the gradual abolition of the *becak* or pedicab. Because these vehicles are slow moving, they can obstruct motorised traffic. As a result, they have for some years been banned from using main roads, and now operate mainly within local residential areas. The authorities, however, recently decided to eliminate the *becak* altogether.

Becak drivers generally do not own their own vehicles but have to hire them on a daily basis from owners who may possess many machines. The work involved in driving a *becak* is very strenuous. Because *becaks* are only allowed to operate in such limited areas, there are often not enough customers, so drivers have to be available for long hours to earn enough to live on.

Trials of the becak

JAKARTA (JP): The world seems to be unequally divided. That's what Pak Taryadi a becak driver by trade, meant when he said: "It isn't fair. The area we are allowed to enter is getting gradually smaller and smaller."

The three-wheeled pedicab has been going through a difficult patch over the last few years. As the traffic in the city becomes more modernized, the pedicab and their drivers are pushed aside. They are forced to give way to modern means of transport: big buses, taxis, mini buses and the motorized cab or *bajaj*."

In the fifties, when traffic in the city still ran at a slow pace the citizens didn't need to travel very far, the pedicab was a very convenient form of transport. It is a two seater vehicle with the driver pedalling at the back. It offers a door-to-door service to clients for a relatively small fee. In those days when the cabs were the main means of public transport they ruled the streets of the city.

A recent Governor's decree has ordered that pedicabs are to be banned from operating in the city starting from 1985. This means that this will be the last year that citizens of Jakarta can enjoy this door-to-door service.

Of the 80,000 pedicabs, only 7,828 are regarded as legal. To legally operate a pedicab service it is necessary officially register with the authorities, pay annual taxes and have a driving license.

When asked whether he knew about the elimination of pedicabs, Pak Taryadi answered: "Yes I heard about it earlier in 1981. But then it was said that the regulations were postponed for a number of years. If the regulation is really carried out, quite a few of us will be unemployed. We are quite well-off compared to other road traders, though we only earn Rp 3000 a day. But as we haven't had any education, we may be forced to sell vegetables or ice cream in future, even if it means a drop in income."

The days of the pedicab are numbered. The vehicle which according to chronicles dates back to 1936, will soon disappear from city life along with a trade for the many pedicab drivers.

Source: Retno K Djojo, *Jakarta Post*, 1 January 1984

Figure 25 *Becak* drivers awaiting customers

?

1 Read the article about *becaks*. Do you think *becaks* should be abolished? What may be some of the consequences of implementing such a policy?

2 The article 'Trials of the *becak*' gives an indication of how much a *becak* driver earns. (£1 = approx. *Rupiah* 3,000). Do you think this is enough to live on? Why do you think that they continue to do such a hard job for so little reward?

3 Write a speech for a *becak* driver to make to protest to the city authorities about the decision to stop the use of *becaks*. Write another speech for a visiting Green Party representative from Europe to make in support of the *becak* drivers' case.

Kampung improvement

As in the cities of many developing countries, a large proportion of Jakarta's housing can be regarded as 'informal': in other words, it has been built without official approval. During the colonial era the city itself was reserved for Europeans. Indonesians, therefore, built their houses on the surrounding farm land. These 'unofficial' settlements are known by the term *kampung*, which literally means a compound. As the city grew, more and more people settled in these *kampungs*, so that today around half of the city's population lives in such areas.

The *kampungs* are not really 'squatter' settlements, inasmuch as most of the residents have some legitimate tenure rights, although some *kampungs*, such as those alongside the railway lines and canals, may be constructed illegally on state-owned land (Figure 27).

Unlike many cities, Jakarta does not have clearly defined wealthy areas and poor areas. Certainly there are many wealthy people and many palatial houses, particularly in central and southern parts of the city – in areas like Menteng, Kebayoran, Kemang and Simpruk; but in most cases, there are areas of *kampung* housing tucked in behind the expensive private housing. The poorer *kampungs* tend to be more concentrated in the northern parts of the city, especially on the land prone to flooding (Figure 26). Within *kampungs*, one can often find substantial properties, as those who have prospered often prefer to remain in the same area and improve their houses, rather than relocate.

Nevertheless, housing conditions in the *kampungs* are often very poor, with severe overcrowding, non-existent infrastructure, and often makeshift buildings. In some areas of the city, densities of up to 1,000 people per hectare have been recorded. Because of the low-lying land on which Jakarta is built, *kampungs* suffer regularly from flooding.

In the late 1960s, the Governor of Jakarta initiated a programme to improve the *kampung* housing areas. The aim was to install basic infrastructure – roads, footpaths, surface-water drainage, water supplies, public washing facilities and latrines, schools and clinics.

This was a massive task, since there are numerous *kampungs* covering a vast area (more than 100 km^2 in all) and usually they are so densely built-up that there is little room to insert the infrastructure. Inevitably, therefore, some houses had to be demolished, and others cut back, to make space available (Figure 28).

During the ten years from 1969, the *kampung* improvement programme upgraded the facilities in nearly 8,000 hectares of the city, accommodating over three million people. The improvements were very modest: only narrow access roads and footpaths, rather than major traffic routes; public taps and latrines rather than

Figure 26 Flooding is a recurring problem in most *kampungs*

private house connections and water-borne sewerage. Indeed, the infrastructure provided in the early phases was often inadequate, especially in the case of water supplies and surface-water drainage (which often had nowhere to drain to and became clogged with rubbish as in Figure 32). Although the project did not involve the improvement of individual houses, it has stimulated households to improve their own housing.

The construction work was carried out by contractors, and residents were not generally involved in any 'self-help', except for maintenance of the facilities provided and improvements to their own houses. No charge was made to the residents for the new infrastructure, but at the same time, no compensation was paid to those whose houses were demolished or cut back during the works.

Most of those who had to cut their houses back to make way for a road were still happy enough with the scheme, as it gave them proper vehicular access. For those whose homes were completely demolished, it was left to the rest of the community to make a donation by way of compensation, although it is not clear to what extent that actually occurred.

Table 10 shows some of the results of the project during this ten-year period. The project generally has been highly popular, especially since it confers a degree of security on the areas concerned, which might otherwise have been demolished. Property values in improved *kampungs* increased substantially. For some tenants this was bad news, since rents increased, and they were sometimes forced out so that the property could be reconstructed or let to richer tenants.

Figure 27 For those living beside the railway tracks there are few prospects of an improved environment

Figure 28 Houses cut back to make room for the new road

Figure 29 The owner of this house will have to cut it back to the position of the arrow (below the window) to provide a route wide enough for vehicles

Table 10 The *kampung* improvement programme, 1969–79

Area covered	7,676 hectares
Population	3,040,000
Total cost	Rp 52 billion (approx. £70 million*)
Cost per hectare	Rp 6.8 million (approx. £9,000*)
Cost per person	Rp 17,000 (approx. £22*)
Construction	
Roads	925 km
Footpaths	950 km
Drainage channels	410 km
Public taps/wells	1,505
Public toilet blocks	277
Pit latrines	14,045
Health centres	89
Schools	150

* Based on the exchange rate which applied at the time

On the whole, though, there does not appear to have been a great deal of movement of people into or out of the improved *kampungs*, and 'gentrification' (the process of richer people moving in and displacing poorer residents) does not appear to have occurred to a significant degree.

Figure 30 New road under construction

Figure 31 A new footpath raised above the normal flood level

Figure 32 The improvements carried out in the early years of the programme have been used heavily and have not always been well maintained – for instance the drainage channels beside the access routes may become blocked

Figure 33 Public stand-pipe and washing facilities

Debate

There are many people who disagree with the policy of *kampung* improvement, usually on the grounds that such areas are so badly constructed, without proper planning, that they can never provide a 'proper' housing environment. Added to which, by improving such areas close to the city centre, proper redevelopment of the city, and the expansion of the commercial centre, are prevented. Thus, it is argued, such areas should be demolished and new housing constructed according to proper standards and a planned layout.

Organise a debate on the motion: 'Complete redevelopment is the only solution for the *kampungs*.'

(*Note*: In Britain in the 1970s there was a similar debate about the demolition of older neighbourhoods under the slum clearance programme.)

Since 1979, the *kampung* improvement programme has been extended into areas of the city not previously covered, as well as returning to some of the areas improved during the early phases, in order to make up for deficiencies in the original upgrading. The programme has also now been adopted in other cities in Indonesia.

Acknowledgement Nick Devas would like to acknowledge the valuable comments made on the draft of his part of the chapter by Richard Phillips and K.H. Morris of the Geography Department of Handsworth Grammar School, Birmingham.

Role play

You are residents of *Kampung Indah* which is scheduled for upgrading in a few months time. Look at Figure 34 which is a diagram of part of *Kampung Indah*, showing the main improvements proposed. The following are some of the people present at a meeting between the residents and city officials to discuss whether or not this *kampung* should be improved, and if so, how.

First, assign the roles below to members of the group; then each person should consider carefully what the likely attitude of the person he/she is playing would be towards the proposed improvement scheme; finally act out the meeting, with Pak Johannes as chairman.

Characters

(Note: There are 14 characters in this role play, but it can be played with as few as five; take characters from the top of the list first.)

Pak Johannes
The administrator for this district of the city, who is concerned to see the project implemented

Pak Priyono
An official of the city's *Kampung* Improvement Department, who has come to discuss the city authority's plan with the residents

Pak Ali
The elected 'head' of the *kampung* and hence spokesman for the residents, and the owner of house marked A

Ibu Hassan
Owner of house marked B, half of which will be demolished to provide road access

Pak Dede
Tenant of a room marked E which might be marginally affected by the road access

Pak Wayono
The landlord of several houses in *Kampung Indah*; he can foresee that he could charge rather higher rents once the area is improved

Ibu Endra
Tenant of a dilapidated house marked D (owned by Pak Wayono), who fears that her rent might go up

Pak Rusli
A water vendor operating in *Kampung Indah*, who fears that his business might come to an end once water connections are provided in the area

Pak Sutomo
The owner of a house in the area to the south of *Kampung Indah*, who wants to be able to drive to his house from the industrial area to the north of *Kampung Indah*

Pak Ibrahim
A property developer who is hoping to redevelop much of the area as a shopping centre and considers the present housing should be demolished, not improved

Pak Harun
The owner of shop marked G, who expects trade to increase if the area is improved

Ibu Tina
Owner of house marked C, which would gain improved access under the scheme

Pak Busri
Another official of the city's *Kampung* Improvement Department, who has come to discuss the plan

Ibu Ida
The owner of house marked F, which would have to be demolished to make way for the washing and toilet facilities

(Note: Pak is the Indonesian term for Mr, Ibu for Mrs.)

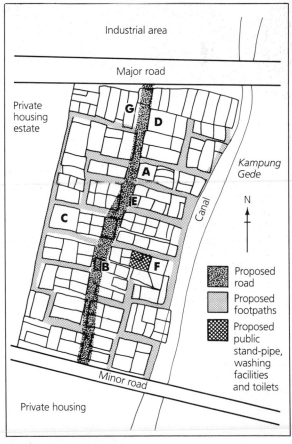

Figure 34 *Kampung* Indah

PART V

MANAGING HUMAN ENVIRONMENTS

What is the 'tragedy of the commons'?

Let's pretend we are looking at a picture. It shows a London cab driver polishing and shining his black London cab. He's working hard. He can see his reflection in the polished bodywork. The cab is parked alongside the kerb in a fairly narrow street.

The cabbie is actually ankle deep in scraps of paper and other litter as he polishes away. *His* eye is on his cab. This story is yet another example of the 'tragedy of the commons'. Read through the adapted article printed here and list further examples.

The tragedy of the commons

Many of the problems facing the world today are related to what might be described as 'the tragedy of the commons'; where tragedy is defined as 'the remorseless working of things'. Imagine a common pasture open to all. It is expected that each herdsman will try to keep as many cattle as possible on it. This arrangement will work well until the sustainable population begins to near its maximum. Each herdsman will rationally conclude that the advantage to himself of keeping one extra animal outweighs the shared disadvantage of overgrazing of the commons. If all the herdsmen pursue this course the commons will eventually be unable to support any animals at all. Therein is the tragedy. Each person is locked into a system which will eventually bring about their own ruin.

This may seem an obvious conclusion but it has only been understood in special cases in the course of history. Even today, cattlemen leasing national land on the western ranges of the United States constantly pressure the federal authorities to increase the head count to the point where overgrazing produces soil erosion and weed dominance. The concept of the 'freedom of the seas' lays the oceans open to the same kind of over exploitation, in which maritime nations profess beliefs in 'the inexhaustible resources of the oceans' whilst bringing species after species of fish and whales closer to extinction.

National parks present another instance of the working of the tragedy of the commons. At present they are open to all, without limit, whilst they themselves are limited in extent. There is only one Yosemite Valley, but the population wishing to use it continues to grow, and as it does so the values that visitors seek in the park are steadily

eroded. Plainly, it is necessary for the world to stop treating its parks as commons or they will be of no value to anyone.

One solution might be for the parks to be sold off as private property, or they could be kept as public property, but the right to enter them might be allocated. The allocation could be on the basis of wealth, or of merit – as defined by some agreed-upon standards – or a lottery system should be used. A first-come, first-served system could be administered to long queues. None of these possibilities are pleasant but, if nothing is done, then the national parks will disappear for everyone.

The problem of pollution provides an example of the tragedy of the commons in reverse. The rational man finds that his share of the cost of the wastes he discharges into the commons is less than the cost of purifying his wastes before releasing them. Since this is true for everyone, we are locked in a system of 'fouling our own nest' as long as we behave only as rational, independent, free-enterprisers. Little progress can be made until we reverse the tendency to assume that decisions reached individually will, in fact, be the best decisions for an entire society.

The ownership of private property can help to prevent overuse of food producing resources but it tends to favour pollution. The owner of a factory on the bank of a stream – whose property extends to the middle of the stream – often has difficulty seeing why it is not his natural right to muddy the waters flowing past his door. Only difficult-to-administer laws can provide a partial solution. As with the overuse of land, the problem of pollution only becomes critical when the population reaches a high level; when there are few people fouling the environment, it was large enough to purify and renew itself.

This analysis of the pollution problem leads to a principle of morality, namely: *the morality of an act is a function of the state of the system at the time it is performed.* Using the commons as a cesspool is not harmful under frontier conditions, but in a metropolis it is unbearable behaviour. This principle is difficult to put into an unchanging law and, so, often the task of protecting our environment is put into the hands of bureaus which are notably liable to self-interest and corruption.

Population tends to grow exponentially, and in a finite world this means that the per capita share of the world's goods must steadily decrease. Until quite recently the world's resources were treated as if they were infinite, but there is now an increasing realisation they are not. If population growth continued until it reached the maximum the earth can support, the amount of energy available to each individual would be so little that people would be able to do nothing more than sleep, eat and work. Even if such things as nuclear power provided limitless energy, it would be impossible to dispose of the waste.

Nowadays it is assumed that most of the problems that the world faces have some technical solution – that, a solution that requires only a change in the technique of the natural sciences and little or nothing in the way of change in human values or ideas of morality. However, not all problems have technical solutions, and the questions of over use of resources, pollution and world population are some of them. Fundamental changes in attitudes and decision-making processes will be necessary if we are to tackle these issues successfully.

Source: Adapted from Garrett Hardin, 'The Tragedy of the Commons', *Science* 162, 13 December 1968

After reading the article, you probably will have no difficulty explaining what Hardin meant by the phrase, 'tragedy of the commons'. Indeed you could go through all the chapters of this book and list further examples. Every day newspapers provide us with many more and give a voice in these issues to those whose attitudes and values place them in one group or another in relation to the environment. At heart, the tragedy of the commons is about our efforts to maximise advantage for our own individual selves at the expense of others.

In all the examples of the tragedy of the commons given, it is interesting that we have aspects of the two categories I mentioned in the introduction to Part II. We have a scientific sort of evidence which points to a degradation of the commons and are therefore confronted by the moral question: 'Ought we to be behaving like this?' We can answer 'yes' or 'no' to this moral question (that is we can ground our response in a belief that 'yes' or 'no', based on certain values, is the appropriate response).

If we do this we perhaps imply that we either give priority to a collective sense of responsibility for the environment, or no priority to it at all. In fact like many, I like to think I give some priority to a collective sense of responsibility towards our environment. But while I continue to drive my car, empty except for myself, I'm fooling myself in relation to that piece of environmental destruction.

The ideas in this final introductory piece are, in my opinion, among the most powerful you'll ever come across. Will our education in geography ever make a difference, not just to our points of view but to our behaviour?

We can read each of the chapters in this section by asking, again, *what is at issue here*? Each of the case studies is, on the surface, about something completely different – transport, development in the M4 corridor, and industrialisation in Hungary. But at depth what is at issue in each case study? The concept of the tragedy of the commons will help you answer my question incisively. Geography is not about accumulating a vast knowledge of case studies. It is about *reading the meaning at depth* in the case study and *developing concepts*, such as individual and collective actions and responsibilities, which actually *explain* why our world is like it is.

15

The impact of industrial change in the M4 corridor

Geoff Squire

New industrial development near the M4 at Reading

The M4 corridor stretches from West London westward along the M4 motorway through Slough, Maidenhead, Bracknell, Reading and Newbury towards Swindon, Bristol and South Wales (Figures 1 and 2).

Towns and villages along the M4 corridor have experienced rapid economic and social changes during the 1970s and 1980s, but Berkshire's location and its proximity to London have given rise to issues which are not present to the same degree in some other parts of the corridor. This chapter focuses on these developments in the *Berkshire* section of the M4 corridor. It investigates four main questions:

- What evidence is there of social and economic change in this part of the M4 corridor?

- What factors have brought about these changes?

- What are the issues raised by living with success?

- What are the prospects for the future? How shall we plan for future development within the South-East region?

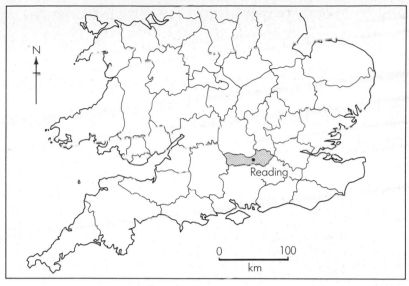

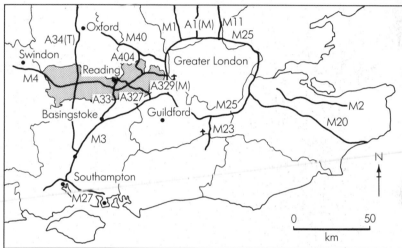

Figure 2 Berkshire in its regional setting showing connections to the motorway network

Population census 1981

Bristol 420,234
Cardiff 266,267
Reading 198,341
Swansea 175,172
Swindon 128,493
Newport 116,658
Slough 106,882
Newbury 31,894
Bridgend 31,579

Proportional circles 0.25 cm diameter per 100,000 population

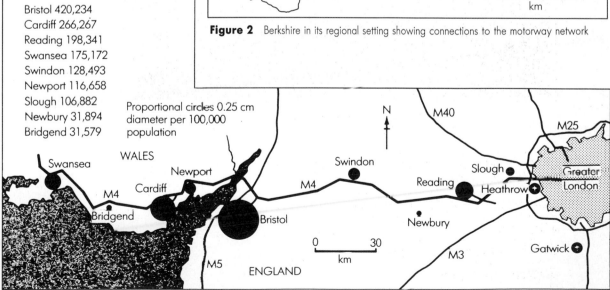

Figure 1 The M4 main urban centres

The growth of industry and employment in Berkshire since 1970

Electronics

By the mid 1980s Berkshire had over 500 electronics firms employing 30,000 people. This was about 10% of all jobs in the county. In Bracknell 30% of employment was in the electronics industry (Figure 3). Nationally, employment in this industry was under 4%.

Often called *high-technology* firms, these plants are spread across the county with some specialisation of

- defence-related electronics employment in Bracknell
- computer software in Maidenhead and
- video-technology in Newbury.

Figure 4 shows the location of new firms in more detail.

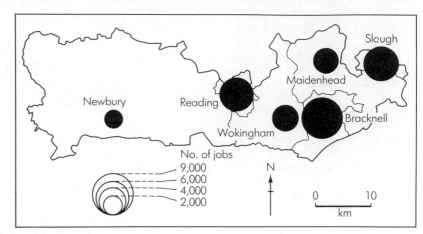

Figure 3 Location of electronics firms in Berkshire
Source: Berkshire County Council, *Development Trends in Berkshire*, 1985

Other features of the industry in Berkshire:
- Employment falls into three groups:
  i manufacturing,
  ii wholesale distribution and
  iii office-based activities which include software production, research and development (R & D) and the marketing of products.

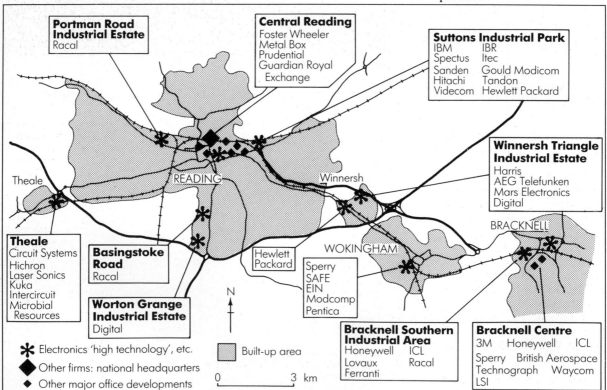

Portman Road Industrial Estate
Racal

Central Reading
Foster Wheeler
Metal Box
Prudential
Guardian Royal Exchange

Suttons Industrial Park
IBM   IBR
Spectus   Itec
Sanden   Gould Modicom
Hitachi   Tandon
Videcom   Hewlett Packard

Winnersh Triangle Industrial Estate
Harris
AEG Telefunken
Mars Electronics
Digital

Theale
Circuit Systems
Hichron
Laser Sonics
Kuka
Intercircuit
Microbial Resources

Basingstoke Road
Racal

Worton Grange Industrial Estate
Digital

Hewlett Packard

Sperry
SAFE
EIN
Modcomp
Pentica

Bracknell Southern Industrial Area
Honeywell   ICL
Lovaux   Racal
Ferranti

Bracknell Centre
3M   Honeywell   ICL
Sperry   British Aerospace
Technograph   Waycom
LSI

READING
Theale
Winnersh
WOKINGHAM
BRACKNELL

* Electronics 'high technology', etc.
◆ Other firms: national headquarters
◆ Other major office developments

▨ Built-up area

0   3 km

Figure 4 The location of new firms, 1970s and 1980s, in Reading and central Berkshire

- Some electronics firms choose Berkshire for their non-manufacturing activities (administration, R & D, and marketing) and manufacture their products in other regions of Britain or overseas. This is often the case where the firm is a multinational enterprise with investments in more than one country. For example, Honeywell (Figure 5), Hewlett Packard and Digital Equipment Company (DEC) have located their R & D, marketing and office activities in Berkshire, but production takes place elsewhere, in particular in Scotland.
- It is likely that production employment suffers most in periods of low growth during periods of recession, so the R & D and office activities in Berkshire may be better protected against employment loss when times get hard.

?

1 Study Table 1 (Employment change in Berkshire 1971–81). Can you suggest reasons for the changes shown in the statistics?

2 Rank the industrial groups from highest to lowest in terms of percentage change in employment.

The multiplier effects of high-technology industry

As Table 1 shows, most of the employment growth has come from service industries rather than high-technology industry itself. During the period 1971–81 services produced a net gain of 49,000 jobs compared with a much more modest increase of about 7,500 jobs in high technology.

It is likely that the growth of service employment is closely related to high-technology growth in several ways.

1 The local economy provides goods and services for high-technology firms.

Figure 5 Honeywell head office, Bracknell, Berkshire

Table 1 Employment change in Berkshire, 1971–81, for selected sectors (1968 SIC, employees in employment)

SIC		Change 1971–81	Percentage change
1	Agriculture	−1,630	−32.6
3	Food	−2,103	−21.6
5	Chemicals	−978	−11.1
7	Mechanical	−4,505	−21.5
8	Instrument engineering	127	4.0
9	Electrical	7,283	60.2
11	Vehicles	−230	−4.1
12	Metal goods	−582	−7.9
18	Paper, etc., printing	−827	−8.4
19	Other manufacturing	336	9.1
20	Construction	−731	−5.0
21	Utilities	540	12.8
22	Transport	−1,858	−12.4
23	Distribution	12,391	34.4
24	Banking	11,672	104.1
26	Miscellaneous services	12,137	45.8
28	Private, professional and scientific services	7,536	86.1
29	Public services	9,734	11.7

Source: P. Hall, M. Breheny, R. McQuaid and D. Hart, *Western Sunrise*, Allen & Unwin, 1987

2 Employment in high-technology industry (much of it skilled) provides incomes which are spent in the local economy on goods and services, boosting the local economy and increasing the demand for education, health and other services.

3 These links are strong in the case of high-technology industry because many of the workers are in professional, managerial and technical posts with high salaries and spending power.

4 As Berkshire has become known for its opportunities and attractive facilities, more firms have been drawn to the county and have located there. Some are high-technology firms, but others provide financial, scientific and managerial services, boosting service employment in Berkshire to higher levels.

?

1 Draw and label a diagram to represent these links within the system.

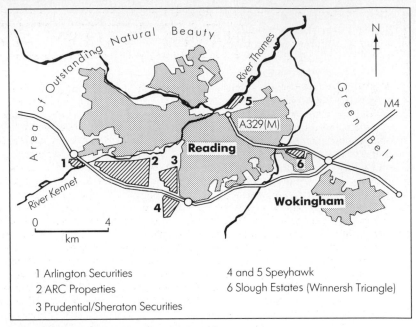

1 Arlington Securities
2 ARC Properties
3 Prudential/Sheraton Securities

4 and 5 Speyhawk
6 Slough Estates (Winnersh Triangle)

Figure 6 Business parks, existing and planned
Source: *Financial Times*, 22 February 1988

The business parks of Berkshire

To accommodate the growing demand for space, a number of new business parks have been planned in central Berkshire. Figure 6 shows the existing and planned parks in the Reading/Wokingham area.

Hemmed in between the Area of Outstanding Natural Beauty (AONB) on the west and the Green Belt on the east (where development is prohibited) these parks are providing the sites, buildings and environments needed by expanding industries.

Figure 7 shows the location and features of the newest business park. The Thames Valley Park (Number 5 on Figure 6) is being developed by Speyhawk on the site of an old power station.

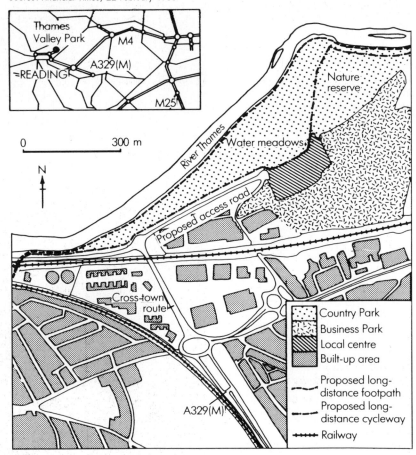

Figure 7 The location of Thames Valley Park
Source: *Reading Chronicle*, 22 June 1988

THAMES · VALLEY · PARK

TODAY, an opening ceremony marked the start of the Cross Town Route stage one.

As work begins on the first stage of the new road, so progress gets under way on the new business park in north Earley, Speyhawk's 'Thames Valley Park.'

Both the road and the park will bring great benefits to Reading. Here we tell you what the business park being built by Speyhawk has to offer not just to major companies but to local residents too.

Speyhawk have made a huge contribution to the cost of the first stage of the Cross Town Route, amounting to nearly £8 million out of a total cost of £10 million.

Time and money is being spent on making good use of the old Earley Power Station site. Speyhawk have recently received planning consent to construct a dual carriageway, 1,050,000 sq ft of B1 Business Use, a 150-bedroom hotel, a local centre and an Information Age Project (IAP) computer museum.

Of the 200-acre park, 80 acres fronting the Thames will exploit the natural advantages of the area and will be sanctioned as a Country Park and Nature Reserve, which will be open to the general public. An option has been given to the District Council to take it over after fifteen years.

The hotel will be situated in a prime location overlooking the Country Park and Thames, and will incorporate a leisure centre offering a variety of sports facilities both to the workforce and local residents.

Also included in the scheme is a proposal to establish Britain's first computer museum for which Berkshire County Council heads the steering committee, responsible for raising funds. Thames Valley Park Ltd have donated the land upon which the museum will be built.

Thames Valley Park is an ideal location for the high-technology industry to display to the world their latest 'state of the art' products and ideas for the future. The displays are to be designed to have a 'hands on' approach that should appeal to the thousands of children expected to visit the museum each year.

The Local Centre will comprise retail units and a food court to cater to both business and leisure visitors.

The direct access to the M4 and Reading town centre clearly enhances Thames Valley Park, and the recent sale to Digital demonstrates the requirements by businesses for ease of travelling and parking and a pleasant environment in which to work.

Faircloughs, the contractors chosen to carry out the work, start on site immediately, and are expected to have completed by Christmas next year.

Source: *Mid Week Chronicle*, 22 June 1988

?

1 Read the description of the Thames Valley Park. What are the locational advantages of this park for new industry?

2 What are the other environmental attractions of this business park?

3 The article has been written from a particular point of view. Write a letter to the paper pointing out this out and detailing some of the likely negative impacts of the so-called 'Park'.

A case study: The Winnersh Triangle
(Number 6 on Figure 6)

In 1985 Wimpey Construction UK wrote an account of their experience of developing the Winnersh Triangle Business Park (Figure 9).

Figure 8 Basingstoke Road business park, Reading

Once the 100-acre landscaped site was finished, Slough Estates, the developers, began to advertise its attractions.

?

---

1 What problems did Wimpey encounter and how were they overcome?

2 You are to head the development team of a firm looking for a site in the M4 corridor. Using the maps and publicity material on the Winnersh Triangle, write a report summarising the advantages of this location for your firm using these headings:

● Location and communication.
● Site, style and layout of buildings.
● Environmental quality, amenity and leisure facilities for your staff.

As you will have seen, Mars Electronics, a US-owned company, was one of the first arrivals at the Winnersh Triangle Business Park. It was founded in Slough, but expansion led the company to look for a new site 'down' the M4 motorway.

By 1988 Mars Electronics employed 750 people making coin-operated machines, marine radar sets and testing equipment for printed circuits. A large percentage of their output is exported, and in 1988 Mars Electronics won one of the 145 Queen's Awards for Industry as a result of its success as an exporting company.

Slough Estates are attracting more investment into the Winnersh Triangle, pointing to the presence of companies such as Mars Electronics, Hewlett Packard, Digital, AEG Telefunken and ICL. Other companies are likely to follow, strengthening the claim that the Winnersh Triangle is a proven business location in the UK.

Agglomerations of electronics companies and their associated services in business parks like those of central Berkshire are likely to become even more important to the UK economy in the

---

Rapid construction, total flexibility and very high levels of accommodation have been the basis of the work for the Southampton office of Wimpey Construction UK in the development of Winnersh Triangle.

The site was a marsh in 1980. But was identified by Wimpey as a promising location for a high-tech 'Sunrise' business park and, undeterred

HOW TECHNOLOGY IS SINKING ITS TEETH INTO SOMETHING WIMPEY FIRST SANK THEIR FEET INTO.

by the unfavourable site conditions, Wimpey went ahead with development. One kilometre of culverting and two kilometres of drainage pipes were needed to drain the 100 hectare site and 176,000 tonnes of sand fill to raise the surface level. On top of this, 150 mm of railway ballast capping was laid to provide a hard surface. The infrastructure was completed with the installation of main services and the construction of service roads. Four blocks of warehouse and office accommodation have been built. Block F, the most recently completed, was occupied by Mars Electronics in August 1983. The entire building was constructed and delivered in the fast-track time of just one year, the design period being concentrated from the usual nine months into four. Rapid construction was made possible using Wimpey's 'integroup project' system. Special techniques and high levels of co-operation between contractors allowed different stages of construction to proceed in parallel, saving time and money. The two-storey, pre-cast

concrete framed building, provides over 8,000 square metres of floor area, built and equipped to a very high standard. A key feature of the building is 5,000 square metres of 'computer floor', a special design of elevated flooring which allows large volumes of cabling to be accommodated under-floor, out of sight and out of harm's way, yet accessible for maintenance and extension. Other occupants of the site are Mars Money Systems, Knickerbocker, Clark and Eaton, Hewlett Packard Ltd. and the new European Headquarters for Modular Computer Services Incorporated.

The rapid conversion of an unpromising marsh into one of Britain's leading high-tech business parks has put Wimpey's capabilities to the most severe of tests. Wimpey Construction (Southampton) has used the latest techniques and systems in this demanding task. This demonstrates clearly that fast-track, high quality construction is what is needed in today's competitive business environments. Winnersh is just one major construction project carried out by the Southampton Office of Wimpey Construction UK which is responsible for all Wimpey contracts in an area stretching from Reading to the South Coast and from Wareham in the West to Newhaven in the East. Other major current contracts by this office include a superstore for Sainsbury in Brighton, major hospital extensions in Southampton, office developments in Basingstoke and various contracts for DOE/PSA.

Further information from:
JOHN HAMPSHIRE. MARKETING MANAGER.
WIMPEY CONSTRUCTION UK LIMITED.
HIGH STREET, WEST END.
SOUTHAMPTON SO3 3TT.
TEL: 0703 476711.

 **WIMPEY** CONSTRUCTION UK **WHERE THERE'S A WILL, THERE'S A WIMPEY**

Figure 9 Wimpey advertisement
Source: Royal County of Berkshire Planning Department, Berkshire *Industrial and Commercial Handbook*, 1985

1990s when the Channel Tunnel is opened, and the EEC becomes a single market with no trade barriers between the member states. With its prime location in southern England, it is likely that Berkshire and the M4 corridor will experience further development pressures during the 1990s.

Foster Wheeler

Foster Wheeler is an example of

a different type of development in central Berkshire. One of Britain's leading engineering companies, it was founded in 1920 to build refineries for the expanding oil industry. Its headquarters, now in central Reading opposite the mainline railway station, employs over 1,500 people.

Foster Wheeler's head office (Figure 10) moved from London to Reading in 1974, so like Mars Electronics it is one of the many

Royal award for export success

WINNERSH-BASED Mars Electronics are breathing the sweet smell of success having won one of the 145 Queen's Awards for Export and Technology for 1988.

The company, related to the American-owned confectionery firm, is the winner of an award for export achievement having sold its electronic equipment all over the globe.

This is the second such award for the company, which employs 750 people at its Winnersh Triangle headquarters and is the world leader in coin-handling technology.

The firm's speciality is the design and manufacture of coin and card payment systems for snack and drink vending machines, payphones, ticket dispensers and many other applications.

Over the past three years Mars Electronics has nearly doubled sales of over £40 million and has increased its exports, which are now more than half of all sales, by 250 per cent.

Export sales are mainly in Europe, North Africa and, increasingly, to the Far East and Pacific, where last year saw the first major orders in New Zealand, Singapore and Taiwan.

Following orders from London Transport for new ticketing machines, Mars Electronics has now sold ticketing systems to the Koreans for this year's Seoul Olympics, to the Madrid Underground and the French State Lottery.

Last year saw the 125,000th coin mechanism shipped to Spain. New Italian payphones incorporate the company's coin-sensing electronics and the Norwegians buy their bingo cards using a Mars Electronics card system.

In Holland, the company has installed a cashless payment system at Schiphol Airport and the Justice and Interior Ministry.

The Queen's Awards for Export Achievement are awarded for 'substantial and sustained' increases in export earnings.

Source: Reading Chronicle, 22 April 1988

Figure 10 UK headquarters of Foster Wheeler Engineering Ltd, Reading

Rejected plans

Sometimes even giant multinational firms find that their expansion plans are rejected by planning authorities. For example, Digital decided to move their UK headquarters from central Reading to a new 33-acre site in the Speyhawk Thames Valley Business Park (Figure 11).

The company submitted plans for a £35 million development to the local council, but the proposed design of the five flat-topped low-roofed buildings was not acceptable.

firms that moved west into the Reading area. Foster Wheeler chose their location in relation to the mainline railway station on a site which gave good access to Heathrow Airport (30 minutes away) and the South Coast.

From Reading the firm manages its worldwide operations in designing and constructing oil refineries, petrochemical, steel, fertiliser, pharmaceutical and other processing plants. The Reading headquarters covers the marketing, financial, commercial and personnel aspects of the company's operations. It employs engineers, designers, drawing office and construction staff as well as commercial, financial and office personnel.

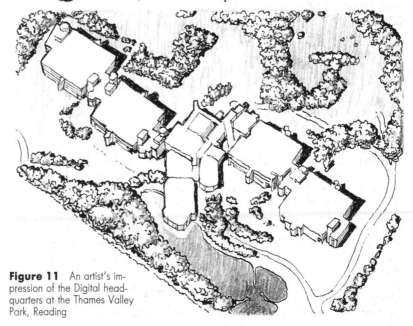

Figure 11 An artist's impression of the Digital headquarters at the Thames Valley Park, Reading

?

Read the article 'Industry giants to appeal in HQ fight' and the other clippings provided.

1 How did Digital react to the council's refusal to grant planning permission?

2 If a large company considered relocating in another region or another country as a result of planning permission obstacles, what factors would it have to take into account?

3 What would be the effects on the region it leaves?

4 In groups of three or four, describe the characters you would put into a role play on the Digital affair. Write role descriptions for each character based on the newspaper cuttings provided. Compare your characters and their descriptions with other groups in the class. Think about the differences which become apparent.

5 Write under examination conditions an account of the Digital affair in a balanced and reasoned manner. In the final paragraph state what your decision would have been if it had been up to you. Explain your decision.

These case studies have revealed some of the reasons for the remarkable growth of high-technology and related industries in the Berkshire section of the M4 corridor:

- The close proximity of Heathrow Airport.

- Access to London and other markets in the UK via the well-developed rail and road system.

- The presence of a large and suitably skilled workforce – an attraction for firms moving out of London and for those arriving from abroad.

- The provision of suitable sites and accommodation for business and commercial activities.

- The environmental quality of the area.

Firm angered by rejection of £35m plan

Industry giants to appeal in HQ fight

COMPUTER giant Digital will appeal against a town hall block on its new UK headquarters.

The company claims Wokingham District Council's suggestion that it has not listened to ideas for improving the building's design is 'absolute rubbish'.

Digital wants to construct its new-look 500,000 sq ft office with a 2,000 space car park at Thames Valley Park between Earley and Sonning.

But on Monday night Wokingham's planning committee refused to allow the £35 million development because it does not like the proposed buildings.

Disappointed

Vice-chairman Rosemary Hudson pointed out the committee is not against Digital using the land.

She said: 'We would like Digital to move on to the site very much indeed, but not in those buildings.'

Digital's estates manager Graham Roberts said: 'We are extremely disappointed by this decision, which was made by the planning committee despite positive comments expressed by the Royal Fine Art Commission.'

The Commission, set up by the Queen and the Prime Minister to advise on matters of taste and aesthetics, told the planning committee it was not against the buildings.

Listened

But it advised the council to control the materials used.

Mr Roberts said: 'We now plan to appeal to the Secretary of State for the Environment against this decision, but it will be a long process.'

He added: 'I think it is absolute rubbish to say we haven't been listening to them.

'We can show in cost and physical terms that we have actually listened to what they said.'

He said Digital is prepared to make changes costing £2 million in a bid to please the council.

Digital has been in Reading since 1964 and Mr Roberts said it wanted to remain in the area.

He said: 'It would be a terrible disappointment to have to move out of Berkshire after all this time and I don't think it will be necessary.'

Source: David Nicolle, *Reading Evening Post*, 8 February 1989

HIGH-TECH GIANT MAY QUIT TOWN

PLANNERS who rejected a scheme by computer giant Digital for a massive new multi-million pound headquarters near Reading will not be 'bullied' into submission, a councillor has warned.

Now the company, which employs thousands of people, has warned it may have to move out of the area after failing to win planning permission for the huge development from Wokingham District Council.

But Councillor Margaret Gimblett, a member of the committee that opposed the scheme, has vowed not to bow to pressure from the American-owned giant.

And Wokingham MP John Redwood has also come out in support of the council decision.

Councillor Gimblett said: 'It is easy to keep people happy by making a quick and easy decision, and being bullied about the possible loss of employment.

'But we expect these buildings to be on the site for a long time and we have a responsibility to do the right thing for the public at large.'

The Reading-based multinational aims to build a new £100 million UK headquarters with 500,000 sq ft of offices and 2,000 car parking spaces at Thames Valley Park.

Planners turned Digital's application down because they did not like the design of the proposed development and car parking layout. Councillor Gimblett said they were trying to preserve the country environment and the Digital designs did not fit in.

She added: 'We are in a difficult position. We want to see industry prosper but we have an absolute duty to protect the environment.' She hopes Digital will now come up with an improved design to reach a compromise with the council.

Mr Redwood welcomed the council decision in the face of criticism and said it should 'stand up for architectural and aesthetic standards' despite commercial interests. Digital spokesman Alan Smith said: 'We are not out to threaten the council. We have to work with them if we are going to stay here. But we have bent over backwards and spent £2 million to accommodate their requirements and still haven't found any common ground.'

Source: Steve Marshall, *Reading Evening Post*,

Defence spending

Recent research has drawn attention to another important set of factors, namely the benefits that local economies have derived from defence spending and the impact of the increasing proportion of defence spending in high-technology aerospace and electronics industries. These industries are well represented in the high-technology activities of Berkshire and the eastern section of the M4 corridor. Companies receiving these payments are likely to produce large multiplier effects in their local economies. This means that the high-technology companies create employment on their own premises and in other firms which supply them with goods and services. This expansion of employment creates more purchasing power, which in turn generates further employment in other firms.

?

1 Study Table 2 and comment on the regional distribution of defence spending in the UK, including the changes during 1977–8 and 1983–4.

Table 2 Defence expenditure

Region	Expenditure £	1977–8 per cent	Expenditure £	1983–4 per cent
South-East	1,175.6	41.6	3,747.1	54.0
South-West	410.2	14.5	763.3	11.0
East Anglia	111.7	3.9	208.2	3.0
East Midlands	213.2	7.5	346.9	5.0
West Midlands	189.2	6.7	277.6	4.0
North-West	242.8	8.6	763.3	11.0
Yorks/Humber	61.9	2.2	138.8	2.0
Northern	174.2	6.2	138.8	2.0
Scotland	195.0	6.9	416.3	6.0
Wales	25.6	0.9	69.4	1.0
N. Ireland	27.9	0.9	69.4	1.0
Totals	**2,827.3**	**100.0**	**6,939.0**	**100.0**

Source: P. Hall et al, *Western Sunrise*, Allen & Unwin, 1987, p. 131

Defence and the Great Divide

WESTLAND and Nimrod did more than demonstrate the importance of defence spending to Britain's industrial base. They also illustrated how much defence expenditure now contributes to the prosperity of the south of England – and thus, it might be inferred, to the electoral prospects of the Conservative Party.

No one can doubt the enormous significance of defence spending in Britain's economy in the 1980s. Between 1978/79 and 1984/85 Mrs Thatcher increased defence expenditure by 29 per cent, while other public expenditure programmes, including the universities and civil R&D programmes, were being cut back. Currently half of government R&D spending goes to defence, and this proportion, which is already higher than in any other West European country, is planned to rise to 54 per cent by 1989.

According to Mr George Younger, the Defence Secretary, his current £8 billion procurement budget accounts for half of the output of the aerospace industry, and 20 per cent of the output of the electronics industry. An enormous number of jobs are therefore supported directly or indirectly by the defence budget.

As an increasing number of research studies are showing, this growing area of public expenditure has been a major factor in the prosperity of the south of England. The first indications of its importance came in regional accounts for 1977/78 prepared by John Short. Mr Short found that in that year 56 per cent of defence expenditure was taking place in just two regions: the South-East and the South-West.

Recently, geographer Michael Breheny of the University of Reading has obtained Ministry of Defence estimates which support Mr Short's calculations. As Table 3 shows, these suggest that in 1983–84 no less than 68 per cent

of defence spending occurred in the south.

As Mr Breheny pointed out, delivering his paper at last year's British Association Conference: 'The South-East and South-West are not only receiving the largest government payments to industry; they are also receiving these payments to those very companies – in electronics and aerospace – who are likely to produce the greatest spin-offs to the local economies.' Regional aid is dwarfed by the scale of defence expenditure.

In 1977–78 (the last year for which suitable information is available) the northern region received £142 million in regional aid and won defence contracts worth £174 million. But the South-East, which of course received no regional aid, benefited from defence contracts worth £1,175 million.

Table 3 Regional defence expenditure 1983/84

	Expenditure (£M)	% of total
South-East	3,747	54
South-West	763	11
East Anglia	208	3
East Midlands	346	5
West Midlands	278	4
North-West	763	11
Yorks/Humberside	139	2
Northern	139	2
Scotland	416	6
Wales	69	1
N. Ireland	69	1
Totals	**6,939**	**100**

At present nearly 300,000 out of 420,000 service personnel live in the south. Much of the MoD's 600,000 acres is also south of a line between the Severn and the Wash. A survey carried out for Mr Heseltine by a firm of chartered surveyors in 1985 estimated that the larger southern

bases alone had a market value of between £600 million and £700 million.

In response to Mr Heseltine, who was anxious to move the military bases north, service chiefs were said to have argued that there were sound strategic reasons for being based in the south. The RAF, for example, argued that its bases must be in the south to meet the Soviet threat, while the Navy is historically southern based.

But the main explanation seems to be simple inertia. Why else is the Navy's admiralty ships division in Bath, which is not even a port?

Inertia is also the main explanation for the concentration of military industries in the south. In the early 1950s, another period of high defence expenditure, government spending on atomic weapons and military electronics grew fast. Much of the basic research was carried out by the Defence Research Establishments (DREs) like Aldermaston.

Gradually the DREs contracted out both research and production to the private sector. But the nature of the procurement process meant that contractors and subcontractors needed to be located close to a DRE or some other MoD contact point. Defence procurement in the UK has involved detailed and regular negotiation with the contractors and extensive lobbying. Indeed, it is said that MoD officials have advised companies that it would be unwise to locate too far from these contact points. And 23 of the 24 official contact points are located in the south of England.

The effect of all this is clear enough: whether by accident or by design the south's economy is now heavily subsidised by military spending. Set against this, the effects of regional aid – which is planned to fall from £842 million in 1978–79 to only £400 million by 1987–88 – pale into insignificance.

Source: Ian Wray, *Guardian*, 23 April 1987

2a Read the article 'Defence and the Great Divide'. Set out a series of headings which give the message of each paragraph. Your first heading might, for instance, be 'Defence expenditure brings prosperity to the South-East'.

b Now read the paragraph above which lists some of the reasons for the growth of the M4 corridor. What additional reason for growth would you now add?

Profound changes

The last twenty years have brought profound changes to the industrial geography of Berkshire and to the lives of people living in the county. These changes have had a marked effect on the Reading area, where nineteenth-century growth was based on 'beer, biscuits and bulbs'. Now only the beer remains: Sutton's Seeds moved to Torquay in 1976 and Huntley and Palmer's closed their biscuit-making operations in Reading in 1977 (Figure 12). Table 1 (page 383) shows large decreases in the percentage of

employees in agriculture and food production in Berkshire between 1971 and 1981.

In the 1980s these traditional forms of employment have been replaced by high-technology related activities, with jobs spread across small companies as well as large ones. Berkshire has become one of the fastest-developing counties, but with this new prosperity have come pressing problems: shortages of land for houses, shortages of skilled people and serious traffic congestion. In these respects, Berkshire is now the victim of its own success.

Figure 12 Huntley and Palmer's biscuit factory, and Sutton's Seeds in Reading

The issues of living with success

1 Before reading the rest of this chapter, brainstorm in groups and make a list of the likely consequences for Berkshire of recent developments.

The high economic growth rates in Berkshire have led to questions about the ability of this section of the M4 corridor to cope with the increasing pressure for land and infrastructure, and concern about the effects of development on the quality of life in the area.

Towns and villages have expanded into the surrounding countryside in the search for new 'greenfield' sites for industry and warehousing, offices, shops and housing. These sites are restricted because development is prohibited in 60% of Berkshire. Western Berkshire is an Area of Outstanding Natural Beauty and eastern Berkshire is in the Green Belt (Figure 14 on page 392).

Expansion is therefore confined to the areas around Bracknell, Wokingham, Reading and

Newbury (Figure 13).

In these areas development adds to the existing noise levels, traffic congestion and pollution. By the late 1980s firms were finding it difficult to recruit skilled workers.

This section of the chapter looks at the ways in which these pressures have affected housing, skilled labour and traffic congestion and examines some of the responses to these issues.

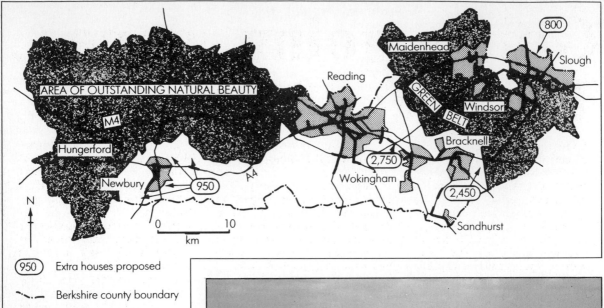

AREA OF OUTSTANDING NATURAL BEAUTY

M4

Hungerford

Newbury

950

A4

Reading

Wokingham

2,750

Maidenhead

GREEN BELT

Windsor

Slough

800

Bracknell

2,450

Sandhurst

N

0 10
km

950 Extra houses proposed

∿·∿ Berkshire county boundary

━━━ Congested roads

⌒ Roads

Figure 13 Planned housing development in Berkshire
Source: Berkshire County Council Structure plan and Mr Ridley's comments

Housing

Between 1951 and 1981 the population of Berkshire increased by nearly 70% and the housing stock doubled. Since 1976 the county's population has increased by 6.3% compared with 0.4% in the South-East region as a whole.

The movement of firms into the county and the expansion of employment in high-technology industry and its related activities has been responsible for much of this growth. In 1988 the OPCS (Office of Population Censuses and Surveys) forecast that by 2001 Berkshire's population will rise by another 90,000 to 814,000, a prediction regarded as 'horrific' by NORPAG (Northern Parishes Action Group), a group representing those parishes north of Bracknell already earmarked for further housing development. Their spokesman said, 'Central

Figure 14 Lough Down, near Streatley, western Berkshire

Berkshire cannot handle any more people. We can't possibly have 90,000 more. Where are we going to put them? We are already nearly full up. How will the roads and hospitals cope? We will end up as one vast urban conurbation. It is a horrific thought.'

House prices

The people who work in Berkshire's new industries and services want to live near their work, so this pressure has increased the demand for land and pushed up house prices. In 1983

it was possible to buy a house in Reading for £20,000. By March 1988 the cheapest terraced house in Reading was priced at £50,000, with three-bedroom semi-detached houses from £90,000 to £100,000. In the more rural areas, family houses with four or five bedrooms could cost as much as £300,000. In the spring of 1988 house prices in Berkshire were 70% above the national average and the average price of a detached house was £132,000. Prices fell in 1989 and 1990, but they are still be well above the national average.

Going, going, gone...
The £50,000 barrier

Estate agents no longer expect to be able to offer properties below this. Yet only five years ago, you could still buy a property in Reading for under £20,000.

And, our poll also suggests, there is little if any difference in basic property prices between the traditionally 'cheaper' areas to the west of the Thames Valley and those of houses in and around Reading – and that Newbury may be becoming the costliest of all.

Graham Hallett, who has recently opened his own estate agency, Halletts, in Thatcham, and was recently with Parkers of Caversham, said: 'It is no cheaper round here than in Reading, and to think otherwise is a myth.

'Anyone wanting to come and live here for no other reason than that they think they can get something at a lower price is in for disillusionment.'

The cheapest home currently on the books of Halletts is a two-bedroom property at £60,000. In the last few days, Halletts have sold a one-bedroom property at £51,250.

'Obviously, this kind of property sells instantly,' said Mr Hallett, who added that in Thatcham, you would expect to have to pay £75,000 for a good semi, and that the real price difference is not between Thatcham and Reading, but between Newbury and elsewhere.

'Newbury has become quite a pricey area. I would say that good semis there cost quite a bit more, maybe £85,000 or £90,000. It is a desirable place to live, now that it has come second in the national property ratings.'

At Robinson and Company in Winnersh, the cheapest property currently on their books is £61,500, for a one-bedroom starter home that is one year old.

The cheapest property they have recently handled was a studio apartment in Twyford at £48,500: 'But anything like this is a complete one-off. We do not really expect to handle anything under the £50,000 mark now.'

At Robinson and Company in Lower Earley, where young couples flock to begin married life in the cheapest homes in the area, prices too are shooting up, ready to smash the £50,000 barrier.

A starter home which three years ago was around £21,000, is now selling for £49,000. Of the starter homes at Lower Earley, there is a price difference of around £2,000 between a Pye and a Barratt. The former commands the higher price because it has a built in double bed and a garden.

Anyone wanting a little more room than that afforded by a studio starter unit which is basically one room, bathroom or shower room and kitchen, has to pay more. A maisonette with one bedroom is around £52,000, and a one-bedroom house is anything up to £58,000 at Lower Earley.

Needless to say, all such starter homes coming on to the market are sold so quickly that often the agents barely have time to draw up the particulars. And the outlook? 'Prices are going up and up. We have never had such a busy start to the year as this one,' they told us at Robinson's.

It was the same story in Bracknell, where Parker's estate agents said that the cheapest property on their books was a £56,500 one-bedroom flat on a first floor.

In Reading town centre, Whiteknights estate agents came up with a £43,950 studio property on the ground floor, with a lounge/bedroom, kitchen and bathroom.

'However, most properties for first-time buyers are around the £55,000 mark,' said Mr John Pundek of Whiteknights, who said that prices are being stimulated by several factors.

'Mostly, it's the sheer number of people coming to the South-East of England to live. Of first-time properties we sell, three out of ten go to people moving here from the north. But the trouble is that there aren't three people already here going the other way, and the result is a shortage of properties and a lot of buyers.

'Property prices are related to salaries. There would have to be extreme conditions before house prices came down. In fact, they would only do so if salaries came down too, and I can't see that.'

?

Read the article by Jane Howard.

1 How do you explain the high cost of housing in Berkshire?

2 What problems are firms and other employers likely to encounter when they try to recruit labour?

3 Who gains and who loses from these high house prices?

Source: Jane Howard, *Property Week*, No. 91, 5 March 1988

Houses for the future – the great debate

In order to cope with the increasing demand, about 5,000 houses have been built in Berkshire since the late 1970s. In the mid-1980s some important changes affected housing policies in the county.

The County Council, concerned about the impacts of the rapid growth of population and businesses, decided to reduce the rate of new house construction to 1,600 each year in the 1990s. County planners thought that this was the maximum that should be allowed.

This target had to be sent to Mr Nicholas Ridley, the then Secretary of State for the Environment, for approval. He decided that the County Council's figure was too low and that 3,000 houses would be required each year to satisfy the future demands for housing in Berkshire. This meant that by 1996 Berkshire would have to find room for 7,000 more houses than it wished.

At the same time Mr Ridley limited the number of reasons that planners could give for turning down applications for the development of out-of-town shopping centres.

Study Figure 13 on page 392. Which areas of Berkshire were chosen for these 'extra' houses? How do you explain their distribution?

Reactions to Mr Ridley's proposals

The Minister's proposals for Berkshire unleashed furious opposition on three main grounds:

1 They would worsen the existing traffic congestion problems.

2 The built-up areas of Reading would be extended south of the M4 motorway into green field areas around the villages of Three

Figure 15 New housing estate, Lower Earley, Berkshire

Mile Cross, Spencers Wood and Swallowfield.

3 There would be a zone of continuous urban development across central Berkshire from Reading to Bracknell.

In February and March of 1988 there was a period of six weeks for comments and objections to the Minister's proposals. The objections fell into three main groups:

The County Council

1 Read the article 'A bitter reaction' on page 396. Write a paragraph on the ways in which the Tory, Labour and Alliance spokesmen emphasise different aspects of the issue.

2 Study the County Council's leaflet 'Planning Berkshire, your chance to comment', and the form for objecting to the proposals (Figure 16). Respond as if you were *either* someone who wishes to use the form to make objections *or* someone who supports the proposals and writes to Mr Ridley to that effect.

Department of the Environment

PART 1

1 Name and address _____
(block letters)

_____

_____ Postcode _____

Telephone _____ (Other) _____

2 Title of structure plan proposals _____

_____

PART 2

State here the number of the proposed modification to which you object:

_____

PART 3

State here the full grounds on which your objection is made. The clearer and more complete your statement, the less likely will be the need to ask you for more information.

Figure 16 Form DP 101, Department of the Environment

Figure 17 Planning Berkshire leaflet
Source: Department of Highways and Planning, Berkshire County Council

SECRETARY of STATE ANNOUNCES CHANGES TO THE BERKSHIRE STRUCTURE PLAN

7000 MORE HOUSES

Berkshire County Council's plans for slowing down the rate of housebuilding in the County have been rejected by the Secretary of State for the Environment. He considers that the reduction in housebuilding rates proposed by the County Council goes too far and could lead to local housing needs not being met and damage to the local economy.

Consequently land for an additional 7000 houses will need to be released. This will increase the number of houses to be built in Berkshire between 1984 and 1996 from 36,500 to 43,500.

These changes are included in the Proposed Modifications to the Draft Replacement Structure Plan.

THIS LEAFLET SUMMARISES THE MAIN POINTS OF THE PROPOSED MODIFICATIONS

HOUSEBUILDING RATES

The additional housing is proposed to maintain an average housebuilding rate of 3000 houses a year between 1991 and 1996

- this is 1900 houses a year lower than the past average rate
- but 1400 houses a year greater than the Council's proposals.

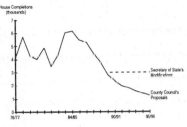

The additional houses will increase the strain on public services including those provided by the County and District Councils, and organisations such as the Health Authorities, at a time when public expenditure is restrained.

LOCATIONS FOR DEVELOPMENT

- 950 houses in the Newbury-Thatcham area
- 2750 houses in Wokingham District including to the south of the M4 at Reading
- 2450 houses in Bracknell District including to the north and north east of Bracknell
- 800 houses in Slough

The increase in houses is contrary to the views expressed during two rounds of public consultation on the draft plan.

PAYING FOR DEVELOPMENT

The Council's ability to ensure that adequate contributions are obtained from private developers for the infrastructure, services and facilities made necessary by their development has been greatly restricted.

In the present financial climate, unless additional funds are forthcoming from Central Government or from private developers, conditions in Berkshire will deteriorate.

EMPLOYMENT

No change is proposed to the overall amount of employment generating development but policies which aim to control the pace of development and the size of sites have been dropped.

The Plan has not been modified to reflect the change in legislation which has done away with the distinction between offices and light industry.

The removal of controls could lead to a fast rate of development in the early years and pressures to exceed the overall level of provisions. Additional confusion and uncertainty has been created by not changing the policies in the light of new legislation.

SHOPPING

Restriction on the overall amount of shopping floorspace and the pace of development have been removed.

This could lead to an excessive amount of new floorspace being permitted which could undermine existing centres.

TRANSPORT

The Secretary of State has recognised existing transport problems in the area, particularly in Reading, and has supported the Council's strategy for dealing with them.

However, unless additional funds are made available, and the amount and pace of development is controlled, traffic conditions will deteriorate still further.

THE ENVIRONMENT

The Secretary of State supports strong restraint on development in

- the Green Belt
- the Area of Outstanding Natural Beauty
- important gaps between settlements.

This is welcomed but strong policies are also required in the remainder of the County.

WHERE TO SEE THE PROPOSED MODIFICATIONS

The Secretary of State's Proposed Modifications to the Structure Plan, and the Report of the Panel on which they are based, can be seen at the following Council offices:

Dept. of Highways and Planning, Shire Hall, Shinfield Park, READING
Newbury District Council, Market Street, NEWBURY
Reading Borough Council, Civic Offices, READING
Wokingham District Council, Shute End, WOKINGHAM
Bracknell District Council, Easthampstead House, BRACKNELL
R.B. Windsor and Maidenhead, Aston House, MAIDENHEAD
R.B. Windsor and Maidenhead, York House, WINDSOR
Slough Borough Council, Town Hall, Bath Road, SLOUGH

Copies of the documents may also be seen at public libraries throughout the County.

MAKE YOUR VIEWS KNOWN

This leaflet has summarised the main changes to the Structure Plan. It is important, whether you object to these proposals, or support them, that you make your views known to the Secretary of State. Please use the forms available at the offices listed above.

Please send your comments, to:

Department of the Environment
South East Regional Office
Room 501
Charles House
375 Kensington High Street
LONDON W14 8QH

CLOSING DATE FOR COMMENTS
31st March 1988

Designed by Department of Highways and Planning, Berkshire County Council
Shire Hall, Shinfield Park, READING RG2 9XG

A bitter reaction

The leader of Conservative controlled Berkshire County Council, Mr Ron Jewitt, said the Secretary of State's modifications would place a 'tremendous burden' on the whole of the county and the central area in particular.

'As Berkshire has taken more than its fair share of development in the South-East over the last few years the county council had hoped to scale down growth – particularly in house building – by the mid 1990s to a level which would allow the infrastructure, roads, schools and public transport, to catch up whilst at the same time preserving the environment of our towns and countryside.

'The county council recognises the need to continue to play a role in the economic recovery but did not wish Berkshire to become the victim of its own success,' he said.

Alliance leader at Shire Hall John Leston said: 'The rape of Berkshire is set to continue now Mr Ridley has decided to take more notice of the housebuilders' public relations agencies than the clearly expressed wishes of the people of Berkshire.'

He added that the Alliance is particularly alarmed by the Department of Environment statement that any land in the county which is not Green Belt or an Area of Outstanding Natural Beauty may come under consideration for development.

Labour leader on the council, Lawrence Silverman, said the government's support for 'get-rich-quick developers' was one reason why an extra 7,000 houses were planned which local people would be unable to afford.

'Just as important is the local Tories' couldn't-care-less attitude to the new generation of Berkshire people who are looking in vain for homes they can afford. The Tories have made a complete mess of things.'

Leader of Conservative-controlled Wokingham District Council, Iain Brown said: 'My concern is that the Secretary of State has not recognised the enormous growth that has occurred within the district in the last ten years, and the pressure this places on the countryside, already congested roads, and the provision of an adequate level of public services.

'I know that I speak for everybody in the community when I say that what the district most needed was a period to assimilate the recent growth. The obvious opportunity for catching up with the provision of services and facilities seems to have been ignored.'

Wokingham MP John Redwood said he would be asking for an adjournment debate so that he and other Berkshire MPs could have the opportunity to question the Minister about his proposed changes: 'I am extremely angry about these proposals. I don't believe that central Berkshire can cope with the extra houses easily,' he said.

He added that he thought it was unlikely that the Minister would change his mind at this stage but the Berkshire MPs would 'leave no stone unturned'.

Source: Reading Chronicle, 5 February 1988

The CPRE (Council for the Protection of Rural England)

?

1 What points did the CPRE make in its objections? (Figure 18)

Pressure groups set up in the villages and rural areas earmarked for more houses under the Minister's proposals

A good example of such a group is NORPAG, the Northern Parishes Action Group. Representing residents in the parishes north of Bracknell (Winkfield, Warfield and Binfield), areas earmarked for another 2,500 houses, this action group launched a bitter attack on the proposals, a reaction parallelled in the other Berkshire villages affected by the proposals (Figure 19).

NORPAG pointed out that the new houses would:

- fill in the green spaces between villages with new estates

- increase the pressure on roads which cannot cope with existing traffic

- destroy the strong sense of community in the area and the settlement pattern which dates back to Saxon times

- place further additional strains on schools and hospitals

- provide housing at £100,000 to £200,000 which could not be afforded by local people.

The group's case was covered by Panorama on BBC TV and a mass lobby of Parliament was organised. Its arguments were taken up by local Conservative MPs who organised a debate in the House of Commons to show that the government's proposals would cause havoc on the county's roads, damage the environment of villages and market towns and produce an urban sprawl across Berkshire.

The object of all this activity was to get the Minister to change his mind. However, he did receive some support.

Figure 18 Council for the Protection of Rural England leaflet ▶

OBITUARIES

Thousands of acres of Berkshire's beautiful countryside are due to be sentenced to death, buried under tons of concrete.

They will be sadly missed.

HELEN HARRIS

Don't let part of our national heritage be *written off* like this.

Berkshire's countryside is now threatened on three fronts. 43,500 new houses in central Berkshire. A proposed huge shopping complex in the Green Belt at Wraysbury. The Newbury By-Pass.

Unless we act now, yet more of Berkshire's finest scenery will be decimated to make way for these developments and another piece of our national heritage will be lost forever.

Why the death threat *must* be stopped.

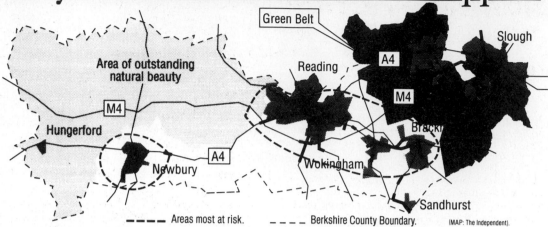

Green Belt

Slough

Area of outstanding natural beauty

Reading

A4

M4

Bracki

M4

Hungerford

A4

Wokingham

Newbury

Sandhurst

- - - - Areas most at risk.   - - - Berkshire County Boundary.   (MAP: The Independent).

The writing is on the wall for some of Berkshire's finest scenery.

An extra 7,000 new houses, 20% more than originally planned, are now threatening to engulf the rural areas of Berkshire, along with a by-pass and a massive new shopping complex.

If we stand by and allow these proposals to go ahead, a dangerous precedent will have been set and further areas of precious countryside could well be doomed.

We at the CPRE are committed to protecting the countryside for future generations and are fighting a hard campaign to reverse these proposals.

But we can't do it alone.

If we are going to make the Secretary of State see sense, we have to make him aware of the full force of public feeling.

We already have many top celebrities behind us, but we desperately need your help and support too.

That's why we're asking you to sign this leaflet and send as much as you can afford in support of CPRE's campaign to help keep Berkshire looking just the way it should. Beautiful.

CPRE
Council for the
Protection of Rural England

✂ -

We the undersigned call upon the Government to think again about their plans and to pledge themselves to keep Berkshire beautiful.

Tim Brooke-Taylor   Julian Pettifer   Peter de Savary   Ernie Wise   The Hon. Gordon Palmer

Sir Michael Hordern   Fred Winter   Wendy Craig   Robert Hardy C.B.E.

George Harrison M.B.E.   Olivia Harrison   Jenny Hanley   Terry Wogan

Name_____

Address_____

_____

_____Postcode_____

Signed_____

Signed_____

I/We enclose a donation to CPRE's "Keep Berkshire Beautiful" Campaign Appeal.

£100 ☐   £50 ☐   £25 ☐   £10 ☐   Other £_____
Please tick appropriate box. Please make cheques payable to CPRE.

CPRE, FREEPOST, LONDON SW1W 0BR. Tel: 01-235 9481.

F G

NORPAG Northern Parishes **Action** Group

Dear Householder,   Feb. 1988

<u>Mass Lobby of Parliament</u>

As you probably know, at the end of
January 1988 the Secretary of State
published his proposed modifications to
the Berkshire Structure Plan.

They are disastrous. He has added
7,000 extra houses to Berkshire, 4,000 of
which (representing a town the size of
Henley-on-Thames) are coming to Winkfield,
Warfield and Binfield.

* He has ignored our MPs, the County
Council, the District Councils and the
Parish Councils; and he has ignored your
own direct pleas, made in petitions and
objections over the past three years.

* Instead he has published a Developers'
Charter for Ridleyville. He has minimised
all the normal restraints and extra costs
which help keep developments in check.
The developers can do virtually what they
like.

We have until 31 March 1988 to voice
our objections. We ask for your help for
the last time. In the past you have
responded magnificently, showering our MP
and the County and District with more
objections than they had ever received
before.

We ask for your support again by:

1. <u>Joining our Lobby of Parliament on
Wednesday 16 March 1988 at 1 p.m.</u>
The more peopel who come, the more power
is given to our MPs and to the local
Peers who also support us. Our anger
must be seen this one and last time. If
you can bring a banner or poster, please
do so.

2. <u>Completing the attached Form of
Objection</u>, stating your views in the
strongest terms. You may well have your
own objections, but the following
suggestions may help:

<u>Part 2 of the Form</u>: Modifications 1, 19,
23 and 34

<u>Part 3 of the Form</u>: Mod. 1 adds 7,000
extra houses; Mod. 19 - major office
development will be allowed; Mod. 23 -
will cause traffic jams; Mod. 34 - the
countryside might be built upon.

Figure 19   NORPAG campaign leaflet

?

1   Read the article 'Berks bosses back
Minister on homes' (page 400). Why
did the Berkshire Business Group support
the Minister's proposals? How did they
view the issue of environmental quality?

Developers reacted quickly to
Mr Ridley's proposals. For example, by late March 1988, in response to the Minister's plans to
allow houses in greenfield sites
south of Reading, developers had
set out plans for 2,750 houses on
350 acres around the villages of
Three Mile Cross and Spencers
Wood. This settlement would be a
dormitory suburb for existing and
new employment centres in
Reading and Bracknell.

As in the case of NORPAG,
local residents reacted against
these proposals, joining the
county-wide chorus of protests
against them.

Mr Ridley's decision

There was a great deal of speculation about the way in which Mr
Ridley would react to the views
expressed. In November 1988 he
announced his verdict.

He no longer insisted that
2,750 new houses should be built
south of the M4 motorway. This
was heralded as a great victory for
the protestors who had challenged
his earlier plan for the future of
this rural area.

He confirmed that the area
around Bracknell should take
another 2,500 houses and that the
extra houses planned for Newbury and Slough should be retained in the plans. This decision was
greeted with dismay and disappointment in those areas. The
NORPAG action group had won
its fight to prevent development
north of Bracknell but the
Minister was still insisting on

43,500 new houses in Berkshire
by 1996.

1   Read the article 'Council split on
Ridley decision' (page 400). How did
the various groups in the county council
react to Mr Ridley's final decision?

Call for action on roads

Berks bosses back Minister on homes

The Berkshire Business Group has requested an urgent meeting with the Environment Secretary, Nicholas Ridley, to discuss the transport problems of Berkshire.

In the meantime the group is giving its backing to the Minister's proposed modifications to the county council's structure plan, in recognition of the buoyancy of Berkshire's economy and its strategic location within the emerging single European market.

The group represents business in Berkshire and consults with Berkshire County Council on its policies affecting businesses in Berkshire. The Newbury Chamber of Commerce is one of the organisations represented on the group.

Mr Peter Gibson, chairman of the group, said: 'The structure plan rightly encourages continued employment growth, but nevertheless reduces the rate of housing expansion of the last decade by some 39 per cent down to the realistic and justifiable levels proposed by the Secretary of State over the next ten years.'

However, the business group would not wish housing provision to drop below that proposed by the Minister. 'Otherwise,' said Mr Gibson, 'local people's housing needs will not be met, and the county's economy and prosperity will be held back. A balanced approach to planning is essential and it is vital that new housing keeps pace with new employment.

'Equally, a proper balance between housing development and the provision of roads and other services, is essential. Serious traffic problems already exist in the county, worsened because transport infrastructure has lagged so far behind other developments. This is already discouraging some companies from expanding or locating in Berkshire.

'We share the county council's concern about finance for new road schemes,' said Mr Gibson. 'That is why we are seeking an early meeting with Mr Ridley, and why we will be consulting even more closely with the county council.'

'The business group is prepared to campaign to make sure Berkshire can develop its economic potential without harming its environment.'

Mr Gibson went on: 'The group recognises that much will depend on how expansion is planned in each area, and the timing of supporting infrastructure. The investment in roads, etc., must come with, or preferably before the houses are built.

'We want to help the dialogue between central and local government, and show the willingness of the business community to help secure adequate financial investment in the county's transport systems,' said Mr Gibson.

Source: Newbury Business Review, 31 March 1988

Council split on Ridley decision

THE Government has railroaded the county council, stuck to its guns, and opened the doors to the over-development of Berkshire, Opposition leaders claim.

But ruling Tories at Shire Hall insist they have brought back peace with honour in the county's long-running development war.

Environment Secretary Nicholas Ridley yesterday unveiled his final decision on the county's structure plan, the document that maps out development rates in Berkshire.

At least 43,500 new homes will have to be built in Berkshire between 1984 and 1996.

Up to 4,000 homes have been forced on the countryside around Bracknell, but Mr Ridley, in a surprise move, has spared the green fields south of Reading.

Labour's Pete Ruhemann said: 'This is not peace with honour, but concrete in our time.'

Alliance leader Tom Heydeman said at yesterday's special county council meeting: 'We now have more development forced upon us with greater uncertainty as to its size and location.'

But Conservatives claim their long campaign to make Mr Ridley back down from his original changes last January, has been successful.

Tory leader Ron Jewitt said: 'We were told we were trying to change an inflexible mind, but Mr Ridley has changed his mind.

In a scale of 10, I say we've got 8 out of 10, and it has been well worth it.'

Opposition leaders claim Mr Ridley has handed power over to the district councils.

Labour leader Lawrence Silverman said: 'He has left the county council with virtually no powers of implementation.

'He has handed it all over to the district councils, who are vying with each other to get developers' contributions by giving them office space and so increasing the demand for homes.'

Source: Kate Ironside, Weekend Post, 12 November 1988

Role play

As the case study has shown, attitudes to the housing debate in Berkshire vary in accordance with such factors as professional roles, political persuasion, class and social backgrounds and self interest in relation to the proposed developments.

Divide into interest groups on the basis of the information provided. Study your role and work out your reactions to the Minister's proposals for house building in Berkshire and the revisions he made in November 1988.

County council planners
Major concerns – To control the overall scale and pace of development. To preserve the Green Belt and AONB and control the spread of settlements in other parts of Berkshire. To ensure that there are sufficient funds for adequate infrastructure, services and amenities. To protect and enhance the environment.

Berkshire business people
Major concerns – To establish plants and increase employment in the most favourable locations, taking advantage of Berkshire's buoyant economy with its access to the M4, Heathrow Airport, London, the Channel Tunnel and the emerging Single European Market. The provision of adequate housing and infrastructure for these developments without harming the environment.

Housing developers
Major concerns – To respond as quickly as possible to the Minister's plans to allow development in new green field sites. To acquire land and form consortia which would finance the development of large numbers of new houses in dormitory suburbs to existing and new employment centres in Berkshire.

Residents' association members
Major concerns – The threat to the quality of life and to the rural character of existing villages. Opposition to plans for new housing estates which would bring noise, congestion on the roads and increased pressure on services such as shops, schools and hospitals. To draw attention to the likely increases in house prices, which would put houses beyond the financial means of most local residents. To organise a mass lobby of parliament in opposition to the Minister's proposals.

Conservation group members
Major concerns – To protect the scenery and rural landscapes of Berkshire and to 'Keep Berkshire Beautiful'. Opposition to the destruction of woodland and other wildlife habitats. These would be threatened and destroyed by the plans for more houses, roads and amenities.

County councillors
Conservatives Major concerns – To organise a campaign to make Mr Ridley back down on his original proposals, on the grounds that they would place excessive and unacceptable burdens on a county which had already taken more than a fair share of development in the South-East. Publicise the view that the Minister's revised proposals of November 1988 represented success for their campaign.

Alliance Major concerns – Alarm over the level of housing growth in Mr Ridley's original proposals, especially at the suggestion that any area outside the Green Belt and AONB may be considered for development. Opposition to the revised proposals of November 1988.

Labour Major concerns – Strong opposition to the original proposals. Local people would not be able to afford the houses, which would be built in the interests of 'get rich quick' developers. Concern about the possibility of an unbroken corridor of housing and development across central Berkshire. Dismay at the revised proposals which were seen as a victory for central government over the Tory-controlled County Council.

Your role play will have brought out some of the conflicts and dilemmas involved in the debate over housing development in Berkshire. It may have given you insights into questions such as these:

- Will there be a continuing war of attrition with local residents and planners on one side and developers and landowners on the other?

- Who will gain and who will lose from Mr Ridley's decision?

- How can a balance be achieved between the need for houses and free market forces on one hand and concern for environmental quality on the other?

- Will Berkshire become a congested conurbation hemmed in between two areas where development is prohibited – the AONB and the Green Belt?

What are the prospects for dispersing some of the development beyond Berkshire and the M4 corridor to those regions of the North which are in need of jobs?

Skilled labour shortages

Economic growth in Berkshire has resulted in rising demands for labour and a fall in the levels of unemployment, so by 1988 the skills shortage facing firms and services in the area had escalated to crisis level for some firms and business organisations.

A survey by the Association of British Chambers of Commerce showed that, by late 1988, 75% of manufacturing firms in the Thames Valley area were reporting difficulties in recruiting skilled labour (in 1986 only 29% had reported difficulties). The service sector reported a similar level of shortages for professional and managerial staff. This survey questioned nearly 13,000 companies in 13 regions. The Thames Valley staff shortage figures were higher than those for other regions.

?

Read the articles on careers, skills and recruitment (pages 402-7).

1 What kinds of skills are in short supply?

2 Why have these shortages arisen in this area?

3 How are the shortages affecting firms and what are they trying to do about them?

4 What difficulties is a firm likely to encounter if it decides to move north to find the labour it needs? Are there stronger reasons for moving?

5 The article 'Moving south for a job' (page 407) refers to one way in which the labour shortage in Berkshire might be solved. What factors would you take into account if you were in the position of one of the unemployed young people from Sunderland?

Workers demand pay linked to house-prices

SOUTH HIT BY SKILLS CRISIS

COMPANIES are now being forced to offer sophisticated financial packages to lure new recruits to the high-priced south, claims a Berkshire relocation company.

Bigger pay packets and moving expenses are no longer enough to woo employees from other less expensive parts of the country to a region with rocketing house prices, according to ARC Relocation of Newbury.

But a recent review by the Advisory Conciliation and Arbitration Service has revealed that the cost of the skills shortage in the south may be too great for some firms, who could be forced to move employees out of the area.

It shows that some employers are considering relocating their employees elsewhere because of pressures for higher pay due to the problems in recruiting and retaining skilled staff.

They are also choosing to take on older people and housewives to strengthen their workforce instead, according to the autumn review by ACAS, the body which helps solve industrial disputes.

General Manager of ARC Relocation, Sean Eastman, says some of their client companies are moving workers out to other offices due to increasing overhead costs for salaries, rent and rates.

Mr Eastman claims house price differentials in the region are now so great that a housing-linked financial inducement is often the only way to persuade an employee to move.

And, as the Thames Valley economy faces an increasing shortage of skilled labour, Mr Eastman predicts that the trend of some companies offering financial 'carrots' for workers will continue.

He said: 'With the current shortages of skilled personnel in the south of England, people's expectations of relocation will continue to rise.

'And, as the price of property increases elsewhere, these sophisticated relocation packages will become more common in other parts of the country.'

Unpaid

Modern relocation packages can mean employers shouldering part of the burden of a new, higher mortgage.

Mr Eastman pointed out that new types of mortgage which require some form of employer commitment are emerging and these are custom-made for relocation companies.

Other inducements include counselling to help new employees find the right schools for their children, and help with settling into new areas.

Source: Steve Marshall, *Reading Evening Post*, 11 October 1988

a What advantages and disadvantages do you think you would find if you moved to a job in Reading Post Office?

b What does the article tell us about the economic and social differences between Reading and Sunderland?

Bosses elated as the jobless total falls again

Skill shortage in Valley boom

BOOMING Thames Valley has hit full employment, according to the employers' organisation, the Confederation of British Industry.

It made the claim as Britain's dole queues were slashed by 34,400 – the largest single fall since similar records began in 1948.

Richard Griffiths, the CBI's southern region director, said: 'We have a situation in the Thames Valley where there is no unemployment, the labour market is so tight.

'Our problem is one of skill shortages. These could hold us back. That is why we must emphasise the need to overcome them.'

According to the CBI, if you have a skill, trade or profession you should be able to find a job in Berkshire.

The claim is backed up by the overwhelming demand for labour, especially in the engineering, machine service and craft fields.

Worry

The latest unemployment figures represent a massive boost to industry in the face of the US dollar crisis.

Mr Griffiths said: 'It is a very good way to start the new year. There is the worry that investors will lose confidence because of the unstable financial markets.

'This will improve confidence and help the economy considerably. It shows the broad thrust of the Government's policies are right.'

Economic growth has produced a big cut in unemployment in all regions.

Fall

It dropped to 2,614,000 in December, putting the national total at 9.4 per cent – the lowest for nearly six years. This compares with 11.2 per cent at the start of 1987.

In the South East, the unemployment rate is 6.6 per cent at 603,500.

Across Berkshire the monthly figure fell in all major towns except Reading.

Source: David Oakley, *Reading Evening Post*, 15 January 1988

Booming county's great expectations

BERKSHIRE needs another baby boom to keep its thriving economy growing, say industry chiefs.

Bosses fear buoyant Berkshire could be hit by a desperate shortage of youngsters in 15 to 20 years' time.

David Coles, president of the Central Berkshire Chamber of Commerce, Trade and Industry, made the claim as Reading's monthly dole queues were slashed yet again.

He said: 'This area is incredibly stable. We are set to have a commercial and industrial influx in central Berkshire.

'The problem is not so much unemployment, but employment.

Training

'With people having children much later in life, there is simply going to be a terrible shortage of labour. We have one now, but it will get much worse.

We cannot start demanding people have more children, so the only way to tackle the problem is by making sure firms put emphasis on training.

'They must use every youngster there is. The 16 to 19-year-olds in 20 years' time will be a valuable breed.'

Rise

In Reading the monthly job figure for January fell by 39 to 4,204 from a December total of 4,243.

The figures for the other major Berkshire towns were:

Bracknell – a rise of 25 from 1,873 in December to 1,898 in January; Newbury – a fall of 72 from 1,839 to 1,767; Slough – a rise of 41 from 3,372 to 3,413; Windsor and Maidenhead – a fall of 22 from 2,104 to 2,082; Wokingham – a fall of 19 from 1,658 to 1,639.

The national unemployment rate fell to 9.2 per cent compared to 11.2 per cent a year ago – the lowest it has been since November 1981.

The numbers out of work normally soar in January as part-time Christmas workers are laid off, but last month the seasonally adjusted adult jobless total – the best guide to underlying trends – fell by 50,800 to 2,563,100.

This is the lowest since April 1982 and represents the 18th consecutive monthly fall.

The national unadjusted figures went up by more than 26,000 to 2,722,154 last month – but the increase was the smallest January rise for 15 years.

Source: David Oakley, *Reading Evening Post*, 19 February 1988

Careers are there to be snapped up

BERKSHIRE's job-hunting school-leavers have never had it so good, say the county's careers officers.

And today's teenagers are taking full advantage of the increasing labour shortages to get good jobs.

The job market for youngsters has completely turned around in the last few years, according to assistant principal careers officer Mike Beadsley.

Seven years ago there were 1,500 school-leavers and only 140 vacancies for young people in the area.

Last year there were more than 1,000 empty jobs, although 400 school-leavers were unemployed.

He said: 'Youngsters can now be more selective, and more and more we advise youngsters to look carefully at job training prospects and not just the pay.'

Mr Beadsley added that skill shortages meant many youngsters were getting more than one job offer, and could afford to go for more highly-paid work.

The demand from firms for school leavers has rocketed in recent years as school rolls have dropped, and the proportion of students going on to higher education has increased by 50 per cent.

Mr Beadsley said: 'Assuming the economic situation remains good one would expect the opportunities for young people to continue.'

Growing numbers of school-children now see their best option as staying on to get better qualifications which will pay dividends when they enter the job market.

Juliet Smith, head of the sixth form at Reading's largest secondary school, Highdown, said school-leavers were in a very fortunate position.

'There is far greater opportunity for the young now and they are taking advantage of it.'

She said high-tech jobs, computing and engineering were more common, more attractive and more available to school-leavers.

Highdown and other schools are building closer ties with industry.

Where are all the workers?

A BERKSHIRE engineering company is on a crest of a trading wave – but says it is held back by the severe labour shortages in the area.

Adwest Engineering, of Headley Road East, Woodley, wants to create up to 45 jobs at its plant. But bosses say they are facing a recruitment crisis which could thwart growth.

Commercial manager Derek Barnett said: 'Our problems are much the same as other companies in the area. Finding workers is such a problem.'

There were fears the company could be forced to move out of the area and expand its other base in Sunderland – due to skill shortages.

One machine worker at the plant said: 'We believe the management is set to lay off a number of workers and expand operations in Sunderland where they can get labour more easily.'

But Mr Barnett denied the claim, saying: 'It is an irrespon-

Bosses 'importing' to beat skills gap

STAFF-starved Berkshire firms are being forced to search far and wide in their desperate bid to find skilled workers.

Skill shortages in the county are rocketing as a new survey shows that 75 per cent of Thames Valley firms are now facing recruitment problems.

Despite booming Berkshire's thriving economy, falling school rolls, and high housing prices

mean there are just not enough workers to fill the jobs.

Now, British Telecom and Reading Post Office are leading the way in efforts to bring workers into the area from as far afield as Ireland and the north of England.

BT's Thamesway division has just drafted in more than 100 skilled technicians from their Irish counterparts Telecom Eireann.

And more than 40 unemployed northerners, some without jobs for five years, were transported to Reading for interviews last week in a bid to fill more than 100 vacancies.

The Post Office admits one of the biggest problems for anyone trying to get a job in Berkshire is the vast cost of accommodation.

Source: Simon Jones, *Reading Evening Post*, 2 February 1989

County businesses put out staff SOS

BERKSHIRE is facing a major labour crisis.

Department of Employment spokesman Frank Crook said firms are struggling to attract any workers – not just skilled staff for high-tech industries.

More than half of the area's firms are affected.

The top five areas hit, according to Mr Crook, and the jobs going include:

■ MANAGEMENT – accounts, marketing and sales reps and computer programmers;

■ SCIENCE and TECHNOLOGY – electronic and electrical engineers, design engineers and draughtsmen;

■ CLERICAL – secretaries, receptionists, computer operators and accountancy clerks;

■ CONSTRUCTION – bricklayers, electricians, plasterers and plumbers;

■ TRANSPORT – heavy goods vehicle drivers, mechanical engineers, tool makers, fitters and general machinists.

sible statement. We are desperate to find workers and this kind of nonsense will do nothing for morale at the firm.'

Adwest, which supplies components to car giants Jaguar and Landrover, says business has never been better.

The Woodley company, part of the Adwest Group, hopes to increase the workforce by up to 15 per cent from the present level of 300.

It also plans to create up to 40 jobs at its 90-strong plant in Sunderland.

Adwest boosted its turnover by more than a million to £12m last year – and predicts another increase at the end of this financial year.

JOBS SHOCKER
Over 1,000 workers could face axe

TWO of Reading's largest employers are poised to quit the town.

And the combined effects could lead to the loss of over 1,000 jobs.

The Intervention Board for Agricultural Produce (IBAP) – a government department which administers the Common Agricultural Policy for the whole of Great Britain – is currently reviewing its position in Reading.

Civil servants are looking into relocating the department, which employs 850 people in Queens Walk, Oxford Road, in a cheaper part of the country where staff would be easier to recruit.

Like many Reading employers, IBAP finds it difficult to find enough staff in the booming Thames Valley. Now, under government guidelines, they have been asked to look at ways of shifting their operations elsewhere.

And unions at the DHSS computer centre, which employs over 400 people, also fear their department could be forced to move to Swindon when the ageing computer system is due to be replaced in 1992.

The centre prints and distributes benefit payments for half the country and unions have so far been unable to get an answer on the question of a move from management.

Christine Borgars, branch chairman of the National Union of Civil and Public Servants, said: 'The effect of not knowing whether we continue to pay benefit from Reading in the 1990s has been upsetting to staff and has aggravated the normal losses of staff in what is after all the Silicon Valley.'

IBAP spokesman, Stephen Briggs, said its review was in its 'very early stages' and that any final decision would be made by the Ministry of Agriculture Fisheries and Food.

A circular has been sent to staff asking them which of many locations, including places in Northern Ireland, Wales, the North, the West Country and the Midlands, they would prefer.

'The move would take place over a period of time and the staff that did not come would be reassigned to other departments in the Reading area,' added Mr Briggs.

All government departments are being asked to review their locations but IBAP could be a prime contender because, unlike tax and unemployment benefit offices, it does not need to be locally based.[...]

Will Waite, branch secretary of the Civil and Public Services Association, which represents many of the clerical grades of staff at IBAP, said he thought the chances of the department moving were 'very high'.[...]

'The wages paid are so low compared to other employers in the area they simply cannot recruit staff. At the moment they have a 45 per cent turnover in staff. I don't think the Intervention Board can exist in its present state in Reading,' he added.

Source: Derek Holmes, *Reading Chronicle*, 9 December 1988

County needs to boost skills pool

■ 1992 message – Lord Young with Gareth Gimblett and Baroness Elles

BERKSHIRE's high-tech industry needs a pool of resources which must be provided by the county's schools, said Trade and Industry Secretary Lord Young.

Speaking to the county's business community at Shire Hall as part of a publicity drive for the 1992 European free market, he said trained people, not jobs, would be in short supply.

Mr UK 1992 Plc, as he was called by Thames Valley Euro MP Baroness Diana Elles, appealed to businesses in Berkshire to go into schools and prepare pupils for 1992.

Lord Young said: 'I hope very much that industrial companies, particularly in this part of the world, will play their part in going into schools.

'Berkshire is a very high-tech area. It is going to require very skilled people working here.'

Shortage

Lord Young said youngsters who wouldn't normally think of going into a high-tech career should be encouraged.

He predicted a shortage of people to fill the available vacancies because the number of school-leavers will drop by a third. ·

'There is going to be a shortage of people, not a shortage of jobs,' he said.

Baroness Elles, who is patron of the single European market information service, Link '92, said: 'It is a great boost to Berkshire that Lord Young has found the time to come.'

Director of Legal Services with Digital in Reading, John Boyd, told Lord Young his company's preparation for the open market started in the last 20 to 30 years.

Mr Boyd said to Lord Young: 'We are fairly well-prepared in Reading for 1992 because we have been working on it for a number of years.'

He told the Post the reason for this was because the company started business in 1957 – the year the European Community opened.

Welcomed

He said: 'We have been able to structure all our operations on the basis of a community.'

He pointed out Digital already has successful operations right across Europe.

Chairman of Berkshire County Council, Gareth Gimblett, also welcomed Lord Young's visit.

Source: David Nicolle, *Reading Evening Post*, 6 February 1989

Moving south for a job

CHRONIC manpower shortages in Berkshire post offices are giving hope to hundreds of unemployed people in Sunderland.

Reading's main sorting office was the first to welcome the job hunters when they were interviewed for some of the 146 vacancies at the office.

Manpower shortages at Berkshire post offices follow the same pattern of all businesses in the area, with centres at Maidenhead, Henley and Reading being the worst hit. There are altogether 370 vacancies at the county's post offices.

Penny Reid, head of personnel at the Reading sorting office, launched the recruitment initiative in Sunderland because there are over 26,500 unemployed in the town.

'It seemed crazy really,' she said. 'Here we were, threatened with cutting operations through labour shortages, while up in Sunderland there is 15 per cent unemployment.'

Advertisements in a local paper in Sunderland asking people to come and work in 'one of the loveliest counties in Southern England' brought 450 replies from would-be postmen, willing to leave family and home town, in their search for employment.

Forty-five applicants, who had passed the initial tests up in Sunderland, came down to Reading for further interviews, and to have a look round the town, on Wednesday.

Some of the job applicants from the Sunderland area being shown round the sorting office at Caversham Road

Some were teenagers, not wanting to hang around waiting for work along with thousands of others. Some were older men who found no more use for their manual skills in manufacturing. Some were couples who wanted to start afresh in a new town.

Typical are Joan Sawyers (36) and David Dawson (41). Joan had been bringing up her two teenage sons, aged 17 and 18, and David, an ex-motor-mechanic, lost his job in 1985. They are both going through divorce procedures and want to start afresh in Reading. Both have applied for a job at the post office.

Although they are hopeful, they are by no means starry-eyed about the south. They know that they will have to pay much more on living expenses. At present Joan pays £27 a week for her large three-bedroom flat.

Joan will have to leave her sons behind with her parents, but she is desperate for a new start, and a job. 'I know it will be hard,' she said, 'but you've got to go where the work is.'

Bran Lathlan is 19, and apart from a few odd jobs as a painter and decorator, he has been unemployed since he left school.

'I had to get out before I lost hope altogether,' he said. 'I'm young and I think I can make a go of it.' He said his mum would miss him, 'but she understands.'

The Department of Employment has given the scheme its full support and co-operation.

Source: *Reading Chronicle*, 3 February 1989

Traffic problems

The economic success of the Berkshire section of the M4 corridor has resulted in increased traffic pressure on the county's roads, with adverse effects on firms, villages and towns and residents.

Read the articles on the traffic problems (pages 408–12) and write short statements to answer the following questions.

1 What are the consequences of traffic pressure on the roads for:

- motorists travelling to and from work?
- residents?
- villages and towns in the region?
- firms?

2 What solutions have been put forward?

Traffic growth puts county on road to chaos

BERKSHIRE's creaking road system is being swamped by an ever-increasing volume of traffic.

The problems are so bad, the county's chief road expert admits there seems to be no acceptable way to deal with the chaos.

His shock report claims: 'Unless the rate of growth in Berkshire is substantially slowed down, the M4 will cease to perform its role as a regional motorway linking London and South Wales, and be relegated to a local distribution road.'

Bob Clarke, Berkshire County Council's director of highways and planning, is aware that major highway improvements are essential.

But he says any improvements that are environmentally acceptable will not be enough to cope with the forecast increase in private motoring.

And unless development slows down, new forms of transport, such as a monorail may have to be considered. This is the result of 30 years' growth in the county, its proximity to London and high car ownership.

Reading, Newbury, Wokingham and Windsor are the worst-hit areas, but even Bracknell's modern road network is approaching saturation point.

In these towns, traffic growth of between 40 to 60 per cent is predicted and cannot be accommodated by highway construction of an acceptable scale.

Among the worst problems caused by the pressure on the road network are:

■ 7.5 per cent of principal roads surveyed have less than a year's life remaining.

■ Limited resources mean efforts to improve the situation will be at the expense of smaller, rural roads.

Source: Paul Nelson, *Reading Evening Post*, 13 June 1988

Heseltine warns of sprawl

MR MICHAEL Heseltine stepped up his defence of the rural South-east by warning that the combination of the Channel Tunnel and Tory adulation of the market place would turn the area into a 40-mile urban sprawl, akin to Tokyo.

The former Environment Secretary predicted that the deteriorating environment within the South-east would increasingly dominate British politics, especially if the Government failed to take practical steps 'to share more generously and more fairly the nation's growing affluence'.

Speaking in Ashford, Kent –

which he described as the epicentre of the growing political storm – Mr Heseltine said: 'It must be a central priority of government to encourage more of our economic growth in the less prosperous, less congested parts of our country.'

The Government had to change the assumption that 'we are going to build houses in the South-east for all those people, presently living in Scotland, Wales, the Midlands and the North, who come South. Every effort must be made to stimulate work where people live.'

On the call by the Transport Secretary, Mr Paul Channon, for

a privatised rail link between London and the tunnel, Mr Heseltine said only overwhelming arguments could persuade Parliament to support anything other than existing corridors.

He also attacked Mr Nicholas Ridley, the Environment Secretary, for not rejecting more planning appeals.

At Andover in Hampshire yesterday, Mr Peter Brooke, the Tory chairman, rejected state regulation as the best means of conservation. His party wished to protect the environment without harming business.

Source: Patrick Wintour, *Guardian*, 22 October 1988

Traffic jams costing firms a fortune

THE ROADS TO RUIN

READING-BASED computer giants Digital are losing up to a million pounds a year – thanks to traffic jams which keep employees in their cars when they should be at work.

And the company's managing director says they would never have come to Reading if they had known what was in store.

Geoff Shingles, who is boss of Digital's 2,500 Reading employees, told TVS's Head To Head programme on Monday that 'unbearable' traffic jams are costing his firm a fortune.

'Knowing what we know today we would not come to Reading,' he said. But he insisted that Digital will maintain existing levels of employment in the town.

In an interview with the *Chronicle*, Mr Shingles explained how he calculates the loss. 'It's just a question of people sitting in traffic jams when they would otherwise be at work,' he said.

'Obviously I can't come up with an exact figure, but it's somewhere between half a million and a million pounds a year. That's just the financial cost – we pay a heavy price in sheer frustration as well.'

Mr Shingle says he does not regret Digital's decision to base its administrative HQ in Reading. But he wishes the manufacturing and engineering staff could have gone somewhere else – possibly north of London – where they would spend less time trapped in traffic.

'What worries us is that even when all Reading's new roads are finished they will only be enough to cope with existing traffic, not the traffic levels of the future,' he said.

'When I come to work in the morning at 7.45 they are already jamming up. I find it extraordinary that some people are actually planning to make that worse by building another 6,000 houses south of the M4.'

The director of Reading's chamber of commerce, Frank Stroud, said: 'Mr Shingles has obviously done some research and I'm sure his estimates are right. We're getting more and more complaints from businesses about traffic jams.

'The answer is for central government to spend some money on our totally inadequate infrastructure, because at the moment plenty of money is being taken out of here and none is being put back in.'

Source: Damian Thompson, *Reading Chronicle*, 21 October 1988

Road network at crisis point

OVERLOADED roads in booming Berkshire cannot cope with the sheer weight of traffic – and the problem can only get worse.

That is the stark warning from the county's highways chief Bob Clarke, who says the situation provides extreme concern for the future.

Ratepayers could be landed with a massive bill for road repairs and construction as new business and residents pour into Berkshire.

In the next financial year, highway maintenance in Berkshire alone will cost an estimated £15.8 million.

In his Transport Policy for 1989, just published, Mr Clarke, Berkshire's Director of Highways, warns that major repairs and improvements are essential.

And while these are likely to focus on the major roads throughout the county in a bid to keep the traffic moving, Berkshire's minor roads will be the ones which suffer most.

He says: 'Preliminary indications arising from transportation studies give rise to extreme concern for the future.

'The county has served as a growth area for some 30 years, as a result of which the capacity of its transportation system has been reached and indeed exceeded.

'Although there has been considerable highway investment in Berkshire over these years, including the M4 motorway, it has been impossible for this provision to keep pace with demand.

'Unless the scale of development being accommodated in the county is reduced, it is considered that not only will acceptable limits of overload be grossly exceeded, but that a limit will be reached beyond which new forms of transport – for example, rapid transport systems – may be required.

'Such solutions could be unacceptable in environmental or financial terms.'

Mr Clarke said Berkshire had the second largest car ownership in the country.

He says the M4 between Theale and Langley is already overloaded during peak periods, but explains that the Department of Transport is considering widening this stretch of the motorway to four lanes in each direction.

Mr Clarke adds: 'Unfortunately the consequences of this spending on the principal roads is that there will be less spent on the more minor roads.'

Drivers warned of M-way delay

ROADWATCH

MOTORWAY drivers on the M4 in Berkshire are being warned of possible delays as a result of £3.5 million resurfacing work which started on Saturday.

The work, expected to last nine weeks, is taking place along the eastbound carriageway between junctions 12 and 13.

The westbound carriageway will be converted to a contraflow system with two traffic lanes in each direction.

A mandatory 50mph speed limit will be enforced throughout the duration of the work.

Drivers are also being asked to allow more time for their journey and to take particular care through the contraflow.

There are also lane closures on the M4 between junction 15 and Newbury services.[...]

Work is also continuing on a new roundabout at Theale which will provide access from the A4 to Arlington Business Park.

The roundabout is sited on the Theale by-pass west of the M4 at junction 12 and the work is likely to take six months.

Source: Tim Boone, *Reading Evening Post*, 13 June 1988

Computer hope for bea[...]

Bill for lost £1.1 millio[...]

FUMING Reading motorists cost their employers more than £1 million every year when they get stuck in the town's notorious traffic jams.

For the first time a report puts a price on the motorists' misery in Reading – and reveals that the town is paying through the nose for bumper to bumper blues.

Much of the blame lies with the county's outdated Highwayman traffic computer. The near-obsolete system broke down again this week, plunging some areas into more jam chaos.

Meanwhile a conservative estimate from county traffic experts this week reveals that 30,000 motorists are two minutes late for work in Reading every day, costing employers 1,000 hours labour daily.

Estimate

Assuming a working year of 250 days, that's a whopping 250,000 man hours of work lost [...] Reading each year.

Using government figur[...] which put average wages at £4.[...] per hour, county experts estima[...] the total cost to Reading busine[...] and industry in lost work [...] £1,167,500 per year.

That's the saving Berksh[...] County Council estima[...] Reading will make every ye[...] after a new £1.2 million compu[...] system is introduced.

Source: Tim Boone, *Reading Evening Post*, 11 February 1[...]

ic chaos

vork tops

As reported in yesterday's Post, uncillors on Berkshire County ouncil's transportation sub-mmittee voted to bring in a new ate-of-the-art computer system to update Reading's road etwork.

Savings

They agreed that spending on ew systems – £974,300 on a com-uter, £120,000 on car park management and £105,000 on closed circuit television – will save the town money in the long run.

The report to committee members adds: 'The estimate takes no account of savings made from reduced fuel consumption and vehicle wear and tear, poten-tial accident savings, reduced pollution levels and reduced driver frustration.'

Welcoming the prospect of a new traffic control computer system, transport sub-committee chairman Joe Slater said: 'This is another move forward, and another step towards solving Reading's traffic problems.'

TRAINS TO TAKE AWAY TRAFFIC STRAIN?

Space-age cure for road chaos

A FUTURISTIC railway on stilts looks set to solve Reading's transport nightmare by the 1990s. The multi-million-pound scheme, similar to the system in London's Docklands, is a major initiative planned by Berkshire County Council.

The introduction of the hi-tech electric network to cover Reading, Bracknell and Wokingham, is thought to be an essential move to cope with the enormous growth in the area.

It would, by the 21st century, have taken the strain away from the hard-pressed road system which the county council now ad-mits cannot cope with the increas-ed traffic.

Bob Clarke, director of highways, said the ultra-modern 'mass transit system' was designed for the commuter.

'It would be an attractive train consisting of small, light railway units with open plan seating. The idea is to have trains running fre-quently like buses without the congestion associated with them. Mass numbers could be transported as they are on the tubes.'

The cost of the project would be 'enormous'. Mr Clarke said: 'The financing of the scheme would have to be shared because it's so big. It is anticipated the Government, British Rail, private industry and ourselves would have to be involved in this investment in Berkshire's future.'

But Mr Clarke promised the idea was one of the best long-term options open to the council and said that by the end of the century the system could make Berkshire the leader in transport and com-munications.

'We ought to be in this position because the Thames Valley is a very important factor in the economy,' he said.

Tory leader Ron Jewitt was all in favour of the silicon valley super train.

He said he looked forward to the scheme progressing and on Tuesday told members of the en-vironment committee: 'There is nothing I would like better than to walk to the bottom of my road and jump on a tube – or monorail.'

And looking towards the development of the area, Mr Jewitt took into account the latest proposals in the Berkshire Struc-ture Plan.

'If we do get a large mass of housing in the south of Reading, one of the most effective ways of dealing with those who will look towards Reading for employment would be to have some form of docklands-type railway,' he said.

The council will begin a feasibility study into the new railway next month. It will be con-sulting with project managers already familiar with similar schemes and hopes to prepare a tailor-made scheme to meet the needs of Reading.

Source: Margaret Cole, *Reading Evening Post*, 4 March 1988

Prospects for the future

Studies have shown that the South-East region as a whole is the most prosperous of Britain's regions and, within the South-East, the M4 corridor stands out as a zone of economic success and prosperity.

The opening of the Channel Tunnel and the removal of trade barriers to create a single market in the EEC will give further boosts to these prosperous regions of Britain, placing further strains on the roads, social services and settlements of Berkshire and the western part of the South-East region.

There is agreement that the South-East will remain the most productive region and the engine of economic growth for the national economy of the UK. This means that there will be some important issues concerning the need for new planning strategies which will allow further wealth creation but limit the penalties of development which are already being experienced in Berkshire and other congested parts of the South-East.

?

Review the evidence and arguments put forward in this chapter and work out separate cases for and against stronger planning controls on development in South-East England and the M4 corridor. The articles 'How green is our valley' and 'Heseltine warns of sprawl' should help you.

For the case in favour of planning you could start with these points:

- Planning could produce a clearer, more logical development pattern which firms and people could understand more readily.

- It would be easier to resolve conflicts about such matters as the allocation of land for further development and the resolution of conflicts between local and national interests.

- Planning could even out development in the South-East, for example, by directing growth away from congested areas like central Berkshire to relatively undeveloped areas in the Lower Thames Valley, east of London.

- It could advise central government on the investment of public funds (for example on roads) and undertake research into the detailed economic structure of the region. A better-organised planning system could attract more foreign investment.

The arguments against planning include:

- Firms know most about where they should locate and expand. Economic growth in the South-East region and in the UK as a whole would suffer if firms were not allowed to make their own decisions. Multinationals might decide to move to other countries if they came up against planning barriers in South-East England. When the Channel Tunnel is open, northern France could become a more attractive location for some firms.

- Planning authorities are not properly representative of all interests. They could impose decisions that people dislike and they would undermine local government.

- A planning authority for the South-East would be in favour of more growth in that region, but what Britain really needs is less growth there and more in those poorer, northern regions which are badly in need of new jobs and improved economic prospects.

HOW GREEN IS OUR VALLEY?

BOOMING Thames Valley towns are at the top of Britain's prosperity league as the north-south divide widens even further.

But top councillors warn the area has paid a bitter price for success.

Services are suffering and a clampdown on the development is vital to the Thames Valley's survival, they say.

In a study out today, leading geographers rank Newbury second only to Milton Keynes among the nation's winners in the 1980s with Didcot, Bracknell and Reading close behind.

Dr Tony Champion of Newcastle University and Anne Green of Warwick University studied 280 towns, using unemployment figures, the number of jobs in high-tech industries and house prices to draw up the list.

Their paper, Local Prosperity and the North South Divide: Winners and Losers in 1980s, is to be presented at the annual conference of the Institute of British Geographers which starts today.

But Tory leader of Berkshire County Council Councillor Jewitt said: 'Berkshire is paying the price of its own success in attracting industry, commerce and people. We are beginning to pay the penalty.'

The county's roads are groaning, social services are at full stretch and local hospitals are floundering.

Councillor Jewitt said: 'We are not hostile to development but we do need a slow-down period to help us to catch up.'

Source: Kate Ironside, *Reading Evening Post*, 6 January 1988

Channel rail link: 'Heathrow rival'

READING will become an international centre on the scale of London's Heathrow Airport if a proposed £3 billion rail link is given the go ahead.

Business and political leaders are backing bold proposals, which would provide the town with a direct rail line to the Continent.

They say it could turn Reading into another commercial hub to rival Heathrow in the sheer volume of people and freight traffic passing through it.

It would put the town on the international map and boost the already booming area.

British construction group Costain has put forward the plans which could open the way for international commuting.

A trip from Reading to Paris or Brussels would take only two hours, with Madrid six hours away and Rome seven.

Peter Gibson, chairman of the Reading and Central Berkshire Chamber of Commerce, Trade and Industry, said: 'The rail link would be like setting up a Heathrow in Reading, making the town an international centre.

'It is the only way forward into the 21st century. It will boost firms in the area and create more jobs.'

And Sir Gerry Vaughan, MP for Reading East, said: 'It is tremendous news for the town. This is what Reading needs and deserves.

'It will make Reading one of the major towns in the country, possibly on the scale of Manchester or Birmingham.

> We have to sort out our traffic problem. Once that is dealt with then we can go ahead with the plans.
>
> Berkshire commerce chief
> Peter Gibson

'There are going to be problems. But the town has to make it happen. This brave new world is totally feasible, and it is in everyone's interest to make it so.'

However Richard Griffiths, director of the Southern Region of the CBI, sounded a warning note. 'We have to be careful not to create an even worse situation in an already overcrowded Thames Valley.'

Reading put firmly on the map as the centre of an international rail link

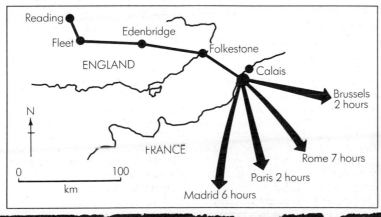

Source: David Oakley, *Reading Evening Post*, 6 January 1988

Plea from Heseltine

FORMER Environment Secretary and Henley MP Michael Heseltine is urging the present incumbent Nicholas Ridley to use his powers to slow down development in the South-East of England.

In a letter to Mr Ridley he says that the Government should use its influence to channel development away from the overcrowded areas of Southern England to areas in the North and Midlands.

He says there is a 'grave and growing anxiety in the south of England about the self-evident ravages of the countryside that the pace of development there is causing.'

Speaking to the *Chronicle* he said: 'Berkshire is a crucially important area, one where pressure is intense. We know there's going to be development in areas like this.' [...]

He added that he well understood the balance the Environment Secretary had to achieve and was not attacking anybody.

But, he says, wherever he drives in Southern England the place is being torn up and torn apart.

Source: *Reading Evening Post*, 18 March 1988

This chapter has shown that the Berkshire section of the M4 corridor has attracted investment from British and foreign companies, bringing in new employment opportunities. As a result, the area has become one of the most successful and prosperous concentrations of high technology and its associated industries in Britain. The county is now faced with the need to match this growth and affluence with the preservation of the quality of life and the maintenance of good social conditions. The pressing issues of traffic congestion, housing costs and skill shortages in this section of the M4 corridor raise questions about the future of development in this area and its place in the wider regional context of South-East England.

16

Transport

John Whitelegg

Traffic congestion near Tower Bridge, London

Transport networks

Geographers are experienced in the description and analysis of transport networks but are also aware of the wider significance of these networks and the social and economic structures which they reflect. The network map or diagram is a powerful tool for geographical analysis and is a familiar form to most people. The London underground map is a classic 'mental map' which many carry around in their head, influencing their view of the geography of London. Similarly maps of rail networks, whether of the whole country or parts like the South-East of England or the Rhine–Ruhr region, figure prominently in discussions of regional identity and attempts to market a region's resources.

1 Refer to two types of map of your local area: a diagrammatic map and a topological map (e.g. an Ordnance Survey one). Then list the differences between the two types of map.

Networks are a clear spatial manifestation of the complexities of movement and organisation within particular social and economic contexts. Their significance lies in four main areas:

● They are remarkably effective data-capture devices. They summarise a mass of data in a very concise format. Without the network diagram we would need a large number of words to describe all the individual links and nodes in the system and their relationship to each other, the degree to which nodes connect with each other and the degree to which the available space is 'packed'.

● They can be subjected to a vast array of analytical techniques which can be used to describe their evolution over time, their efficiency in terms of providing good access to facilities, their cost characteristics and their status given the addition or withdrawal of a node or a link. Networks are mathematical statements about reality which can be manipulated to reveal more information about what is going on.

● They influence (some would say control) a wide range of important social and economic variables: access to jobs and schools, the availability of recreational opportunities, the feeling of well-being which derives from knowing an area, travelling around without encountering insurmountable obstacles and attachment to place. Variability in these characteristics can enhance or detract from quality of life and income and can redistribute income and wealth from rich to poor or poor to rich. No network is neutral in its social and economic impact.

● They influence the way we build up a picture of reality and the image of places. Geographers have contributed specifically to this theme by studying perceptions of place and the image of the city. For example, if pedestrian networks are lightly used because of heavy traffic and fear of accidents, then places become 'non-places' and sources of concern for residents and visitors. Places rapidly become perceived as dangerous for personal safety and quarters of cities are categorised as violent and to be avoided. The use made of networks is a determinant of social well-being and quality of urban life.

This chapter uses three transport issues as examples to show the importance of networks in various ways and, more importantly, to show how networks are part of a much wider social and economic structure. These structures are important in themselves and in the way they determine who wins and who loses when a conflict over additions and subtractions to the network emerges. The examples are:

● The traffic problems of the city of Lancaster and the proposals for a new road through its historic core.

● The proposed closure of the Settle–Carlisle railway line.

● The proposal for transporting nuclear spent fuel to a store at Heysham near Lancaster.

The traffic problems of Lancaster

Lancaster is a city of 42,473 inhabitants (1981 Census) in the north of England. It is part of a local authority area (Figure 1) which includes the seaside resort of Morecambe (population 39,371) and a rural hinterland stretching up the valley of the River Lune to North Yorkshire.

In 1981 the total population of the local authority area centred on Lancaster was 118,589. The city of Lancaster serves a wide area, stretching from Preston in the south to Kendal in the north, and acts as a service centre to a population of about 250,000. Lancaster City Council describes the city in the following terms:

'Lancaster is an historic city with a compact commercial centre and a fine heritage of 18th century buildings. It is the business centre of the District and the focus of administrative, health and educational services for the county.'

Like most urban areas in Britain Lancaster has a traffic problem (Figures 2 and 3). The general increase in travel by car throughout Britain from 309 billion passenger kilometres in 1976 to 424 billion passenger kilometres in 1986 has produced serious problems of congestion in cities and a state of permanent disruption on motorways (as, for example, on the M25 around London). The traffic problem exists in cities of all population sizes and brings with it excessive noise, pollution, damage to health (diesel exhaust emissions are carcinogenic), fear of injury, actual injury and death, and visual blight on a massive scale.

In Lancaster the 1981 Census revealed that 50.9% of Lancastrians has access to a car, a number which is lower than the national average of 61% in 1981. In spite of this lower level, Lancaster experiences a degree of traffic congestion at peak periods and, increasingly, in the off-peak periods. It also produces an

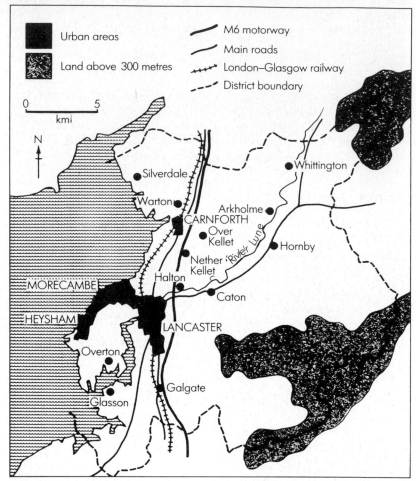

Figure 1 Lancaster District

Figure 2 Traffic on Greyhound Bridge Road

Figure 3 Traffic congestion in Cable Street. The Castle is just visible in the background

unpleasant environment for those on foot trying to gain access to the shopping centre and those who live in residential areas which are used by car drivers as short cuts.

1 Study Figure 4 (pages 418–19) and describe Lancaster's transport network.

2 List the features you think would pose problems for traffic planners.

3 Rank these features in order of severity.

Lancaster's traffic difficulties are very much the result of its geography and network structures. Every part of the traffic system has a particular set of problems. The basic problem in Lancaster is clear: too many vehicles circulating in a city centre and creating both a polluted environment and one that is dangerous for pedestrians and cyclists.

The analysis of these problems by Lancaster City Council has been superficial and has been influenced by three factors:

1 A long-standing land use allocation for a new road – the Eastern Relief Road.

2 A belief that bringing cars into the city centre is good for the economy.

3 A belief that building more space for roads is a solution to a traffic problem.

The City Council has proposed several road schemes over the last 20 years. They are:

- the Western by-pass,
- the Western Relief Road,
- the Eastern Relief Road,
- Morecambe Link Road to the M6 motorway,
- St George's Quay Link Road.

These are shown in Figure 5 on page 420.

Figure 4 Lancaster's one-way system and some of its problems

CATON ROAD–BULK ROAD
Again this junction is most stretched during morning peaks when the tailback of traffic waiting to cross into Bulk Road (much of it short-cutting) prevents the necessary weaving movements on Kingsway.
Morning peak traffic carrying out this manoeuvre is 76% higher than during average hours.

SKERTON BRIDGE
Frequently exceeds its capacity: at its most congested (morning peaks) traffic is unable to carry out necessary weaving movements.

KINGSWAY–PARLIAMENT STREET
Constant streams of traffic from Skerton Bridge along with tailbacks from Caton Road constrain the merging and weaving of northbound traffic approaching from Parliament Street. The new Kingsway Recreation Centre sits in a virtual traffic island and is very difficult and dangerous for pedestrians to reach.

BULK ROAD–BACK CATON ROAD
Is considered to be the most saturated junction on the system. Tailbacks on Back Caton Road are typical at most times of the day and are particularly severe in the morning peak, whilst in the evening peak there is a regular tailback on Bulk Road. This in turn prevents access and egress from St Leonard's Gate. Caton Road at this point presents a particulary unsightly and depressing entrance to the town.

PARLIAMENT STREET–GREYHOUND BRIDGE
The Parliament Street approach to the traffic signals has a limited space for queueing: when the approach is full, the queuing traffic interferes with the access to Greyhound Bridge to the city centre. This in turn leads to traffic backing up at the Fire Station on Cable Street. Again, pedestrian movement in this vicinity is very difficult and dangerous – this has almost certainly led to the decline of Parliament Street as a secondary shopping centre.

CABLE STREET–DAMSIDE STREET
A difficult and dangerous junction for traffic emerging onto Cable Street from St George's Quay. The problems here can lead to substantial evening peak queues on Damside Street. At the top of the hill, pedestrians have real difficulties in crossing flows of traffic to and from Mitre House and its substantially underused car park (typically 3,100 crossings daily).

GREAT JOHN STREET–LOWER CHURCH STREET
Traffic queueing for the Great John Street car parks frequently stretches back onto the one-way system. Its effects will often lead to tailbacks in Rosemary Lane and to North Road. Here, heavy traffic also coincides with considerable pedestrian traffic (6,000 crossings per day).

MEETING HOUSE LANE
Again this light-controlled junction is saturated for much of the day and long queues will back up on King Street. The tailbacks are particularly severe during the evening peak. This junction is also well used by pedestrians (almost 10,000 crossing daily) particularly since King Street–China Street is a secondary shopping centre. Conditions for shoppers are noisy, uncomfortable and dangerous; again the heavy traffic passing through this area conflicts with the conservation and tourist aspirations of the Council.

DALTON SQUARE
This light-controlled junction is working at 89 to 90% of its capacity for much of the day. Waiting queues will stretch back down the hill on to Great John Street making driving and pedestrian conditions both difficult and dangerous. There are over 10,000 pedestrians crossing the road daily in this vicinity. The constant streams of traffic on Great John Street and circulating around Dalton Square also clash with the conservation efforts in this area.

PENNY STREET BRIDGE
Is becoming increasingly congested in the evening peak when heavy traffic flows coincide with frequent use of the pelican and zebra crossings (4,000 crossings recorded daily) at this junction. The recent opening of a B&Q store on Aldcliffe Road increased the queues of traffic waiting to cross the South Road and added to the problems at this junction. It is now typical for queues to stretch back on Thurnham Street.

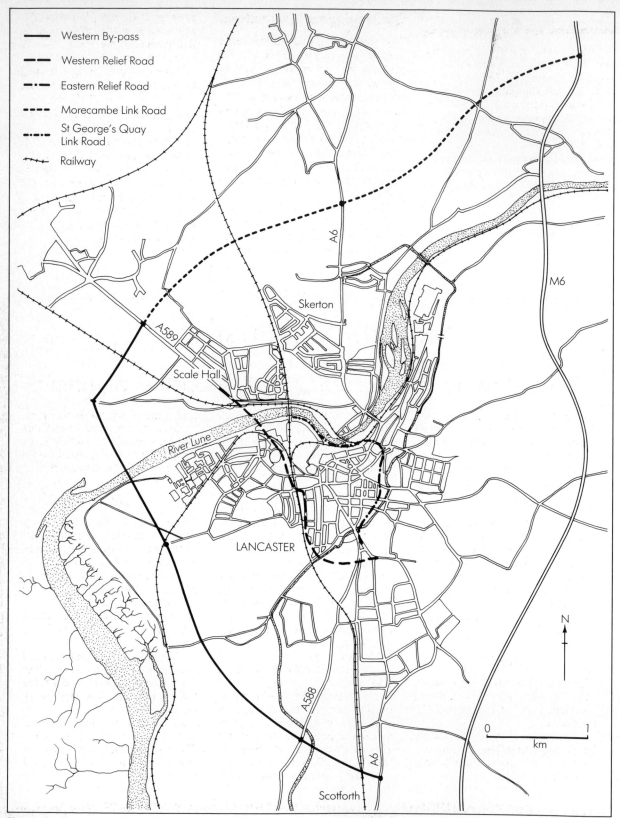

Figure 5 The routes of the five road improvement schemes

?

1 After you have worked through the rest of this section (up to the end of page 425), write roles for people for and against the five proposed schemes listed above. Act out the roles in small groups, with people challenging any assumptions made (see the commentary below).

Challenging the assumptions

The assumption that adding more links to a network solves a traffic problem has not gone unchallenged and is frequently the object of fierce argument at inquiries into new road proposals. If a situation exists where there is a *constant* number of vehicles then adding more capacity should, in theory, spread that constant number over a bigger area and so relieve congestion.

The flaw in this argument is that there is never a constant number of vehicles. Not only does vehicle ownership and use rise from year to year, but there is also evidence that new roads actually create new traffic. This has been the case with the M25 motorway, with the Los Angeles freeways and with the autobahns of the Ruhr area of West Germany (particularly the A430/B1 road).

There has been an intensive debate in Lancaster over these issues, a major public inquiry into development proposals and widespread opposition to the new roads, in particular to the Eastern Relief Road (renamed the Central Area Access Road).

U-turn on road plan

Dual flow is the answer to snarl-ups — planners

A FOUR-LANE highway has been suggested as a solution to Lancaster's chronic traffic problems.

The £7m route would follow the path of the controversial city centre access road but carry traffic in both directions.

A new bridge would cross the Lancaster canal near Granada TV's White Cross studios to prevent bottle-necks at the city's Southern end.

To the North, two traffic lanes would turn right off Skerton Bridge at a new traffic light-controlled junction.

Public

The latest proposals were drawn up following meetings of a joint working party of county and city officials.

Before they go to the county highways committee on June 24, the authority plans a public consultation exercise.

Over 18,500 explanatory leaflets have been sent out, and an exhibition at Palatine Hall in Dalton Square will open to the public from Saturday to Wednesday.

Explaining the plans, county chiefs said the city's blueprint for a single-direction road would do little to relieve Northbound traffic congestion.

They revealed that 20,000–24,000 vehicles used the clogged one-way system each day, far more than it was ever built for.

As a result, two accidents per month occurred on average — one involving pedestrians.

Lancaster had the county's worst record for shoppers getting hurt.

The hoped-for Western bypass to Heysham, excluded from recent government spending plans and not expected to be built for another decade, would only cut traffic by 1,500 vehicles per day.

A new computerised traffic management scheme is to be introduced this year. But relief this will provide will be swiftly eaten away because traffic levels are set to grow by at least two per cent per year.

Short

County traffic chief, Mr Terry Carter, said unless something was done, more visitors would turn their backs on Lancaster.

Local residents would also compound problems on back streets by taking more short cuts.

He said the new highway would cut accidents by one-third, and added:

"We are trying to build a road which fits into Lancaster, does not split the city in half, and helps the people who live and work there."

At least three years' preparation would be needed if the county gave the go-ahead, and it could be five to ten years before the road was build.

Source: Reproduced by kind permission of the *Lancashire Evening Post*, 13 May 1987

Congestion 'well into the Nineties'

LANCASTER City centre's traffic congestion is set to continue well into the Nineties, it became clear at the Local Plan inquiry on Wednesday.

Even if the Inspector, Mr Anthony Moscardini, comes down in favour of reserving land for the proposed city centre access route, construction of the four-lane, two-way road would not be expected to start for another five to seven years.

"That is the earliest it could start, assuming the county council has a commitment to it," said the county's principal engineer, Mr Terry Carter.

Two phases

The road from Skerton Bridge to White Cross to the east of the city centre, would cost £6 million to £7 million as proposed by the county, with the cost split between the county and the Government.

The inquiry heard that the first two phases of the city centre retail redevelopment scheme were planned to be completed about 1991–92 — a year before work was expected to start on the road.

Objections to new road building, including the Damside Street link road, will continue until Tuesday. The rest of next week will be devoted to conservation policies before the inquiry adjourns on Friday after hearing four weeks' evidence.

Because all parties involved are not available at the same time, it will not resume now until Tuesday, October 20. Another 3½ weeks' evidence is scheduled to be taken then, before the inquiry is completed and the Inspector considers his report, which should be received by the city council before the end of the year.

As well as being the city's Golden Jubilee Year, this should be "Golden Opportunity Year" to get the future of Lancaster right. argued Mr Chris Whitehead, of Gerrard Street, representing Landlife. He would prefer to see a canalside park with housing instead of the road.

Headmaster of Lancaster Royal Grammar School, Mr Peter Mawby, pressed for increased road safety measures in the area of the school. He estimated that

his 900 pupils already made 4,000,000 road crossings a year.

Anti-plan campaigner, Mr Jon Catt, of Bradshaw Street, Lancaster, urged other solutions to the city's traffic problems instead of a new road. He claimed a county questionnaire contained questions which were loaded in favour of the new road.

Demolition

Principal city planning officer, Mr Reg Haslam said that for the road to avoid the Polish Church in Nelson Street would involve demolition of other buildings. "We believe we have selected a line that results in the least amount of demolition," he said.

A resident of Park Road, Lancaster, Mrs Ann Milston, submitted that Lancaster's traffic problems were over-exaggerated and they should call in independent transport consultants.

West Road Residents' Association member, Mr John Angus opposed the Damside Street link road, as it would lead to more industrial traffic.

Source: Alan Sandham, *Lancaster Guardian*, 24 July 1987

?

1 Read the extracts 'U-turn on road plan' and 'Congestion "well into the Nineties" '. Use box-and-arrow diagrams to represent the main issues involved.

The public inquiry produced over 1,500 objections, the largest number ever to a statutory local plan outside London. The Central Area Access Road was justified by the local authority on the grounds that it would relieve flows elsewhere in the system and bring

with it consequent environmental gains. These arguments can be followed in a series of network diagrams. Study these carefully.

Forecasting the future

Figure 6 shows the existing flows of traffic in June 1986. The flows are 16-hour weekday flows. Flows of over 20,000 vehicles per day (vpd) are clearly unacceptable in a central area of an historic city and there is a problem to be resolved.

Figure 7 shows a forecast for

1996 without any new roads and a much worsened situation appears. A high and low forecast is given because of the uncertainty involved in the forecasting operation. (However, see the comments below about forecasting as a basis for new road justification.) The King Street 'leg' of the one-way system has increased from 23,000 vpd to 29,900 vpd and the Thurnham Street 'leg' of the A6 from 24,600 to 30,700 vpd (high forecast).

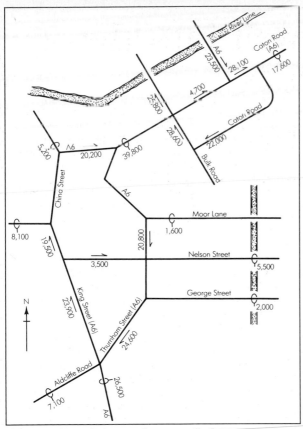

Figure 6 Network diagram of existing traffic flows in Lancaster city centre, June 1986

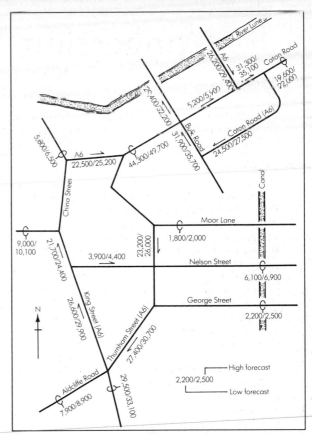

Figure 7 Projected traffic flows in 1996

Forecasting of this kind simply extrapolates past trends in the growth of car ownership and use towards a theoretical saturation point where most families own at least one car. This builds growth into the system, so that roads are built to cater for the demand. In effect, we have a self-fulfilling prophecy. This forecasting process does not question the desirability of the trend; it merely serves to accelerate it. Forecasts are carried out nationally and then appear in public inquiries, as at Lancaster, to justify the 'need' for new roads. It is not possible at these inquiries to question the forecasts themselves.

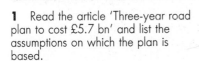

1 Read the article 'Three-year road plan to cost £5.7 bn' and list the assumptions on which the plan is based.

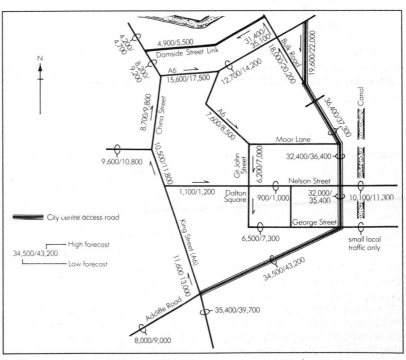

Figure 8 Projected traffic flows in 1996 with the two-way access road

Three-year road plan to cost £5.7 bn

A FULL commitment to an expansive road building programme was delivered by Mr Cecil Parkinson, the Transport Secretary, yesterday in a new report on improving the roads network throughout England.

Although Mr Parkinson has attempted to soften the impact of the proposals by announcing several new environmental measures, the scale of the programme will arouse renewed controversy over the Government's increasingly unpopular transport policies.

In the report, Trunk Roads, England: into the 1990s, Mr Parkinson firmly dismisses the growing demand for curbs on road building and commits the Government to the largest ever road building programme planned for the country.

His aim "is to achieve a balance between the various forms of transport so that each of them can make its proper contribution to a safer, more efficient transport system. The nation wants a national road system which meets its expectations. The Government aims to provide it."

Expenditure over the next three years, calculated in 1987 prices, is put at £5.7 billion — a large slice of the proposed £12.4 billion earmarked by the Government for road spending in the next 10 years.

The report says increased public transport investment will not solve the problems of congestion on the main inter-urban roads. Its assessment was carried out against a background of last year's national road traffic forecasts, which predicted traffic demand would rise by between 83 and 142 per cent by the year 2025.

It says, "The mobility, flexibility and convenience afforded by a car is greatly prized by the private motorist.

"Road and rail for the most part serve different markets and for most journeys one mode cannot readily be substituted for the other. Even a 50 per cent increase in rail traffic would be equivalent to only 5 per cent of present road traffic — about one year's growth in recent years."

Total spending on the road trunk network over the next three years will increase to £5.7 billion, compared with £3.35 billion in the previous three-year cycle.

According to the document, spending on new roads will be over £4 billion, compared with £2.3 billion in the previous three years, while spending on capital maintenance will grow in real terms by 42 per cent to £1.3 billion.

The current programme embraces over 500 schemes covering 2,500 miles of existing or planned roads, including 170 miles of new motorway, the widening of almost 600 miles of existing motorway and the conversion of 43 miles of all-purpose sections of the A1 to motorway.

Completion of the programme will mean that nearly one third of the motorway network will operate as dual four-lane standard and most of the remainder will be dual three-lane standard. The length of all-purpose dual carriageway trunk road will be doubled, with nearly two-thirds being dual carriageway standard.

The programme will mean improvements to the trunk network in all regions of the country, including widening of 134 miles of the M1, over 80 miles of the M6 and over 100 miles of the M25.

In addition, a further 20 new schemes have been added to the road building programme first outlined in the white paper published last year. These include widening schemes on the M2 and M4.

In the past three years, the Department of Transport has completed 83 national trunk road schemes which added 289 miles of new or improved road.

To help deflect criticism of the road building plans, Mr Parkinson is proposing a series of environmental measures. Consultants would advise on best landscape and environmental treatment of motorway widening, and there would be a substantial increase in the planting of trees, and an increase of £500,000 in the archaeological works grant to English Heritage.

Source: Michael Smith, *Guardian*, 21 February 1990

Lancaster council's response to the forecasts and predictions of doom can be seen in the form of the City Centre Access Road (Figure 8 on page 423). The vehicle flows show the projected effect on all links on the system of this new road in 1996. The new road has a two-way flow of between 34,500 and 43,200 vpd and has brought about a redistribution of traffic in the central area.

There is no behavioural input into these calculations, however, and what we see is a network allocation in the future superimposed on a forecast of traffic volumes. This process produces highly unreliable numbers, but these are routinely used in the planning process for new roads.

The main effect of the new link is to reduce King Street flows from the range 26,000–29,000 vpd to the range 11,600–13,000 vpd and increase the flows on Great John Street–Dalton Square from the range 2,300–2,600 vpd to the range 6,200–7,300 vpd.

These forecasts and allocations were made by computer programs which use networks as their basic tools (for example TRANSYT). Networks and their mathematical analysis have provided a powerful tool in the 'solution' of Lancaster's traffic problems. They have also been used without any consideration for social or behavioural factors to produce a mechanistic solution to a problem that cannot be understood accurately by trend forecasts and allocation routines.

The movement of vehicles and people cannot be separated from the structure of cities and the motivations and aspirations of their inhabitants. In the case of Lancaster, car-based trips have risen in number as journeys to work have lengthened, public transport declined and parents have become more accustomed to transporting children in cars when 20 years ago the norm was walking or cycling. Changes in retailing, medical care and recreational activities have all contributed to the growth in car traffic. Networks alone cannot reflect these complex interactions between behaviour and land use. Nor can they cope with the existence of feedback loops (Figure 9).

Lancaster encapsulates a national problem. How to cope with the car in cities? It shows the application of sophisticated planning techniques and a rejection of criticisms based on experience elsewhere and the gut reaction of citizens who feel their city is being turned into an asphalt car park. If the new road goes ahead, together with the city centre redevelopments of which it is part, then Lancaster will move closer to the Los Angeles or Melbourne model of urban life where the car dominates and the walking and cycling dimension fades away. In this process the town dweller who moves around on foot is the loser and the long-distance commuter from a rural retreat is the winner. A battle about roads is in fact a battle about what kind of city we would choose to live in in the twenty-first century. In Lancaster the dice are loaded in favour of more cars and fewer people and an urban townscape dominated by the needs of motorised transport.

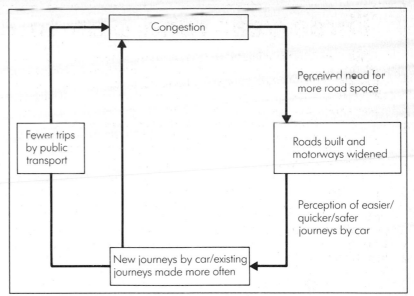

Figure 9 Feedback loops

Role play – planning new roads

Roads are frequently suggested as solutions to city traffic problems in spite of evidence that they can contribute to the creation of more traffic and make the problem worse.

1 See if you can find a proposal for a new road or a road improvement scheme in your local town or area. Try and collect information for and against the proposal from interested groups, such as the local authority, protest groups or perhaps a local branch of Transport 2000 (a pressure group which campaigns against unnecessary road building and for better public transport).

2 Organise the information under the main headings: for example, relieving congestion, improving the environment, improving access, etc. Perhaps you could carry out a traffic survey to discover the traffic use on the existing roads.

3 Divide into two groups to argue the case for the road proposal as at a public inquiry. The teacher or a group of students could act as the Inspector who has to make the final decision on the basis of the evidence presented. Each side should try to present its case covering the following areas:

For:
- Dealing with the increased numbers of vehicles;
- Reducing accidents by diverting traffic onto pedestrian-free roads;
- Economic development, jobs and prosperity.

Against:
- Noise, danger, air pollution and accidents;
- Need for more public transport;
- The quality of life in towns and cities (for cars or people?);
- Community severance (will the road divide communities?).

4 After the groups have presented their case, the Inspector should give a decision whether the road goes ahead.

The Settle-Carlisle railway

Railway closure proposals excite a great deal of interest and emotion in Britain. In the 1980s railways are a rapidly growing sector of the tourist economy, as well as a mode of transport which still penetrates remote areas of Britain not well served by other means of public transport. The Central Wales line, the Cotswold line, lines in the Scottish Highlands and the Settle–Carlisle line (Figure 10) are all routes which have come under the threat of closure but which for various reasons have survived.

Rail closures

Nevertheless the Beeching cuts of the 1960s did result in the loss of hundreds of miles of railway and the loss of several important routes, such as the Waverley line between Edinburgh and Carlisle. The debate about the Beeching cuts is still a live one. It is relevant background to list the arguments for and against rail closure.

For rail closure

● Rail is an outdated technology now largely replaced by motorised transport and well-designed modern roads.

● Rail is too inflexible and does not serve the locations chosen by manufacturing and service industries. These are no longer based in city centres as they were in the nineteenth century.

● Rail is very expensive to run and accounts for less than 10% of the freight moved and 20% of the passengers moved. Therefore it makes substantial financial losses and it is not right that these should be subsidised by car drivers and lorry operators.

● Rail trade unions are very inflexible and frequently resort to strike action. Road transport is

Figure 10 Dent station on the Settle-Carlisle line. The highest station on the route, it is now used as a field centre for Lancashire schools

not so heavily unionised and can be more efficient.

Against rail closure

● Rail is environmentally superior to road. Road transport is now a major contributor to atmospheric pollution, with nitrogen oxides, carbon dioxide, carbon monoxide and hydrocarbons. In 1986 out of 1.937 million tonnes of nitrogen oxide emissions, 40% was from road and 2% from rail. Nitrogen oxide is a major contributor to acid rain and to the development of photochemical smogs. The 'greenhouse effect' and cancers derived from hydrocarbons are major problems

which can only be resolved by reducing emissions. No known technology reduces carbon dioxide, which is a major source of the greenhouse effect.

● Rail is not expensive if all the social, economic and environmental costs of transport are taken into account. If an economic value is placed on noise, pollution, health, injury and death, road transport rapidly becomes a very uneconomic option compared to rail. A study by the German Federal Environment Office in Berlin shows that we should increase vehicle taxation on fuels by at least a factor of three to bring payment into line with the damage caused.

● Rail is much safer than road. Many lives could be saved if we could bring about a transfer of road trips to rail.

● Rail is much more energy-efficient than road. If is is necessary to conserve energy and reduce demand, then rail can transport more people further for the same expenditure of fuel.

● Rail is very economical in the land it uses. For a given capacity in terms of millions of passenger journeys, rail takes less than one-tenth of the space needed by road. Rail is the only form of transport which can support dense commuting flows into the centres of cities and (at the other extreme) can support leisure journeys into national parks without destroying the very thing that visitors are seeking.

In Germany these arguments have been given precise quantitative values in a series of research reports from IFEU and UPI in Heidelberg. In Britain the arguments came into sharp focus in the campaign to keep open the Settle–Carlisle line.

The history of the Settle–Carlisle line

British Rail announced its intention to close the Settle–Carlisle line in 1983 because it was uneconomic and in need of major investment to repair its large, stone-built Victorian viaducts, particularly the Ribblehead viaduct (Figure 12). The closure proposal was met by a storm of local opposition.

The line has had an eventful history. The original builders (the Midland Railway Company) obtained parliamentary approval in 1866, but tried to back out of the scheme in 1869, even before construction had begun. This attempt failed and Parliament insisted that the project go ahead. The line opened in 1876 (Figure 11).

Figure 11 Railways in the North-West

The line is regularly billed as one of the scenic wonders of upland Britain and its construction was a huge achievement. It required civil engineering on a massive scale without the benefits of heavy machinery such as cranes or bulldozers. The scale of the engineering effort involved can be judged from a list of its major structures, including 21 viaducts and 14 tunnels.

The line was first selected for closure in 1963 but consent was refused. In 1968 consent was given by government to the withdrawal of passenger services at all stations on the route apart from Appleby-in-Westmoreland and Settle. In 1976 the through London–Glasgow service was withdrawn, leaving only three inter-city trains each day in each direction between Nottingham and Glasgow. The decline continued into the 1980s, with a further reduction in service. The through trains from Nottingham to Glasgow were reduced to two per day and ran from Leeds to Carlisle. This led to a further drop in income for the line, leaving it in a very precarious financial condition and a suitable candidate for closure.

Reasons for closure

?

1 As you read this section, take the role of a local historian in 1995 who is preparing a book on this area. One section will deal with the arguments for and against the closure of the railway. The views of British Rail and the Transport Users' Consultative Committees (TUCCs) will need to be set out clearly. Before you start this task, read through the section and make notes under the headings: Statements for; Statements against.

The case for closure is financial. British Rail's case was that in 1982 the line was incurring annual costs of £1.3–1.8 million with a revenue of £509,000. This produced an annual deficit of £0.79–1.291 million. In addition to this unfavourable revenue situation British Rail stressed the problems involved in repairing the Ribblehead Viaduct. This is a large structure towards the southern end of the line, 400 metres long and 30 metres high, with 24 arches, and represents an imposing monument to the era of railway construction. British Rail's estimate for the repair of this structure was in the £4–6 million range, but by 1989 had come down to £1.5 million.

At the public hearings into the proposed closure of the line in 1986 British Rail refused to discuss financial matters, even though their case for closure was based on a financial assessment. All the organisations opposing closure disputed the financial details and presented evidence to show that the line, although not

Figure 12 The Ribblehead viaduct

profitable, was as profitable as any other line in the same operational group.

The financial case for the line was certainly much stronger in 1989 than it was in 1983. In this six-year period passenger journeys rose from 90,000 to approximately 500,000 annually and revenue stood at £1.4 million in the 1988–9 financial year. BR argued that this was a 'closure effect' and would rapidly fade away after rail fans had had their 'last' trip. This proved to be inaccurate, as the line attracted more and more passengers, a trend which has continued through 1989.

The growth in passenger traffic has demonstrated that the demand for rail travel exists and, more importantly, that the level of rail usage is a function of the level of marketing effort and quality of the service offered. This fact is important for the future of rail transport. It means that poor levels of patronage can be artificially created simply as a result of inadequate management input and neglect. Closure then becomes a self-justifying procedure and, paradoxically, leads to loss of revenue potential. The case of the Settle–Carlisle line illustrates this in the context of a rural line passing through attractive countryside, but the same concept can be applied to commuter trips in cities.

British Rail used network arguments to support their case

for closure. The map of rail routes in the north of England shows that there is an argument for the Settle–Carlisle route being superfluous to requirements.

British Rail argued that passengers using the route would transfer to alternative services along the West Coast main line or Cumbrian coast line, leading only to a small loss of revenue caused by the closure. In terms of route alternatives and journey times the argument is plausible. However, a Joint Action Committee (JAC) survey of passengers on trains over the Settle–Carlisle route revealed that 80% of passengers would not switch to other lines. They were travelling simply because they liked the route. Once again behavioural considerations show the need for a careful evaluation of network arguments in their wider context.

The reprieve for the line

The Settle–Carlisle closure proposal was subjected to a statutory procedure of public hearings (as required by the Transport Act 1962). A total of 22,000 objections to the proposed closure were received and 20 days of hearings were held to hear evidence. Most of the evidence concerned the damage that would be done to local communities should they be deprived of their rail service. Essential journeys to work, shop or medical facilities would be made difficult or impossible. The damage to tourism in the area would have a serious effect on the local economy. The hearings were conducted by the Transport Users' Consultative Committees (TUCCs), one for North-East England and one for North-West England. Both TUCCs concluded their investigations and reported to the Secretary of State for Transport in December 1986. Their conclusion was clear:

'On the basis of the undoubted hardship that closure of the line would cause, together with the strength of the commercial case presented for its retention, the Committees strongly and emphatically recommend that consent to BR's proposal to close the Settle–Carlisle line be refused.'

The TUCCs had to argue primarily on grounds of 'hardship' to existing users. This is the rather narrow definition laid down by the Transport Act 1962 of the reasons why a line might remain open. Hardship was demonstrated at the hearings, even though it is a difficult concept to define. Settle Town Council presented evidence at the hearings from a survey of 1,400 visitors in 1985. Of these, 36% stated that they would not have come to Settle had there been no trains. Settle is a very small town (population 2,500) and dependent on tourism revenues. The loss of this revenue or a significant proportion of this revenue would have a serious effect on the local economy.

Economic hardship is only one aspect of hardship. The population of Settle would be subjected to many other problems without the line. A county council survey of passengers between Settle and Skipton showed that, of 20,800 existing journeys, 8,400 would not be made after closure of the line. (Note that the line between Skipton, Settle Junction and Morecambe would remain open.) The TUCCs were particularly concerned about the elderly, those with heavy luggage, people with young children and pushchairs and all those without access to a car. Many examples of individual hardship were detailed in the TUCC report.

The TUCC case for retaining the line was extremely sound and clearly influenced the government. On 11 April 1989 (27 months after the TUCC hearings) the minister concerned announced that he had refused consent for closure. He gave his reasons:

- improved traffic (40% higher in 1988–90 than in 1987–88);

- wider social and economic considerations;

- the willingness of local authorities and agencies such as English Heritage to put money into the line;

- the reduced costs of repairing Ribblehead Viaduct;

- the willingness of British Rail and the private sector to co-operate in promoting the line and developing private sector projects.

1 Read the article 'Not so much a train, more a way of life' (page 430). Who stood to gain and who to lose by closure of the line? What alternatives were there for local people if the line had closed?

2 Should local communities be given the resources to oppose national organisations (by paying for consultants and lawyers, for example)? What are the advantages and disadvantages of doing this?

3 One of the ideas for the line, as explained in the article 'Rise in traffic saves Settle rail route' (page 431), was for a privately run railway. Would this have been a good option for the Settle–Carlisle route? Give your reasons. Should the local community itself be given the right to own and run its services (in this case the railway), as opposed to a national or private company?

Not so much a train, more a way of life

FARMER'S daughter Nicola Fryer was in particularly good humour yesterday. The Transport Secretary, Paul Channon, had just done her a good turn.

By announcing the reprieve of the Settle–Carlisle rail link, he had also cleared the way for this fifth-former's future. Without the picturesque but "uneconomic" railway, she would be unable to travel from her home near Kirkby Stephen to take up a place on a new drama course at Carlisle School of Art.

"If the line had closed, I would have had to drop out of Carlisle and do something different at Kendal," she said. "But that's not what I wanted. It would also have left me feeling rather cut off. I am just very, very glad about the news."

She will not be alone. Students travelling to college in Carlisle from Kirkby Stephen and Appleby make up more than half the 60 to 70 commuters who arrive in Carlisle on the early morning train each day.

Even in the driving rain and intermittent sleet yesterday, with low cloud hiding the Pennine peaks, the trip from Settle was stunning: through the dry-stone wall country of the Dales, over the spectacular Ribblehead Viaduct, into Dent – which proclaims itself the highest railway in England – and through the rolling Eden Valley.

Mrs Alice Fisher, 62, has been using the line for 40 years for round trips from her home in Keighley to visit her ageing mother-in-law in hospital near Carlisle. Without the link, the regular journey would be too daunting.

"At my age, it is too far to drive all the way, so if they had closed the line, I would have had to go right across to the west coast by train," she said.

"The return journey would have been impractical to do in a day – I just could not have visited my mother-in-law as often as I do now. It's a tremendous service and I rely totally on it." She is now so familiar with the beautiful scenery that she spent her time intently knitting a cardigan for a grandchild.

Train driver David Parrinder, who started in the days of steam, said: "There is nowhere that compares with this run, I am delighted it has been saved – it is great news for everybody, not just railwaymen."

The route provides a lifeline for people in isolated Cumbrian and Yorkshire communities. With rural bus services sharply cut back and the poor state of road links, for some the train is the only means of reaching hospitals, shops and schools. It takes on extra importance in winter when snow can leave many country roads impassable. This is not so much a train, say locals, as a way of life.

There are half a dozen trains each day; the return fare for the 144-mile round trip is £7.60. Standards are variable: yesterday the train from Settle was spotlessly clean, but on the train from Carlisle grimy windows hid the view and coaches were deep in litter.

Keith Morgan, a picture framer who is also mayor of Appleby, the only stop left on the line, has spent nearly 10 years campaigning to save it. Despite his delight at the decision, he urged caution: "We have still got to make sure the line is not run down. The next stage is to work on developing and marketing it with the local authorities and private business."

Back in Settle, the Union flag was hoisted above the town hall and nearby Castleberg Rock. The mayoress cracked a bottle of champagne on the platform to celebrate the tiny North Yorkshire town's victory over mighty and obdurate British Rail.

In the ticket office, a listed building with freshly-cut flowers in the waiting room, stationmaster Ken Keen had no doubt what Channon's decision meant for the town.

"If this line had closed, people would have been devastated – it is as simple as that. Everyone is delighted."

Source: Philip Sherwell, *Daily Telegraph*, 13 April 1989

The Settle–Carlisle line has survived its severest test to date. This is an outcome which has benefited local communities, benefited the environment of an upland area which would otherwise come under even greater pressure from car-based leisure trips and benefited all those who can now gain access to this region and walk or cycle from station to station. No-one has lost.

British Rail will, on the contrary, improve their revenues from an outcome that they resisted for six years. Any lingering doubts which remain to cloud the issue must concern the characteristics of a political and economic system which can impose such stress on local communities and pursue objectives which are so narrow and perverse.

Rise in traffic saves Settle rail route

THE future of the 72-mile Settle to Carlisle railway was secured yesterday when the Government announced a change of heart and refused British Rail permission to close it.

Mr Paul Channon, the Transport Secretary, said the reprieve stemmed from the line's recent popularity. Revenue has risen by 40 per cent over the past year and the number of passengers increased fivefold to 450,000 since 1980.

Mr Channon said last year that he would accept BR's case for closure and opened negotiations with the private sector to find a suitable bidder.

This proved unsuccessful but the year's breathing space convinced the Government that the line could be viable. Mr Channon said that if repairs were counted, it was still likely to make a small loss, but would probably be profitable on the operational side.

He was concerned at the hardship facing local people, who accounted for 100,000 of the 450,000 journeys last year.

Mr Channon said BR will now seek private sector and local authority co-operation to promote and develop the line. This may include a railway museum to celebrate what has been called a symbol of Victorian ingenuity and engineering skill and, along with York Minster and Hadrian's Wall, one of the three wonders of the North.

The line has recently been one of the best performers in BR's provincial sector, but the board based its case for closure on the cost of repairing the centre-piece of the line, the 24-arch Ribblehead viaduct.

When BR first announced closure plans in November 1983, it estimated the cost of repairing the viaduct to be more than £5 million, but Mr Channon said yesterday it would be much lower.

Latest estimates suggest the bill will be between £2 million and £3 million. Much of the money will come from English Heritage and local authorities.

The line, built between 1869 and 1876, was the last to be built by traditional navvy methods. Hundreds of men died during work on the 325 bridges, 21 viaducts and 14 tunnels.

Yesterday's decision also means a reprieve for the associated Blackburn–Hellifield line. It is a triumph for the many protesters and railway enthusiasts who fought a prolonged battle, and the local authorities which pumped money into the line three years ago, enabling regular stopping trains to run for the first time since 1970.

The interest generated by the closure fight and better marketing by BR has meant that the number of trains has increased from two to five a day, with stops for local residents and hikers at picturesque halts such as Dent station, the highest in England and five miles from the Dales village from which it takes its name.

BR welcomed the decision because it ended the uncertainty. It will now look at ways of cutting costs, including radio signalling, different rolling stock, and turning the line into a single track.

Source: Larry Elliott, *Guardian*, 12 April 1989

Transport to a proposed nuclear waste 'dump' at Heysham

The purpose of this part of the chapter is to show how transport issues are central to major planning controversies. Transport issues are frequently considered in isolation from the land use context with which they are closely associated, and the intention here is to show the intimate links between a major land use issue and its transport implications. The issue chosen is the proposed siting of a 'dump' for spent nuclear fuel at Heysham near Lancaster in the North-West of England.

When considering this example you should try and make connections with other land use issues that have arisen in recent years and describe their transport implications. Good examples include out-of-town shopping centres and hypermarkets, new towns in Green Belts, and proposals for leisure developments in National Parks or areas of great scenic beauty outside the Parks.

The transport issues which these developments raise are central to the viability and the credibility of the scheme itself and are often the source of much local concern and opposition.

Plans for the store

In 1988 the Central Electricity Generating Board (CEGB) announced a plan to construct a 'dry fuel buffer store' at the Heysham nuclear power plant near Lancaster. The purpose of the store would be to receive spent nuclear fuel from all the AGR nuclear power stations in Britain and to store it until reprocessing was thought to be necessary. Reprocessing currently takes place at Sellafield (formerly called Windscale) in Cumbria, but there are serious problems with the disposal of high-level (i.e. very toxic) waste from this site. In addition, the CEGB is less convinced than in former times about the need to reprocess. The CEGB is also concerned about the costs of reprocessing, and a store at Heysham keeps their options open. If the operators of the plant at Sellafield (British Nuclear Fuels Ltd – BNFL) increase their price, the CEGB at the moment has little alternative but to pay. With a store they can hold the waste for at least 50 years and probably longer. This is bound to put a downward pressure on reprocessing costs and save the CEGB money.

The idea of a central store is a major departure from current practices. At the moment each nuclear power station stores its own spent fuel for approximately 100 days until it cools sufficiently to be transported to Sellafield. The present system is compared with the system with a store in Figure 13.

The proposal for a store has excited a great deal of local opposition and is a classic example of a locational decision bringing serious environmental hazards to a community and stimulating the formation of opposition groups and a campaign to have the plan scrapped.

The purpose of this part of the chapter is to unravel the transport elements of the argument and to emphasise, as before, the intimate relationships between transport and other layers of argument which cloud the transport issue. As in the case of the Lancaster relief road and the Settle–Carlisle line, a transport issue usually signals the existence

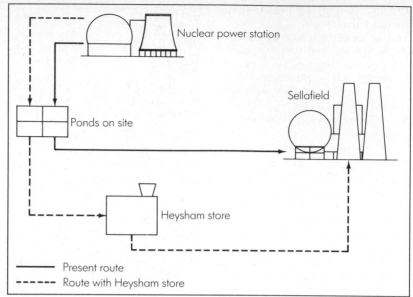

Figure 13 The circulation of spent nuclear fuel in Britain

of deeper issues about choices and preferences, concerns about health and environment and problems with political decision-making processes.

The nuclear fuel cycle

Before proceeding further it will be necessary to describe the basics of the nuclear fuel cycle and nuclear activities in Britain. With this as background we can look at the transport arguments against the store and spell out the connections between these arguments and the more general concerns about any nuclear activity.

The map in Figure 14 shows nuclear Britain. Each of the locations is involved in a flow of nuclear materials which is both national and international. This flow follows a particular sequence of operations and is known as the 'nuclear fuel cycle'. It covers the whole range of operations from the origin of nuclear fuels as a rock (uranium) to be mined through to its final destination as waste in storage at Sellafield or as waste emptied into the Irish Sea and vented to the atmosphere.

The nuclear fuel cycle is

essentially a transport process which involves highly dangerous toxic elements. Uranium ore is extracted in Canada, the USA, Namibia, Australia and France and processed into uranium oxide ('yellowcake'). One tonne of yellowcake produces 100 tonnes of waste which accumulates in tips at the source or at the site of processing. The wastes are

Figure 14 Nuclear Britain

radioactive and are a documented health hazard both to workers and to local residents. Uranium oxide arrives in Britain by sea (usually via Liverpool) and is transported to BNFL Springfields near Preston. This is the start of the fuel cycle in the North-West. The concentration of facilities (significant on a global scale) in the North-West is one of the arguments put by protesters against the store at Heysham. The diagram right (Figure 15) shows the North-West's concentration of nuclear facilities in relation to population centres and transport routes.

After Springfields, the uranium mixture is enriched to increase the proportion of uranium 235 in the fuel. This process is carried out at BNFL's Capenhurst plant near Chester (see Figure 15). Enriched fuel is then transported back to Springfields for fabrication into fuel rods. The completed fuel rods are then despatched to all power stations.

Once in the reactor core, nuclear fuel begins to disintegrate into many different radioactive fission products and gives off a

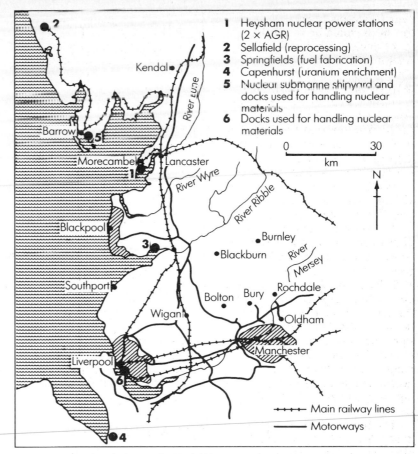

1 Heysham nuclear power stations (2 × AGR)
2 Sellafield (reprocessing)
3 Springfields (fuel fabrication)
4 Capenhurst (uranium enrichment)
5 Nuclear submarine shipyard and docks used for handling nuclear materials
6 Docks used for handling nuclear materials

Figure 15 Nuclear facilities in the North-West

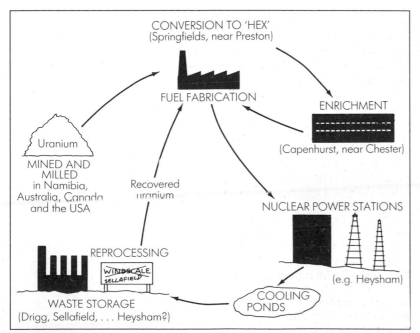

Figure 16 The nuclear fuel cycle in the North-West

good deal of heat. It is this heat which is used to produce steam, drive turbines and generate electricity. In this process the fuel rods degenerate and need replacement. Once removed from the reactor core they are both highly radioactive and very hot, and they stay that way for decades. Once outside the reactor they must be heavily shielded and handled by remote control. After removal they are stored on the site of the nuclear power station for up to 100 days whilst they cool (usually under water). After cooling they move to Sellafield for further storage under water and eventual reprocessing. This process is summarised in Figure 16.

Physical movements of nuclear products can be summarised in a network diagram (Figure 17).

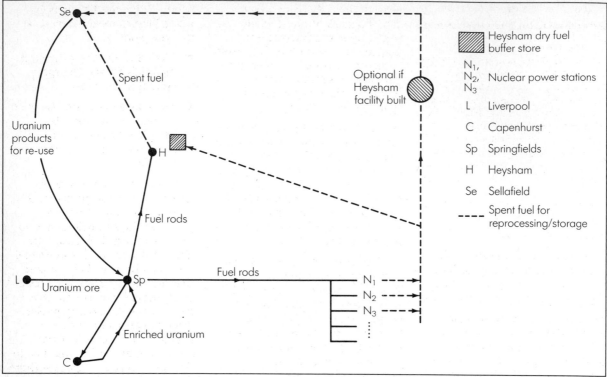

Figure 17 Network diagram of the flow of nuclear products in North-West England

Heysham 'a nuclear dustbin' says county's leader

BUILDING a store for spent fuel rods at Heysham would turn Lancashire into the nuclear dustbin of Britain, the leader of the county council has claimed.

Coun. Mrs Louise Ellman urged the county policy and resources committee to press their officers to arm themselves with the expertise needed to be able to evaluate properly CEGB's proposal for a £220 million national store.

She argued that it was important that the county remained the environmental watchdogs and that she could see no justification for building a store which would be the equivalent of 17 storeys high and 30 times bigger than a football pitch.

Backing the stand already taken by Lancaster City Council, Coun.

Mrs Ellman said there were six key points of concern.

● Why should Lancashire be singled out to house the spent fuel rods from all of Britain's advanced gas-cooled reactors?

● Were there any guarantees that no international waste would be brought to the store?

● What were the dangers of transporting the rods?

● If they were transported by sea would this increase the risk of accidents or nuclear pollution along the coast line?

● Had the economics of double handling been considered?

● And what were the implications for the emergency services?

But at the same time MP for Morecambe and Lunesdale, Mr Mark Lennox-Boyd, said in a

letter to constituents that it would be irresponsible of him not to give a qualified welcome to the proposals.

"I would never advocate for anyone something which I felt to be remotely unsafe and I would never support anything which I did not consider to be in the interests of my constituents," he wrote.

He said the rods would not be permanently stored at Heysham and added that the British nuclear industry was one of the safest if not the safest in the world.

And he gave notice of his intention to attend any public meetings that were called saying that CEGB would also send an expert representative in a bid to allay public concern.

Source: Lancaster Guardian, 14 October 1988

?

1 From the article 'Heysham a "nuclear dustbin" says county's leader' pick out the transport issues mentioned by Mrs Ellman. As you read through the next section, make notes of ways that her questions can be answered or if they produce further queries. Using your notes, draft a short letter from her to her MP, bearing in mind the views that are attributed to him in the article.

The movement of this radioactive material presents specific transport problems:

● The material is intrinsically dangerous and presents special problems for emergency services should an accident occur.

● There is a risk to human health from the movement of these products under normal circumstances (i.e. without an accident). This is difficult to quantify and there is argument about the effects of low-level radiation on human health.

● Transport problems are exacerbated by specific difficulties on the route, especially where there are embankments, tunnels or viaducts. Where these occur near centres of population, the consequences of an accident would be particularly severe. Galgate to the south of Lancaster is such an example. A high-level rail viaduct already carrying spent nuclear fuel crosses the centre of the village.

● Rail is the preferred means of transport for nuclear cargoes, but spent fuel from Chapel Cross in Dumfriesshire does travel by road to Sellafield. Given the enormous disparity between road and rail accident rates, the movement of nuclear cargoes by road gives rise to special concern.

● Transport represents a linear extension of a point-base hazard. Whilst we are reasonably familiar with emergency planning and coping with hazards at a point, we are very ill-prepared for moving cargoes, especially cargoes that pass through densely populated areas and share the track with inter-city trains carrying over 500 people. In effect we have a constantly-changing hazard that creates a danger zone one kilometre wide and several hundred kilometres long.

Opposition to the 'dump', as it is described by its opponents, has been vociferous. Two closely-related issues have emerged as the key points:

● The extra loading of nuclear materials on the transport system of the area.

● The concentration of all spent nuclear fuel at one site (Heysham) rather than storage at source and/or storage at Sellafield.

The first of these is an interesting transport problem. If we refer to the map of nuclear power stations in Britain and to the rail system, it is clear that most, if not all, of the spent fuel from English and Welsh power stations already travels through Lancashire. If we assume that all the spent fuel currently passes through Lancaster, then the construction of a store does not make all that much difference to the area's current exposure (from the transport chain) to hazardous materials. The exposure from the actual storage operation is another matter. In effect, Lancaster already has the spent fuel. The store, it could be argued, will not make much difference to the transport of material, only to the length of time it stays there.

Figure 18 Crash between an empty train and a nuclear container (filled with water and steel bars), staged by BR in 1984. The container was undamaged

'Nuclear trains would use resort's station'

Trains carrying high-level radioactive material will stop at Morecambe's Promenade station on their way to the proposed reactor and store at Heysham it was revealed by a protestor on Tuesday.

About seven trains per week would arrive at Heysham carrying spent fuel from Britain's 14 AGR reactors – and would have to be routed through Morecambe to use the branch line to Heysham, county councillors heard.

Veteran railwayman, Mr Bert Farrar, told CEGB officials and councillors at the board's presentation to the county council that each train carrying nuclear flasks would have to stand in Morecambe station for at least half an hour while the locomotive was switched to take the train on to Heysham.

"How can you tell us that is safe? Everything is safe until a disaster happens – we have seen that in London this week. You want to put profits before safety and before the wishes of the community and that is deplorable."

Mr Farrar, a lifelong Morecambe Tory and an active LAND campaigner, said thousands of people from Crewe, up to Whitehaven and in the Isle of Man had signed a petition against the store.

CEGB transportation expert, Mr Richard Pannett said it was up to British Rail how it organised the movement of trains. If the trains were routed through passenger platforms that gave him no cause for concern, as the fuel flasks were scrupulously tested for safety.

A party of LAND members travelled from Lancaster to lobby the meeting. Some blew cascades of soap bubbles which drifted down from the public gallery, to symbolise the CEGB's promises, which, they said, were like froth which vanished into thin air.

County Coun. Keith Roach said the thought of holiday makers getting off trains at the Promenade station alongside trains carrying nuclear fuel was "diabolical". And he warned, "You made your announcement on September 15, that is the anniversary of the Battle of Britain. I was in the RAF and I can promise you that this plan will be fought with the same commitment as we fought then."

Former County Council leader, Mr Jim Mason said the people of Silverdale were horrified at the prospect of nuclear trains passing within a quarter of a mile of their homes. And he accused the CEGB of underestimating the number of train movements involved in delivering the fuel to Heysham and transporting it back north to Sellafield.

Earlier, CEGB planning manager Mr George Johnson, said that local opposition was not enough to deter the board from their plans. "If all you are saying is just 'Go Away', that isn't a sufficient reason." He said he was very disappointed by the negative attitude being shown by local people. The local community had not benefited enough in the past from the building of the two power stations at Heysham because local firms had lacked entrepreneurial skills, he added.

Rejecting the charge that to store spent fuel for up to 50 years amounted to permanent storage, Mr Johnson said it would take a national catastrophe for things to get that far. The proposed extension of the store, enlarging it seven times, would only be needed if reprocessing was halted. After 50 years any fuel left in the store would not be left there, but transported to another store or a foreign reprocessing plant.

CEGB health and safety spokesman, Mr Stan Rodcliffe, said that leukaemia was not a product of the nuclear age, but had existed for centuries.

Mr Johnson freely admitted the prime reason for the store was commercial. Many councillors urged the Board to go back to BNFL and negotiate a better price for reprocessing rather than spend 220 million on a national store.

Source: Lancaster Guardian, 10 February 1989

Interestingly for the Galgate residents and their proximity to a railway viaduct, the store does not in itself make a great deal of difference. The issue of the store has given the residents an opportunity to voice long-standing opposition to the transport issue, something which was not well articulated before the proposal.

?

1 Read the article 'Nuclear trains would use resort's station'. Make notes of the CEGB's responses to the transport protesters. Add other arguments in favour of the proposal. Draft a short letter to the local MP, saying why you think the proposal should go ahead.

A store located at Heysham may not increase the number of spent fuel 'units' passing through the area, but it does increase the amount of time spent in transit because of the need to leave the West Coast Main Line (WCML) and transfer to a minor branch line which connects Lancaster (on the WCML) with Morecambe and

Heysham (see Figure 19).

Let us assume an arbitrary number of 25 flasks per week from all power stations passing through Lancaster in a northerly direction and heading for Sellafield. Let us further assume:

- No stops for any reason
- A constant speed of 30 km/h.
- A 30 minute transit time for a 15 km journey.

Note: The speed chosen may be too low. If it is, the effect is to make the difference between the store and no-store options smaller. A faster speed means the nuclear materials clear the area much more quickly, heightening the time difference between the transit traffic and the more circuitous local traffic en route to Heysham. This means the bias (if any) is in favour of the CEGB.

On the basis of these assumptions we can calculate that each nuclear 'unit' or flask stays in the area for 30 minutes. This produces 25×30 units of exposure or 750 units. This represents the existing situation with no central store at Heysham.

Let us now assume that the store is in place. A calculation of exposure units must be done in two parts. The first covers the shipment of flasks into the store and the second the shipment out of the store to Sellafield. The CEGB has declared its intent to carry out the latter operation. The store is not a permanent facility.

A comparison of the present situation with the proposed store arrangement shows the following. Units of exposure under present transport arrangements are 750. If the store is built, they will total 2,400 (bigger by a factor of 3.2).

These calculations do not take into account any periods of time when flasks are left in sidings, delayed at signals or held in the open whilst waiting for docking at the store. Nor do they take into account the differences between Magnox and AGR fuels and the reorientation of flows of nuclear

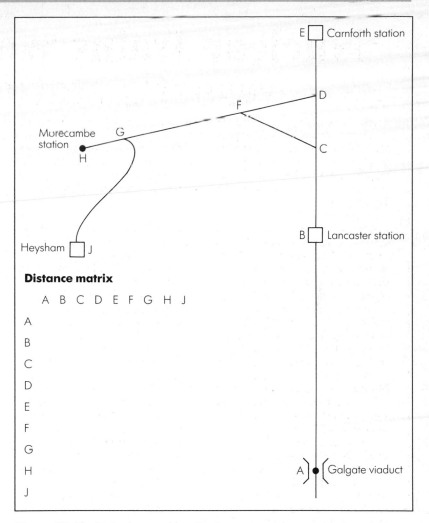

Distance matrix

A B C D E F G H J

A

B

C

D

E

F

G

H

J

Figure 19 The local rail system serving Heysham

---

1   Inward transport

Main line length = 9km; junction length = 11km

Passage time for main line length (9km at 30km/h)	= 20 minutes
Passage time for junction (11km at 20km/h)	= 32 minutes
Total	= 52 minutes

Units of exposure = $25 \times 52 = 1,300$

2   Outward transport

Junction length = 11km; main line length = 6km

Passage time for junction length (11km at 20km/h)	= 32 minutes
Passage time for main line length (6km at 30km/h)	= 12 minutes
Total	= 44 minutes

Units of exposure = $25 \times 44 = 1,100$

Figure 20 Heysham nuclear power station

materials from Scottish power stations and Hartlepool from Sellafield to Heysham should the store proceed. More importantly, the calculations have nothing at all to do with the most important issue – the long-term storage of these flasks at Heysham. These are important issues but beyond the scope of a chapter on transport.

Opponents of the store have suggested that spent fuel should be kept at the nuclear power station where it was produced under exactly the same circumstances as have been proposed for the central store in Heysham. This has been rejected by the CEGB, but the choice poses some interesting problems for the transport geographer. The arguments of both sides can be summarised in Table 1.

In this matrix of alternatives there are clear winners and losers. The CEGB is convinced that the facility will be better because this is the least-cost option for them. The groups fighting the plan argue that this is to ask too much of the local communities which will have to live with the facility. As there is no mechanism in society for putting costs on what the local community must endure (for example on fear, stress or health risks under normal operation and on the enormous costs should an accident occur) these costs are not considered. Nevertheless they are real. Given this imbalance, which is also a feature of the Lancaster relief road and the Settle–Carlisle railway line, there is a strong likelihood that the CEGB will get its store at Heysham.

A planning application was to have been made in autumn 1989 but has been delayed by uncertainties over electricity privatisation. Any planning application will almost certainly be followed by a public inquiry into the proposal. The outcome will be awaited with great interest.

Table 1 A comparison of the LAND and CEGB positions on the store issue

	CEGB	LAND
Store at Heysham	There is a lot of land available at Heysham already in CEGB ownership and room for expansion. There will be economies of scale in handling all the waste at one site (for example only one set of expensive handling equipment).	There is already enough nuclear activity at Heysham. To concentrate more is to increase the level of risk to an unacceptable level. Heysham is badly sited because of its proximity to population centres.
Store at each station	Too costly. There would have to be expensive duplication of facilities.	Spreads the risk and avoids the possibility of a major disaster should something go wrong with either the power station or the store.

CEGB = Central Electricity Generating Board   LAND = Lancashire against the Nuclear Dump

?

1 Let us suppose that a planning application has been made. A public inquiry is taking place. You have decided to prepare a paper of 1,500 words to road at the inquiry. You should take up a viewpoint (for or against the planning application) and select points and arguments to support your stance. Your paper will need to be persuasively written as well as factually correct. This may be a case where you deliberately create a bias for your own point of view (see the introductory section on bias, pp. 4–5).

2 Assume that you have to organise the shipment of a very hazardous cargo across a large urban area you know. Select a route and a means of transport which minimises the damage to the local population should anything go wrong.

You should consider any mode of transport and more than one in combination, the density of population and its proximity to transport routes or terminals (for example, airports, railway stations, sidings) and the risks of accidents for any particular mode. You should also consider the time of day. The numbers of people exposed to this hazard will vary enormously depending on the time of day. These risks are independent of the load carried and accident rates for road, rail and air can be found in *Transport Statistics Great Britain, 1979–1989*, published for the Department of Transport by HMSO. You should map your chosen routes in some detail and select the least risky route from all the alternatives.

You can build into your analysis a further constraint such as the necessity to avoid all schools and hospitals on your routes and all other sites of hazardous chemical or nuclear activity.

Conclusion

The three case studies in this chapter were chosen to illustrate the complex interrelationships between transport problems, environmental impacts and the needs and aspirations of local communities. Each of the issues discussed has clear winners and losers and illustrates the political problems associated with the resolution of these conflicts in a democratic society. In the case of the Settle–Carlisle line the local communities won. The result in the other two cases is not yet known. The case studies show the degree to which transport problems are embedded in wider societal problems and the degree to which simplistic arguments about networks and structures fail to grasp the richness of social and behavioural modifications of these structures. The three proposals are summarised in Table 2.

Table 2 Summary of the three case studies

	Lancaster's road plan	Settle–Carlisle railway	Nuclear store at Heysham
Originator of scheme	Lancaster City Council Lancashire County Council	British Rail	CEGB
Local opposition	Very large LPAG[1]	Very large FOSCLA[2] SCJAC[3]	Very large LAND[4]
Main arguments of opponents	Environmental damage Loss of city centre land Loss of safe walking routes Community severance	Loss of transport in rural areas Loss of recreational opportunities Economic damage	Danger from radioactive waste in long term store Transport dangers
Benefits seen by proposers	Solve traffic problems by building more roads Increase use of shopping centre by encouraging cars	Save money	Save money More security for electricity generation
Gains to local community	Some gains to car users, but soon overtaken by traffic growth	None	A few jobs, CEGB claim tourism benefits
Overall gainers	'Technocratic' planning Out-of-town car users	None (the marginal gain to BR would not be noticed)	Electricity industry

[1] Lancaster Plan Action Group
[2] Friends of the Settle Carlisle Line Association
[3] Settle–Carlisle Joint Action Committee
[4] Lancashire Against the Nuclear Dump

17

Socialist industrialisation: in Hungary

Alan Dingsdale

Small and large tractors produced at the Rába Hungarian Wagon and Machine factory, Györ

What is socialist industrialisation? What is market socialism?

In this chapter you will be investigating four main themes about the impact of socialist industrialisation in Hungary, so you will be able to begin to answer the questions in the heading above. The themes are:

● Industrialisation and the national development strategy
● Industrialisation and the firm
● Industrialisation and regional change

Remember that Hungary is a specific example and that (from the mid-1960s to the late 1980s) each Eastern-bloc country followed its own distinctive path to socialist industrialisation.

Nationalisation, central decision making and planning – the three great pillars of the communist economic system – lasted in most Eastern European socialist countries until the collapse of communist power in late 1989. Consequently, privatisation, the transfer of ownership from state to private citizens, has become a sudden and crucial issue. In Hungary, however, moves to privatise businesses have been occurring with increasing speed throughout the 1980s. This has taken several forms, all of which are mentioned in this chapter. They include increasing freedom for small private businesses, the break-up of large state companies and trusts, the rapid growth of joint ventures with Western corporations, and the joint actions of local authorities and private firms. All of these processes were boosted by legal changes which allowed new forms of economic organisation to be created. As a result, though privatisation is an important aspect of economic change it is not the critical issue that it is elsewhere.

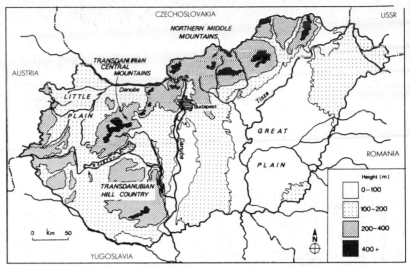

Figure 1 Hungary: physical regions

Major economic regions

CENTRAL	NORTHERN GREAT PLAIN
Budapest	Szabolcs-Szatmár
Pest	Hajbu-Bihar
	Szolnok
NORTH-WEST	
Györ-Sopron	SOUTHERN GREAT PLAIN
Komaron	Békés
Fejér	Csongrád
Veszprém	Bács-Kiskun
Vas	
	SOUTHERN TRANSDANUBIA
NORTH	Tolna
Borsod-Abaúj-Zemplén	Baranya
Heves	Somogy
Nógrád	Zala

Figure 2 Hungary: counties and economic regions

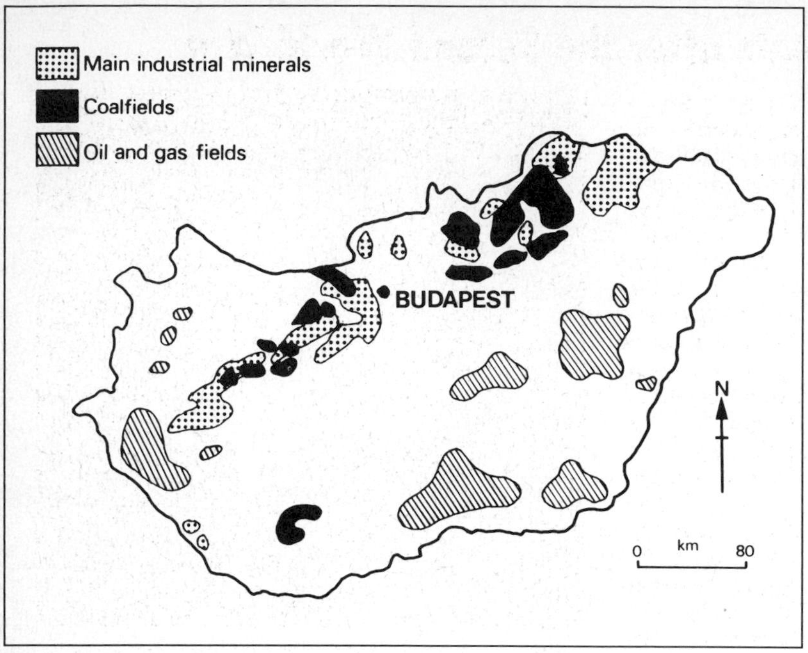

Figure 3 Distribution of industrial raw materials

Hungary (Figures 1 and 2 on page 441) is poorly endowed with industrial minerals and energy resources (Figure 3). There are small deposits of a wide range of non-ferrous metal ores, but only bauxite is abundant. Several small coalfields yield mainly brown coal, but they are technically difficult to work. There are some small oil and natural gas fields.

?

1 Using Figures 1, 2 and 3 draw a sketch map showing the distribution of mineral and energy resources in Hungary, relating them to their place names.

Industrialisation and the national development strategy

In 1947 under the leadership of the Hungarian Socialist Workers Party (we call it the Communist Party) the Hungarian government set about the task of developing and modernising Hungary by building a socialist economy. The economic management of this process we can call the *national development strategy*. In this strategy decisions were made about the ownership and organisation of production, which sectors should grow, how work should be organised and who should decide about economic and social development.

The period of central planning, 1947-68

Gyurkò is a Hungarian writer who experienced the post-war development of Hungary. Read his description of the first phase of development. You may have heard the term *centrally planned economy*. In this article you will find the main features of the system that is given this name.

?

1 Using Gyurkò's article opposite, note down references to nationalisation, planning, central control and self-sufficiency.

2 Do you think Gyurkò thought that the strategy of a centrally planned economy was a good one?

3 What part did industrialisation play in this strategy and how does Gyurkò measure the success of its role?

4 In your opinion, what were the positive aspects of this strategy and what were the negative aspects for Hungary at this time?

5 How had historical circumstances affected the government's assessment of the situation?

6 Why do you think Hungary adopted the policy of a centrally planned economy?

Developments after the Second World War

From the end of the forties, Hungary lived in the atmosphere of the Cold War, with a siege mentality. This also explains why she aimed to be 'a country of iron and steel'. It was not an easy task for a primarily agricultural country poor in natural resources. Hungary was the bread basket of the Austro-Hungarian Monarchy while industry developed mostly in Austria and Czechoslovakia. The roles were the same in the German-Italian-Hungarian alliance during the thirties.

Yet Hungary became an industrial-agricultural country within fifteen years. But at what a price! The great projects, first of all in heavy industry, were completed at a forced pace beginning at the end of the forties. The result was that industrial production grew by 50 per cent between 1950 and 1952 and the standard of living decreased by 20 per cent.

The totally centralised management of the economy was not a fortunate matter either. All production quotas were set centrally; they thought it was possible to determine at a desk in the capital what and how much every production unit of the country had to produce. This structure was organically linked to the power structure in which all significant decisions were centralised in the hands of a few people.[...]

With slight exaggeration, I could say that the ideal picture the leaders of the time had in mind was of a single foundry, a single bakery, a single food trading company, a single cooperative in the whole country which then could be managed centrally at the press of a button.

It was another peculiarity of the period that quantity was the sole consideration in production. There was a realistic basis to this as it was impossible to mine as much coal, to produce as much steel, to make as many clothes and bake as much bread as was needed to satisfy the suddenly increased demands. Quality was not a consideration even in the case of export products because the other socialist countries had the same shortage problems and there was a buyer for everything in every quantity, irrespective of quality. Yet Hungary, ideology notwithstanding, tried in vain to become self-sufficient as she had to import the indispensable raw materials and pay for them with products.

Although this centrally managed gigantic machinery did work, it was creaking all the way ... the whole structure was threatened with collapse. Incentives were essentially eliminated from economic life, which did not exactly boost people's enthusiasm for work. On the one hand, fantastic one thousand per cent overfulfilment of norms was achieved – those who worked in the trade knew best that it was a lie – and, on the other hand, as soon as performance increased the norm was raised, too, and overfulfilment became compulsory. This led to a situation whereby the factories, production units, brigades, and workers aimed at a 103 per cent fulfilment

Figure 4   The giant Lenin Metallurgical Works, Diósgyör, built in 1864, divided into two parts in 1948, and for decades the pride of socialist industry

which was enough to gain praise for overfulfilment, but not enough to lead to the revision of the plans and norms. The slogan of the day said that "Work is a matter of honour and glory" which eliminated the very fundamental Marxist category, interest, from economic life.

These changes were accompanied by an unbelievable increase in red tape. [...] Although the most striking faults of economic life diminished somewhat during the sixties, the structure remained essentially unchanged and new problems appeared. First of all, there was a shortage of manpower. The rapidly developing industry had two great reserve pools of labour: rural Hungary and women. The number of people employed in industry doubled between 1950 and 1965, while the number of agricultural workers fell by half. During these fifteen years, the number of working women increased by a million and many of them were in industry. By the mid-sixties, however, these reserves were exhausted and industrial expansion could no longer be attained by quantitative factors.

It was also a considerable problem that by then the population's basic needs had been met and people were unwilling to buy just any sort of product. The enterprises were also unwilling to buy shoddy goods, and the foreign markets even less willing to accept them. Nevertheless, the factories were churning out products because they had a vested interest primarily in quantitative production and it did not matter to them whether or not the products could be sold. The warehouses were packed to the roof as more and more unmarketable goods accumulated.

Source: Jànos Kàdàr, *Selected Speeches and Interviews*, with an introductory biography by L. Gyurkò, Akadèmia Kiadò, Budapest 1985

The new economic mechanism (NEM), 1968

The NEM was intended to create a system of market socialism which would combine micro-economic efficiency, indirect government regulation and socialist ethical principles. It involved key changes to the original strategy.

In detail the NEM aimed at:

1 Removing the following aspects of the centrally planned economy:
- obligatory plan targets
- incentives for managers and workers based on the quantity of production
- centrally controlled resource allocation and investment.

2 Replacing the above aspects with:
- market forces (referred to as economic methods)
- price and wage flexibility
- incentives based on efficiency and quality
- more responsibility for company managers in business decision-making and investment.

J. Kádár (Figure 5) was the leader of Hungary from 1956 to 1988. Read the extract from his speech to Parliament in 1965 and his reply to an American journalist's question in 1966 about the essential aspects of the reform of the economic management system the government was proposing to introduce at the beginning of 1968. Then consider the following questions.

1 What problems does Kádár see in the original economic strategy which he thinks need to be changed?

2 Which detailed features of the aims of the NEM does Kádár stress?

3 What does he see as the purpose of reform?

4 What are the key words used to describe the changes that the government wants to introduce?

J.Kádár: *Extract from speech to Parliament in 1965*

Except for the agglomeration of industrial plants, we've made no radical change in economic organisation, or in economic management in the past few years, in part because we quite rightly wanted to achieve stability. Now, however, there are more and more indications that we must thoroughly re-examine our system of economic management, and work out the means of its rational development. A strongly centralised economy is slow and cumbersome. It is partly on this account that a portion of the goods produced with considerable labour using costly raw materials has failed to meet the demands of the market, domestic and international, and has remained on stock. It is particularly important to produce goods that are up-to-date now that, under the circumstances of peaceful coexistence, competition between the two social systems is growing, economic competition included. We have to present goods that are modern and competitive in price and quality alike on the international markets if we are not to lose out. On the Western markets, that is. But I must add that the times are over when the socialist world accepted poor-quality, useless goods from us, just as the days are over when we accept such goods from anyone. Unfortunately, the economic incentives we have at the moment are more likely to promote the quantitative overfulfilment of the plans, rather than economical production and improved quality. The fact is that the system of incentives and bonuses often works counter to considerations of quality.'

J.Kádár: *Extract from interview, 1966*

HS: What is the importance of the reform of economic management in Hungary?

JK: We can be satisfied with the achievements if we look back on the path which has been covered. But we are encouraged to make new efforts, to increase work efficiency if we look ahead at our more distant objectives and into the future. The fact that we have entered a new stage of socialist development calls for a reform of our economic mechanism. What do we mean by this as far as economic activities are concerned?

In the past twenty years, when the ruins had to be removed, when centuries of backwardness had to be made good through the industrialisation of the country, the top priority issue was to make a certain quantity of products available. Questions like economic efficiency, how much the goods cost, whether our articles met international standards and whether they were competitive or not were not in the focus of attention. When we completed laying the foundations of a socialist society the initial stage of development ended. Today our construction work at home also calls for the better utilisation and more rapid development of the forces of production, and this is what is demanded by the international market as well. A strict and high degree of centralisation in management was necessarily a characteristic of the stage of economic development which has ended.

The economic mechanism must be changed so that it will be capable of meeting new demands. Companies will be given a larger measure of independence; there will be more scope for taking the initiative and for the realisation of the democratic rights of the working people.

As a result of the reform, socialist property relations will grow stronger in Hungary along with the systematic development of the national economy. The pace of technological progress will be accelerated, production and productivity will increase, the assortment of goods will become wider and their quality will improve.

Source: Jànos Kàdàr, *Selected Speeches and Interviews*, with an introductory biography by L. Gyurkò, Akadèmia Kiadò, Budapest 1985

Figure 5 János Kádár addressing a party meeting in Györ, 1969

1 There will be less direct government involvement in economic structural change and that there should be a further decentralisation of economic and political power.

2 Full employment should be maintained, but the changing employment demands should be met by re-deploying workers in local labour markets.

3 Firms should no longer be protected from bankruptcy.

These were the key points in the process of socialist industrialisation, as they increased the possibility of structural change in the organisation of industry.

Reform must go on

Speedy though change seemed in the 1970s to many an old Party conservative, the pace of change hotted up in the 1980s. As a new round of reforms got under way, even more bastions of socialist thinking were challenged. On all sides it seemed the very vitals of the old system were being swept away. The giant industrial enterprises were being broken up whilst small, private – and increasingly the emphasis is on private – firms were encouraged. Success on the world market and co-operation with foreign corporations rose high on the agenda. But most significantly of all the financial sector, neglected since the beginning for ideological reasons, was overhauled and made to look and act suspiciously like those in the West. In 1980 a bond market. From 1985 the monopoly National Bank created commercial credit departments which competed with each other in an almost Western style. In 1990 a stock exchange was set up to cope with the many new forms of business organisation now permitted. In 1990 the first multiparty political elections took place. 'Reform must go on' was the call of all but the most entrenched Party stalwarts.

Socialist bloc integration and its impact on Hungarian industry

Hungary has been a member of the Council for Mutual Economic Assistance (CMEA), often referred to as Comecon since its foundation in 1949.

CMEA was inactive for years, many years.

The Comprehensive Programme of 1971 best set out the purpose of CMEA, which was closer economic co-operation and socialist integration, by:

a coordinating the medium- and long-term plans of members
b specialisation within sectors
c inter-enterprise co-operation
d joint investments
e scientific and technical co-operation
f improvements in the socialist division of labour.

By these means it was intended that each member would make the most efficient use of its natural resources, productive capacities and labour force. Examples are: the international Friendship gas pipeline; integration of CMEA countries' electricity grids; concentration on manufacturing vehicles, telecommunications and technology in Hungary. Co-operation has also affected the chemicals industry, food and agriculture, and the transport networks.

Reform in the 1980s

Until the mid 1980s the process of socialist industrialisation guaranteed full employment for all workers. This meant that unprofitable firms were subsidised by the state, which hindered modern, efficient industries.

In 1965 new laws resolved that:

Read the articles on this page.

1 What outside influences affected the progress of economic reform in Hungary?

2 What economic reforms were introduced at the beginning of the 1980s? What did the government hope to achieve by these reforms?

3 Why does Mr Nemeth want to introduce Plan A?

4 How do the articles assess the success of the reforms?

5 What are the likely problems?

Hungary has had to go further with its economic reforms and stick with them more tenaciously than the other Soviet block countries because it is small, highly dependent on foreign trade and has hardly any natural resources except its people and its agricultural land. Like most small countries, Hungary cannot produce everything it needs, and must specialise in certain exports (over 40 per cent of Hungary's national income comes from exports). Exports often have a high import content, so for exporting to be worthwhile raw materials and other inputs must be used sparingly. Unlike the Soviet Union, Hungary simply cannot afford the wastefulness of the centrally planned system.

This is particularly true for energy. Unlike its neighbours, Hungary has to import 60 per cent of its energy needs.

According to a Polish economist who drew up Solidarity's economic reform proposals in 1981, there are three pillars of central control over the economy in a Soviet-type system:

● the hierarchical subordination of managers to the central economic administration, which hires and fires them;

● the right of the Government to raid the coffers of firms (e.g. by special taxes or price controls), and to subsidise other firms from the proceeds as they wish;

● central control over essential raw materials and investment funds, which means that planners can prevent particular firms from producing as much as they wish or from expanding, and can thus affect earnings and bonuses.

It is only when all three pillars are removed that you have a market form of socialism rather than a centrally planned economy.

Source: Jan Rostowski, *Guardian*, 31 October 1985

The implementation of the Government Programme

The 1988 National Economic Plan already gives effect to two of the basic objectives; to start with restoring economic equilibrium within a few years, and secondly, reliance on livelier technological progress, the gradual transformation of the product structure.

The state of the world, in particular the recognition of the interdependence of international security, as formulated by Mikhail Gorbachev, created favourable outside conditions for this implementation which started in January this year. The improvement in Soviet–American relations palpably reduced international tension. In this connection it ought to be said that it has seldom happened before that the outside world should show so much sympathy for what Hungary is trying to do. This is not only true of the other socialist countries but also of states whose social system differs. They are all anxious that Hungary should succeed, and the common interest has prompted them to lend a helping hand more than once.

I am not arguing that the intention is always above board in every case but it is certainly true that those forces in the capitalist world which believe that the future belongs to cooperation between the two systems tend to identify Hungarian ways as a suitable form for such common action.

Source: K. Grosz, *New Hungarian Quarterly*, Summer 1988

Miklos Nemeth presented the case for Plan A, arguing in an open and highly critical analysis that the economic situation was dire – the economy's reserves were exhausted, infrastructure neglected, the debt burden severe and export performance inadequate. The main problem lay in the economy's isolation from the western economies, despite a high level of trade in that direction. Because of this, he said, 'the gap between Hungarian and foreign technological development continues to widen.'

Plan A will include a wide range of measures designed to establish real capital, money, labour and commodity markets in Hungary. When asked if Hungary was moving towards capitalism, Mr Grosz replied that he was not concerned with labels. Whether a system worked or not was the main criteria.

This law seeks to establish equal rights for all types of enterprises including state, co-operative and private. It also will encourage the formation of joint stock holding companies and private capital will be allowed to bail out loss-making state enterprises.

Source: Financial Times Newsletters, *East European Markets*, 23 July 1988

Effects of the development strategy

?

Re-read Gyurkò's article on page 443. Refer to it when you answer questions 1 3.

1 Using the above figures, on a piece of graph paper make two sets of bar charts showing changes in the employment structure: (a) grouping the sectors together by years, (b) grouping the years by sectors. You will need to choose a suitable scale. Comment on your findings in the light of Gyurkò's penultimate paragraph.

2 What is meant by the terms *producer goods* and *consumer goods*? Classify the products in Table 2 into these categories.

3 To what extent do the data in Table 2 suggest that, in the early phase of socialist industrialisation, the emphasis was on producer goods and in the later phase consumer goods? What other evidence have you found to support this interpretation?

4 Which are the most important branches of industry shown by Table 3? Which branches increased their share of gross output and which decreased?

5 Study the resources in the box on page 448. What is meant by the term extensive development?

6 What is intensive development?

7 At which periods were these different kinds of growth important for socialist industrialisation in Hungary? Compare the processes, economic and social effects of the three periods, 1950-60, 1960-74, 1974-84 and relate them to changes in the National Development Strategy.

Table 1 Number of workers employed in major sectors of the Hungarian economy 1950-1987

	1950	1960	1970	1980	1987
Agriculture	1950	1650	1245	1064	947
Industry	900	1450	1804	1690	1525
Services	670	910	1940	2320	2412

Source: Magyarország: Nemzeti Atlasza (National Atlas of Hungary) 1967; *Statistical Pocket Book of Hungary*, Central Statistical Office, 1987

Table 2 Output of raw materials and basic products

	1949	1960	1970	1980	1987
Hard coal ('000t)	–	–	4151	3065	2360
Iron-ore ('000t)	339	516	629	426	–
Pig-iron (000t)	400	1300	1822	2214	2109
Steel ('000t)	900	1900	2038	3043	2825
Natural gas (million m^3)	372	342	3469	6142	7118
Crude oil ('000t)	506	1217	1937	2031	1914
Machine tools:					
Milling machines	374	1177	985	248	114
Drilling machines	983	3054	4834	3468	5529
Radios ('000s)	67	212	206	271	75
Televisions ('000s)	–	139	364	417	414
Tape recorders ('000s)	–	–	60	459	862
Washing machines ('000s)	–	144	165	233	239
Refrigerators ('000s)	–	9	242	499	399
Semi-conductors (millions)	–	2	26	144	199

Source: Statistical Yearbooks of Hungary and T. Bernàt (ed.) *An Economic Geography of Hungary*, Akademiai Kiadò, 1985

Table 3 The sectoral pattern of socialist industry, 1950-87

Industry	Percentage of gross output				
	1950	1960	1970	1980	1987
Mining	11.2	7.8	5.5	8.1	6.9
Metallurgy	13.5	13.6	10.7	9.1	8.1
Electric generation	4.3	4.3	3.5	5.7	6.1
Engineering	20.6	22.9	26.5	23.6	25.7
Chemical	3.5	6.8	10.9	18.6	19.6
Building materials	3.3	3.7	3.3	3.5	3.3
(Heavy industry total	**56.4**	**59.1**	**60.4**	**68.6**	**68.5)**
Light industry	19.9	21.3	19.7	14.7	13.8
Food industry	23.7	19.6	19.9	16.7	18.6
	100.0	100.0	100.0	100.0	100.0

Source: Statistical Yearbooks of Hungary

Major effects

The process and consequences of industrialisation during the phase of extensive* development 1950–60

Processes	Economic effects	Social effects	Other effects
Initially a very high, later a moderate growth rate with the absorption of new manpower. Quantitative production objectives and a mainly autarchic type of development.	Rapid change in economic structure. Forced investment policy, large number of new plants. Slowly improving productivity, inadequate economic efficiency.	Rapid changes in social and occupational structure favourable to industry	Excessive migration from the less developed areas to the north of the country, the main scene of industrialisation. Rapid urbanisation in the above areas causing overcrowding in certain places, primarily in Budapest.

The process and consequences of industrialisation during the transition phase from extensive to intensive production 1960–74

Processes	Economic effects	Social effects	Other effects
Moderate growth rate; less new labour included in production; still surviving extensive growth in certain areas, important substitution, later to be replaced by export-oriented development	Slow transformation of the economic structure; a decreasing number of new industrial investments; greater emphasis on the existing plants; increase in productivity although still slow, was faster than during the previous phase; improving economic efficiency.	Slowdown in social and occupational restructuring, but still movement towards industry.	Decreasing migration; more balanced urbanisation regionally, acceleration of the development of infrastructure.

The process and consequences of industrialisation during the phases of intensive and selective development (fourth and fifth phases) 1974–84

Processes	Economic effects	Social effects	Other effects
Low growth rate. Growth is covered by increased productivity. Fall in the number of industrial manpower. Sectoral development by selective methods, and more marked export-oriented industrial development.	New industrial investments minimised. Development is directed decisively towards changes in the product structure of existing plants. Growth in productivity is speeding up with improving efficiency.	Beginning of the transformation of the occupational structure and consolidation of the tertiary sector.	Low migration rates; urban development separated from industrialisation.

* The terms 'extensive' and 'intensive development' are used generally in socialist countries. The former means the high utilisation of labour relative in capital and technology in economic growth. The latter is designed to achieve economic growth by a higher input of capital and technology relative to labour and by a more efficient organisation of production.

Source: T. Bernát (ed.), *An Economic Geography of Hungary*, 1985, pp 104–105

Industrialisation and the firm

In the first part of this enquiry you have investigated the economic and social environment of socialist industrialisation in Hungary. We now turn to industrial organisation and investigate the development and characteristics of the industrial firm.

In socialist industry firms are owned by the state sector, that is central ministries and local councils and by industrial co-operatives (Figure 6). Their names often just describe the products they make and the place where they are located. Few have distinctive personal names that characterise privately owned industries. Generally speaking in Hungary firms are known as enterprises. Co-operatives are owned by their members, not the state.

Figure 6   Wine co-operative, Eger: loading 'Bull's Blood' for bulk export to West Germany

Table 4   The distribution of industrial companies by ownership

	1965	1970	1975	1980	1982
Ministerial	30	32	34	38	43
Local Council	20	18	16	12	10
State Sector	50	50	50	50	53
Co-operatives	50	50	50	50	47

Source: G. Barta 'The Spatial Impact of Organisational changes in Industrial Companies' in Enyedi, G. and Pecsi, M., *Geographical Essays in Hungary*, M.T.A. Budapest 1984

Table 5   The changing structure of Hungarian state firms and industrial co-operatives 1983–8

	1983	1984	1985	1986	1987	1988
Large firms	1363*	716	750	974	1009	1050
Small firms	–	156	184	n.a.	n.a.	n.a.
Subsidiaries	–	23	–	52	96	108
Industrial co-ops	*	626	601	956	1126	1408
Small co-ops	80	159	244	n.a.	n.a.	n.a.
Subsidiaries	–	–	–	15	35	46
Trusts	11	8	8	8	8	8
Firms in trusts	173	145	146	128	131	115
Firms with foreign partners	3	8	13	21	24	59

* State and co-operatives together.

Source: *Statistical Pocket Books of Hungary*, 1983–8

?

1   Study Table 4 Which is the most important form of company ownership?

2   What has happened to the structure of state firms and co-operatives in the period 1983–8? Summarise the main changes refering to the information in Table 5.

3   How far do these figures support the points made about the reforms of the 1980s (on pages 445–6)?

The automotive industry

HUNGARY'S AUTOMOTIVE EXPORT TRENDS

In the sixties when the long-term development programme for Hungarian industry was launched, no signs of a world-wide economic recession were predicted.

At that time executives were induced by a lot of considerations to elaborate a project which concentrated efforts on the large-series production of buses and their main parts, preferably typified components that could be used also in heavy lorries.

These decisions were passed by the Government in 1964. It has been proved in recent times that even in a period of recession, the concept will hold its own.

The yearly output of the IKARUS Coach and Body Works is about 14,000 vehicles: at the RÁBA works the number of Diesel engines runs to 30,000, the axles to more than 100,000. To these come vehicle components such as gearboxes, power steering, auto-electricity, etc.

The major industrial plants: IKARUS, the RÁBA Wagon and Machine Works, the CSEPEL Automobile Factory.

Another 25–30 medium and minor factories participate in the production of automotive goods.

Dynamic progress is reflected in the turnover of MOGÜRT (handling the export of the automotive goods) during the past 30 years:

Year	Export/Import $m	Bus export unit
1950	2.8	313
1970	115.1	4772
1982	1282.7	11240

MOGÜRT are set up in a network of 12 after-sales bureaux in 23 countries and the company has local representatives in 24 countries.

Besides their dealings, **MOGÜRT** have for some years now acted as main contractors, supplying full-scope service/repair plants in turn-key state; they also undertake the planning and establishing of public transport systems.

MOGÜRT/IKARUS are setting up assembly plants either as their own undertaking or else in co-operation with foreign manufacturers, such as SAAB-SCANIA, RENAULT-SAVIEM etc., undertaking the entire implementing of these assembly plants, the professional training of the local staff, etc.

MOGÜRT/IKARUS supply the complete vehicle of the bus bodies in **SKD or CKD** state.

MOGÜRT establish the after-sales service in all important markets, within which training is provided for the local technical staff.

Among the export markets the developing countries play an important part, particularly in the **Middle East** e.g. Kuwait, Jordan, Syria etc. Also the first assembly plant established with Hungarian assistance was erected in Iraq in 1973 and has been in continuous operation ever since.

The African markets, Egypt, Tunisia and Algeria are regular customers. Assembly plants set up by the Hungarian party are operated in Mozambique, Malgas and Angola.

Multiple relations link Hungary's automotive industry to several countries in Europe: IKARUS buses are operated in the FRG, Sweden, Greece, Turkey. Special bus models have been designed and built e.g. Volvo/Ikarus, Scania/Ikarus, Ikarus/MAN/Volkswagen, Renault/Ikarus and Ikarus/Bedford.

It is considered a success for Hungary's bus trade that the United States have become one of the export markets. The model IKARUS 286, an articulated city bus, has been specially designed to meet all U.S. regulations of safety, pollution, specific dimensions, etc.

MOGÜRT/IKARUS obtained orders upon their tender bids from the public transport organisations of the cities Louisville (Kentucky), San Mateo (California) in 1979, Portland (Oregon) in 1980. Santa Clara (California) in 1981, Albany (NY); Jacksonville (Florida) and Milwaukee (Wisconsin) in 1982. The buses for these orders total nearly 200.

Looking back upon professional traditions of nearly a hundred years, fully equipped for production by methods of the latest technology, Hungary's automotive industry proposes making increased efforts and even greater versatility in order to fight recession.

HUNGARIAN TRADING COMPANY FOR MOTOR VEHICLES
H 1391 Budapest 62, POB 249
Telex: 22–5357; 22–5358

Source: *Financial Times*, 10 May 1983

Note: SKD = semi knock down
CKD = complete knock down

IKARUS
by Sándor Béres

The story of Ikarus begins in 1949 when the Ikarus Body and Coach Building Works was established by amalgamating the Ikarus Machine and Hardware Corporation and the Uhri Brothers Body and Vehicle Company. Both were old established companies which had earlier been nationalised and put under the control of the Ministry of Heavy Industry to save them from insolvency, keep their skilled employees in work and their machines and factories operating.

In 1949 the Budapest authorities ordered 150 buses for their public transport system and so began a profitable business with public transport companies throughout Hungary. New type ranges of buses were introduced and in 1958 cooperation began with the General Mechanical Engineering Works at Székesfehérvár.

In 1962 the Economic Committee of the Council of Ministers decided that in preparation for a major government investment programme Ikarus should merge with Székesfehérvár firm, and the headquarters of the new company should be in Budapest.

In 1964 a Resolution of the Hungarian government gave priority to investment in bus production. In 1967 the building of new specialist facilities began. In 1970 Ikarus took over the workshops of a coal mine at Pusztavám-Mor which was being closed down. A new factory was opened at Szeged. Currently Ikarus operates 5 manufacturing plants, but its national and international linkages are very complex.

COMECON agreements have played a special role in the development of Ikarus. By these arrangements Hungary does not manufacture cars but instead specialises on bus production. This ensures a large market for Hungarian buses which are exported to all the socialist countries. By 1985 Ikarus had supplied 100,000 buses to the Soviet Union. The German Democratic Republic is the second largest customer and Czechoslovakia buys Ikarus articulated buses – 25% of all articulated buses operating in the world are of Ikarus manufacture. Ikarus has supplied buses to China since 1952. The COMECON programmes allowed volume production and the introduction of new type ranges which have achieved world wide sales, but did not entirely go as planned or meet all Ikarus' needs.

Ikarus employs 11000 workers. It ensures they are well trained but through its social fund provides many services. Between 1980 and 1985 10% of Ikarus employees received, low, some no interest loans for home building or flat purchasing, or were provided with company flats. Ikarus provides 700 creche and nursery places and spends 30 million forints ($30000) per year on education, culture and sports facilities for its workers. Ikarus organises holidays for 4000 employees and their families each year at its holiday centres, every employee can have a company holiday at nominal cost every two years.

Source: Ikarus company brochure

Figure 7 Ikarus promotional leaflet

?

1 Use the advert placed by Mogurt/Ikarus in the *Financial Times* to find out about Ikarus's world-wide services.

2 Plot these services on an outline world map. How would you describe the overall pattern

NEWSFLASH

In February 1989 Ikarus was offered for sale to Western businessmen along with fifty-two other companies. Rába was not included in the list.

Source: East European Markets, 10 March 1989

RÁBA

by Ede Horwath – President

Rába – the Hungarian Railway Carriage and Wagon Works was founded in Györ in 1876. Before World War Two it developed connections with many foreign companies and manufactured automotive engineering products in partnership and licence agreements, with great success. Rába was nationalised in 1947 as part of the policy of the new government.

From 1947 to 1961 growth was moderate, but in 1964 a new era began. The Hungarian government adopted a centrally designed industrial programme to develop a national vehicle industry with investments of billions of forints. Rába had a leading role to play.

After 1968 with government help and encouragement Rába management embarked on a programme of modernisation of equipment, special training of skilled workers and managers in order to improve efficiency, productivity and the quality of its products. Rába now employ 20,000 workers and operates 11 plants using the most up to date methods of management and production, which are constantly under review.

Rába specialises in the production of front and rear axles, diesel engines, heavy duty trucks and tractors.

Licence and cooperation agreements disrupted by the war were taken up again:

1968 agreement with a consortium of Renault, M A N, and Ferrostaal to manufacture diesel engines known as Rába-M A N. At first supplied Ikarus but later generation engines now fitted to railway rolling stock, ships, earth movers, tractors and heavy duty trucks. The Hungarian International Road Transport Company 'Hungarocamion' in a major customer for these trucks.

1974–1978 cooperation agreements with Steiger Tractors (US), International Harvester Corporation (US), Eaton Corporation (US) and General Motors for the production and supply of automotive products.

COMECON agreements led to Hungary specialising in truck production and 70% of Rába's specialised rear axle output is sold to socialist countries.

Most recently Rába has diversified into large scale poultry farming equipment, in cooperation with the Babolna State Farm which is a world leader in mechanised poultry farming. Products from this association have been supplied to socialist and middle eastern countries.

Like other Hungarian companies Rába has a large social fund. This provides 150 creche places and 40 nursery places at Rába headquarters plant. The company provides holidays for 4,500 people each year at its own holiday homes and by subsidising its employees holidays. Rába sponsors the Rába-Györ football club in the Hungarian First Division.

Source: Rába sales brochure

Figure 8 The Rába Hungarian Wagon and Machine Factory, Györ: among its successful products are rear-driven running gears

League table of enterprises. There was no major change in the top ten Hungarian enterprises – the Danube Oil Refinery was first, followed by Rába, Ikarus, Videoton and the Tisza Chemical Combine.

Source: Financial Times Newsletters, *East European Markets*, 12 August 1988

?

1 Which are the most important Hungarian enterprises in the automotive industry? What are their main products?

2 How is the export of these products arranged?

3 What led to the increased pace of expansion in Ikarus and Rába in the mid 1960s?

4 In what ways have Ikarus and Rába co-operated with corporations and firms outside Hungary? How successful do you think that this co-operation has been?

5 What advantages have Ikarus and Rába gained through their co-operation with Western corporations?

6 List the features of Ikarus and Rába that you think are the most important aspects of their common ownership, organisation and development.

COMECON and the Ministry cause difficulties for Ikarus and Rába

According to the original concept of the road vehicle program, Hungary was only supposed to introduce the production of large category buses and to import for them not only propeller shafts, front axles, driver's seats and windscreen-wipers but also, for example, gearboxes and shock absorbers from other CMEA countries. It was presumed to import the first ones from Poland and the latter ones from the Soviet Union. The Hungarian industrial management also planned to satisfy the demand for small and medium category buses from CMEA imports.

First: according to the original plans, Hungary should not have manufactured small and medium categories of buses and Ikarus set to it only because it was forced to. Namely, against expectations, it was not possible to import such buses from other CMEA countries; either the amount of the supplied GDR, Polish or Romanian buses was not sufficient or the quality of the vehicle was below the Hungarian requirements. And so they happened to start the production of small and medium category buses without proper preparations.

The Soviet manufacturer of the imported front axles turns out enormous series of front axles for trucks and is willing to consider only part of the aspects of adaptation for buses. The same was to happen with the Soviet shock absorbers but in that case the compromise was beyond what could be accepted and therefore the use of Soviet shock absorbers had to be given up. A Hungarian medium-size enterprise undertook the production of shock absorbers. Under British licence they manufacture top quality shock absorbers in very small batches.

In other cases contemplated imports failed to come because of the lack of export capacities of the partner country (Polish gearboxes). Thus it became necessary to continue to manufacture and use the existing obsolete product in Hungary (AS gearbox) which spoils the quality of the whole bus, and later on to introduce a new product under a licence but only for domestic needs (ZF gear).

Ikarus does not have the right to get front axles from Rába Works in spite of the fact that the imported Soviet front axle is practically produced in a single version and is not the most suitable one for all the Ikarus buses (mostly the long-distance ones). When the Soviet imports started Rába Works were actually forbidden to manufacture front axles. Then it was allowed – but not for domestic sale. At present Rába Works produces swing-axles (suitable for long-distance buses) for exports to Czechoslovakia. If they wanted to fit such axles in some of the Ikarus buses, the reduction of Soviet imports could entail trade balance problems; especially if Rába Works undertook to produce not this but really an advanced type of swing-axles it would need investment. So perhaps here one might argue that the price would have been too high for allowing a domestic and foreign supplier to compete. Another similar case could have been a much simpler decision: to substitute for the not too up-to-date Polish windscreen wiper motors an up-to-date appliance of the Factory for Automobile Electricity. Here the investment requirements were much smaller and the amount of missed import much smaller too; economical serial production would have been guaranteed by the demand stated by the GDR. But the windscreen-wiper motor was deleted from the factory's plan by the Ministry of Metallurgy and Engineering, when the plan was 'judged'.*

* Judgement of enterprise plans by ministries: a system of indirect approval of enterprise plans which became a custom in the mid-seventies in Hungary. According to the 1968 reform which abolished the system of plan-instructions, plans are drawn up by the enterprises independently and need not be referred to any higher authority for approval.

Source: T. Bauer, K. A. Soòs, 'Inter-firm Relations and Technological Change in Eastern Europe – The Case of the Hungarian Motor Industry', *Acta Oeconomica* **23**, 1979, p. 285

1 How did the original Comecon programme change, and why? Was the change planned or did it arise because of difficulties experienced by Ikarus which then responded?

2 What problems did Ikarus experience at this time?

3 How did the Ministry impose its control after 1968?

Figure 9 The Ikarus plant in Székesfehérvár

Aluminium, steel and coal

Hungarian bauxite mining in the Bakony region

THE possibility of a major aluminium industry in Hungary was envisaged some 50 years ago, as evidenced from the cutting (right) from the *Mining Journal*, of March 28, 1925. In fact, 1926 may be considered as the starting point for this industry, when bauxite production began. The manufacture of alumina started in 1943, smelting in 1940 and fabrication in 1942.

A number of important changes in the industry took place between 1946 and 1954, leading to the present day structure of the industry. These changes were mainly concerned with alumina production; manufacture of semi-finished and finished products; and the signing of alumina/aluminium agreements with neighbouring countries such as Czechoslovakia, Poland and the Soviet Union.

The industry is controlled by the Hungarian Aluminium Corporation (Magyar Aluminiumpari Tröszt – MAT), the head offices of which are at Pozsonyi ut 56, Budapest XIII. This corporation embraces the activities of mines, smelters, alumina plants, fabricating works and bauxite prospecting. MAT was founded in 1963.

During the 1920s as noted, geological surveys revealed important bauxite reserves in Hungary. The main mining areas which grew up as a result of these discoveries are the Bakony Region bauxite mines north of Lake Balaton, centred around the town of Tapolca; and the Fejer county bauxite mines near the town of Kincsesbanya. When production began in 1926 about 3,700 tonnes a year was produced and by 1943 this had reached 1 million tonnes. By 1972 this had risen to almost 2.4 million tonnes.

The Mining Journal   March 28, 1925

'There are two considerable bauxite fields in Hungary: the one around the northern shores of the great Lake Balaton, between the villages Szöc and Halimba; the other in the Vértes mountain, between the towns of Csákvár and Csákberény. Both the quantity and the quality of the ore deposits are highly satisfactory; Government figures estimate about 30,000,000 tons of bauxite ore to be found there. The starting of a great aluminium industry would be, therefore, within the limits of a sound speculation, and the by-products of the aluminium industry would be of great benefit for the already existing chemical and ceramic industries of the country. But these are to-day merely dreams, because here is no capital, and business on a large scale cannot be carried on.'

The Felix II open-pit mine in the Bakony region

Source: Mining Magazine **5**, 1975, p 350

Efficient key supplier

Aluminium

A SIZEABLE contributor to Hungary's hard currency trade surplus last year was Hungalu (the Hungarian Aluminium Corporation), which boosted convertible currency exports earnings from $149m in 1983 to $168m, while keeping its hard currency import bill to about $26–28m.

Dr Ervin Ernest, Hungalu's commercial director, says the surge in exports was a very conscious effort to capitalise on high aluminium prices which started 1984 at about $1,500 a tonne, but have fallen substantially since then.

Equally, the expected slowdown in the U.S. market, on which Hungalu focused after meeting complaints – quite unjustified, says Dr Ernest – in 1982–83 that it was dumping aluminium foil in the EEC, is likely to reduce Hungalu's export growth this year.

But Hungalu remains a key supplier to such parts of domestic industry as Ikarus buses, and the refrigerator and white goods sector, as well as supplying some components to Western carmakers (General Motors, Volvo, Fiat), an activity which would greatly increase if Hungary were ever to set up its own car assembly plant.

Hungalu virtually *is* the Hungarian aluminium industry. But unlike other monopolies on quasi-monopolies which were horizontally integrated and are now being broken up by the government to create greater competition. Hungalu's structure is being left untouched. This is because its vertical integration is considered to promote efficiency.

Hungalu has 16 member enterprises, with activities ranging from bauxite mining, to smelting, to research, to foreign trading (since 1982).

The proportion of exports differs with each stage in the production process. Bauxite is one of the country's few mineral endowments, and 3m tonnes are mined every year and there are 50 years of proven reserves. Bauxite exports are negligible but two-thirds of alumina, the next stage in the refining process, is exported, mostly to the Soviet Union which returns some of it as aluminium.

Some 10–20 per cent of the aluminium is sold abroad, while the rest (about 200,000 tonnes a year) is made into semi-finished or ready-made products.

Source: David Buchan, *Financial Times*, 14 May 1985

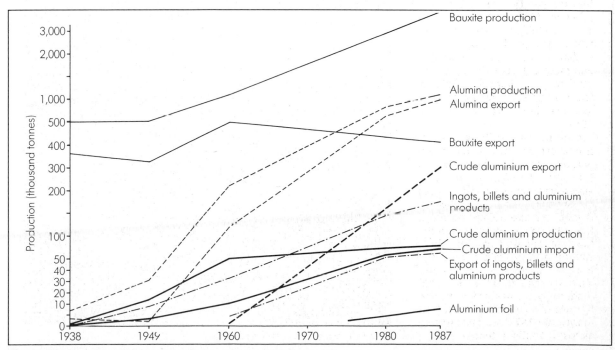

Figure 10 Production in the Hungarian aluminium industry 1938–87
Source: G. Bova and S. Koves, *Foldrajz*, 1986

PLANTS AND COMPANIES OF THE HUNGARIAN ALUMINIUM CORPORATION

HUNGALU BAKONY MINES
Tapoica, Halimba, Ajka, Szöc, Nyirad
Bauxite

HUNGALU FEJER MINES
Kincsesbanya, Fenyofö, Iszkaszentgyörgy
Bauxite

HUNGALU MOTIM WORKS
Mosonmagyarovar
Calcined alumina, alumina hydrate, vanadium
compounds, aluminium sulphate, polishing
grains, electro-fused corondum products,
refactories

HUNGALU AJKA WORKS
Ajka
Calcined alumina, aluminium ingots and billets,
gallium metal, gallium oxide, aluminium die-
castings

HUNGALU INOTA SMELTER
Inota
Aluminium ingots and billets, continuous cast
wires, Properizi/, continuous cast strips, slugs

HUNGALU TATABANYA SMELTER
Tatabanya
Aluminium ingots and billets, continuous cast
wires/Properzi/, high-purity aluminium ingots
and billets

HUNGALU SZEKESFEHERVAR LIGHT METAL WORKS
Szekesfehervar
Rolled sheets, strips and discs, extrusions,
pressed and drawn rods, tubes, forgings, bent
profiles from strip, welded tubes

HUNGALU ALMASFUZITO REFINERY
Almasfuzito
Calcined alumina, alumina hydrate, special
alumina brands

HUNGALU KOBANYA LIGHT METAL WORKS
Budapest
X. Cserkesz u. 42.
Thin strips, foils, aluminium pigments

HUNGALU METAL WORKING CO.
Balassagyarmat
Aluminium building structures, castings,
containers, mining installations

HUNGALU STRUCTURES
Hodmezovasarhely
Aluminum tanks, vessels and barrels, aluminium
transportation facilities, aluminium siding
systems for the building industry, garages

HUNGALU MACHINERY CO.
Zalaegerszeg
Machines for the aluminium industry, spare
parts for the mining, aluminium smelting and
mills

HUNGALU ENGINEERING AND DEVELOPMENT CENTRE
Budapest
XIII. Pozsonyi ut 56.
Design research and technical development in
the following areas: prospecting, mining and
concentration of bauxite and other ores; production of alumina and its by-products; aluminium
smelting; production of electrocorundum, high-
purity and rare metals; semi and finished products; application techniques of aluminium;
mechanization and automatization; performing of
plant trial operations; main contracting inside
and outside Hungary; technical consultancy services; manufacture of prototypes

HUNGALU PROSPECTING CO.
Balatonaimadi
Drilling of large-diameter shafts, shaft sinking

HUNGALU TRADING CO.
Budapest
XIII. Pozsonyi ut 56.
Export of semifabricated and finished products,
purchase of basic materials and equipment,
warehousing for the plants and companies of the
Hungarian Aluminium Corporation.

HUNGARIAN ALUMINIUM CORPORATION
H-1387 Budapest, P.O. Box 30
Phone: 494-750, 494-790
Telex: 22-5471/22-5473

Source: Hungarian Aluminium Corporation

Figure 12 Advertisement for Hungalu

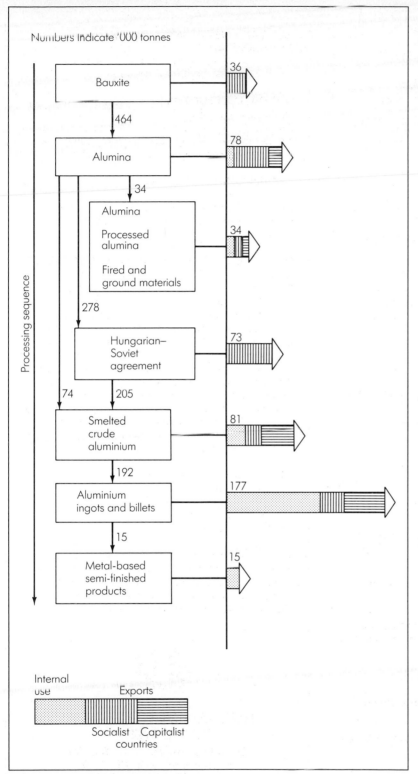

Figure 11 The production process in the Hungarian industry, 1986
Source: based on F. Probald, *Foldrajz*, 1988

1 Compare the products which Hungary supplies to other socialist and to capitalist countries. Note that exports to socialist countries occur under Comecon agreements.

2 You are a project development manager for Brital Industries, a transnational corporation operating in the aluminium industry. Your company is interested in developing links with Eastern-bloc countries and sees Hungary as a good starting point. You are sent to Hungary to assess the industry there. Write a report for your managing director on the Hungarian aluminium industry. Include sections on:

a the development of the industry,

b the organisation of the industry,

c the spatial structure and linkages of the industry,

d the output of aluminium products,

e your assessment of the prospects for the industry, bearing in mind the changing economic situation in the country the features of which you must outline in your report.

Steel production to be cut

Hungary's output of iron and steel is to be reduced by the early 1990s, some years earlier than originally planned. The decision to bring forward the cuts came following a report by Swedish consultant, Scandiaconsult, working on behalf of the World Bank.

The industry, says the report, was over developed in the 1950s and has been facing financial and sales difficulties for years, mainly because of a fall in world market prices, structural tensions and inefficient production.

At present Hungary produces 2m tonnes of iron, 3.6m tonnes of steel and 2.8m tonnes of rolled stock goods as well as 270,000 tonnes of more highly processed output.

Large state subsidies to the industry have not helped to speed up modernisation of production or improve the financial health of the sector. In 1986 the Government adopted a comprehensive programme, cancelling the debts of the three largest enterprises. This cost the Government Ft 17bn. At the same time the three enterprises were given credit repayment preferences.

In exchange the three drew up a programme to convert facilities, reduce obsolete open-hearth steel production and increase the production of more highly processed output.

Last year the three reduced costs. The Danube enterprise, using better quality iron ore, improved efficiency and made a profit, as did the Lenin iron and steel enterprise, LKL and the Ozd works, (OKU).

Nevertheless, the Government has decided to accelerate restructuring, particularly at Ozd. LKM and OKU are to merge, working as a trust, with steel production decreasing, elimination of parallel capacities and increasing the range of modern products.

If the plan is carried out, Ozd will reduce and then stop production of metallurgical basic materials, replacing them with more advanced capacities at the LKM plant. Closure of three furnaces at OKU will save $18m but 6,000 jobs will be lost at Ozd by 1992.

In a region where the Ozd works provides the main employment, the job losses are expected to be resisted, even though the Government has promised to provide some help in creating investment projects and expanding other enterprises in the area.

As a result of the restructuring, production of crude iron will fall from 3.5m to 2.9m tonnes and rolled stock from 2.8m to 2.3m tonnes.

Source: Financial Times Newsletters, *East European Markets*, 10 February 1989

Coal restructuring may be dangerous

The Government has decided to cut off completely subsidies to two of the biggest loss making coal mines this year and to eliminate all subsidies to the industry, starting next year. If the Government sticks to its plans, a number of mines will close, coal production will decrease and unemployment will increase.

Since the late 1970s Hungary's coal mines have been producing less coal at increasingly greater cost. In 1981 Hungary's mines produced about 24m tonnes of coal, 3m tonnes of which was hard coal. By 1987 it had fallen to 22m tonnes. Over this period subsidies from the state grew, reaching Ft 11bn last year.

The Government first decided to cut subsidies to Ft 5bn for 1988, forcing several mining companies to go through rehabilitation schemes involving the closure of a number of individual pits, without any bankruptcies.

Following the May conference, the Government began to take a tougher stand. All government subsidies to the coal industry will stop on January 1 1989. Coal prices for producers will be raised by 15 per cent, while production costs at mines are to be reduced by 2.5 per cent. Any coal mine that cannot make a profit under these circumstances will face bankruptcy.

Rather than wait until next year to take action, the Government – under pressure to reduce its own deficit – decided to cut the 1988 subsidy level to Ft 4.3bn,

The Ft 700m subsidy cut will fall on two of the most inefficient coal mining companies – Tatabanya and Nograd – which have combined losses and debts of about FT 5bn. Nograd, must pay back Ft 76m in subsidies it has already received this year.

According to Nograd's director, Miklos Zsuffa, the company may be forced to close this year, with a loss of 600 jobs. The Tatabanya company, which is much larger (but also deeper in debt), may survive by closing a number of uneconomic pits.

The Government intends to make up for the shortfall in coal production, which its policy will bring about, by importing coal from other socialist countries, particularly East Germany, or from the West.

Greater emphasis will be placed on other sources of energy, too. Hungary has plans to develop further its nuclear power industry and intends to increase imports of natural gas from the Soviet Union, doubling domestic consumption by the mid-1990s.

The Government is coming under pressure from industrial consumers of coal, who have benefited from the heavily subsidised prices and now face rapidly rising energy costs as coal prices are brought in line with actual production costs.

Since the announcement, the Government appears to be standing firm, but it would not be surprising to see new and more complicated forms of subsidies cropping up to placate irate industrial managers. This is something the Government should avoid.

Source: Financial Times Newsletters, *East European Markets*, 29 July 1988

Joint ventures with Western companies

?

1 What problems face the steel and coal companies and how have these problems arisen?

2 How does government policy towards the two industries differ?

3 What do you think that the outcome of the government's policy will be?

4 How does the policy differ from that of the first period of industrialisation for these two industries?

5 How does the policy fit in with the strategy of the 1980s?

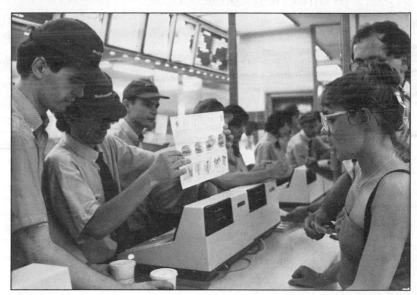

Figure 13 Hungary's first McDonalds opened in Budapest in 1988. By 1990 its turnover was the largest of any McDonalds restaurant in the world

Joint ventures on the rise

The number of joint ventures with Western companies in Hungary has doubled in the past two years to more than 70 separate companies.

The majority of the new ventures are small. But there are some exceptions, for example the recent venture between Hungarian companies and Siemens and the ITT European subsidiary, SEL. McDonalds has recently signed a joint venture with Babolna and will sell its first Hungarian hamburger this spring. The reason for the recent increase in western investment in Hungary – which still only amounts to about $100m – is the January 1986 change of the laws governing foreign investment.

Joint ventures with Western companies have been possible in Hungary since 1972, but because of high profits taxes and stifling regulations, only a handful of Westerners ventured into such deals. The joint venture law was amended in 1982, but the general response was disappointing.

In an effort to bring more foreign working capital and expertise into the country, a major liberalisation of the regulations on joint ventures began in January 1986. The changes included:

● A reduced profit tax from 40 per cent to 20 per cent

● Further concessions in priority fields, such as no profit tax for the first five years

● The possibility of Western majority participation

● Simplification of licensing, registration and accounting

The response from the West has been surprisingly positive. Although most of the enterprises established so far have been between Hungarian and either West German or Austrian companies, joint ventures have also been agreed with Japanese, Indian, Portuguese and Greek companies.

As Hungary's hard currency earnings on traditional exports is way down, this new influx of western capital, however limited, is greatly appreciated. The transfer of technology and know-how – and access to new markets – is a definite plus for the Hungarian partners.

For their part, Western companies are attracted to Hungary by the well-educated and relatively inexpensive workforce. The new Hungarian entrepreneurial spirit, at least in some enterprises, has also played an important role in bringing some Western companies to Hungary. Also, despite numerous snags, Hungary's market-oriented economy makes it a somewhat easier country for western businessmen to manoeuvre in than other Comecon countries.

But Hungary still faces serious obstacles to attracting Western investment. Although it has made progress towards liberalising the joint venture regulations, profit taxes are still relatively high. Hungary does not provide a coherent package of incentives, nor does it 'sell itself' as professionally as many of its Western competitors. Furthermore, its small domestic market and the difficulty of access to the larger Soviet market are factors Hungary can do little about.

►

Maybe some changes. Nevertheless, this last point may be about to change. Moscow is now encouraging direct contact between enterprises within Comecon. The first Soviet–Hungarian joint venture was formed this year.

Further, more radical changes are under discussion. So, if Soviet–Hungarian trade becomes more open, then Hungary's attractiveness to Western companies as a possible entry point to the enormous Soviet market would be definitely enhanced.

More joint ventures

Two new joint ventures have been agreed between Hungarian enterprises and Western companies.

Maier (Parma, Italy) reached an agreement in January with the Sopiana machine factory of Pecs on the joint production of packaging machinery. After initial imports of machinery from Italy, the new joint venture, Somak, hopes to develop products for export to third markets.

Dutch company Daniko and an agricultural cooperative in Retsas teamed up in January to form a joint venture specialising in the production of frozen French fried potatoes. The Hungarian Agrarian Innovation Bank and the Pannonia Csepel Foreign Trading Company are also partners.

Using Western machinery imported with the help of the Dutch partner, the new joint venture hopes for a turnover of about Ft* 40m this year. Half of the company's output will be exported through the Dutch partner, the other half will be for domestic consumption.

Source: Financial Times Newsletters, *East European Markets*, 6 February 1987

* Ft = forint, Hungarian unit of currency

?

1 What advantages do you think there are for Hungarian firms in joint ventures with Western companies?

2 What advantages can you think of for the Western companies?

3 What are the specific intentions of Italian and Dutch joint ventures?

4 List some of the difficulties you foresee occurring in the setting-up of joint ventures between Western and Hungarian firms. How have these been reduced recently?

Small is beautiful

'Big is Best' seems to have been an appropriate slogan for early socialist industrialisation. For Hungary in the 1980s 'Small is Beautiful' captures more accurately the mood.

There has always been a small private business sector in socialist Hungary, made up of craftsmen and retailers; a *second economy* providing services that the socialist sector could not has flourished for many years. Since 1982 many new small firms have been founded in manufacturing and services. Changes in government regulations have made it easier for private individuals to set up in business. In detail several different forms of business association exist but all are perceived as small co-operatives by the government. This is an important point because it allows the government to regard them as a socialist form of organisation. However the latest regulations permit these firms to employ up to 500 workers. None actually employ this number, but many have moved beyond small scale operations. Despite this official encouragement such firms must pay extra high taxes. Many firms rely on work done as a 'second job' in addition to the official employment of the workers.

'If someone wants to set up a small business, a textile factory or a grocers shop he should be allowed to do so, encouraged, supported.'

'Profits and exports – these are the priorities.'

'Wages should be increased only for better productivity.'

Hungarian Ministers 1984

Hungary is shedding its taboo about the private sector. Only it prefers to call it the 'second economy'

So, new laws of 1982 have spawned many little industrial co-operatives and "economic partnerships" – more than 4,000 people have formed 900 such partnerships in the Budapest area alone. They involve individuals pooling their savings into a common fund to do such diverse things as make calculating machines, translate languages and manage sports fields.

Part of the Government's aim is to foster small enterprises to plug gaps in the market left by big companies. But the latter are changing in this regard too. Groups of workers can now strike bargains with their factory managers whereby, after regular hours or at weekends, they leave plant equipment and facilities for special contract work, either for themselves or for the company. This legalises what many workers were doing anyway unofficially.

Source: *Financial Times Survey*, 10 May 1983

Cutting them down to size

Many Hungarian executives are fed up with the number of large firms wished on their economy by 30 years of state socialism. More than two thirds of all companies employ a workforce of 2,000 or over. Small industrial firms employing 50 or fewer people, on the other hand, account for only 0.1% of the total.

These executives argue that smaller firms would respond more quickly to rapidly changing market conditions. They quote the example of western European neighbours where modest-sized firms employ a much larger share of the total industrial workforce and where they do very well. Many Hungarians are impressed by the co-operation that exists between a western multinational like Fiat and thousands of smaller firms. Why could not Hungary's own industrial giants show more interest in providing orders for smaller concerns?

While big enterprises like Raba Engineering in Györ spend millions of forints on maintaining production in their own workshops, the country as a whole is short of nuts, bolts, metal and plastic fittings, general-purpose tools, springs, electrical fittings and a host of other things. It is, as ordinary Hungarians will tell you, often necessary to traipse for hours from shop to shop for a single screw.

Small companies might – it is argued – also be more adventurous than the bureaucratically shackled giants. The Hungarian national bank has recently set up a special innovation fund to help them. And then on July 1st, the government disbanded the three so-called 'trusts' running Hungary's wine, tobacco and sugar industries.

Another large 'trust' – that running Hungary's confectionery industry – is to disappear next January 1st. These trusts prevented competition between individual plants by imposing prices and wages in their industries. Now individual enterprises may get more independence. What they will do with it will largely depend on whether the more distant master – the so-called branch ministry in Budapest – will let them get on with it without too much interference.

The government has also promised more aid for industrial co-operatives. Hungary had some 900 of these at the end of last year, with a workforce of 300,000. These co-operatives are the industrial counterparts of the agricultural co-operatives on the land, and some began their lives as ancillaries to them. Last year their turnover was just over 71 billion forints ($3.1 billion). This is not a large sum, but some of these co-operatives produce quite sophisticated goods; Radelkis of Budapest has formed, for example, a joint venture with Corning of the United States for the production of blood-gas analysers.

But years of bureaucratic socialism have taken their toll. Raise with a senior Hungarian official the idea of a small private firm under an entrepreneur, and he will start to hum and haw. He will tell you that it is not easy to see who would form such a company because, of course, in socialist Hungary a private individual could not. An enterprise under the sponsorship of an institution, yes; a small industrial co-operative, yes; but a full-blooded private enterprise even under a party member, well no.

In the 1960s the late Professor Imre Vajda, one of Hungary's most famous Marxist economists, launched the idea of a socialist entrepreneur. A decade and a half later Hungary has not yet realised that without true entrepreneurs the kind of success that the formidable Asian free-enterprise economies have achieved and that many Hungarians secretly admire is not possible.

Source: Chris Cviic, *Economist*, 20 September 1980

Figure 14 The Politoys co-operative in Budapest

Read the three extracts above.

1 What advantages might small firms have over large firms?

2 Who do you think wants small firms to grow, and why?

3 Why is there a taboo about private enterprise?

Table 6 Small business development in Hungary

Form	Number of workers										
	1982	1983	83/82 (%)	1984	84/83 (%)	1985	85/84 (%)	1986	86/85 (%)	1987	87/86 (%)
In company economic partnership	36 173	103 484	286	200 074	193	241 258	121	266 661	111	304 220	114
Private economic partnership	12 708	25 357	200	42 516	168	54 742	129	66 317	121	101 050	152
Industrial/co-op special team	17 232	46 282	269	79 800	172	87 885	110	100 777	115	121 600	121
Other	1 463	1 018	70	844	83	900	102	863	98	3 400	385
Total	**67 576**	**176 141**	**261**	**323 234**	**184**	**384 785**	**119**	**434 637**	**113**	**530 270**	**122**

	Number of partnerships										
	1982	1983	83/82 (%)	1984	84/83 (%)	1985	85/84 (%)	1986	86/85 (%)	1987	87/86 (%)
In company economic partnership	3 531	9 966	282	18 178	182	20 270	112	21 490	106	28 685	134
Private economic partnership	2 289	4 831	210	7 873	163	9 311	118	10 941	118	15 921	146
Industrial/co-op special team	536	1 387	259	2 424	175	2 523	104	2 768	110	4 630	167
Other	227	216	95	190	88	154	81	168	109	527	313
Total	**6 593**	**16 400**	**249**	**28 665**	**175**	**32 258**	**113**	**35 367**	**110**	**49 763**	**141**

Source: World Economy Weekly, 6 August 1988

1 Which is the most important new form of partnership?

2 What is the average number of workers in each type of partnership?

3 What has been the pattern of increase in the various partnerships?

Management changes in the 1980s

HUNGARY'S NEW management and wage reforms introduced last month are among the most wide-ranging since the New Economic Mechanism was launched in 1968. They aim to achieve a greater degree of company self-management and wage differentials than in any other Comecon country.

Managers in 50 per cent of Hungarian enterprises are to be elected, subject to industry ministry approval, by newly-formed company councils representing management and employees.

The councils, which resemble the supervisory boards of West German companies, will determine a company's 'strategic' goals including investments, products, pay and may recommend closure if all else fails.

In other 25 percent of companies, mainly smaller ones, managers are to be directly elected by employees. The remaining companies – operating in defence, essential goods and services and so-called monopoly trusts such as oil and aluminium – will continue to be under direct ministerial supervision.

From 1986 to 1990 there is to be a spurt in national income growth with an annual rise projected at 3 per cent according to Mr Lajos Faluvegi, Deputy Prime Minister.

Industrial production is also expected to increase at an annual rate of 3–4 per cent while agriculture is to grow by 2 per cent annually. Productivity, he said, is to expand by 4 per cent to 5 per

Source: Leslie Colitt, *Financial Times*, 1985

Problems implementing reforms

There are two main points to the next stage of reform: the expansion of worker democracy and the breaking up of the huge industrial conglomerates in the state sector, with a view to making factories more profitable and more flexible. A decision on the changes is expected from the Politburo in spring.

Under the present plans, smaller factories will have worker directors elected to their boards, while larger plants will have boards composed equally of managers, citizens nominated by the state to monitor profitability and workers chosen by trade unions or directly elected by the workforce.

The second part of the latest reform is to "deconcentrate" state industry. This should in the view of some influential economists, be carried out by managers on the spot rather than by state bureaucrats, who have too vested an interest in keeping industry large and unwieldly, for this is their power base.

Smaller units will be able to react more quickly to shifts in demand and to increase profits.

If the authorities can overcome the innate conservatism of the state bureaucracy and the entrenched directors of the largest plants (all of whom are afraid of losing power), they will still face at least two problems.

First, the workers have to be persuaded to increase productivity without large financial incentives. It is significant that the one strike in Budapest last year was organised by lorry drivers protesting at a productivity scheme which paid them less for the same work.

Unions used their veto right – blocking management decisions without having to resort to the strike weapon – in 45 disputes in Budapest alone and most of these were wage and productivity-related issues.

The second hurdle, the banking system. If the reform is to work, banks must be allowed to declare state-run factories operating in the red as bankrupt.

Only the pressure of the market will force managers to work out ways to profitability.

The logical extension of profit-seeking, and bankruptcy for failures, is that state factories are sold into private hands. Theoretically this is possible, but to do so would be to rip into the fabric of the socialism that Hungary still espouses.

Source: *Time*, 7 February 1984

cent annually as a result of the latest reforms.

While the company councils will be responsible for broader corporate strategy managers are companies much as before on a daily basis.

Concurrent with these changes to increase participation by employees in state companies, Hungary has begun wage reforms which are to allow considerable differentials in profitable companies. This device is designed to both attract labour to more efficient firms and to base wages on performance and not mere atten dance as in the past.

Plans have also been unveiled to turn some Hungarian foreign trade organisations (FTOs) into trading houses taking part in production, company organisation, financing and product development of the domestic companies they represent. Until now the FTOs have had virtually no say in what domestic companies produce.

Changes

As of last month some 250 Hungarian companies conducted their own foreign trade and in the engineering sector half of the foreign trade turnover is handled by the producers themselves. Necessity fostered these changes as Hungarian state companies were inherently complacent together with their workers.

Innovation was much discussed but seldom practised and industry, as in other Comecon countries, took months to gear up for production in the first half of the year and then spurted to complete delayed work in the last quarter.

In the same period investments and real wages are to level off or increase only slightly – more belt tightening for the Hungarian consumer. Throughout the next five year plan Hungary plans to achieve an annual surplus of $600m to $700m on its hard currency trade account.

Beginning next year he explained it is planned 'to import more machinery and technology from the West.

According to this scenario, Hungary's external debt is to be substantially reduced between 1988 and 1990 with the debt service imposing a smaller burden. Several hundreds of millions of dollars are expected to be freed annually to plough back into the economy which Mr Faluvegi said could result in a strong 4 per cent annual growth in national income.

Does all this fine-sounding theory work in practice? The answer is no, or at least not yet. There is a risk of 'overwriting' the Hungarian reforms, fascinating though they are. Not because there is temporary backsliding by the Government into restrictive, administrative measures, such as its September 1982 import curbs; many well-run economies have to impose these from time to time, and Hungary is only slowly recovering from its external liquidity crisis of a year ago. The real reason is that, at the present state, the market mechanisms are still in some areas only a skin graft on to a state-controlled structure, concealing the body of the economy.

The core problem is the inadequate flow of labour and capital resources from inefficient companies to efficient ones. Workers in money-losing enterprises are naturally reluctant to search elsewhere for employment, and local party bosses and the equivalent of union shop stewards resist layoffs. Oddly, for what is a fairly dynamic economy, the ratio of Hungarian industrial workers who change their jobs in any one year is declining. Yet, there are labour shortages in expanding sectors, remedied in a few instances by hiring Poles or Czechs.

The industrial wage structure does not spur structural change. Basic pay rates for comparable skills differ little between money-making and money-losing companies or sectors. The Kadar Government, and the IMF for that matter, want to see wider differentials in basic pay, but the effect of the "second economy" has been perverse.

Those in second jobs can double their money, providing plenty of incentive for after-hours work. But, in regular industry where the incentives should be, income differentials have narrowed, as most workers can take advantage of the new contract work system but most managers cannot.

The cross-flow of capital is still nearly as sticky as that of labour. Under pressure from the IMF this year to reduce the budget deficit to 1 per cent of Gross Domestic Product, the Government has cut back subsidies to money-losing companies a little. Companies wishing to expand, on the other hand, bump up against the pretty tight credit policy of the National Bank. Not surprisingly, they are in the van of those wanting to see some competition introduced into Hungarian commercial banking.

What is needed is to capture some of the cash washing around in the second economy, where it is being used to buy Mercedes cars at 100 per cent import duty, and put it to good use. One means is to improve the tax system. A better way would be to allow companies to sell bonds to individuals, which the Government says it is contemplating.

Source: Financial Times Survey, 10 June 1983

1 How do the proposals in these articles extend the NEM aims with regard to company management?

2 What difficulties do you see as the main obstacles to structural change in a company organisation?

3 What steps must be taken if good companies are to grow and inefficient companies weeded out?

What the workers say

Elizabeth Locsi - Marketing Assistant

I have worked for Ikarus for 11 years and liked every minute of it. I started as a graduate trainee in the production control office at Szèkesfehèrvár. After three years I married and moved to Budapest where my husband lived. I transferred to the marketing department of Ikarus shortly after I had a baby. I could have received a state salary for three years, staying at home with my baby, but I wanted to make a career. My baby went to the firm's crêche at the office and I worked hard. I am attached to the World Marketing Section and deal with many countries – I speak English and Russian as well as Hungarian. I have been on sales visits to America and China. I could never have done this for holidays or if I had worked for a small firm.

Zoltan Toth – retired lathe operator

I worked all my life for Ikarus, even before it became a state-owned firm. Before World War 2 things were terrible: poor wages, old equipment, bad management, not knowing from day to day if there would be work. In the early socialist days we were being constantly urged to increase output, but we didn't get extra wages. Mind you, prices in those days kept steady and basic foods were cheap, but there were very few household goods to be bought. When they started the big investment in the mid 1960s, things became much better. We got better machines to work with and our wages went up. Because prices stayed the same we had more money to spend on luxuries, and they were available too. Another advantage of the socialist government was that we knew we couldn't get sacked. That was very important for me with a growing family to provide for.

I retired in 1978 and it's been hard since then. My pension has not risen much but prices have shot up. My children are grumbling that it's more difficult to get an official job and some firms are being closed. The unions have persuaded the government to set up an unemployment fund, but there's not much money to go round. It seems odd, but some people now have two or three jobs. They say it's the only way they can make ends meet.

Janos Szabo – Middle Manager in Technical Development – Rába

Rába is an exciting place to work. The company is very keen to improve its technical capacity and the quality of its products. I am given plenty of scope to work on my ideas. I had thought of moving to work in Budapest – Rába has a technical/sales unit there, but living in Györ is pleasant and the company headquarters is here. Working for Rába is better than for most firms because many don't have their forward-looking management. We ensure good training for all grades of workers and aim to make the company strong for the future. Too many companies have managers who were appointed by the ministry because they would do as they were told and not because they could do the job. When managers and directors kept their jobs, whether or not they made a profit, the lazy or the incompetent couldn't be ousted. Rába has never been held back because managers were not prepared to innovate, but many Hungarian companies have relied too much on subsidies and feather-bedding by the Ministry. When you depend on the Ministry for investment funds, good managers and workers are held back. In Hungary firms have some say in how they raise and invest money, but still the Ministry interferes.

Ilona Micsek – Factory Worker

I like working for a state firm. The firm helped us to buy a flat and runs lots of sports facilities and holiday homes. We feel secure because we know the state ensures our jobs and doesn't measure success just by short-term profits. There is a very strong social awareness of workers' needs.

Tomas Köszegi – Factory Director

I manage a state factory and I think people don't realise that many of the changes made recently are going to pose problems. Some industries need enormous amounts of capital and can only make small profits or don't make profits for a very long time, but the items they manufacture are essential – like, for example, machinery. If the state did not subsidise these factories, we would have to import the equipment – we are short of hard currency already and we have a big debt to Western banks. On the other hand, the quality of goods from our Comecon partners is not always so high and they often miss delivery dates.

We might not be as efficent as every Western producer, but we have control over supply and, furthermore, the ministry knows what the needs are for our products because it has an overview of the whole of our economic sector, so it can judge much better the needs for our product, and give us a stable environment in which to plan and organise our production, for the benefit of everybody. Small firms are often more flexible than bigger ones and respond more quickly to changes in demand, but what do they do when they need to invest in new equipment? Raising capital is not easy and it is certainly expensive.

Many people have got very little experience of management. They think it is easy, but they soon find it's not. And workers aren't guaranteed job security as they were in the old system. They are just a factor of production. It's fine having a lot of money today, but what if you are thrown out of work next week because there is an unforeseen fall in demand for your skills or your company's products? Big firms can weather such storms; little ones cannot. Centrally planned economies can avoid them completely by planning ahead.

If Hungary is not careful it will become dependent on Western banks and Western corporations. Hungary will just supply cheap labour – raw materials will come from abroad, be manufactured here then sold in Western markets, all under the control of Western corporations. This sort of thing is happening in Romania and we don't want that here. That's dependence, not development.

Ferenc Gardi – Organiser of a v-gmk* (in-company economic partnership)

Since 1982 in Hungary groups of workers have been able to set up a variety of small enterprises. The Government wants to encourage individual initiative because it thinks that people work harder and more efficiently when they work in a small unit with some independence. In my group there are eight of us. We hire machinery from our state firm and at weekends and evenings we manufacture special valves which we sell to numerous firms on contract. We keep the profits we make and share them among ourselves. I like this because it means I am in a way running my own business. It gives me management independence.

You see, we could have set up our own business forming a *special team* which did extra work for the state firm. The arrangement would have been similar: we would have worked in the evenings and at weekends doing special contract work for the firm. We would have got extra pay but less independence.

On the other hand, we might have formed a *private economic partnership*. Then we would probably have had to borrow money to hire or buy equipment. We could have done this, but it was a much bigger risk and would not have been balanced by extra profits or greater independence. I think the v-gmk gives us the best of both worlds. In time, if things keep going well, then we might go wholly private.

* v-gmk vállalati gazdasági munkaközösseg

1 Read the comments of the Hungarian workers about the firms they work for. Draw up a balance sheet of the advantages and the disadvantages according to them of:

a big firms in socialist industry
b small firms
c private ownership of firms.

2 Think about the situation in Hungary today and discuss with your class what you think is the best way forward from the workers' point of view.

Industrialisation and regional change

Regional development in Hungary in 1949 was described by a leading Hungarian geographer, G. Enyedi:

'The regional economic structure of the country was of a very simple form. Budapest was the only dynamic centre that influenced the whole country. Outside the capital an advanced manufacturing industry existed only in Györ (Figure 15) and a heavy industry only in Miskolc-Diosgyör (Figure 16). There was hardly any connection among countryside towns or the different regions of the country. Natural resources were hardly utilised, farming was most backward on the most fertile loess soils of the Great Plain and the national utilisation of water was unimportant.'

Figure 15 Györ: the city hall and surrounding area (top right)

Figure 16 Miskolc: view over the city, with the heavy industry of Diosgyör in the background (right)

Table 7 Changing regional distribution of the industrial workforce

	1949 Share of workers	1969 Share of population	1969 workers	1987 Share of population	1987 workers
Central	55.7	27.2	41.3		
North-West	16.5	17.5	18.7		
North	13.0	13.4	13.2		
Great Plain	7.9	29.2	17.9		
S. Transdanubia	6.9	12.7	8.9		

Source: T. Bernàt (ed.), An Economic Geography of Hungary, Akademiai Kiadò, 1985

?

1 Look at the map of industrialisation (Figure 17) in 1949, and at the regional distribution of industrial workers shown in Table 7 together with the above statement.
Which of the following statements best summarises the pattern?

a There is an even regional distribution of industry.

b There is a single industrial core region surrounded by peripheral regions.

c There is a north/south contrast in regional industrial development.

d There is an east/west contrast in regional industrial development.

Explain your choice.

2 Using the information in Table 8 complete Table 7 and then comment on the changes in the distribution of the industrial work force in the relation to the regional share of population between 1969 and 1987.

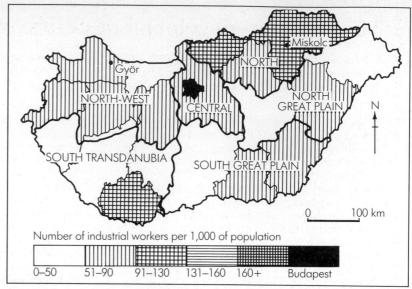

Figure 17 Regional pattern of industrialisation, 1949

Number of industrial workers per 1,000 of population

| 0–50 | 51–90 | 91–130 | 131–160 | 160+ | Budapest |

Table 8 Population and industrial labour force by countries 1987

	Population ('000s)	(%)	Labour force ('000s)	(%)
Central Region				
Budapest	2105	19.8	327	22.6
Pest	988	9.3	86	5.9
North-West				
Fejer	426	4.0	72	5.0
Györ Sopron	426	4.0	67	4.6
Komaron	320	3.0	57	3.9
Vas	277	2.6	39	2.7
Veszprém	387	3.6	64	4.4
North				
Borsod-Abauj-Zemplen	779	7.3	133	9.2
Heves	338	3.2	49	3.4
Nógrád	229	2.1	37	2.5
North Great Plain				
Hajdu-Bihar	549	5.2	62	4.3
Szabaks-Szatmar	570	5.4	56	3.9
Szolnok	429	4.0	57	3.9
South Great Plain				
Bács-Kiskun	553	5.2	62	4.3
Békés	415	3.9	53	3.6
Csongrad	456	4.3	59	4.1
South Transdanubia				
Baranya	433	4.1	63	4.3
Somogy	349	3.3	30	2.1
Tolna	263	2.5	33	2.3
Zala	311	2.9	44	3.0

Source: Regional Statistical Yearbook 1987, Central Statistical Office

The regional development policy of the Government

The main principles of regional development policy and long-range trends in the regional development of productive forces

Regional development policy in Hungary forms part of general government policy as well as economic policy. It contains the main long-range aims of regional development and determines how they can be attained.

Change in society and the territorial structure of the economy are determined partly by the current organization of productive forces, and partly by the trend, rate and structure of socio-economic growth. In addition to the objective factors that influence the development of territorial structure, well-defined demands and requirements are also generated by the different strata, groups and individuals in society. Regional development policy harmonizes the existing conditions and means, as well as the social demands made on them.

According to the government, the most important guiding principle of regional development is to statisfy the territorial requirements of effective growth of social production. In conformity with natural and socio-economic conditions, this can be attained by:

- the realization of the optimal spatial distribution of productive forces, i.e. the most expedient territorial division of labour, and in accordance with this
- territorial specialization, i.e. mutual co-operation between regions,

- the attainment of the optimal territorial balance between manpower and the means of production.

This can be realised by locating the productive forces in areas that are optimal from every viewpoint, while ensuring the growth of economically underdeveloped areas as far as possible. The viewpoints to be considered in the development of each branch of the national economy result from this most important guiding principle:

In the regional development of industry the location of industrial plants should only be carried out after a thorough scientific examination of the balance between social and sectorial (factory) interests, and demands regarding factory optima and rentability.

In addition to this, the industrial structure of individual settlements and economic planning districts must promote the development of the settlement network, and must ensure economic co-operation and the most comprehensive utilisation of raw materials, energy and natural- economic-social conditions. It is absolutely necessary that plants should complement one another with regard to manpower utilization, for instance, the balance between males and females in the labour force and the reduction of seasonal employment. Opportunities must also be provided for the collective use of the incidental infrastructure of establishments and institutions.

The present economic system regulating regional development

Every element of the system regulating the national economy has a direct or indirect influence on regional development. Within this system the attainment of regional development objectives is expressly served by the undermentioned direct regulators.

a) The central regional development fund, which consists of three separately administrated parts:
- the industrial development fund for state-subsidized areas,
- the fund for the alteration of the industrial structure of coal-mining districts,
- the fund for encouraging the movement of industry from the capital.

b) Financial regulators, namely:
- credit preferences connected with the central regional development fund,
  credit discounts connected with state-subsidized areas,
- other credits, e.g. for the construction of flats for mobile workers,
- other discounts for the investing company and its labour force.

c) Regulators connected with the acquirement, ownership and use of land:
- the charges for developing land and for its use,
- the contribution to communal (town and village) development.

Regional planning

The regional effectiveness of national economic policy is ensured by a system of regional planning and plans. The objectives of the system are to promote the more effective use of national resources, the more rational spatial organisation of the aims of sectorial development and regional co-ordination. In this way we can ensure:

- the co-ordination of development trends with national economic objectives in the individual territorial units of the country,
- the co-ordination of productive and non-productive sectors within the individual regions,
- the narrowing of regional disparities in living standards and the level of services.

The system of regional planning and plans consists of two complementary fields of activity namely: physical plans and regional development plans.

Source: J Korodi, ''Regional Development and Regional Planning in Hungary'' in P. Compton and M. Pecsi (ed.) *Regional Development and Planning*, Akademiai Kiadò 1976, p. 25

Hungarian regional policy

In Hungary, the main objective of current regional policy is to promote the exploration of the natural, socioeconomic resources of the regions and to put them into the service of the national economy and to improve the efficiency of social production and simultaneously level living conditions of the population.

In the period following liberation the objectives of regional policy were formulated even more unequivocally. The structure of the country was characterised by districts and regions at different levels of economic development and having different economic structures. In the backward regions, the rate of employment, living standard, the cultural-educational facilities and sanitary supply were low, and the way of life traditionally backward. In 1949, at the end of the post-war reconstruction period, half of all industry was concentrated in Budapest. Of the 19 counties, the number of persons employed in industry was about 100 per 1000 inhabitants in only three counties. In the others it was considerably lower. Thus, the aim of regional policy was the promotion of development of the backward regions by the proper management of industrialisation on the one hand and restraints on the capital city. However, efficient industrial development was possible primarily where industry was already located and a great part of the objectives (industrialisation of the Great Plain) remained only a declaration for a very long time. Even natural gas and oil discovered in the Great Plain were used and processed in the traditional industrial region. In the fifties and sixties rural industry developed more rapidly in backward areas and new industrial centres came into being in an island-like manner alongside rural traditional industrial centres.

An important regional objective of the 1960s was the infrastructure supply to the population at a higher level. In its entirety, this effort yielded even fewer results than industrial location policy primarily because the proportion of the infrastructure investments (although volume continuously increased) remained below that of productive investments throughout the whole decade. In 1971 the Government adopted three fundamental resolutions which have become the determining factors of regional policy, planning and development activity.

The government resolution containing the guidelines of regional development outlined the aim in the following dual task.

It should ensure the efficient utilisation of the resources of the national economy and the individual regions and the modernization and rationalization of the settlement network and at the same time, by the levelling of employment and productivity levels in the regions and the supply levels of settlements, it should reduce the differences existing in the material and cultural levels of the population of the individual regions.

The government resolution outlining the National Settlement Network development concept determined the basic urban centre system of the settlement network while the counties established a hierarchy of settlements at a lower level.

The government resolutions indicate that by the early 1970s it was possible to harmonize the processes of: 1) the expansive force of regional differences; 2) the load-bearing capacity of the country (in connection with the new system of economic management and with the termination of the socialist transformation of agriculture); 3) the manpower shortage in industry (in the traditional industrial districts); 4) the socioeconomic expansive force of infrastructure shortage; and 5) the general acknowledgement of regional policy and its upgrading to a government level which used incentives and orientations as well as planning.

Regional policy and development – even if they were not free from contradictions – yielded much more spectacular results in the 1970s than earlier. The transformation of industry is indicated by the fact that while in 1949 the number of industrial employees per 1000 inhabitants was 9 to 130 in the three most industrialized counties, in 1981 the proportion of industrial employees was similar in the four least developed counties. In the other counties considerably higher proportion was recorded. It is characteristic of the rate of levelling that the difference between the most industrialised and least industrialised counties was four-fold in 1970 and only two-fold in 1981. The importance of the capital city in the industry of the country radically decreased: measured in industrial employees, it fell from 50 percent in 1949 to one third by 1970, and to a quarter by 1980.

Regional policy has not been able to handle in every respect the rapid changes taking place. Thus, for example, besides the significant industrial deconcentration and rural industrial location, there was a considerable manpower (population) flow in the opposite direction. Consequently 70 percent of the industrial employees work in the traditionally more industrialised northern and North-Transdanubian regions. Thus, in certain respects, today infrastructure in the industrially more developed regions can be regarded as more backward. Consequently, the contrast exists between the same regions, but since full employment was realised, it is in the other direction. The situation is similar with regard to towns and villages: extensive urban development resulted in overcrowding and now the living conditions in some villages may be considered better than the urban ones.

Another great problem of regional policy is that it has not been able to overcome the problems of the agglomeration ring around Budapest. It has not been able to eliminate the conflicting interests of locally competent councils (for example, the council of Budapest and the council of Pest County), and has not brought about directed and coordinated development.

Source: L. Lacko, 'An assessment of regional policies and programs in Eastern Europe', G. Demko (ed.) *Regional Development Problems and Policies in Eastern and Western Europe*, Croom Helm, 1984

Government regional development policy

At first the government paid no attention to the regional distribution of industry. The First Five Year Plan stressed the need to industrialise the Great Plain but only in general terms.

In 1959 at the Seventh Congress of the Hungarian Workers Party the following measures were adopted:

a Five regional cities were designated as 'counterpoles' to Budapest

b Government funds to be directly invested in local industries and setting up new ones in the cities.

c Industries to be encouraged to move out of Budapest.

d New industrial plants in Budapest to be prohibited.

e Specific industrial plants (employing 20,000 workers in all) to be removed from Budapest.

Budapest factories were assigned to one of three catagories. Those which had to move – broadly those of low technology, little growth potential and polluting branches. Those which could stay but not expand. Those which could stay and expand, generally those of higher technology and with growth potential.

In 1968 six Economic Planning Regions were designated. They were amalgamations of counties and were given no administrative staff or powers. County authorities have proved unwilling to cooperate with each other and so these regions have been ineffective for the purpose of planning integrated regional development.

In 1971 the government adopted four basic resolutions for regional policy.

1a To ensure efficient use of resources from all regions and modernise the network of settlements.

b To level out employment and economic differences between regions by equalising services and infrastructure in towns and reducing differences in standards of living between regions.

2 To establish a National Settlement Development Strategy to guide the long term development of 130 towns in a planned hierarchy through which investment funds would be channelled.

3 To give local and county councils the task of preparing economic and physical plans for their territories.

4 To begin work on a National Regional Plan Conception to plan regional development integrated across all the country.

New laws of 1985 affected regional policy:

a There would be a withdrawal from direct involvement in regional structural change.

b High technology industries should be encouraged. Investment should be focused on the energy sector. Both measures likely to favour more developed regions especially Budapest.

c Central redistribution of funds to be reduced. Local councils to raise own taxes from citizens and private businesses and be responsible for spending of own resources.

Source: after E. Enyedi, *Regional Development Policy in Hungary*, International Social Science Journal **112**, 1987, p. 255

?

Working in groups of three, each member of the group read one article that gives an account of government regional development policy then answer the following questions.

1 What have been the government's main regional policy objectives in relation to industry?

2 What measures has the government taken to achieve its policy objectives in relation to industry?

3 Why do you think the government restated its commitment to regional policy in 1971?

4 What would you say that the government's regional policy is mainly characterised by:

a Direct spatial measures which differentiate between regions and give selected assistance

b Indirectly assisting regions by investment through different economic sectors

c The idea that each region is a part of the whole and its industrial development should reflect its distinctive mineral and human resources as they most effectively contribute to the wider national objective of rapid economic development and industrialisation?

If you think all of these features are found in regional policy and industrial development, what is their relative importance?

5 What other sector policies have been associated with regional development policy in addition to industrialisation?

6 What has been the relative importance of industrialisation as against these other sectors?

7 Has the relative importance of industry changed with different stages of regional development policy?

Discuss your views within your group then write together a statement which summarises your combined assessment of ths situation.

Under the New Economic Mechanism firms had more freedom to locate new plants and investment where they chose and so changes began to occur which were based on the strategies of specific firms and not government policy.

We have seen that Ikarus and Raba originally operated as single plant firms, but today they both operate several plants. This kind of development has been typical or large Hungarian firms. Particularly important in this form of development is the geographical separation of headquarters from production plants.

Table 10 Plants belonging to firms with headquarters in Budapest. The plants are outside Budapest

1963	1970	1975	1980	1985
857	1121	1234	1446	1968

?

1 One objective of Hungarian government regional policy was to set up the regional cities as counterpoles to Budapest. Do the figures in Table 9 suggest this has been achieved?

2 To what extend does the regional distribution of small firms follow the general pattern of industrialisation in Hungary?

3 What proportion of Hungarian firms have headquarters in Budapest? What is the relative ranking of regions according to the regional distribution of headquarters?

Source: Calculated from figures in J. Nemes-Nagy and E. Ruttkay, *Geographical Distribution of Innovation in Hungary*, 1985

Table 9 Industrial locating activity of regional cities 1972 and 1982

City	1 1972	1 1982	2 1972	2 1982	3 1972	3 1982
Budapest	431	536	51	81	47	43
Miskolc	47	49	48	65	3	3
Debrecen	43	44	42	39	2	3
Szeged	49	67	43	58	2	2
Pécs	59	63	71	65	3	3
Györ	73	75	37	67	3	4

1 Number of settlements outside the city where parent companies have branch plants
2 Employees in branch plants outside the city as a percentage of employment in city HQ offices
3 Employment in city HQ offices as a percentage of national industrial employment

Source: Barta, G. 'Spatial Impacts of Organisational Change in Hungarian Industrial Enterprises,' in F. E. I. Hamilton (ed) *Industrial Change in Advanced Economics*, Croom Helm, 1987

Table 11 Regional distribution of company headquarters 1985

Central	525	Northern Great Plain	151
North West	212	Southern Great Plain	199
North	114	South Transdanubia	139

Source: *Industrial Pocketbook of Hungary 1985*, Central Statistical Office

Table 12 Regional distribution of new forms of small firms (%) 1985

Central	45.4	Northern Great Plain	8.7
North West	16.7	Southern Great Plain	11.0
North	8.9	South Transdanubia	9.3

Source: Calculated from figures in J. Nemes-Nagy *Regionalis Folyamatok A Nyolcvanas Evek Elso Feleben*. (Regional Processes in the First Half of the 1980s [in Hungary], 1988

Table 13 Regional pattern of research and development and innovation 1982

A *The location of research institutions, universities and firms R & D departments as a percentage of the national total*

Central	54.1	Northern Great Plain	9.6
North-West	9.1	Southern Great Plain	12.7
North	6.4	South Transdanubia	8.4

B *The location of patents registered nationally and internationally, and innovations as percentages of the total*

	National	International	Innovations
Central	80.8	85.4	75.8
North-West	8.3	4.8	7.2
North	1.8	5.8	8.1
N. Great Plain	3.8	2.9	4.1
S. Great Plain	3.4	1.0	3.2
S. Transdaubia	1.3	0.0	0.1
Hungary	100.0	100.0	100.0

The emergence of a plant economy

Study Figure 18 and use this information to answer these questions.

1 Which counties have the greatest proportion of industrial plants controlled from outside in:
a 1963?
b 1970?
c 1980?

2 What is the highest category found in:
a 1963?
b 1970?
c 1980?

3 How many counties are in the highest category found in:
a 1963?
b 1970?
c 1980?

4 Describe their location.

5 Do you think that the emergence of a branch plant economy has led to greater integration of the regional industrial structure and a levelling of old regional contrasts, or has it strengthened the traditional dominance of Budapest?

Study Table 14.

1 Which regions have received consistently the greatest share of industrial investment?

2 Do the figures suggest any evening-up of the distribution of industrial investment?

3 Since 1968 firms and councils have played an increased role in industrial investment. Central government has concentrated on large-scale projects. How do you think this may have affected the regional pattern of industrial investment?

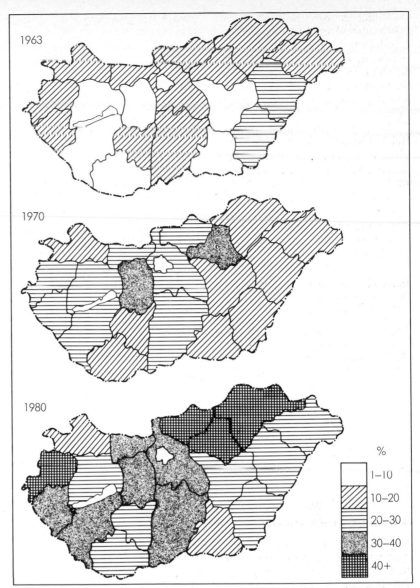

Figure 18 The proportion of plants with headquarters outside the county area of Budapest
Source: G. Barta, 'The spatial impact of organisational changes in industrial companies', in G. Enyedi and M. Pecsi (eds) *Geographical Essays in Hungary*, 1984

Table 14 The regional distribution of industrial investment by 5-Year Plan periods 1956–1985 (%)

	1956–60	1961–65	1966–70	1971–75	1976–80	1981–85
Central	34.4	31.8	29.6	29.6	24.2	25.7
North-West	25.6	22.9	24.8	23.6	21.9	22.1
North	17.7	19.7	20.8	21.0	18.8	12.6
N. Great Plain	4.2	7.0	7.1	7.3	10.7	9.3
S. Great Plain	3.3	7.2	9.6	9.1	9.0	10.1
S. Transdanubia	14.8	10.6	8.1	9.4	15.4	20.1

Source: *Regional Statistical Year Books* and Z. Tatai, *25 Years of industrialisation of the Great Plain*, Teruleti Statsztika **2**, 1984

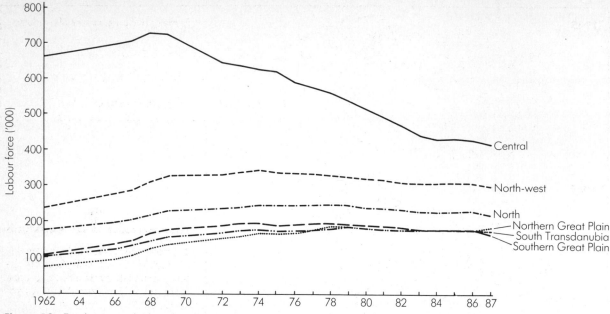

Figure 19 Trends in regional industrial employment, 1962–87
Source: County Statistical Yearbooks, Central Statistical Office

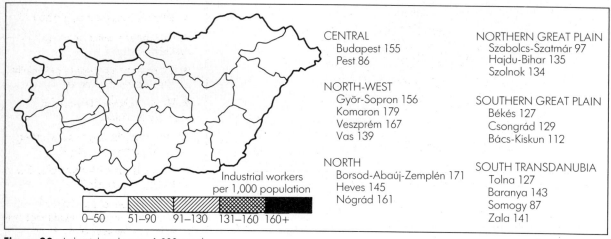

CENTRAL
  Budapest 155
  Pest 86

NORTH-WEST
  Györ-Sopron 156
  Komaron 179
  Veszprém 167
  Vas 139

NORTH
  Borsod-Abaúj-Zemplén 171
  Heves 145
  Nógrád 161

NORTHERN GREAT PLAIN
  Szabolcs-Szatmár 97
  Hajdu-Bihar 135
  Szolnok 134

SOUTHERN GREAT PLAIN
  Békés 127
  Csongrád 129
  Bács-Kiskun 112

SOUTH TRANSDANUBIA
  Tolna 127
  Baranya 143
  Somogy 87
  Zala 141

Industrial workers
per 1,000 population

0–50 51–90 91–130 131–160 160+

Figure 20 Industrial workers per 1,000 people

?

1 Does Figure 19 suggest

a convergence in industrial employment between regions?
b a reduction in the importance of the central region, but little change in other regions?
c a similar pattern of change in all regions?
d an evening out of north-south contrast?
e an evening out of east-west contrasts?

2 Using the county data given in Figure 20 make a map of the distribution of the industrial workers. Use the categories indicated. Comment on the pattern and compare it with the map for 1949.
3 Make a scattergram of the number of industrial workers per county and select suitable categories. Make a map and comment on the results shown by these categories.
4 Study Figure 21 and then describe the changes in the pattern of industrial

centres between 1945 and 1986. What factors do you think were the most important causes of industrial development in the major regions:

a direct government assistance through regional policy,
b government policy through sectoral investment policy,
c local initiative in forming industrial firms,
d firms responding to changes in the economic environment?
Give your reasons for your view.

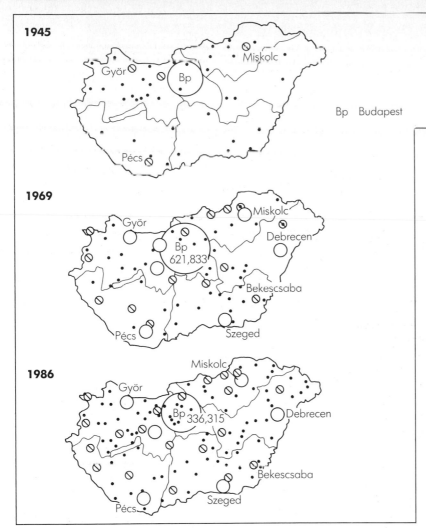

Figure 21   Industrial centres in Hungary, 1945, 1969, 1986

1   Having investigated the material in this section, do you think these conclusions accurately summarise the changes in Hungary? Give your reasons for your decision.

2   Now consider again the questions we began with:

● What is socialist industrialisation?

● How does it differ from capitalist industrialisation?

● What was the purpose of socialist industrialisation in Hungary?

● What problems did socialist industrialisation meet?

● What was its role in transforming and modernising Hungary?

● How did socialist industrialisation itself change and why?

● What impact did socialist industrialisation have on the management of firms and the lives of workers?

● How did socialist industrialisation affect regional patterns of industry and development?

3   What is market socialism? How has it affected ideas which underlay the original ideas of the Hungarian government? How has it affected socialist industrialisation?

4   Has socialist industrialisation brought prosperity and equality to people and places in Hungary?

5   Write down a summary of your findings on 'Socialist Industrialisation in Hungary', mentioning the above points.

Comments by Hungarian geographers on regional changes in industrial patterns:

'Despite the reduction in spatial differences in production the most dynamic control elements of industry remain in Budapest. Even though industrial control also increased in some other cities, its significance fell far behind that of Budapest. A perceptible differentiation has come about among the counties according to their scale of dependency.'
Dr G. Barta

'In spite of a trend of regional decentralisation in the Hungarian economy (especially in manufacturing) in the 1960s and the early 1970s, no profound change took place in terms of the regional distribution of the sources of innovation. What is more the above trend of decentralisation in the sphere of production occurred with a growing level of concentration of economic management, control and research functions in the hands of company centres and headquarters in the capital.'
Dr J. Nemes-Nagy

Preservation of a wetland environment: Prespa National Park, Greece

Sheila Bradford

View of the Park   Inset: the Dalmatian pelican, an endangered species

Introduction

What is a wetland environment?

Wetlands can be found in a wide range of environments. They exist in areas of marsh, fen and peatland, where the soils are either continuously saturated with water or subjected to periodic saturation. They also exist in areas of static water as well as flowing water. The water may range from fresh to brackish or salty. They include lakes, river banks in tidal zones near river mouths, and freshwater areas upstream. Coastal zones of both islands and continents also provide important wetland environments. The wet conditions result in a predominance of water-loving vegetation. The specific species depends, of course, on variations in climate, soil characteristics, pH, salinity, and human activity.

Examples in Britain range from the peat bogs of Kinderscout in the Peak District National Park and the Southern Uplands of Scotland, to the wide, tidal river estuaries of the Thames and the Mersey.

Why are wetlands important?

The particular environmental conditions that exist have a significant effect on the life cycle of various plant and animal species. In particular, wetlands provide feeding and breeding grounds for many species of birds. The birds make up a part of a complex food web, along with aquatic plants, fish and other species. This community of plants and animals and their associated physical and chemical environment is an example of an ecosystem.

Wetlands, when drained, often provide a productive environment for people, particularly for agriculture. Unfortunately, such activity may alter the ecosystem and threaten the extinction of both plant and animal species. Thus conflict arises. Careful control and management may be required to ensure that human activity remains in harmony with nature.

Prespa National Park, Greece: characteristics, conflicts and conservation

The background information and exercises which follow were compiled as part of a Worldwide Fund for Nature (WWF) mission to Prespa National Park in the autumn of 1988. The aim of the mission was to propose a viable management plan for the Park. The plan would attempt to resolve conflicts that have arisen between human activity in the Park and conservation of rare species. This case study is divided into four sections.

1 General background information

This provides a basic setting for the issues related to characteristics, conflicts, and conservation.

2 The physical and human geography of the Park

This provides a fairly comprehensive examination of the geography of the Park and its people. You are required to use a variety of geographical skills in the completion of the exercises in this section.

3 Proposals for the development and management of the Park

This section explains some basic proposals for conservation measures, agriculture, fishing and related secondary industries, mining and quarrying and related industries, and tourism, that have been made for the Park. This section also contributes to the role play exercise which follows it.

4 Role play exercise

You are asked to assess the issues involved and attempt to reach a compromise solution for the management of the Park and its resources in the same way as the actual WWF team was asked to do. This exercise draws upon information from the previous three sections.

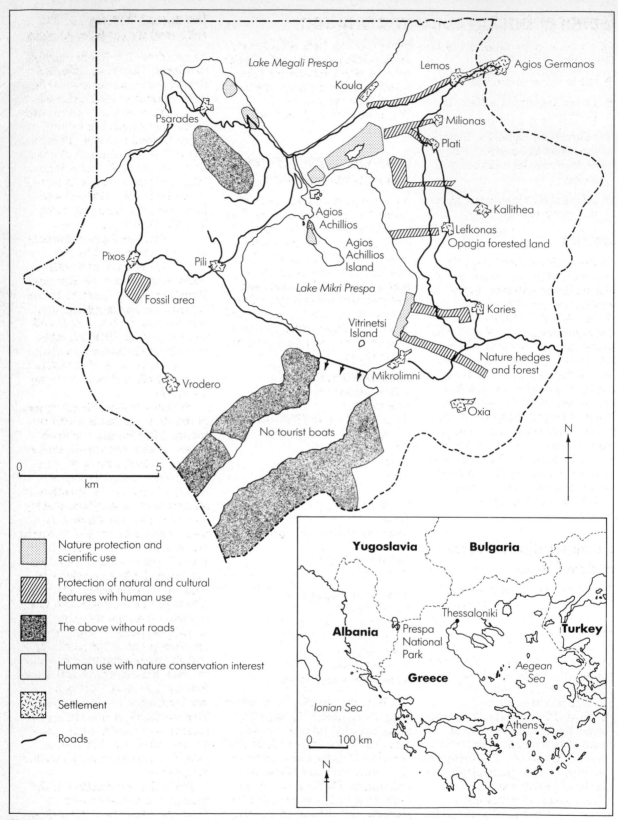

Figure 1 Location and uses of Prespa National Park

General background information

This section gives detail about the following:

- the location of the Park;

- its designation as a National Park;

- information about the important species, biotopes and legislation which relates to these;

- information about the lake and its catchment area.

Location

Prespa National Park (see Figure 1) is located in the Prefecture of Florina in the extreme north-western corner of Greece (40°41′ N, 21°37′ E). Its boundaries are formed by Yugoslavia to the north, Albania to the west and the Prefecture of Kastoria, Greece to the south. The Park contains two lakes: Megali (big) Prespa and Mikri (small) Prespa. Much of Megali Prespa is located within Yugoslavia. A portion of Mikri Prespa, at its south-western end, is in Albania. The catchment area for the two lakes is formed by a watershed, part of which lies within each of the three countries.

The designation of Prespa National Park

Prespa was declared a National Park in January 1974 (Presidential Decree 46/14.1.74). The National Park Authority of Greece, which governs the Park, is part of the Ministry of Agriculture. The Park covers an area of 19,470 ha, of which 11,095 ha is land and 8,375 ha is water surface (4,735 ha, Mikri Prespa; 3,640 ha, Megali Prespa). The area was elevated to national park status mainly because of the presence of rare bird species, particularly two species of pelicans and one cormorant species (pygmy cormorant) and botanically important flora, such as juniper forest. The nucleus of the Park was defined as lake Mikri Prespa and a buffer zone of 200m around the lake which includes an area of juniper forest near the village of Psarades, reed beds and wet meadows.

Important species, biotopes and related legislation

As mentioned above, the area within Prespa National Park is important because of the endangered and rare species that exist within it. During the WWF mission, a list was made of the specific species of animals and biotopes that needed special protection. A biotope is a small part of an ecosystem which supports its own community of interrelated living things.

Important species
White pelican (*Pelicanus onocrotalus*)
Dalmatian pelican (*Pelicanus cripus*)
Pygmy cormorant
Bear
Otter
Wolf
Eagle owl
Egret
Endemic species: fish, plants, invertebrates
Narcissus poetica
Dwarf cow

Important biotopes
Juniper forest
Fagus (beech) forest
Lake
Reed bed
Wet meadows
Mixed, deciduous forest

There are specific international laws that should help to protect these endangered species and biotopes. These laws include EEC laws, the Ramsar Convention on the Conservation of Wetlands, and others. The lack of any co-ordinating body in Greece to implement and enforce these means that they have been ineffective.

The recent 'history' of the lake and its catchment area

At one time, it is likely that the two lakes, Megali and Mikri Prespa, were not separate. There is an isthmus of land between the two lakes, which may have been formed by deposition by the Agios Germanos River. There is a channel which connects the two lakes, but surface flow is from Mikri to Megali Prespa at highest water level only. Groundwater flow probably occurs at all times into Megali Prespa.

In 1936, the Agios Germanos Torrent, which used to flow across the isthmus into both lakes, was diverted to flow into Megali Prespa in order to try to control flooding of agricultural meadowland in late winter and early spring. In 1965, an extensive irrigation/drainage system was constructed on the eastern shores of Mikri Prespa covering 1,450.8 ha.

Forestry within the catchment of the drainage basin which surrounds Mikri Prespa has been rather loosely controlled. There has been clean cutting of trees for building materials and firewood, without much attention to afforestation. In addition, grazing and, perhaps, overgrazing by sheep and goats has led to barren and eroded areas on some hillsides. There is evidence of large expanses of rills and gullies on some of these hillsides. The effects of this erosion mean that topsoil is lost and, therefore, the fertility of the land is affected. In addition, there is the possibility that the sedimentation rate within the lake has increased, and therefore the lake may infill more quickly than it would naturally. This would affect the ecological balance and would, as a consequence, affect the fish and, in turn, the fish-eating birds, such as the pelicans.

Since the construction of the irrigation/drainage system in 1965, the intensity of agriculture on the flat land on the eastern shores of the lake has been increasingly used for cultivation and arable farming rather than grazing. In the last few years the land has been used, in particular, for the cultivation of giant white beans (Figure 2), which are sold as a cash crop. This has been true especially since 1986. There are guidelines and recommendations for the use of chemical fertilisers and pesticides, but there is no real control on what is used. There is some indication that there is an increasing nutrient input into Mikri Prespa, leading to the lake becoming more eutrophic, with large algal blooms in summer. There is no evidence as yet, however, that the level of eutrophication is having any adverse effect on the ecosystem.

Details about other aspects of the physical and human geography of the Park are included in the next section.

Figure 2 Giant white beans drying in the fields and ready for harvest

The physical and human geography of the Park

In this section, a series of exercises is presented. These relate to the physical and human geography of the Park. You are asked to use a variety of geographical skills to complete the exercises using the maps, graphs, tables and the written information provided in the introductory section and within the exercise itself.

It is interesting to note that, within the context of this study, the roots of many geographical words come from the Greek language. Use a dictionary to identify the Greek root of the following words: limnology, hydrology, geology.

The climate

The area is described as having a climate on the 'boundary' between the warm, temperate west coast (Mediterranean type), with hot dry summers (less than 30mm in the driest summer month) and the cool, temperate continental climate (temperature of the coldest month is less than 4°C) (see Table 1).

Table 1 Climatic data (averages) for Prespa National Park (1969–85)

	Jan	Feb	Mar	Apr	May	June	July	Aug	Sept	Oct	Nov	Dec
Temperature °C	2	3	6	10	14	19	21	20	17	13	8	4
Precipitation mm	60	49	48	47	48	51	27	26	38	48	60	71

1 Use Table 1 to describe the annual seasonal pattern of temperature and precipitation. Use specific figures to support the statements you make.

2 What basic agricultural problems could arise from the fact that the highest temperature corresponds to the time of lowest precipitation?

Relief and drainage, geology and geomorphology

Two large-scale maps are provided for you: relief and drainage (Figure 3) and geology (Figure 4). These will help you become familiar with the basic geomorphology of the Park.

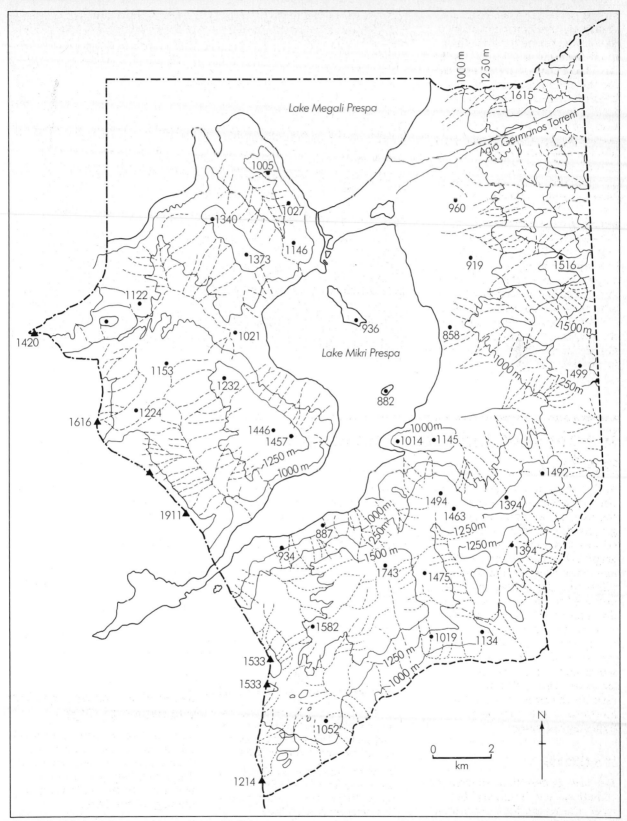

Figure 3 Relief and drainage of Prespa National Park

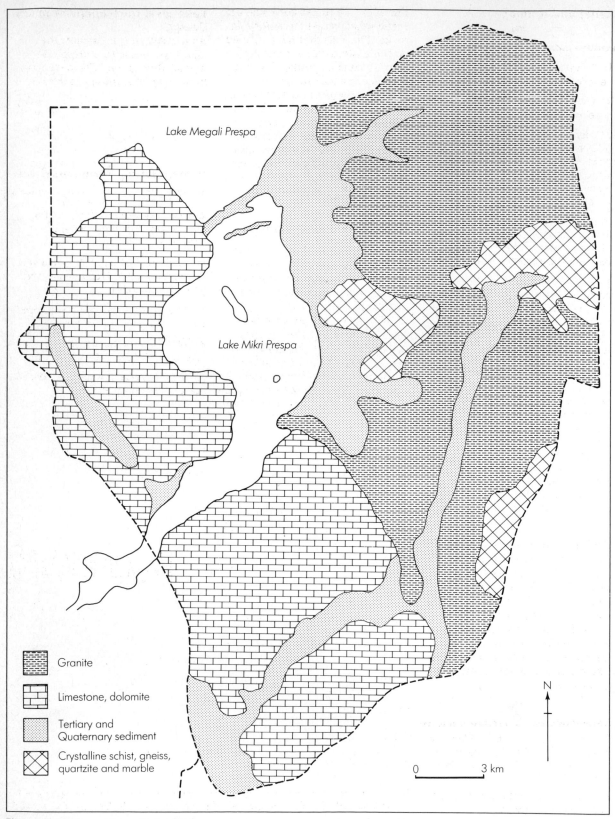

Figure 4 Geology of Prespa National Park

Relief and drainage

1 What is the highest point shown on the relief and drainage map (Figure 3)?

2 Give the average lake level shown, in metres above sea level.

3 Identify the watershed on the map. (Watershed: high land which separates the streams that flow into the Mikri and Megali Prespa system from those flowing away from these lakes.)

4 Note that some of the streams are intermittent, meaning that they only contain water for part of the year. Give two reasons why this might be the case. (Clues: climate and geology.)

5 Find the main river, the Agios Germanos, on the map. This river is probably responsible for the deposition of the isthmus that separates the two lakes. The river used to flow into both lakes, but in 1936 a large drainage channel was constructed so that the river now flows into Megali Prespa only. In addition, a drainage/irrigation network was constructed in 1965 on the eastern side of the lake on the gently sloping land adjacent to Mikri Prespa.

Describe the pattern of drainage shown by the rivers, both permanent and intermittent streams, within the catchment of the two lakes.

Geology and geomorphology

Figure 4 is a simplified geology map. The lake occupies a karst basin. The rocks are overlain by sediment, which helps to make the floor of the lake relatively impervious. The area is within the Alpine earthquake zone and is, therefore, tectonically active. The lake basin is probably continuing to subside.

1 Refer to Figures 3 and 4. Name the rocks which form the lake basin and the hills to the western side of the drainage basin.

2 Name rocks which form the eastern side of the drainage basin.

The rocks on the eastern side are acidic igneous and metamorphic rocks. The soils that have formed on the eastern side are mostly alluvial (river deposits), deriving from these acidic rocks, and therefore the pH of the soils is low and they are lacking in calcium, soluble salts, potassium and phosphorus. On the western side of the catchment, there are also limestone-derived terra rosa and red Mediterranean soils that are richer in calcium and with a higher pH.

Limnology and hydrology

Limnology is the study of lakes. Hydrology is the study of river systems, including the water cycle, streams, drainage, watersheds and catchment areas.

This section deals with lake level changes of Mikri Prespa, streamflow of the Agios Germanos Torrent, and the interrelationship between climate and discharge. You are asked to interpret information from a variety of graphs.

Lake level fluctuations of Mikri Prespa

As a result of the climate, the lake level tends to undergo an annual fluctuation. The next questions deal with these changes.

1 Study Figure 5.

a Using Figure 5 and Table 1, give reasons why the fluctuation of water level occurs.

b Between 1954 and 1988 what was the highest level recorded and in what year did this occur?

c What was the lowest level recorded and in what year did this occur?

d What was the general trend of the lake level between 1963 and 1978?

e What has been the general trend of the lake level since 1978?

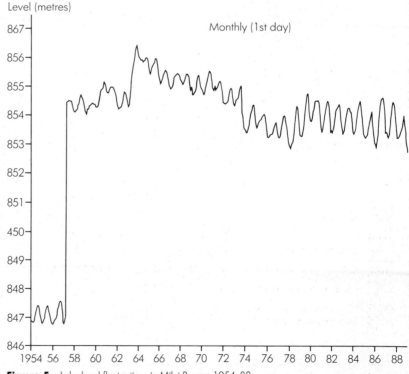

Figure 5 Lake level fluctuations in Mikri Prespa 1954–88

?

2 Most farmers, fishermen and fish experts seem to agree that the lake level should be maintained at a fairly high and steady level during the fish spawning season of May and June. It is suggested that the best spawning years have a low May/June range of lake level and a high June maximum lake level. Study Figure 6.

a In which years was the May/June range less than 0.2m and the maximum June water level greater than 854.5m?

b What is the position of these years on the graph?

c In which years was the May/June range greater than 0.3m and the maximum June water level less than 854.5m?

d What is the position of these years on the graph?

e From the information in the introduction to this question, which of the two sets of years would have been the best for fish spawning?

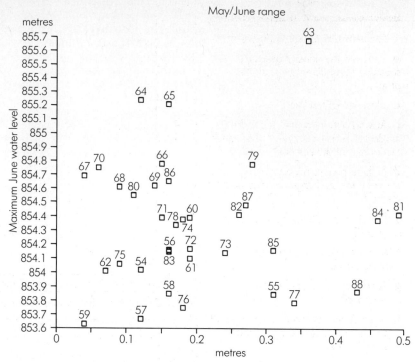

Figure 6 Ratio of May–June range of water level to June maximum water level minus 853.5m (mean lake level) 1954–88

Hydrographs for the Agios Germanos Torrent

A hydrograph is a graph which shows stream *discharge* (velocity multiplied by cross-sectional area) plotted against time. A hydrograph is provided for the main stream in Prespa National Park, the Agios Germanos Torrent (Figure 7). As mentioned in the limnology section in the 'Introduction', the river rises on the eastern side of the catchment, mainly on granite rock, and flows towards the west, entering Megali Prespa through an artifical channel constructed in 1936. It used to flow across the isthmus into both lakes.

Interrelationship between climate and discharge

Climate data and a detailed hydrograph for the Agios Germanos Torrent for the water year 1978–79 is provided in Figures 8, 9 and 10. A *water year* runs from October to October. The questions which follow relate to these graphs and the interrelationship between them.

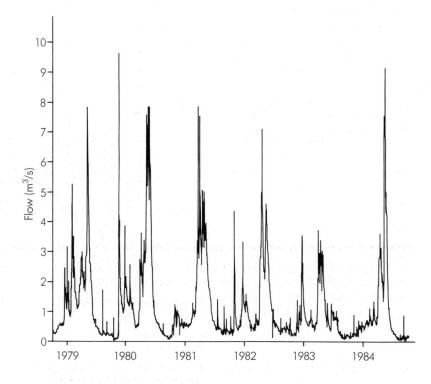

Figure 7 Daily hydrograph for the Agios Germanos Torrent 1979–84

?

1 Study the hydrograph (Figure 7).

a Describe the general pattern of seasonal fluctuation shown by the graph.

b How is 1983 different?

c At what time(s) of year does the maximum discharge appear to occur? Is there any definite pattern?

d Is there a correlation between the time of peak discharge and maximum rainfall?

e What would be the significance of snowmelt?

f At what time of year would snowmelt occur?

g Is snowmelt reflected in the hydrograph?

h In what way do peak discharge and maximum rainfall relate to lake level (see Figure 5)?

2 Using the information that has been provided, answer the questions which relate to the potential impact of a scheme to redivert the Agios Germanos Torrent into Mikri Prespa.

a Between 1979 and 1984, what might have been the impact on lake level had the water of the Agios Germanos Torrent been allowed to flow into Mikri Prespa?

b In what way might the rediversion of the Agios Germanos into Mikri Prespa be significant in the management of wet meadows on the shores of the lake?

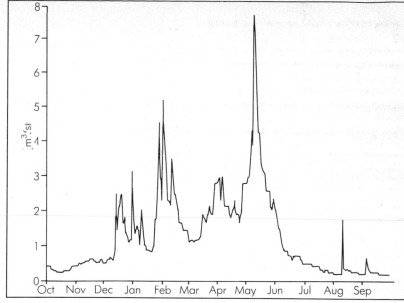

Figure 8 Detailed hydrograph for the water year 1978–79

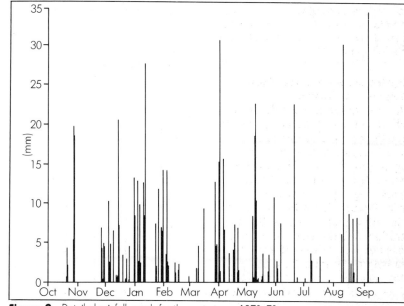

Figure 9 Detailed rainfall graph for the water year 1978–79

1 Study all the data for the 1978–79 water year carefully before you answer the following questions:

a What is the peak discharge shown?

b In what month did peak discharge occur?

c In what other months did discharge rise?

d What month was notable for especially heavy precipitation?

e What is the lowest discharge shown?

f In what month did the lowest discharge occur?

g Suggest reasons why the high rainfalls at the end of October 1978 produced no appreciable increase in the discharge of the river.

h Suggest reasons why the high precipitation in August and September of 1979 produced such small increases in discharge when a similar amount of precipitation in February 1979 produced a series of large flows.

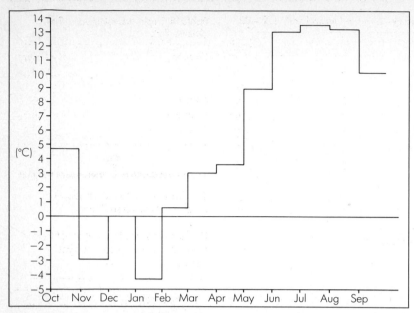

Figure 10 Mean monthly temperature at Florina, October 1978–October 1979. Florina is the capital of the Greek province which includes Prespa.

Population, settlement, and employment

The people who live in the Park are dependent upon Mikri and Megali Prespa for domestic, agricultural and fishing purposes. Until 1965, the people drank the lake water. Some say that they would still be prepared to drink it if they did not have their piped supply. There is no proper sewerage system for the villages. In Agios Germanos village, for example, only 5% of the houses have a septic tank. There is, therefore, a potential problem of pollution in the lake. High priority should be given to sewage treatment and waste disposal within the Park. On the WWF mission in 1988, one lady from the village of Agios Germanos was seen, at midday each day, dumping her domestic rubbish into the Agios Germanos Torrent. She is unlikely to be the only one who uses the stream in this manner.

The following exercises focus attention on the people, settlement and employment within the Park.

Population
The total population in the Park in 1988 was approximately 1,200. Table 2 shows the population changes from 1944 to 1981.

Table 2 Population change, 1940–88

Year	Population
1940	6,880
1951	1,464
1961	3,284
1971	2,225
1981	1,545
1988	1,200 (approximately)

1 Draw a line graph to show these figures.

2 Describe the pattern shown by this graph.

Many people moved away to countries such as Canada and Australia or other parts of Greece (emigration and rural-to-urban migration leading to rural depopulation) as a result of the

civil war between 1946 and 1952. There was a slow drift back to the area. Now, however, there seems to be another decline, with mainly older people staying in the area. Most people live in 12 small villages that lie within the Park. The largest of these villages is Agios Germanos.

Settlement

Refer to Figures 1 and 3.

1 Study the site and situation of the villages. Make a general comment about the relationship of these villages to relief and drainage.

2 Describe the site and situation of any two named villages in detail.

Study Table 3.

3 Calculate the total number of births from 1973 to 1982.

4 Calculate the total number of deaths from 1973 to 1982.

5 Calculate the difference between the two figures.

6 What is the average loss of population per year on the basis of simply deaths minus births?

7 What would be the result of a continuance of this trend?

8 Calculate the total number of marriages.

9 What is the average number of marriages per year in the Park?

10 Comment on the overall impression you have of future population change from the figures in this table.

Employment
The results of a recent survey of the employment structure (1979) are shown in Table 4.

The main occupations in the primary sector are agriculture and fishing. Psarades is the main fishing village located on the shores of Megali Prespa. Koula, on the isthmus, is another fishing settlement. Forestry is also practised by a number of inhabitants of the Park.

Table 3 Marriages, births and deaths in ten villages in Prespa National Park, 1973–82

Villages	Marriages	Births	Deaths
Agios Achillios	18	1	7
Agios Germanos	23	1	31
Vrodero	12	0	9
Kallithea	14	2	9
Karios	6	1	12
Lemos (Laimos)	14	3	30
Mikrolimni	6	0	6
Plati	3	0	10
Psarades	15	1	29
Lefkonas	2	0	7

Source: Pyrovetsi, *Ecodevelopment in Prespa National Park*, 1984

Table 4 Employment structure in Prespa National Park

Category	% of active population
Primary	84.3
Secondary	7.4
Tertiary	8.3

?

1 Draw a horizontal, divided bar graph to show these figures.

2 Does this employment structure surprise you? Give reasons for your answer.

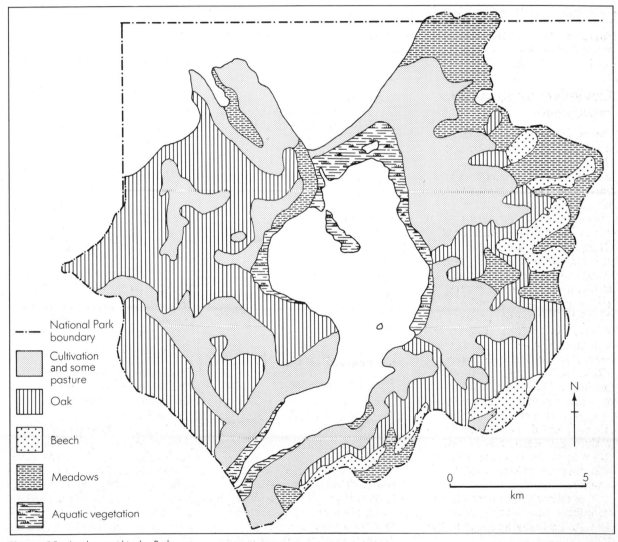

National Park boundary

Cultivation and some pasture

Oak

Beech

Meadows

Aquatic vegetation

N

0   5
km

Figure 11 Land use within the Park

Land use within the Park

The following exercises look at all the land use within the Park, particularly related to human activities; these have been the main source of conflict with conservationists.

Land use – some general observations

The following questions relate to Figure 11 on page 487.

1 Describe the location of the cultivated land.

2 Until 1986, a small percentage of the irrigated agricultural land was being used. By 1988, approximately 50% of this category of land use was being used, mainly to grow giant white beans, a cash crop. If the lake level is allowed to rise in order to extend the area of wet meadow, as in one proposal put forward as part of a conservation plan within the Park, what conflict might arise between the conservationists and the farmers?

3 Describe the relationship between the general relief and altitude, and the main terrestrial (land, non-aquatic) vegetation types (oak, beech, pine and alpine meadow). Is this the relationship that you would expect? Explain your answer.

4 The main aquatic vegetation consists of reeds such as *Phragmites* (Figures 12 and 15) and *Typha*. These are the main areas which provide the breeding and nesting sites for fish-eating birds. With raised water levels in late winter and early spring, these reeds provide the spawning grounds for fish such as carp.

Describe the location of the main areas of aquatic vegetation.

5 What conflict may arise from any changes in land use such as a decrease in the reed beds and an increase in agricultural land?

Land use and land use changes

The following questions relate to Table 5 which shows land use and land use changes.

Table 5 Land use in the Park, 1945–84

Land use category	Area (ha) 1945	Area (ha) 1984	Change (1945–84) (ha)	Change (1945–84) %	% of total terrestrial land
Forests	10,903.6	10,881.8	−21.8	−0.2	63.69
Rangeland	3,794.8	2,932.7	−862.1	−22.7	17.17
Wet meadows – marshland	117.3	89.0	−28.3	−24.1	0.52
Agricultural land, non-irrigated	2,171.1	1,353.9	−817.2	−37.6	7.92
Agricultural land, irrigated	0	1,450.8	+1,450.8	–	8.49
Agricultural land, abandoned	0	214.9	+214.9	–	1.26
Barren-eroded land	19.8	86.7	+66.9	+337.9	0.51
Urban areas	81.5	75.3	−6.2	−7.6	0.44
Water	8,106.0	7,985.0	−121.0	−1.5	–
Reed beds	495.8	619.8	+124.0	+25.0	–

Sources: Pyrovetsi and Karteris 1986; Karteris and Pyrovetsi 1986

Figure 12 *Phragmites* along the eastern shore of the lake. This photograph shows part of the area of wet meadow and *Phragmites* which some of the farmers would like to see drained for more agricultural land. (Taken looking north-westward.)

?

1 Draw a pie chart to show the land use in the National Park in 1984 (last column in Table 5).

2a Which category of land occupies the greatest number of hectares in 1984?

b What is the percentage of the 1984 total terrestrial land in this category?

3a Which category shows the greatest number of hectares lost between 1945 and 1984?

b What is the value in ha of this land lost?

4a Which category shows the greatest percentage loss from 1945 to 1984?

b What is the percentage of this land lost?

5a Which land use shows the greatest number of hectares gained?

b What is the value of this land gained?

6a Which land use shows the greatest percentage gain from 1945 to 1984?

b What is the value in ha of this land gained?

7 In the summer of 1988, a fire destroyed 1,800 hectares of the forest land. Calculate the percentage loss of forest land from this fire. (Subtract the amount of forest lost in the fire from the total forest [1984]. Divide this difference by the 1984 total. Multiply your answer by 100%. This gives you the percentage loss).

8a What has happened to the number of hectares of wet meadow between 1945 and 1984?

b The area of wet meadow has decreased by 24.1% between 1945 and 1984. What other figure in the table might help to explain why wet meadow area has been lost?

9 Why do you think the percentage of barren, eroded land has increased between 1945 and 1984? [Clues: agricultural/pastoral practices and forestry practices.]

10 Compare the values for number of hectare change for water area and reed bed area from 1945 to 1984. What is the fairly obvious relationship between these two categories?

Table 6 Percentage of crops grown, by area, in 1984 and 1988

Crops	1984	1988
Barley	48	–
Wheat	15	–
Alfalfa	10	–
Dry beans (giant white beans)	9	85
Meadows	5	–
Rye	3	–
Potatoes, vegetables and fruit trees	10	–
Others	–	15

Table 7 Animals raised in Prespa National Park

Animal	Kept on farm	Wild grazing
Sheep	–	8,633
Goats	53	2,790
Sows	201	–
Cows	–	227
Bulls	–	79
Poultry	6,560	–

Agricultural land use

The next section deals specifically with agriculture in the Park.

Agriculture includes both arable and pastoral forms. Crops grown include white beans (fasolia), wheat, barley, rye, maize, alfalfa, potatoes, grapes, orchard fruit and vegetables. Animals include: sheep, goats (Figure 13), pigs, cattle and poultry.

Study Table 6.

Not all of the sheep belong to farmers within the Park. Some sheep are brought into the Park from Thessaloniki in the summer months, which obviously puts additional pressure on the resources of the Park.

Figure 13 A goat herder and his flock. Sunflowers were being harvested in the field behind his goats. This picture was taken near the village of Karies (looking northward).

?

1 Use Table 6 to draw two horizontal, divided bar graphs to show these sets of figures for comparison.

2 What is the dominant change that you notice between the two years?

3 There is an EEC subsidy for growing giant white beans, which are sold within Greece as a cash crop. What problems would arise from having what is effectively monoculture?

4 How might the farmers try to overcome the problem of growing the same crop without rotation?

5 How do you think that the government and the EEC might encourage the farmers to rotate or to grow other crops, for example, sunflowers?

6 Use Table 7 to draw a bar graph to show the numbers of animals raised by the farmers.

7 Comment on the effects that grazing may have on the natural vegetation of the Park.

Proposals for development and management of the Park

This section provides details about the proposals for development and management within the Park as well as a proposed management structure. The information will prove useful for the role play exercise which follows.

Conflicts of interest in Prespa National Park result mainly from the fact that people live and work in the National Park, yet there are endangered species there. The main conflicts arise because conservationists wish to restrict human activities and development, but the people who live there need to subsist and find a way to earn a living. Each group of people (or 'actors') within the system, therefore, will perceive development in their own particular way and will wish any developments to further their own interests. Listed below are some of the proposals related to the management and development of the human and natural resources within the Park.

Some of the opinions of the 'actors' involved in these developments are expanded in the role play section.

The list which follows contains suggestions for developments within the Park. A few of these have been implemented in some form or other as indicated in the brackets. Many of these suggestions/schemes are controversial and may result in conflict between the 'actors'.

Conservation measures

- Re-divert the Agios Germanos Torrent across the 'delta' so that it flows into Mikri as well as Megali Prespa, as it had done before the construction of a diversion system in 1936.

- Create a National Park Authority to operate within the Park to include the following people or groups of people: a warden of the fields; a village federation; a department of forestry warden; and a WWF representative. These would be overseen by a Park Warden or Director. Responsibilities would include biological monitoring, monitoring agricultural activities, and development of tourism.

- Extend the wet meadowland and control cutting and burning of the reed beds in order to provide more space for the breeding and nesting grounds of endangered fish-eating bird species and to extend the spawning grounds of fish. Control the lake level so that it remains high in May and June during the fish breeding season.

- Control tree cutting and afforestation within the catchment.

- Control grazing within the forest area.

- Develop a hydro-electric power station on the Agios Germanos Torrent upstream of the village for electricity and to help with water level control and irrigation on the northern section of irrigated land.

(HEP station multipurpose scheme: This scheme has been proposed to be built upstream of the village of Agios Germanos. The environmental impact of it would have to be carefully considered.)

- Reconstruct the steps on the main pelican observation tower which had fallen into disrepair.

- Provide septic tanks for all new houses and eventually for all houses.

- Create an area where household waste could be disposed of.

Agriculture

- Extend the area of drainage/irrigation to provide more land for arable agriculture.

(Irrigation/drainage scheme (1965): This system was first proposed in 1957 and finally began to operate in 1965. The area, which covers 1,450.8 ha on the eastern shores of the lake, has begun to be used more fully since 1984, and particularly since 1986. Some of the concrete conduits are broken, but the system is being used for irrigation in the hot, dry summers. The money for the construction of this system came from the Greek government and from gifts. The pumps were provided by the Ministry of Agriculture. The farmers have to pay 75% of the costs of water supply and pumping. The upper zone (northern section) has water provided from the Agios Germanos Torrent; the lower zone (southern section) receives water pumped from the lake. There are four pumps, each of which provides 250 litres per second.)

- More crop control with advice on variety of crops to grow, rotation of crops, and intensity of agriculture.

(Grain storage silos (1986): These were built at Kallithea on the assumption that growing maize would increase cattle feed. They are not in use now, because not much maize is grown. These silos do not blend with the existing landscape.)

- Control on the type and quantity of fertilisers and pesticides used in agriculture. This would help control chemical pollution of the lake.

Fishing and related secondary industries

- Construction of a better sluice culvert connecting the two lakes to allow boats to move between the lakes.
- Control the size of the fish catch and the size of the mesh

used for nets, so that only fish above a certain size are caught.

- Develop the fish farm which has been built by EEC money and has not yet been used.

(Fish farm (1983–84): This area on the eastern side of the lake below the 'viewpoint' (1,022m) was finished in 1983–84. EEC money was provided for its construction. The lake level has not been sufficiently high enough for the fish farm to be used. The main fish raised would be carp. The lake itself is too eutrophic and warm for trout. Problems apart from the unreliable lake level are that there are fewer and fewer fishermen and fishing, in general, should be more closely regulated.)

- Re-open the fish canning factory, which is now derelict because it was causing a high degree of pollution.

(Fish canning factory (1970s): This factory was constructed on the western side of the lake to the north-east of Pili. The factory was built with money from the EEC, at a time when Greece was an associate member. There was so much pollution from the factory that it was shut down in 1980. The buildings are now derelict and are rather an 'eye-sore' on the edge of the lake. Re-opening such a factory would have to be carefully considered.)

Mining and quarrying and related secondary industry

- Re-open the stone quarry at Mikrolimni.
- Develop a bauxite mine. There are bauxite deposits within the Park, which could be exploited. This would provide a further source of employment. The method of extraction would have to be carefully

considered so that the environmental impact could be assessed.

- Develop a granite quarry. There are extensive granite areas near Agios Germanos which could be exploited, thereby providing some additional employment. The problems of the impact of extraction would have to be weighed against the economic arguments.
- Extend the development of the marble quarry and marble finishing plant at Pyli (Pili).

Tourism

- Encourage tourism. The following activities would be allowed within the Park as long as tourist numbers were controlled to prevent too much pressure on the land: hill walking, nature trails, canoeing and pony trekking. (Measures could be taken to prevent the sort of extreme footpath erosion that has taken place in Britain.)

(Ski lodge (Just outside the park): This lodge was built to encourage tourism in the winter. The duration and timing of snow in this area is very uncertain.)

- Allow construction of a hotel on the isthmus. (A local farmer has submitted a planning application to build a hotel on the isthmus. This proposal would have to be seen in the context of what sort of buildings are allowed in the National Park.)
- Allow the building of small hotels and guest houses to help attract more tourists to the Park. (Perhaps some of the derelict farmhouses could be developed in this way, as in Figure 14.)

Figure 14 Agios Germanos village. Some renovated farm buildings used for tourists are shown in the foreground

Who might help to run the National Park?

As part of the proposed plan for the Park, it would be necessary to create a management structure for the control, monitoring and development of human and natural resources within the Park. It has been suggested that the following people should play a part in such a scheme.

- **Park Warden or Director**: The Park Warden (one already exists) should be paid a salary which would allow for him or her to co-ordinate a team of people who would be responsible for various activities in the Park: biological monitoring, tourist development, waste disposal/sewage, arable agriculture, grazing/pastoral agriculture, conservation, forestry, and fishing.

- **Warden of the Fields**: The agricultural/rural police officer (one already exists), who is employed by the Ministry for the Interior, could be part of the Park Warden's team. The role would be to supervise and control land use and prevent abuse of the irrigation system, for instance, control use of water. He or she should also be given authority to protect grazing land from the effects of overgrazing.

- **Village federation**: The 12 villages would each have a representative (these already exist in some form) and they would elect an overall president (one already exists). These people would meet with the Park Warden and perhaps the president would be part of his or her team. Consultation and discussion would occur, and information about 'legislation' and other relevant issues would be passed on to the representatives and thus to the other villagers. This would give the people who live in the Park a say in their internal affairs.

- **Department of Forestry warden**: This warden (one already exists, but lives in Florina), should be required to live in Prespa (therefore, he or she should be a 'local'). The warden could help to monitor and manage the forestry plantation, including afforestation and cutting programmes.

- **WWF representative**: This person (one already lives in the Park) could:

  a work directly with the inter-ministerial committee to help see that suggestions are implemented;

  b implement the purchase of some of the Park land by WWF, particularly the areas where rare/endangered species live (especially the isthmus including Vromolimni, the areas of juniper forest, etc.) which they could specifically control;

  c help resolve conflicts of interest, for example between local farmers (proposed village federation) and conservationists.

Acknowledgements This study was written as part of WWF Project 3535 in the autumn of 1988 while the author was a C.B. Fawcett Fellow in the Geography Department at University College London. The data used in the project was derived from references, some of which are listed (see Further reading). The opinions expressed were based on actual statements made by the WWF 'experts' and the people living in Prespa National Park during the WWF mission to Prespa in October 1988. The observations and synthesis of information is the author's own work. Special thanks are due: to WWF for their sponsorship; to Dr G.E. Hollis and to the Geography Department at UCL for encouragement and for allowing the project to take place; and to Dr M.G. Bradford for his invaluable comments on the text.

Role play exercise

This section provides you with instructions on how to carry out the exercise in which you are asked to take the part of 'actors' who have an interest in Prespa National Park. It then gives some detailed comments expressed by the 'actors' that will help you play your particular role. The information provided in the previous three sections should help you in this exercise. You should find the section 'Proposals for development and management of the Park' particularly helpful. Enjoy the role play!

Instructions for the role play exercise

1 Divide into groups.

2 Each group should take the role of one particular 'actor' or set of 'actors': arbitrators; scientific advisers; National Park advisers; Worldwide Fund for Nature representatives and conservationists; Greek government ministers and other observers; farmers; and fishermen.

3 Each group should familiarise itself with the opinions and comments made by the group it represents and appoint a spokesperson to put their views across in discussion and debate.

4 Hold a 'public meeting' to discuss the issues involved and the conflicts that may arise associated with any developments within the National Park. The arbitrators should organise the discussion and debate in the manner that seems most appropriate to the group involved. Each group should put forward its views to the whole assembly.

5 On the basis of the discussion, try to come to a compromise solution, with the arbitrator in charge. Take into account the views of the various 'actors' aiming:
- to protect species and biotopes;
- to allow non-environmentally damaging land use within the Park by humans; and
- to decide which developments you would allow to take place, with reasons for your decisions.

Comments from the 'actors'

To help you play your roles, detailed views and opinions of each 'actor' or group of 'actors' are expressed in the paragraphs which follow. They are grouped together as outlined in 2 above. The names are fictitious, but the viewpoints expressed are very real.

In playing your part, do *not* simply read out the text. Use the information in order to allow you to play your role with competence and conviction.

Arbitrator(s)

Mr/Ms Peacemaker (the person who organises and controls the discussion and debate):
'I shall try to arrive at a good, compromise solution.'

Scientific advisers

Dr Hydrollis (consultant hydrologist):
'The main river within the drainage system, the Agios Germanos, was diverted in 1936 by the construction of a large drainage channel. This river formerly drained into Mikri Prespa, but with the construction of the channel, it flows into Megali Prespa only. This diversion has had an effect on the deposition of sediment and also in the fluctuating water levels in the lakes. The water level in the lakes will change because of the climate of the area; for example, the lake levels will fall in the hot, dry summers. The water level affects the area at the lake margins which is inundated by water seasonally. On the margins of the lakes are reed beds in permanently or semi-permanently waterlogged conditions as well as wet meadow land, which is usually waterlogged in spring after the wetter winter and snow melt.

I propose that eventually the Agios Germanos Torrent is rediverted to its original course, that is, onto the isthmus and across into both lakes. For the time being, however, the lake level could be controlled by an improved sluice culvert during May and June. This will ensure that the lake level is high enough to provide adequate breeding grounds for endangered bird species as well as providing increased spawning ground for the fish which live in the lake upon which the birds feed. During the rest of the year, the lake level would be allowed to fall so the that a wet meadow area could be used for grazing. This area would be referred to as a "multiple-use" zone. I feel that these variations in lake level are desirable and necessary.'

Dr Goldfish (ecologist):
'The whole system is in an equilibrium at present. I do not think that the lake level should be controlled. If it is, then the natural balance that has been established at present will be disturbed. We don't know what effect a fixed lake level during May and June would have on the present balance. Perhaps some sort of lock and weir system could be constructed to help with the movement of fish between the two lakes for spawning purposes.'

Mr/Ms Meadows (ecologist):
'Maximum bird usage occurs on inundated wet meadow. Spawning of the fish in this inundated wet meadow is also important. This area continues to be lost due to conversion to cultivated land and due to encroachment of reed beds and woodland. Mowing or topping is probably necessary to help keep the meadow in a suitable state for both cattle and wildlife.

Remedial action could be implemented swiftly, if a monitoring system is set up at appropriate time intervals. This would include monitoring of: forestry operations; bird numbers and behaviour; fish catches; vegetation; and water quality. Local people should be used as much as possible.'

Figure 15   Dr Aviari and Dr Boatman with the WWF mission boat at Mikrolimni village. Note the *Phragmites* behind Dr Boatman

Dr Aviari (ornithologist and fish expert):
'Although the lake is moving towards becoming eutrophic (high nutrient content) from a mesotrophic (medium nutrient content) state, there is no evidence that the lake has any problems with this eutrophication. Raising the lake level during the spring would extend the area of reeds and wet meadows, which would help increase the rate of spawning of fish such as carp.

At present, the fishermen use net sizes which are too small. This has a tendency to trap younger fish which might have the effect of disturbing the population structure and the future of the fish population. The fish in the lake are very important for fish-eating birds, particularly the two breeds of pelican (Dalmatian (*crispus*) and white (*onocrotalus*)) and the pygmy cormorant, all of which are endangered species. To help with fish spawning, high water levels should be maintained during May and June.

I would suggest the following measures to help maintain fish numbers within the lake: licences to fish granted only to those whose entire income comes from fishing; a closed season on fishing from the beginning of May to the end of June; strict regulations on the mesh sizes allowed on fishing nets; limitations on the fish yields, including limiting the number of fishermen and restricting the number and length of nets that can be set in a day.'

Dr Boatman (palaeoecologist and limnologist):
'There is no strong scientific evidence that the lake is becoming more eutrophic (nutrient-rich) nor is there evidence that the lake is rapidly filling with sediment that would lead to the destruction of the lake. The likelihood is that this lake lies in a slowly subsiding basin, which is probably sufficient to cope with any increase in sediment load, which does appear to have increased since 1950 with the use of the irrigation system. There is some indication that the root zone of the reed beds acts as a type of filtering mechanism on any phosphate and nitrate runoff from the agricultural land. There does not appear to be any significant detereoriation of water quality between 1838 and 1988 based on sediment core analysis carried out. Any management plan, however, should aim to prevent practices which promote soil erosion and additional use of fertilisers on the soils within the catchment.'

Mr/Ms Delta (lecturer in ecology and agriculture):
'The villagers could form a federation by which agriculture could be managed within the Park. Perhaps Integrated Mediterranean Programme (IMP) money could be used to initiate a suitable structure and plan for the Park. Any agricultural co-operatives that are set up would have to be managed by local people, as should any other jobs created within the Park. Otherwise resentment results. More control needs to be exerted by the Forestry Commission, which in the past has been rather ineffective.

I am against construction of a ditch for the collection and treatment of pollutants from the agricultural land on the shores of the lake. This sort of system would be expensive and ruin the landscape. I would favour, instead, implementing a scheme that would educate the farmers to use less harmful fertilisers and insecticides leading to protection of agriculture as well as the natural ecosystems of Prespa.'

National Park Advisers

Mr/Ms Stonewall (co-ordinator, English National Park):
'It would be desirable to obtain a nationally accepted definition of the objective of National Parks in Greece.

Human activity such as agriculture is an integral part of Prespa National Park. Farmers can be encouraged to manage the land and to engage in activities that are helpful rather than destructive to the existing environment. Grants and other incentives may be paid to farmers for them to use more conservation "friendly" practices. An effective National Park Authority needs to be established. This should consist of a whole team co-ordinated by a head warden or director who would oversee all activities going on within the Park. Tourist activities could include nature trails, footpaths for walking, canoeing and pony trekking. If the numbers of tourists were controlled, none of these activities would be environmentally damaging.

The National Park Authority would be responsible for scientific monitoring, wardening, supplying advisory and educational information to the people, and making planning proposals. Small-scale developments would be preferred. Particular villages could also be selected to be centres where higher order services might be made available. This may eventually attract some people from the smaller villages to move into these rather than any "forced" movement which has been suggested.'

Dr Wayne (National Park Service, US Department of the Interior):
'The International Union for the Conservation of Nature and Natural Resources (IUCN) has adopted the principle that although human activity that exists within the National Parks has to be allowed, future plans should aim to curtail agricultural and associated irrigation activities.'

(National Parks in the USA consist, on the whole, of land that is not cultivated. There are large areas of land in public ownership. Within many of the parks of the western USA are Indian Reservations. These are usually in isolated parts of the parks. This is the only land within the parks which is cultivated. This contrasts with National Parks in Britain where most of the land is in private ownership. This is also true in Prespa.)

Worldwide Fund for Nature people and other conservationists

Mr/Ms Strakis (ornithologist studying pelicans):
'Prespa National Park is the only place in the EEC where the white pelicans breed. If the breeding grounds are destroyed by the draining of the wet meadows in order to create more agricultural land, then these birds will inevitably become extinct.'

Mr/Ms Dukakis (WWF representative in Prespa National Park):
'Conservation and life should be one and the same thing. In the National Park there are many endangered species of plants and animals as well as important biotopes within which these species exist. It is important that the activities of people do not destroy these ecosystems or the plant and animal communities. A detailed soil survey of the Park would be helpful.

It is necessary, however, to consider the feelings of the people who live and work in the Park, who are mainly farmers or fishermen.'

Mr/Ms Poulis (WWF representative for Greece):
'WWF should buy land within the Park so that it could be managed and controlled in the best way possible relating to the protection of the endangered species and threatened biotopes within the Park.'

Greek government ministers and other officials

Inter-ministerial committee (three ministries – Agriculture, Environment, and the National Economy):
'We would like to see the following:

- agreed priorities for action to be taken within the Park using the employees of the Ministry for Agriculture, National Parks division to protect the Park;
- human activities within the Park should be controlled;
- rubbish should be collected and there should be an effective sewerage system including, perhaps, septic tanks for all homes;
- the development of tree plantations within the Park which would ensure controlled afforestation and cutting of trees;
- maintenance of the natural landscape;
- controlled development around the villages.'

Mr/Ms Stavros (person from the Agricultural Bank, Florina):
'IMP money is available for suitable proposals for development within the National Park. If an acceptable plan is put forward, under the IMP, the money would consist of a "gift" of 55% and a loan of 45% at 5% interest. Such a plan might include:

- fixing the broken wooden steps on the pelican observation tower;
- constructing a lock system by which fishermen could go between the two lakes;
- paying the fishermen not to work for two years while the fish numbers are allowed to increase again; the fishermen would be allowed to cut the reeds systematically to assist spawning of the fish;
- the farmers could be hired to repair derelict farm houses and rebuild the pelican tower for their money;
- facilities could be set up for tourists including fishing holidays and an "animal farm".

Other observer

Mr/Ms Bradford (teacher):
'Conservation of nature and the natural environment is a middle-class luxury. If you are a poor farmer in a National Park such as Prespa and you want to make a meagre living to support your family, it is not really important to you that species will become extinct or that

Figure 16 A farmer pumping water for irrigation from the lake into a tank on the back of his tractor near the village of Mikolimni. People from the WWF mission are sorting out the fuel for the boat engine.

biotopes are destroyed. It is not viewed as relevant to their lives. They have not been educated to understand that all parts of ecosystems interact and that their activities may actually be detrimental to the environment in the long term, which may affect their lives adversely in turn. They need to be educated and also to be given incentives to do things that are not damaging to the environment.'

Farmers and fishermen:

As seen in the employment exercises, a large percentage of the people are either farmers or fishermen. These people are the ones who are most likely to come into conflict with conservationists.

It was thought that pelicans and other fish-eating birds were leading to an overall reduction in the fish population of the lake. In the mid-1960s a local government agency gave an order for pelican destruction. People were paid 50 drachmas per adult pelican killed and 5 drachmas per egg destroyed. Pelican shooting was organised by groups from Florina and Prespa. By 1968, the pelicans were exterminated in this area. This law was then revoked and numbers of pelicans have gradually increased again as they fly in from elsewhere in Europe during annual migration.

Fishermen used to use the open water in Vromolimni to breed *Lutra lutra*. With increasing awareness of conservation, at least in part through WWF pressure, in 1971 an ordinance was issued by the Forest Service which prohibited fishing in Vromolimni. Gradually the passage through the reed beds closed and fishermen were effectively excluded from this zone. The pelicans gradually began to return to this area for nesting and breeding.

The following are opinions expressed by various farmers and fishermen within the Park. It should be noted that a few farmers are now aware of some of the environmental impact of their farming practices.

Farmers (The men and women who live in the Park's villages. In general, they do not want restrictions on what they grow or on their grazing rights.)

'I would not give you two (giant white) beans for a pelican!'

'I don't see why I should not continue to use pesticides and fertilisers to help my crops grow better and therefore allow a higher yield per hectare. These substances, nitrates and phosphates, do not have any affect on the lake that I can tell.'

'I want the lake drained for more agricultural land. Well, perhaps not all of the lake, as I need water for irrigation.'

'I would like a better sewerage system for houses in my village that will cope with waste. I would also like to see a rubbish collection service that would dump all household waste into a tip that could not be seen from the villages.'

'I would like to see the development of tourism. Perhaps some of the old, derelict farmhouses could be converted into bed-and-breakfast accommodation. My wife could run this to supplement our agricultural income.'

'I want to grow more and more giant white beans (fasolia) as a cash crop. I have extended the area planted to white beans in the last few years. I used to grow more cereals, particularly alfalfa and wheat.'

Figure 17 The channel through the isthmus between Mikri and Megali Prespa. Bleak rafts are floating on the water.

'I grow potatoes because I think the price of white beans will decline as more and more are grown. There must be a limit to the market for these, as they are all sold within Greece.'

'I grow a small amount of sunflower seed as a cash crop. I do not like pelicans at all, since I think they eat my sunflower seed.' (Can you imagine a big pelican sitting on a sunflower plant? It is really the smaller birds that eat his seed. Actually, he grows too little of this crop. A farmer has to assume with any crop that there will be a certain percentage loss. If he grows a larger amount of this crop, the loss would not be as bad.)

'I have cattle which graze on the wet meadow land. I find that the annual flooding of the lake margin (wet meadows) in spring and early summer is a nuisance.'

'Bears come down from the mountains and trample on my crops. In the Park we managed to shoot and kill 14 bears last year, so we farmers are pleased.' (There is no real evidence that the bears do any real damage.)

'I am a farmer who owns land around Mikri Prespa. I do not wish to live in the Park and, therefore, I live in Florina. I rent some of my land to another farmer to cultivate his crops. On the rest of the land, I have hired a manager to grow giant white beans for me.'

'I have proposed to build an attractive, big hotel on the isthmus to attract tourists to the lake. I do not see why tourist development of this kind should not be allowed.'

Fishermen (The men of Psarades and a few from other settlements. This is generally their only income.)

'I do not wish to see any restrictions on the amount of fish that I catch nor on the size of the mesh on the fish nets that I use. Fish are my only income.'

'I built some bleak rafts out of juniper branches, and I float them in the channel which links the two lakes. The bleak spawn under these rafts and shelter under these during the winter.'

'Controlled cutting of the reeds helps some species of fish to get to their spawning grounds, and we must be allowed to cut and burn the reeds.'

'I would like a widened and improved sluice culvert between the two lakes through which I could take my boat, since I fish in both lakes.' (fisherman from Psarades)

'With an improved sluice channel between Megali and Mikri Prespa, fish could swim between the two lakes. I would like to see movement of fish allowed from Megali to Mikri Prespa, but not the other way around.' (fisherman from Plati)

'I think that pelicans and other fish-eating birds lead to an overall reduction in the fish population of the lake. In the mid-1960s a local government agency gave an order for pelican destruction. We were paid to kill pelicans and to destroy their eggs. By 1968, the pelicans were exterminated. This pleased some of us.'

'Some of my fellow fishermen and I used to use the open water in Vromolimni to breed *Lutra lutra*. In 1971 fishing was prohibited in Vromolimni. Gradually the passage through the reed beds closed, which prevented us from fishing there. The pelicans gradually began to return ot this area for nesting and breeding. I am not happy about this.' (fisherman from Koula)

FURTHER READING

1 Coastal management

Chorley, R.J. et al, (1985) *Geomorphology*, Methuen, Chapter 15.

Clark, M.W. 'Marine processes' in Embleton, C. and Thomes, J. (eds) *Process in Geomorphology*, Edward Arnold, Chapter 11.

Clayton, K., *Coastal Geomorphology*, Macmillan.

Davis, R.A., 'Beach and nearshore zone' in Davis, R.A. (ed.) *Coastal Sedimentary Environments*, Springer, Chapter 5.

King, C.A.M. (1972) *Beaches and Coasts*, Edward Arnold.

Naish, M. et al, *Coastal Management*, 16–19 Project, Longman.

Pethick, J. (1984) *An Introduction to Coastal Geomorphology*, Edward Arnold.

Skinner, B.J. and Porter, S.C. (1987) *Physical Geology*, Wiley, Chapter 14.

2 The delicate balance

Goudie, A. (1982) *The Human Impact*, Blackwell.

Myers, N. (ed.) (1985) *The Gaia Atlas of Planet Management*, Pan Books.

3 Disaster in the arid realm

Agnew, C.T. (1983) 'Pastoralism in the Sahel', *Third World Studies U204*, Open University.

Curtis, D., Hubbard, M. and Shepard, A. (1988) *Preventing Famine*, Routledge.

Franke, F. and Chasin, B. (1981) *Seeds of Famine*, Osman & Co.

Garcia, R.V. (1981) *Drought and Man*, Pergamon Press.

Glantz, M.H. (1987) 'Drought in Africa', *Scientific American* **256** 6.

Huss-Ashmore, R. and Katz, S. (eds) (1989) *Anthropological Perspectives on the African Famine*, Gordon and Breach, New York.

Goudie, A. (1986) *The Human Impact*, MIT, Mass.

Harrington, J. (1987) 'Climatic change', *Canadian Journal of Forestry Research* **17** 1327.

Heathcote, R.L. (1983) *The Arid Lands: Their Use and Abuse*, Longman.

Hewitt, K. (ed.) (1983) *Interpretations of Calamity*, Allen & Unwin.

Mortimer, M. (1989) *Adapting to Drought*, CUP.

Timberlake, L. (1985) *Africa in Crisis*, Earthscan.

Wijkman, A. and Timberlake, L. (1985) 'Is the African drought an act of God or of Man?', *Ecologist* **15** 1/2, pp.9–18.

4 Glacial environments

Grove, J. (1988) *The Little Ice Age*, Methuen.

Swiss National Tourist Office, *Switzerland and Her Glaciers, from the Ice Age to the Present*, Kummerly and Frey, Berne, 1981.

Tufnell, L. (1984) *Glacier Hazards*, Topics in Applied Geography, Longman.

5 The energy question

Soussan, J. (1988) *Primary resources and energy in the Third World*, Routledge, London.

Foley, G. (1987) *The energy question* (3rd edition), Penguin, Harmondsworth.

Commoner, B. (1976) *The poverty of power*, Alfred Knopf, New York.

Ramage, J. (1983) *Energy: a guidebook*, Oxford University Press, Oxford.

Chapman, J.D. (1989) *Geography and energy: commercial energy systems and national policy*, Longman, London.

Leach, G. and Mearns, R. (1988) *Beyond the fuelwood crisis*, Earthscan, London.

6 Forests

Mather, A.S. (1987) *Global Trends in Forest Resources*, *Geography* vol. 72.

Myers, N. (ed.) (1985) *The Gaia Atlas of Planet Management*, Pan Books.

Simmons, I.G. (1979) *Biogeography: Natural and Cultural*, Edward Arnold.

Simmons, P. (1988) 'Costa Rica's Forests are Reborn', *New Scientist*, 14 October.

7 Oceans and seas

Barston, R.P., Birnie P. (eds) (1980) *The Maritime Dimension*, Allen & Unwin.

Beresford, A., Dobson, H.W. (1989) *Lloyds Maritime Atlas*, Lloyds of London Press.

Bird, J. (1971) *Seaports and Seaport Terminals*, Hutchinson.

Chapman, K. (1976) *North Sea Oil and Gas: A Geographical Perspective*, David & Charles.

Couper, A.D. (1971) *The Geography of Sea Transport*, Hutchinson.

Couper, A.D. (ed.) (1989) *The Times Atlas and Encyclopaedia of the Sea*, Times Books.

Earney, F.C.F. (1989) *Marine Mineral Resources*, Routledge.

FAO (1982) *Atlas of the Living Resources of the Seas*, 4th edn, FAO.

Hutcheson, A.M., Hogg, A. (1975) *Scotland and Oil*, 2nd edn, Oliver & Boyd.

Lee, A.J., Ramster, J.W. (eds) (1981) *Atlas of the seas around the British Isles*, Fisheries Directorate, Ministry of Agriculture, Fisheries and Food.

Pethick, J. (1984) *An Introduction to Coastal Geomorphology*, Edward Arnold.

Smith, H.D. (1985) *Oceans and Seas*, Bell & Hyman.

Tait, R.V. (1981) *Introduction to Marine Ecology*, 3rd edn, Butterworth.

Turekian, K.K. (1976) *Oceans*, Prentice-Hall.

Wise, M. (1984) *The Common Fisheries Policy of the European Community*, Methuen.

8 The aid business

Bauer, P. (1984) *Reality and Rhetoric*, Weidenfeld and Nicolson.

Cassen, R. (1986) *Does Aid Work?*, Clarendon Press.

George, S. (1988) *A Fate Worse Than·Debt*, Penguin.

HMSO (1987) *Bilateral Aid Country Programmes*, Observations by the Government on the Second Report from the Foreign Affairs Committee, Cmnd 225.

ODA (1987) *British Overseas Aid 1986, Annual Review*.

ODI (1985) *UK Aid to Africa Agriculture*, All Party Group on Overseas Development.

OECD (1987) *DAC Aid Review of United States*.

World Bank (1987) *World Development Report* (published annually) OUP.

9 Is tourism good for development?

de Kadt, E. (ed.) (1979) *Tourism – Passport to Development?*, Methuen/UNESCO.

Krippendorf, Jost (1987) *The Holiday Makers: understanding the impact of leisure and tourism*, Heinemann.

Lea, J. (1988) *Tourism and Development in the Third World*, Routledge.

Mathieson, G. and Wall, T. (1983) *Tourism – its economic, environmental and social impacts*, Longman.

Murphy, P. (1985) *Tourism – A Community Approach*, Macmillan.

O'Grady, R. (1982) *Third World Stopover*, World Council of Churches.

Prosser, R. (1982) *Tourism*, Thomas Nelson.

Walter, J.A. (1979) *A Long Way From Home*, Paternoster.

Walter, J.A. (1982) *The Human Home*, Lion Publishing.

10 Women and development

Afshar, H. (ed.) (1983) *Women, Work and Ideology in the Third World*, Tavistock.

Commonwealth Secretariat (1989) *Engendering Adjustment for the 1990s*, Commonwealth Secretariat.

Cornea, A., Jolly, R. and Stewart, F. (1987) *Adjustment with a Human Face*, Oxford University Press.

Moser, C. and Peake L. (eds) (1987) *Women, Human Settlements and Housing*, Tavistock.

Momsen, J. and Townsend, J. *Geography and Gender in the Third World*, Tavistock.

Rogers, B. (1980) *The Domestication of Women*, Kogan Paul.

11 Refugees: problems and prospects in the late twentieth century

Gallagher, D. (ed.) (1986) *Refugees: Issues and Directions*. Special issue of the *International Migration Review*, Vol. 20.

Gorman, R. (1987) *Coping with Africa's Refugee Burden: A Time for Solution*, Martinus Nijhoff, The Hague.

Kibreab, G. (1985) *African Refugees: Reflections on the African Refugee Problem*, African World Press.

Norwood, F.A. (1989) *Strangers and Exiles: A History of Religious Refugees*, Abingdon Press.

Proudfoot, M. (1956) *European Refugees, 1939-52: A Study in Forced Population Movements*, Northwest University Press.

Rogge, J.R. (1985) *Too Many, Too Long: Sudan's 20-Year Refugee Dilemma*, Rowman and Allenheld, Totowa, NJ.

Rogge, J.R. (ed.) (1987) *Refugees: A Third World Dilemma*, Rowman and Littlefield, Totowa, NJ.

Rogge, J.R. and Akol, J.O. (1989) 'Repatriation: Its Role in Resolving Africa's Refugee Dilemma', *International Migration Review*.

Zaryevski, Z. (1987) *A Future Preserved: International Assistance to Refugees*, Pergamon Press.

Simpson, J.H. (1939) *The Refugee Question*, Clarendon Press.

12 Britain's housing environment

Balchin, P.N. (1989) *Housing Policy: An Introduction*, Routledge and Kegan Paul.

Burnett, J. (1989) *A Social History of Housing, 1815–1985*, Methuen.

Knox, P. (1988) *Urban Social Geography*, Longman.

Land Use Research Unit, Kings College (1985) *Utopia on Trial*, Hilary Shipman.

13 West European cities

Burtenshaw, D., Bateman, M. and Ashworth, G.J. (1981) *The City in West Europe*, John Wiley.

Herbert, D. and Smith, D. (1989) *Social Problems and the City: New Perspectives*, OUP.

White, P.E. (1984) *The West European City: A Social Geography*, Longman.

14 Asian cities

Angel, S. et al (eds) (1983) *Land for Housing the Poor*, Select Books, Singapore.

Ballard, J.G. (1984) *Empire of the Sun*, Gollancz.

Fei Hsaio Tung (1986) *Small Towns in China*, New World Press.

Gilbert, A. and Gugler, J. (1982) *Cities, Poverty and Development: Urbanisation in the Third World*, OUP.

Howe, C. (ed.) (1981) *Shanghai: Revolution and Development in an Asian Metropolis*, CUP.

Mochtar, L. (1983) *Twilight in Jakarta*, OUP, Kuala Lumpur.

Sethuraman, S.V. (1976) *Jakarta: Urban Development and Employment*, ILO, Geneva.

Yeung, Y.M. and Lo, C.P. (eds) (1976) *Changing South-East Asian Cities – Readings in Urbanisation*, OUP, Singapore.

Zhang Xinxin and Sang He, (1987) *Chinese Lives, An Oral History of Contemporary China*, Macmillan.

15 The impact of industrial change in the M4 corridor

Breheny, M. and McQuaid, R. (1985) *The M4 Corridor: Patterns and Cause of Growth in High Technology Industries*, Paper 87, Department of Geography, University of Reading.

Breheny, M. (ed.) (1988) *Defence Expenditure and Regional Development*, Mansell.

Hall, P., Breheny, M., McQuaid, R. and Hart, D. (1987) *Western Sunrise: the Genesis and Growth of Britain's Major High-Tech Corridor*, Allen & Unwin.

Williams, A.M. (1987) *Western European Economy*, Hutchinson.

16 Transport

Adams, J. (1981) *Transport and Planning: Vision and Practice*, Routledge, London.

Hanson, S. (1986) *Geography or Urban Transportation*, Guildford Press, New York.

OECD (1988) *Cities and Transport*, Paris.

TEST (1989) *The Big Choke. Short and long term approaches to London's transport problems*. TEST, 177 Arlington Rd, London NW1 7EY.

Whitelegg, J. (1985) *Urban Transport*, Macmillan Educational, Basingstoke.

17 Social industrialisation in Hungary

Barta, G. 'Spatial impacts of organisational change in Hungarian industrial enterprises' in Hamilton, F.E. (ed.) (1987) *Industrial Change in Advanced Economies*, Croom Helm.

Barta, G. and Dingsdale, A. 'Impacts of changes in industrial company organisation on peripheral regions: a comparison of Hungary and the United Kingdom' in Linge, G.J.R. (1988) *Peripheralisation and Industrial Change: The Case of Hungary*, Croom Helm.

Bora, G. 'International division of labour and the national industrial system: the case of Hungary' in Hamilton, F.E. and Linge, G.J.R. (1981) *Spatial Analysis, Industrial and the Industrial Environment*, John Wiley.

Compton, P.A. 'Hungary' in Dawson, A. (ed.) (1987) *Planning in Eastern Europe*, St Martin's Press.

Compton, P.A. (1989) 'Social and economic change in Hungary', *Geography* 74 1, January.

Dingsdale, A. (1984) 'Hungary's energy crisis and nuclear power', *Geography* 69 4, October.

Turnock, D. (1989) *The Human Geography of Eastern Europe*.

Afterword The preservation of a wetland environment: Prespa National Park, Greece

Athanassiou, H. (1987) *Past and Present Importance of the Greek Wetlands*, International Waterfowl Research Bureau, Slimbridge.

Crivelli, A.J. (1984) 'Lakes-Fisheries'. In Pyrovetsi et al (eds) *Integrated Environmental Study of Prespa National Park. Greece. Final Report.* Commission of the European Communities DG XI, pp.46–86 and 144–55.

Hollis, G.E., et al (1989) *A Management Plan for the Prespa National Park, Greece: Phase 1*, Vol. I and II, Worldwide Fund for Nature, Project 3535.

Karteris, M. and Pyrovetsi, M. (1986) 'Land cover use analysis of Prespa National Park, Greece, *Environmental Conservation*, 13, pp.319–30.

Newbold, C. (1986) *Wetland Conservation: British Council Visit to Greece*, Nature Conservancy Council.

Phillips, A. (1987) *Report on a Visit to Greece*, British Council.

Pyrovetsi, M.D. and Karteris, M.A. (1986) 'Forty-years land cover/use changes in Prespa National Park, Greece, *Journal of Environmental Management*, 23, pp. 173–83.

Pyrovetsi, M.D. and Gerakis, P.A. (1987) 'Environmental problems from practising agriculture in Prespa National Park, Greece', *The Environmentalist*, 7 (1), pp. 35–42.

Pyrovetsi, M.D. and Crivelli, A.J. (1988) 'Habitat use by water-birds in Prespa National Park, Greece, *Biological Conservation*, 45, pp. 135–53.

THE AUTHORS

Sheila Bradford, *Head of Geography, Withington Girls' School, Manchester*

Dr Clive Agnew, *Lecturer in Physical Geography, University College, London*

Nick Devas, *Senior Lecturer, Development Administration Group, School of Public Policy, University of Birmingham*

Dr Alan Dingsdale, *Senior Lecturer, Department of History and Geography, Nottingham Polytechnic*

Dr Colin Fenn, *Senior Hydrologist, Southern Science Ltd. (part of the Southern Water Group)*

Nicholas Foskett, *Lecturer in Geographical Education, University of Southampton*

Rosalind Foskett, *freelance writer and a former Head of Geography*

Kate Harris, *freelance editor and writer*

Dr Paul Machon, *Division Head, Wyggeston and Queen Elizabeth I College, Leicester*

Dr Roger Millman, *Director, Centre for the Advancement of Responsive Travel, Tonbridge*

Dr Caroline Moser, *Lecturer in Social Planning in Developing Countries, Department of Social Science and Administration, London School of Economics*

Raymond Pask, *geography teacher, Melbourne High School, Melbourne, Australia*

Dr Robert Prosser, *Principal Lecturer in Geography, Newman and Westhill Colleges of Education, Birmingham*

Dr John Rogge, *Professor of Geography, University of Manitoba, Canada*

Dr Frances Slater, *Senior Lecturer in Education, University of London Institute of Education*

Dr Hance Smith, *Lecturer, Department of Maritime Studies, University of Wales, Cardiff*

Dr John Soussan, *Lecturer in Geography, University of Reading*

Geoffrey Squire, *Senior Lecturer in Education, Faculty of Education and Community Studies, University of Reading*

John Tanner, *freelance writer*

Dr Paul White, *Senior Lecturer in Geography, University of Sheffield*

Dr John Whitelegg, *Senior Lecturer and Head of Department of Geography, University of Lancaster*

INDEX

ACKNOWLEDGEMENTS

Every effort has been made to contact the holders of copyright material, but if any have been inadvertently overlooked the publishers will be pleased to make the necessary arrangements at the first opportunity.

Photographs The publishers would like to thank the following for permission to reproduce the following photographs:

University of Aberdeen, Figs 1.18, 1.19;
Aerial Photography/University of Cambridge, Fig 7.11;
Aerofilms Ltd, Figs 1.24, 7.13, 16.20, p. 380;
Andes Press Agency, Fig 9.3;
Ardea Ltd, p. 476;
Associated Press, Figs 3.1, 4.2, 8.5, p. 61;
Barnaby's Picture Library, Figs 9.13a, 13.7a, p. 332;
Berkshire County Council Library Service, Figs 15.12a, 12b, 12c;
Biwater, Fig 8.10;
Sheila Bradford, pp. 476, 480, 488–97
David Brenchley, p. 14;
Paul Brierley, Fig 7.26 (inset);
C.J. Gilbert/British Antarctic Survey, Fig 7.21;
Canadian High Commission, p. 165;
J. Allan Cash Photolibrary, Figs 2.12, 3.21, 7.8, 13.7b, 7c, 15.14;
John Cleare Mountain Camera, Fig 4.5;
Cloud 9 Photography, Fig 15.8;
Bruce Coleman Ltd, Fig 2.12 (inset), p. 47, p. 65, p. 155, p. 159;
D. Ford Connolly/Colorific!, p. 56;
Countryside Commission for Scotland, Fig 1.21;
Prodeepta Das, Fig. 9.12, p. 233;
Nick Devas, p. 354, Figs 14.19–33
Devon and Exeter Press Service, p. 305;
Mark Edwards/Still Pictures, p. 2, Figs 3.5, 6.10, p. 134, p. 153;
Dr Colin Fenn, Figs 4.8, 4.11, 4.14;
Financial Times, p. 196, p. 197;
Maggie Murray/Format, p. 226, Fig 9.11, p. 251;
Sheila Gray/Format, p. 253;
Foster Wheeler Energy Ltd, Fig 15.10;
Sally & Richard Greenhill, p. 304;
Holt Studios Ltd, Fig 2.2;
Honeywell Control Systems Ltd, Fig 15.5;
Impact Photos, p. 118;
Interfoto MTI (Hungary), Figs 17.8, 17.9, 17.13, p. 440, p. 443, p. 454, pp. 464–7;
Lancaster City Council, p. 416, p. 417
Frank Lane Picture Agency, Fig 2.4, p. 154 (left);
Serge Lucas, Fig 7.23;
MMG Civil Engineering Systems, Fig 2.18;
Paul Machon, p. 307;
Paul Fusco/Magnum Photos, p. 171;

Dr Caroline Moser/P. Sollis, Figs 10.5, 6, 8, 9, 10
Dr Brian Moser, Figs 10.3, 10.4, 10.7
John Markham/Nature Conservancy Council, Fig 2.5;
Peter Wakely/Nature Conservancy Council, Fig 2.6;
Nature Conservancy Council, Fig 1.14, p. 156;
E.A. Janes/NHPA, Fig 1.22;
National Museums and Galleries on Merseyside, p. 180;
Mike Abrahams/Network, p. 297;
Norfolk Library and Information Service, Fig 2.15;
Government of Ontario, Fig 11.18;
Overseas Development Administration, Fig 8.13;
Vincent Banabakuntu/Oxfam, Fig 8.6;
Wendy Shattil & Bob Rozinski/Oxford Scientific Films, p. 36;
Patridge Films/Oxford Scientific Films, p. 146;
Ron Giling/Panos Pictures, Figs, 3.14, 3.23, 6.9, 8.8, p. 237;
Sean Sprague/Panos Pictures, p. 202;
Paul Harrison/Panos Pictures, Fig 8.16;
R. Berriedale-Johnson/Panos Pictures, Fig 9.7;
Tom Learmonth/Panos Pictures, Fig 8.7;
Parkfield Environmental Services, Leicester, Fig 2.7;
Ray Pask, Figs 14.2–6, 14.8–10, 14.15–17;
Peterborough Development Agency, p. 333;
Julia Martin/Photo Co-op, Fig 15.15;
Picturepoint Ltd, Fig 9.13c;
Planet Earth, Fig 7.26;
Popperfoto, Fig 17.5, p. 168, p. 268;
Dr Robert Prosser, Figs 1.6, 7, 8, 9, 11, 12, 17;
Reading Evening Post, p. 406, p. 409;
Reading Newspaper Co. Ltd, p. 407;
Prof. John Rogge, Fig, 11.2, p. 288;
Dr M Romeril, Fig 1.25;
Claude Sauvageot, p. 248;
Science Photo Library, p. 120;
Scottish Wildlife Trust, Fig 2.1;
David Hoffman/Select Photos, p. 324;
Tim Sharman, Figs 17.6, 14;
Dr John Soussan, pp. 108, 122, 123, Figs 5.8, 9, 10, 11
South American Pictures, Fig 8.14, p. 138;
Syndication International, Fig 16.18, p. 305 (inset);
Caroline Thompson, Figs 12.4, 5, 6;
Topham Picture Source, p. 265;
Camilla Toulmin, p. 63;
United Nations High Commissioner for Refugees (London), Figs 11.7, 11, 12, 14;
UNHCR/M Vanappelghem, p. 274;
Simon Nicholson/VSO, Fig 8.9;
US Air Force (source: Syndication International), Fig 7.24;
Simon Warner, Figs 16.10, 12, p. 180 (inset);
Paul White, Figs 13.3, 4, 5, 8, 9, 12, 13, 14, 15, 16;
David Wise, p. 326;
ZEFA, front cover, Fig 9. 13b, p. 242, p. 414